Get the eBook FREE!

(PDF, ePub, Kindle, and liveBook all included)

We believe that once you buy a book from us, you should be able to read it in any format we have available. To get electronic versions of this book at no additional cost to you, purchase and then register this book at the Manning website.

Go to https://www.manning.com/freebook and follow the instructions to complete your pBook registration.

That's it!
Thanks from Manning!

Hugo in Action

Hugo in Action

STATIC SITES AND DYNAMIC JAMSTACK APPS

ATISHAY JAIN
FOREWORD BY STEVE FRANCIA

MANNING
SHELTER ISLAND

For online information and ordering of this and other Manning books, please visit
www.manning.com. The publisher offers discounts on this book when ordered in quantity.
For more information, please contact

> Special Sales Department
> Manning Publications Co.
> 20 Baldwin Road
> PO Box 761
> Shelter Island, NY 11964
> Email: orders@manning.com

Manning Publications Co.	Development editor: Katie Sposato Johnson
20 Baldwin Road	Technical development editor: Louis Lazaris
PO Box 761	Review editor: Ivan Martinović and Adriana Sabo
Shelter Island, NY 11964	Production editor: Deirdre Hiam
	Copy editor: Frances Buran
	Proofreader: Keri Hales
	Technical proofreader: Taylor Dolezal
	Typesetter: Gordan Salinovic
	Cover designer: Marija Tudor

ISBN 9781617297007
Printed and bound by CPI Group (UK) Ltd, Croydon, CR0 4YY

To Ritika, my lifeline.

brief contents

contents

10 *The power of JavaScript* 275

foreword

Hugo was born out of two beliefs: 1) website maintenance (authoring, hosting, securing, etc.) could be dramatically simplified, and 2) the Go programming language and its ecosystem would provide the right base for a fast, straightforward, and productive website engine.

As I write this in late spring of 2022, we're approaching the ninth anniversary of Hugo's first public announcement (June 2013). Reflecting back to the months leading up to Hugo's first release, I had recently begun investigating a new programming language from Google, the Go programming language. It had just reached 1.0 status, and I was looking for a project so I could learn through building. Simultaneously, I was becoming increasingly frustrated with my WordPress-powered blog that was growing in cost and complexity. I calculated that I had spent more time doing maintenance and security patches than authoring new posts.

I had begun playing with the static site generators available at the time; Jekyll and Pelican being the two most prominent. Installing was complicated, however, taking me a few hours each because they both required me to first install the entire toolset for each programming language and then all the language dependencies. After that, I needed to install the software and all of its dependencies, requiring hundreds of packages to be fetched and resolved.

I began porting my content to Markdown and building my blog in Jekyll. Rendering my small blog of maybe 200 posts and the most basic template still took over five minutes! I would tweak the template and then rerun the builder and wait another five minutes before I could see how it was rendered. Five minutes is far too long for a feed-back loop to be productive.

I recognized that these tools didn't fix the maintenance issues I experienced with WordPress; they just shifted it to the dev machine. I thought it must be possible to write a better and simpler static site generator and was looking for a project to learn Go anyway. I spent the next couple of days writing a small prototype. The prototype confirmed that a website engine in Go could be magnitudes faster than the existing ones, and it would fix my installation experience as well. I spent the next few months designing and writing Hugo, incorporating my 20 years of experience working with and building CMSs and taking inspiration from everywhere.

I ported my blog to Hugo and announced my first Go project to the world in July 2013. At the time, I had no idea how this personal project, which I simply wrote for my own blog, would change my life and change the world. To build Hugo the way I wanted to design it forced me to invent new libraries in Go, several of which (notably Cobra, Viper, and Afero) have gone on to be some of the most popular in Go's ecosystem, with adoption from Kubernetes, Docker, GitHub, and thousands of others. The experience of writing Hugo ultimately led me to join the Go team as the product lead in 2016 to help shape the future of the language.

Hugo's simple and accessible design, combined with its unparalleled performance and productivity, immediately gained attention. Hugo continued to grow in adoption and popularity, ultimately becoming the most popular static site generator and one of the most popular open source CMS systems. It's currently rated as #13 based on a number of websites (https://trends.builtwith.com/cms/open-source). Along with this growth came a small but dedicated contributor base, including Bjørn Erik Pedersen who succeeded me as the lead developer of Hugo.

Hugo also attracted the attention of Atishay Jain, an innovative software engineer who had a part in developing many of Adobe's technologies that we're all familiar with. He's written this book, *Hugo in Action*, which is straightforward and approachable. It explains not only how to use Hugo but also explains the history of how things came to be and the context of each decision you make through the process.

Beginners will deeply appreciate chapter 2's "Live in 30 minutes" section, which provides plenty of guidance to make even people who are new to command-line applications and websites feel comfortable. All readers will benefit from the breadth and context that this book provides. I personally appreciated chapter 9's recipes to extend Hugo using external APIs, which expand the functionality of Hugo to include dynamic features while retaining Hugo's security and performance advantages.

—STEVE FRANCIA
creator of Hugo

preface

The World Wide Web was initially a document delivery mechanism. Early web pages were documents that presented the same contents to everyone and were present as a file on disk. Early web browsers were more like a printer that would deliver the documents on the screen. The significant achievement of the web was document delivery from a server far away, managed by someone else, and the ability to navigate across documents via hyperlinks. Developers always wanted to do more. They wrote scripts to generate all combinations of web pages to make the system appear dynamic. As the number of combinations increased, we found that we could support an infinite number of variations by dynamically generating the web pages on a server. This approach brought a lot of complexity that the mainstream web community has been dealing with ever since.

My first website had a total of 10 pages. It lasted on the internet for eight months. When it was defaced the first time, I tried to set it up again. But I had neither the skills nor the perseverance to keep it running for a long time. This whack-a-mole game continued across multiple technology stacks, frameworks, and approaches. Either pay someone to keep your system secure or dedicate yourself to keeping it up. The cycle of redoing the website continued until I landed on the Jamstack. Very few websites need infinite combinations of pages. For the rest, the run-time content generation approach is suboptimal both from the maintenance and performance perspectives. The Jamstack is a flashback to the generate-all-combinations era with just one catch—we can still do infinite combinations using JavaScript for the cases where there is a need. For the significant portions of most websites, we can be free of all the complexity.

When I first picked up Hugo, I didn't realize how much of it was unlearning the web development conventions used in the run-time development model. Although images should always get stored with the rest of the document, static and dynamic content constraints forced this to be different. The more I used Hugo, the more I found about its way of doing things. The lack of structured learning resources caused a lot of rework. That is what triggered me to write this book. Hugo is an engineered product, not a mashup of multiple technologies to catch up to the trends or a solution covering years of cruft under a set of buzzwords. Hugo deserves a proper learning resource that presents the most straightforward web development approach and showcases how we can use Hugo to do much more than what it humbly advertises. That is what this book is about—setting up for simplicity and success.

As I wrote this book, my website has been sitting patiently. I do not have to spend a single second to maintain it. After a hiatus of two years, I can pick it up from where I left it, whenever I want, to make incremental improvements. This book is about fast websites that can last without continuous monitoring, unlike the approaches I tried in the past.

acknowledgments

This is my first book, and I when I signed up for it, I had no idea what I was signing up for. What was planned as a six-month project took two years to complete, thanks to changing personal circumstances (arrival of kids) and changes all around the globe (the COVID-19 pandemic).

I would sincerely like to thank my wife, Ritika, who went through a tough pregnancy, premature delivery, and a month-long stay in NICU—all while I was writing this book! Without her constant support and inspiration, this book would never have happened. This book also required continuous support from my parents, work colleagues, and friends who made time for me to get it done.

Next, I would like to thank my editor, Katie Sposato Johnson, for helping me comb through the entire set of guidelines to complete the book in the right format. She had answers with additional resources and guidelines for everything. I really appreciate the accommodation that the entire Manning team provided with my slippage of deadlines again and again, specifically, Deirdre Hiam my project editor; Frances Buran, my copyeditor; and Keri Hales, my proofreader.

This book would not have been the same without the readers and reviewers on the livebook forums and the structured reviews. They, with their sharp critiques, changed the direction of the book multiple times. The first two chapters have been redone almost 20 times with major and minor tweaks based on places where the readers got stuck. It was great to see the roadblocks getting removed, albeit slowly, with each change as more and more readers could get through the initial hurdles and get into enjoying Hugo. To all the reviewers: Al Norman, Alberto Ciarlanti, Alex Lucas, Amit

Lamba, Anton Rich, Cena Mayo, Clive Harber, Darrin Bishop, David Jacobs, David Pardo, Guy Ndjeng, Hilde Van Gysel, Jeff Smith, Jerome Meyer, Joseph Houghes, Joshua White, Jürgen Hötzel, Lakshmi Narasimhan, Marjorie Roswell, Michael Bright, Milorad Imbra, Riccardo Marotti, Sander Zegveld, Sau Fai Fong, Taylor Dolezal, Theofanis Despoudis, and Vidhyadharan Deivamani, your suggestions helped make this a better book.

Of course, nothing was possible without @spf13, @bep, and the entire team that has made Hugo the ultimate static site builder. The thought and care that has gone into making Hugo is evidenced in the way its core structure and ideas have survived unchanged as the Jamstack concepts and services have matured. The Hugo community is a marvel, and it is a pleasure to have had healthy discussions on the Hugo forums for not only problems and solutions, but also for approaches, pros and cons, and performance considerations for doing things in a certain way.

Lastly, I would like to thank the service providers, GitHub, Netlify, Formspree, Stripe, and SendGrid, for having stable backbone services for us to be able to build upon. These services are affordable, reliable, and have allowed us to focus on what we love the most—creating new websites.

about this book

Hugo in Action guides you through building a fast and low maintenance website using the Hugo static site builder. It enables you to understand the core concept of the Jamstack and the profound impact of its compilation step on the website's architecture. This book provides a step-by-step walkthrough for laying out content, organizing templates, and managing assets in a Hugo-based website. It provides the best practices for building a quick-to-compile, quick-to-load, and easy-to-maintain website, along with the means to debug issues, optimize existing template files, and set the website's architecture for optimal usage of Hugo.

Who should read this book

Hugo is a tool for web developers looking for a powerful static site builder to create feature-rich websites without compromising run-time performance, developer experience, and maintainability. This book expects its readers to understand HTML, CSS, JavaScript, and version control using Git and GitHub-based code hosting. The readers should also be familiar with the basic usage of the command line, including navigating through the filesystem and running simple commands. Both beginner and experienced web developers will benefit from this book.

How this book is organized: A road map

The entire book runs through a single example website for a fictional company called Acme Corporation. We'll build the site and add new features to improve its behavior while introducing approaches to development.

The book has two distinct parts. The first part focuses on the core functionality of Hugo, which we will run in isolation from the rest of the internet. The second part centers on how Hugo provides the means to communicate with various services and how the JavaScript ecosystem furnishes the functionality that is not possible during Hugo's compilation step.

- Chapter 1 introduces the Jamstack and explains the ideas behind it. This chapter also lays out the parts of the Jamstack and how these work together. It also introduces the Hugo static site builder and discusses when it is sensible to use Hugo and when it is inappropriate to use Hugo or the Jamstack.
- Chapter 2 provides a brief overview of a Hugo project's working directory. It also sets up web hosting and creates a simple Hugo-based website that is live on the internet, which offers outstanding performance and a manageable set of dependencies.
- Chapter 3 lets us play the role of the content author. This chapter provides an in-depth overview of Markdown and YAML, the two main languages used to create content and provide metadata for a Hugo website. It also compares these languages with other available options and provides an overview of the standard metadata properties we can use in the front matter of a Hugo web page.
- Chapter 4 allows us to play the role of the website editor. This chapter shows how to organize pages in a Hugo website into sections, menus, and Hugo taxonomies, how to bunch contents into a page bundle, and how to effectively use Hugo's built-in and community-provided shortcodes to enable and extend Markdown features.
- Chapter 5 offers our first glimpse of the Go template language that provides the means to control the rendering of a web page. We will explore how to build custom pages in Hugo, how to render content with the Go template language, how to access Hugo's variables, functions, configurations, and front matter, and how to read from the filesystem using Hugo.
- Chapter 6 explores the critical components of a Hugo theme and the tools Hugo provides for building custom web pages. It teaches us how to organize templates for easy maintenance and reuse, to improve productivity by sharing template code and snippets between multiple page types, and to tackle resource management issues with Hugo pipes.
- Chapter 7 allows us to take full ownership of the website. It shows how the building blocks of Hugo's content system (the leaf and branch bundles, the taxonomy system, layouts, and types) all map to template code.
- Chapter 8 dives deep into Hugo Modules, which are a powerful, widely misunderstood, and underused feature of Hugo. Hugo's modules allow the creation and consumption of plugins (from themes and templates to shortcodes and even content) from all the components of a Hugo-based website.

- Chapter 9 steps outside of the bounds of our project folder and showcases Hugo's support for the second pillar of the Jamstack—APIs. This chapter moves us into Web 2.0 with support for dynamic features like comments and contact forms. It also presents some simple solutions to historically more challenging problems such as dynamic surveys and RESTful GET APIs.

- Chapter 10 shows why Hugo goes to great lengths to ensure that it plays nicely with JavaScript (the "J" in Jamstack). This includes customizing and integrating with one of the fastest JavaScript bundlers. Hugo clarifies concerns between the compile-time and run-time environments while still keeping tight integration and providing unified control. This chapter uses client-side scripting for dynamic features like background form submissions and the npm ecosystems for client-side searches. It also sets up a hybrid website with Hugo and JavaScript that takes ownership of the pieces they excel in.

- Chapter 11 introduces the Jamstack way of building low-maintenance APIs to extend Hugo with features that it does not natively provide. We do this without losing the key performance benefits of Hugo. This chapter also explores web-hooks—the server-to-server API communication mechanism that integrates with independent API providers—to enable our website to act as a unified back-end with little operational overhead.

- Chapter 12 dives into a capstone project where everything from the book is put into practice. This chapter busts some of the most popular myths of the Jam-stack by building an e-commerce website with end-to-end support from the shopping cart to checkout to order fulfillment.

- Chapter 13 takes the existing website and stretches it in multiple directions. This provides support for numerous (human) languages and many views of the same content with different themes. It also makes our website even faster with offline support, instant pages, and Turbo techniques and libraries. It also discusses scripting to reduce the work done manually in the browser and participation in the Hugo community for support, appreciation, and contribution.

The chapters in this book should be read in order: what you learn from previous chapters is built upon in the following ones. Each chapter improves the example website from where it was left in the last chapter. If the reader, by chance, wants to understand a topic out of order, it is advised to look at the code checkpoint at the end of the previous chapter to understand where the next chapter starts.

About the code

This book contains many examples of source code, both in numbered listings and in line with normal text. In both cases, the source code is formatted in a `fixed-width font like this` to separate it from ordinary text.

In many cases, the original source code has been reformatted; we've added line breaks and reworked indentation to accommodate the available page space in the book. In rare cases, even this was not enough, and listings include line-continuation markers (➡). Additionally, comments in the source code have often been removed from the listings when the code is described in the text. Code annotations accompany many of the listings, highlighting important concepts.

The book has over 128 code checkpoints and more than 94 chapter resources present on GitHub with links to the exact checkpoint associated with any section immediately after the section. You can get executable snippets of code from the liveBook (online) version of this book at https://livebook.manning.com/book/hugo-in-action. The complete code for the examples in the book is available for download from the Manning website at https://www.manning.com/books/hugo-in-action, and from GitHub at https://github.com/hugoinaction/hugoinaction.

The resources provide easy-to-use copies of the code samples embedded throughout the book and assets like CSS files and the images used to build the example website. Code checkpoints provide working code up to the point in the book where it is referenced and are presented as branches in the GitHub repository. We can compare two checkpoints between any sections in the text to see the changes between those two sections. For example, https://github.com/hugoinaction/hugoinaction/compare/chapter-03-06...chapter-04-11 provides all the changes as commits messages between code checkpoints chapter-03-6 and chapter-04-11. It also provides a diff between the two checkpoints. Each checkpoint can also be viewed live on the book's website in a subdomain like https://chapter-04-11.hugoinaction.com, which offers a working version of the website at chapter 04, checkpoint 11. The readme file for the repository also provides summaries and links to additional chapter resources and checkpoints. You can clone the code repository locally and use `git checkout <checkpoin or chapter resource name>` to get to a specific code checkpoint or to a specific chapter's resources.

> **TIP** Code checkpoints are a vital tool in debugging issues. Some details with light documentation can be gleaned from code checkpoints. Readers can compare their code to a checkpoint to figure out and fix misunderstandings and mistakes.

liveBook discussion forum

Purchase of *Hugo in Action* includes free access to liveBook, Manning's online reading platform. Using liveBook's exclusive discussion features, you can attach comments to the book globally or to specific sections or paragraphs. It's a snap to make notes for yourself, ask and answer technical questions, and receive help from the author and other users. To access the forum, go to https://livebook.manning.com/book/hugo-in-action/discussion. You can also learn more about Manning's forums and the rules of conduct at https://livebook.manning.com/discussion.

Manning's commitment to our readers is to provide a venue where a meaningful dialogue between individual readers and between readers and the author can take place. It is not a commitment to any specific amount of participation on the part of the author, whose contribution to the forum remains voluntary (and unpaid). We suggest you try asking the author some challenging questions lest his interest stray! The forum and the archives of previous discussions will be accessible from the publisher's website as long as the book is in print.

Other online resources

The official documentation website for Hugo is https://gohugo.io/documentation/. It provides a complete list of all available Hugo parameters and features. The Hugo community at https://discourse.gohugo.io/ can be of immense help in figuring out best practices, asking for help, or providing feedback.

about the cover illustration

The figure on the cover of *Hugo in Action*, "Femme de cracovie," or "A Woman from Krakow," is taken from a collection by Jacques Grasset de Saint-Sauveur, published in 1797. Each illustration is finely drawn and colored by hand.

In those days, it was easy to identify where people lived and what their trade or station in life was just by their dress. Manning celebrates the inventiveness and initiative of today's computer business with book covers based on the rich diversity of regional culture centuries ago, brought back to life by pictures from collections such as this one.

about the cover illustration

The figure on the cover of *Hugo in Action*, "Femme de cracovie," or a woman from Krakow, is taken from a book by Jacques Grasset de Saint-Sauveur, published in 1797. Each illustration is finely drawn and colored by hand.

In those days, it was easy to identify where people lived and what their trade or station in life was just by their dress. Manning celebrates the inventiveness and initiative of today's computer business with book covers based on the rich diversity of regional culture centuries ago, brought back to life by pictures from collections such as this one.

Part 1

Static Hugo websites: Loading fast, building to last

Are you looking for a website that is fast, flexible, fully automated, and fun to build? Part 1 of *Hugo in Action* gives you a static website that loads instantly across the planet and works with minimal operational overhead.

Chapter 1 introduces Hugo and the Jamstack, and provides an understanding of the unique approach to website development practiced by Hugo users.

Chapter 2 discusses setting up the build environment and deploying a functional website to production. We will also discuss how to keep tabs on its performance and to keep our maintenance work low.

Chapter 3 takes us deep into authoring with Markdown and YAML for content and metadata, respectively. We will use Markdown's formatting capabilities and Hugo's extensions to prepare our pages for presentation on the internet.

In chapter 4, we don the hat of the website editor. The content organization with Hugo is different than most other approaches for building websites, and there are solid reasons for that. Chapter 4 also shows how intuitive and maintenance friendly Hugo's page bundles are.

In chapter 5, we shift gears and move into the developer role. The Go template language is powerful, and Hugo's function library massively amplifies that power. We will see how we can use Hugo templates for everything—from extending Markdown to automating repetitive work for the content author.

In chapter 6, the development moves from a single web page to an entire section and also provides the ins and outs of sharing templates and content within a website.

In chapter 7, we become independent of the external theme we have used since chapter 2. Here we dive into the internals of Hugo's model for web development. We write code enabling all the features we used as a content editor in chapter 4.

Finally, chapter 8 adds a new direction, where we go beyond a single website into sharing content, templates, and code across multiple websites.

As you will see, Hugo Modules is a plugin system for everybody—from content authors to editors and from user interface to business logic developers.

At the end of part 1, you will have a fast and flexible website. You will also have experience using some of the best techniques to ensure it remains fast, without a heavy investment in operations.

The Jamstack and Hugo

This chapter covers

- Jamstack basics for building websites
- Principles of static site generators
- Understanding the Hugo static site generator
- Benefits of the Hugo static site generator
- Use cases best suited for Jamstack and Hugo

If you have been associated with websites recently or have friends in similar situations, you must know how much work is involved in maintaining a website. It needs DevOps engineers, system administrators, and database architects to keep a website running on the internet. It is a full-time job for an entire team, not just an individual. The upkeep of content is so time-consuming that the creators move at an unprecedented rate to managed hosting services like WordPress.com or even to give away their content to platforms like Medium or Facebook.

Jamstack is a web development architecture that minimizes the day-to-day overhead of maintaining websites by moving the complicated pieces out of run time or by encapsulating them into easier-to-manage services. The term *Jamstack* was coined by the cofounder and CEO of Netlify, Matt Biilmann, in 2016. Jamstack forgoes databases by storing all the content into files compiled during deployment and then distributing them over a content delivery network (CDN). Application programming interfaces (APIs) provide dynamic, server-based content, maintained by third parties or hosted by cloud service providers with minimal day-to-day involvement by the website owner. This way, developers are freed from the tasks of handling security updates, denial-of-service (DoS) attacks, and constant monitoring to keep hackers at bay.

Jamstack is heavily reliant on the core web technologies of HTML, CSS, and JavaScript. It offers the ability to get up and running on the modern web quickly so we can build websites with outstanding performance, low cost, and little maintenance. It can create websites for various use cases like individual blogs, business websites, and e-commerce solutions. Jamstack works in harmony with a server-based framework by providing full support for static content. We can, however, still use a traditional framework to offer user-generated, server-based content.

Hugo is among the most popular of the current Jamstack frameworks and provides the best build speeds. It helps us enjoy web development without the annoyances of setup, upkeep, or day-to-day maintenance. There is no waiting for compilation, updates, or deployment! Hugo takes a template and a website in markup format and converts that to HTML, so the site is ready to be hosted. I congratulate you for picking up this book and embarking on the journey to radically simplify your approach to web development.

1.1 The stack in Jamstack

To understand Jamstack fully, we first need to understand the concept of a web stack. The *web stack* is a collection of software used for web application development. Some popular web stacks include LAMP (Linux Apache MySQL PHP), Microsoft .NET (IIS, ASP.NET, MS SQL Server), MEAN (MongoDB Express Angular Node.js), and MERN (MongoDB Express React Node.js). Figure 1.1 shows a typical web stack for a non-Jamstack-based website.

A web page consists of static as well as dynamic assets. Different servers serve these assets in the stack. A web server like Apache or IIS primarily hosts static assets such as images, JavaScript, and CSS in a traditional web stack. These files do not change across multiple users. A second set of assets is dynamic content, which can be different. It is based on the supplied request parameters, which include the URL, request headers, cookies, or associated HTTP POST data. An application server with software like PHP, ASP.NET, or Express takes these parameters and creates a response. It might need to do a series of requests to the database server (like MySQL or MongoDB) that holds the website's content. The application server takes this content and uses the application logic to stitch it into a JSON response (in MEAN/MERN) or, with an HTML template, into HTML content (in LAMP), which it then serves to the web browser. The web page is assembled in the browser by executing the JavaScript and styling the provided content and images with CSS.

This web architecture has been mostly the same since the beginning of the internet, but growth and increased traffic have stressed this architecture. Increasing the CPU and RAM in the servers (called *vertical scaling*) cannot handle the amount of

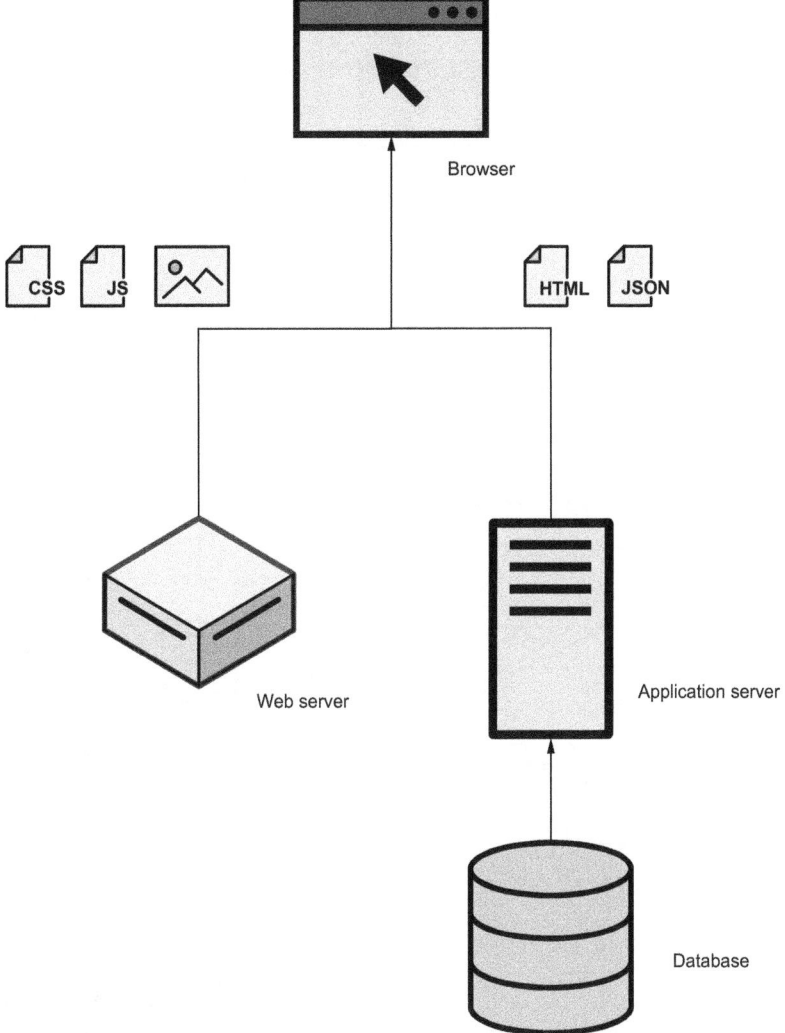

Figure 1.1 A traditional web stack used for development. Non-Jamstack websites have a stack with web servers that provide static assets. Application servers provide dynamic content, generated by using the data stored in the database server and assembled and rendered in the web browser.

traffic moving through the modern internet. This load requires us to add multiple machines (called *horizontal scaling*) to the stack.

Web servers are easy to scale. Because the content does not change, we can replicate it across multiple machines that share the load. CDNs perform the task of copying these assets across nodes geographically closer to the end user and provide internet scaling of all network traffic at faster speeds for the end user. Figure 1.2 shows the scaling strategies for the web server on the left.

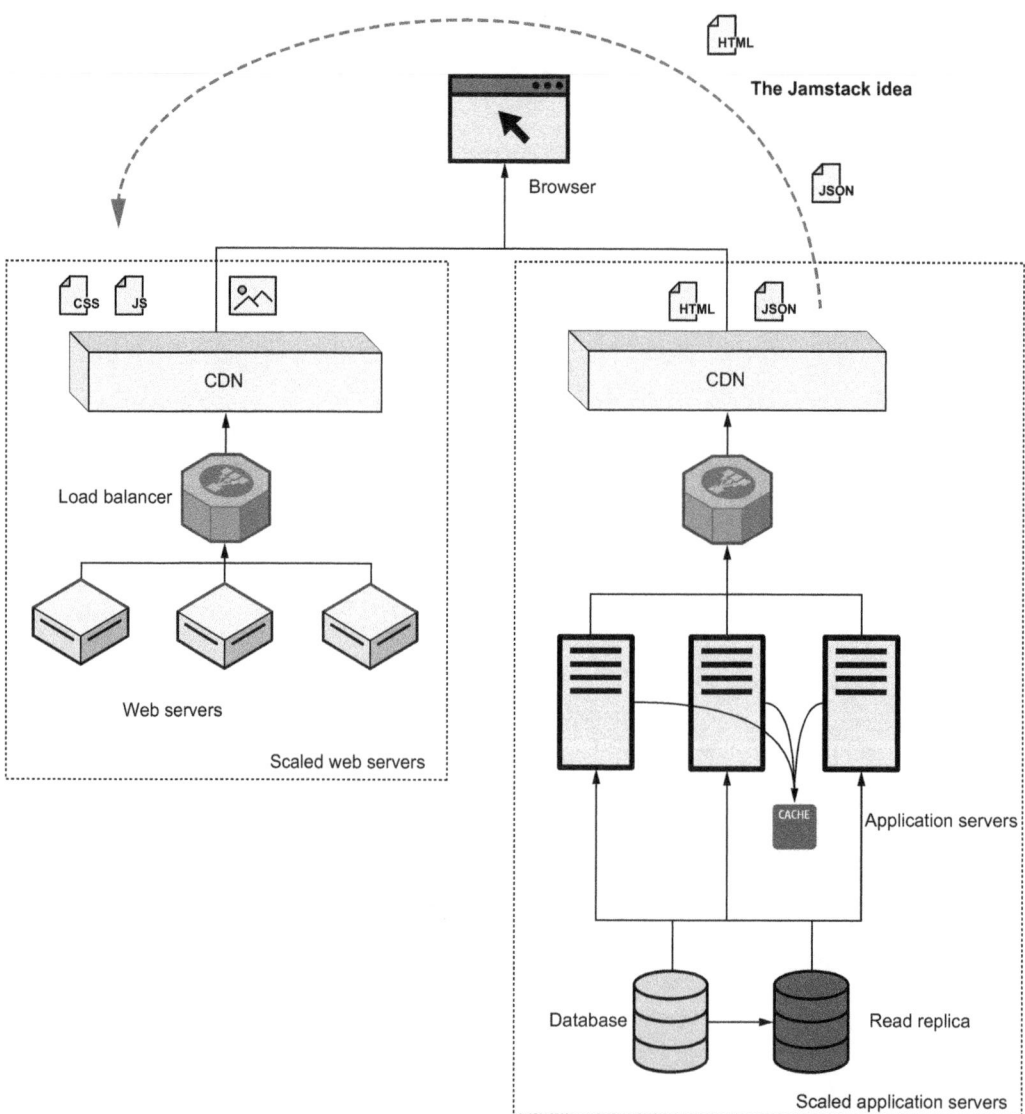

Figure 1.2 **The traditional web stack needs scaling to handle the load on the web. Horizontally scaling the web servers (left) is easy. We can add as many web servers as needed to handle the load. Scaling the application stack (right) is difficult. We cannot have hundreds of database servers (horizontal scaling), and there is a limit to the RAM and CPU capacities (vertical scaling) we can have in these servers. A variety of caching techniques are needed to solve this problem. Jamstack suggests (top) moving as much work as possible from the application servers to the web servers.**

The application layers (application and database servers) are a lot harder to scale. If we keep the requests stateless by managing the user's state on the client (via JavaScript or cookies), we can scale the application servers horizontally. Because these servers handle the application logic, it is harder to move these to a CDN.

The database layer is the hardest to scale. The *CAP theorem* tells us that scaling a regular database is not possible at the internet scale. (We cannot horizontally scale to thousands of MySQL servers.) The theorem states that in a distributed database, we can simultaneously have, at maximum, two of the three CAP properties:

- *Consistency*—Every read receives the most recent write or an error.
- *Availability*—Every request gets a (non-error) response.
- *Partition tolerance*—The system continues to operate despite an arbitrary number of messages being dropped (or delayed) by the network between nodes).

Workarounds such as eventual consistency are present in the application stack, where the database is not consistent but becomes so after some time. These workarounds lead to difficulties in the application logic and force constraints on some of the things we can achieve with server technology.

Despite the problems, the traditional web stack has survived the internet scale. One of the biggest reasons why the stack has worked despite database scalability problems is the type of load. Database changes are an order of magnitude less, in most cases, than the retrieval of that data. We can relieve the database retrieval load by adding layers of caching. Read replicas for the database and RAM-based caching on the application servers are both solutions for this. We have even found that many web pages do not change across multiple requests. Many websites can add CDNs over the application layer to ease that load. Figure 1.2 on the right shows this solution.

Looking at figure 1.2 closely, the application layer is similar to the web server layer. It is a lot harder to manage the caching layers in the application servers built for dynamic calculations. Jamstack upends the traditional web stack by moving most of the logic out of the application into the web server layer.

> **NOTE** Jamstack is not a web stack in the traditional sense. It does not prescribe any specific technology for use in developing websites. It provides an approach to web development where most of the website is prebuilt and client-side scripting adds dynamicity. This changes the nature and arrangement of software in the traditional stack.

Being explicit about trying to cache everything makes cache management a lot simpler. We can precompute and cache a lot of the work that needs dynamic computation. This *precomputation* (also called *compilation* and *prerendering* in Jamstack) provides an added benefit of enhanced performance because no calculation is needed in the server when the user requests data.

Jamstack does not prohibit server-side or client-side processing. It advises using these only when required. Precomputation during deployment is more efficient, and web servers have fewer security issues and maintenance needs than application servers.

Figure 1.3 provides a comparison of the Jamstack with the traditional web stack at run time for the first issued request that fetches the HTML page. For the initial HTML in the classic approach, the query needs to go through to the service's origin server across the internet. The load balancer then selects an application server. The

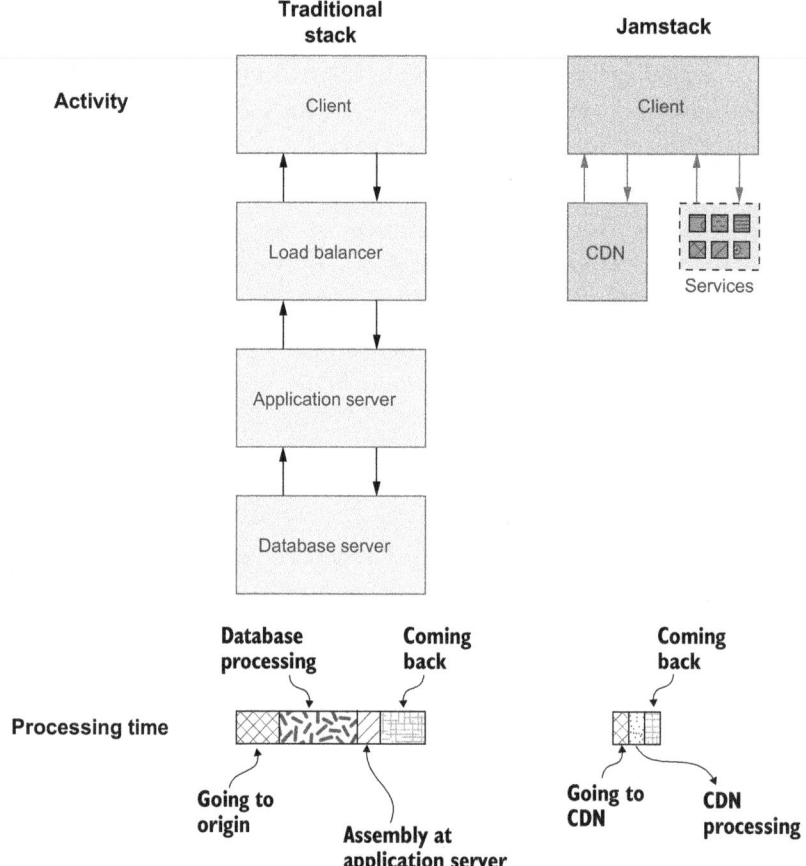

Figure 1.3   A comparison of the first request's run-time impact in a traditional web stack with the Jamstack architecture. In the conventional approach, when we request the initial HTML page, it goes through the load balancer to the application server. The application server does multiple database calls to get the data and then creates the HTML page based on the template. In the Jamstack approach, the HTML is precomputed and comes from a CDN.

application server may send multiple requests to the database to get the data it needs. It assembles the response based on the application logic and the HTML template that is a part of the application code to create the final HTML passed on to the client for rendering. With Jamstack, the compilation step has already performed database processing and application logic-based stitching. This HTML generation does not happen for every request. Therefore the request does not need to go across the internet to the origin server. A CDN location geographically close to the client serves the content.

Note that figure 1.3 shows only the initial request for data. Normally, there are additional calls for images, JavaScript, and CSS files. These requests might ask for more data from the origin server or from third-party services.

1.2 How does Jamstack work?

The simplified stack that Jamstack provides has a lot of processing going on behind the scenes. Jamstack's emphasis on the compilation process is something new for the web platform. Figure 1.4 explains the various parts of the Jamstack.

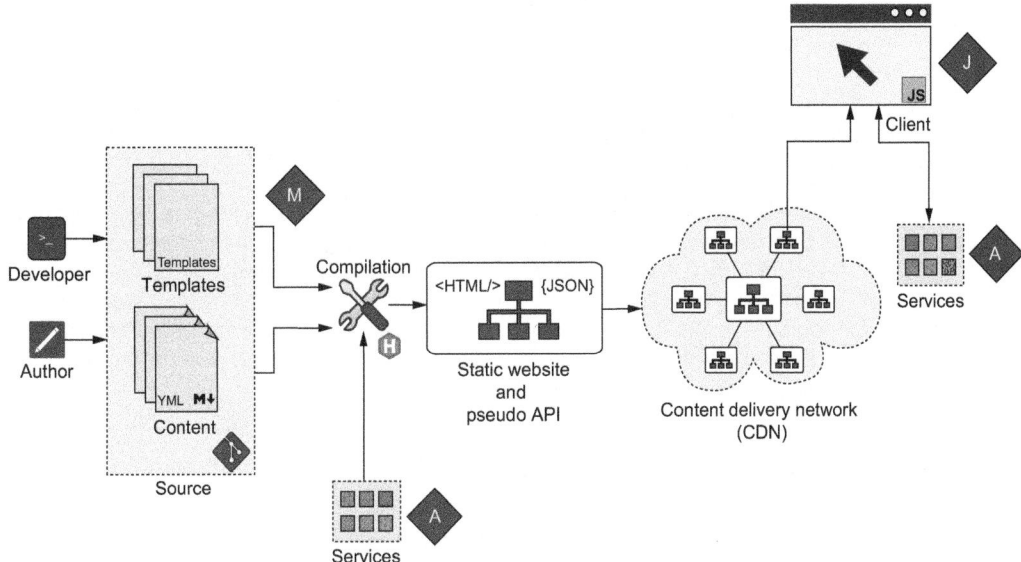

Figure 1.4 Viewing the inner workings of the Jamstack. The development and content teams maintain the source code for a Jamstack-based website. This code consists of the website data and a set of templates. A Jamstack builder picks up the code in the compilation process to create the static website's HTML/CSS/JS contents. The builder might also call services during compile time and output JSON documents that serve as an API. This output is given to the CDN to distribute geographically. The client gets the website from the closest CDN endpoint. The client executes the JavaScript code that can ask for additional data from the services.

A considerable portion of the world wide web consists of websites managed by a CMS. A *content management system* (CMS) is a tool used for creation and management of digital content. The content in most websites is kept separate from the presentation logic and can be managed by different individuals, requiring a different skill set to develop and maintain than the business logic. In a Jamstack-based website, we store the content in markup documents instead of in the database. Unlike a cell in a database table, a markup document allows for viewing and editing the page contents with a regular text-based editor. The content authors or editors can directly edit those files or use a graphical CMS if they so desire. The developer maintains the templates and the business logic to combine the data and create the website. These files can be managed in a version control system like Git and hosted on a cloud-based repository system like GitHub to manage the changes. This forms the *markup* (M) layer of the website.

A website builder like Hugo uses the data stored in markup files to compile the website into HTML and CSS files, JavaScript, and image-based assets. The builder can

Doing it old school

The approach of writing content and saving it in a folder on a disk and then uploading it to a shared hosting provider that manages the content looks a lot like the early web, where we used to upload HTML and PHP files over an FTP connection. The parallels are easy to see. These similarities raise the question, what is different this time?

The web has matured a lot since we moved away from controlling full servers. Frontend technology now performs many features that required server code back then. Additionally, shared hosting has upgraded itself to the cloud, where you can scale hosting and computation to the internet scale. Even the traditional web stack-based services are cloud-hosted.

The other significant change from that era is tooling. Tools like FrontPage originally targeted designers and end users, making the website a mesh of copy-pasted scripts that even the website author did not understand. Modern tools target developers and help in optimization, maintenance, and performance. Now we engineer websites with these tools rather than mashing them up together. We've learned from the early days of the web. We have a much better system with enough power and flexibility to build any application desired without compromises.

communicate with both external and internal services via APIs to fetch the data to compile into the website. The builder can also build the website content into a machine-friendly format like JSON. JSON files act as APIs (called *pseudo APIs*) for the markup data that the JavaScript code or native mobile apps consume.

The geographically distributed machines of a CDN host the compiled website for consumption. The CDN node closest to the end user serves this content to the end user. All the static content is user-agnostic and fast to produce. For dynamic data, JavaScript code can take over. JavaScript is the *J* layer of the Jamstack. JavaScript provides interactivity and personalization to the website.

The JavaScript layer can communicate with various services to provide dynamic content. These services expose APIs that form the *A* layer of the Jamstack. These APIs encapsulate the remains of the application servers of the traditional stack. Jamstack recommends using managed services like those owned by third parties or those hosted on a FaaS (function as a service) cloud solution to minimize maintenance.

Exercise 1.1

In Jamstack, where should most of the logic reside?

- a. Server
- b. Microservices
- c. Compiled templates
- d. Client
- e. JavaScript

1.3 The JAM in Jamstack

The *JAM* part of the Jamstack stands for JavaScript, APIs, and markup. Let's take a look at each of these components.

1.3.1 JavaScript

JavaScript in Jamstack refers to all the approaches to client-side scripting that provide interactivity and dynamic functionality, which is personalized to the user and cannot be precompiled. This enables developers to react to user actions and modifies the user interface at run time. Jamstack leaves the specifics of the JavaScript framework and its management to the web developer.

In traditional stacks, the server plays a prominent role in handling user interactions. It generates new pages even when just a part of the page needs to be modified. That is unnecessary and suboptimal. Modern JavaScript is fully capable of storing the user state in the browser. It can communicate with the server and update the interface without the user needing to reload or see a flicker in the interface. Jamstack prescribes using JavaScript for use cases where it shines the best—providing interactive interfaces to the end user and communicating from the client to the server.

1.3.2 Application programming interfaces (APIs)

Application programming interfaces (APIs) provide a well-defined contract for communicating with a web service. APIs abstract the entire server functionality so the client does not need to understand the server internals to consume the service. In Jamstack, precompilation and client-side JavaScript take over a lot of the work usually done on the server, but the server still has its use cases. These include storage of the application state across machines, computations that require more processing power than a single machine, and data that must be transmitted back from the website viewer to the servers.

Many traditional systems expose APIs to communicate with the underlying functionality. Although this approach fits in the Jamstack definition, Jamstack advises minimizing the building of APIs to reduce maintenance overhead. A lot of operations that need APIs in other stacks are handled differently in Jamstack. Instead of content creation, update, or deletion APIs, you can place, update, or remove files on disk. Only dynamic updates based on user actions in the website (like purchases and comments) need dedicated APIs.

There are third-party API providers that provide high-level APIs, which developers can use without going through the overhead of building everything themselves. From handling comments to full-text searches, a lot is available at scale without writing custom code. When we need to write a custom backend, cloud service providers make that task easier than building it from scratch. With FaaS, the cloud service providers take over the ownership of uptime, ongoing security updates, and scaling with user load. The service provider maintains performance and availability across the globe. The developer writes code and hands it over to the service provider to deploy. The ongoing work is minimal. Developers can then work to enhance functionality or update any dependencies at the function level.

1.3.3   *Markup*

The traditional definition of *markup* includes a set of annotations (like XML tags in HTML documents or stars around the text in Markdown) in a text document that provides further information on how to understand or render the text. Jamstack considers the entire markup document as markup. This consists of the textual data, the annotations, and the structured metadata.

Markup forms the data layer of the Jamstack. Unlike traditional databases, we store markup in text files. It is readable and editable by humans in its raw form without using a tool to convert it to a readable format. Markup languages provide a way to write formatted documents in a terse and readable way. Markdown is the most popular markup language for writing content in the Jamstack. (We will examine Markdown in detail in chapter 3.) Various metadata languages that we use for additional information associated with the document can accompany this content. One of these is YAML (Yaml Ain't Markup Language), which we will also discuss in chapter 3.

> **NOTE**   HTML (HyperText Markup Language) is also a markup language, and you are free to choose that for writing your data in Jamstack. Human-readable languages like Markdown, however, make it easier to read and maintain our data. This is converted to HTML during rendering, keeping the layout (template) and presentation (CSS) out of content.

There are many advantages to using a markup-based document to store data. Most of the web page is unstructured. A regular database keeps it in a single cell. This approach, however, is not a good use of database technology. We can use a version control system like Git to monitor the data changes if the data is managed as individual files. Having the data along with the code eases migration across services and build environments. We can store all configuration files together. Optimization and testing are more straightforward with the ability to create new build environments (stage, production, etc.) on demand. With unstructured content, most of the organization and querying capabilities of the databases are not helpful. Hosting blogs or generic web pages based on a database is not the best use of their resources.

With the popularity of Git and GitHub, many developers are already familiar with markup languages, especially Markdown. Most developers write readme files in a markup language. These languages are stable, standardized, easy to learn, and easy to understand. There is a lot of tooling available to write in these languages or migrate data to them. They also work well with diff and merge tools (used for comparing changes in a file), and most programming languages have libraries to parse these languages. This tooling provides extreme flexibility for programmers to manipulate data the way they like.

> ### Exercise 1.2
> What does the M in Jamstack stand for?
>
> a. markup
> b. Markdown
> c. MySQL
> d. MongoDB

1.4 Why use Jamstack?

Prebuilding HTML content presented to the user has unique advantages—from minimal operations to outstanding performance and cost reductions. We'll look at these advantages and more in the following sections.

1.4.1 Minimal operations

Because content is prebuilt before publication, the number of moving parts in a site is reduced. The service provider takes care of security updates, hardware failures, and network issues. The cloud host provides almost 100% uptime without any active involvement from the website owner. There is no need to be on call, no need to think about servers, scaling, load balancing, uptime across continents, or any other operational overhead. The developer can focus on the joy of building, and the business can focus on its core competency rather than setting up a DevOps team.

1.4.2 Great performance

CDN hosts in its entirety the prebuilt HTML provided as a static website. This way, every file is cached and served from a server geographically close to the end user. There is no round trip to an application server and no database query, which can become a bottleneck. Most site generators targeting the Jamstack generate the HTML at compile time. It is already available to render when the user requests it. The website is functional, even with a single HTTP request. A simple website built with Jamstack can provide a 90%+ performance score on most audits. If the developer is sensitive to performance while building the theme, the Jamstack-based website can meet all the criteria for a 100% score in these audits.

1.4.3 Lower costs

The removal of the database and the application servers from the hosting stack reduces the hardware costs. With the operations becoming automatic, most DevOps requirements are not present. All this translates to significant cost savings. You can have a website for free using static-site hosts like GitHub Pages and Netlify. All major cloud providers like AWS S3, Google Cloud Storage, and Azure Storage provide low-cost static hosting. There is no need to have an IT or a DevOps team for managing the fleet of servers.

1.4.4   *Developer productivity*

A version control system like Git manages a Jamstack-based website. There is no need to have complicated development environments. Running the code on the developer machine is one command away. Most websites can be deployed by a simple push to a server many times a day. These features give the developer the time and flexibility to focus on the content of the website.

1.4.5   *Longevity*

HTML/CSS is the most stable technology built. Today's browsers bend over backward to continue to support all features that they have supported since the 1990s. If you host a Jamstack-based website and vanish from the internet for a decade, it will still be there when you come back in the same state (mostly) where you left it. The internet is not forgiving to any technology stack outside of plain HTML, CSS, or JavaScript hosted on a static server. You can even continue to use the static site generator in a virtual machine without updating the version. Because the generator is local, security vulnerabilities in the generator do not impact the website. You do not need to go online and expose these vulnerabilities to the internet.

1.4.6   *Tooling*

With fewer moving parts and a well-defined structure, the tooling for Jamstack is much more advanced and powerful than other web stacks. One-click deployment is readily available with hands-off support for scaling through Netlify, GitHub Pages, and so on. Having the entire website present as code also means that there is nothing to hide. There are no complicated configurations for security or performance, no extra management overhead for different layers in the stack, and no IDE (integrated development environment).

> **Updating on the fly**
>
> When new to the Jamstack, it may seem to be a limitation that we cannot update the website on the fly. Most traditional systems provide an admin mode to update the website. The Jamstack does not prescribe anything. With the Jamstack, there is no need for any special tooling to update a Jamstack-based website.
>
> The markup language is friendly and easy to use. We can provide updates in any text editor. Most version control providers like GitHub, GitLab, and Bitbucket can commit new changes from the browser. Continuous integration can automatically build and deploy this to production. We get the benefits of having an entire version control system for our content. We also can choose our text editor freely. As a bonus, we can update the theme wherever and whenever desired. Textual content, automatic deployment, and continuous integration ensure that we do not miss WordPress's admin mode, but admin tools are also available if needed. We'll discuss the Netlify CMS in appendix C.

1.5 *When not to use the Jamstack*

One assumption of the Jamstack is that the content is available at compile time and does not change rapidly. The Jamstack does not offer a lot if this assumption turns out to be false. The following sections provide use cases for when not to use Jamstack.

1.5.1 *When there is dynamic data with no historical significance*

If we are building a dashboard-type application with ever-changing data, then precompilation as a concept does not provide great value. Sensor-based data can change within milliseconds. In many cases, no one reads this data. Jamstack does not work well with this type of application. A major exception is reporting, where some data needs to live for a long time, is read frequently, and is rarely, if ever, changed. This type of report is a perfect case to be pre-generated and saved. There is no point in doing this on the fly. The Jamstack fits the reporting use case perfectly.

1.5.2 *Building based on user-generated content with transient data*

Websites like Twitter and Facebook have tiny posts that we rarely read as individual pages. These get compiled into feeds, which are different for each user and which change over time. The users may not read the feed at any given time, so pre-generation can prove to be wasteful. These use cases do not fit into the write once, read many times scenarios the Jamstack excels at. While we could theoretically compile often-used pages, the traditional web stack can also do that. One thing to remember here is that the story changes considerably if the data has value in permanence. If we have user-generated blog posts, product pages, or articles that are written once and read many times, this comes back to the write once, read many times use case that the Jamstack is great at.

1.5.3 *Having user-specific web pages*

There are websites where the developers personalize each page for the user. This data is different because it's based on the user ID. Therefore, it might not make sense to precompile. Most users might not log in. There is no public access to bots that can cause increased load. The whole concept of many reads and a single write for the data is false. An example of this would be a calendar application. Because each user's calendar is different, it does not make sense to pre-generate everyone's daily calendar.

1.5.4 *When there is no data to compile*

Web apps are websites where the user is a creator and a consumer. For a document editor (think Google Docs), there is no data to present. In these cases, the Jamstack approach does not help.

Note that the Jamstack is helpful in all the previous cases for building the static parts of the website. These include the Privacy Policy page and the Terms of Use page. Even the About Us page and the company blog can be built optimally using the Jamstack. These pages could be set up using the Jamstack approach, while a different stack can serve the rest of the website or web application.

Exercise 1.3

Which website from the following list would be best to build with the Jamstack?

  a. A search engine
  b. A shopping website
  c. A social network
  d. An image editor

1.6 Selecting the builder

The Jamstack does not prescribe a specific technology. The developer is free to choose the technology of their liking to build the website. There is an extensive list of static site builders with various tradeoffs. These are made in different programming languages, provide integrations, and support many plugins.

Jekyll, built in Ruby, is a popular static site builder that seamlessly integrates with GitHub Pages. GitHub can automatically deploy Jekyll-based websites from a repository without writing a custom build step. Many Hugo users started their journeys with Jekyll and moved to Hugo looking for better build performance.

Hugo is among the fastest static site generators with a deep feature set. Hugo's development team has focused on building a system that can render a complicated website with hundreds of pages in less than a second. Written in Go (Golang), Hugo comes as a single binary with all batteries included. With no plugins, the core team has standardized most of its features. This standardization allows building the elements with a lot of thought focusing on maintainability and performance. Its template language is a complete programming language that we can use to create anything. The documentation is well maintained, and the community is active in the forums. Many popular websites with millions of monthly users have Hugo as their generator. The core of Hugo is stable, and while it does rapidly evolve, it has compatibility with the older versions.

There is a crop of popular JavaScript framework-based static site builders like Gatsby, Nuxt, and Next.js. These force you to follow their choices of how to write and use JavaScript. Frameworks like Next.js include features to build the API backend. If you are looking to develop a JavaScript-heavy application and agree with the decisions made by these frameworks, these might be great choices. Due to the nature of the JavaScript ecosystem, and the relatively small amount of time these frameworks have been in existence, expect some churn.

There is another set of static site builders like Pelican in Python and mdBook in Rust. These are much smaller in feature sets and popularity. Use these if you are tied to a language and want to write custom features.

1.7 Why choose Hugo?

Hugo is one of the oldest static site generators and has continued to rise in popularity over time. Its creator, Steve Francia, has extensive experience with CMS and technical writing needs. His background includes building a closed-source CMS (Supersite) that's used by Major League Soccer and Priceline. He has deep experience with Magento and WordPress and has served on Drupal's board of directors. He led the technical writing departments of both MongoDB and Docker. He took all of that experience, using the strengths of each of these systems, and channeled that into designing Hugo.

Hugo lies at the sweet spot between a tool like WordPress, which is built primarily for a nontechnical audience, and Rails or Express.js, which provide the power to generate generic software but require ongoing maintenance. With Hugo, you get the flexibility of a custom theme with less maintenance than most other options and excellent performance. Hugo is for users who don't mind getting their hands into the code and for those who need to have a life outside of their project.

> **You are not alone**
>
> Hugo is extremely popular in the industry. Websites like Bootstrap (https://getboot strap.com), Let's Encrypt (https://letsencrypt.org), Smashing Magazine (https://www.smashingmagazine.com), Netlify (https://www.netlify.com/), and 1Password Support (https://support.1password.com/) use Hugo at scale. Smashing Magazine migrated its website with thousands of pages from WordPress to Hugo because of Hugo's performance and ease of use.

1.7.1 Hugo is fast

Hugo is the fastest feature-rich static site builder available. While we may not appreciate this when starting a project, this is extremely important in our day-to-day lives. Waiting for compilation or refreshes is a significant reason for developer frustration and can mean a project's death if it's a hobby. Performance becomes even more critical when technology modifications force us to go through a substantial change in our website template. For example, the advent of mobile devices brought death to many WordPress themes, where updating every aspect was so painful that developers gave up. Moreover, a Hugo-based website continues to provide a respectable development performance even with a decade worth of content. A Hugo-based website's facelift or rewrite is easier and more enjoyable than with any slower framework.

> **Hugo and the Go language**
>
> One concern people have is that adopting Hugo means learning the Go language. While this is true for other static site generators written in scripting languages, this is not true for Go-based applications. *There is no need to learn Go or to understand how it works to be successful with Hugo.* Just like people don't need to learn C++ to use Windows or Photoshop, Hugo does not require any Go programming knowledge. This book does not have a single line of Go code. The Go programming language has built-in support for concurrency. Writing code with parallel execution is easier in Go than in many other programming languages used to build website generators. Hugo benefits immensely from Go's speed without additional complexity.

(continued)

Hugo's users use the Go template language, which, despite the name, is a different language from Go itself. It allows us to write anything we want, including modules and functions, without dealing with a lot of complexity with multithreaded code. You may not even need the Go template language if you don't plan to write a custom theme or a shortcode. You can write content in a markup language and pick a theme off the shelf to build your website.

Most other Jamstack-based website builders have a single-threaded, sequential-flow source language. This approach allows them to have plugins, but you pay massively in the form of performance. With the most significant features available in Hugo, there is no need to compromise on build performance and developer experience with a slow framework.

Go is among the newer languages (publicly released in 2009), but it has broken into mainstream development. It is a top-10 language in terms of adoption. Major projects including Docker and Kubernetes are written in Go. Also, most of the cloud is written in Go, including AWS, Azure, and Google Cloud Platform (GCP). Major enterprises including Google, American Express, and Dropbox use Go extensively.

Conveniently, Hugo's creator, Steve Francia, also serves as the product and strategy lead for the Go programming language at Google. Consequently, Hugo is a project that is well understood by the Go team. It influences the programming language itself and can adopt the best of its features.

1.7.2   Hugo is stable

The core features of Hugo have been supported for a long time and are not likely to break. Any new additions make sure that these features are not disturbed and continue to work as-is. In the early days of Hugo, development moved slowly as the team focused on getting the architecture right. This approach has paid off. Hugo is flexible and extensible to new features, and most releases do not break the thousands of websites built with it.

The Hugo development team believes in the continuous evolution of Hugo while maintaining backward compatibility. Hugo attempts to be backward-compatible across releases and guides us in upgrading if something needs to change. If you pick an old theme and get the latest version of Hugo, you might get some warnings, but most of it should continue to work.

1.7.3   Hugo is built for performance

The Hugo community has a tendency to look for performance gains in everything they do. There is a lot of advice on improving your website's performance in easy-to-do steps in the community forums. If you find a random script from the internet for doing something with Hugo, there is a high likelihood that its author has optimized it for performance.

The core performance of Hugo also impacts its output. The performance primitives are available for other uses. Developers can learn from the approach that Hugo uses for optimizing their workflows.

1.7.4 *Hugo is self-contained*

A plugin-heavy system appears to provide a lot of flexibility and capabilities until maintenance rolls around. Your site can get into a bad state even if one plugin is abandoned while the framework is being actively maintained! Plugin abandonment has been a classic problem with frameworks like Rails, where each major version became a massive pain for migrating all the plugins. We can see the same in the ecosystems like Backbone and Angular, where there are many stale plugins. Even Jekyll, which is extremely popular and actively maintained, has a considerable problem of *plugin rot.*

Being self-contained has allowed Hugo to bypass issues that have plagued other projects. The core team has standardized optimal approaches to perform tasks that are available natively. The Hugo team has optimized Hugo without needing lower-level API compatibility. They continue to write complicated multithreaded logic for the standardized workflows to eke out the few extra milliseconds that their users can spend elsewhere. Hugo's users get a lot more support than they would from the plugin authors and have less fear of abandoning their core workflows.

Being self-contained does not mean Hugo is not extensible. The Go template language is potent, and users can share snippets of code as modules that can be reused and that can perform complicated logic using this language.

1.7.5 *Hugo is a single file*

Hugo packages all its core dependencies and resources in to a single executable file. A single file makes downloading Hugo, transferring it to another machine, and backing it up extremely simple. In systems where each file has a lot of scrutiny due to security concerns, a single binary file with no other dependencies shines. Developers can merge the Hugo binary with their source code to use it in a restricted environment. With a single file taking care of everything, there are no dependencies to update and no build systems to manage. The full web stack with custom APIs can be built with a handful of dependencies. This freedom is in stark contrast to JavaScript-based static site builders, which have hundreds of dependencies, each of which might need to be vetted by a security team for usage in an enterprise environment.

1.7.6 *Hugo can be extremely low maintenance*

With fewer moving parts (plugins and operating system dependencies), a tiny installation footprint, no database, and no complicated hosting steps, the maintenance churn with Hugo can be a lot less than with other web development approaches. Each dependency needs to be maintained. You can get a compelling website with low maintenance with just Hugo and a hosting provider. While Hugo has had updates where backward compatibility has broken (for valid performance, extensibility, and maintainability reasons), you are free to take the updates when you have time, and you do not have to fix arcane plugins. We cannot say this about most other ecosystems in the web development world.

1.7.7   *Hugo can save you from analysis paralysis*

Hugo is opinionated and built with a lot of techniques to get up and running quickly. While the powerful template system allows you to roll out a custom solution to a problem, the Hugo team has already solved the most common ones. Hugo has generic implementations for pagination, categorizing content into unlimited types of categories, and getting core website elements like menus. Getting up and running is easy with Hugo because there is a well-documented and widespread approach to solving most problems readily available.

1.7.8   *Hugo is powerful*

Despite being opinionated, Hugo is versatile. The Go template language that Hugo extends is powerful and flexible. This power provides the ability for developers to write proper programs with Hugo. The standard library provided by Hugo is enormous and growing. It comes with outstanding performance right from the start. Even if you write terrible code, the core performance of the built-in functions ensures a relatively good performance for the website's compilation. With access to APIs during website generation, Hugo provides a lot of power without losing the generated output's performance.

You can write functions anywhere in your website with Hugo, including while developing content (as custom shortcodes embedded in the markup) to do some special processing. You can encapsulate that into something that you can reuse or leave as one-time snippets of code on specific pages.

Hugo has lots of web development primitives. Still, not using them does not seem like fighting the framework. If you don't want to use a feature provided by Hugo and build your own using the template language, the experience with the rest of Hugo does not deteriorate. Hugo provides good support for interacting with APIs and JavaScript that can provide extensibility and dynamicity where needed.

1.7.9   *Hugo is scalable*

Hugo already caters to websites with multilingual content, having thousands of pages and millions of monthly active users. Hugo has a proven record of handling the scale of some of the biggest and most heavily used websites on the internet. There are already enough primitives and capabilities to scale the Hugo-based website from a developer to a team. Hugo supports a wide variety of input and output formats. It has various features to enable the automation of the day-to-day work for a nontechnical member of the team.

1.7.10   *Hugo is a community project*

A community of volunteers maintains Hugo with no commercial interest in the project. This voluntary nature allows for the direction of the project to be in the community's best interest. Hugo cannot pivot, get acquired, or shut down at the whim of a corporation.

Figure 1.5   DevOps and the Jamstack: Alex, the web developer, talks to Bob, who works as a system/IT admin. Bob convinced management to use a cloud-based solution with the existing technology and drop the investigation into the Jamstack.

1.8   Is speed really important?

We cannot emphasize enough the importance of build performance. Hugo employs many techniques to speed up build times, like having a multithreaded core with support for caching at all layers to prevent as much rework as possible. Speed frees the developer from the burden of waiting for the build to complete after every small change.

If you launch Hugo in watch mode (a special mode for development), the website comes up in less than a second. It reloads with your edits without having to go through the entire step of setting up fancy hot module replacements for live reloads. This feature is not just for the themes but for the whole of the website! We get the flexibility to edit the website in the 5 minutes that we might have between other chores. In other frameworks, getting up and ready is in itself a task.

Because you don't need to recompile your site after changes, the developer can make changes or experiment and see results quickly. The same is the case with data entry. A significant burden with static site builders and slow build times is that committing data is something that the content writer needs to plan for because getting up and running itself can take time. The flexibility of WordPress and the performance of the Jamstack are not either/or with a framework like Hugo.

With performance at Hugo's core and all the primitives exposed, as a developer you start to rethink your website-building strategy. Does this code need to go into JavaScript that has to run on every one of the billion customer machines that visit this page, or can we write this so it runs once and saves the results as SVGs or precomputed

HTML so that our customers don't have to re-execute? These minor tweaks while building go a long way in improving the website's performance.

> ### Exercise 1.4
> Hugo is built using which programming language?

1.9   What can we build with Hugo?

The Jamstack is a versatile concept, and we can apply it to a variety of problems. Hugo has been a poster child for the success of the Jamstack with its ability to handle scale. Hugo shines when information flows from the server to the client, then the users can focus on consumption rather than creation. This approach fits the traditional definition of publishing, where content creators provide content via a medium like the web to consumers. The following sections introduce us to the things that Hugo specializes in.

1.9.1   Personal websites and blogs

Hugo is well suited for getting up and running with a personal website. Big goals for personal websites are low maintenance, low costs, and the flexibility to showcase your tastes. Throughout this book, you will see how we can build something with little supervision, almost free hosting, and enough flexibility to customize as much as you desire. You get outstanding performance, the ability to update when and where you want, full SEO support, and a quick start.

You can pick up any publicly available Hugo theme to get started and be up and running with a decent website in minutes. (You will be surprised at how many features are available without any customization.) Once there, it is straightforward to fork the theme and start customizing it to leave your unique impression on the internet.

1.9.2   Nontechnology business websites

Hugo scales to teams updating content in parallel without any problem. Businesses whose core competencies do not include building websites need something easy to maintain, with low cost, and outstanding performance. They also want flexibility and control. Hugo ticks all of these boxes. It is well thought out and easy to understand for any vendor team. Hugo provides few places where a developer could write harmful code that would slow down the website. The entire mechanism is flexible enough to add the one custom page that the business needs immediately without going through and ripping apart the whole website.

With the JavaScript and API layer of the Jamstack, you can extend Hugo websites to provide features reserved for dynamic websites updating on the fly. You will see in this book how we can build low-cost, low-maintenance features like shopping carts while statically managing the rest of the website.

1.9.3　Documentation websites

Hugo has excellent support for reading structured data from a CSV or JSON files and then creating a website from those, and you can still apply custom themes! It has built-in support for syntax highlighting and can scale to a large number of pages quickly. These make it well suited to write custom websites that can read from the API docs and prepare a neatly formatted version from the specification.

1.9.4　Hybrid Jamstack-based websites

All websites have pages for displaying content. These pages include, for example, a privacy policy, a generic About Us page, a blog, a product listing page, and a newsroom where the company releases press statements. Hugo and the Jamstack can help keep that content running at a low cost with high availability and good performance. The server technology-based pages can be delivered separately or can be built-in JavaScript, communicating with the servers using APIs exposed by them.

> **Exercise 1.5**
> True or False: Hugo-based websites require the full setup to be present locally to write content.

1.10　Cases that don't map to Hugo

Like all tools, Hugo has its use cases. Apart from all the Jamstack limitations that apply to any of the Jamstack frameworks, we need to understand that Hugo's focus is on the markup portion of the Jamstack only. While Hugo provides the fastest available JavaScript bundler and has good support for the npm ecosystem, it takes a hands-off approach to the JavaScript and the API layers of the Jamstack. If you want to build a tool which requires a lot of JavaScript to intermingle with the static pages, or you want to have an API that shares code with the website template, Hugo's approach of having these pieces independent falls short.

Hugo might not be optimal when we need some functionality that Hugo does not have, and we cannot achieve that with an API. Hugo keeps its core inaccessible to the templates and modules to maintain its flexibility and to keep its performance intact. Hugo is likely not the right choice for developers wanting to build a customized static site builder with lots of plugins catering to an uncommon use case. For example, if we need to interact with the SOAP or FTP protocols at compile time, that may not be possible with Hugo (as of v0.91.2).

1.11　How to be successful with Hugo and this book

In this book, we will build the website for Acme Corporation, a leading manufacturer of digital shapes. The website will have regular company pages, a blog with support for dynamic comments and searches, a JavaScript-based shape editor, and a storefront to purchase your shapes delivered over email. The final version of the website that we will build in this book is hosted at https://chapter-13-09.hugoinaction.com/.

We will start with the markup layer of the Jamstack, which Hugo excels in. We will talk about creating and organizing markup-based documents in a Hugo website, how to use those to render web pages, creating themes that share the web templates, and how to use modules to create reusable content and template code. In the second part of the book, we will delve into Hugo's support for the JavaScript and API portions of the Jamstack. We will see how to call APIs at compile time and run time, build simple Jamstack-based APIs, and use JavaScript to enhance the user experience. We will also compile and bundle a complex JavaScript application with a Hugo-based website.

To succeed with this book, you need a machine with a modern operating system, access to the internet, a web browser, and an understanding of tools and programming languages familiar to a web developer. These include HTML, CSS, JavaScript, Git, GitHub, any template engine such as Mustache, Jade, or Embedded Ruby (ERB), and optionally npm. The code samples are all available on GitHub and hosted at https://hugoinaction.com. We recommended using the diff between the various files to compare the changes done locally to those present in the code samples.

> **Exercise 1.6**
> Hugo works on the _____ layer of the Jamstack.

Summary

- Jamstack is an approach to web development where most content is stored along with the theme as files and compiled into the website during deployment.
- The static content in Jamstack is written in a markup language, which compiles to HTML. The dynamic pieces are available in the form of APIs accessed via JavaScript.
- The Jamstack architecture provides massive savings in cost, operations, and maintenance. We also get a fast website.
- Hugo is a framework to help build these so-called static websites, which provide outstanding build performance, and Hugo is available as a single binary.
- Hugo meets the promise of low ongoing maintenance and a great developer experience, and it scales to a large team.
- Hugo especially shines at places where the information flow is from the server to the client, such as personal or company websites, news posts, blogs, documentation, and so forth.
- For places where the information flow is from the client to the server or personalized based on the user, Hugo follows the Jamstack approach. The JavaScript layer is responsible for communicating with the servers over an API.

Live in 30 minutes: You now have a website

This chapter covers

- Running the Hugo command line
- Setting up a Hugo website with themes and content
- Outlining the structure of a Hugo-based website
- Setting up a continuous deployment pipeline
- Measuring performance and analyzing website maintainability

Hugo is quick and easy to get started with. You can download Hugo and get going using just a basic text editor and a web browser. This chapter navigates through the entire length of Jamstack's flow as figure 2.1 illustrates. We will create a website for a company named Acme Corporation. Acme Corporation is a leading manufacturer of shapes like lines, circles, squares, and triangles in digital form. We will use the Hugo command line to bootstrap the website (section 2.1) with a prebuilt theme (section 2.2) and some ready-to-use content (section 2.3). We will also host the website on the internet (section 2.4) and analyze the decisions made in this

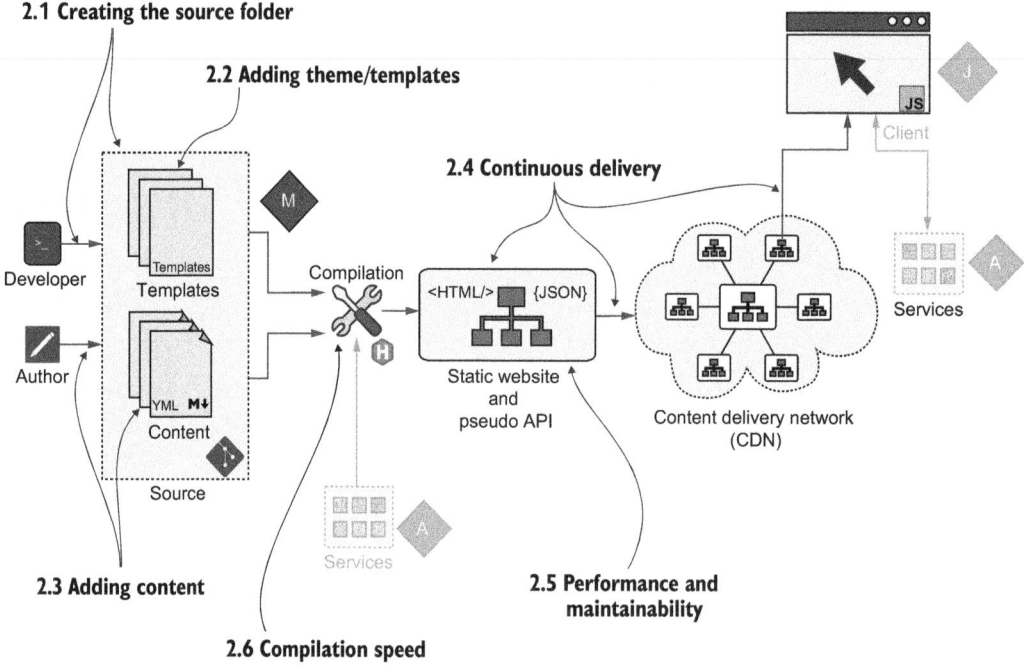

Figure 2.1   This chapter runs through the entire flow of the Jamstack—from the developer to the published website.

chapter for performance and maintainability (section 2.5). Note that we will enhance this website throughout the book.

Appendix A provides the information to get up and running with Hugo. You can also use the official website at https://gohugo.io/ to download Hugo as well as to refer to its documentation. Hugo is available on all major platforms. For this book, you need Hugo with a version greater than or equal to 0.91.2.

2.1   Your first Hugo website

Hugo offers an extensive command line that exposes all of its functionality, including bootstrapping a new website. This section introduces you to Hugo's command line.

2.1.1   The Hugo command line

Hugo is a command-line tool that's well designed and provides all of Hugo's functionality. It helps by migrating data, creating placeholders, and analyzing performance, along with the core task of building your website. The Hugo command line has two distinct parts:

- *Commands*—Determine tasks that you want Hugo to do. You can supply commands and subcommands by using `hugo [command]` on the command line. Hugo's commands are hierarchical. A plain `hugo` call runs the default command to build the site. Issue `hugo new` to create new things. The default for `hugo new` creates new content pages. You can use `hugo new site` to build a site skeleton, and `hugo new theme` to generate a theme.

- *Flags (also called command-line parameters)*—Specify options that modify the result of the command by providing a different configuration. Flags are specific to the command, and each command can have independent flags. For example, `--format yaml` in the `new site` command changes the metadata format from the default TOML to YAML.

An intuitive way to learn the Hugo command line is to use the `--help` flag. Help with Hugo is hierarchical: `hugo --help` provides help for the `hugo` command and lists `hugo new` as a subcommand; `hugo new --help` provides documentation for the `new` command and mentions `site` as a subcommand. Hugo's help also shows all the flags available for each command. You can also generate the Hugo command-line documentation in the man pages format (as used by the `man` command in UNIX-based operating systems). For this, use `hugo gen man` or use `hugo gen doc` for Markdown files.

Let's see how all this fits together by creating our first website. To create a new website in Hugo, we'll use the command in the following listing.

Listing 2.1   Hugo command to create a new website

```
hugo new site acme-corporation --format yaml
```

This command creates the Hugo skeleton folder structure with YAML as the metadata language in a subfolder called acme-corporation in the current folder. The various parts of this command are labeled in figure 2.2. Note that we'll use YAML (https://yaml.org/) instead of the default TOML (https://toml.io) metadata language for this book. YAML is more prevalent in the general programming community, less verbose than TOML, and GitHub has better support for it. It is an easier language to get started with and a better choice for users new to the entire Hugo ecosystem. We will discuss YAML as a metadata language for Hugo in chapter 3. Appendix B discusses TOML as the metadata language option. Note that the official Hugo documentation provides metadata in all supported languages.

**Command and
subcommand to execute**

```
hugo new site --format=yaml
```

**The Hugo
command line**   **Parameters to pass
to the command**

Figure 2.2   The `hugo` command provides access to the Hugo command line. We can use all of Hugo's functionality via this command line. You can use it to compile Hugo websites, run the development server, measure build performance, and access modules.

Exercise 2.1

Which of the following allow you to get help on Hugo?

  a. `--help` flag
  b. `man` command
  c. Hugo website
  d. All of the above

2.1.2   *Adding to source control*

The first step in any project is to commit the changes to a version control repository. The command-line interface does not have native undo/redo support. If you accidentally delete a file, it does not go to the recycle bin or to the trash folders. Any running script has the potential to cause data loss, including the `hugo` command. There is no turning back unless you have versioned the source code.

Version control systems allow for recovering deleted files and reverting to older versions. The version control system used in this book is Git. Git is the most popular system, and GitHub has tight integration for it. This also includes GitHub Pages, the most popular host for static websites on the internet. It is a good idea to commit each checkpoint to version control. You can use the `git` command or a GUI client like SourceTree or Fork to perform these tasks. On the command line, you can perform this using multiple Git commands as the following listing shows. To help with version control, take note of the code checkpoints where you can pause to check your code.

Listing 2.2   Git commands to create a new repository

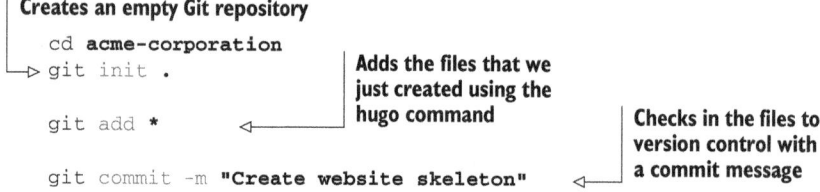

Creates an empty Git repository

```
cd acme-corporation
git init .
```
Adds the files that we just created using the hugo command
```
git add *
```
Checks in the files to version control with a commit message
```
git commit -m "Create website skeleton"
```

Even though we created a website skeleton, that does not mean we have a working website. Most of the skeleton folders created by the `hugo` command are empty. At the bare minimum, we need to provide some content and a theme to render it on our website.

CODE CHECKPOINT   https://github.com/hugoinaction/hugoinaction/tree/chapter-02-01

NOTE   Extra files (Readme.md, License.md, and .gitignore) were added to the repository on the server for better GitHub support.

Migrating to Hugo

Hugo supports importing content from Jekyll and automatically converts content from that format to a format that Hugo understands. You can use the `hugo import jekyll <source jekyll folder> <target hugo folder>` command to import the `folder`-equivalent content from Jekyll into a Hugo website. This command does not provide synchronization, but we can use it for a one-time import.

2.1.3 *Structure of the Hugo source folder*

Before adding a theme or some content, let's look at what makes up a Hugo website. A Hugo source folder is more than templates and content. The hugo new command generates six folders, and we will create more as we use Hugo's features. The critical folders in our website, as figure 2.3 shows, include the following:

- *archetypes*—Contains the templates for the content files. Hugo tries to minimize the copy and paste work needed to create content. We can create templates for Markdown files or folders in this folder, and Hugo uses them to create a basic content file. We will get to archetypes in chapter 5.
- *content*—Contains all the content that traditionally goes into the database. We can organize the content into files and folders as we desire. By default, Hugo generates the website output directly, based on this folder's structure, although we can override that using the metadata in each file (called *front matter*, which we will discuss in chapter 3). We will work with the content folder throughout the book.
- *data*—Stores structured content in the form of YAML, TOML, CSV, or JSON files, which are made available as global variables throughout the website. A traditional database houses more than just web page content. There can be tables associated with structured data, which have no place in the content folder, so this folder comes in handy when we generate content from outside of Hugo and pass that information in as a JSON or a CSV file for Hugo to consume. We will read from the data folder in chapter 5.
- *layouts*—Overrides parts of the theme. Hugo gives us the flexibility to mix and match pages from themes and to write our own custom pages. In this folder, all customization of the theme occurs. We can use this directory to store these overridden theme layouts. The line between a theme and layout is blurred, and Hugo gives us total flexibility to create a theme slowly by overriding pages one by one. We will use the layouts folder to update the home page in this chapter and go into layouts in detail in chapters 6 and 7.
- *themes*—Contains the code that we use to make the content in the content folder presentable. We can use the Go template language to write themes. We will add themes in this chapter and create our own in chapter 7.

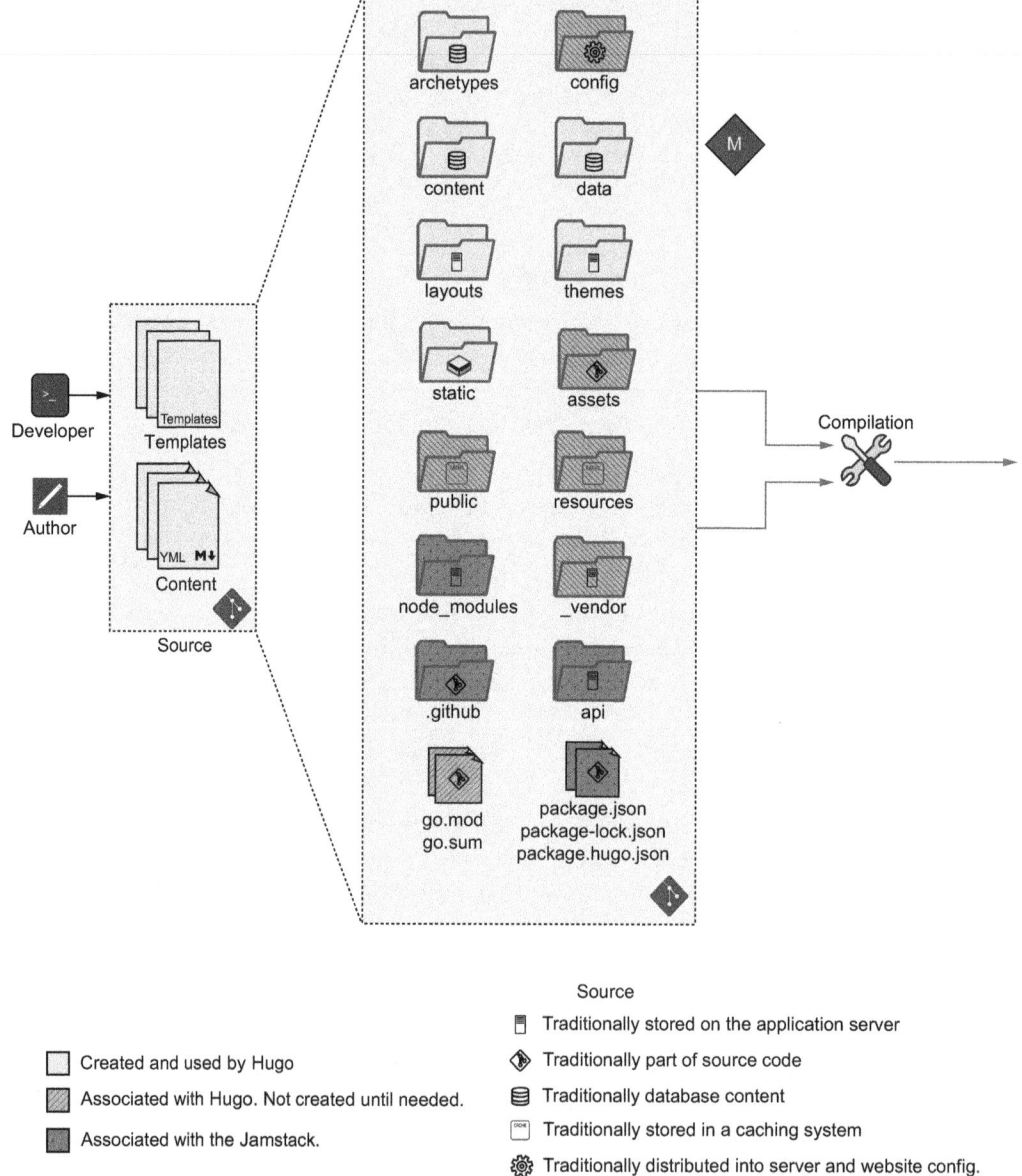

Source
- Traditionally stored on the application server
- Traditionally part of source code
- Traditionally database content
- Traditionally stored in a caching system
- Traditionally distributed into server and website config.

☐ Created and used by Hugo

▨ Associated with Hugo. Not created until needed.

▧ Associated with the Jamstack.

Figure 2.3 The website source code and content in Hugo lies in the source folder. The `hugo new` command creates a basic set of folders, which designates the various parts of a Hugo website: the archetypes folder (for the content templates), the content folder (for the textual content), the data folder (for structured content, and key-value pairs), the layouts and themes folders (for templates and individual page designs), and the static folder (for additional content that needs to be hosted but does not fit into any other category). Other folders and files that show up during usage include assets (for unprocessed images and JS/CSS files), config (for settings and metadata, initially generated as a single file), resources (for caching processed assets), public (to hold the output), vendor and go.sum/mod (for Hugo Modules), package*.json and node_modules (for JavaScript), .github/netlify.toml (for continuous integration), and api (for custom first-party APIs).

- *config*—Houses the website's configuration. This directory contains the metadata shared across the website, including the theme's name and any parameters that need to be passed to Hugo or to the theme to render content. By default, Hugo creates a single config.yaml file. Hugo supports splitting this configuration file into multiple files and having different environments for testing and production. That turns the configuration into a folder. We will go into the configuration in detail in chapter 4.
- *static*—Stores static content like fonts or PDF files. Hugo copies this content as is to the output directory. This folder is somewhat equivalent to the Apache/Nginx web server root folder, where you can place any HTML file for rendering. It is advisable to put as much content as possible in the content, data, themes, and layouts folders to have programmatic access to it and to benefit from Hugo's render pipeline. In the static folder, we can store binaries files like .pdf, .woff (for web fonts), and .zip files for downloadable content that does not belong anywhere else. We will put some files in the static folder in this chapter.

Of all these folders, the content folder is where we usually spend the most time adding content to the website. The themes folder contains the theme that the developer can manage outside the website. In contrast, we change the other folders (except for the data folder for the data-driven web pages) infrequently, only when something significant needs to be added.

Exercise 2.2

Which of the following folders contains the text displayed on a web page?

- a. markup
- b. markdown
- c. content
- d. data
- e. text

When building your Hugo-based website, here are some other files and folders that you will encounter:

- *assets folder*—Places images, JavaScript, and CSS files as unprocessed source code to be consumed globally from the website. This folder allows us to process these files during compilation. Hugo can resize images, bundle and minify JavaScript files, and convert SCSS to CSS via its asset pipeline (Hugo Pipes). We will learn about image manipulation and asset bundling in chapter 6 and work with JavaScript assets in chapter 10.
- *public folder*—Hugo's default output directory, where the `hugo` command generates the HTML output to be deployed and cached at the CDN.

- *resources folder*—When processing data, Hugo caches the results of heavy operations in this folder. We should put this folder into our version control and reuse its data across builds. This folder is one of the critical ingredients for getting outstanding performance with Hugo. Processing images is a CPU-intensive operation and takes time. Most assets don't change across builds, and caching the processed images for as long as they do not change provides Hugo with a significant performance boost.

- *go.mod and go.sum files*—Hugo Modules uses these files to synchronize project dependencies. We rarely look into these files, but we do need to put these files in version control. We will introduce these files in chapter 8.

- *vendor folder*—Stores third-party dependencies that we can include via Hugo Modules. We will create this folder while working with Hugo Modules in chapter 8.

- *node__modules, package.json, package-lock.json, and package.hugo.json files*—Associates and integrates Hugo with the JavaScript ecosystem. We will discuss using JavaScript with Hugo in detail in chapter 10.

- *.github folder and netlify.toml files*—Associates Hugo with the continuous integration services GitHub and Netlify. We will use these services throughout the book.

- *api folder*—Although not standard, we'll create this folder to house custom APIs in chapter 11.

Exercise 2.3

Match the file type to the most likely folder to place the file.

1. YAML   a. assets
2. Markdown   b. static
3. PDF   c. content
4. HTML   d. config
5. CSS   e. themes

2.2 Adding a theme

Coming back to Acme Corporation's sample website, before that website can see the light of the day, it needs a theme and some content. A *theme* in Hugo represents all the logic that converts markup documents into presentable web pages. It consists of template code, JavaScript, and CSS assets and images used for common elements like icons and backgrounds. Creating a Hugo theme is time-consuming, and it is a good idea to try out some prebuilt themes to begin with.

NOTE If you plan to use a theme created by someone else, you may not need to learn the Go template language to use Hugo.

You can create a website by learning a markup language like Markdown and a meta-data language like YAML. You can always modify the theme to customize the UI, but if you want to get a website up and focus on the content, you only need to know a content markup and a metadata language. For Acme Corporation, we will start with a pre-built theme that's ready to use. There are multiple ways to get a theme:

- *Use Hugo Modules to integrate the theme.* Hugo Modules is Hugo's package management system that allows themes to have dependencies. Hugo can automatically fetch dependencies required by a theme when building your site using Hugo Modules. Themes with dependencies will not work with other integration methods. Hugo Modules have setup requirements that we will discuss when introducing it in chapter 8.
- *Use Git Submodules to reference the theme in the themes folder.* The Git version management system can set this up for you. This allows one Git repository to include another repository as a module within it. The dependencies can be linked to another server location and built independently. While the submodule feature is a part of Git and needs no separate installation, it still needs to be set up.

   This feature is less potent than Hugo Modules. Theme authors who have not updated their themes to support Hugo Modules mention Git Modules as the integration method for their theme. However, over time, the use of Git Submodules will diminish in the Hugo world, and we do not recommend using it in newer themes and websites.

- *Download and copy the theme to the themes folder.* The download-and-copy approach is the simplest of techniques. Because the theme code is available locally, we can easily read it to understand what the theme is doing, modify it, and view our website's updates. When developing a new theme, this approach allows for making changes quickly and saves us from the overhead of managing different repositories. To simplify getting started, we will use the download-and-copy approach for the book's first seven chapters.

2.2.1 Adding a theme to the website

We can find themes on the Hugo website at https://themes.gohugo.io/. While most themes work with the download-and-copy approach, some may have dependencies for which Hugo Modules are necessary. We will use the Eclectic theme, which has no such requirements. A copy of the Eclectic theme is provided in the code samples accompanying this book (https://github.com/hugoinaction/hugoinaction/tree/chapter-02-resources/01). It is also available at https://github.com/hugoinaction/Eclectic.

We need to download and paste the Eclectic folder into the themes folder for our website for it to be made available. The files are present in the proper subfolder so that you can place them in the root folder of the website. Each listing comes with the path to the file and the filename where the changes need to be made. For loading

Eclectic as the theme for our website, we need to specify it in the website configuration file using the theme key. Listing 2.3 tells Hugo to look for a folder named Eclectic in the themes folder and to load the theme from that folder.

NOTE   In the chapter resources throughout the book, the files are provided in the proper relative paths from the website root and need to be placed in the exact same relative location for your website.

Listing 2.3   Updating the theme in the config file (config.yaml)

```
...                    ⊲────── Existing data that's generated
theme: Eclectic               by the hugo new command.
```

CODE CHECKPOINT   https://chapter-02-02.hugoinaction.com, and source code: https://github.com/hugoinaction/hugoinaction/tree/chapter-02-02.

NOTE   You can compare various GitHub branches by navigating to https://github.com/hugoinaction/hugoinaction/compare/chapter-02-01..chapter-02-02, where chapter-02-01 and chapter-02-02 are branch names. The Readme file at https://github.com/hugoinaction/hugoinaction provides every code checkpoint (along with its respective section), a link to the hosted version, and the diff from the previous code checkpoint. It is a good idea to view the hosted version of a code checkpoint before reading the corresponding section of this book.

2.2.2   *Running the dev server*

We can run our Acme website in development mode using the command hugo server on the command line (we could also use hugo serve). This command creates a development server that provides local content. The development server mode compiles the code automatically when changed. It has near real-time updates to the website's locally-hosted version (popularly called *live reload*) with content changes. The default port (the location in the machine where we can find the website) for Hugo is 1313, and unless something else is running at that port (in which case, it can be changed by --port <number> flag), the development mode website should be available there. You can open http://localhost:1313 in your browser to find the default website as figure 2.4 shows. The default home page is unique to most themes but needs configuration to be used.

Listing 2.4 shows how we can run the Hugo development server by using the hugo server command. This command hosts the Hugo-based website locally at http://localhost:1313/ by default. It automatically rebuilds the server as the content changes so that we can view it in the web browser.

There is no default website logo.

By default Hugo gives each website the name My New Hugo Site.

Eclectic applies a default background.

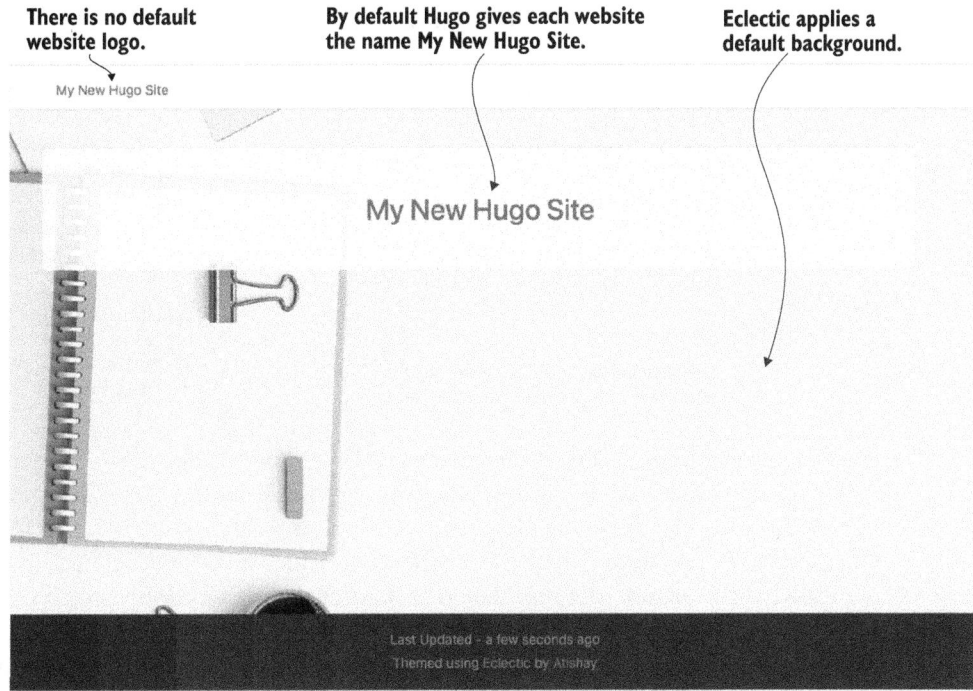

My New Hugo Site

My New Hugo Site

Last Updated - a few seconds ago
Themed using Eclectic by Atishay

Figure 2.4   Default website with the Eclectic theme. When we chose the Eclectic theme for a Hugo-based website, Hugo created an index page based on that theme, which the website can render even if we provide no content for the page. (It will look better when we configure the page, but it still works without anything.) This page can be used as a starting point to develop the rest of the website. (Background image by theglassdesk on Pixabay.)

Listing 2.4   Running the Hugo development server

```
> hugo server
Start building sites ...

WARN 2021/04/06 22:51:34 Page.Hugo is deprecated
and will be removed in a future release. Use the
global hugo function.

                     | EN
---------------------+-----
     Pages           |  7
     Paginator pages |  0
     Non-page files  |  0
     Static files    |  3
     Processed images|  2
     Aliases         |  0
     Sitemaps        |  1
     Cleaned         |  0
```

Displays warnings when you use any deprecated feature. This output also shows how to fix this. (This warning may not be present when you run this command.)

Indicates the number of pages Hugo has compiled

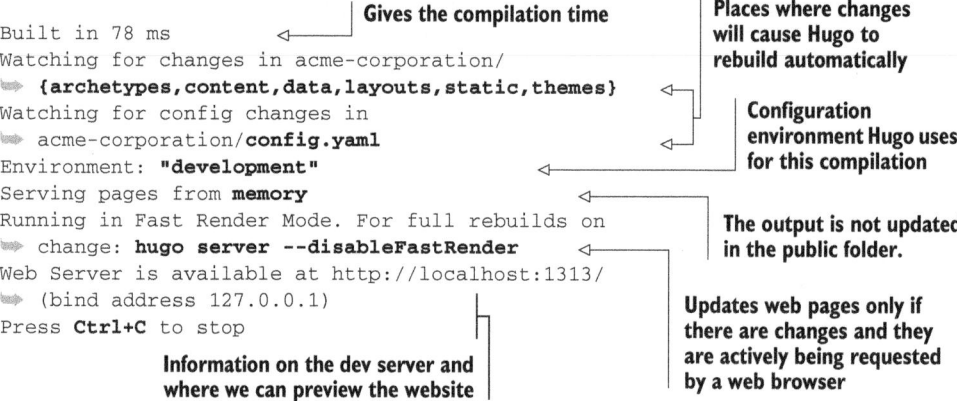

```
Built in 78 ms
Watching for changes in acme-corporation/
  {archetypes,content,data,layouts,static,themes}
Watching for config changes in
  acme-corporation/config.yaml
Environment: "development"
Serving pages from memory
Running in Fast Render Mode. For full rebuilds on
  change: hugo server --disableFastRender
Web Server is available at http://localhost:1313/
  (bind address 127.0.0.1)
Press Ctrl+C to stop
```

Gives the compilation time

Places where changes will cause Hugo to rebuild automatically

Configuration environment Hugo uses for this compilation

The output is not updated in the public folder.

Updates web pages only if there are changes and they are actively being requested by a web browser

Information on the dev server and where we can preview the website

If we run hugo without additional arguments, Hugo compiles the entire website and places the files in the public folder. We also refer to development mode as *server mode* or *live reload mode*. It listens to changes in the filesystem and rebuilds the website with the update. Hugo also supports fast rendering in development mode, which involves building only the page requested on demand. Because Hugo is blazingly fast, we don't notice the delay in rebuilding the web page. We can disable fast rendering or live reload if it interferes with the JavaScript state by using the command-line flags --disableFastRender and --disableLiveReload, respectively. Note that you can run the website's production version in development mode using the --environment command-line flag. Chapter 4 discusses the difference between the various build environments.

There is no need to quit the Hugo development server through most of this book as it supports live reload so we can easily switch content. But you are free to abort it at any time by pressing Ctrl-C and running the hugo server command again.

TIP   The Hugo development server optimizes for refreshes with content changes. Theme changes affecting multiple files are error-prone when reloading. If you change a theme's contents, it's possible that caching in the browser or incrementally building with the development server will get in the way of viewing updates. Restart the dev server, clear the browser cache, and use hugo server --noHTTPCache --disableFastRender to help in these cases.

Exercise 2.4
The default port for Hugo is _____.

When you run the website in development mode for the first time, the images provided by the theme and its JavaScript and CSS files are optimized by Hugo and cached in the resources folder we discussed earlier in this chapter. This process may cause a slower build. It is OK to commit the resources folder to source control to prevent Hugo from generating it again.

NOTE Most Hugo themes need some configuration and content to be functional. You might get a blank screen if you try replacing Eclectic with a different theme and have not provided Hugo with the appropriate configuration.

2.3 Adding content

We will convert the empty page generated with the Eclectic theme into a fully functional website. This conversion includes configuring the theme by providing it with some settings and metadata, adding pages like the privacy policy and terms of use, and overriding the theme's landing page with a custom version.

NOTE Custom data for a theme is not portable. You will have to look at the theme's documentation to figure out the theme-specific configuration. If you are still judging the theme as you develop the website, it is recommended to focus first on the standard template-based content pages (like posts) rather than the unique pages (like the landing page and Contact Us).

Exercise 2.5
The _____ command runs Hugo in development mode.

2.3.1 Configuration

The fact that the website ran so well with two lines of code is the magic of the well-thought-out defaults in Hugo. We can do better by passing it the right options for our website. The configuration file has two distinct parts: the top-level configuration, which is common across themes, and the theme-specific `params` section, which differs across themes. Let's add some data to the configuration file, config.yaml. This is needed to be successful with the Eclectic template in Hugo. These changes provide the information to fill up the menus, the footers, copyright notices, and the title and author information, per the requirements of the Eclectic theme for Acme Corporation.

The updated configuration file is present in the chapter 2 resources folder that accompanies this book (https://github.com/hugoinaction/hugoinaction/tree/chapter-02-resources/02). You do not need to understand the entire file yet. We will be working with these settings in the following chapters, where they will become clearer. Listing 2.5 shows the configuration file that we'll use for the Acme Corporation website. A typical Hugo configuration file contains:

- Configuration options that are standard across all themes (such as the URL of the website, its name, and language)
- Options for specific Hugo features (like `menu`)
- Theme-specific parameters (like `params`)

Listing 2.5 Setting up Acme Corporation's configuration file (config.yaml)

Website language. Hugo supports multilingual websites so we
should use this option when building for only one language.

URL of the website. Change this
to your website location.

Name of the folder that
contains the theme

```
baseURL: http://example.org/
languageCode: en-us
title: Acme Corporation
theme: Eclectic
author:
    facebook: " https://facebook.com/example"
    twitter: " https://twitter.com/example"
    email: "contact@example.org"
    name: "Acme Corporation"
    location: New York
    phone: (999) 999-9999
    hours: "Mon-Fri: 9:00AM - 6:00PM, ET"
```

Name
of the
website

Author section in Hugo, a top-level
section that applies to all themes. If
there is one author, this is the right
place to provide author information.

```
menu:
    main:
        - identifier: about
          name: About
          url: /about
          weight: 100
        - identifier: contact
          name: Contact
          url: /contact
          weight: 200
params:
    color: "#4f46e5"
    copyright: "Copyright &copy; 2022 Acme Corporation.
    All Rights Reserved."
    footer:
        - title: About
          content:  >
            Acme Corporation is the world's leading
            manufacturer of digital shapes. From squares and
            circles to triangles and hexagons, we have it
            all. Browse through our collection of various
            forms with different thicknesses and line styles.
            We shape the world. You live in it.

        - title: Recent Blog Posts
          recents: blog
          recentCount: 7
        - title: Contact Us
          contact: true
```

Main menu of
the website

The theme
parameters

Hugo supports multiple authors via a feature called *taxonomies* (discussed in section
4.4). Hugo also provides a standard way to define menus. The menu section in the configuration file has keys, each of which specifies a menu name. Each menu has a list of
entries, which can have a unique identifier, a name to display, a URL, and a weight to

sort menu items. In the configuration file, the `params` section is theme-specific; its contents can differ across themes.

We wrote the configuration file in listing 2.5 in the YAML metadata language, which we will discuss in chapter 3. It provides structured information using keys and values separated by colons. YAML is human-readable and case-sensitive, but changes in spacing can cause problems with the YAML parser.

Hugo also supports the more "spacing-friendly" TOML format. The resources with this book also contain the TOML version of the configuration file. If you use that as an alternative, config.yaml should be removed.

> **NOTE** Update the actual `baseURL` of the website instead of `http://example`
> `.org/` in the configuration file before publishing. Leaving the file example
> .org breaks absolute links in the website.

The Eclectic theme allows us to provide our logo and even control the website background image by placing these in the assets/image folder (not in the themes/Eclectic/ assets/image folder). We will place logo.svg and background.svg in this folder to personalize the website. We will need to create this folder if it does not exist. (You may need to restart your development server for the changes to take effect.) These files are present in the code bundle for chapter 2 (https://github.com/hugoinaction/hugoinaction/ tree/chapter-02-resources/03).

> **CODE CHECKPOINT**   https://chapter-02-03.hugoinaction.com, and source
> code: https://github.com/hugoinaction/hugoinaction/tree/chapter-02-03.
> ↻ Restart your dev server.

Hugo standardizes some previously specified parts (like `menu` and `title`) in the configuration file. We will cover those parts in chapter 4. Other parts (like `params`) are different for each theme. Even image locations like that of the logo.svg are theme-specific.

Exercise 2.6

Which of the following is used to provide the website endpoint for Hugo to compile?

- a. baseURL
- b. endpoint
- c. website
- d. url
- e. host
- f. domain
- g. server

You can see the impact of providing the metadata on the Acme website instantly. With the configuration mentioned previously, the site should look similar to figure 2.5.

Custom logo   Provided menus   Site name updated   Custom background
                                         based on config

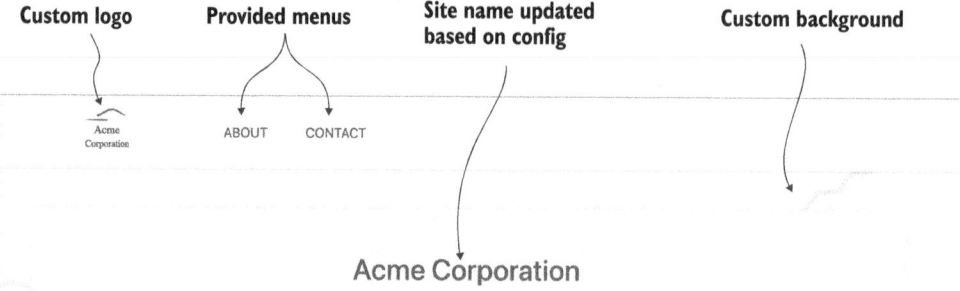

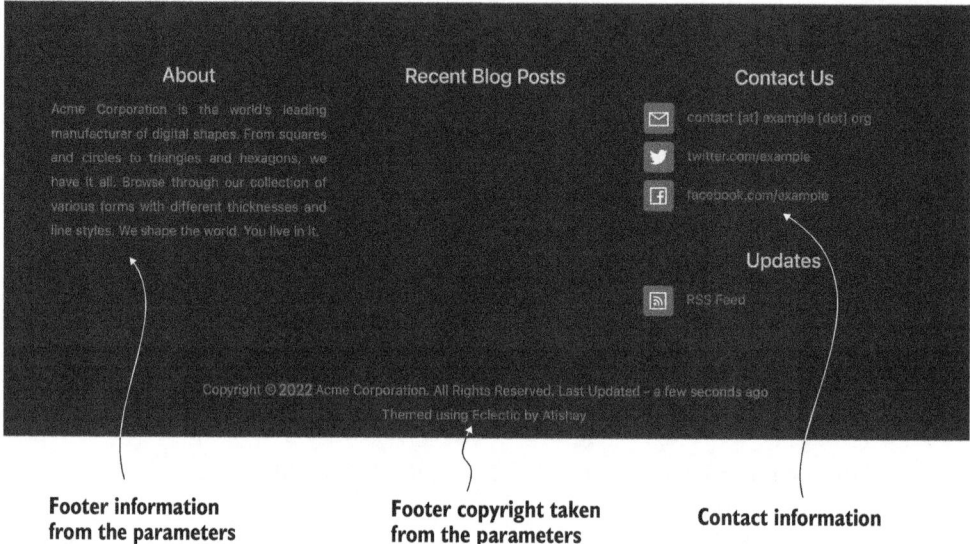

Footer information   Footer copyright taken   Contact information
from the parameters   from the parameters

Figure 2.5   The Acme Corporation website looks much more complete after configuring the theme. Now the main menu and the footer section added in the configuration file are available on all pages. The logo and background images are updated as soon as we place the image files. (Abstract vector created by BiZkettE1 at www.freepik.com.)

2.3.2   Content pages

A website's objective is to serve content, and we have none on our beautiful website so far. The entries added at the top menu of the website link to pages that do not exist! We need to create pages on the website to make it functional. We will begin by adding content to the pages linked to in the menu in this chapter and then will format the content in chapter 3.

We can create content pages as text or markup files in the content folder. We can place a privacy.md file in that folder with Markdown-based content to get the https://localhost:1313/privacy URL. Similarly, we can add the about.md, credits.md, terms.md, and contact.md pages (https://github.com/hugoinaction/hugoinaction/tree/chapter-02-resources/04). Hugo automatically applies the theme, and the page should render as soon as you add the document. This way, we can add as many pages as we desire to generate the website's core structure. Markdown provides a variety of formatting options that we will study in chapter 3.

2.3.3 Index page

The *index page* (also called the *home page* or the *landing page*) is the first page of the website and is responsible for orienting the user on what to expect. Its content is unique and different than all other pages. A text-based content works well for some pages, but many websites implement custom content for the index page. Websites even have tailor-made carousels and sections with extensive imagery that would need a custom implementation. Hugo recognizes this and provides a unique template for the index page, which is called the *index template.* In many themes, the index template is customized in a theme-specific way, and the index page configuration is not portable across themes.

> **NOTE** Most Hugo themes provide a folder called `exampleSite`, which contains a starter website using that theme. This folder is extremely useful in exploring theme-specific configurations and customization options.

Hugo's templates are HTML files, but these can be in any text-based file format (for example, JSON, XML, or even plain text), with additional template tags that participate in the compilation step. For users trying to build custom Hugo templates, it is a good idea to start with the index template because it impacts only one page of the website. Hugo templates can be overridden using the layouts folder. In this chapter, we will not be using any template tags and will start with a plain HTML template that we will place as layouts/index.html. It is still a Hugo template and has access to all the variables, which are optional.

For Acme Corporation's index page, we will override the theme's index page with a custom page, hardcoded in HTML and CSS, as figure 2.6 shows. This page will contain the website logo, title, subtitle, a button with a call to action (telling the reader to explore more), and a footer with links to additional pages.

In the layouts folder, we will place a new file named index.html with custom HTML content (https://github.com/hugoinaction/hugoinaction/tree/chapter-02-resources/05). Because we are not using Hugo's template language, we will be hardcoding all paths and using relative locations to various support-hosting locations.

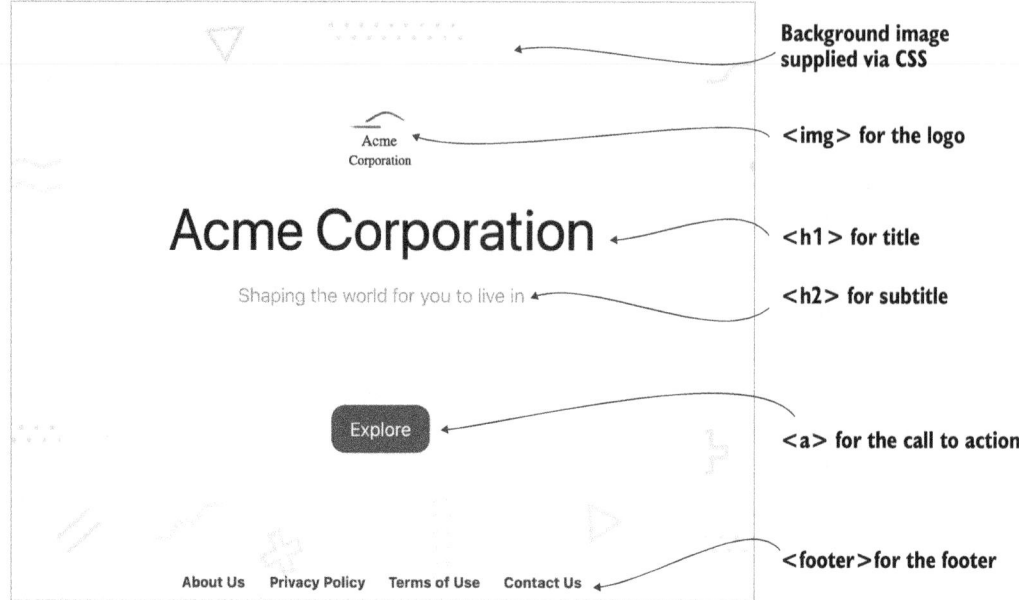

Figure 2.6   **We can create a custom landing page in a Hugo website by placing a file called index.html in the layouts folder. This page overrides the home page provided by the theme. For Acme Corporation, we used a landing page with hardcoded HTML and CSS and eschewed the theme-specific features of Eclectic to create pages based on structured data.**

We can override templates in a Hugo theme by placing an HTML template file in the layouts folder as listing 2.6 demonstrates. Doing that provides someone who understands HTML with a quick way to customize a website without learning Hugo. Custom HTML can be unique to a particular website. Until we use Hugo's template language, we have to be careful with the HTML we are writing as the custom HTML page does not change automatically when the content it links to changes.

Listing 2.6   Overriding Hugo's themes (layouts/index.html)

```html
<!DOCTYPE html>
<html lang="en">
  <head>
    <meta charset="UTF-8">
    <meta name="description" content="Welcome to the
      website of Acme Corporation, the leading creator
      of digital shapes on the planet, providing
      precise shape creations that are ready to use.">
    <meta name="viewport" content="width=device-width,
      initial-scale=1.0" />
    <link rel="stylesheet" href="./index.css">
    <title>Acme Corporation</title>
  </head>
  <body class="home">
```

Relative paths for resources. Absolute paths cause problems when we publish this code with subfolders in a hosting environment.

```
<section>
  <img src="./image/logo.svg" alt="Acme Logo"
    width="64"/>                              ◄───────────
  <h1>Acme Corporation</h1>
  <h2>Shaping the world for you to live in</h2>
  <a href="./blog">Explore</a>
</section>
<footer>
    <a href="./about">About Us</a>
    <a href="./privacy">Privacy Policy</a>
    <a href="./terms">Terms of Use</a>
    <a href="./contact">Contact Us</a>
</footer>
</body>
</html>
```

Assets from the static folder. Assets referred to in the HTML should be provided in the static folder for correct links in the final website.

Hardcoded menus. In plain HTML, we have to assume that the URLs of the menu entries and their names match what is specified.

NOTE Hugo does not modify the HTML provided inside the template.

The plain HTML file needs images and an index file to function properly. The images in the assets folder, which we placed for the Eclectic theme, require the use of Hugo Pipes. (We will discuss Hugo Pipes in chapter 6.) For content that does not need processing, we have to use the static folder. Until we start using Hugo's assets-processing pipeline, we will need to place a second copy of the assets in the static folder. This includes static/index.css, static/image/background.svg, static/image/logo.svg, and static/favicon.ico. These assets are provided with the chapter resources (https://github.com/hugoinaction/hugoinaction/tree/chapter-02-resources/06).

Exercise 2.7
For theme independence, it is advisable to customize which page in plain HTML?

- **a.** privacy
- **b.** index
- **c.** robots.txt
- **d.** English
- **e.** settings

CODE CHECKPOINT   https://chapter-02-04.hugoinaction.com, and source code: https://github.com/hugoinaction/hugoinaction/tree/chapter-02-04.
↻ Restart your dev server.

2.4   *Continuous delivery*

A huge benefit of Hugo and the Jamstack is the ability to have low maintenance and cheap and efficient hosting readily available. We get this power through continuous delivery from the code repository. *Continuous delivery* is the concept of deploying the changes to our code in an ongoing manner. Good continuous delivery pipelines are automated and require minimal manual effort.

There are many ways to achieve continuous delivery with Hugo, such as writing a script to push our code to a storage provider like Amazon S3 or to place it with Apache/Nginx at the web server layer as with any other web stack. We will focus on the approaches most popular within the Hugo community. You can find more hosting information on the Hugo website (https://gohugo.io/hosting-and-deployment/), which maintains a running list of various popular hosting providers and scripts to set up Hugo-based hosting.

Although deploying a Hugo-based website on a public cloud provides access to many other services and immense power, the simplicity of Netlify and GitHub Pages is the best approach to get started with learning Hugo. These approaches also support *continuous deployment*, where changes are made live as soon as we submit the code to the code repository. We will focus on Netlify and GitHub Pages as our hosting solution in this book.

> **NOTE** The following sections assume that the website's source code has been uploaded to GitHub. Every code checkpoint in the book is a good time to commit changes and deploy it to get a new build.

2.4.1 *Netlify hosting*

Netlify, whose founder coined the term *Jamstack*, is a leading hosting service for static websites. Netlify provides deployment services with built-in support for Hugo. Netlify takes care of continuous integration and provides APIs for websites to utilize. We can connect our GitHub repository and get static hosting on Netlify (even for private repositories) for free, until we reach its bandwidth limits. Netlify provides a handy command-line tool to perform tasks without leaving the terminal. We can also offer our build instructions via a configuration file called netlify.toml. Netlify additionally supports domain purchases, DNS, and CDN management with things like custom headers.

> **TIP** If you use Netlify, make sure to check out the branch domain feature. Netlify builds and hosts each pull request in a different website and can maintain different versions via branches. We'll use this feature to host the various versions of the website that we demonstrate in this book. You can navigate to https://chapter-02-04.hugoinaction.com to see a live website with content up to this chapter so far.

Once we sign up for Netlify (https://app.netlify.com/signup), it provides a step-by-step wizard to host our website. If we have already pushed our website's source code to GitHub, we can click New Site from Git as figure 2.7 shows, after signing into Netlify to begin deployment.

The New Site from Git button takes us to https://app.netlify.com/start, where we can connect with our hosting provider (figure 2.8). Once we select the hosting provider, we need to log in and authorize Netlify to access our code repositories.

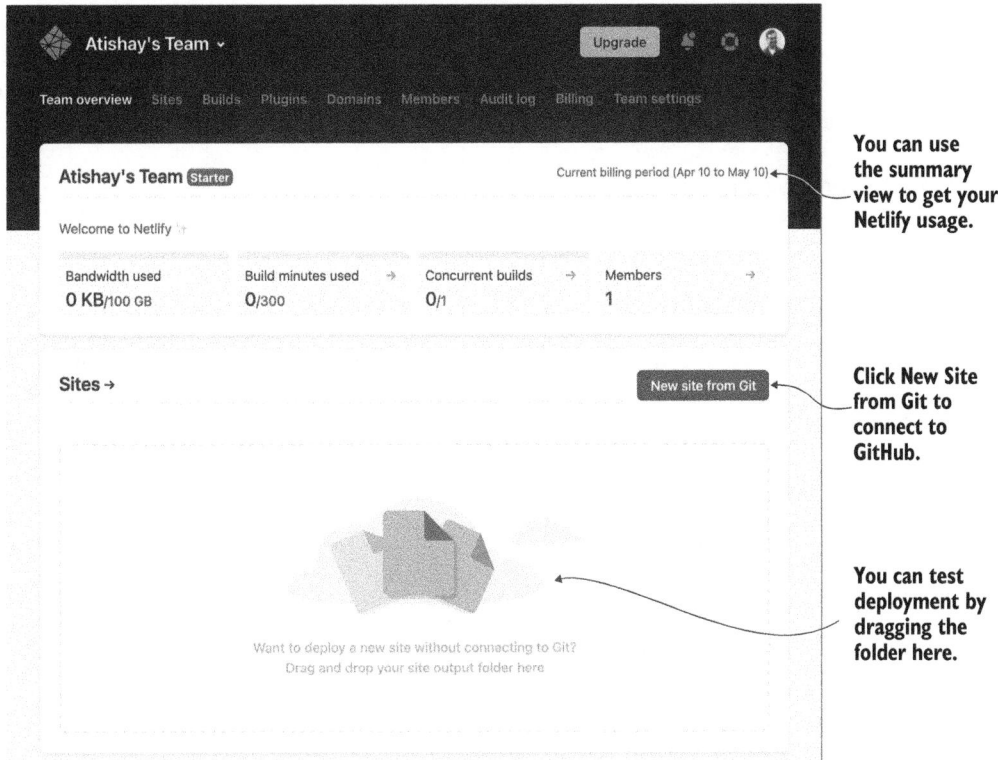

Figure 2.7 After signing up, Netlify presents us with a screen that lists a summary of our Netlify usage and provides the means to set up a new Netlify website. We can connect to a hosting provider or upload our website directly. Connecting to a provider is recommended to get continuous deployment when pushing code.

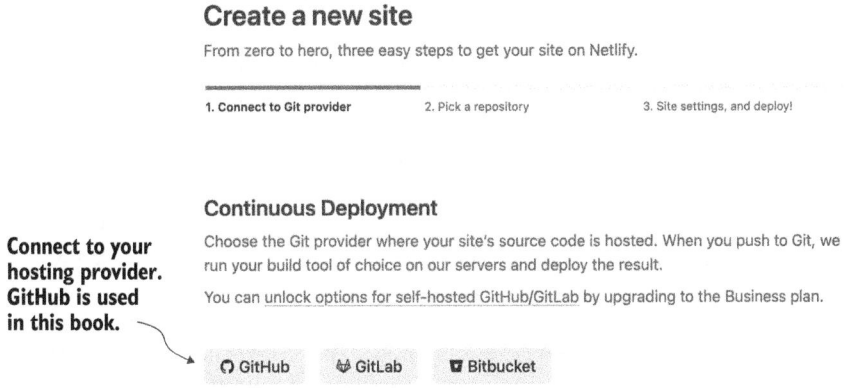

Figure 2.8 Netlify supports connections with multiple hosting providers. Connecting to them is as simple as clicking a button and then logging in.

Once we provide the credentials, Netlify can browse our repository list and provide all repository names in Netlify's UI for us to select the one we want to deploy (figure 2.9). Note that Netlify does not read GitHub organizations by default, so we need to configure Netlify by using a link on the bottom to provide access.

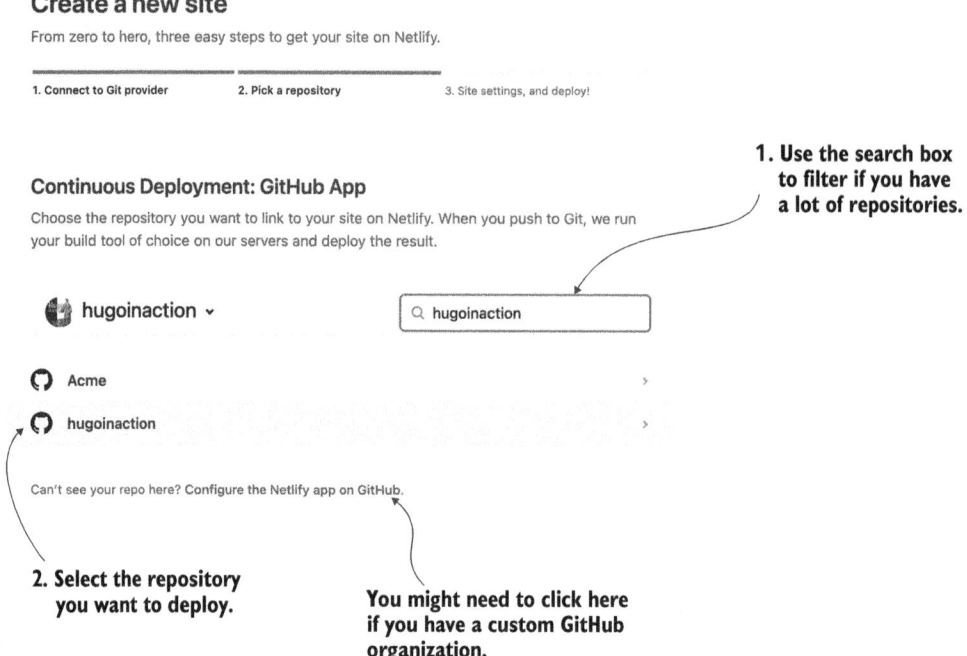

Figure 2.9 Once logged in, we can search for the code repository for the code we want to host via Netlify.

Next, we can specify the branch to build, the build command, and the output directory (figure 2.10). We provide the website URL to Hugo with the command-line arguments hugo --minify --baseURL $DEPLOY_PRIME_URL. The baseURL flag overrides the setup in config.yaml with the one Netlify uses for building branches. If we use pull request previews and branch deploys, it might be better to give each deployment a proper URL. We can also specify build parameters in a file called netlify.toml (https://docs.netlify.com/configure-builds/file-based-configuration).

> **NOTE** To specify the exact version of Hugo, we can click the Show Advanced button when we specify the build command and then add the environment variable HUGO_VERSION with the correct value, which is the version of Hugo we want to use (for example, 0.91.2). Netlify does not guarantee setting up the latest version of Hugo if the version number is not specified. It is better to have control over the build version by providing it manually.

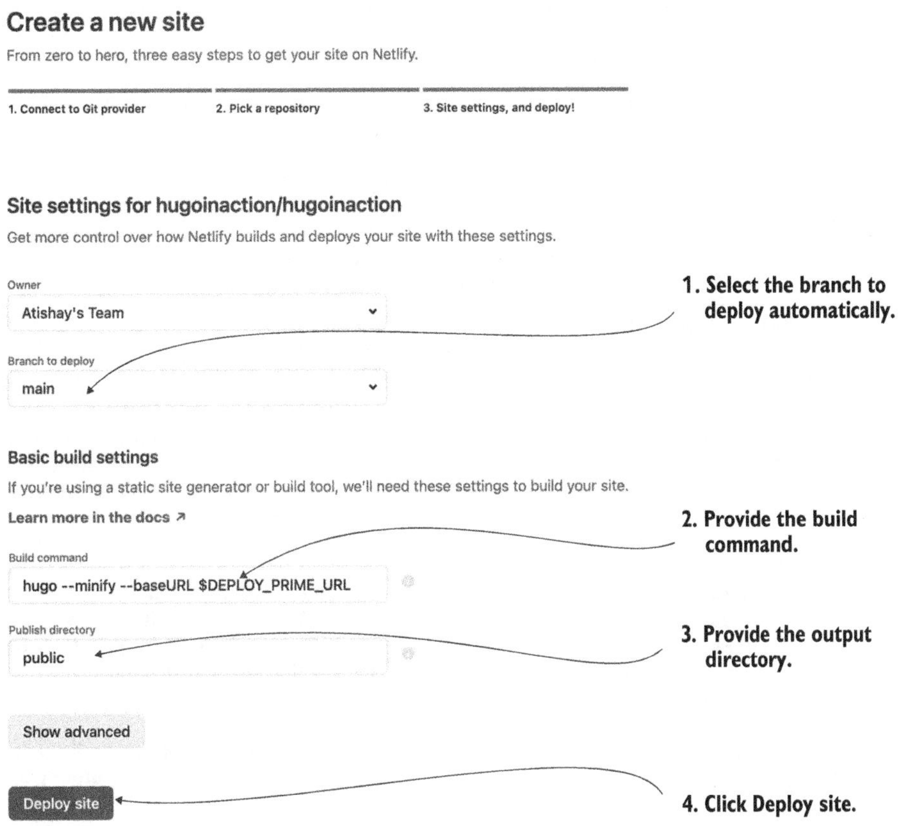

Create a new site

From zero to hero, three easy steps to get your site on Netlify.

| 1. Connect to Git provider | 2. Pick a repository | 3. Site settings, and deploy! |

Site settings for hugoinaction/hugoinaction

Get more control over how Netlify builds and deploys your site with these settings.

Owner

Atishay's Team

1. Select the branch to deploy automatically.

Branch to deploy

main

Basic build settings

If you're using a static site generator or build tool, we'll need these settings to build your site.

Learn more in the docs ↗

Build command

hugo --minify --baseURL $DEPLOY_PRIME_URL

2. Provide the build command.

Publish directory

public

3. Provide the output directory.

Show advanced

Deploy site

4. Click Deploy site.

Figure 2.10 Specifying the branch for continuous integration and providing the build command and the output folder to deploy our website. We can designate the Hugo version to use with advanced options by clicking the Show Advanced button.

2.4.2 GitHub Pages

GitHub is the Swiss army knife of development. With its extreme popularity in the developer community and its ability to have unlimited free hosting for open source code, GitHub is a perfect place to get started with static hosting. The Pages service can render static HTML from a branch or a folder in our source code repository. GitHub Actions perform continuous integration. There are multiple actions available in the GitHub Actions marketplace for Hugo. We will be using Hugo setup (https://github .com/marketplace/actions/hugo-setup) in this section.

The steps for hosting our Hugo-based Acme Corporation website on GitHub Pages follow. Listing 2.7 provides the code for enabling GitHub Pages.

1 Create the GitHub Actions file at .github/workflows/gh-pages.yml, which tells GitHub the actions to take (https://github.com/hugoinaction/hugoinaction/ tree/chapter-02-resources/07). When these changes are pushed to GitHub, these

actions automatically execute, creating the gh-pages branch with the compiled version of our website.

Listing 2.7   Enabling GitHub Pages (.github/workflows/gh-pages.yml)

```
name: GitHub Pages        ◁──┐  We can name this
                              │  workflow what we want.
on:
  push:                          ┌── Triggers this workflow when a push
        branches:                │   happens on the main branch
            - main    ◁──────────┘
    workflow_dispatch:   ◁──┐
                            │   Enables workflow dispatch
jobs:                       │   for manual triggers
  deploy:
    runs-on: ubuntu-18.04            ┌── The checkout action gets the source code.
    steps:                           │   We use fetch-depth to keep some Git
      - uses: actions/checkout@v2  ◁─┤   history for Hugo's .Gitinfo (more on this
        with:                        │   in chapter 4).
          fetch-depth: 0

      - name: Setup Hugo                            "true" specifies that we want to use the
        uses: peaceiris/actions-hugo@v2             extended flavor of Hugo version 0.91.2
        with:                                       for this action, or you can use "latest"
          hugo-version: '0.91.2'   ◁──────────      to get the latest version.
          extended: true

      - name: Build                        ┌── Command to compile code. We
        run: hugo --minify --baseURL=  ◁───┘   can specify the output page here.
--> https://hugoinaction.github.io/GitHubPages

      - name: Deploy                              ┌── The Deploy action pushes to the gh-pages
        uses: peaceiris/actions-gh-pages@v3   ◁──┘   branch for GitHub Pages to deploy.
        with:
          github_token: ${{ secrets.GITHUB_TOKEN }}
          publish_dir: ./public
```

2   In the GitHub settings for the repository, enable GitHub Pages from the gh-pages branch repository (see figure 2.11). Once enabled, the URL of the website will be visible in the interface.

3   After deployment, change the base URL in the GitHub Actions file and in the config.yaml file from the sample value to the correct one provided in the GitHub Actions, then push it again. We can view the updates on the Actions tab on GitHub as figure 2.12 shows.

An example website using GitHub Pages is hosted at https://hugoinaction.github.io/GitHubPages/ with the source code at https://github.com/hugoinaction/GitHubPages/. We can navigate to the Actions tab in the GitHub UI to see the results of running GitHub Actions, which deploys the website.

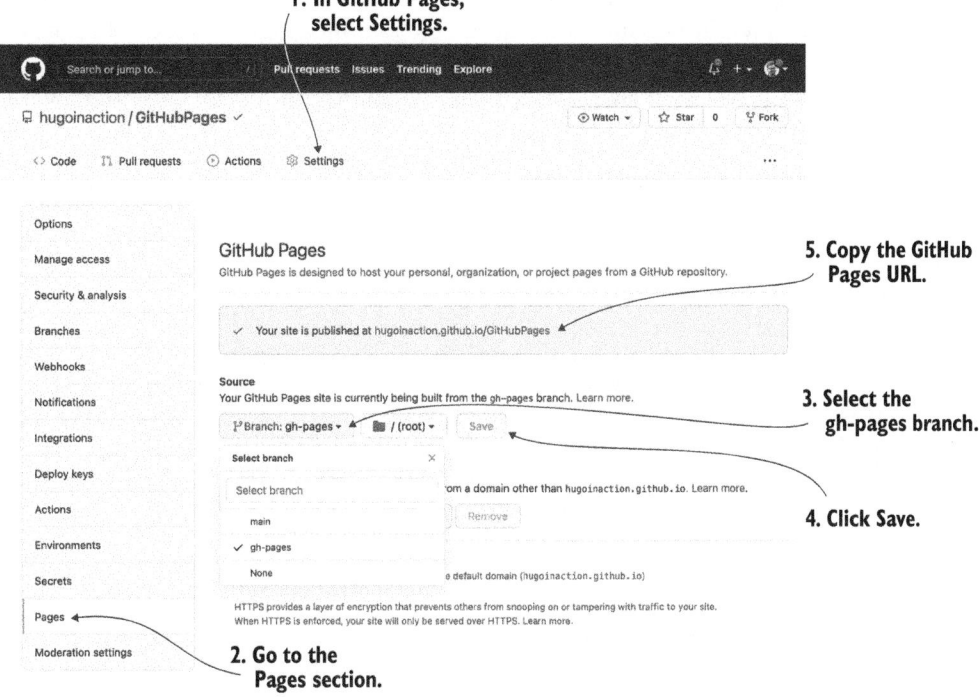

Figure 2.11 Options for GitHub Pages as a host for a static website. Use the Branch: gh-pages option for Hugo.

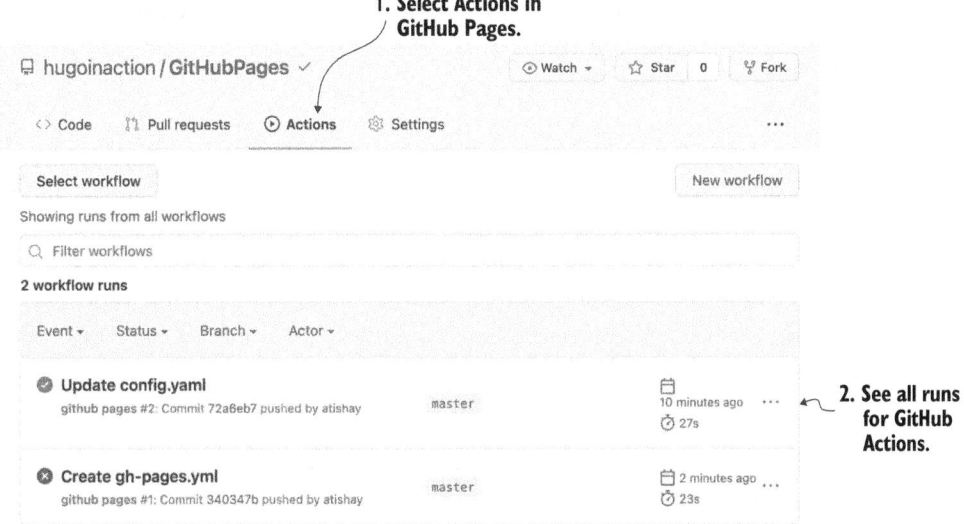

Figure 2.12 The Actions tab on GitHub shows all executed actions. Each code push can potentially run a GitHub action.

Now the website should be available on the web, and we should be able to navigate to the link provided by GitHub in the pages section once it goes live. GitHub provides a CDN that distributes websites across the planet and is free for a website under its quota limits (size less than 1 GB, a monthly bandwidth of 100 GBs, and around 10 builds per hour as of writing this book). This is a good place for a personal website or for test-driving the Jamstack. Many GitHub Pages document source code already on GitHub, and Hugo is one popular tool for generating that.

Editing on the go

There is a popular misconception that websites built with the Jamstack architecture are difficult to edit unless you have the development environment set up. Most modern Jamstack websites have a continuous environment setup, and we can push it to production with a simple check-in. This system makes Jamstack more flexible than a traditional database-based website stack. We can change not only content but also designs, configurations, and even business logic without setting up a development environment. With scaling not a concern, it is easier to edit on the Jamstack than with the traditional web stack.

In case of minor edits, GitHub's web interface is a valuable tool that provides the ability to edit the website from anywhere. There are applications like *CodeHub*, *Pocket-Hub*, or *Working Copy* (available on both mobile and tablet) to create or modify Markdown documents from a Git repository. We can make our changes anywhere we want, and the continuous integration system ensures they go live within seconds of being committed. Unlike traditional stacks, setting up the local development environment for the Jamstack is much easier, and when we have to, it does not take days.

2.4.3 *Vercel, Cloudflare, AWS Amplify, and other dedicated Jamstack hosts*

Like Netlify, other dedicated Jamstack hosts provide similar feature sets like branch/commit previews, automatic continuous integration and deployment, and API creation support and management. Vercel provides robust support for managing JavaScript and can be an advantage if our website is getting JavaScript-heavy. Cloudflare Pages are built by one of the biggest CDNs on the planet and provide unlimited bandwidth, better performance than most other services, and a well-defined means to create our APIs (with Cloudflare Workers and Cloudflare Workers KV). AWS Amplify is an AWS service that provides excellent integration with the rest of AWS. The Hugo hosting setup for Cloudflare, AWS Amplify, and Vercel is similar to Netlify, and one cannot go wrong in choosing any of these providers.

2.4.4 *AWS, Azure, and Google Cloud file storage*

If you are using the public cloud features for the other parts of the Jamstack or desire more fine-grained control than that provided with standardized hosting, deploying from Hugo to the cloud is also available. Hugo comes with a built-in command, `hugo deploy` (https://gohugo.io/hosting-and-deployment/hugo-deploy/), to deploy the website to an AWS S3 bucket, Google Cloud Storage, or Azure Storage. Once we set up the authentication credentials on our machine, we can specify the link to the specific service in the `deployment.targets.URL` section in the config.yaml file. For example, to deploy to AWS S3, you would enter `s3://<Bucket Name>?region=<AWS region>`. Hugo automatically identifies the changes between the cloud and the current build and synchronizes those when we run `hugo deploy <target name>`. We can also specify the caching policies that the cloud exposes to the website's users in the same section.

Figure 2.13 Publishing with the Jamstack. Alex does not give up on the Jamstack even after Bob gets additional resources to continue with the existing stack.

2.5 *Meeting the goals for performance and maintainability*

Hugo and the Jamstack promise solid performance and low ongoing maintenance. Both of these are not absolutes in themselves. There is a gradient: we need to choose the right balance of features, ease of development and use, maintenance, and performance to get the best benefit. A website with no images would likely be faster to load than one with hundreds of them, but that does not mean that it would be the best website for all use cases. Therefore, when analyzing performance and maintainability, we need to consider the use case.

2.5.1 *Performance*

Performance is one notable metric that Hugo's development team uses to benchmark its builds. We should be able to get good performance for a typical use case without any significant difficulties. We are hosting all the web pages for Acme Corporation on a CDN (prerendered), and the client does not need to do much processing to display the site. While we should find the website quick to load, it is vital to get the performance as a number and tabulate that across builds to be able to compare changes and to fix regressions.

The standard tool for measuring performance is the Audit tool called Lighthouse (https://developers.google.com/web/tools/lighthouse/). It's built into Google's Chrome browser (figure 2.14). For Acme Corporation, the About page represents a regular page of the website, which we will measure for performance.

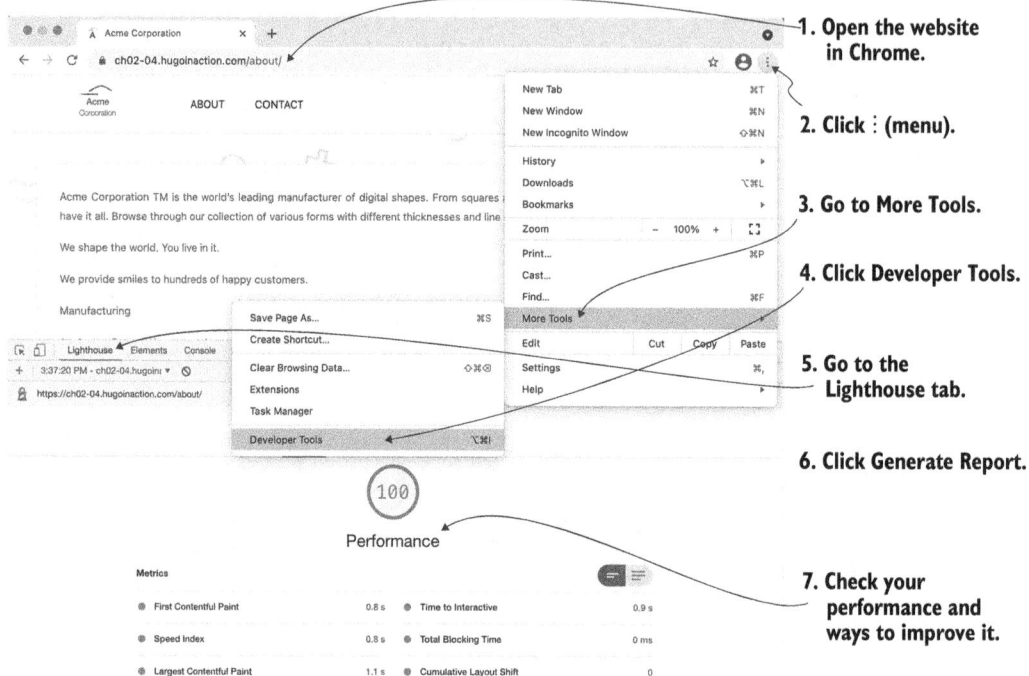

Figure 2.14 Performance audit for the About page for Acme Corporation using the Google Chrome Lighthouse performance test.

> **NOTE** Chrome regularly updates the Lighthouse tool with new tests, so the measurement results might not exactly match the screenshot shown.

It is essential to measure the hosted site's performance on the CDN as the development server from Hugo is not what the users get in production. It is built for development and does not provide the right results. To measure the hosted site's performance,

1 Go to the View > Developer > Developer Tools menu in Google Chrome to open the web inspector.

2 Go to the Lighthouse tab and run an audit. You should be able to achieve a decent audit score for performance on most Hugo websites.

Lighthouse may suggest issues in the theme. If so, there is an option to clone the theme or to create a bug for the theme developer to fix.

2.5.2 *Maintainability*

The maintainability of the web setup is difficult to measure directly. There is no tool to tell whether a stack is maintainable. One way to check how much effort it would take to maintain a system is to list each of its dependencies and figure out which dependencies require ongoing security updates, which need to be abandoned by the developer, or which can become difficult to update due to nested dependencies. We should also measure the effort to remove a dependency in case it is not actively maintained. Luckily, for the Hugo-based setup we just discussed, we have few dependencies. In our measurement system, we can consider a rewrite, huge updates, or partial rewrites as high risks, and tweaks that do not involve many changes as medium risks. At the same time, a low risk would refer to no minimal manual intervention. Let's try to assess this for the website we have built so far, right after the next exercise.

Exercise 2.8

What is the primary reason to benchmark the performance of a website?

  a. Find overall performance issues.
  b. Plot a graph to show on our website.
  c. Compare performance across multiple builds of our website and multiple builds of Hugo to find faulty behavior.
  d. Find bugs in our website.

- *Our Acme Corporation's website created in this chapter depends on Hugo.* Hugo has had breaking changes in the past releases, but most of them have been minor. We do not need to update for security fixes because it is a development-only dependency. This could be rated as low in an ongoing effort if we are happy with the website or as medium for an upgrade.

- *The hosting on GitHub Pages requires no ongoing effort to maintain.* This is among the most critical services for developers on the internet. We can, therefore, rate both ongoing maintenance and upgrade as low. If we use Netlify, it manages the upkeep for us, and the effort there is also low. Because it is a lot less popular than GitHub, there is an inherent risk of Netlify pivoting to a new business model or shutting its doors. Migration to GitHub is easy for the type of website built here, and its overall risk is low.

- *The Eclectic theme chosen for Acme Corporation is dependent on a few JavaScript-based plugins.* These plugins are stable, however, and haven't had significant changes in years. Still, Eclectic is not heavily used, and if it gets abandoned, the team at Acme Corporation will have to pick up the task of adding fixes to support newer Hugo versions when they want to update the website. That would be a medium effort commitment (unless they want new features).

Overall, the ongoing work to keep the website we built in this chapter alive is meager. If we need to upgrade it, the effort would be low to medium, depending on the breaking changes in Hugo and the theme developer's ability to adapt to those. Note that as we progress further along with this book, we will add more dependencies to our website, especially in part 2. This will increase the maintenance overhead. While an attempt has been made to look for dependencies that are self-contained, readers are advised to weigh the pros and cons of adding dependencies independently every time something is needed in their own projects.

2.5.3   *Choose the theme wisely*

The performance and maintenance risks of a website depend heavily on the theme selected. If the theme is not good, Hugo's hard work maintaining its performance will not show in your website's build time. The main maintenance risk to a Hugo-based website is the risk of depending on a theme that stops being compatible with the newer versions of Hugo. We can continue to use the older version of Hugo and the theme indefinitely without worrying too much about security issues because the content is static. But if we ever want to update Hugo and the theme is not supported anymore, we would be on our own to maintain the theme. It is a good idea to be theme agnostic, at least early on in a website project, so that if we find a problem with the theme we are using, we can move to a different one quickly.

Themes can also be an excellent source for learning how to use Hugo best. Many developers using Hugo choose the themes as the starting point rather than the absolute solution. One big reason to choose Hugo is to customize everything, and forking the theme is a powerful way to perform that task. We will be moving out of the Eclectic theme into our custom theme by the end of chapter 7.

If we want to continue to build our website with a theme maintained by someone else, it is a good idea to investigate portability. Hugo provides standardization across themes, and switching Hugo themes is not difficult (see listing 2.8). We will be adding another theme to Acme Corporation's website to make sure our code is portable. We provide a copy of the Universal theme for Hugo in chapter resources (https://github.com/hugoinaction/hugoinaction/tree/chapter-02-resources/08) and also host it at github .com/hugoinaction/Universal. You can copy that theme to the themes folder and enable it with the website configuration. You may need to restart the development server.

Listing 2.8   Changing a theme to Universal (config.yaml)

```
theme: Universal
```

While the previous code works and renders the website, there is more configuration that we need to do to get the maximum benefit of the Universal theme. For that, place logo.png in the static/image/logo.png folder and update the configuration to include the parameters in the following listing (below the existing `params` for `footer`) for Universal to be able to parse them (https://github.com/hugoinaction/hugoinaction/tree/chapter-02-resources/09).

Listing 2.9 **Changes to support the Universal theme (config.yaml)**

```yaml
theme: Universal
params:
  footer:
  ...
  style: blue
  logo: /image/logo.png
  logo_small: /image/logo.png
  about_us: >
    Acme Corporation is the world's leading manufacturer
    of digital shapes. From squares and circles to
    triangles and hexagons, we have it all. Browse through
    our collection of various forms with different
    thicknesses and line styles. We shape the world.
    You live in it.

  recent_posts:
    enable: true
```

The configuration file for Universal is available in both TOML and YAML format in the code resources with this book (https://github.com/hugoinaction/hugoinaction/tree/chapter-02-resources/10). Note that the configuration for Eclectic has not been removed, and we can switch between the two themes easily.

CODE CHECKPOINT https://chapter-02-05.hugoinaction.com, and source code: https://github.com/hugoinaction/hugoinaction/tree/chapter-02-05.

Because each theme has a unique home page, switching themes will be considerably easier if we choose our own customized HTML-based home page. That way, if we render now or with a live reload, the home page remains the same. Because the About page is styled, it will match the Universal theme (figure 2.15) if we switch to that theme.

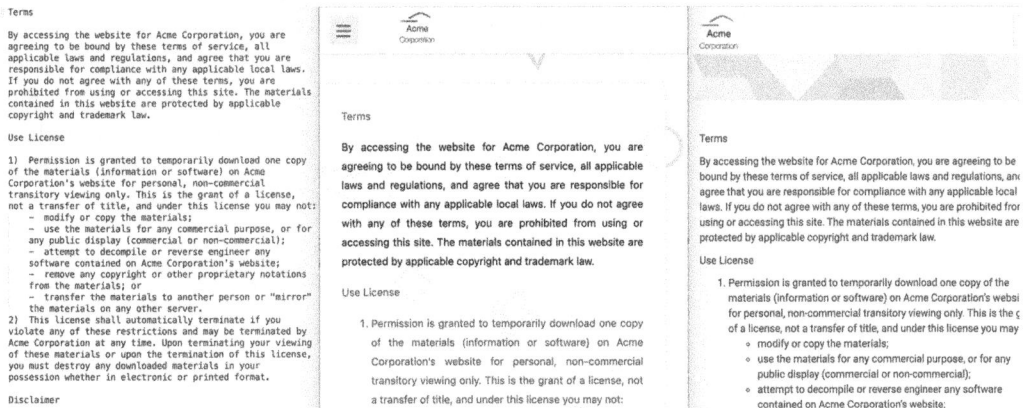

Figure 2.15 Terms of Use page for Acme Corporation in code (left), Eclectic (middle), and Universal (right). When we switch themes in Hugo, most of the content that we provide as Markdown still works. Only the parameters provided in places like the configuration file need to be reworked.

We will be reverting to Eclectic for the rest of the book. With a running website, it is time to add some more content, so we will do that in chapter 3.

Summary

- Hugo is available for installation in most major package managers on Linux, macOS, and Windows.
- Hugo has extensive command-line functionality to minimize the work that its users need to do. It has handy options that help build all parts of a website, from adding module dependencies to creating new Markdown-based documents.
- A Hugo project consists of folders beyond the content and themes folders: static for static content, data for structured data, layouts for theme overrides, resources for Hugo's internal caching, assets for images, JavaScript, and CSS files, and public for the generated output. It also includes archetypes for posted templates and a configuration file for global settings.
- Hugo themes can be added in various ways, the simplest of which is to directly copy a theme to the themes folder. We need to configure these with standard and theme-specific parameters and file placements before using.
- Content can be added as Markdown, theme-specific structured data, or in an overridden HTML template.
- Hugo websites can be hosted easily across the planet via GitHub Pages and Netlify, which provide continuous delivery support without making the developer do much work.
- We can switch themes, but if we use a lot of theme-specific data (like data supplied via params in the configuration), then that work needs to be redone. We should investigate theme switching early on so that we can switch out quickly if the Hugo theme gets abandoned.
- We can use Google Chrome's Lighthouse feature for measuring performance. We should also do a full dependency audit to check maintainability.
- Every website needs to be monitored for maintainability and performance regularly during development to ensure quality. Hugo offers excellent performance and has a small set of dependencies, but the website performance and maintainability still depend on the chosen theme.

Using markup for content

This chapter covers

- Creating content using Markdown
- Using Hugo's extensions to Markdown
- Understanding the markup languages supported by Hugo
- Using YAML for metadata in a Hugo-based website
- Playing with the various elements of the front matter

Most documents in the content folder of a Hugo website consist of textual content in a markup language and its associated metadata in a metadata language. Markdown is the most popular markup language and the most widely used. YAML is among the most popular languages for writing key-value configurations, where human readability is essential.

Figure 3.1 (top) shows the focus area for this chapter. In sections 3.1 to 3.3, we will focus on the Markdown language to provide content, and from section 3.4 onward, we will study the YAML language that adds the metadata. We will also look at the typical metadata entries in the front matter of a website. In this chapter, we

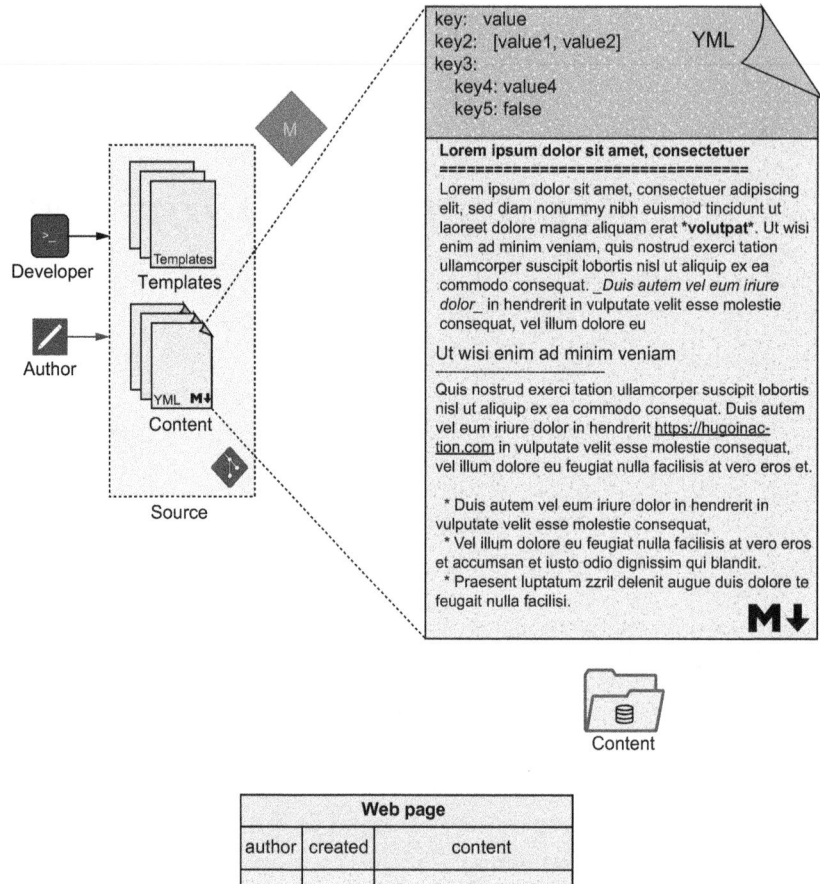

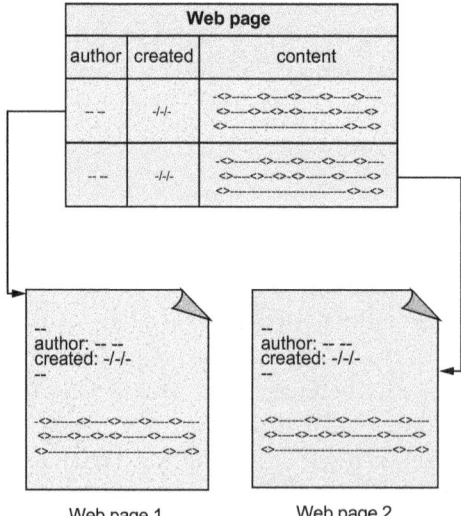

Figure 3.1   Most content documents in a Hugo-based website consist of markup in some metadata language like Markdown and structured metadata in a metadata language like YAML. The focus of this chapter is to format a single Markdown document (on the top). The bottom shows a comparison of database storage versus file-based storage for our content.

will format the pages we created for the website we built for Acme Corporation in chapter 2.

In the traditional web stack, the content of a web page is stored in a single database cell, whereas the associated metadata fills up other columns in the content table or other tables in the database. In the Jamstack, the content (called the *front matter*) is of prime importance and is placed in a separate file with the rest of the metadata moved from the header section (as figure 3.1 shows on the bottom).

3.1 Writing content in Markdown

So far, we have used plain text to provide content for our web pages. With plain text, however, we get no structure, and a blob of text is not fun to read. Markdown is a lightweight document format for writing easy-to-read and easy-to-write documents with support for basic formatting and for structuring content using text-based constructs. In 2004, John Gruber and Aaron Swartz created Markdown as a human-readable, text-based formatting language. It standardizes on a text-based mechanism for specifying formatting. Although a compiler and a renderer improve readability, the language is easy enough to understand without it. This readability has made Markdown popular as a formatting language from the command line to Git commit messages, README files, plain text boxes, and chat pods.

Original Markdown had a limited set of features, extended by CommonMark (https://commonmark.org/) and further developed as GitHub Flavored Markdown (GFM), which is the popular variant (see https://github.github.com/gfm/). Hugo supports most of GFM and extends it even further. Hugo parses files created with the filename extension .md or .markdown as Markdown. The privacy, credits, terms, and about files in chapter 2 already have the .md extension and are ready to use with Markdown's formatting capabilities.

Markdown editors

Markdown is a language that can be read and written in a plain-text editor without any support for this format. Many users don't have a special editor for Markdown. Simple text editors like Sublime Text and VS Code provide color coding to help identify special formatting in Markdown. They also support a live preview of Markdown content in the output format.

If you are looking for a dedicated Markdown editor, tools like Typora (https://typora.io/) and iA Writer (https://ia.net/writer) provide many capabilities for helping create good Markdown documents. These tools support keyboard shortcuts and inline as well as live previews. Online tools like Dropbox Paper (https://www.dropbox.com/paper) also support a subset of Markdown. Apart from these, pandoc (https://pandoc.org/) can take many file formats including Microsoft Office, Open Office, Latex, and MediaWiki and convert them to Markdown.

3.1.1   *Paragraphs in Markdown*

Markdown already formats blobs of text with an empty line between paragraphs (the <p> tag in HTML). The various pages we provided in chapter 2 did not look very ugly because of this feature. Figure 3.2 shows how the paragraph and line break elements render.

If we provide more than two line breaks, rendering content collapses them. The rendering also ignores single line breaks during this process. We can also use Markdown in text boxes where automatic text wrapping is not available, and we can add line breaks without impacting output, thereby keeping readability intact. To create a regular line break (
 tag in HTML), add two spaces at the end of the line and then add a new line character using the Enter (Return) key.

```
I am a paragraph in Markdown with line
wrapping so it fits in this width.
I am a continuation of the first paragraph
as there is no empty line before me.

I am in the second paragraph.


I am the third one. Even though there are
two line breaks before me, this does not
create any newline characters. After me there
are two spaces before the newline character.
I have line break before me and even though
I am not a new paragraph, I start on a
new line due to the manual line break and
spaces before the newline character.
```

I am a paragraph in Markdown with line wrapping so it fits in this width. I am a continuation of the first paragraph as there is no empty line before me.

I am in the second paragraph.

I am the third one. Even though there are two line breaks before me, this does not create any newline characters. After me there are two spaces before the newline character.
I have a line break before me and even though I am not a new paragraph, I start on a new line due to the manual line break and spaces before the newline character.

Figure 3.2   Elements in Markdown, part 1: Paragraphs and line breaks

3.1.2   *Headings, lists, and other block elements*

We need headings, lists, and other block elements to provide proper structure for the Terms of Use and the Privacy Policy pages for the Acme Corporation website. Figure 3.3 shows these elements and how they are rendered in the browser. To create top-level headings,

- *Before the heading text, use a hash mark (#).* The single # sign creates a level 1 (H1) heading, and two ## signs make the level 2 (H2) headings. We can use hash marks like this to reach six levels of headings in most parsers (##, ###, and so forth).
- *Under the heading text, add a row of equal signs for a level 1 heading or add hyphens (dashes) for the next level headings (H2, H3, and so forth).* This underlining (created from the equal signs and dashes) highlights the headings, making them not only more readable but also easier to locate.

GFM requires a space after the hash mark to be considered a proper heading to distinguish between hashtags that have become popular for labeling issues. For headings, hashes need to begin the start of a new line, preceding the text that we want to use for the heading. The in-between text (from one heading to the next) does not create headings but, rather, is our content.

```
Top Level H1
=============
H2
---

#Just a tag
\# Not a heading
Also a # tag
# Alternate H1
## Alternate H2
### H3
###### H6

* This is a list element
+ This is also a list element
- This is also a list element
    - This is a sublist element
    + Also a sublist element
        + Sublist level 2
        1. Numbered sublist
        2. Next item
            1. Next indent level

1) Numbered list
2) Next item
        1. Next indent level
            * Sublist not numbered
3. Back

Horizontal lines:

------------------------------
.

******************************
.

***
.

---

> Block Quote

        Preformatted text
```

Top Level H1

H2

#Just a tag # Not a heading Also a # tag.

Alternate H1

Alternate H2

H3

H6

- This is a list element
- This is also a list element
- This is also a list element
    - This is a sublist element
    - Also a sublist element
        - Sublist level 2
        1. Numbered sublist
        2. Next item
            1. Next indent level

1. Numbered list
2. Next item
    1. Next indent level
        - Sublist not numbered
3. Back

Horizontal lines

> " *Block Quote*

```
Preformatted text
```

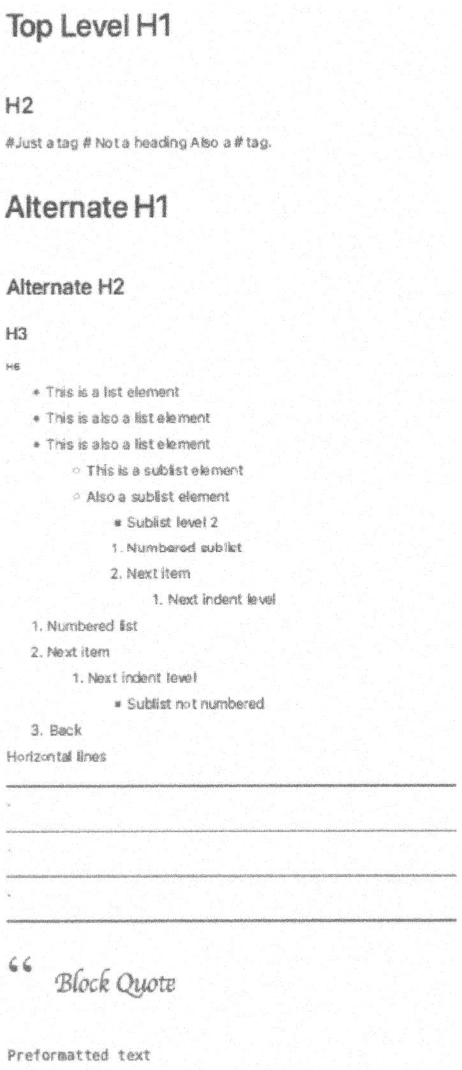

Figure 3.3 Elements in Markdown, part 2: Headings, lists, and horizontal lines

We can add bulleted lists (the <ul> block element) by using either *, -, or + at the start of the sentence. Sublists are added by inserting four spaces before the bullet character. A number followed by a dot (.) or a closing parenthesis ()) creates numbered or ordered lists (the <OL> block element). We can nest different lists in Markdown.

We can create horizontal lines (the `<hr>` tag) using a series of dashes or asterisks (with a minimum of three). To add a blockquote, we prefix the text with > as the first element in the line. Any text starting with four spaces or a tab character is considered a preformatted code block, which displays exactly as you write it with no line wrapping.

Figure 3.4 shows the Terms of Use page for Acme Corporation (on the left) with the corresponding block elements for headings and lists (on the right). The block elements highlighted in the image are an exercise for the reader. For that, the reader should update the Privacy Policy page with these elements. You can tally your changes

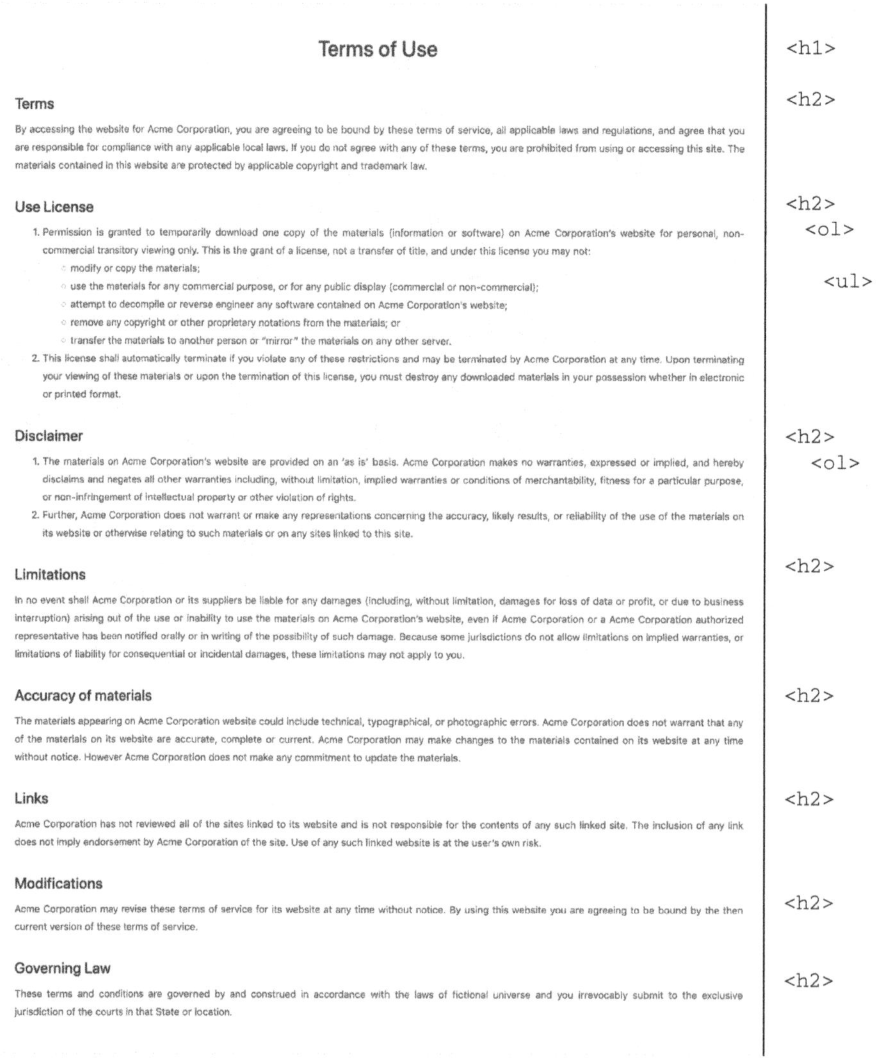

Figure 3.4   Addition of headings and lists and the corresponding block elements to the Terms of Use page for the Acme Corporation website

with those provided in the chapter resources (https://github.com/hugoinaction/
hugoinaction/tree/chapter-03-resources/01).

> **CODE CHECKPOINT** https://chapter-03-01.hugoinaction.com, and source code:
> https://github.com/hugoinaction/hugoinaction/tree/chapter-03-01.

Exercise 3.1

Which symbols from the following list can help identify a heading in Markdown?
(Select all that apply.)

- **a.** Asterisk (*)
- **b.** Underscore (_)
- **c.** Hyphen/dash (-)
- **d.** Equals sign (=)
- **e.** Plus sign (+)
- **f.** Hash mark (#)

3.1.3 *Formatting, inline links, code, and images*

While block elements give the page its structure, inline elements emphasize vital parts
of the page. Figure 3.5 shows these inline elements (on the left) and how they are rendered in the browser (on the right).

Note that Hugo automatically formats hyperlinks on the page and converts them
to HTML anchor tags. This auto-linking is a feature provided by Hugo's Markdown
parser, so we do not need to write anything special to enable it. We can also create
links using a `[visible text](http://example.org/path/to/file)` format. We can
also use the `[visible text](http://link "Title")` format, where `"Title"` is available as a tooltip.

We can share links across text by writing a reference to them as `[visible
text][target 1]` and then adding a footnote with the value of the reference by using
the format `[target 1]: https://example.org/path/to/target`. Shared links also
work in footnote locations directly; for example, `[target 1]` autolinks to the `target
1` link that we just set.

Markdown provides basic formatting support using text-based markers. We can surround the desired text with an `_`(underscore) or an `*`(asterisk) for italics, or a `__`(double
underscore) for boldface. For both bold and italics, we can use `**_<text>_**` or
`__*<text>*__`. Double tildes (`~~`) are used for strikethroughs.

We can specify inline code by surrounding it with backticks like this, `` `inline
code` ``, and we can place it in free-flowing content. It gets formatted with a monospace
font in the HTML `<code>` tag.

Markdown creates `<img>` tags to show images inline with the content. There is no
support for specifying block images, image dimensions, or other details; that is left to
the theme to implement. We can inline images using a similar syntax to links and

	Inline formatting
`## Inline formatting`	**Inline formatting**
`*Italics*`	*Italics*
`_Italics_`	*Italics*
`__Bold__`	**Bold**
`__*Bold+Italics*__`	***Bold+Italics***
`**_Bold+Italics_**`	***Bold+Italics***
`this_is_not_emphasis`	this_is_not_emphasis
`~~strikethrough~~`	~~Strike-through~~
`Content with a -- (dash) and a --- (long dash).`	Content with a – (dash) and a — (long dash).
`[link](http://link/path/to/target)`	link
`[link](http://link/path/to/target "TITLE ON LINK")`	link
`[Shared links with footnotes][target 1]`	Shared links with footnotes
`[Second shared link][target 1]`	Second shared link
`[target 1]`	target 1
`[target 1]: http://footnote.com`	
`Sample inline code `a++` can be specified here.`	Sample inline code `a++` can be specified here.
`![Alt Text](/path/to/image "Optional Tooltip")`	Acme Corporation

Figure 3.5 Elements in Markdown, part 3: Inline elements including bold, italics, underline, links, and images

prefix those with an ! (exclamation mark, commonly called a *bang*). To render an image inline in the text, we'd write `![alt text](/path/to/image "optional tooltip")`. We can use relative paths in the image tag as well.

Using these features, we can properly format salient parts of the privacy policy for the Acme Corporation website. The formatted Privacy Policy page looks much more complete and professional now. Figure 3.6 shows a part of the completed Privacy Policy page on the right with the inline elements marked on the left. Updating the Privacy Policy page to match this design is an exercise for the reader. The completed Privacy Policy

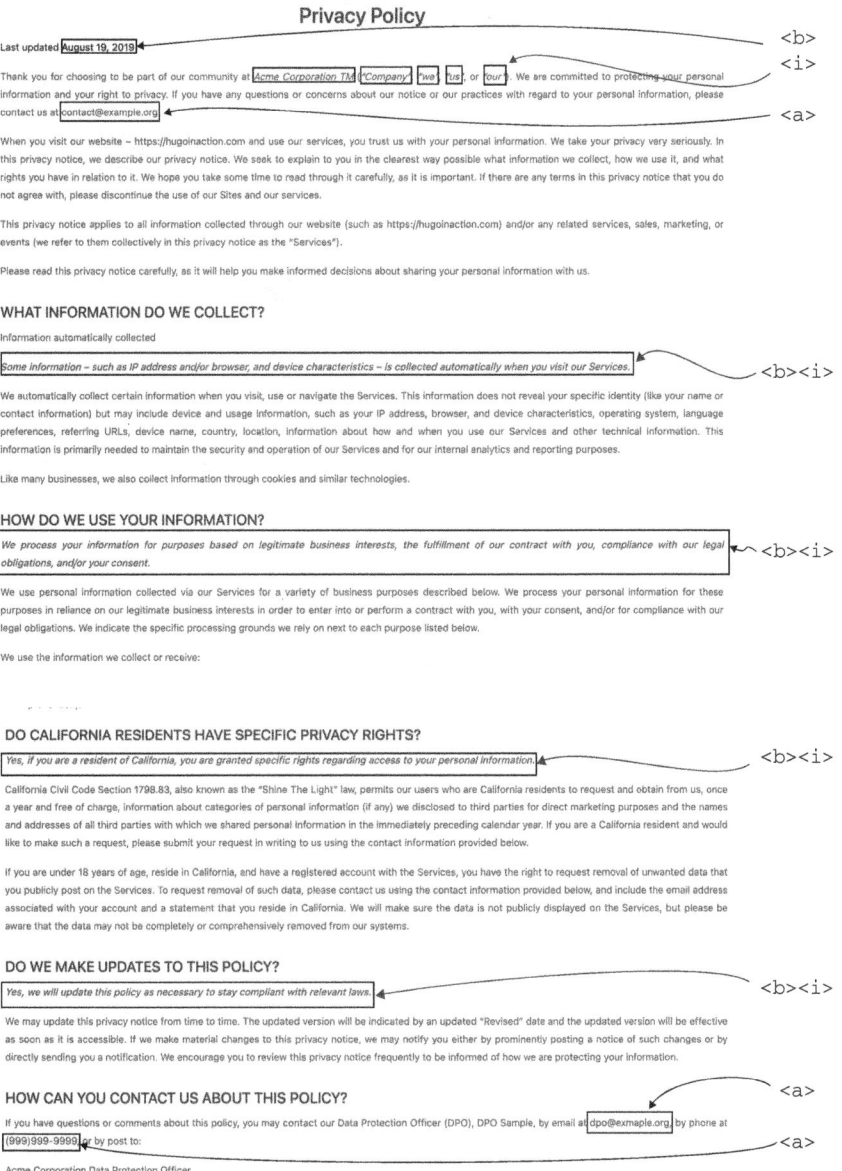

Figure 3.6   The Privacy Policy page for Acme Corporation using block elements, inline links, and other formatting. Note that HTML uses `mailto` URLs for email links such as `contact@example.org` and `tel:` for phone numbers. The image only labels inline elements but the headings also need to be labeled.

page is available in the code checkpoint as well as provided in the chapter resources (https://github.com/hugoinaction/hugoinaction/tree/chapter-03-resources/02).

CODE CHECKPOINT   https://chapter-03-02.hugoinaction.com, and source code: https://github.com/hugoinaction/hugoinaction/tree/chapter-03-02. ↻ Restart your dev server.

3.1.4   *HTML*

While we can do a lot in plain Markdown, pure HTML and CSS are even more powerful. There is no way to represent a lot of HTML features with Markdown. Fortunately, Markdown recognizes this problem. If a Markdown document contains an HTML tag, the Markdown parser outputs the HTML tag as-is, and it will be present in the generated output. For example, if we use `bold with <em>emphasis</em>`, it's converted to `<strong>bold with <em>emphasis</em></strong>`. Markdown, therefore, is a superset of HTML.

Technically, any valid HTML is also valid Markdown. We can use HTML tags with Markdown to pass those tags to our content. We can also write Unicode characters using the escape syntax common in HTML and XML documents. This feature provides access to the entire set of Unicode characters, including localization letters, emojis, symbols, and so on. Figure 3.7 shows these elements and how they are rendered in the browser.

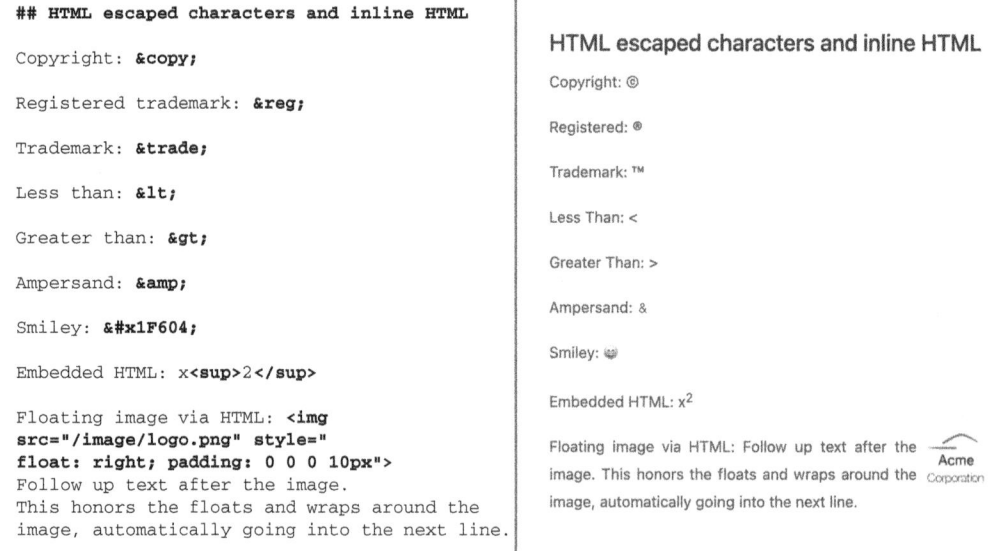

Figure 3.7   Elements in Markdown, part 4: Escaping HTML and inline HTML

Although we can use any HTML to provide additional features that are unavailable with Markdown, it is not a great practice to do so. In fact, *it is strongly advised to minimize the use of embedded HTML in Markdown content.* Inline HTML can turn into a security risk if we do not trust the content creators because they can add arbitrary

JavaScript and CSS. Having little control of the embedded HTML in the hands of the theme creator can turn into a big problem when attempting to update a theme. Additionally, when we have the freedom to be creative with HTML, adding layouts, alignment, color, and other stylistic features to the content, it becomes difficult to clean up.

Hugo disables inline HTML by default. We can enable it in Markdown via the unsafe key in the markup/goldmark/renderer section) of the config.yaml file as the following listing shows. Note that Unicode characters are not disabled. Also, there is little need for inline HTML with the shortcodes feature that we will discuss in chapter 5.

> **Listing 3.1 Enabling inline HTML for Hugo's Goldmark renderer (config.yaml)**

```
markup:
  goldmark:
    renderer:
      unsafe: true
```

When we created the configuration file for Acme Corporation's website, we specified the copyright directive as Copyright ©. In figure 3.7, you can see the escaped HTML for the Unicode-based copyright symbol. The text that is entered for any key in config.yaml is plain text by default, but the theme authors have the option of treating that as Markdown (more details on this in chapter 6). Many themes support Markdown-based configuration parameters, giving us the power to customize formatting for our content.

In the Privacy Policy page, we used TM in the first line to indicate Acme Corporation's trademark. Now would be a good time to replace it with ™ to get the HTML trademark symbol. Note that you can also insert direct Unicode characters like ™ for the trademark symbol.

3.1.5 Tables, task lists, and code blocks

Hugo supports the extensions to Markdown popularized by GitHub as GFM, including the syntax for tables, task lists, and code blocks. Figure 3.8 shows these extensions and how they are rendered in your browser.

To create tables, we can write one row per line, separating each column with the pipe (|) character. We can write a row of dashes (-) to underscore the table header row. Hugo also supports a shorter form of Markdown tables where we can ignore the pipe characters at the outer edges of the rows. You can use colons and dashes in the table to define the column alignment. For example, :-- is left-aligned, :-: is center-aligned, --: is right-aligned, and --- is undefined (the default is based on language and theme).

Task lists follow the GitHub style, where we write a dash (-) followed by square braces ([]) to declare a task. You can even add a cross (x) between the brackets for a completed job. Task lists in Hugo render as disabled; there is no automatic enabling because updating content by clicking the "checkbox" is impossible without involving a server to edit the files.

```
## Tables, task lists, and code blocks

    Name  | Job
--------|------
    Alex  | Web Developer
    Bob   | Sys Admin
    Gabby | Technical Writer


### Alternate table


 |  Name   | Mantra
 |  ---    | ---
 |  Alex   | There must be a better way.
 |  Bob    | Play it safe.
 |  Gabby  | Try everything, but do what you like.

### Table alignment

 | Index  | Product  | Edges |
 | --:    | :--      | :-:   |
 | 1.     | Circle   | 0     |
 | 2.     | Line     | 1     |
 | 3.     | Square   | 4     |

## Acme website task list

- [x] Get the home page up
- [x] Update Privacy Policy and Terms of Use
- [ ] Add the About page
- [ ] Start the blog
- [ ] Enable Contact Us page

## Code block

```javascript
var x= 10;
x++;
console.log(x);
```

With highlighting:

```javascript {linenos=true,hl_lines=[2,"4-6"],
linenostart=199}
while (!success) {
  tryAgain();
  attempt++;
  if (Dead) {
    break;
  }
}
```
```

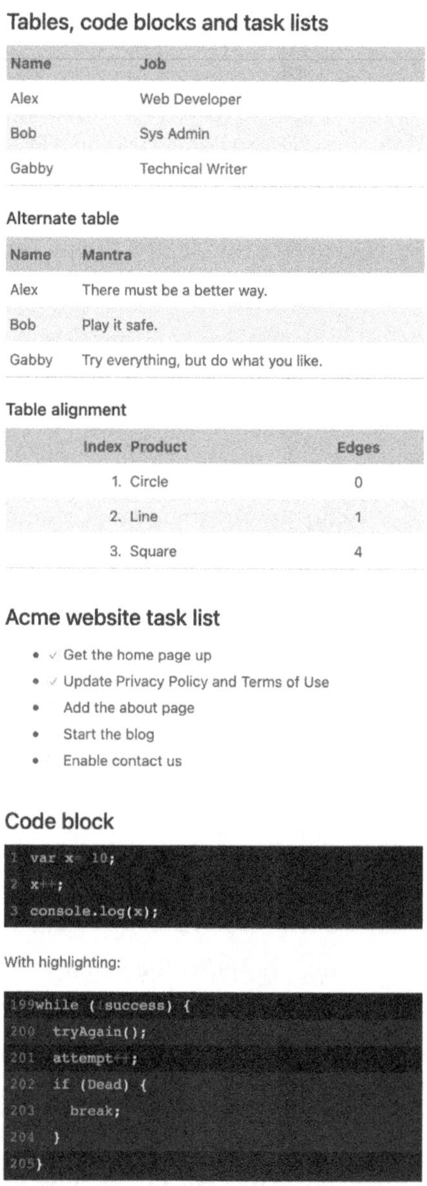

Tables, code blocks and task lists

Name	Job
Alex	Web Developer
Bob	Sys Admin
Gabby	Technical Writer

Alternate table

Name	Mantra
Alex	There must be a better way.
Bob	Play it safe.
Gabby	Try everything, but do what you like.

Table alignment

Index Product	Edges
1. Circle	0
2. Line	1
3. Square	4

Acme website task list

- ✓ Get the home page up
- ✓ Update Privacy Policy and Terms of Use
- Add the about page
- Start the blog
- Enable contact us

Code block

```
1 var x  10;
2 x++;
3 console.log(x);
```

With highlighting:

```
199 while (!success) {
200   tryAgain();
201   attempt++;
202   if (Dead) {
203     break;
204   }
205 }
```

Figure 3.8   Elements in Markdown, part 5: Tables, task lists, and code blocks

Markdown supports blocks of code using three back ticks (```), popularly called *code fences*, at the start and end of the code block. The language name can follow the beginning code fence to get language-specific code highlighting. Hugo does not enable line numbers in code by default. We can allow these by setting `markup/highlight/lineNos` in the global configuration file to `true` as the following listing shows.

Listing 3.2 Enabling line number highlighting in Hugo (config.yaml)

```
markup:
  highlight:
    lineNos: true
```

Hugo supports highlighting code snippets or overriding code sections by passing additional options to code fences. For example, passing {linenos=true, hl_lines=[2,"4-6"],linenostart=199} tells Hugo to override the line number configuration, allowing those to be present, to start the line numbers at 199, and to highlight lines 2, 4, 5 and 6.

3.1.6 Emojis, IDs, and other Hugo extensions

Hugo extends Markdown with added features that make our day-to-day use of Markdown easier and more fun. *Emojis* or *emoticons* are symbols used to depict an idea or emotion. Emojis are not enabled by default, and you need to add an entry in the configuration file to use them. The following listing shows how to enable these.

Listing 3.3 Enabling emojis in the Hugo configuration (config.yaml)

```
...
theme: Eclectic
enableEmoji: true
```

With this change in config.yaml, we can use emojis in our content by surrounding the emoji name with colons (for example, :smile:). The syntax is similar in Slack, GitHub, Basecamp, Trello, Gitter, and Bitbucket, and Hugo supports the same set of emojis. You can use the emoji cheat sheet from https://www.unicode.org/emoji/charts/emoji-list.html for a list of supported emojis.

Hugo automatically converts headers to IDs so that we can link directly to them. We can add custom classes, IDs, or attributes to any Markdown element by supplying them after the text in curly braces (for example, ## heading {#id .className attribute="value"} creates a second-level heading with the text "heading", the id attribute as "id", the CSS class "className", and a custom attribute named "attribute" whose value is "value").

Hugo also supports HTML *definition lists*, another type of list in HTML (besides ordered and unordered) that are relatively less used. To declare a definition list, you can specify the term on one line, followed by a : (colon), and a definition on the next line. Figure 3.9 shows these elements and how they are rendered in the browser. Apart from this, Hugo supports custom shortcodes by which we can extend Markdown by adding custom elements that render HTML, which we will discuss in chapter 4. You can read more about Hugo's extensions to Markdown on the official website at https://gohugo.io/getting-started/configuration-markup.

```
## Direct Emojis
Smile please :smile:

I :heart: Hugo

Wink :wink:

A link to [Emojis](#direct-emojis)

## Smart conversion

This will convert to a dash --

This is followed by ellipses ...

## This is highlighted text{style=
    "background: yellow"}


## Definition lists

Alex
: Hippy Web Developer
: Technophile

Bob
: Classic SysAdmin
: Conservative

Gabby
: Cool Content Master
: Cautious
```

Direct Emojis

Smile please 😊

I 🖤 Hugo

Wink 😉

A link to Emojis

Smart conversion

This will convert to a dash –

This is followed by ellipses …

This is extra highlighted

Definition Lists

Alex

    Hippy Web Developer

    Technophile

Bob

    Classic SysAdmin

    Conservative

Gabby

    Cool Content Master

    Cautious

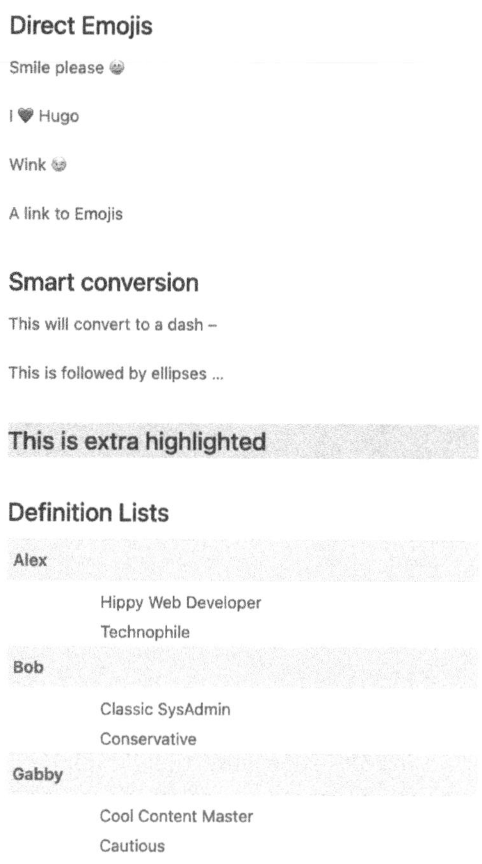

Figure 3.9   Elements in Markdown, part 6: Emojis, smart conversions, and definition lists

NOTE Not all themes have support for all Markdown features. If you plan on relying on something from a third party, we advise that you first check for support for all the Markdown features that you want to use. To figure out Markdown support in a new theme, the markdown.md in the code content with this book can act as a good sample of all Markdown features.

Exercise 3.2

Which of the following features is not supported natively in Hugo's Markdown?

    a. Bold

    b. Smaller font size

    c. Italics

    d. Table

    e. Headings

    f. Horizontal lines

3.2   *Markdown in action*

Using all these content features, we will now update the About Us page for the Acme Corporation website to make it more presentable. Figure 3.10 shows the completed

Figure 3.10   The About Us page for Acme Corporation using advanced Markdown features: 1) block elements like headings and lists, 2) inline elements like bold, italics, and links, 3) inline HTML and character codes, 4) the tables, and 5) definition lists and an emoticon. (Font by Peax Webdesign; image under Creative Commons CC0 from PxHere.)

page. The core elements of the About page are already present in the sample text from chapter 2. The following changes will make the page more presentable.

1 Block elements
   a Add a top-level title with the text `About Us`.
   b Make Manufacturing, Products, and Team second-level headings.
   c Make the following a blockquote: We shape the world. You live in it.
   d There is a numbered list in the Manufacturing section. Make some bulleted sublists for it.
2 Inline elements
   a Format the text "three different" and the item names in the numbered list in the Manfacturing section as bold.
   b Format the text "200 shapes" in the Products section as both bold and italicized.
   c Convert text in the Products table to links.
3 Inline HTML and character codes
   a Add a trademark sign after Acme Corporation at the top of the page.
   b The character code for a circle is ? and for a triangle it's ?. Add these to the Design column of the Products table. Note that two dashes automatically convert to a line.
   c Add the embedded HTML for a right-floating image with a 20 px margin pointing to /image/draw.jpg in the Manufacturing section. (You'll find draw.jpg in the resources for this chapter, but you need to move it to the static/image folder.)
4 Tables
   a Convert the comma-separated list to the Products table.
5 Emojis and definition lists
   a Convert the text "smiles" to the emoji (`:smile:`).
   b Convert the description of team members in the Team area to an HTML definition list.

The completed About page is provided in the chapter resources (https://github .com/hugoinaction/hugoinaction/tree/chapter-03-resources/03) and as a code checkpoint for comparison.

CODE CHECKPOINT   https://chapter-03-03.hugoinaction.com, and source code: https://github.com/hugoinaction/hugoinaction/tree/chapter-03-03. ↻ Restart your dev server.

3.3 Other markup languages

Hugo natively supports Markdown and HTML for content markup. The parsers for these languages are written in Go and are embedded in Hugo, receiving the love and care from the Hugo team to ensure outstanding performance. Hugo also supports AsciiDoc, pandoc, and reStructuredText for providing content. These languages are not available natively in Hugo but instead are supported via *external helpers.* External helpers are software programs that Hugo calls over the command line to get some content parsed. Because they are outside Hugo, Hugo cannot guarantee their performance. Table 3.1 compares the different markup languages supported by Hugo.

Table 3.1 Content markup languages in Hugo

	Markdown	HTML	AsciiDoc	pandoc's Markdown	reStructuredText
Hugo support	Native	Native	External	External	External
Performance	Fast	Fast	Slow	Slow	Slow
Human readability	Good	Bad	Good	Good	Good
Primary target	Regular documents	Browser-readable content	Long-form documents	Regular documents	Code documentation

- *Markdown* trades simplicity and ease of use over features. It is the perfect language for website content that does not span beyond a couple of pages. Hugo's Markdown parser is fast and powerful. For users new to Hugo, it is recommended to begin with the Markdown format unless they already know a different markup language.

- *HTML (HyperText Markup Language)* is also a markup language. Because this is the format that web browsers understand, no translation is needed when we provide content in this language. HTML is more human-readable in its native form than a format like DOC or PDF, and it offers more power than most other markup languages. We can write HTML directly in Hugo and still take advantage of Hugo's template features that we will discuss in the upcoming chapters.

  Writing plain HTML does come at a disadvantage, though. While writing basic HTML, we tend to mix up the page layouts and structure with content. Languages like Markdown force us to focus on content, but a strict disciplinarian can eke out better performance by using plain HTML with Hugo.

- *AsciiDoc* focuses on documents with hundreds of pages and is the most popular of the markup languages among book authors. It provides more features than Markdown, although that comes at the cost of not supporting many programming languages and frameworks. The source code for this book is in AsciiDoc.

- *pandoc* is a file format converter that supports a superset of Markdown, which Hugo can convert to HTML using its command line.

- *reStructuredText* focuses on generating documentation projects. It is formally defined and has a stricter language providing easier parsing at the cost of simplicity.

Note that Hugo constantly adds support for new formats. As of writing this book, there were active discussions to support AsciiDoc in Hugo natively. With native support, AsciiDoc would get a performance boost, and we will have an option for choosing that language for content with minimal downsides.

3.4   Metadata

By embellishing the raw textual data with formatting elements and structure, the pages individually look complete when rendered with the Eclectic theme, which forms the template and code associated with the Markdown data. While there is ample content on the pages to form a website, we need to provide information that we can use to organize content and structure it in lists, menus, and so forth. Markdown is not the best language to offer structured data for this. Hugo supports another set of languages that we call *metadata languages*. We can use these languages to provide this information. One of these is YAML (https://yaml.org/), which we use in this book. It is a popular language for software configuration and the easiest to read among the metadata languages.

YAML stands for *YAML Ain't Markup Language* (the *Y* of the YAML stands for YAML, recursive acronym). It is a language for structured data with keys and values separated by a colon (:). The definition of YAML highlights the fact that the core use case of YAML is around structured data and not marking data like we do in Markdown or HTML. YAML is sensitive to spaces. We use YAML for the configuration file for the Acme Corporation website. YAML supports plain key-value pairs as its primary data structure and also has support for individual data elements and lists. In this section, we will go over the syntax and features supported by YAML in detail.

3.4.1   Comments

We use hash marks (#) for comments in YAML. Comments are single lines and can appear anywhere in a YAML document. The following listing shows the syntax for YAML comments.

> **Listing 3.4   Adding YAML comments**

```
# This is a comment.
```

3.4.2   Basic data types

For human readability, YAML automatically guesses data types based on content. It supports strings, numbers, and Boolean data types. It also supports nil (also called *null*) types. If a key or a value is true or false, YAML automatically coerces it to the

Boolean data type. It guesses numbers as numbers, and everything else becomes a string. The following listing provides examples of YAML's data types.

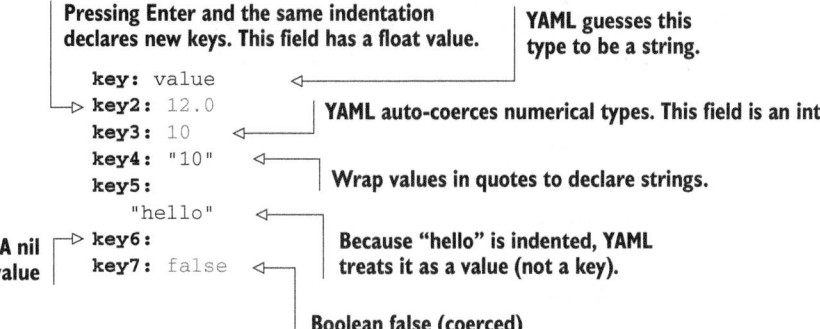

Listing 3.5 Basic data types in YAML

3.4.3 Multiline strings

YAML is sensitive to indentation, and newline characters define the beginning of a new YAML key-value pair. We can use the pipe character (|) to create multiline strings that honor new lines and the greater than sign (>) to create multiline strings insensitive to new lines. The following listing provides examples of this.

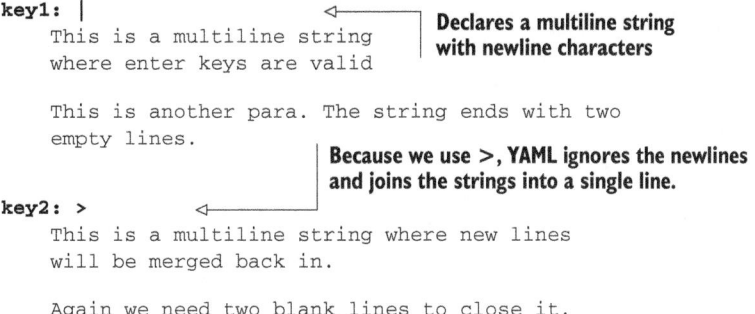

Listing 3.6 Using multiline strings with YAML

3.4.4 Lists

We can declare lists in YAML using dashes (-) or square brackets ([]). The following listing shows how to add lists.

Listing 3.7 Representing lists in YAML

```
key1:
  - a
  - b
```
Adds a list using a dash

```
    - c                     | Adds a list using
key2: [d, e, f ]            | square brackets
```

3.4.5   *Dictionaries*

Dictionaries, also called *maps* or *objects*, are key-value pairs. The top-level YAML object is also a dictionary. We can create dictionaries and subdictionaries in YAML, and they can contain all types. The next listing shows how to add dictionaries with YAML.

Listing 3.8   **Representing dictionaries in YAML**

```
Dictionary key-value pair
 └─▷ key1:                         | The order of elements in the
        key11: value13     ◁────┘   dictionary does not matter . . .
        key12:             ◁──┐
          - List Item 1        | . . . but indentation does.
          - List Item 2
        key13: 10          ◁──┐
 ┌─▷ key14: {key14: value14}    | Keys and values can
 |                              | be of any type.
 | Alternate dictionary
```

Exercise 3.3

YAML does *not* support which of the following data types?

- **a.** Date
- **b.** Boolean
- **c.** Map
- **d.** List
- **e.** Numbers

3.4.6   *Revisiting config.yaml*

Now would be a good time to revisit config.yaml, which we created in chapter 2 and have been modifying since. It contains key-value pairs for elements such as baseURL and title. The order of these does not matter.

The author, menu, and params elements are dictionaries, while footer and main are lists in the params and menu dictionaries. Because types are automatically inferred, recentCount is a number, recents is a string, and true automatically converts to a Boolean. Listing 3.9 shows the most recent use of YAML elements in the configuration file.

NOTE   The dashes before identifier in the main section in config.yaml are needed because the main menu is a list, where each list item is a dictionary.

Listing 3.9   **YAML configuration for Acme Corporation (config.yaml)**

```
baseURL: http://example.org/   ◁──┐ Key-value pair for the
                                   | top-level dictionary
```

```
languageCode: en-us
title: Acme Corporation
theme: Eclectic
author:
  facebook: "https://facebook.com/example"
  twitter: "https://twitter.com/example"
  email: "contact@example.org"
  name: "Acme Corporation"
  location: New York
  phone: (999) 999-9999
  hours: "*Mon-Fri*: 9:00AM - 6:00PM, ET"
menu:
  main:
    - identifier: about
      name: About
      url: /about
      weight: 100
    - identifier: contact
      name: Contact
      url: /contact
      weight: 200
params:
  color:
  copyright: "Copyright &copy; 2022 Acme Corporation.
--> All Rights Reserved."
  footer:
    - title: About
      content: >
          Acme Corporation is the world's leading
          manufacturer of digital shapes. From squares and
          circles to triangles and hexagons, we have it all.
          Browse through our collection of various forms with
          different thicknesses and line styles. We shape
          the world. You live in it.


    - title: Recent Blog Posts
      recents: blog
      recentCount: 7
    - title: Contact Us
      contact: true
  style: blue
  logo: /image/logo.png
  logo_small: /image/logo.png
  about_us: >
    Acme Corporation is the world's leading manufacturer
    of digital shapes. From squares and circles to
    triangles and hexagons, we have it all. Browse through
    our collection of various forms with different
    thicknesses and line styles. We shape the world.
    You live in it.


  recent_posts:
    enable: true
```

Annotations:
- **Subdictionary** (pointing to `author:`)
- **Quotes are optional.** (pointing to `name:` / `location:`)
- **Main is a list where each element is a dictionary.** (pointing to `main:`)
- **Multiline string** (pointing to `content: >`)
- **Numeric values (integral)** (pointing to `recentCount: 7`)
- **Boolean values** (pointing to `contact: true`)
- **URL and paths are strings.** (pointing to `logo_small: /image/logo.png`)

```
markup:
  goldmark:
    renderer:
      unsafe: true
  highlight:
    lineNos: true
enableEmoji: true
```

3.5   *Other metadata languages*

YAML also has the same tradeoff as Markdown: human readability over a strict specification. This tradeoff comes with complexities in parsers and weird edge cases that might not be easy to understand. We have chosen YAML in this book for the configuration file due to its popularity and ease of readability. Hugo supports TOML and JSON as other metadata languages apart from YAML. Appendix B goes over TOML and JSON in detail, and table 3.2 provides a quick comparison of their features.

Table 3.2   Metadata language comparison

	YAML	**[T]**	**○**
Name	YAML	TOML	JSON
Overall popularity	Medium	Low	High
Usage in Hugo community	Low	High	Low
Readability	High	Medium	Medium
GitHub support with Markdown	Present	Absent	Absent
Objective	Human readability	One way of doing things	Information interchange
Data types supported	number, string, boolean, null, list, dictionary	number, string, boolean, date, list, dictionary	number, string, boolean, null, list, dictionary

- *TOML (Tom's Obvious Minimal Language)* has the objective of ensuring that there is one standard way of writing a particular data item. YAML's automatic guessing of data types makes it easier to read but can lead to cases where YAML infers a wrong type. For example, plain text is a string, but if the plain text is the word *true*, it becomes a Boolean. TOML avoids that confusion with a strongly defined system where we have to enclose every string in quotes.
- *JSON (JavaScript Object Notation)* is a popular format for exchanging information and is much easier than YAML and TOML for generation and machine parsing. The most significant advantage of JSON is the availability of high-performance parsers in most programming languages and familiarity with this format among developers. Graphical editors and CMS solutions typically use JSON for Hugo interaction.

NOTE You will find a lot of resources from the Hugo community in the TOML format. TOML is more straightforward to copy and paste due to its nonstrict spacing policy. If you happen to write a parser, TOML will be much easier to parse. For an advanced Hugo user, TOML is an excellent language to know.

3.6 *Front matter*

Apart from the global site-wide configuration, we also need page-specific metadata like creation date, tags, URLs, author name, and so forth. Hugo needs this information to organize the page in the website and to provide information about this page to the broader internet, such as search engines and social networks. We can also show some metadata in the sidebar of the page.

To provide page-specific metadata, Hugo has the concept of front matter. The *front matter* is a set of key-value pairs that define the metadata for the content provided right before the content. With the front matter, we can provide metadata on the same file as the main content. The front matter is also called the *page metadata section* (*page metadata* or *metadata* in short) as well as the *page configuration*. Those terms are used interchangeably in this book.

To place YAML content in the front matter of a page, we need to wrap it with three dashes (---) and place it at the top of the page. The following listing shows how to use the three-dash format to identify YAML as the content metadata language.

> **Listing 3.10   Identifying the YAML metadata for a markup page in Hugo**

```
---                                    ◁─────────────────┐
                                                         │  Wraps a YAML
# Note that the file extension is .md                    │  grouping block
<metadata section in YAML>                               │
---                                    ◁─────────────────┘
<data section in Markdown>
```

Hugo is clever with the metadata and provides a reasonable set of defaults. That is why we have been able to get along so far, providing little metadata and still being able to render content. By default, Hugo receives the information from the filename, the Git version control system (if used), and the OS attributes like the modified date. We need to deal in the front matter only if we need to do something that Hugo cannot guess itself or need to override it to perform specific tasks.

> **Metadata before content**
>
> The concept of having metadata before the content has been present in computers since the beginning of programming. Pascal represents strings by a length followed by raw binary data of that length. Many binary file formats start with a signature that is the metadata associated with the file. For example, if you open a .pdf file in a text editor, it starts with %PDF, a .png file begins with .PNG, and a .gif file with GIF. Jekyll, the first modern static site builder, introduced metadata in the front matter for all static site builders, and Hugo adopted the concept.

3.6.1 *Common metadata elements in the front matter*

The front matter consists of all the metadata properties that are associated with the specific page. Just like a website has a configuration file (config.yaml), we can place page-specific YAML content on the page itself. We can override these properties in the front matter. Table 3.3 presents some of the most common properties.

Table 3.3 **Common front matter properties in Hugo. Examples shown are for the About Us page in Acme Corporation's website.**

Name	Default	Use	Example
title	Name of the file	Used in summary pages and RSS feeds provided to search engines. We may want to show these properties on the page itself.	About Us
description	<empty string>	Provided to search engines; can be used in listing pages.	World's leading manufacturer of digital shapes. We shape the world. You live in it.
date	Git-modified date if enableGitInfo is true in config.yaml, otherwise it's January 1, 01 AD.	The date is associated with this page. This field helps in sorting the pages by the creation date.	January 01, 2020
keywords	<empty list>	Keywords used in the metadata passed on to bots and search engines.	Acme Corporation, Acme Line Company, Circle, Line, Triangle
type	Name of the subfolder containing the current file; default if this file is present directly in the content folder.	Content type for the theme. Each type can render differently (we discuss content types in chapter 6).	<absent>
slug	<folder>/ <title or filename if not title>	The URL of the file in the web browser. Hugo also provides the url field for this task. The slug is the final part of the URL and honors the localization for multilanguage content as the URL ignores it. If we use slug and later add languages, the page may get the language prefix.	<absent>

Table 3.3 Common front matter properties in Hugo. Examples shown are for the About Us page in Acme Corporation's website. *(continued)*

Name	Default	Use	Example
draft	false	`draft` marks content that is committed but is not complete. Hugo does not render draft content by default. We can set `buildDrafts: true` or pass in `buildDrafts` to build these pages (which we can do in the Acme project in development mode).	<absent>
aliases	[]	Alternate URLs can point to the same content, allowing us to retain our links. Use for migration from an old system to Hugo.	<absent>
layout	<depends>	This field marks the layout that Hugo uses to render the page. A single page has a single layout, while an index page with a list of pages has a list layout. We will go into layouts in chapter 7.	<absent>
cascade	<absent>	Lets us set a front matter property on all child pages in a folder. Chapter 7 discusses cascade in detail.	<absent>
outputs	<gets from config>	The formats this page needs to be rendered in HTML or JSON, for example. We will use outputs in chapter 9.	<absent>
tags	<absent>	Used to supply tags with the default Hugo config. There can be multiple keys that may or may not include `tags`. We will discuss taxonomies and tags in chapter 4.	<absent>
<others>	<absent>	Theme-specific parameters for the page.	<absent>

To update these properties in the About Us page for the Acme Corporation website, we can add the code in listing 3.11 to the top of the page (https://github.com/hugoinaction/hugoinaction/tree/chapter-03-resources/04). We can supply the front matter in YAML format, enclosing it in three dashes (---).

Listing 3.11   Adding front matter to the About page (content/about.md)

```
---
title: About Us
date: 2020-01-01T00:00:00Z
description: World's leading manufacturer of digital shapes.
    We shape the world. You live in it.
draft: false
---

<page content>
```

The Eclectic theme places the title on the page so we do not need to add it manually. Other than that, there seems to be no significant changes. You should see the updated description and the document title should also show up in the tab bar (see figure 3.11), when you view the generated HTML (see figure 3.12).

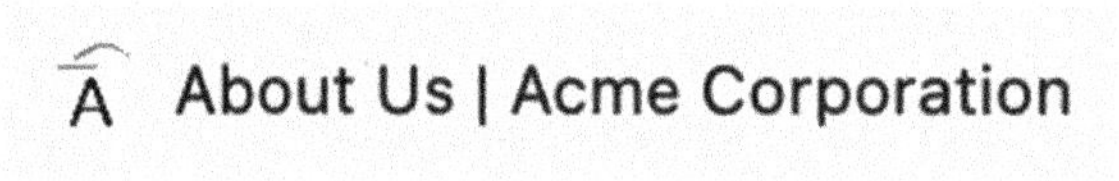

Ā About Us | Acme Corporation

Figure 3.11   Address bar update with the front matter content

CODE CHECKPOINT   https://chapter-03-04.hugoinaction.com, and source code: https://github.com/hugoinaction/hugoinaction/tree/chapter-03-04.

NOTE   The rest of this book discusses more front matter entries and use cases. One crucial feature missing in this chapter is the cascade front matter entry addressed in chapter 7.

Exercise 3.4

We can use the _____ front matter entry in Hugo to define a custom URL endpoint for the web page.

We can enable only some of the features such as draft via the front matter. The front matter will get more important once we start getting into taxonomies in chapter 4. The front matter and the content form the updates that a content creator has to work on regularly. With a working knowledge of these two areas, we can design as many pages of content as we want in a website. GitHub supports rendering front matter and Markdown when we use YAML in the front matter, making it easy to navigate the content. Figure 3.13 shows the About Us page on GitHub.

Title updated   **Metadata and description for FaceBook, Twitter, and Google**

```html
1   <!DOCTYPE html>
2   <html class="no-js
"   lang="en">
3   <head><script src="/livereload.js?mindelay=10&amp;v=2&amp;port=1313&amp;path=livereload" data-no-instant defer></script><meta charset="utf-8">
4   <meta name="apple-mobile-web-app-capable" content="yes">
5   <meta name="viewport" content="width=device-width,initial-scale=1.0">
6   <meta name="theme-color" content="#4f46e5"><meta name="generator" content="Hugo 0.82.0" />
7   <meta name="robots" content="index, follow">
8   <title>About Us | Acme Corporation</title><link rel="canonical" href="http://localhost:1313/about/" />
9   <meta name="description" content="World&#39;s leading manufacturer of digital shapes. We shape the world. You live in it."
10  />
11  <meta name="author" content="Acme Corporation">
12  <link rel="manifest" href="/manifest.json">
13  <meta property="og:title" content="About Us" />
14  <meta property="og:site_name" content="Acme Corporation" />
15  <meta property="og:description" content="World&#39;s leading manufacturer of digital shapes. We shape the world. You live in it."
16  />
17  <meta property="og:type" content="article" />
18  <meta property="og:url" content="http://localhost:1313/about/" /><meta property="article:published_time" content="2020-01-01T00:00:00&#43;00:00"/>
19  <meta property="article:modified_time" content="2020-01-01T00:00:00&#43;00:00"/>
20  <meta property="article:author" content="https://www.facebook.com/https://facebook.com/example" />
21  <meta property="article:publisher" content="https://www.facebook.com/https://facebook.com/example" /><meta name="twitter:card" content="summary"/>
22  <meta name="twitter:title" content="About Us"/>
23  <meta name="twitter:description" content="World&#39;s leading manufacturer of digital shapes. We shape the world. You live in it."/>
24  <meta name="twitter:site" content="@https://twitter.com/example" />
25  <meta name="twitter:creator" content="@https://twitter.com/example" />
26  <script type="application/ld+json">
27  {
28      "headline": "About Us",
29      "publisher": {
30          "@type": "Organization",
31          "logo": {
32              "@type": "ImageObject",
33              "url": "/image/logo.min.svg"
34          },"name": "Acme Corporation"
35      },
36      "author": {
37          "@type": "Person",
38          "name": "Acme Corporation"
39      },
40      "description": "World\u0027s leading manufacturer of digital shapes. We shape the world. You live in it.",
41      "name": "Acme Corporation",
42
43      "@type": "Article",
44      "wordCount": 263 ,
45      "mainEntityOfPage":{"@type":"WebPage","@id":"http:\/\/localhost:1313\/about\/"},
46
47      "@context": "http://schema.org",
48      "dateCreated": "2020-01-01T00:00:00+00:00",
49      "dateModified": "2020-01-01T00:00:00+00:00",
50
51      "url": "http://localhost:1313/about/"
52  }
53  </script>
54  <link rel="preload" href="/index.json" as="fetch" crossorigin importance="low">
55
56  <link rel="stylesheet" href="/css/index.min.8adf14be89b870d3e35eea06c25c3fa429e531e82ee10f933ac146e949c5e529c07a3b24fd43e7251cfa99c238e1453af2c143425
57  <noscript>
58      <link rel="stylesheet" href="/css/index.min.8adf14be89b870d3e35eea06c25c3fa429e531e82ee10f933ac146e949c5e529c07a3b24fd43e7251cfa99c238e1453af2c1434
59  </noscript>
60  <style>
61      html {
62          opacity: 0;
63      }
64  </style>
65  <script type="text/javascript" src="/js/main.js" defer></script>
66  <script>
67      if (window.localStorage.color) {
68          document.documentElement.style.setProperty("--theme-color", window.localStorage.color);
69      }
70
71      if(window.localStorage.dark === "true") {
72          document.documentElement.classList.add("dark");
73      }</script>
74
75  </head>
```

Figure 3.12 Metadata updates with the front matter content

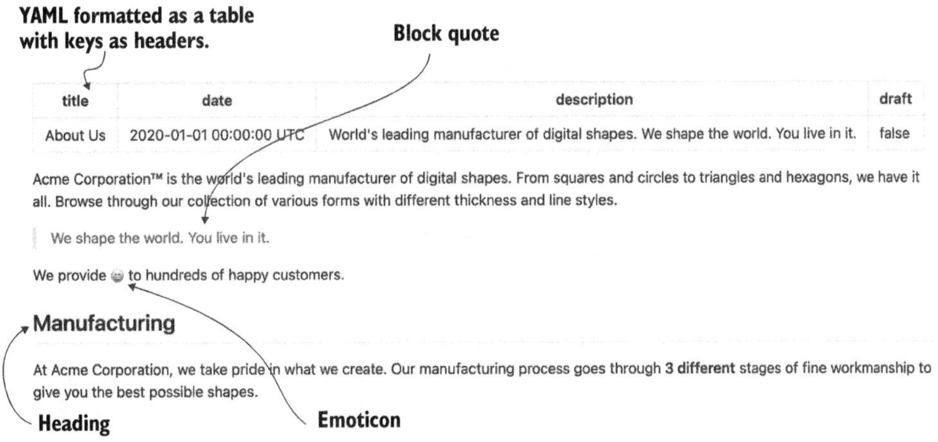

YAML formatted as a table
with keys as headers.   **Block quote**

title	date	description	draft
About Us	2020-01-01 00:00:00 UTC	World's leading manufacturer of digital shapes. We shape the world. You live in it.	false

Acme Corporation™ is the world's leading manufacturer of digital shapes. From squares and circles to triangles and hexagons, we have it all. Browse through our collection of various forms with different thickness and line styles.

> We shape the world. You live in it.

We provide 😀 to hundreds of happy customers.

Manufacturing

At Acme Corporation, we take pride in what we create. Our manufacturing process goes through **3 different** stages of fine workmanship to give you the best possible shapes.

Heading   **Emoticon**

Figure 3.13 GitHub's default rendering of the front matter along with Markdown

Front matter language conversion

Hugo supports all metadata languages in parallel. Different documents can use other metadata languages, and Hugo parses these correctly. Hugo can also convert content between metadata languages. We can use the Hugo command line to convert the content to TOML by entering `hugo convert toTOML <content file>`. We can similarly convert to JSON/YAML by updating the command with `toJSON` and `toYAML`, respectively.

There is no real reason to do this conversion because Hugo supports all of these languages in the front matter. Most users stick with the choice of metadata language they began with, but there is a straightforward command-line interface available if you need to switch to a different one.

3.6.2   *Data-driven landing page using the front matter*

Front matter is not just for metadata; we can use it to specify the data of the page. The theme authors are free to use the structured data supplied in the front matter with any page. Some elements like carousels benefit from structured data. We can provide individual pages for the carousel as key-value pairs. Theme authors can embed these in the right places in the template much more easily than they can do with Markdown, which acts as one big blob.

   The Eclectic theme, for example, has support for photo and text carousels, icon-based lists, testimonials, client icons, etc., all driven by data that we can provide in the page's front matter. You can place the provided data-driven.md file (https://github.com/hugoinaction/hugoinaction/tree/chapter-03-resources/05) in the content folder to try out this feature. You can view the corresponding page at http://localhost:1313/data-driven to get a page similar to that shown in figure 3.14.

   CODE CHECKPOINT   https://chapter-03-05.hugoinaction.com, and source code: https://github.com/hugoinaction/hugoinaction/tree/chapter-03-05.

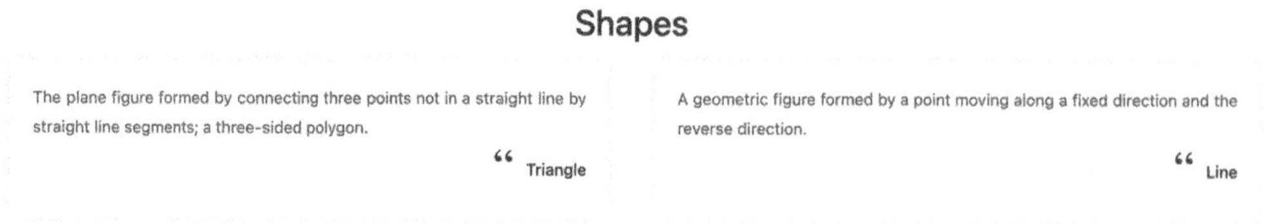

Shapes

The plane figure formed by connecting three points not in a straight line by straight line segments; a three-sided polygon.

A geometric figure formed by a point moving along a fixed direction and the reverse direction.

"   Triangle

"   Line

Figure 3.14   A carousel for the Acme Corporation website that makes use of the data-driven approach and uses the front matter with the Eclectic theme. We can place data-driven.md in the content folder to get this page.

Some themes (like the Universal theme) can also take the information in the global config.yaml or read it from the data folder. You should read the documentation for your theme to figure out how to use these features.

The approach of providing structured metadata in the front matter, as a global configuration, or in the data folder comes at a cost. Because structured data is specific to the theme, your custom data does not get picked up automatically if you switch themes. For many users, using a prebuilt theme and providing structured data are best suited to their needs because they likely chose that theme for those features. It is also easier to maintain data in a format like YAML rather than plain HTML.

Themes provide many built-in features and complicated logic to enable compatibility across screen sizes when presenting our data. We will create our structured data-based web pages in chapter 6.

> **Exercise 3.5**
> True or False: Theoretically, we could build a Hugo website with all the content in the front matter and nothing in the Markdown body of the web pages.

3.7 Benefits of using markup and metadata languages

In the Jamstack, we use markup and metadata languages across multiple files to replace the role of the database in the traditional web stack. The benefit of giving up on the database is not obvious when we move to the Jamstack. Databases have been optimized for over 30 years and provide vast storage optimizations and querying capabilities. Databases (both SQL and NoSQL) require some structure to the data they store. Databases expect some schema, even if it is different in every document. They are not very useful if there is no schema/structure at all, as in the case of formatted text.

In most database-oriented content management systems, the formatted content of the web page gets shoved into a single column or assigned to a single key. With textual content stored as files on disk, we get access to a massive set of utilities that work on text files, from standard bash tools like grep to general-purpose software like version management systems (Git).

3.7.1 Content versioning

When we write and commit text content alongside code using a version control system, we inherit the robust versioning scheme built for source code and can use it for versioning content. With Markdown, the formatting updates are easy to understand in the diff view. We get full support for forks, branches, and pull requests for content. We can have a proper software life cycle for the website content, including staging, branch views, and versioned content releases. If we want, we can write scripts to validate content, check spellings, or fix structure, which can trigger code commits, just like we built the website for GitHub deployment in chapter 2.

This support is present not only in Hugo but in the entire Jamstack. Jamstack enables this by moving content from databases to markup. We can see the diff view in action on GitHub by navigating to the commit pages for the changes we make to the Acme Corporation website. A sample diff view is shown in figure 3.15.

Addition (green)   Deletion (red)   Highlight has color/bold formatting.

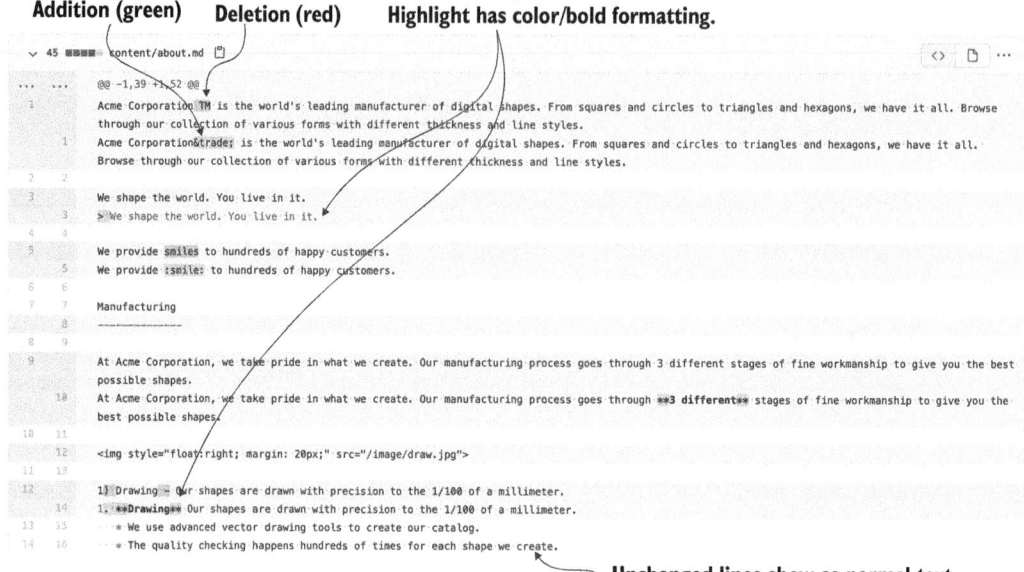

Figure 3.15   A sample diff view for the About page on GitHub. We can view, review, and manage each content change as code.

Figure 3.16   Content language over web forms: Gabby, the lead editor for the Acme Corporation website, tries to understand what moving from a web form to a document for content entry entails.

3.7.2   *Theme independence*

A lot of moving of the website from Markdown to the configuration is standardized. Content authors put things like text colors and HTML spacing in Markdown. The elements that we move make the content stable across multiple themes. We can switch themes and see our page render almost correctly. While Hugo generates the correct

HTML for all Markdown, it is still up to the theme author to provide good styling for all of the Markdown features.

If you are interested in checking the portability of your code across themes, it is not a bad idea to try out the functionality across themes. The About Us page for the Acme Corporation website (figure 3.17) does not look shabby in the Universal theme.

CODE CHECKPOINT   https://chapter-03-06.hugoinaction.com, and source code: https://github.com/hugoinaction/hugoinaction/tree/chapter-03-06.

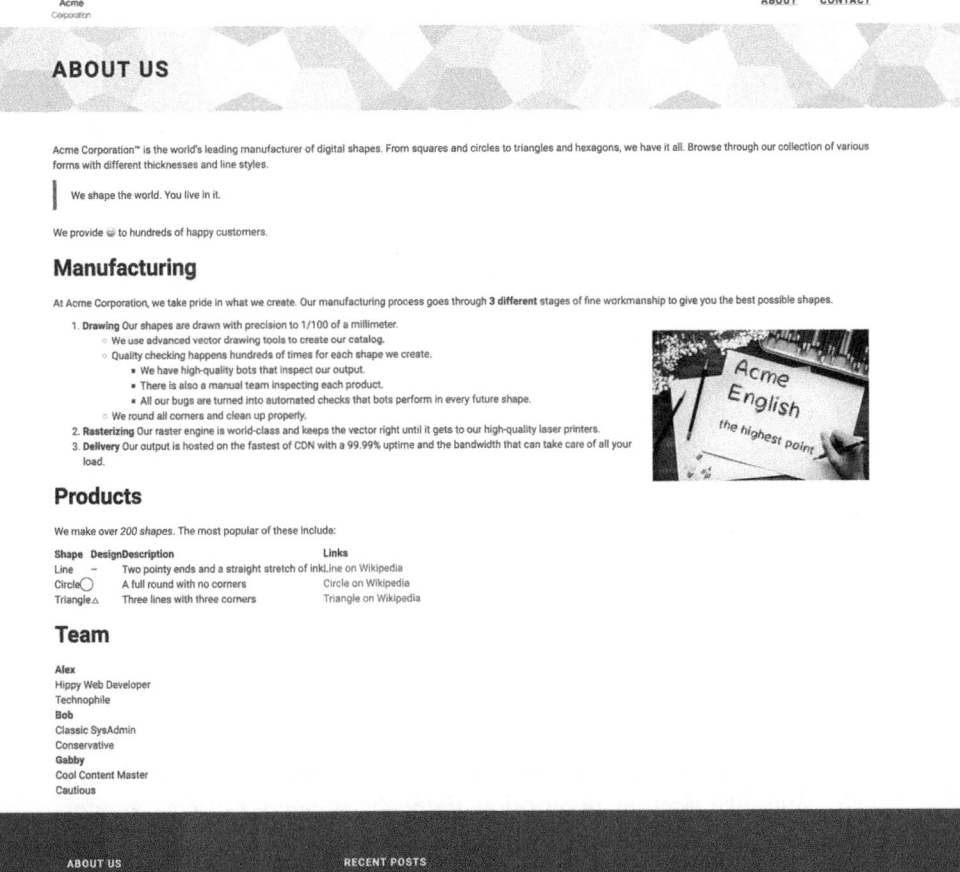

Figure 3.17   The About Us page for Acme Corporation website rendered using the Universal theme for Hugo

3.7.3   *Cleanliness*

The HTML markup generated by the WYSIWYG (what you see is what you get) editors present in tools like WordPress can be overly complicated and unreadable. We are also at risk of the WYSIWYG creators pasting arbitrary JavaScript into the content, which can turn into a security issue. Markdown is a much cleaner language than HTML. The likelihood of extra tags and mistakes is much lower when we write readable text. Similarly, with Markdown, we have forms to enter metadata in traditional content management systems. There are many websites where the admin section is shoddily prepared, and a plain-text metadata language provides more flexibility and power than any of those forms ever could.

Summary

- Markdown has all the features that we need for formatting regular web pages and blog posts.
- Markdown supports block elements like headings, various types of lists, and sublists.
- We can provide inline images, links, basic formatting, and code blocks to Markdown-based content using text-based constructs.
- GitHub Flavored Markdown (GFM) is supported by Hugo, which adds task lists and tables to Markdown.
- Hugo's rendering engine also supports features like emoticons, automatic fractions, and definition lists.
- Hugo supports multiple languages for content, including AsciiDoc for long-form content, pandoc for extended Markdown, and reStructuredText for documentation.
- Apart from data, a web page also needs metadata supplied in Hugo using YAML, TOML, and JSON.
- YAML is easy to read and provides a mechanism to deliver structured data to Hugo.
- While Hugo has sensible defaults, and we can build websites without writing a single metadata item, Hugo provides the ability to override most metadata items like the title, description, date, and theme-specific parameters.
- Most of the Markdown features are native to Hugo and can be used across all themes.
- With the approach of managing content as files instead of as databases and the readability of Markdown, we get sensible diff views and versioning support for content using a code versioning software like Git.

Content management with Hugo

This chapter covers
- Organizing pages into sections and menus in a Hugo website
- Grouping related content using Hugo taxonomies
- Bundling page contents into a page bundle
- Using Hugo's built-in and community-provided shortcodes for more Markdown features

A website is not just a bundle of web pages scattered at random URL locations. The pages need to be discoverable, organized into meaningful sections, and there needs to be a way to navigate to them for a reader to be successful. Content in most websites is laid out with a strategy; grouped, tagged, and navigation cues are present in pages for the reader to navigate to others.

There are two distinct roles in a website's development team: the content owner and the theme developer. The *content owner* decides the content that shows up on the website, and the *theme developer* focuses on surfacing content. In this chapter, we will be playing the role of the content owner (also called *author* or *website editor*) for the Acme Corporation website.

We will look into content organization and management in this chapter (see figure 4.1). In section 4.1, we will organize the configuration in the config folder. In sections 4.2 to 4.4, we will discuss the means to manage and associate content on a Hugo website. Section 4.5 will go into shortcodes, which live in the layouts folder. *Shortcodes* provide the means to extend Markdown and share content between different pages in Hugo.

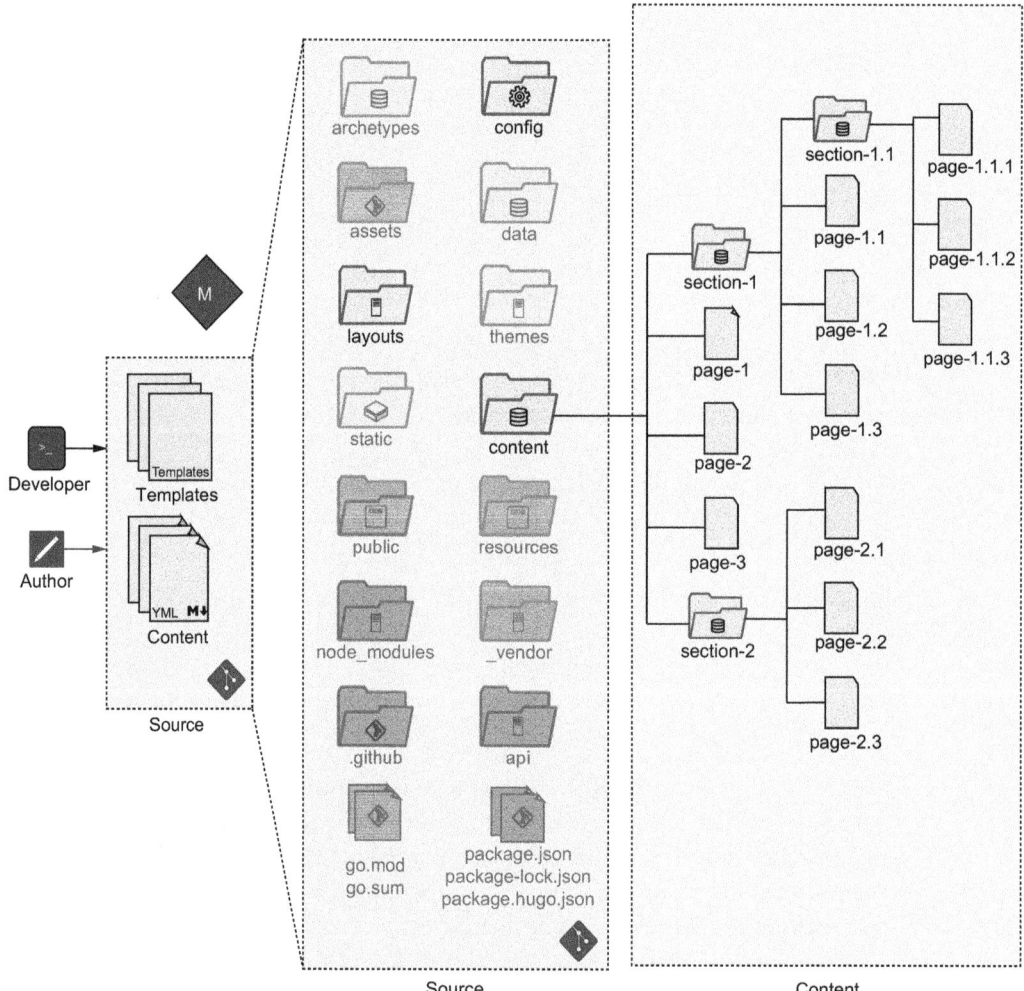

Figure 4.1 The author and the developer organize the website's contents into files and folders that are then stored in the content directory. This chapter focuses on the organization of the content directory for optimal resource management. We will also organize the configurations in the config folder and will create shortcodes in the layouts folder to extend Markdown.

4.1   Customizing with the Hugo configurations

On the Acme Corporation website, so far we have had only one configuration file, config.yaml, where we have been piling our configurations. If we look at the Hugo documentation, we notice that many configuration parameters can be changed, which can quickly get overwhelming. A single configuration file is bound to become a bottleneck.

Another problem with our configuration file is that we cannot have different settings for development and production in one file. An essential practice for web development is to have different environments. This way, many teams can contribute independently. To debug easily, a web developer needs HTML that has not gone through *minification* (processing to reduce the file size for faster serving over the internet). In a testing environment, we may need more logging to enable the development team to reproduce issues quickly and to fix bugs. The content team needs a website as stable as the production team.

Hugo recognizes these problems and supports splitting the configuration files with environment-specific overrides to the base configuration via a config folder. In this section, we will split the configuration file into multiple files, building separate files that override the default configuration. To do that, we will create a folder called config and add a folder called _default in the config folder and move the Acme Corporation website to those folders. The _default folder is special; Hugo refers to the default content in that folder. This name is used not only for configurations but also for templates, as we will see in chapter 7.

If we move the config.yaml file to the config/_default folder, the website will continue to behave the same. But now that its contents are in a folder, we can divide the configuration file into multiple files for multiple properties. We can now move the author section in the configuration file to config/_default/author.yaml, and we can move the params and the markup sections to separate files. The filename is automatically mapped to a key when Hugo parses the configuration. This way, this information is isolated and more manageable. We will also split the menu in menu.yaml and extend this in section 4.2. The split files are also provided in the resources for this chapter (https://github.com/hugoinaction/hugoinaction/tree/chapter-04-resources/01).

Hugo supports environment-specific configuration overrides using folders for each environment in the config folder. These environments take the values from the _default folder and override the environment-specific values. We can now create a folder called production and put production-specific overrides in the configuration parameters in that folder. Similarly, we can add a folder called development for development-specific configurations. Listing 4.1 provides the code to split the configuration directory for the Acme Corporation website. (The listing's .yaml file document icon is by IYIKON from the Noun Project; the folder icon is from flaticon.)

When Hugo runs with a live reload server via hugo server, it defaults to the development configuration (the names "development" and "production" are hardcoded in Hugo as defaults). When built by the hugo command, by default, the mode changes to production. We can override the configuration to any name we want by specifying it in the environment variable HUGO_ENV or using the --environment flag in the Hugo command line. This override can be used, for example, to debug production-only bugs in the development server mode.

Listing 4.1   Splitting the config.yaml file into multiple files

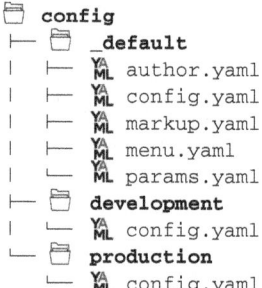

```
config
├── _default
│   ├── author.yaml
│   ├── config.yaml
│   ├── markup.yaml
│   ├── menu.yaml
│   └── params.yaml
├── development
│   └── config.yaml
└── production
    └── config.yaml
```

The world of environments

Most hosted software has the concept of environments. If we need to ensure that there is no downtime as we develop, we need to have a methodology to ensure only stable releases go live. It is crucial to label stable builds and move them to a higher environment tier for further testing before going live. The number of environments depends on the number of people involved and the degree of independence needed for independent tasks. A standard set of environments in a large project can include:

- *Development*—This is where active development happens. Developers may have separate branches or branch-specific environments, but we need a shared branch where all development teams merge their code and resolve conflicts. Development mode is the default when Hugo runs in live server mode.

- *Testing*—An environment with all completed features currently under automated and manual testing.

- *Staging/Alpha*—Stabler environment for testing across teams in the company. The companies might also provide access to this environment to some selected customers who are helping to fine-tune the software.

- *Beta*—A public prerelease that is ready to go live, and the company invites everyone to verify their workflows.

- *Production*—The current live/active environment served to the end users. Production is the default environment when you run Hugo without the live server.

Each team is different and can decide to use a different set of environments. Hugo provides total flexibility to name the environments and to have settings specific to them. The code changes for features under development should be managed by a version control system like Git.

In the development environment, let's update the settings to disable minification by setting `minify` to `false`. (You can control minification settings for individual file types using this setting as well.) Additionally, the Eclectic theme supports a debug bar (created initially by JugglerX), which provides the front matter in a visible section on the web page as figure 4.2 shows. We can enable this by setting `DebugMenu` to `true` in the `params` section for development and can be launched by clicking the red wrench icon on the bottom right in the debug bar. In chapter 8, we will show you how to integrate this debug bar in other websites using Hugo Modules.

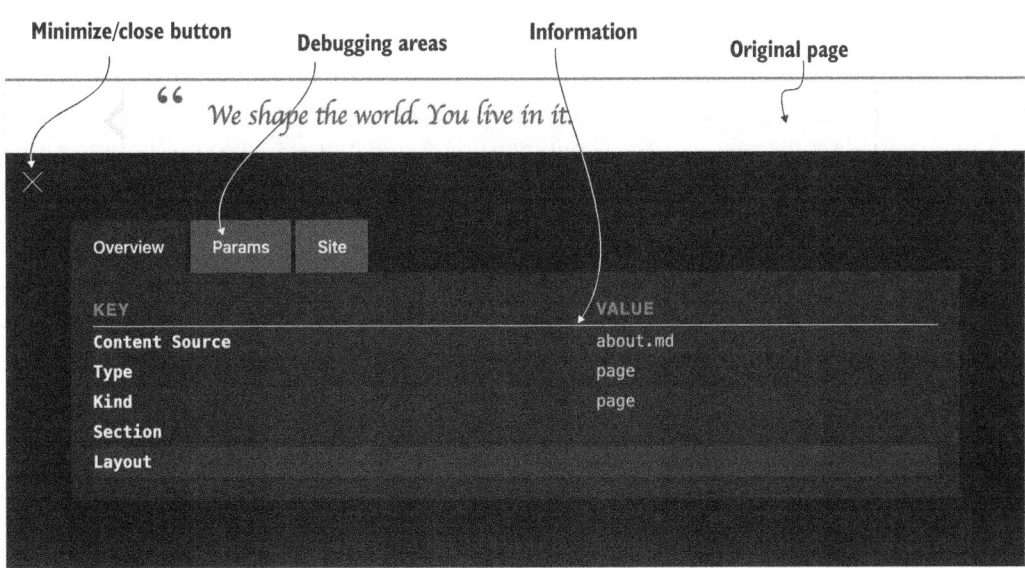

Minimize/close button   Debugging areas   Information   Original page

Figure 4.2   The debug bar in Eclectic (only when running in the development environment)

Listing 4.2 sets the overrides for the development environment to enable the debug bar, to disable minification, and to build drafts. Then listing 4.3 sets the overrides for the production environment to enable robots.txt and minification.

Listing 4.2   Enabling the debug bar (config/development/config.yaml)

```
buildDrafts: true
minify: false
params:                         Enables the Debug
  DebugMenu: true   ◁────┘      menu via params
```

Listing 4.3   Enabling robots and minification (config/production/config.yaml)

```
enableRobotsTXT: true
minify: true
```

Defaults in Hugo are specific to the environment; Hugo understands development and production natively. Therefore, many websites that use Hugo do not need separate environment-specific configurations.

CODE CHECKPOINT   https://chapter-04-01.hugoinaction.com, and source code: https://github.com/hugoinaction/hugoinaction/tree/chapter-04-01.

Exercise 4.1

The two default environments in Hugo are development and _____.

You can also use environment variables to provide configuration options for Hugo. For example, if you set the environment variable HUGO_ENABLEGITINFO to true, that overrides the enableGitInfo configuration setting in the Hugo configuration, forcing it to be true. We can use the ability to override the configuration settings using environment variables to set up Hugo on the build server via a configuration system outside of Hugo. Note that environment variables are different from command-line flags. These can be set in the running shell and are accessible to all programs that run after they have been set. You can read more about environment variables at https://help.ubuntu.com/community/EnvironmentVariables.

Figure 4.3   Configuration as code. Bob learns that, due to its expense, configuration as code is not as flexible as the actual code.

4.2   *Organizing content with sections and menus*

The essential tool to lay out content is the desired structure of the website that we will create from it. If we can physically represent the content we want to express on the sitemap logically, it makes our lives easier. This section provides some insights on how to go about laying out your content.

4.2.1 Sections

When a website has a lot of content, placing all of that in top-level pages makes managing the content challenging. Therefore, we can classify content into *sections* like blog, news, or products. We can use the path component of a web page's URL to identify its section. For example, in the URL `https://example.org/blog/community/welcome`, the page named welcome belongs to the community subsection of the blog section of the website example.org. A *subsection* is not really a special construct in Hugo; it's just a section in a section. Sections also have an index page like `https://example.org/blog` that introduces the sections and provide a list of subsections and pages in them.

We can list all the areas in the website in the main menu or on the home page. To create a section in Hugo, we create a subfolder in the content folder. You can have nested subfolders for nested sections. Technically, the content folder (also called *content root*) that contains the *home page* (also called the *root page* or the *index page*) for the entire website is also a section, and all website sections are subsections of the content root. We can override the front matter of the home page using the content/_index.md file. The content root is the only section whose _index.md is optional. Because we override the index template with a plain HTML file in the Acme Corporation website, adding front matter specific to the page in content/_index.md has no effect.

> **NOTE** We need to create a markup file named _index.md, even if empty, at the root of every section. Hugo uses this file to identify a website section. Hugo does not consider a folder to be a section without this file and might not display its contents.

Each section can have multiple pages that form its content. The sections have a template for the index page where we have access to all the pages and subsections. We use the section's index page to help the user navigate the section. Custom parameters and data can customize the index template via the _index.md file in the section folder. We are free to choose the organization of pages as we desire to get the content structure we want.

Let's add a news and a blog section to Acme Corporation's website. In the blog section, let's also add a community subsection for blog posts from community members using Acme products. Also, we will enable the automatic setting for the Git author dates for the content by setting `enableGitInfo: true` in the configuration file. The following listing enables access to Git commit information while building the website.

Listing 4.4 Accessing Git commit information (config/_default/config.yaml)

```
...
enableGitInfo: true
```

The content for these sections is provided in the chapter resources (https://github.com/hugoinaction/hugoinaction/tree/chapter-04-resources/02). Figure 4.4

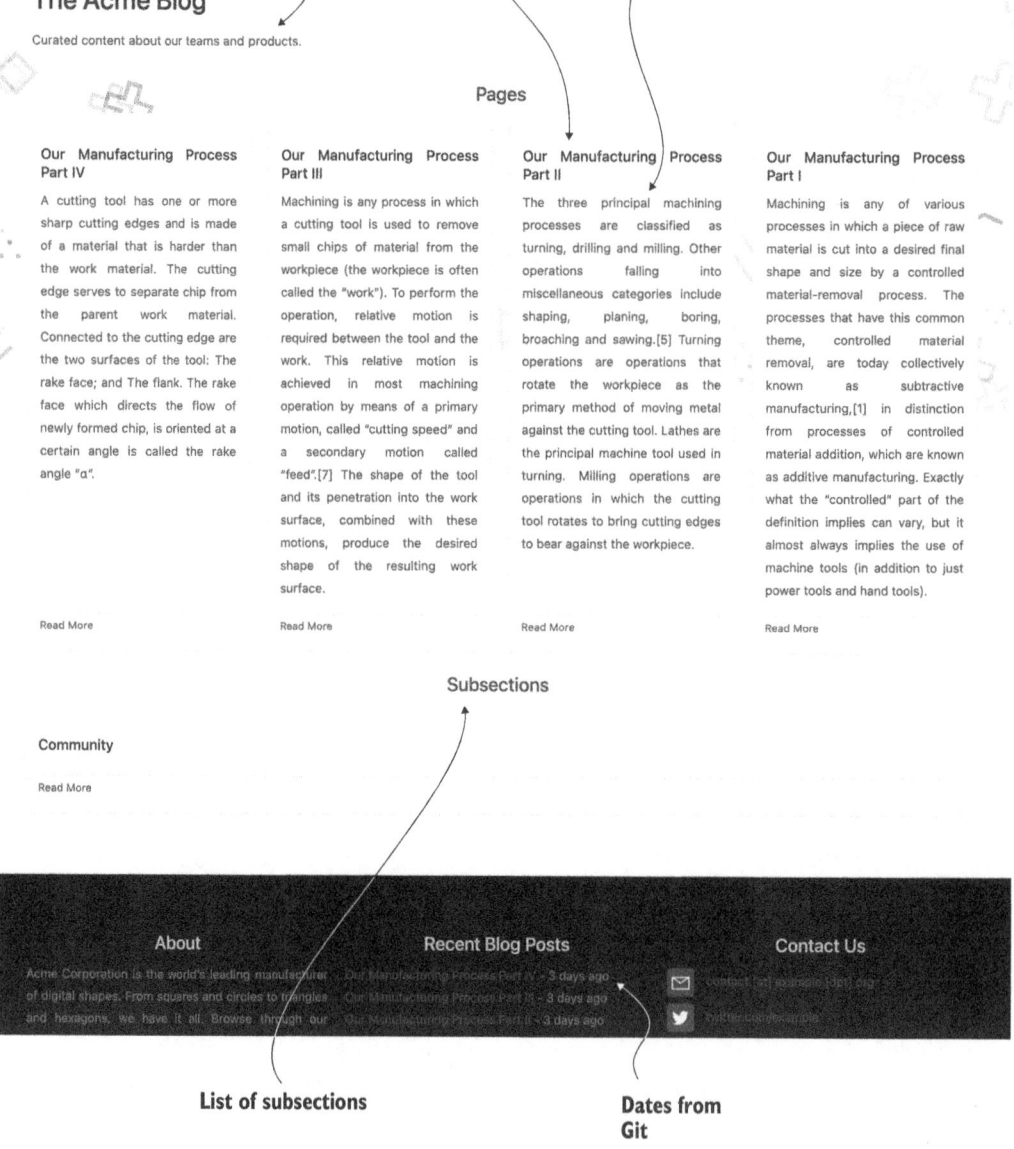

Figure 4.4   The blog for Acme Corporation's website showing summaries from the different pages (top) and the subsections (bottom)

shows the corresponding Blog page. The sections present on the Acme Corporation website are shown on the right as filenames. The following listing provides the code for organizing the content in sections for the Acme Corporation website. (The listing's Markdown icon is from octoicons; the folder icons are from flaticons.)

Listing 4.5   Organizing content in sections

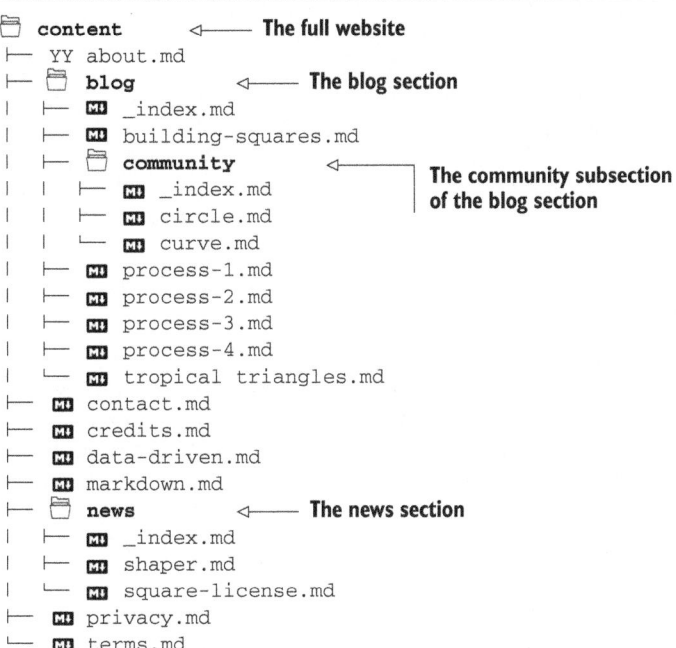

We can navigate to http://localhost:1313/blog to view the entries in the blog section, to http://localhost:1313/blog/community to see the posts in the subsection for community-provided entries, and to http://localhost:1313/news to see those in the news section.

> **NOTE**   You need to commit the files to a Git repository for the dates to be read from Git by Hugo.

We can use the _index.md file in the blog folder to provide the settings and the content that show up on the /blog page. We can also add Markdown content for the index page to pick up and then use the front matter to override the settings. The index page has access to all the pages and subsections in the blog section.

> **CODE CHECKPOINT**   https://chapter-04-02.hugoinaction.com, and source code: https://github.com/hugoinaction/hugoinaction/tree/chapter-04-02. **Note:** The changes are not reachable from the home page yet.

Content summary

The index pages of the sections in the Acme Corporation website automatically provide a summary and titles of the posts in the section. Hugo generates the summary information automatically if we do not provide it. Although the index pages are the most common places where we can use a post's summary, it can also be used elsewhere by the theme. Here are the ways to provide the summary:

- *Automatic*—By default, Hugo picks up the first 70 words of the content as the summary for the theme. The `summaryLength` variable in the website configuration file controls the number of words in the default summary.
- *Manual*—We can specify the summary length with the marker `<!--more-->` at a location in the content to clip the summary if desired. Note that `<!--more-->` is matched verbatim by Hugo. Adding spaces, changing to uppercase, or not having a proper HTML comment is not understood by Hugo. You can see this in use in the content/blog/tropical triangles/index.md file.
- *Front matter*—We can use the `summary` variable in the front matter to supply the summary text.

Note that the `summary` variable is different than the `description` variable. The `summary` variable in Hugo is a teaser into the content, while the `description` variable is more about the content sent to search engines. The `description` field can only be supplied via the front matter and does not have an automatic value based on content. Some themes like Eclectic give a higher priority to `description` and fall back to `summary` in the index pages.

4.2.2   Menus

The sections that we added to Acme Corporations's website are not linked and, therefore, not discoverable from the home page or from any content pages. Hugo provides a generic way to enable content to show up in the menus. We can include multiple menus on a website, and each theme defines its own set of menus and submenus. Each menu has a name, like main for the main menu, in the Eclectic and Universal themes. Each menu consists of a list of entries that form the whole of the menu.

We have already split the menu created in chapter 2 in the configuration file in section 4.1. Listing 4.6 shows the configuration that we created in menu.yaml. Let's go over some of the fields in that configuration. Each menu entry has multiple fields:

- The `identifier` field uniquely defines the menu so Hugo can find it.
- The `weight` field orders the entries.
- The `url` field provides the relative path to the page from the website's base URL defined in the configuration.

Hugo is flexible with the other fields and their purpose. Some themes use the `name` field for the menu's display text, and others use the `title` field. To create a submenu, we need to provide the `parent` field with the identifier of the parent menu (see listing 4.9 for an example submenu).

Listing 4.6   Menu entries in the config file (config/_default/menu.yaml)

```yaml
main:
  - identifier: about
    name: About
    url: /about
    weight: 100
  - identifier: contact
    name: Contact
    url: /contact
    weight: 200
```

Hugo provides two ways to include pages in the website menus. First, we can add menu items for the page in the configuration file. This approach helps localize and tightly monitor the menu. The second way is to specify the page menus in the front matter. This way, the menu becomes more dynamic and controlled by the content. If we delete a page, the menu automatically gets trimmed, and we do not have to worry about cleaning up stale links. The choice of which approach to use depends on our use case. If the objective is to have the menu in one place, the configuration file is the way to go. If we want to split the ownership of menus among the owners of different content sections for the website, then using the front matter is the way to go. Both can be mixed and matched as needed.

The Eclectic theme has two menus: the main menu and the footer menu. So far, we have only used the main menu. Let's add a menu entry in the front matter of the _index.md file for the blog section to allow the blog to show up in the main and the footer menus. Listing 4.7 shows the configuration for this. We will also add a News submenu to the main menu. Listing 4.8 shows this configuration, and figure 4.5 shows the result of enabling all the menus.

Listing 4.7   Menus for the blog section (content/blog/_index.md)

```yaml
---
menu:
  main:
    name: Blog
    identifier: blog
    weight: 110
  footer:
    name: Blog
    weight: 100
---
```

Listing 4.8   Menu for the news section (content/news/_index.md)

```yaml
---
menu:
  main:
    name: News
    identifier: news
    weight: 120
---
```

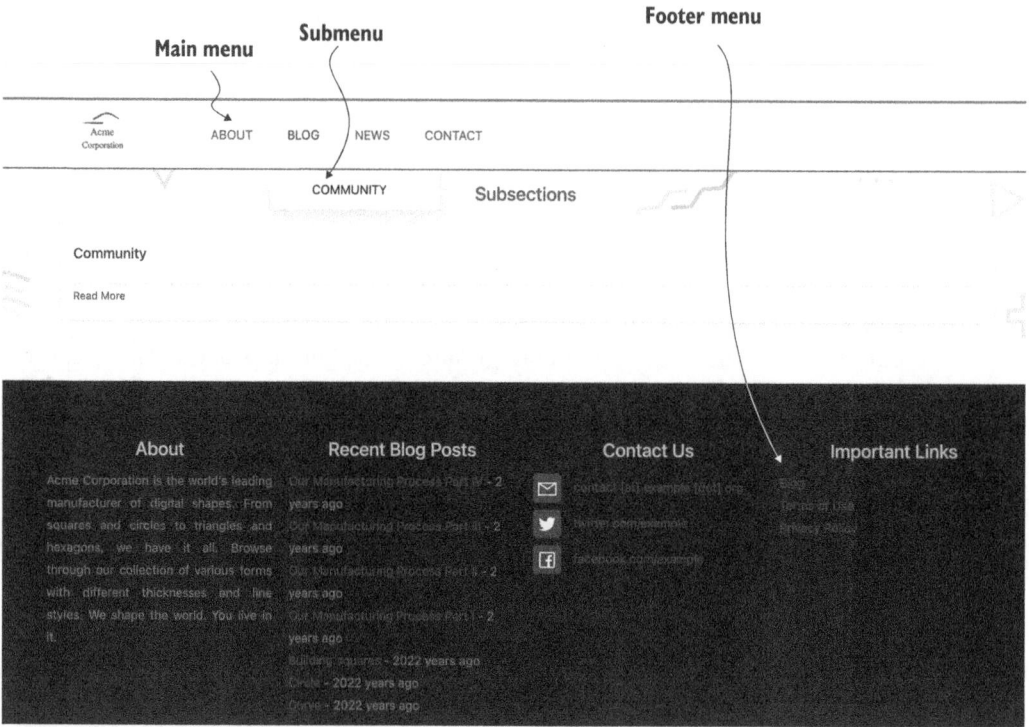

Figure 4.5   The Blog page for Acme Corporation's website showing the main menu, a submenu, and the footer menu

The community section's _index.md enables a submenu for that section in the Blog menu. The following listing shows its configuration.

Listing 4.9   Menu for the community blog (content/blog/community/_index.md)

```
---
menu:
  main:
    name: Community
    parent: blog
---
```

We also need to add the terms of use and privacy policy to the footer menu. The following two listings show these configurations.

Listing 4.10   Menu for the terms of use (content/terms.md)

```
---
menu:
  footer:
    name: Terms of Use
    weight: 200
---
```

Listing 4.11　Menu for the privacy policy (content/privacy.md)

```
---
menu:
  footer:
    name: Privacy Policy
    weight: 300
---
```

While the footer menu has content, Eclectic does not show it until we explicitly enable it by adding `menu: true` in the config/_default/params.yaml file for the `footer` section. The following listing shows how to do that. Note that you may need to restart your development server for these changes to take effect.

Listing 4.12　Enabling the footer menu (config/_default/params.yaml)

```
...
footer:
  ...
  - title: Contact Us
    contact: true
  - title: Important Links
    menu: true
...
```

Because the home page does not use a menu yet, we will need to manually update the website's home page to change the Explore button to link to the Blog page and then add an entry for the Blog and News pages in the footer in layouts/index.html. The following listing enables direct links to the `blog` and `news` section in the website footer and changes the Explore button to link to the Blog page in the index page of the website.

Listing 4.13　Enabling direct links and changing a button (layouts/index.html)

```
...
<a href="./blog">Explore</a>
...

<footer>
  <a href="./blog">Blog</a>
  <a href="./news">News</a>
...
</footer>
```

CODE CHECKPOINT　　https://chapter-04-03.hugoinaction.com, and source code: https://github.com/hugoinaction/hugoinaction/tree/chapter-04-03. ↻ Restart your dev server.

Exercise 4.2

Which menu placement is better if we want to cut and paste pages from one Hugo website to another?

a. Layouts

b. Front matter

c. Theme

d. Config

Content management with a GUI

For authors and editors that require a graphical environment to manage content without losing performance benefits with static site builders like Hugo, there are wrappers like Forestry.io, Hokus CMS, and Netlify CMS. These content management systems have graphical forms instead of YAML and Markdown. Tools like these can help teams with a diverse set of requirements to come on board and get the benefits of using Hugo. Nontechnical team members who prefer a graphical form can benefit from the Jamstack with a comfortable GUI on top. These forms place the files in suitable locations and update the appropriate entries in the front matter and the configuration files. We can use them interchangeably, along with directly editing the files.

Appendix C goes over integrating Netlify CMS with your website as the administrative interface for the content management system. The corresponding changes are present in all code checkpoints from chapter-04-03 onward.

4.3 *Better together with page bundles*

A common problem with website source code is the scattering of the content across databases, filesystems, and third-party locations. Additionally, the images associated with the page live in a different place. That makes it difficult to properly clean up after we remove a page from the website. Because pages are not portable across websites, the authors need access to multiple places to create them. Hugo, however, attempts to make the contents of a web page more self-contained. The menu field in the front matter (that we just learned about) is one of the features that Hugo uses to do this.

Front matter menus allow each page to own its menu entries and lets us add and remove them independently. Another feature to enable this independence is page bundles. *Page bundles* are a collection of resources, both textual and nontextual (like images, PDF files, and fonts), which are sufficient to represent individual or a group of related pages. Page bundles can be independently placed or removed from a Hugo website to add the associated web pages. They help content authors localize changes to a web page or section to a specific folder on disk. There are two main types of page bundles: the leaf bundle and the branch bundle. Apart from these, we also have the less commonly used headless bundles.

4.3.1 Leaf bundles

Leaf bundles are a collection of textual and nontextual elements needed to independently represent the core contents of a single web page. The folder for leaf bundles contains the markup, the metadata, and the resources (images, PDF files, etc.) specific to the page. These may also include page-specific CSS and JS files.

We can convert any web page in Hugo to a leaf bundle by creating a folder at the same location as the markup file and with the same name (without the extension), then moving the markup file in this new folder and renaming it to index.md. We should move all the specific resources to the web page in this folder as well. The web page can use any assets in this folder and its subfolders, including images, PDF files, and metadata (YAML, TOML, or JSON) files.

We can move a leaf bundle independently to a different Hugo website, which provides everything needed to render it correctly. A leaf bundle can have multiple markup files, but during the rendering process, it's treated as a single web page and will not have direct access to any other markup files from the bundle apart from index.md.

---

index.md vs. _index.md

While _index.md and index.md are similar names, they are two very different files: index.md represents the content of a *single web page*, and _index.md represents a section's root, which is a *set of web pages*. To understand this better, let's look at an example.

Think of a website with the following URL endpoints: / (the root), /about, /blog, /terms, /blog/process-1, and /blog/process-2. In this website, the /about, /terms, /blog/process-1, and /blog/process-2 pages do not have child pages and represent individual web pages. These pages can be represented by index.md. The / and /blog endpoints have child pages and, therefore, need to be represented by _index.md.

Note that for single-page endpoints like /about, we can create about.md if we do not want to use page bundles. For /blog and /, we do not have such a choice.

The independence of the leaf bundle provides content creation and management capabilities that are not present in most other static site builders. Two authors can work on content independently in their branches, and the likelihood of a merge conflict is minimal. A stripped-down version of the website can easily be created by emptying the content folder and then using it for content creation with minimal compilation overhead and full support for previewing. Contractors can be assigned to develop content using a generic Hugo theme, and they can submit their leaf bundle to the main website. The integration effort would be minimal.

The About page in the Acme Corporation website is the perfect page to turn into a leaf bundle. The draw.jpg image is used in the page, not anywhere else, and we should localize it to that page. We will create a subfolder named about in the content folder and move draw.jpg from the static/image folder and about.md from the content folder to this about folder, renaming about.md to index.md. For a proper page bundle, the image should now be relative to the web page, and we should refer to it from the page. The path in the `img` tag needs to be replaced with the local one: from /image/draw.jpg to draw.jpg. We could have alternatively created an image folder in the leaf bundle and set the path to image/draw.jpg if we want to keep the image resources in such a folder. We can navigate to http://localhost:1313/about and verify that the page looks the same as before.

Leaf bundles don't need to have any files other than index.md. We can convert any page to a page bundle by creating a folder, moving the .md file to it, and renaming the file index.md. For example, we can convert content/blog/tropical triangles.md to a page bundle by creating a folder and moving the original file as index.md to the folder.

CODE CHECKPOINT   https://chapter-04-04.hugoinaction.com, and source code: https://github.com/hugoinaction/hugoinaction/tree/chapter-04-04.

Which image files go where

We have already mentioned three places to store images: a page bundle and two folders called static and assets. This can get confusing early on when we try to decide which image goes where. The decision is actually straightforward. The images specific to a page bundle belong to the page bundle. As we create more web pages, we should try to stay in the content folder and rarely update anything outside of this folder. The images used by the theme to render the website do not belong in that folder.

The folders static and assets are similar in their type of content with just one difference: images in the assets folder can be preprocessed and optimized by Hugo (via Hugo Pipes, which we'll cover in chapter 6). We need to use the images in the static folder as-is. Ideally, we should move as many images as possible to the assets folder to utilize the complete set of Hugo's image optimization features for these files. The static folder, in this case, should only be used for images that are accessed directly from HTML without being processed by Hugo.

4.3.2   *Branch bundles*

Branch bundles form a collection of both textual and nontextual resources that represent a website section. Technically, the section folder created for the blog, the `news` section for the Acme Corporation website with its subpages, and an _index file fit the definition of a branch bundle. To meet the definition in spirit, however, all the resources required by the index page should also be present in the folder. An ideal branch bundle contains page bundles for all the pages in the section, the _index file, and the resources referred to in the index page.

The objective of the independent branch bundle is the same as that of a leaf bundle: to allow sections to be dropped into the website and to become functional with no other change in the site. A branch bundle should ideally set its menu entries and provide all the assets referred to in the branch and then be good to go. Figure 4.6 shows the various branch and leaf bundles in the Acme Corporation website so far.

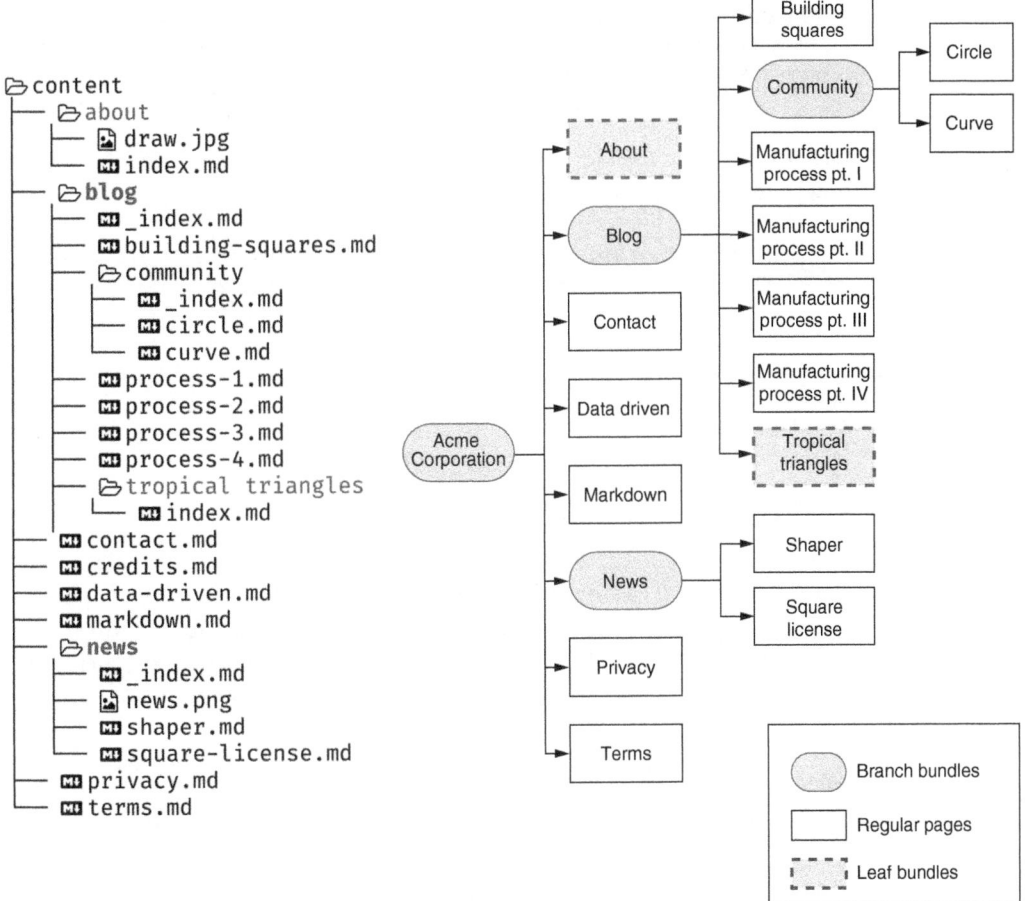

Figure 4.6 Branch and leaf bundles in Hugo. On the left is the folder structure after creating page bundles. The right side shows the sitemap. Branch bundles show up as nodes with children in the sitemap (rounded corners), while leaf bundles are end nodes in the sitemap, just like a regular page.

We do not have any resources on any of the _index.md pages for Acme Corporation's website. We will add an image (news.png) to the news section and turn that into a proper branch bundle by referencing it. The images and the corresponding _index.md for the news section are provided in the chapter resources (https://github.com/hugoinaction/hugoinaction/tree/chapter-04-resources/03). Note that we cannot add subfolders for assets associated with a branch bundle. For this exercise, we will force the

Reusing page bundles

Page bundles are meant for isolation and not reuse. If the desire is to reuse images, we need to place them in the top-level assets folder or the static folder. We can use page bundles along with shared images. One-off images used for specific pages should be present in page bundles, and we should ideally place the shared images (used across a vast set of pages) in the top-level folders. Sharing resources leads to extra cleanup and integration effort, however, but reusing these resources provides both bandwidth and storage savings. The tradeoff is a choice left to the web developer, who should evaluate this on a case-by-case basis.

news image to center on the News page using Markdown attributes. The following listing shows how to add this image.

Listing 4.14   Adding an image to the news section (content/news/_index.md)

```
---
menu:
  main:
    name: News
    identifier: news
    weight: 120
---
![News](news.png){style="text-align:_center_"}
---------------------------------------------
```

Branch bundles are places from where the website branches into one or more pages. Note that in an edge case, where a branch bundle is yet to add pages, it will show up in a sitemap as a leaf, although Hugo treats it as a branch and shows an empty list of child pages when it renders. See table 4.1 for a comparison of branch and leaf bundles.

Exercise 4.3

Which of the following files are suitable to be placed in a page bundle?

1. The logo of a section
2. A unique border image used in the theme
3. The website logo
4. The website font

CODE CHECKPOINT   https://chapter-04-05.hugoinaction.com, and source code: https://github.com/hugoinaction/hugoinaction/tree/chapter-04-05.

Table 4.1 Branch vs. leaf bundles

Area	Branch	Leaf
Used for	Section	Single web page
Contents	Header and (as a part of the theme) a list of pages in the section	Contents of the web page
Index Page	_index.md	index.md
Template layout page (chapter 6)	list.html	single.html

4.3.3 *Headless bundles*

Headless bundles are leaf bundles where the index file's front matter has the property headless set to true. Headless pages do not have separate URLs, and Hugo does not render these bundles. Some themes use these for storing shared data. For example, instead of choosing the parameters for a structured footer, the theme author can use a headless page bundle for a more unstructured footer. The headless page with the name footer could store the markup-based content for it and its associated assets. This bundle provides the advantage of having assets associated with the footer together with the markup. Not many themes use headless page bundles, and we will not be investing in them for the Acme Corporation website.

Clever uses for page bundles

The page-specific assets linked in page bundles allow for the theme to standardize on the naming convention for these assets, which lets us use them without writing code. Eclectic supports creating a file called cover.png (or cover.jpg) in the page bundle and picks this up to use as the cover image for the page. This, however, does not provide any less discoverability of the front matter entry (banner, for example) than themes like Universal use. To make things easier, we can put a default image in the archetypes (discussed in chapter 5) for a page.

The cover images for all the pages on the Acme Corporation website are included in the chapter resources (https://github.com/hugoinaction/hugoinaction/tree/chapter-04-resources/04). You can use these to make your blog posts presentable. Note that the version of the Universal theme provided with this book supports cover images via page bundles, but this is not standard in Hugo, and most themes do not support it.

CODE CHECKPOINT   https://chapter-04-06.hugoinaction.com, and source code: https://github.com/hugoinaction/hugoinaction/tree/chapter-04-06.

4.4   *More than tags: Taxonomies*

To organize content into sections in Hugo, we need to physically organize the files. It is easier to have individual files for each web page neatly organized into folders and subfolders. In many cases, the logical organization of the website matches the physical organization on the disk. That is why Hugo, by default, generates the URLs with the section name as a part of the URL. But that alone may not be enough for good content discovery. There are infinite ways to organize content, and each use case is different.

As we organize content, we quickly realize the need to group pages such that the same page is a part of multiple categories. For example, we can place a web page about the differences between iPhone and Android in both the iPhone and Android sections. Having two copies is terrible for maintenance. Two different URLs would cause many problems because we will need to synchronize comments, social media appearances, and search engine content. In this case, it would be ideal to have one URL for the actual content, which could show up in the index pages for both the iPhone and Android categories.

Apart from categories, there may be other needs to have groups with unique index pages. Our users need support for tags to find similar content. Websites may need pages that have links to all the author's posts. There could be a series where readers should read the posts in a specific order that's predefined by the author.

Hugo understands the need for infinite ways to organize content and provides a generic solution. At the top level of content organization, Hugo allows us to define what is called *taxonomies*. Taxonomies are higher-level constructs that we can use to group the pages that describe relationships between web pages. In chapter 1, we moved the content from the database to the markup files. We gained the ability to represent unstructured content better but lost some of the capabilities to provide structured relationships. Taxonomies attempt to build relationships between web pages.

Figure 4.7 shows the mapping of concepts between a relational database approach of defining relationships and Hugo's approach. In a relational database, the content lives in table cells. These tables have an identifier cell. Identifiers from two tables are placed together in a third table to build many-to-many relationships between the content in those tables. In Hugo, each row in a table corresponds to a separate file in the filesystem. To define a relationship, we can provide the names (which act as the identifiers) of the related files in the front matter of the content files, and Hugo takes care of creating those relationships. We do not have to create a join query to get these relationships. They are available as variables in both pages.

Taxonomies have two parts: the lists and the terms. Each *taxonomy list* is a collection of *taxonomy terms*. A page can be associated with many taxonomy terms, and a taxonomy term can be associated with many pages. Hugo builds many-to-many relationships between pages and taxonomies. We are free to define taxonomies and have our content organized by whatever field we desire. For example, if we are building a website about movies, we would want pages with a list of movies in groups like genre or actor names. We would also want to list movies by director, actors, music director, and so

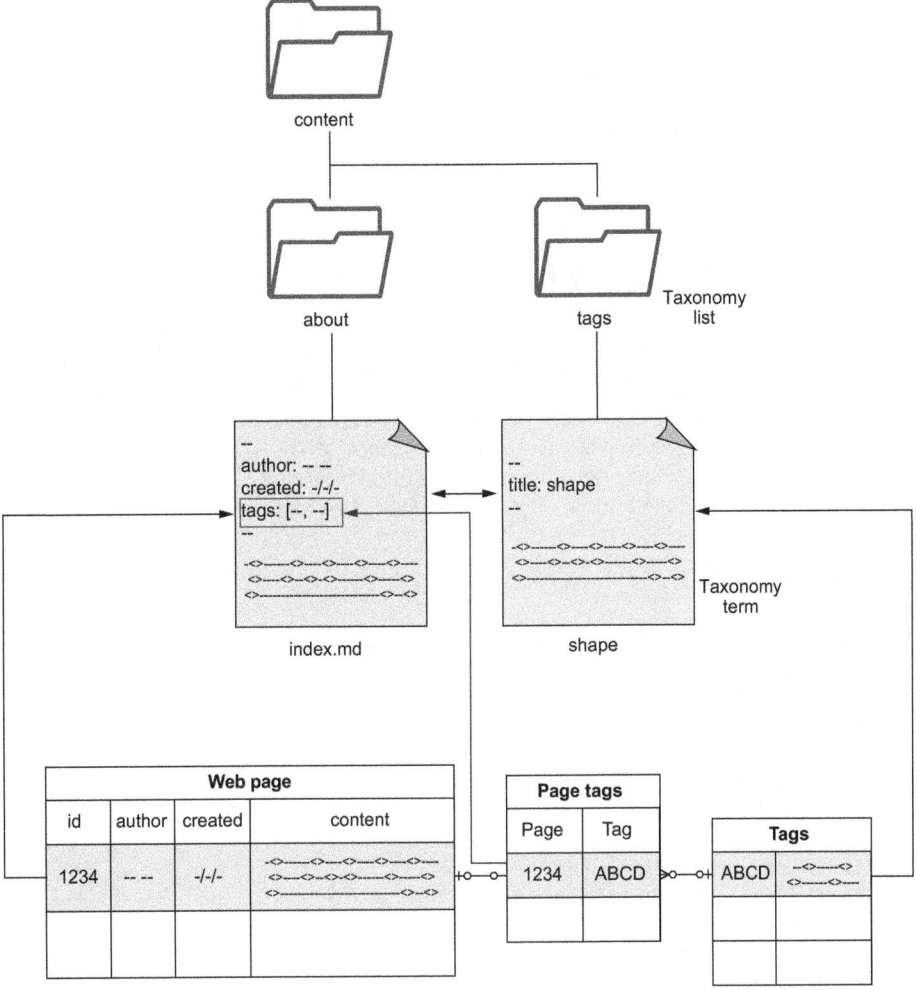

Figure 4.7 Mapping from the traditional database structure to a Hugo taxonomy to define relationships between web pages

forth. In Hugo, these would turn into taxonomy lists, where each particular genre or actor name becomes a taxonomy term with its index page.

By default, Hugo defines categories and tags as taxonomy lists. We can group content into categories and tags. Because tags and categories are logical constructs (they do not match with the filesystem), we can have web pages in numerous categories with multiple tags. Note that we do not need to create separate pages for every taxonomy list or term we use if we have no additional content to supply. During compilation, Hugo figures out the lists and terms used in the website and create pages for them.

Let's work on taxonomies for the Acme Corporation website. First, we'll add tags and categories for its posts. We can add these directly in the front matter of the page.

Multiple renditions of a single page

A page can have multiple URLs. Aliasing using the front matter allows us to render the same content many times. Template authors can implement the user interface (UI) for the page differently for different renditions. The power to have multiple copies of a page does not mean it is a good idea:

- Search engines penalize copies.
- Comments from one page do not flow into another.
- There is confusion among users about the absolute correct page of the website.

We should use this feature to have multiple renditions for cases like backward compatibility. If you are coming from a different URL scheme or something that supported various URLs in the past and would like to maintain links, then aliases come in handy. Theme creators provide canonical references in their theme's head section to prevent the search engine penalty across these aliases. The other management problems with multiple copies of content remain, but Hugo provides a mechanism to have a unique template for each handle even though it may not be present in many themes. Note that we do not advise creating multiple copies of a single page.

This addition would auto-populate tags in the content and also generate a Categories page. In the index.md for tropical triangles, we will add the tags and categories to get a view similar to figure 4.8. The following listing shows the syntax for this.

Listing 4.15   Adding tags and categories (content/blog/tropical triangles/index.md)

```
---
title: Tropical triangles
tags: [triangle, shape, product]
categories: [shape, design]
---
```

The Eclectic theme displays the tags in the bottom right of the page and the categories in the index page with the summary. Hugo also creates an index page (e.g., /tags/shape) for every tag on the website and a top-level /tags web page that lists all the tags on the website. The corresponding files are available in the chapter resources (https://github.com/hugoinaction/hugoinaction/tree/chapter-04-resources/05).

> **CODE CHECKPOINT**   https://chapter-04-07.hugoinaction.com, and source code: https://github.com/hugoinaction/hugoinaction/tree/chapter-04-07.

We will also add the top-level Categories page to the footer menu. Although we can do this using the configuration file, we can create a branch bundle for the Categories

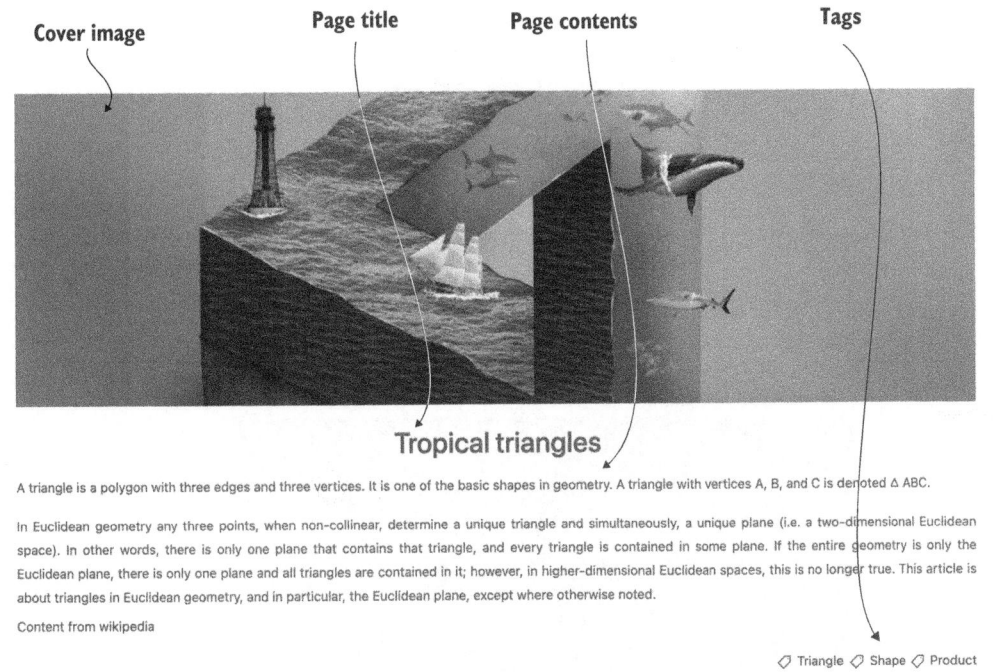

Figure 4.8 Elements of a page after adding tags. The figure shows the cover image, the page title, its contents, and the tags. (Image by Alexandr Nebesyuk on Pixabay.)

taxonomy list to keep this information isolated. The following listing creates a top-level Categories page that shows up in the footer menu.

Listing 4.16 A top-level Categories page (content/categories/_index.md)

```
---
title: Categories
menu:
  footer:
    weight: 150
    name: Categories
---

At Acme corporation, we produce shapes and love to talk about them.
Here are the various categories of content we have at Acme.
```

The corresponding file is present in the chapter resources (https://github.com/hugoinaction/hugoinaction/tree/chapter-04-resources/06). The generated Categories page should look like that shown in figure 4.9. You might need to restart your dev server for the changes to take effect.

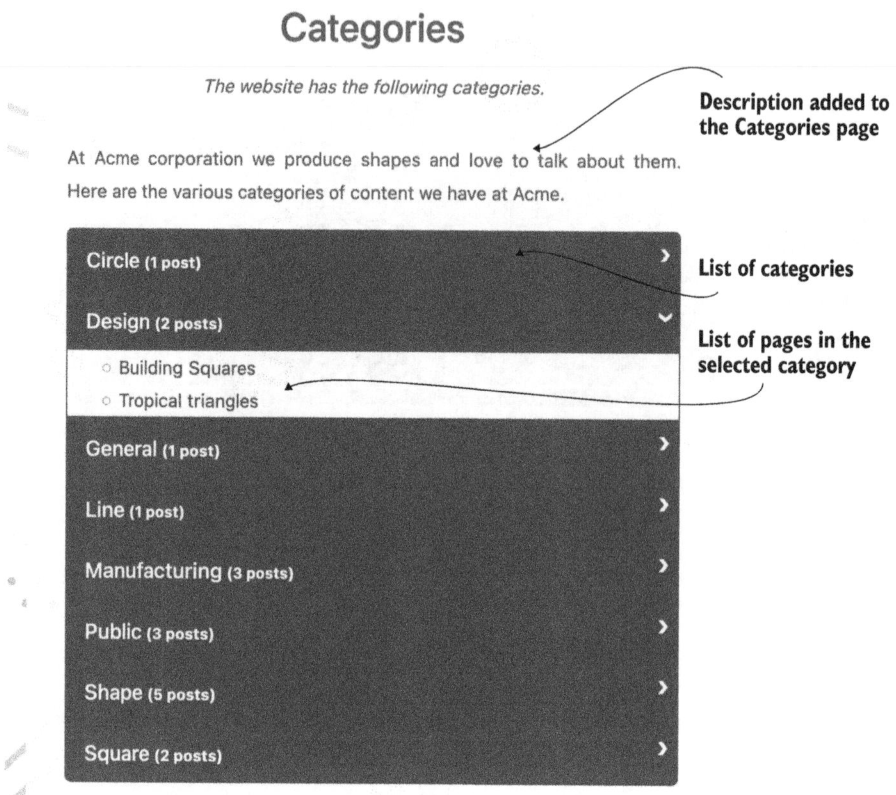

Categories

The website has the following categories.

Description added to
the Categories page

At Acme corporation we produce shapes and love to talk about them.
Here are the various categories of content we have at Acme.

List of categories

List of pages in the
selected category

Circle (1 post)   ›

Design (2 posts)   ⌄

  ○ Building Squares

  ○ Tropical triangles

General (1 post)   ›

Line (1 post)   ›

Manufacturing (3 posts)   ›

Public (3 posts)   ›

Shape (5 posts)   ›

Square (2 posts)   ›

**Figure 4.9   Categories taxonomy list page for Acme Corporation, which lists all the available
categories and their pages in the website**

We can also create Markdown pages for each category. We can use these pages to provide Markdown content that describes the category. For this, we'll create a branch
bundle at content/categories/<term>. By placing the _index.md file in the content/
categories/design folder, we can provide information to the page generated for the
Design category.

> **CODE CHECKPOINT**   https://chapter-04-08.hugoinaction.com, and source
> code: https://github.com/hugoinaction/hugoinaction/tree/chapter-04-08.
> ↻ Restart your dev server.

Tags and categories are the default taxonomies. For our example website, Acme Corporation has a series of posts around its manufacturing process. We need to migrate
this to the new website. For that, we need to create a new taxonomy called `series`
(see figure 4.10). To create a new taxonomy, we can modify the `taxonomies` option
in the site configuration (config.yaml) or create a new file called taxonomies.yaml

Series

The website has the following series.

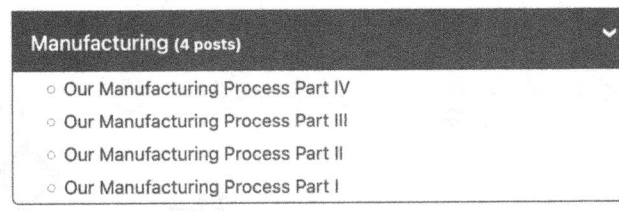

Figure 4.10 The `series` taxonomy for Acme Corporation lists all the series available on the Acme Corporation website.

(https://github.com/hugoinaction/hugoinaction/tree/chapter-04-resources/07) in the config/_default folder with the content in the following listing.

Listing 4.17 Creating taxonomies (config/_default/taxonomies.yaml)

```
category: categories
series: series
tag: tags
```

Hugo requires both plural and singular values for taxonomies. With this information, Hugo creates pages at <domain>/<plural value> for the index page and at <domain>/<plural value>/<term> for the individual terms in the taxonomy list. Hugo uses the singular value in the template when rendering it.

We can update the manufacturing process-related posts on the Acme Corporation website and assign them the manufacturing series. Once we add `series: [manufacturing]` to the front matter for the posts, we can see the index page for a series at http://localhost:1313/series and the manufacturing series at http://localhost:1313/series/manufacturing/. (You may need to restart the live server to view this.) We can add as many series to the website as needed. It is as valid a construct for grouping content as are tags and categories.

Exercise 4.4

In a multi-author website, we want to represent the author using Hugo taxonomies. Which of the following options are best suited to list the works of a single author?

- **a.** Taxonomy list
- **b.** Taxonomy term
- **c.** Single post page
- **d.** A list/index page
- **e.** The website index
- **f.** We need to create a new page

CODE CHECKPOINT   https://chapter-04-09.hugoinaction.com, and source code: https://github.com/hugoinaction/hugoinaction/tree/chapter-04-09. ↻ Restart your dev server.

4.5   *YouTube, Gists, and other snippets via shortcodes*

As powerful as Markdown is, it does not have all the possible features that we might require in our content pages. Elements like those required for YouTube videos, GitHub Gists, Tweets, etc., are not a part of plain Markdown. While we can add these as HTML, Hugo provides a better, cleaner solution—shortcodes. *Shortcodes* are snippets of templates that we can include in the content files. These get replaced with the actual contents at compile time. They are equivalent to functions in the programming world.

With shortcodes, we can wrap reusable pieces of HTML into functions compiled during the page compilation. This way, content creators do not have to deal with the generation of the perfect HTML for a particular case that the shortcode author handles. Shortcodes can take arguments that can be processed in the template code. Shortcode authors have access to the entire website configuration and all its variables, Hugo's built-in functions, and the entire theme to generate the HTML.

Shortcodes can be used in markup using double curly braces followed by HTML-like angle brackets: ({{< … >}}). The space between the angle brackets and the content inside is optional. Shortcodes take the name of the shortcode, followed by some arguments. Shortcodes support both named arguments (if supported by the shortcode) or unnamed arguments. The following listing shows how we call a shortcode called `myshortcode`.

> Listing 4.18   Using custom shortcodes in a Hugo website

```
{{< myshortcode arg1 arg2 >}}              ◁————   Creates a shortcode
                                                   using angle brackets and
  ▷ {{<myshortcode name1=arg1 name2=arg2>}}        unnamed arguments
Uses named arguments
```

The Acme Corporation website has a teaser video that the company wants to incorporate in the About page. In the About page, we can add `{{< youtube nLAVanlu5js >}}` or `{{< youtube id="nLAVanlu5js" >}}` to get a YouTube video with the embedded ID, `nLAVanlu5js`. Fortunately, Hugo provides a built-in shortcode to render a YouTube video. Note that a YouTube video's ID is available as the parameter after *v* in the YouTube URL (e.g., https://www.youtube.com/watch?v=nLAVanlu5js is the URL for the Acme Corporation video). You can also pass parameters like `autoplay` to the YouTube shortcode (see figure 4.11).

NOTE   There are active discussions to move shortcodes built into Hugo out of Hugo's core into a separate repository. That will allow us to link to specific versions of the shortcodes and to update outside of a Hugo release cycle.

You'll find a copy of the bundled shortcodes like youtube and highlight used in this book in the layouts/shortcodes folder for the Acme Corporation website (https://github.com/hugoinaction/hugoinaction/tree/chapter-04-resources/08) to prevent incompatibility issues.

CODE CHECKPOINT https://chapter-04-10.hugoinaction.com, and source code: https://github.com/hugoinaction/hugoinaction/tree/chapter-04-10.

```
## Shortcodes

*Youtube*
{{< youtube nLAVanlu5js >}}




*Highlight*

{{< highlight js
"linenos=table,hl_lines=3-4,linenostart=1080" >}}
// Enjoy your work
if (!tired()) {
    keepCoding();
} else {
    drinkCoffee();
}
{{</ highlight >}}


{{< highlight html
"linenos=table,hl_lines=2 ,linenostart=1080" >}}
<!-- Generated Youtube source code for video -->
{{</* youtube nLAVanlu5js */>}}
<!-- Output -->
{{< youtube nLAVanlu5js >}}
{{</ highlight >}}
```

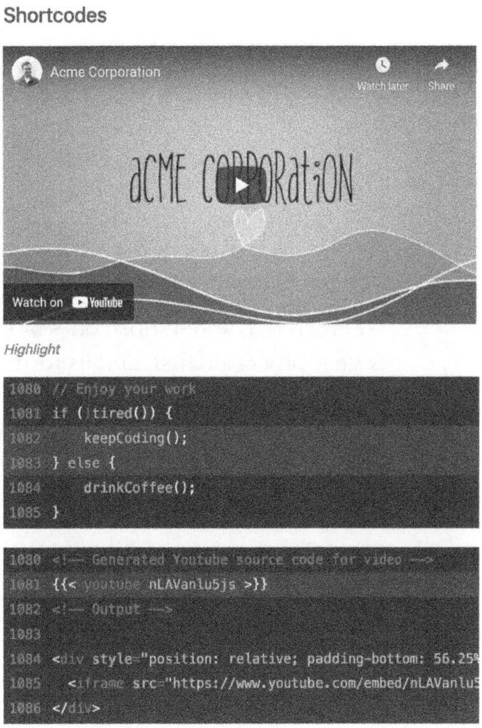

Figure 4.11 There are multiple ways to use built-in shortcodes in Hugo. You can directly call the youtube **shortcode, pass content to the** highlight **shortcode, or nest shortcodes.**

4.5.1 *Shortcodes with content*

Shortcodes can also take content as an argument that the shortcode author can process using the Go template language. This way, shortcode creators can do processing on the passed content before rendering the final HTML. The content we give to a Hugo shortcode can be in the form of HTML or markup.

We can use HTML-like opening and closing angle braces inside the double curly braces to provide the opening and closing tags for the shortcodes. Hugo passes the content in the boundaries of the shortcode as-is to the shortcode, and the shortcode author can then do any processing on the supplied content as they wish.

One popular shortcode used in Hugo is the `highlight` shortcode, which provides syntax highlighting. This shortcode is an alternative to code fences and provides the same functionality (see figure 4.11). The following listing shows the syntax to add the `highlight` shortcode.

Listing 4.19   Using the `highlight` shortcode

```
{{< highlight js
    "linenos=table,hl_lines=3-4,linenostart=1080" >}}    ⟵── Opens shortcode

if (!tired()) {
    keepCoding();
}
else {
    drinkCoffee();
}
{{</ highlight >}}    ⟵── Closes shortcode
```

4.5.2   Nested shortcodes

We can build nested shortcodes by inserting a shortcode in another. The innermost shortcode is processed first, and its results pass on to the outermost shortcode. One clever use of this feature is to see the result of shortcode processing by passing it to the `highlight` shortcode. The following listing shows how to do this. Note that `{{</* … */>}}` is the comment syntax for Hugo shortcodes; Hugo does not process the content in this block as a shortcode (see figure 4.11).

Listing 4.20   Using nested shortcode to highlight the generated code

```
{{< highlight html "linenos=table,hl_lines=3-4,linenostart=1080" >}}

{{</* youtube nLAVanlu5js */>}}    ⟵┐  Generated YouTube
    {{< youtube nLAVanlu5js >}}       │  source code for a video
{{</ highlight >}}                    ┘  (passed as a comment)
```
Output

4.5.3   Built-in shortcodes

Hugo comes with its own built-in generic shortcodes. Some themes may come bundled with shortcodes for the users. We also have community-built shortcodes available that we can add to our website and use as needed. We are free to create custom shortcodes in the shortcodes subfolder within the layouts folder. Some of the built-in Hugo shortcodes include the following:

- `gist`—Takes the user and gist ID as parameters and renders a GitHub gist. You can also pass a filename if the gist has multiple files.
- `ref`—Takes a file path in the Hugo website and provides an absolute link to that file. If the `url` or `slug` is overridden in the front matter of a page, the ref shortcode follows the newly provided location.

- relref—Provides the relative link to the file in the Hugo website. This shortcode works similar to ref.
- figure—Renders an image with a caption.
- tweet—Renders a Tweet with the given ID.
- instagram—Embeds an Instagram image with the given ID.
- vimeo—Renders a Vimeo video with the given ID.
- youtube—Renders a YouTube video with the given ID.
- highlight—Adds syntax highlighting for the provided source code.
- param—Prints a passed parameter (useful for debugging purposes as well).

4.6 Content sharing using custom shortcodes

While sharing complicated logic is one use of shortcodes, we can also use shortcodes to minimize our copy and paste efforts and to keep our content clean. Shortcodes can be as simple as snippets of HTML or even Markdown content that needs to be shared to prevent duplication. With one source of truth, managing content gets a lot easier. While creating content, if we find that we are copying and pasting some text repeatedly, it is a good idea to wrap that text up in a shortcode, then call the shortcode to provide the content. For content sharing, we can create two types of shortcodes as described in the following sections.

4.6.1 HTML shortcodes

We can use custom shortcodes for placing inline HTML in our Markdown files by adding an HTML file in the layouts/shortcodes folder. Then we can use that filename as the shortcode to render it in the document.

We will embellish the About page for the Acme Corporation website by adding dividers via a shortcode (figure 4.12). To do that, we'll create a file named divider.html in the layout folder and add the content provided in the chapter resources (https://github.com/hugoinaction/hugoinaction/tree/chapter-04-resources/09) to create a beautiful divider in plain HTML. Then we can use this file anywhere in our website to place a divider on the page. The following listing shows how to add this divider to multiple places on the About page. Note that you may need to restart your dev server for the changes to take effect.

> **Listing 4.21   The divider shortcode (layouts/shortcodes/divider.html)**

```
<div style="background-image:
    linear-gradient(to right, transparent, #4f46e5, transparent);
    margin:15px 0;height:2px;position:relative">
  <!- Additional trick: We can add Unicode
characters as-is in HTML to render them. ->
  <span style="position:absolute;
    left:calc(50% - 10px);
    line-height:2px;
```

```
    font-size:30px;
    padding: 0 5px;
    background: white;
    color:#4f46e5">😃</span>
</div>
```

CODE CHECKPOINT https://chapter-04-11.hugoinaction.com, and source code: https://github.com/hugoinaction/hugoinaction/tree/chapter-04-11. ↻ Restart your dev server.

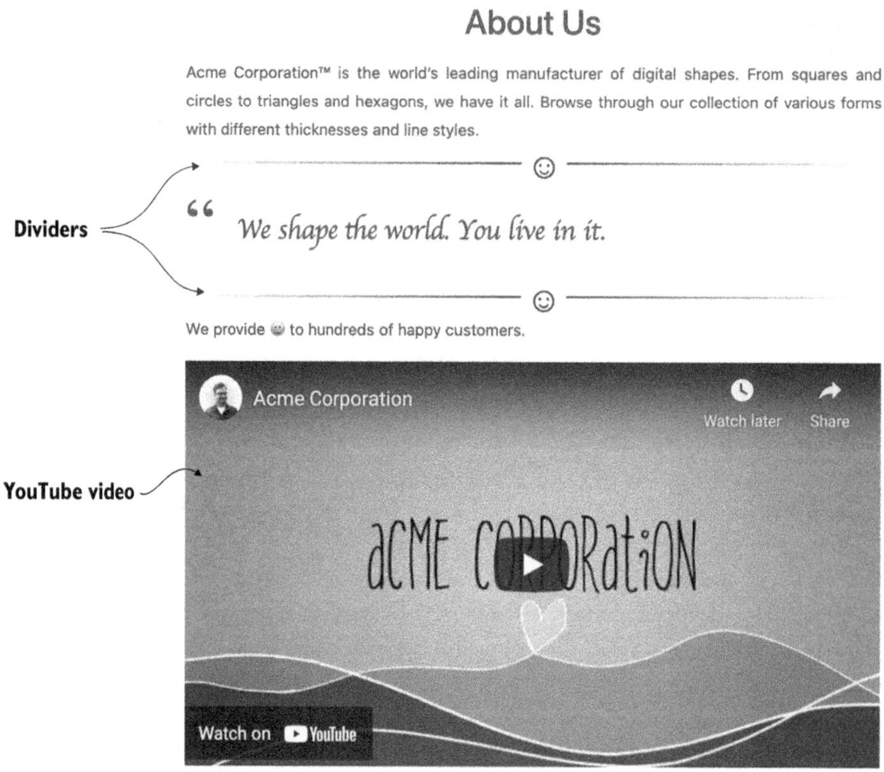
About Us
Acme Corporation™ is the world's leading manufacturer of digital shapes. From squares and circles to triangles and hexagons, we have it all. Browse through our collection of various forms with different thicknesses and line styles.
Dividers
We shape the world. You live in it.
We provide to hundreds of happy customers.
YouTube video
Acme Corporation
Watch later
Share
Watch on YouTube

Figure 4.12 Using custom shortcodes in the About page for Acme Corporation to create a personalized divider

4.6.2 *Markup-based shortcodes*

While most shortcodes are HTML, we have the option to write shortcodes in markup languages like Markdown. Hugo converts the Markdown shortcodes to HTML if we call them using percent signs (`%`) instead of angle brackets (`<>`) as we do in regular shortcodes. This way, we can move data in a shared place and then use that from everywhere it is needed.

Exercise 4.5

Shortcodes are declared in the _____ top-level folder in a Hugo website and consumed in _____.

We can move the product information table from the About page into a shortcode and
share it in the blog post about the manufacturing process on the Acme Corporation
website. Let's create a file named productInfo.md in the layouts/shortcodes folder and
move the contents of the product information to this page. Then we can place the
string `{{% productInfo %}}` anywhere in our content to get the product information
table. Let's do that for the About page and the manufacturing process page on the
Acme Corporation website (https://github.com/hugoinaction/hugoinaction/tree/
chapter-04-resources/10).

> **CODE CHECKPOINT** https://chapter-04-12.hugoinaction.com, and source code:
> https://github.com/hugoinaction/hugoinaction/tree/chapter-04-12.

4.6.3 *Inline shortcodes*

We have built shortcodes in a separate file (like productInfo.md), which is available
globally and shared in the entire website. Alternatively, if we want to have a shortcode
specific to the page, we can declare the shortcode in the Markdown content of the page
and use it in that page. This shortcode can do everything a regular shortcode can. This
does not create variables outside the page and, therefore, speeds up compilation along
with keeping the global list of shortcodes clean. These shortcodes are called *inline shortcodes* because they are declared inline in the file where we invoke them.

Inline shortcodes are disabled by default because shortcodes can access the entire
website configuration. If all content is coming from a trusted source, this is not an issue.
We can enable inline shortcodes by creating a security configuration file (config/
_default/security.yaml) with the setting `enableInlineShortcodes: true`. Once we do
that, we can declare a shortcode in our content using `.inline` after the name we want
to give to the shortcode.

Inline shortcodes execute as soon as they are declared and cannot be nested. We
can generate both HTML and markup-based inline shortcodes. The following listing
shows how to use inline shortcodes. Unlike regular shortcodes, we declare these inline
with the content.

Listing 4.22 Using inline shortcodes in Hugo

```
{{< reuse.inline >}}

Reused _content_ here
{{< /reuse.inline >}}
```

**Declares an inline shortcode and its first
use that's executed as HTML. We can also
declare it with % to run as Markdown.**

```
{{< reuse.inline />}}    ◁——— Shortcode usage as HTML

{{% reuse.inline /%}}    ◁——— Shortcode usage as markup
```

There is a lot more we can do with shortcodes, so we will explore some advanced shortcodes in chapter 5. This chapter concludes the usage of Hugo as a content management system. Using the features discussed so far and relying on an existing theme like Eclectic, we can build and maintain complicated websites.

Many Hugo users do not cross beyond this point in their journey to learn Hugo. While we can do a lot within the bounds of a Hugo theme, more power awaits in the Hugo template system. In the next set of chapters, we will build pieces of an independent theme that takes data in various ways, including from the front matter, separate files, or over the internet to create custom web pages. Moreover, we're not through with Hugo's content management features just yet. We will introduce some features like the cascade property in the following chapters.

Summary

- Hugo offers the flexibility to override global configuration variables and to manage them via multiple files and in various environments. By moving configuration from a single file to a folder, we can choose options based on numerous conditions.
- We can organize web pages in Hugo into sections by placing the corresponding markup content into folders. These sections can be nested and typically match the URL scheme for the website.
- We can make the content accessible using index pages for various sections and add those pages to menus.
- To enable the portability of content across websites, Hugo offers the capability to have self-contained and isolated data. We can achieve this isolation by placing the menu entries in the front matter and by using page bundles.
- With leaf and branch bundles, we keep all assets closer to the content. We can bundle page-specific images and files in the same folder as the markup content for the page.
- Hugo offers the ability to logically organize the content in any way desired via taxonomies. Each taxonomy consists of terms, and a page can be present in multiple taxonomies and have numerous terms.
- Taxonomies create list pages and provide support for many-to-many mappings between pages and taxonomy terms. We can define as many taxonomies as needed.
- Shortcodes are a means to provide snippets that we can use to extend Markdown with new features. Hugo comes bundled with shortcodes for various use cases, from YouTube videos to syntax highlighting.
- We can define custom shortcodes in both markup and HTML formats and in line with the content to prevent the need to copy and paste rendering logic.

Custom pages and customized content with the Go template language

This chapter covers

- Customizing pages and shortcodes
- Rendering content and accessing variables and functions in the Go template language
- Accessing Hugo's configuration and front matter in code
- Reading from the filesystem
- Creating reusable page templates called archetypes

One strength of Hugo is its clear separation of concerns between content (Markdown) and presentation (HTML/CSS/JavaScript). When we create content, we rarely have to deal with HTML. Team members who are not well versed in HTML or CSS can be successful with Hugo as a content management system using features we've discussed so far in this book. However, we can unlock a lot more power by digging deeper into layouts and HTML generation.

Chapter 2 has a section where we step out of the theme to create the home page in pure HTML. In doing so, we eschewed the role of the content creator and went into web developer mode, while primarily supplying content for the other pages. In this chapter, we will get first-hand experience with Hugo's template language and its rendering mechanism as we improve the home page for the Acme Corporation website. In addition, we will add some features based on the content that a static HTML page cannot provide.

The pure HTML index page we currently have for the Acme Corporation website has an intermingling of content and layout. This approach has a massive set of problems:

- We cannot share parts, HTML fragments, or data between pages.
- Data and layout are interspersed in the HTML file so changing the textual content needs an understanding of HTML.
- HTML is not as easily human-readable as is Markdown and YAML.
- HTML does not have variables, conditionals, and loops, making it difficult to manage pages with a repetition of content.

Even for a single page, writing using the template logic is better than using plain HTML. We can simplify the maintainability of a website by using a template instead of simple HTML. One significant benefit of Hugo is the blurriness of the boundary between the theme and the content. Hugo provides the power to use a theme partially and override parts of web pages or to write our custom pages using all the features available to themes. In the following two chapters, we will move away from the Eclectic theme. Because we do this in a piecemeal manner, our website will still be functional the whole time.

This chapter deals with a single-page template as illustrated in figure 5.1. In section 5.1, we will split the layout and the content for the index page of the Acme Corporation website. In section 5.2, we will enhance the index page with information generated by Hugo based on the content of the rest of the website. Section 5.3 provides a glimpse of data-driven web pages built using structured front matter and data files. Finally, in section 5.4, we will use the teachings in this chapter to help our content editor by contributing as developers to provide some content automation.

5.1 Separating data and design

To control the website's index page with a markup document, we need to create the markup document first. The content folder is the branch bundle for the entire website. We need to place _index.md (https://github.com/hugoinaction/hugoinaction/tree/chapter-05-resources/01) in that folder to represent the /index.html web page. Note that if we use index.md instead, the website's root becomes a leaf bundle and will not use the template we provide in the layouts folder. With the markup document

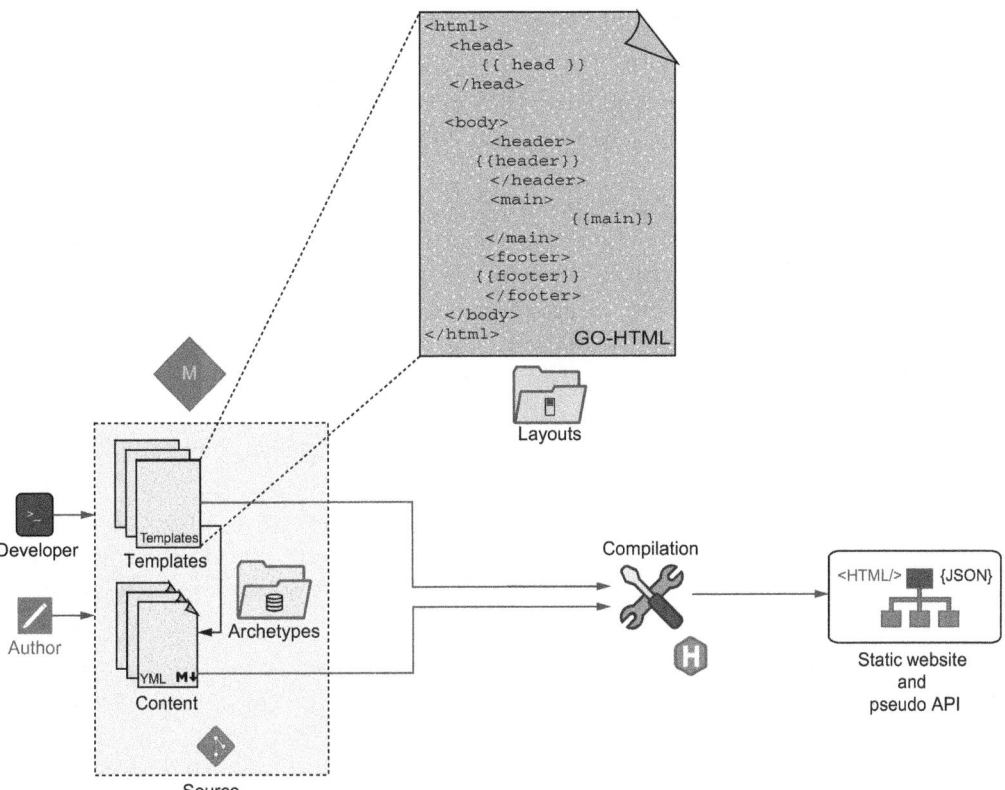

Figure 5.1   Hugo compiles the template file provided in the layouts folder in combination with the markup content to generate the HTML content for the web page. The developer provides the template file and uses some content to ensure that the Hugo build process generates the content for a web page correctly. This chapter goes through the program logic that the developer needs to create between the template and the content to generate a single web page.

present, we can move the data currently hardcoded in index.html into the front matter of this markup document. The following listing shows the contents of the index page using Markdown as the markup language. We'll use this information in the index.html page.

> **Listing 5.1   The contents of the index page in Markdown (content/_index.md)**

```
---
title: Acme Corporation
description: Welcome to the website of Acme Corporation, the
    leading creator of digital shapes on the planet, providing
    precise shape creations that are ready to use.
subtitle: shaping the world for you to live in
explore: blog
---
```

5.1.1   *Accessing the Go template language*

Hugo uses the Go template language, which is different than the Go programming language, for creating templates. The Go template language can be accessed with the HTML in the template pages by using double curly braces ({{ ... }}), which are also called *mustache tags*.

Appendix D provides a short overview of the Go template language. The resources for this chapter also include a folder named template-playground that we can place in the layouts folder and play around with Hugo's template technology. The corresponding changes can be viewed from the /template endpoint if we place template.md in the content folder (https://github.com/hugoinaction/hugoinaction/tree/chapter-05-resources/02). While this book introduces most of Hugo's commonly used features, if you are looking for a more comprehensive list of its features (outside of the appendix), Hugo's official documentation at https://gohugo.io/documentation/ does a great job of listing these.

Hugo treats the content outside of the mustache tags as a raw string that we can pass in to the final HTML as is. All the information present in the content folder is also available via variables in the template. Hugo provides a few top-level variables to access content, including:

- $—This variable represents the top-level context of the template. In the case of a page template, this variable represents the current page. Page-level metadata like the title is available as $.Title, and the description is available as $.Description. A page-level variable links to itself via the Page property, and we can therefore write the website's title as $.Page.Title.
- site—This variable provides data for the whole website. We can use this variable to access configurations in config.yaml, to navigate the website's pages via site.Pages, to move through the taxonomies using site.Taxonomies, and to view custom parameters with site.Params.
- hugo—This variable provides access to the Hugo compiler. The compiler includes methods like hugo.IsProduction (to detect if we are building for production) and hugo.Version (to inform us about the Hugo version).

Exercise 5.1

A shortcode in Hugo also allows for Go templates. What would the top-level context $ represent in a shortcode?

- a. The shortcode
- b. The containing page
- c. The entire site
- d. None of the above

The metadata provided in the front matter is available in the page-level variable accessible as $ or $.Page. In addition, the page-level variable has multiple properties and subproperties that we can use to access user-supplied and Hugo-generated metadata about the page. We can use these in the template for the index page (layouts/index.html) by using the page-level variables $.Title and $.Description. The following listing provides the page-level variables that we'll use to fill the website's <head> section.

Listing 5.2   Using page variables (layouts/index.html)

```html
<head>
  <meta charset="UTF-8">
  <meta name="description" content="{{$.Description}} ">
  <meta name="viewport" content="width=device-width, initial-scale=1.0" />
  <link rel="stylesheet" href="./index.css">
  <title>{{$.Title}}</title>
</head>
```

We can reuse the page title in the body of the index page. That way, we do not need to repeat this information across web pages. The following listing shows how to access the same parameter multiple times in a Hugo template to reuse the page title.

Listing 5.3   Accessing the same parameter (layouts/index.html)

```html
<h1>{{$.Title}}</h1>
```

Hugo standardizes the title and description properties of the web page. These are available in the top-level page object. The custom metadata item subtitle is not available at the top level in Hugo. To access the subtitle variable, we need to use the Params object in the page. That way the Params object holds all the user-defined metadata in the front matter. By moving all the custom metadata to the Params object, the Hugo team was able to add more properties to the page variable without breaking compatibility with older websites. The following listing shows how to access the subtitle variable in the Params object.

Listing 5.4   Accessing nonstandard parameters (layouts/index.html)

```html
<h2>{{$.Params.Subtitle}}</h2>
```

> **NOTE** Although we defined the metadata item as subtitle, in the listing, we accessed it as Subtitle. Variables in $.Params are *not* case-sensitive. The supplied title also exists in Params and can be accessed as $.Params.Title.

> **CODE CHECKPOINT**   https://chapter-05-01.hugoinaction.com, and source code: https://github.com/hugoinaction/hugoinaction/tree/chapter-05-01.

5.1.2 *Existence checks*

Although our code provides the data needed, there are edge cases where the code will fail. One rule of thumb when writing markup-driven websites is to assume all properties are optional. That enables all the content to be portable. If the user switches from a different theme to a more current one, they have an intense desire that the website remains functional at all times. They can slowly provide the data to support theme-specific features. If we do not provide any metadata, the home page we just created renders empty strings in place of all the custom data. But we can do better by providing default values and running existence checks.

Listing 5.5 provides one way to do an existence check using the `if` statement in Hugo. In the listing, the `if` statement checks its arguments for a truthful value for the title, description, and subtitle. When the supplied argument is `true`, the `if` statement executes the template code inside the `if` block. Additionally, the container HTML tags are not present if we do not provide the inner content. The values that fail the `if` check include `false`, `0`, a nonexistent variable (`nil`), a slice, a map, or a string of length zero.

Listing 5.5   Using existence checks (layouts/index.html)

```
...
{{if $.Description}}
<meta name="description" content="{{$.Description}}">
{{end}}
...
{{if $.Title}}<title>{{$.Title}}</title>{{end}}
...
{{if $.Title}}<h1>{{$.Title}}</h1>{{end}}
{{if $.Params.Subtitle}}<h2>{{$.Params.Subtitle}}</h2>{{end}}
...
```

> **CODE CHECKPOINT**   https://chapter-05-02.hugoinaction.com, and source code: https://github.com/hugoinaction/hugoinaction/tree/chapter-05-02.

5.1.3 *Using site variables for defaults*

The page title is also optional. If we do not provide the title for the home page, we can fall back to the website title supplied in the config.yaml file. The following listing shows how we can achieve this by using the `site.Title` variable for the content if the page title is unavailable. We can use the `else` logic for falling back to `site.Title`.

Listing 5.6   Falling back to the website's title (layouts/index.html)

```
{{if $.Title}}
  <title>{{$.Title}}</title>
{{else if site.Title}}
  <title>{{site.Title}}</title>
{{end}}
```

CODE CHECKPOINT   https://chapter-05-03.hugoinaction.com, and source code: https://github.com/hugoinaction/hugoinaction/tree/chapter-05-03.

We can also use `$.Site` for the `site` variable. Because `site` is available globally in the Hugo templates to access all the site variables, it is advisable to use `site` instead of `$.Site`. That's because `$.Site` may not be available across all template types.

5.1.4   *Creating variables for simplification*

Although the page title is needed twice on the home page, that is an unnecessary repetition. We could store the title in a variable called `$title` and use that instead as the following listing demonstrates.

Listing 5.7   Declaring `$title` with a default value (layouts/index.html)

```
{{$title := $.Title}}    ⬅——— Declares a variable called $title
```

Note that all user-defined variables start with a dollar sign (`$`). A declaration also requires `:=` for assignment. We can use a single equals sign (`=`) for future assignment as well. If needed, the following listing shows how we can provide a fallback value to a Hugo variable.

Listing 5.8   Using `if` to provide a fallback value (layouts/index.html)

```
...
{{if not $title}}
{{$title = site.Title}}
{{end}}
```

In the listing, `if not` checks if the page title is not truthful and, if so, resets the `$title` variable to the website title. In the Go template language, `not` is a Boolean function. It takes a parameter and flips its truthfulness.

Note that we can use `=` to reset an existing variable and `:=` to declare a new one. Hugo scopes variables to the code block where they are present. In other words, a variable declared inside an `if` block is not accessible outside of it. Because we defined `$title` with a default value earlier, we did not need the `else` statement to match the `if` statement in the previous listing.

Also note that we cannot use variables without declaring them. Using a variable before declaration fails. Because we declared the `title` variable in listing 5.7, we can now use `$title` wherever we need the page title with the site title as a fallback. The following listing shows this usage.

Listing 5.9   Providing the web page title (layouts/index.html)

```
{{if $title}}<title>{{$title}}</title>{{end}}
```

CODE CHECKPOINT   https://chapter-05-04.hugoinaction.com, and source code: https://github.com/hugoinaction/hugoinaction/tree/chapter-05-04.

5.1.5   *Using standard library functions to reduce the code size*

Although we are not doing anything special to get the title, our code can be needlessly lengthy and challenging to write and understand. Hugo has predefined functions for common code patterns in its websites. These can significantly reduce the complexity of the templates and their code size. We got a taste of Hugo's functions by using the not function in listing 5.8. Let's look at another Hugo function next.

We can use the `default` function to provide a default value if a value is absent. We can replace the `if` check with the usage of the `default` function. The following listing uses `default` as a shortcut to provide a default title for our website.

Listing 5.10   Declaring a default title (layouts/index.html)

```
{{$title := default site.Title $.Title}}
```

Hugo functions separate their parameters with spaces. Function calls can be wrapped with parentheses, `()`. Unless we use multiple nested functions where there is ambiguity, parentheses are optional when invoking Hugo functions. We can write the not call in listing 5.7 as if (not $.Title), and the bracketed version of the default call would be (default site.Title $.Title).

The first argument to the `default` function is the default value, while the second is the value to be checked and used if it exists. One difference between `default` and the regular `if` check is that `default` checks for the existence of a value, whereas `if` verifies the value's truthfulness. Empty strings, `false`, and 0 will not pass the truthfulness test. The `if` statement will also check the `else` code block if such is available. (This is only valid for the subtitle field. Note that Hugo provides Title as a string property and coerces `false` to the string `"false"`, which is truthful for $.Title). To match the default behavior with the `if` statement, we should use the `isset` function. The following listing uses this function to check if a variable is not undefined.

Listing 5.11   Using the `isset` function (layouts/index.html)

```
{{if isset $.Params "subtitle"}}<h2>{{$.Params.subtitle}}</h2>{{end}}
```

If we pass false as the subtitle of the web page (by setting subtitle: false in the front matter of the .md file), Hugo still renders the web page.

Another function worth mentioning here is $.Param. This function is tied to the $ object because it accesses site.Params and $.Params. The pattern of accessing the page variable and falling back to the site variable is so common that Hugo has a built-in method to do this. We can use $.Param when passing just the subtitle call to access the title. The following listing shows how to declare the $.Param function to provide the subtitle. The $.Param function provides the page subtitle and falls back to the site subtitle if the page subtitle is not present.

Listing 5.12 Using the `$.Param` function (layouts/index.html)

```
{{$.Param "subtitle"}}
```

CODE CHECKPOINT https://chapter-05-05.hugoinaction.com, and source code: https://github.com/hugoinaction/hugoinaction/tree/chapter-05-05.

Exercise 5.2

It is a good practice to continue to render a website even if certain front matter properties are absent. The _____ function allows us to fill in a custom fallback value if the front matter entry does not exist.

5.1.6 *Using a context switch via the with conditional for simplifying further checks*

Having deeply nested properties in objects like `site.Params` makes the template lengthy and difficult to read (and write). This verbosity discourages users from properly grouping their keys, which impacts website maintainability. For example, we provided `site.Params.Footer[0].title` as a property to the Eclectic theme. One can easily imagine why we would not want to write this line five times in code. Hugo provides a special context variable, a dot (`.`), to solve this problem.

The context variable can be loosely compared to the `this` variable in object-oriented programming languages, which becomes the method's object. When rendering a page, the context variable represents a page, but if we are rendering a taxonomy, it becomes that taxonomy. If we render a shortcode, the context variable becomes that shortcode. When working in the context of a property, we can override the context variable with that property and access that property with the `.` variable.

Hugo provides the `with` conditional, which overrides the context variable in its code block. Using `with`, we can write a less verbose existence check. That's because `with` calls its inner code block if the variable is supplied with a value. We can pass a variable or an expression to `with`. If it evolves to a truthful value (not `nil`, `0`, `false`, or an empty slice, dictionary, or string) that value is set as the value of `.` (the dot) inside the block contained in the `with` statement. In case the value is not true, the `with` block is skipped. The following listing shows how to override the context variable using `with`. The `.` represents the value of the variable passed to `with`.

Listing 5.13 Overriding the context variable (layouts/index.html)

```
{{with $title}}<title>{{.}}</title>{{end}}
```

Inside the `with` code block, the context variable `.` was replaced with the value of the `$title` variable. Note that if we do not set `$title`, this code does not execute. However, if we provide an `else` code block in the `with` block, Hugo runs that code instead.

CODE CHECKPOINT   https://chapter-05-06.hugoinaction.com, and source code: https://github.com/hugoinaction/hugoinaction/tree/chapter-05-06.

$ is by default the top-level context variable, but we can remove an unnecessary $ sign from our code to convert it into something that a typical Hugo theme developer would write. $ is only needed if we need to access the top-level context in the with block.

Exercise 5.3
When should with be used in a Hugo template?

- **a.** with is among the "bad" parts of Hugo, having a vast negative performance impact, and should not be used.
- **b.** with can be used to check the existence of a value and provide a default behavior or value if one is absent.
- **c.** with can be used to update the context to write less code if it relies only on the subproperties of a variable.
- **d.** with can be used to provide inline handling of map properties without having to write a nested function like index to access the property.
- **e.** both b and c.
- **f.** both c and d.
- **g.** b, c, and d.

5.1.7   Adding content processing

In this section, we will enhance the home page with more Hugo features to make it match the design shown in figure 5.2. The subtitle field we have rendered so far is in plain text. We want to start that with a capital letter and provide the capabilities to use Markdown-based formatting for the subtitle. Because the subtitle is already available in a variable, this task involves passing the subtitle to an appropriate function to do further processing. To enable the subtitle to start with a capital letter, we can give this to the humanize function as the following listing shows.

> **Listing 5.14   Adding the humanize function (layouts/index.html)**

```
{{with .Param "subtitle"}}<h2>{{humanize .}}</h2>{{end}}
```

After "humanizing" the subtitle, we can further use Markdown processing by passing the data through the Markdown parser via the markdownify function. In section 3.1.4, we discussed how the theme authors can parse Markdown from front matter data; markdownify is the function to do this. The following listing shows how to add this function for future Markdown support.

> **Listing 5.15   Adding the markdownify function (layouts/index.html)**

```
{{with .Param "subtitle"}}<h2>{{markdownify (humanize .)}}</h2>{{end}}
```

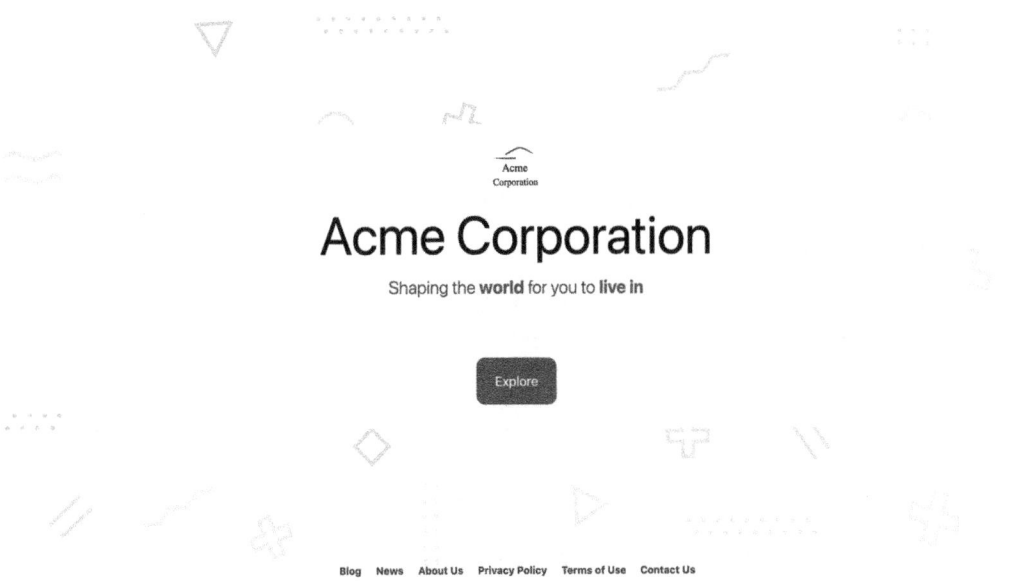

Figure 5.2 The Acme Corporation home page, where we used Markdown on the subtitle, and markup to control the index.html page in the layouts folder

Although calling nested functions using parentheses is a perfectly valid approach, Hugo also supports the pipe operator (|) for a more functional programming style. This allows us to take the output of the previous function and pass it to the next one. The following listing shows how to pipe though functions.

Listing 5.16   Using the pipe operator (layouts/index.html)

```
{{with .Param "subtitle"}}<h2>{{. | humanize | markdownify}}</h2>{{end}}
```

The functional programming-style approach is easier to read and is preferred when the function takes just one argument. We will use this as an opportunity to make the words "world" and "live in" bold in the subtitle by wrapping them with double stars (**) as the following listing shows. We also need to link the Explore button using the explore option in the front matter for the index page to make that page data driven.

Listing 5.17   Highlighting parts of the subtitle (content/_index.md)

```
subtitle: shaping the **world** for you to **live in**     ◁──┐ Highlighting parts
explore: blog   ◁──┐                                           of the subtitle using
              ┌──────┴──────────────────────────────┐          Markdown
              │ The explore option (already in the front matter)
              │ for the data-driven Explore button configuration
```

The ref function in Hugo takes a file or folder name and provides the corresponding URL for this content. We can also use relref for a relative path. The following listing calls the ref function to convert a file to the corresponding URL.

Listing 5.18   **Using the `ref` function (layouts/index.html)**

```
<a href="{{ref . (.Param "explore")}}"
>Explore</a>
```

CODE CHECKPOINT   https://chapter-05-07.hugoinaction.com, and source code: https://github.com/hugoinaction/hugoinaction/tree/chapter-05-07.

5.1.8   *Adding Markdown content*

We have Markdown content in the content file. This content is available in its HTML form via the `.Content` variable on the root context (`$`) variable. We can place this anywhere on the page using `{{.Content}}` in our template to enable a new section on the home page as figure 5.3 illustrates.

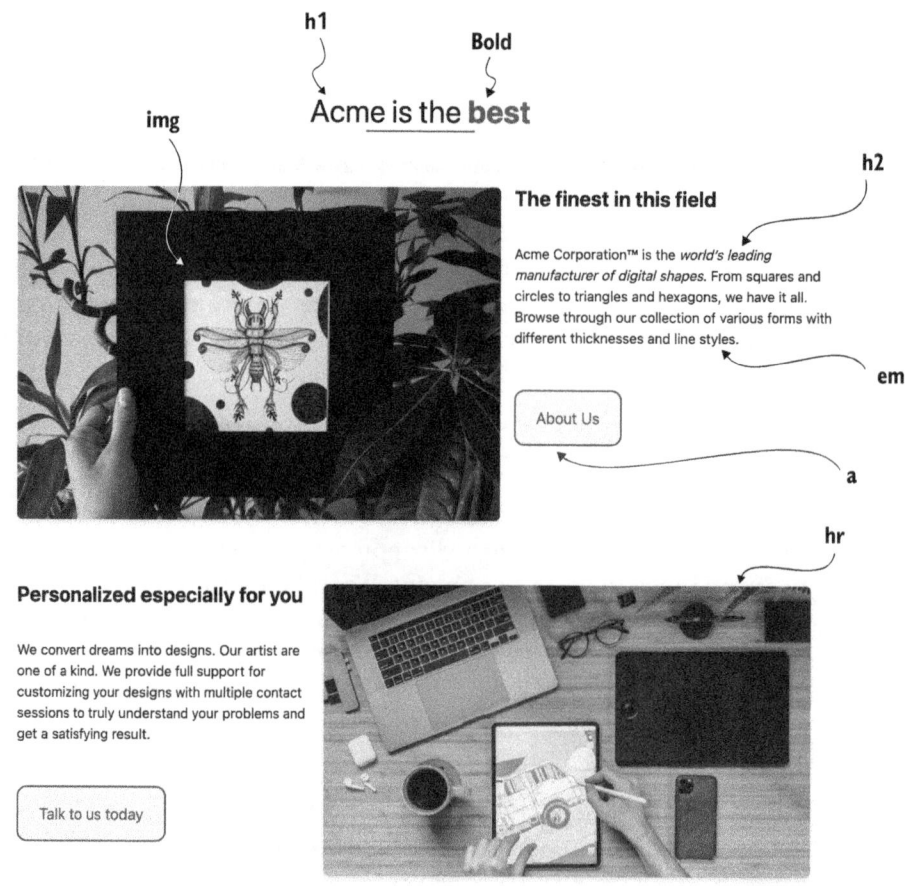

Figure 5.3   Adding Markdown content to the home page. (Photo for the about image by Angela Pencheva on Unsplash; photo for the contact image by Cristofer Jeschkeon on Unsplash.)

Let's add some Markdown data to the Acme Corporation's website's home page (https://github.com/hugoinaction/hugoinaction/tree/chapter-05-resources/03). The following listing provides the data for the index page.

Listing 5.19   Adding descriptive content in Markdown (content/_index.md)

```
Acme is the **best**
==================

![about us](about.jpg)

The finest in this field
------------------------

Acme Corporation&trade; is the _ world's leading manufacturer
of digital shapes_. From squares and circles to triangles and
hexagons, we have it all. Browse through our collection of various
forms with different thicknesses and line styles.

[About Us](./about)

* * *

![contact us](contact.jpg)

Personalized especially for you
-------------------------------

We convert dreams into designs. Our artists are one of a kind.
We provide full support for customizing your designs with multiple contact
sessions to understand your problems and get a satisfying result.

[Talk to us today](./contact)
```

To use this content, we will also need two images, contact.jpg and about.jpg, which can be placed in the page bundle for the website index in the content folder. To fit the design of the current website, we will add the ID intro to the current section and create a new section with the ID description in the Markdown content. The following listing shows how this is done.

Listing 5.20   Rendering the Markdown content (layouts/index.html)

```html
<section id="intro">
  . . .
</section>
<section id="description">
  {{.Content}}
</section>
```

CODE CHECKPOINT   https://chapter-05-08.hugoinaction.com, and source code: https://github.com/hugoinaction/hugoinaction/tree/chapter-05-08.

Hugo automatically runs this content provided in the Markdown file through the Markdown parser and provides an HTML string to place directly in the document.

> **Customizing the generated HTML from Markdown**
>
> While generating HTML from Markdown, Hugo provides the developer with the flexibility to customize the HTML generated for a specific element. Special templates, called *render hook templates*, can control exactly how this rendering happens. For example, we can use the custom templates at layouts/_default/_markup/render-image .html, layouts/_default/_markup/render-link.html, or layouts/_default/_markup/ render-heading.html, and then decide on how to render the inline images, links, and headings provided in Markdown.
>
> These templates have access to the entire set of page and site variables, along with unique variables like .Level, .Text, .Title, and .Destination for the HTML headings, display text, appended title, and the provided URL in Markdown. In chapter 6, we will create custom render hooks to control Markdown rendering.
>
> Note that the templates in the _default folder apply to the whole website. We can limit these to a set of pages by moving these templates to a specific content type. We will discuss content types in chapter 7. Developers can further process the generated HTML string using methods like findRE to replace certain substrings.

5.2 *Using external data to add content*

While we can obtain most web page data from the markup document, we can also get some of it outside the markup document. This data includes menus, other sections, and pages of the website and content generated by Hugo from the website or web page data.

5.2.1 *Adding the menu*

The links for the main pages on the home page break the independence of those pages. If we delete one of those pages, we will have a dangling link. Adding a link to that page involves copying and pasting content and then changing the text in an HTML file. This solution is not scalable. A better and more scalable solution is to have a menu for this content. This way, the pages can independently get assigned to a menu with the configuration or with the front matter.

   While we can create a new menu for this information, a better idea for the Acme Corporation website is to render the main menu used throughout the website on the home page. The main menu is already present in the site.Menus.main variable. We can loop through this to create anchor tags for the various menu entries on the home page. Listing 5.21 adds a new section for the menu under the current context area with this information. Later, we will enhance the menu to match figure 5.4.

Figure 5.4   Our new section in the home page with a rendering for the main menu as a section on the home page

---

Listing 5.21   Rendering the menu on the home page (layouts/index.html)

```
{{with site.Menus.main }}        ◁——  The outer with statement ensures that
                                       Hugo does not render the section if the
<section id="menu">                    main menu is not present.
<h1>Website sections</h1>
  <h2>This website has these major areas</h2>
  <ul>
    {{ range . }}           ┌── Uses the URL of the              The CSS file provides
    <li>                    │   menu entry to navigate           icons based on the
      <a href="{{.URL}}">  ◁─┘                                   identifier.
        <i class="icon-{{.Identifier}}"></i>   ◁──────────────┘
        {{.Name | humanize}}     ◁──
      </a>                               The name is humanized
    </li>                               for proper appearance.
    {{ else }}                     ◁──────────────┐
    {{/* Log for the website editor/developer */}}   range supports an else
    <!-- No menu entries present -->                 block for cases where the
    {{end}}                                          array (slice) is empty.
  </ul>
</section>
{{end}}
```

In listing 5.21, range is the primary looping function in the Go template language. The range function updates the context (.) in each run for the next menu entry. If there are no entries, Hugo does not process the code block inside the range. If needed, we can supply the else code block for this. The range function also has an alternate form to fill variables instead of updating context with a value and providing the index. Still, the context update version is more popular.

site.Menus is a Hugo-generated object with subproperties for each menu on the website, which internally contains all the menu entries sorted on the supplied weight. Each menu entry provides the Name and URL subproperties. Note that the main menu has submenus, which we are ignoring in this case. We can use the humanize function to capitalize the first letter of the name, thereby transparently dealing with all lower-case entries.

The `else` code block introduces comments in the Go template language. We are free to use HTML comments for this, but they do have some gotchas:

- HTML comments are generated and exposed in the output. Unless we strip them out during minification, they will increase the page size.
- Hugo executes any Go Template code in mustaches (`{{...}}`), even in the HTML comment block.

HTML comments are suitable for the theme or page developer to send messages to the content author for the web page. On the other hand, Go template comments are stripped at compile time and are helpful for the theme or layout developer only.

While a menu needs only the name, identifier, and weight, we can add custom `pre` and `post` properties to the menu entry to supply additional data to the template that it can use before or after the menu. In the chapter resources, we've added a `post` property to the main menu (https://github.com/hugoinaction/hugoinaction/tree/chapter-05-resources/04) that can be used to populate the content. We can now use this property in our template as the following listing shows, updating the rendering of the main menu on the home page.

> **Listing 5.22   Adding a post section to the main menu (layouts/index.html)**

```
<li>
  <a href="{{.URL}}">
    <i class="icon-{{.Identifier}}"></i>
    {{.Name | humanize}}
  </a>
  {{with .Post}}<p>{{.}}</p>{{end}}
</li>
```

Wraps .Post in a with statement to allow the template to render even if .Post is absent

---

Creating a new menu

There is nothing special that we need to do to create a new menu in Hugo. All we need to do is to assign pages to the menu. For example, we could add the following to the About page to create a separate home menu:

```
menu:
  home:
    name: About
    identifier: about
    weight: -500
```

With this, instead of looping through `site.Menus.main`, we can run the `range` loop through `site.Menus.home` and leave the rest of the code as-is.

We can also generate the header for the web page using the same main menu. We will move the website logo from the intro section to the header and render it as in figure 5.5. Listing 5.23 provides the code to set up the header.

Figure 5.5 Adding a header with another copy of the main menu to the home page.

```
Listing 5.23   Setting up a header for Acme Corporation (layouts/index.html)
```
```html
<header>

<a href="{{ site.BaseURL | absLangURL }}">
    <img src="./image/logo.svg" alt="Acme Logo"
        height="36" width="48" />
    Acme Corporation
  </a>
  {{with site.Menus.main }}
    <nav>
      <button class="hamburger">☰</button>
      <ul>
        {{range .}}
          <li>
            <a href="{{.URL}}">{{.Name | humanize}}</a>
          </li>
        {{end}}
      </ul>
    </nav>
  {{end}}
</header>
```

Note that when we develop the home page, we can use .Permalink to link to the current page. Using site.BaseURL as the link to the home page ensures that we can reuse this header in other pages (we will do this in the next chapter). We can also update the footer to the website to use a footer menu instead of hardcoded text in a similar fashion. Finally, the absLangURL function converts the URL to an absolute link for the current language. This function will come in handy when we convert to a multilingual website in chapter 13.

Exercise 5.4

Build the footer for the Acme Corporation website to match the view in figure 5.6 by generating the HTML that matches https://chapter-05-09.hugoinaction.com.

a. To fill the social media icons, use the author information supplied in the configuration.

b. The copyright information is present in the website parameters.

c. The footer menu is already available in the website content, and you should use it.

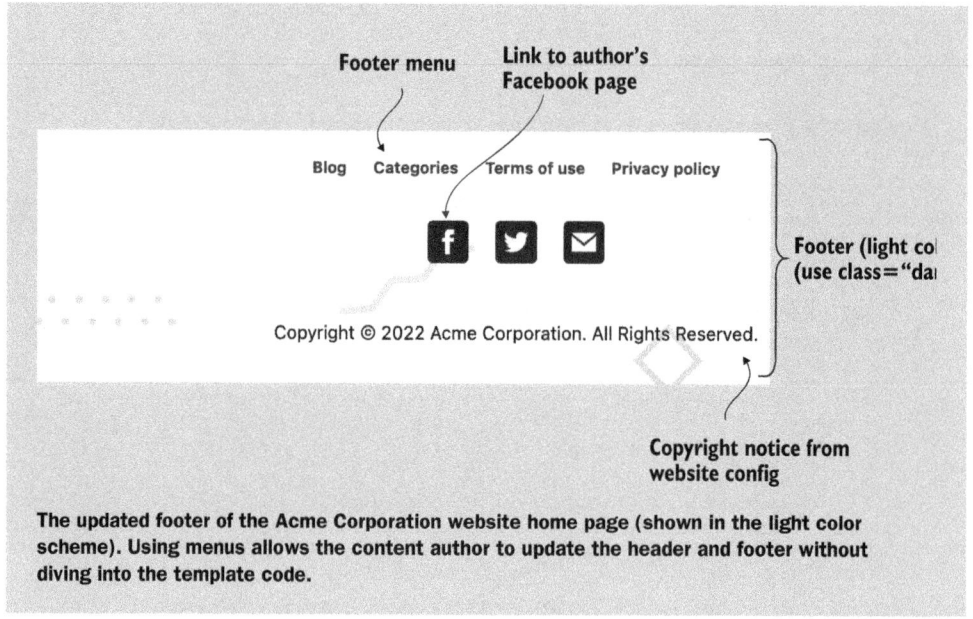

Footer menu

Link to author's
Facebook page

Blog   Categories   Terms of use   Privacy policy

Footer (light co
(use class = "da

Copyright © 2022 Acme Corporation. All Rights Reserved.

Copyright notice from
website config

The updated footer of the Acme Corporation website home page (shown in the light color scheme). Using menus allows the content author to update the header and footer without diving into the template code.

The CSS file makes a light-colored footer by default, but we can make it darker by adding the dark class to the footer tag. We will use the dark footer in the rest of the website. We will also take this opportunity to add the link to the Credits page in the footer. In credits.md, add the following:

```
---
menu:
  footer:
    name: Credits
    identifier: credits
    weight: 400
---
---
```

CODE CHECKPOINT   https://chapter-05-09.hugoinaction.com, and source code: https://github.com/hugoinaction/hugoinaction/tree/chapter-05-09.

Section pages as menus

Writing a menu entry with links to index pages in the sections of a website is such a common task that Hugo has defined this with an easier default. If we add, for example, `sectionPagesMenu: sections` to our configuration parameter `sectionPagesMenu: <name>` (https://gohugo.io/templates/menu-templates/#section-menu-for-lazy-bloggers), then a menu named Sections is automatically created with an entry for each section in the website. We do not need any references to the sections menu in our content and can just use `sectionPagesMenu: sections` in our configuration to populate the Sections menu with a link to the index page of each section.

5.2.2 Adding recent blog posts

The data added so far is mostly static and does not change frequently and, therefore, provides little benefit when using templates. A major benefit of static-site frameworks is auto-updating pages with data that changes. We will add a list of recent blog posts to the home page of the Acme Corporation website, which will auto-update with new entries as we add more blog posts. To do this, we will create one more section on the website's home page with a list of recent blog posts (https://github.com/hugoinaction/hugoinaction/tree/chapter-05-resources/06). Figure 5.6 shows the output of this section.

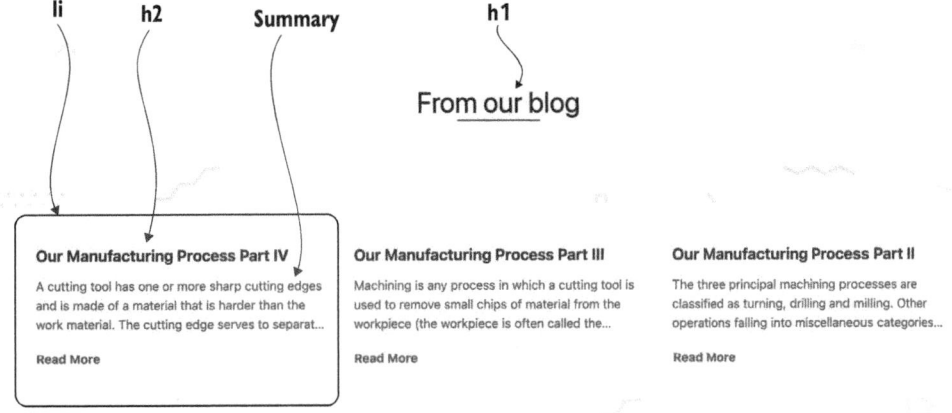

Figure 5.6 Recent blog posts section on the Acme Corporation website home page

To provide content, we will get a list of child pages for the website belonging to the blog section and then render them in a small card layout with the title and the summary (manual or auto-generated). We will add images to the blog posts in the next chapter. Listing 5.24 provides the changes that we'll make on the home page of the Acme Corporation website. These involve filtering the website pages for blog posts and getting the first three. The most interesting code in the template is the filtering logic, which is described in detail in figure 5.7.

Listing 5.24 Changing the recent file list (layouts/index.html)

```
{{with (where site.RegularPages ".Section" "blog")}}        Filters the page based
<section id="blog">                                         on whether the section
    <h1>From our blog</h1>                                   is a blog (more on this
    <ul class="posts">          Loops through the first three shortly)
        {{range first 3 .}}     pages from the context slice
        <li class="post" >      supplied by the first function
          <a href="#{{.Permalink}}">       .Permalink provides
            <h2>                            the URL of the page.
              {{.Title}}
            </h2>
            <article>
```

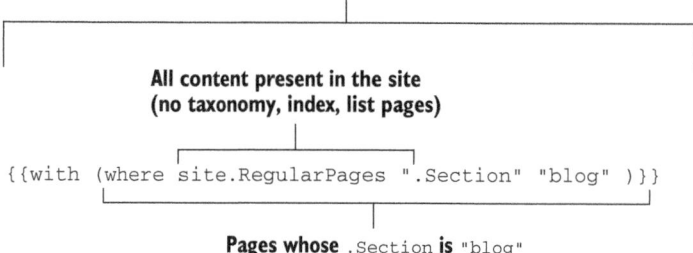

```
            {{.Summary}}
            </article>
            <div>Read More</div>
          </a>
        </li>
        {{end}}
      </ul>
</section>
{{end}}
```

.Summary provides the auto-generated or the manually provided summary of the web page.

Update the context with the slice only if it is not empty

All content present in the site
(no taxonomy, index, list pages)

```
{{with (where site.RegularPages ".Section" "blog" )}}
```

Pages whose .Section is "blog"

Figure 5.7   The filtering logic to find the blog entries to showcase

In the listing, we filtered the page with the `where` statement content coming from the `RegularPages` property on the website. This property gives us a list of all content pages, excluding support pages like taxonomies and indexes, sorted by the date field in descending order. While we can change the sort order with the `sort` function, descending order by date is usually the desired behavior, and we do not need to change it. The `where` function takes a slice (list), a key, and a value. It filters the list based on elements whose value at the provided key (`.Section`) matches the value (`blog`). While the default operator is equality (=), we can override it by passing the custom operator before the value.

> **NOTE** Because `site` is global, `site.RegularPages` is available across all templates.

The outer `with` statement performs two tasks: it updates the context variable so that we do not need to duplicate the `where` check twice and ensures that there is content in the blog section if that section is present. Hugo's template engine is smart enough to identify an empty slice in a `with` statement and does not render in this case.

While the filtering code we are using is functional, we have hardcoded the key `blog` in the template. If we have a website layout with a different section name, this would become a problem. Hugo has a standardized key for this scenario, whose default value Hugo auto-generates.

We can use `site.Params.mainSections` to get the main sections within the website. By default, it contains the section with the maximum number of pages, but we can override this variable to support multiple sections or to add or remove them. Because it is a list, the default equality checks for where the operation does not work, and we will need to supply the in operator for this. The following listing updates the page filtering logic to look for the main section rather than the hardcoded blog section.

Listing 5.25   Updating the page filtering logic (layouts/index.html)

Hugo supports multiline template code.

```
{{with
  (where site.RegularPages
    ".Section" "in" site.Params.mainSections)
}}
```

Filters regular pages

Uses the extended where format, where the "in" operator is specified

CODE CHECKPOINT   https://chapter-05-10.hugoinaction.com, and source code: https://github.com/hugoinaction/hugoinaction/tree/chapter-05-10.

5.3   Playing with structured data

There are two general types of data in a web page: unstructured, free-flowing text (represented by a Markdown document), and structured or grouped data (represented by keys and values or rows and columns traditionally defined in a database). For example, in a shopping cart application, the product description should be unstructured, but if we put the price field in Markdown, extracting the price to show in multiple places would be tedious. There are multiple ways to provide structured data separately. One approach is to read a file from the disk. Another option is to use the front matter to provide structured data along with the metadata.

5.3.1   Using front matter for structured data

The .Params object in the site and the page-level variables belongs to the theme. The theme authors are free to decide what to add to these variables to provide structured data. Let's put the concept to use for the Acme Corporation website home page. We will add a list of testimonials on the website's home page using the front matter as shown in figure 5.8. Then, in listing 5.26, we will add a field called testimonials in the front

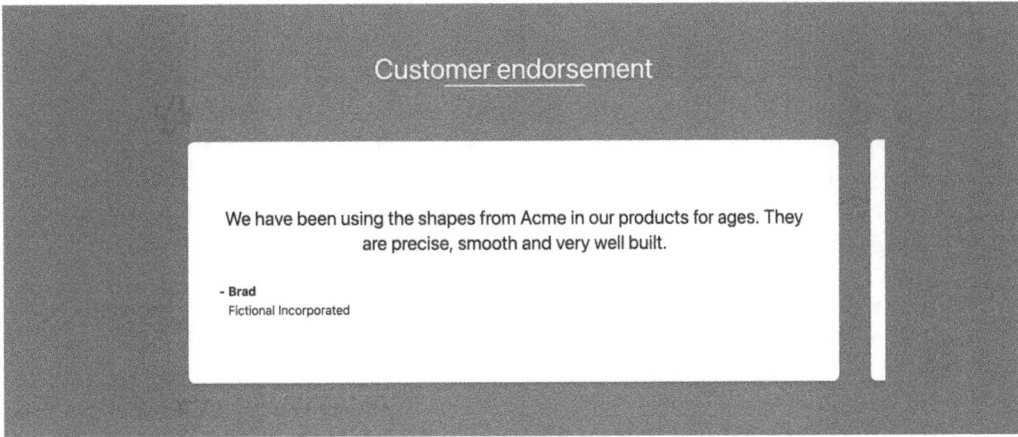

Figure 5.8   Testimonial section on the Acme Corporation website home page

matter and place all the testimonials there (https://github.com/hugoinaction/ hugoinaction/tree/chapter-05-resources/07).

Exercise 5.5

Which of the following are examples of structured data that will benefit from moving outside the Markdown content to structured data and into the front matter or separate files? (Select all that apply.)

- **a.** Music playlists
- **b.** Author biography
- **c.** Reviews of physical products
- **d.** List of top ten most liked blog posts
- **e.** Affiliate link to the product in review

Listing 5.26   Text for data-driven testimonials (content/_index.md)

```
testimonials:
  - author: Brad
    from: Fictional Incorporated
    content: >
            We have been using the shapes from Acme
            in our products for ages. They are
            precise, smooth, and very well built.

  - author: Random
    from: Random Education
    content: >
            Sharp and sturdy - Just like you want them.

  - author: Richter
    from: Richter Measures
    content: >
            Undoubted accuracy. Safety guarantee.
            We love what Acme delivers.
```

Now we can read this variable on the page and render it appropriately. Listing 5.27 provides the changes to display the testimonials. This type of logic enables data-driven custom elements in the HTML, which use structured data provided as a parameter. It is good practice to check for their existence and to not create HTML tags surrounding a list if the list is empty. If it is not empty, we can loop through it and access inner properties like Content, From, and Author.

Listing 5.27   Changes to the testimonials (layouts/index.html)

```
{{with .Param "testimonials"}}

<section id="testimonials">
  <h1>Customer endorsement</h1>
  <div>
```

> ◁—— The with statement provides the outer existence check and context update. It uses the .Param function to read from the front matter, falling back to the site config.

```
           <ol>
Content  ┌─▷  {{range .}}
  loop   │       <li>
         │          <p>{{.content}}</p>
         │          <div>
         │            <h2>{{.author}}</h2>
         │            <h3>{{.from}}</h3>
         │          </div>
         │       </li>
         └───  {{end}}
           </ol>
         </div>
       </section>
    {{end}}
```

CODE CHECKPOINT   https://chapter-05-11.hugoinaction.com, and source code: https://github.com/hugoinaction/hugoinaction/tree/chapter-05-11.

In listing 5.27, the top-level `with` call ensures that we add nothing if there is no testimonial section provided in the front matter. However, if it is present, we loop through the list of testimonials and print each of those in the HTML.

We used the same technique in section 3.6.2 to build a data-driven landing page using the Eclectic template. Theme authors have used structured data to create sidebars, carousels, accordions, and other advanced user interface elements.

5.3.2 *Parsing files for data*

For interoperability with other systems, a file-based approach to data gathering is extremely useful. Hugo supports parsing structured content that we can use to provide raw data from CSV-based spreadsheets, JSON-based API output, or individual YAML files. We can convert this data to slices (arrays) and dictionaries (maps) in Hugo and then use those to present the data as HTML. This feature is extremely useful in creating websites based on another system that provides output in a machine-readable format.

There are many ways to access files. For example, you can drop a JSON, CSV, YAML, or TOML file into the data folder in parallel with the content folder. The data in the file is available as a dictionary in the `site.Data` variable. We can also put the file at a fixed location and use `readFile` to get its contents and then use `transform.Unmarshal` to convert it from raw text to a dictionary. Page bundles can also be used for these files, where we can use `$.Page.Resources.Get` followed by `transform.Unmarshal`.

For Acme Corporation, we have a file called products.csv, which lists the product information for the products sold by the company. A separate inventory management system manages and exports the Excel-supported CSV format. We need to render this as a table in the home page of the website (figure 5.9).

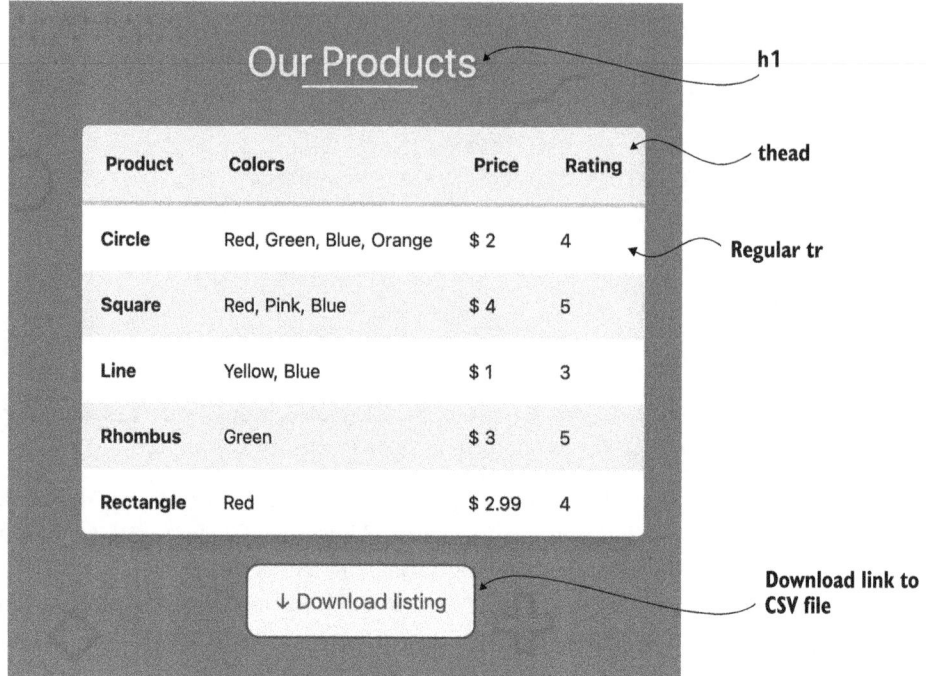

Figure 5.9   Products list on the index page via parsing a CSV file from disk

We can place products.csv in the root of the content folder to make it a part of the branch bundle for the index page (https://github.com/hugoinaction/hugoinaction/tree/chapter-05-resources/08). The code in the following listing loops through the products.csv file and prints the values in a table. We will mark the first row of the table as a header.

Listing 5.28   Looping through products.csv (layouts/index.html)

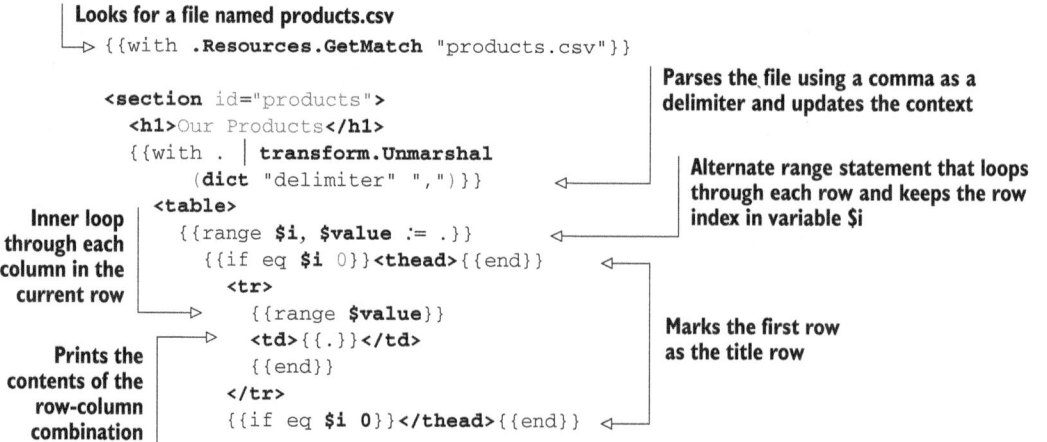

```
      {{end}}
    </table>
  {{end}}
  <a download href="{{.Permalink}}" >        ◁─┐  Provides a link to
    Download listing                              download the resource
  </a>
</section>
{{end}}
```

CODE CHECKPOINT   https://chapter-05-12.hugoinaction.com, and source code: https://github.com/hugoinaction/hugoinaction/tree/chapter-05-12.

We can use the resources API to find the products.csv file in the page bundle for the current page. The resources APIs are a powerful way to access resources and process, manage, and transform them. We will delve more into resource APIs with Hugo Pipes in chapter 6.

In the previous listing, we took the file and parsed it using a comma (,) as the delimiter for CSV, which returns a slice of slices (nested array) representing a two-dimensional array. In the outer loop, we used the alternative form of the range expression. Instead of setting the context variable ., the corresponding value, $value, in the range is returned along with its index $i. Next, we used the index to identify the header row. Finally, we looped through the entries with an inner range to create the table for all rows. At the bottom of the section, we provided a downloadable link to the CSV file using the same resources API.

5.4 Enhancing life with the Go template language

We can do a lot more with the template language than just build web page templates. We can use the Go template language at various places to remove repetitive work and enhance the day-to-day workflows dealing with content. We can invent new shortcodes that enhance Markdown to provide a new feature. We can create archetypes or templates for content so that when we start to write the content later, we have a page with the essential metadata prefilled.

5.4.1 Template code in shortcodes

Shortcodes (which we used in chapter 4) are not just snippets of HTML. They are snippets of templates that have access to the complete template functionality. We can access all the variables of the site in them and can use those along with the passed parameters and the inner content to write our logic to render the shortcode.

Using the Go template language skills we have developed so far, we can write a shortcode that takes a product name, parses the price, and renders it to the website. For the shortcode to work in the whole website, we will need to move products.csv to a more accessible location, such as the assets folder. (The assets folder is the global folder for the content accessible through the Go template language.) Note that we will also need to update the index page template to use this new location (using resources.get instead of .Resources.Get). The following listing provides the custom shortcode to perform these tasks (https://github.com/hugoinaction/hugoinaction/tree/chapter-05-resources/09).

Listing 5.29 Shortcode for the product price (layouts/shortcodes/price.html)

If the shortcode in the context variable is passed, named arguments get the product argument, falling back to the first argument given.

Reads the file products.csv from the global assets; resources (a lowercase "r") refers to global assets.

Loops through the rows of the CSV

Parses as CSV with a comma as the delimiter

```
{{- $product := default (.Get 0) (.Get "product") -}}
{{- if $product -}}
  {{- $products := resources.GetMatch
        "products.csv" -}}
  {{- $parsedProducts := $products |
    transform.Unmarshal (dict "delimiter" ",") -}}
{{- range $r := $parsedProducts -}}
    {{- if eq (index $r 0) $product -}}
      $ {{- trim (index $r 2) " " -}}
    {{- end -}}
{{- end -}}
{{- end -}}
```

The trim function removes any spaces we get from the CSV.

If the first column (index 0) for any row is the exact text as the passed product, prints the third column (index 2) of that row

CODE CHECKPOINT https://chapter-05-13.hugoinaction.com, and source code: https://github.com/hugoinaction/hugoinaction/tree/chapter-05-13.

The main thing to notice in listing 5.29 is that the context variable, ., is different in a shortcode. That's because it refers to the shortcode and not to the page rendering it. Also, in the listing, we use {{- -}} instead of the standard {{ }} Go template mustaches (mustache is another common name for double curly braces). The reason for using {{- -}} (dashed mustaches) is that they remove all whitespace from both sides of the string output. We do not need aggressive space trimming in most cases because we do need a single space, and HTML ignores additional spaces.

In a case like the current example, where we need absolute zero spaces to allow complete space control in the Markdown document, dashed mustaches and the trim function are handy. We can also have single dashed mustaches like {{- … }} or {{ … -}} to trim spaces from the left and the right, respectively.

We can use the index function in Hugo to access the value from a list at a specific index. We can use this shortcode by calling it with the parameter {{< price "Square">}} or with named parameters like {{< price product= "Square">}}. We will add this to the Building Squares and the Circle blog posts as the following code snippet shows. Additionally, by using resources.GetMatch instead of .Resources.GetMatch, we target the global assets folder for content.

```
{{< price "Circle" >}}          $4
{{< price product="Square" >}}  $2
```

Figure 5.10 A developer's gotta do what a developer's gotta do. At coffee, Alex and Bob discuss the most complicated pieces of their codebase.

5.4.2 Inner content in shortcodes

Shortcodes can also take inner content (discussed in section 4.5.1). We can access this and do any processing we need with this information using the Go template language. For example, the shortcode in the following listing repeats the inner content *n* times, where *n* is supplied as a parameter (https://github.com/hugoinaction/hugoinaction/tree/chapter-05-resources/10).

Listing 5.30 Shortcode to repeat a message (layouts/shortcodes/repeat.html)

Like the product argument in the price shortcode, looks for
the count. If nothing is present, it defaults to 5 instead of nil.

```
{{$count := default 5 (default
    (.Get 0) (.Get "count"))}}
{{/* Preprocess to speed up */}}
{{$inner := .Inner | markdownify}}
{{if gt $count 0}}
<ul>
  {{ range seq $count}}
  <li>{{$inner}}</li>
  {{end}}
</ul>
{{end}}
```

Uses markdownify to convert the supplied inner data from Markdown to HTML. We are preprocessing for better performance.

seq takes a number and generates a slice from 0 to that number. We use that to loop $count times to print $inner in an HTML unordered list.

CODE CHECKPOINT https://chapter-05-14.hugoinaction.com, and source code: https://github.com/hugoinaction/hugoinaction/tree/chapter-05-14.

The code in the previous listing should not be difficult to understand. The critical thing to remember with the repeat shortcode is the performance cost of looping. We should avoid heavy processing in a loop and precalculate (like running the Markdown parser in this case) wherever possible. We can use this approach in the about section of the website to remind the team, by repeating five times, "The customer is our **number 1** priority." The following listing uses the repeat shortcode to add this reminder.

> **Listing 5.31   Adding the `repeat` shortcode (content/about/index.md)**

Input

```
{{< repeat 5 >}}
Customer is our **number 1** priority.
{{< / repeat }}
Nothing else.
```

Output

```
<ul>
  <li>The customer is our <strong>number 1</strong> priority.</li>
  <li>The customer is our <strong>number 1</strong> priority.</li>
  <li>The customer is our <strong>number 1</strong> priority.</li>
  <li>The customer is our <strong>number 1</strong> priority.</li>
  <li>The customer is our <strong>number 1</strong> priority.</li>
</ul>
Nothing else.
```

5.4.3   *Save some time with archetypes*

The set of steps involved in writing content is repetitive. It consists of creating folders, filling in front matter and, in many cases, placing cover images. While these tasks are repetitive, they are unique to the theme and its layout. Whatever can be generalized across all websites has already been done by setting good default values for most front matter and other variables in Hugo.

As websites grow complex and more features are added, setting up content for a web page gets complicated. While we started with placing Markdown files in the content folder, we have already moved to page bundles. In the foreseeable future, we can imagine dense front matter with fields like date, draft, etc., which can become required fields.

Archetypes are templates for a Hugo post that we can use to automatically create the folder structure, fill in the front matter, and supply placeholder images for content so that we can get to writing quickly. When we use hugo new <filename>, a placeholder file is created in the content folder. When we made the website for Acme Corporation, the hugo new site command in chapter 2 created a default archetype. We can use this as a template to generate blog posts by issuing the following command:

```
hugo new blog/line.md
```

This command creates a line.md file in the content folder, which is marked as draft. We can start adding content, and when we are ready to publish this page, we can remove the draft field from the front matter. We can preview draft pages using hugo server --buildDrafts.

While the default archetype fills in the essentials, we can add more to the blog template. For regular Markdown posts, we can create a new file, for example, blog.md (https://github.com/hugoinaction/hugoinaction/tree/chapter-05-resources/11) in the archetype folder with the content shown in the following listing.

Listing 5.32 Contents of the blog archetype (archetypes/blog.md)

```
---
date: {{ .Date }}
title: "{{ replace .Name "-" " " | title }}"
draft: true
tags:
  - unknown
categories:
  - general
---

Provide an awesome introduction here

<!--more-->

Here goes the main content.
```

We can now delete content/blog/line.md and generate a new one. This time Hugo automatically picks up the blog template for the content in the blog section.

Exercise 5.6

Archetypes are a means for the _____ to help the _____ with a great set of defaults.

We can also create page bundles in the archetypes. To add page bundles, create a subfolder named blog in the archetypes folder and move blog.md to it, renaming the file index.md. We can also add a cover image if we so desire (https://github.com/ hugoinaction/hugoinaction/tree/chapter-05-resources/12). Now we can create a page bundle for the line blog post by using the kind flag in the new command. To do that, we remove line.md and run the command in the following listing.

Listing 5.33 Creating a new blog post by specifying kind

```
hugo new blog/line --kind blog
```

NOTE Both blog.md and the blog folder should not exist simultaneously.

CODE CHECKPOINT   https://chapter-05-15.hugoinaction.com, and source code: https://github.com/hugoinaction/hugoinaction/tree/chapter-05-15.

Now the blog will have a folder named line with the index.md in it. If we add an image to the archetype page bundle, Hugo copies it to the template. This way, we can define complicated templates with placeholder data for content creators to get started quickly. For example, the Line page shows up when we run Hugo in development mode because we set `buildDrafts` to `true` in our development configuration. Using these features, we can make custom pages or ease our day-to-day activities in a Hugo website by moving repetitive work to shortcodes and archetypes.

Summary

- The Go template language has full support for variables, functions, conditionals, and loops.
- We can use variables to access the site and page metadata, including information like menus and all the pages in the website.
- Hugo can get structured metadata from the front matter as well as from files on disk. Structured data allows for easier use of individual values as variables.
- We can use the Go template language in shortcodes programmatically to create new features for Markdown.
- Archetypes are templates to the content files that can be used to prepopulate specific front matter fields, create the correct folder structure, and provide placeholders for content creators.

Structuring web pages 6

This chapter covers

- Organizing the template for better understanding and reuse
- Using layouts and partials to structure code and improve compilation speeds
- Using content types to organize templates
- Manipulating assets using Hugo Pipes
- Using templates bundled with Hugo

With the Go template language in Hugo, we can build templates for markup-controlled HTML pages in as much detail as needed. In this chapter, we will enable multiple types of pages, sharing template code and snippets between them (figure 6.1). We will also look at how Hugo can help with the JavaScript, images, and CSS files using Hugo Pipes. We will build our foundation to move away from the Eclectic theme and have more control over the entire website rendering using custom template code.

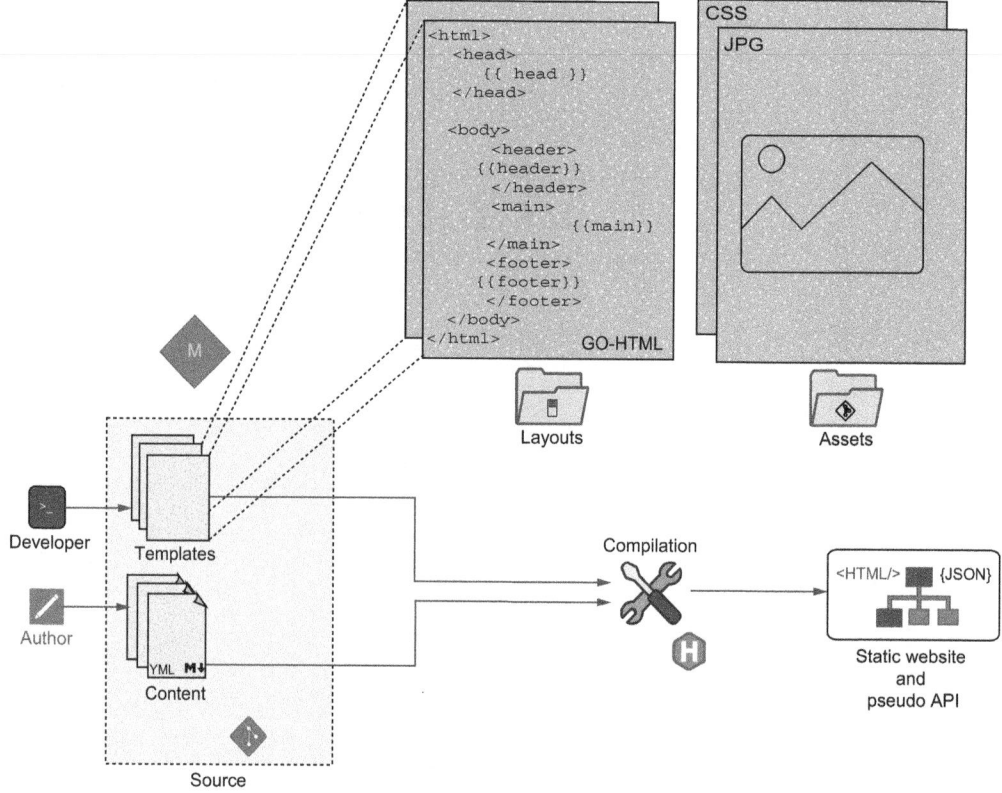

Figure 6.1   Chapter 6 focuses on getting multiple pages to work together, sharing the right set of snippets between them, and using assets like images, CSS files, and HTML optimally.

6.1   *Using content types, base templates, and blocks to structure templates*

So far, we have focused on creating index.html for the home page using the Go template language. While we don't have a large and unmanageable file yet, it can quickly get out of hand if we keep adding code to this file. Also, with one file, we cannot share template code between various web pages that are slightly different.

In this section, we will start to build a template for accessibility beyond the index page. As we make the new template system, we will still have a functional website, albeit with two template designs: one with Eclectic and the other that we are building in parallel. We will migrate the website to the new code slowly to ensure minimum breakage. To do this, we will create a new content type with all the custom template code we are building and will allow the pages to switch between Eclectic and the new template. Then we will create a base layout for code sharing for the reusable pieces between the index page and the data pages using the Terms of Use as a sample page to migrate to the new content type.

6.1.1 Encapsulating templates with different content types

A Hugo *content type* is a collection of templates that can render pages from markup according to a unique design. Conceptually, a content type is similar to a theme, but instead of being the entire website's design, a content type only renders to a section. Each website can have multiple content types, each of which can display content differently. For example, in a typical website, we can have a design for a page associated with news posts and a different one for blog posts, and yet another design for a privacy policy page. We can model each type of page (blog, news, general text, etc.) with its distinct content type. Each content type can have an independent rendering template.

A *theme* is a collection of multiple content types that link to different parts of a website. Not all pages in a website need to look exactly similar, and content types allow for that variety. Each theme defines the default type that all pages revert to, unless they use custom content types defined by the theme for various sections within the website. By placing a file named index.html within the layouts directory, we can override the index template for the default type as defined by the theme. Hugo supports overriding any template in a theme by creating a file at the exact location in the layouts directory as was present within the theme. Hugo redirects all the code paths to the new file.

Unless we study the theme internals and make sure we are not breaking rendering for any code path, there is a high probability of causing unexpected behavior somewhere. We should avoid overriding templates directly, unless we are doing minor bug fixes to the theme. It is much safer to place our template changes within a new content type that does not interfere with the theme. Then we can slowly move all our pages to that type and decommission the theme from the website when our pages no longer use it. This approach allows us to incrementally move from one theme to another or to customized code (like we are doing), thus enabling more control. A new content type defines a new type of rendering for markup-based content different than the theme.

Before adding more template code to the website, we will create a new content type to isolate our changes. We can choose any name for the content type that is unused by the theme to safeguard against collisions. We will name this content type *modern* (for the modern design) and will move the index page to this type definition. To perform this task, let's create a folder named modern within the layouts directory and move index.html to that folder. Next, in the index file for the home page, which is content/_index.md, we will update the type to modern as the following listing shows.

Listing 6.1   Updating the content type (content/_index.md)

```
type: modern
```

> **NOTE** Hugo uses the default template provided by the theme to render content for the index page unless the type field is present.

> **CODE CHECKPOINT**   https://chapter-06-01.hugoinaction.com, and source code: https://github.com/hugoinaction/hugoinaction/tree/chapter-06-01.

Hugo's clever template lookup order

Hugo cleverly assigns a suitable template based on the intent of the website developer. For example, if we create a folder named blog in the content directory, Hugo sets the content type for all files in the folder as `blog`. Then if we create a folder named blog in the layouts folder and begin to define templates for those pages, they will automatically get picked up by the blog section in the website. On the other hand, if no such content type is specified, the default templates are automatically loaded.

This content type selection is made possible by a well-designed template lookup order in Hugo. When Hugo needs to render the page, it goes through an ordered list of files and executes the first one as the template for the web page. This list is huge due to backward compatibility, and it provides many ways to name template files. However, we strongly advise sticking to the straightforward type-to-folder convention in our code with manual overrides using the `type` field in the front matter. Hugo's website provides the template lookup order at https://gohugo.io/templates/lookup-order/.

6.1.2 *Providing the base template for reuse*

Most web pages have a similar HTML structure. There is a head section with metadata and a `header`, `main`, and `footer` that define the interface where the header and the footer reside across the whole website. Hugo has the concept of a base template that can hold these common elements shared across the entire website. The *base template* holds the skeleton of the website. It contains default HTML for the common parts of a web page, which can be overridden for specialized cases if needed. All templates in a type can inherit from and customize the base template for that type. If a type does not provide the base template, we can use the default base template for the entire website.

The base template in Hugo is named *baseof.html*. Let's create a basic baseof.html file in the modern folder. This file stores the Acme Corporation web page skeleton that we will use across all pages that use the `modern` type. By creating baseof.html, we have severed ties to the template provided by Eclectic and can focus on our custom theme.

6.1.3 *Defining blocks of code*

Let's create a skeleton in the base file, baseof.html. The <head> tag in the index page is not specific to the home page, so we can move it to the base template. The content in the <body> tag is page-specific, and we will retain it within the index.html specified template. Then, in baseof.html, we will place the base template (https:// github.com/hugoinaction/hugoinaction/tree/chapter-06-resources/01).

A *block* defines content that we can override in specialized templates. The base template uses blocks for pieces of content that can be overridden by the child templates. We can provide a default value for non-overridden templates. Hugo executes the code inside the block of the base template if the template used by a particular page does not override this block. We can have as many blocks as we desire in a template, including nested blocks. The following listing shows the syntax for creating a block in Hugo.

Listing 6.2 Understanding a block in Hugo (don't add this to your website)

```
<!-- Block creation -->
<!-- In baseof.html -->
{{block "blockname" blockArgument}}
{{end}}

<!-- In derived template -->
{{define "blockname"}}
<!-- The dot (.) refers to the supplied block argument here -->
<!-- We can still access $ if we need the top-level
     template (page) variable access -->
{{end}}
```

The block has two arguments: the block's name and the context variable to pass to the block. Passing the value of context variable replaces the value of . in the block. We will give the current context (which is also the global context $) to the block from the base template.

As we add blocks to allow overriding customizable portions of the template, we also need to ensure that the pages derived from the base template can load properly from all URLs. In listing 6.3, we change the URL to index.css and base it on the website base URL rather than relative to the current page's URL. Note that the base template should be as generic as possible to work with all content in the specific type. Also note that all blocks should have reasonable default values, and all parameters should be optional.

Listing 6.3 Adding the content type base file (layouts/modern/baseof.html)

```
<!DOCTYPE html>
<html lang="en">
  <head>
    <meta charset="UTF-8">
    {{with default .Summary .Description}}        The top-level context refers
      <meta name="description" content="{{.}}">    to the current page.
    {{end}}
    <meta name="viewport"
      content="width=device-width, initial-scale=1.0" />    Sets the absolute base
    <link rel="stylesheet"                                   URL of the website for
      href="{{ site.BaseURL }}/index.css" >                  the CSS file
    {{$title := default site.Title .Title}}
    {{with $title}}<title>{{.}}</title>{{end}}
  </head>
  <body class="home">            Passes the current context to the code
    {{block "body" .}}           block, not hiding any information
      <main>
        {{with .Title}}          Because $title does not work inside the
          <h1>                   block, it needs to be self-contained based
                                 on the provided context.
```

```
            {{.}}
          </h1>
        {{end}}
        <div class="content">
        {{.Content}}
        </div>
      </main>                    Adds a default to the summary
    {{end}}              ◁────┘   if description is not available
  </body>
</html>
```

In the base template, the top-level context refers to the current page. All page types have the `Title` and `Description` properties. However, these can still be undefined, so we need to check for them. We add a default value to the `.Summary` if `.Description` is not available. Because the pages can be at any location, we use the absolute base URL of the website for the CSS file.

The `block` statement is used to define a block that can be overridden in the child templates. We provide default content for the blocks in the base template so that if we create a new template, it will provide a meaningful rendering even if all the blocks are not overridden. The last argument of a `block` statement is similar to the `with` statement, and it becomes the context variable for the block. In listing 6.3, we passed the current context to `block`, not hiding any information. Note that `$title` does not work inside the block, which needs to be self-contained, based on the provided context.

Exercise 6.1

The root template in a Hugo website holding the skeleton of the HTML is called
_____.

   a. root.html
   b. base.html
   c. baseof.html
   d. primary.html
   e. index.html
   f. parent.html

The code in listing 6.3 is almost the same as the `head` portion abstracted from our index page. On the index.html page, we can now fill in the value of `block` by using the `define` keyword as listing 6.4 shows. When we use `define`, we inform Hugo that the template defines blocks within the base template. Hugo will not use the base template if there is no `define` within a template. Also note that `$title` needs to be redefined to be used inside the body.

Listing 6.4   Filling in the block values (layouts/modern/index.html)

```
{{define "body"}}
{{$title := ...}}      <─── Redefines $title

...Contents of the body tag...
{{end}}
```

CODE CHECKPOINT   https://chapter-06-02.hugoinaction.com, and source code:
https://github.com/hugoinaction/hugoinaction/tree/chapter-06-02.

In the previous listing, we defined the body block in the base template. The context variable . is supplied by the base template. When we use the define keyword, the default implementation of the block in the base template is not used. The index page should now look exactly as before, but Hugo composes it from two files instead of one—from the base and the index templates.

6.1.4   Reusing the base template in a different layout

With the base template present, the code is ready to be reused on other pages. We used index.html to represent the index page of the website. The name "index" is not random. Hugo developers chose this to mean the home page of the entire website, whereas in everyday web development, the index file represents the home page of that specific section (or folder). In Hugo layouts, it always means the website's home page. In Hugo, the various types of pages we render are called *layouts*. There are four main layouts supported by Hugo:

- The *list layout* renders index pages of sections within the website. This usually provides a list of all subsections and a list of all pages within the section. Rendering the base page of each branch bundle (_index.html) uses the list layout.
- The *single layout* represents a regular web page with content stored in a markup document or a leaf bundle. All leaf bundles (index.md) and plain Markdown documents (mypage.md) use the single layout.
- The *index layout* renders the home page of the entire website, which is present at the root of the website. This layout is a specialization of the list layout and is present because the home page is generally different than the section list pages. If the index layout is absent, Hugo uses the list layout for the website's home page.
- The *404 layout* forms the basis of all error pages within the website. This layout creates a unique page (/404.html) that we can configure on the hosting server for page not found (HTTP 404) errors. We are free to create more error pages such as 503.html for the 503 server errors, although with static hosting using the Jamstack, the chances of a 500 series error are low. Many developers do not need anything beyond the 404 pages.

Apart from these, we have two more layouts: *taxonomy* and *terms*. These are used to render a list of terms (e.g., the list of tags) and a list of pages associated with the terms (e.g., the list of pages tagged as square), respectively. These layouts can typically reuse most of the work we do for the list layouts. (We will go into these in more detail in chapter 7.) The list and the single layouts are the most critical layouts in Hugo, corresponding to the branch and the leaf bundles, respectively.

Let's add single.html for single pages in the website. We can add code specific to the single pages here. In single.html for the Acme Corporation website, we do not want to override the base template but, instead, use the contents of the base template as-is. Hugo treats a template as an entire web page if a template does not start with a defined block. Hugo renders an empty page if we leave the page blank rather than running the base template. To inform Hugo to load the base template, we need to define a dummy block, which we will not use. The following listing shows how to do this.

Listing 6.5   Adding dummy content to single.html (layouts/modern/single.html)

```
{{define "garbage"}}
<!-- Never gets rendered -->
{{end}}
```

Note that if we put the comment outside of the define block, this does not work. It will fail because only define blocks are allowed in templates that override parts of a template.

Next, we will assign this template to the Terms of Use page. In terms.md, we will add type:modern to the front matter to perform this assignment and then convert it to the design shown in figure 6.2. The contents of the Terms of Use page now use the

Terms of Use

Terms

By accessing the website for Acme Corporation, you are agreeing to be bound by these terms of service, all applicable laws and regulations, and agree that you are responsible for compliance with any applicable local laws. If you do not agree with any of these terms, you are prohibited from using or accessing this site. The materials contained in this website are protected by applicable copyright and trademark law.

Use License

I. Permission is granted to temporarily download one copy of the materials (information or software) on Acme Corporation's website for personal, non-commercial transitory viewing only. This is the grant of a license, not a transfer of title, and under this license you may not:

→ modify or copy the materials;
→ use the materials for any commercial purpose, or for any public display (commercial or non-commercial);
→ attempt to decompile or reverse engineer any software contained on Acme Corporation's website;
→ remove any copyright or other proprietary notations from the materials; or
→ transfer the materials to another person or "mirror" the materials on any other server.

II. This license shall automatically terminate if you violate any of these restrictions and may be terminated by Acme Corporation at any time. Upon terminating your viewing of these materials or upon the termination of this license, you must destroy any downloaded materials in your possession whether in electronic or printed format.

Figure 6.2   The rendered Terms of Use page using the single.html template created within the Acme type

CSS of the home page, which does not provide good formatting. Listing 6.6 shows how to add a layout-specific class override. We will do this in the body tag in baseof.html.

Listing 6.6 Adding support for a class override (layouts/modern/baseof.html)

```
<body class="{{block "bodyClass" .}}{{end}}">    ◁──┤  There's no need to escape
                                                      quotes within the block.
```

We can use code blocks anywhere we want in a template. They perform simple string replacements and do not care about the HTML structure of our web pages. Therefore, if we place bad HTML in some tag (e.g., quotes in bodyClass), the output can be broken. Note that templates automatically XML-encode special characters coming from the markup document, and therefore, we can add them to HTML tag attributes without additional encoding. The following two listings show how to override the bodyClass in index.html and single.html, respectively, to cater to this. Note that after we add a proper define to the single page (listing 6.8), we can remove the dummy define "garbage" (from listing 6.5).

Listing 6.7 Defining a home page with home (layouts/modern/index.html)

```
{{define "bodyClass"}} home {{end}}
```

Listing 6.8 Defining a regular page with page (layouts/modern/single.html)

```
{{define "bodyClass"}} page {{end}}
```

> **CODE CHECKPOINT** https://chapter-06-03.hugoinaction.com, and source code: https://github.com/hugoinaction/hugoinaction/tree/chapter-06-03.

Exercise 6.2

The layout used by Hugo for a regular web page is stored in a file named _____.

We can define as many overrides as needed in a single file. Hugo does not check the validity of the final HTML. We should ensure that we do not cause invalid HTML due to the content of our overrides. Using a quote (") in the class attribute, bodyClass, in our example closes that attribute and produces unexpected results.

Our Terms of Use page is still incomplete. We have a header and a footer on the home page ready to be moved to the base template. We should always create a new block when we do this to allow for overrides as needed. We will generalize the code to cater to all the pages by making the image path absolute, thereby allowing it in any subpage. The following listing moves the header and the footer to the base template to share across all pages.

Listing 6.9   **Moving the header and footer (layouts/modern/baseof.html)**

Wraps parts of the base template into blocks to allow overrides in child templates

```
<body class="{{block "bodyClass" .}}{{end}}">
    {{block "header" .}}
        <header>
            . . .
            <a href="{{ site.BaseURL | relLangURL }}" >
            <img src="{{site.BaseURL}}/image/logo.svg" alt="Acme Logo"
                 height="36" width="48" />
                Acme Corporation
            </a>
            . . .
        </header>
    {{ end }}
    {{block "body" .}}
        <main>
            . . .
        </main>
    {{ end }}
    {{block "footer" .}}
        <footer>
            . . .
        </footer>
    {{end}}
</body>
```

> **Adds link to the home page. We use relLangURL here as we are linking via a relative path to the website root.**

> **Converts the path to logo.svg to an absolute URL to allow loading from all pages**

> **Wraps parts of the base template into blocks to allow overrides in child templates**

CODE CHECKPOINT   https://chapter-06-04.hugoinaction.com, and source code: https://github.com/hugoinaction/hugoinaction/tree/chapter-06-04.

With these changes, the index page template now has only the things specific to that page, and the shared parts like the head and the footer that we can use elsewhere have moved to the shared template. The Terms of Use page looks like a complete web page. We will come back to the home page to improve it further, however.

6.2   *Reusing content with partials*

As we introduced new sections to our home page, it pushed the footer menu down, far away from the top of the website. While those links are not as important as the header, we would like to have them available without scrolling (commonly called *above the fold*, which comes from newspapers where articles hidden under the fold on the front page were considered less important). Ideally, we want to reuse the code to render the footer.

Inheritance (where a template gets or inherits the entire code of the base template with rights to modify or mutate certain parts), provided by the base template and code block, is not suitable for code reuse at arbitrary locations on a web page. For that, we need *composition*, where we have a reusable piece of template code that we can plug in wherever we want. We can use shortcodes to share snippets of shared functionality in the markup data, and we can use partials to share common snippets of code in the templates.

Partials are function equivalents in standard programming languages, which provide support for isolating a piece of computation that generates some output to a rendered HTML file and returns some data. Partials take arguments, do some processing using those arguments, and log data into the output HTML file, returning the computation results to the caller. Partials are among Hugo's most important template features, and understanding the concept of partials is important to being successful with Hugo. Table 6.1 compares using partials versus base template code for reuse.

Table 6.1   Partials vs. base template-based code reuse

Area	Partial-based code reuse	Base template-based code reuse
Primary method for reuse	Using a `partial` in the calling template	Using a `block` in the base template
Can be used multiple times within a page	Yes	No
Defaults are enabled automatically	No	Yes
Can be cached to improve build performance	Yes	No
Can take arguments	Yes	No
Can return computation results	Yes	No
Easily overrides theme-based data in layouts	Yes	No

6.2.1   Moving to a partial

Let's start by moving the footer menu to a partial. To do this, we will create a file called layout/partials/menu.html and move the code to generate the menu-based links used on the home page to that file. Note that we are not using the modern subfolder under layouts. Partials are available across all content types in Hugo. Also, we can override the partials used in a theme locally and change its behavior by creating a file with the same name in the layouts/partials folder.

Partial overrides allow us to replace parts of a page used with a theme and to customize those parts. The partials folder allows subfolders to be used as namespaces, although we don't need one for now (https://github.com/hugoinaction/hugoinaction/tree/chapter-06-resources/02). The following listing shows how to share our code to create the footer menu from a partial.

Listing 6.10   Sharing the code via a partial (layouts/partials/menu.html)

```
{{with site.Menus.footer }}
<nav>
  <ul>
  {{range .}}
  <li>
    <a href="{{.URL}}">{{.Name | humanize}}</a>
  </li>
  {{end}}
  </ul>
</nav>
{{end}}
```

To call a partial, we use the `partial` statement followed by the name and the context variable. The following listing uses this statement to add the footer menu to the hero section of the index page.

Listing 6.11   Calling a partial (layouts/modern/index.html)

```
<section id="intro">
  . . .
  {{ partial "menu.html" . }}
</section>
```

Just like a `block` statement, the `partial` statement also needs to be passed a context variable. Passing the context variable as-is loads menu.html so we can reuse it in the footer. The next listing provides the code for this.

Listing 6.12   Reusing the footer menu (layouts/modern/baseof.html)

```
{{block "footer" .}}

<footer class="dark">
    {{ partial "menu.html" . }}
    . . .
  </footer>
{{end}}
```

> **CODE CHECKPOINT**   https://chapter-06-05.hugoinaction.com, and source code: https://github.com/hugoinaction/hugoinaction/tree/chapter-06-05.

6.2.2   *The partial context*

Partials in Hugo are self-contained and isolated, having access to no variables apart from the ones passed to them. The $ variable inside a partial does not reference the global page object but the top-level context variable passed to the partial instead. While we can pass the entire top-level context from the caller to a partial, it is better to limit this data. This limitation ensures maximum reuse of the partial and performance optimization via caching in a much better way. Otherwise, we pass too much information to the partial, much more than what is needed.

We can reuse the partial between the footer and the main menu if we pass the menu directly. In the following listing, we update the partial to take the specific menu to render instead of the hardcoded main menu for the website, making it capable of rendering different menus.

Listing 6.13 Making the partial more flexible (layouts/partials/menu.html)

```
{{with $ }}
<nav>
  <ul>
  {{ range $ }}          ◁─────  Because partials are self-contained, the top-level $
    <li><a href="{{.URL}}">{{.Name | humanize}}</a></li>        and dot (.) are the same as the argument passed to
  {{end}}                         it. We could have used . instead of $ here.
  </ul>
</nav>
{{ end }}
```

We can reuse the previous listing using the code in the footer menu. The following listing shows this use.

Listing 6.14 Loading the footer menu (layouts/modern/baseof.html)

```
{{ partial "menu.html" site.Menus.footer }}
```

CODE CHECKPOINT   https://chapter-06-06.hugoinaction.com, and source code: https://github.com/hugoinaction/hugoinaction/tree/chapter-06-06.

The `partial` statement in the Hugo is similar in concept to a JavaScript module or a PHP `include`. Now we can use `{{ partial "menu.html" site.Menus.main }}` as the argument for the main menu, and `{{ partial "menu.html" site.Menus.footer }}` would render the footer.

One problem with moving the main menu to a partial is the loss of the hamburger button used to render the main menu on mobile devices. Because it is not needed everywhere, we need to pass additional arguments to the partial to figure out when to render this button.

A Hugo partial takes only one argument. To allow passing multiple values, we can convert that argument to a dictionary or a slice, which have multiple values. Slices cause readability issues as the order of the arguments becomes important, and undefined arguments are hard to support. To avoid these issues, the following listing uses dictionary arguments as an optional element for the menu to reuse the partial for the header.

Listing 6.15   Adding the hamburger button (layouts/partials/menu.html)

```
{{with $.Menu }}
<nav>
  {{if $.Button}}
  <button class="hamburger">☰</button>
  {{end}}
  <ul>
  {{ range $.Menu }}
    <li><a href="{{.URL}}">{{.Name | humanize}}</a></li>
  {{end}}
  </ul>
</nav>
{{ end }}
```

We can now load the header menu with the hamburger button using the partial and passing true for the button option. The following listing provides the code for this. Note that we do not need to pass the Button parameter in the footer because the default value will fail the if check.

Listing 6.16   Loading the header menu (layouts/modern/baseof.html)

```
{{ partial "menu.html"
    (dict "Menu" site.Menus.main
          "Button" true)
}}
```

CODE CHECKPOINT   https://chapter-06-07.hugoinaction.com, and source code: https://github.com/hugoinaction/hugoinaction/tree/chapter-06-07.

6.2.3   *Bringing back the submenu using additional parameters to the menu partial*

We lost the submenu from the header when we moved to our content type. Now would be a good time to bring it back. Hugo supports infinite nesting of submenus in a tree data structure and uses the parent-child terminology to represent a menu and its submenus, respectively. Each menu object has a property called .HasChildren and a slice (array) called Children that we can use to render those objects. The following listing adds the submenus as nested unordered lists in the menu partial. For cases like the footer, where there are no submenus, this call has no impact.

Listing 6.17   Submenus as nested unordered lists (layouts/partials/menu.html)

```
<li>
  <a href="{{.URL}}">{{.Name | humanize}}</a>
  {{if .HasChildren}}
    <ul>
      {{ range .Children }}
        <li><a href="{{.URL}}">{{.Name | humanize}}</a></li>
```

```
      {{ end }}
    </ul>
  {{end}}
</li>
```

CODE CHECKPOINT   https://chapter-06-08.hugoinaction.com, and source code:
https://github.com/hugoinaction/hugoinaction/tree/chapter-06-08.

Hugo's Menu objects provide additional features like highlighting an active menu
when we are on the right page. These extensions are beyond the scope of this book.
Additionally, Hugo's documentation offers a ready-to-use menu template that covers
more cases than we were able to do in our code here.

6.2.4   *Partials and performance*

When a template is present in multiple pages, one template invocation takes place for
every page. Over a lot of pages, this can slow down the website compilation. Partials
allow us to perform caching to prevent duplicate calls. Before we use this feature, let's
spend a few minutes understanding the performance of the code we just wrote.

Hugo provides a build flag, --templateMetrics, which is case-sensitive. When supplied, it measures the impact of each template on the overall build. Note that many
Hugo operations run in parallel. Therefore, the sum of all the times provided is much
more than the time taken to compile the website. The code in listing 6.18 runs performance metrics on the Acme Corporation website. Note that the numbers are highly
dependent on the hardware and software running and may not be the same at all
times. (Hugo and its themes are constantly evolving to improve performance, and
these numbers can change dramatically.) The file, menu.html, that we just created has
run four times already.

Listing 6.18   Running a performance metrics measurement

```
> hugo --templateMetrics
Start building sites …

Template Metrics:

  cumulative          average         maximum
   duration          duration        duration   count   template
  ----------        ---------       ---------   -----   --------
369.675412ms      23.104713ms     147.820628ms    16   _default/single.html
245.782463ms       6.144561ms      146.59241ms    40   partials/core/head.html
239.945001ms       5.998625ms      145.99365ms    40   partials/class.html

  . . .
  1.046679ms        209.335µs       313.026µs       5   partials/menu.html
   939.401µs         46.97µs        260.135µs      20   _internal/alias.html
    807.44µs        807.44µs        807.44µs        1   partials/core/manifest.html
   629.844µs        209.948µs       628.044µs       3   shortcodes/divider.html
```

```
505.491µs      168.497µs      270.374µs    3    shortcodes/youtube.html
411.414µs      411.414µs      411.414µs    1    partials/util/background.html
368.915µs      368.915µs      368.915µs    1    js/sw.js
223.668µs      223.668µs      223.668µs    1    _internal/_default/robots.txt
198.997µs      198.997µs      198.997µs    1    shortcodes/repeat.html
101.654µs       50.827µs      100.908µs    2    shortcodes/productInfo.md
 85.716µs       85.716µs       85.716µs    1    js/main.js
 60.208µs       60.208µs       60.208µs    1    json/manifest.json
```

```
                    |  EN
--------------------+-----
 Pages              |  68
 Paginator pages    |   0
 Non-page files     |  14
 Static files       |   8
 Processed images   |  35
 Aliases            |  20
 Sitemaps           |   1
 Cleaned            |   0

Total in 263 ms
```

The key column to note in listing 6.18 is the count column. The single page template (_default/single.html) is called 16 times to render 16 pages. The shortcodes are reported separately. The menu partial (partials/menu.html) has already called the menu template five times to render the home page and the Terms page. Let's move the Privacy Policy page to the modern template type as well. The menu.html file is called seven times, adding one time for the header and one for the footer for this new page.

> **CODE CHECKPOINT**   https://chapter-06-09.hugoinaction.com, and source code:
> https://github.com/hugoinaction/hugoinaction/tree/chapter-06-09.

To prevent this repetition, we can use partialCached instead of partial. At a minimum, partialCached takes the same arguments as partial. If we replace all partial calls with partialCached without passing another argument, we would see that partials/menu.html executes only once. This execution is an obvious mistake as it forces the header and the footer to have the same menu.

> **CODE CHECKPOINT**   https://chapter-06-10.hugoinaction.com, and source code:
> https://github.com/hugoinaction/hugoinaction/tree/chapter-06-10.

To ensure that the header and the footer have their own menu, partialCached can take an arbitrary number of arguments, each of which is combined to create a unique key. We need to add separate arguments to partialCached, one for each rendered. Listing 6.19 adds the arguments to the index page. Then listing 6.20 adds the arguments to the base template file, baseof.html.

Figure 6.3 Everything's on (the) line: the Jamstack gets its big break, but Alex has to get it online with his reputation at stake.

Listing 6.19 Using `partialCached` in layouts/modern/index.html

```
{{ partialCached "menu.html" (dict "Menu" site.Menus.footer) "footer"}}
```

Listing 6.20 Using `partialCached` in layouts/modern/baseof.html

```
{{ partialCached "menu.html" (dict "Menu" site.Menus.main "Button" true)
➡ "main" }}
{{ partialCached "menu.html" (dict "Menu" site.Menus.footer) "footer"}}
```

We could have added `true` as a cache key alongside `main`, but this is unnecessary. That's because the main menu always has a button, and the `main` key is unique enough.

> **CODE CHECKPOINT** https://chapter-06-11.hugoinaction.com, and source code: https://github.com/hugoinaction/hugoinaction/tree/chapter-06-11.

Now, as we add pages, the count of the partial's execution does not increase. Partials take a single argument (which can be a dictionary object, `dict`, with multiple values) to ensure independence. This allows for efficient caching. The additional arguments in `partialCached` can be added easily to partials without changing the partial code.

> **TIP** The easiest way to reduce the time taken by a template is to move some implementation to a partial and use a `partialCached` for slow processing HTML that is the same across pages.

6.2.5   *A detour to partial returns*

It would have been partiality against the partial function (pun intended) to have not mentioned the `return` statement when introducing partials. So far, we have used partials as equivalents of shortcodes in the template files. Although rendering in HTML is an important use case for `partial` and `partialCached`, partials also act as functions in the Go template language. We can use partials to do string and number crunching or to access the network or the filesystem, and then provide the processed result in a variable. Partials already support caching via `partialCached`.

Exercise 6.3

True or False: The blocks present in the base template are executed by Hugo only once and the output is shared across multiple pages.

For this chapter, let's make the `price` shortcode we created in chapter 5 execute faster. The `price` shortcode reads a CSV file that provides the price of any Acme Corporation product. We will cache the prices for all the products in a single partial (https://github.com/hugoinaction/hugoinaction/tree/chapter-06-resources/03) accessible across all pages. This way, the reading and parsing of the CSV file happens only once.

Because a table is two-dimensional, we can create a dictionary of dictionaries to represent it. The outer dictionary has the product's name (row header) as the key and the product information as its values. The inner dictionary uses the column headers as the key and the product's price and rating as the values. The following listing provides a sample of this function's output in JSON format.

Listing 6.21   Output from the `price` shortcode

```json
{
  "Circle": {
    "Colors": "Red, Green, Blue, Orange",
    "Price": "2",
    "Rating": 4
  },
  "Square": {
    "Colors": "Red, Pink, Blue",
    "Price": "4",
    "Rating": 5
  }
}
```

Hugo's `slice` and `dict` data structures are immutable and cannot be modified. Therefore, we will use the `scratch` data structure for this partial. Hugo's `scratch` structure is a read-write data store that can act as a temporary variable to hold data. It works like a mutable dictionary, where we can add or remove values easily. Listing 6.22 creates a partial to get the product information from the CSV file, which can then be parsed and cached.

Listing 6.22 A partial for product info (layouts/partials/products.html)

Creates a new scratch pad

```
{{$scratch := newScratch}}
{{$products := resources.GetMatch "products.csv"}}
{{$parsedProducts := $products |
  transform.Unmarshal (dict "delimiter" ",")}}        ← Parses the CSV file using a
                                                          comma as the separator

{{$index := index $parsedProducts 0}}   ← Gets the first row as the index row

{{ range $i, $r := $parsedProducts }}   ← Loops through all the rows in the table
  {{ if ne $i 0}}
    {{range $j := seq (sub (len $index) 1)}}   ← Loops through all the columns
      {{ $scratch.SetInMap (index $r 0)
        (index $index $j) (index $r $j) }}   ←   Creates a dictionary (map) in
    {{ end }}                                     the scratch pad that points to
  {{ end }}                                        another dictionary
{{ end }}

{{return $scratch.Values}}   ←  Converts the scratch pad
                                 to a dictionary and return
```

Ignores the first row of the table

The partial in this listing uses no variable from the outside. It returns the same results regardless of the arguments, and we do not need different variants for different inputs. Note that only one return is allowed within a partial in Hugo. Also, when creating a dictionary in the scratch pad that points to another dictionary, the outer dictionary uses the first item in the row ($r) as the index whose value is a dictionary that uses the first entry in each column ($index) as the key. Now we can update the price shortcode to utilize this partial. The following listing shows how to do this. Note that partialCached needs at least one key.

Listing 6.23 Using a products partial (layouts/shortcodes/price.html)

```
{{$product := default (.Get 0) (.Get "product")}}
$ {{index (index (partialCached "products.html" "key") $product) "Price" }}
```

CODE CHECKPOINT   https://chapter-06-12.hugoinaction.com, and source code: https://github.com/hugoinaction/hugoinaction/tree/chapter-06-12.

In the code in the previous listing, we got the product information using the parameters passed to the shortcode. We used partialCached to call the cached partial named products. We gave it a string as an argument because it does not need a variable. Inside the partial, we created a scratch pad with the key as the product name and the value as its price. We can verify that the partial executes only once using the template metrics provided by Hugo. Table 6.2 compares partials and shortcodes and their use in Hugo.

Table 6.2   A comparison of partials and shortcodes and their use in Hugo

Area	Partials	Shortcodes
Use	In templates	In markup data
Access	Only supplied variables	All variables
Caching	Can be cached based on inputs using `partialCached`	Not cached
Returns	Can render to output and return values as variables	Can only render to output

Inline partials

Hugo also supports defining partials inline. If we want to reuse the same code multiple times within the same file, but do not want to generate a separate file, an inline partial can come in handy. Inline partials can also act as private functions, while regular partials act as public functions. We can also use the `define` keyword to define a block that, in turn, defines a partial. The following code shows how to implement these various declarations.

```
{{ $variable := partial "inline-partial" . }}
. . .
{{ partial "inline-partial" . }} {{/* Ignoring return values */}}
. . .
{{ define "inline-partial" }}
. . .
{{return $returnValue}}

{{end}}
```

6.3   *Asset handling with Hugo Pipes*

By moving HTML generation to Hugo's template system, we have significantly eased the job of HTML generation, which we can now do based on a markup document. However, problems remain with images and other assets like JavaScript and CSS. There is a lot of work involved in changing the aspect ratios and resizing images into multiple files for thumbnail, mobile, desktop, etc., which we need to do to get good performance. Also, to be markup- or metadata-based, there needs to be a way for the markup-based information to get into JavaScript or CSS. Hugo Pipes are Hugo's answer to these problems.

Hugo provides utility methods to manage resources from a page bundle, the global assets folder, and any file path supplied. Most of these methods take a single argument, and we use them with the pipe operator discussed in section 5.1.7. Hugo Pipes is a set of Hugo's features for resource management.

6.3.1 Handling textual assets

We are currently using the static folder for background.svg, index.css, and logo.svg assets apart from favicon.ico. (logo.png was used for the Universal theme, and we will remove that when we remove support for that theme.) We can move all of those files to the assets folder and use Hugo Pipes to process them further. Hugo supports using Pipes for all text-based file formats.

Let's start with index.css. The following listing reads the CSS file using Hugo Pipes. Then we need to move the index.css file to the assets folder for this to function. Finally, we can load this file using the resources API.

Listing 6.24 Reading the CSS file (layouts/modern/baseof.html)

```
{{ $css := resources.GetMatch "index.css"}}
<link rel="stylesheet" type="text/css" href="{{$css.Permalink}}">
```

CODE CHECKPOINT https://chapter-06-13.hugoinaction.com, and source code: https://github.com/hugoinaction/hugoinaction/tree/chapter-06-13.

With resources.GetMatch, we can place the default file in the asset folder of the theme to be overridden in the website. Note that we used the same feature in the products.csv file earlier. To get an exact resource, we can use resources.Get, although GetMatch supports wildcards (also called *globs*).

The real power of Hugo Pipes comes with the support for processing. Hugo can process CSS files with the SCSS processor (only in the extended flavor) and the PostCSS postprocessor. SCSS (or SASS) is a CSS superset language that supports nesting, functions, and compile-time variables in CSS. The philosophy behind SCSS is compile-time optimization and code generation. This approach matches that of the Jamstack, and both work well together. Let's rename the assets/index.css file to assets/index.scss and use the SCSS preprocessor via Hugo Pipes using $css := resources.GetMatch "index.css" | resources.ToCSS.

First, we need to verify if the version of Hugo we have installed is the extended version. For that, let's run the command hugo version on the command line. If you have the extended version of Hugo installed, you should see extended in the command-line output:

```
Hugo Static Site Generator v0.91.2/extended
```

The SASS compiler comes in two flavors: the version that is embedded in Hugo, which does not need a separate binary (LibSass), and the version where the SASS compiler runs as an external process (Dart Sass). Dart Sass is newer and feature-rich, but we need an external script to install it. We can configure the SASS compiler that we want to use in the website configuration.

You will need the extended version of Hugo to use the SCSS features. Note that in many platforms (including Chocolatey on Windows), the package manager installs the regular (non-extended) version of Hugo by default. There is no harm in using the extended version because a bigger compiler binary has no impact on the final output size or on performance. Listing 6.25 complies SCSS into CSS for us.

> **NOTE** You do not need SCSS to complete the code examples in this book. If you do not have Hugo extended installed, you can skip this specific code checkpoint and continue along through the rest of the book.

Listing 6.25   Compiling SCSS into CSS (layouts/modern/baseof.html)

```
{{ $css := resources.GetMatch "index.scss" | resources.ToCSS }}
```

CODE CHECKPOINT   https://chapter-06-14.hugoinaction.com, and source code: https://github.com/hugoinaction/hugoinaction/tree/chapter-06-14.

Hugo does not care about the filename extension. We can pass index.css through the SCSS transpiler if we need to. SCSS is beyond the scope of this book. It is not essential to Hugo, and we will not go into it in depth. We only need CSS for styling content, which is the output of SCSS compilation. For readers who do not want to use the extended version of Hugo, we will revert this change, although you are free to continue using SCSS for your websites.

We can use the PostCSS processor for CSS via `resources.PostCSS` (requires installing postcss-cli) without any configuration changes. We can also process JavaScript files through the Babel transcompiler (requires installing @babel/cli and @babel/core) for getting access to future JavaScript features via the pipe `babel` for older versions of web browsers. A much better approach is to use Hugo's built-in JavaScript bundler, js.Build (we'll discuss js.Build in chapter 10).

> **NOTE** Hugo has a special integration with the JavaScript ecosystem. Chapter 10 is dedicated entirely to using JavaScript within Hugo-based websites.

When using a CSS/JS processor with Hugo Pipes, we can run the JavaScript or CSS files through the Hugo template parser with full access to the entire system of variables, functions, and partials, and make their contents data-driven just like the HTML. The theme color for the Acme Corporation website currently is blue. If we move this to the template system, we can control this from the Acme configuration file. We already defined this color in config.yaml as `color` in the parameters. We can access the parameter via `{{site.Param "color"}}`. Remember from chapter 5 that `site` is the global variable provided by Hugo for the site variables. It is available in all partials as well as templates. Using `site` instead of `$.Site` provides maximum flexibility when using this template across partials.

While the color value is present in the configuration, we do not use it inside index.css and background.svg, which currently use the hardcoded value, `"#4f46e5"`. We need these values to be dynamic so that we can change them in one place in the configuration. To do this, we need to convert these files to a template. Then we can run Hugo's template rendering through this and generate the actual files for the website at compile time. Hugo provides a function called `resources.ExecuteAsTemplate` to process any resource file as a Hugo template. To do this, we will start with logo.svg and background.svg.

Let's create a copy of these files and add a .tpl extension to them. While not required, it is a good idea to rename the template files and add the .tpl extension to help in identification. Next we need to replace all occurrences of "#4f46e5" with `{{site.Params.color | default "#4f46e5"}}` in these files (https://github.com/hugoinaction/hugoinaction/tree/chapter-06-resources/04). Note that we will not be removing the older background.svg and logo.svg until chapter 8, where we completely move out of the Eclectic theme. Listing 6.26 provides the code to change to the background.svg template so we can use the supplied theme color. Then listing 6.27 changes the logo.svg template.

Listing 6.26 Changing background.svg (assets/image/background.svg.tpl)

```
<style type="text/css">
   . . .
   .st2{fill:none;stroke:{{site.Params.color | default "#4f46e5"}};
   stroke-width:4;stroke-miterlimit:10;opacity: 0.2}
   . . .
   .st6{fill:{{site.Params.color | default "#4f46e5"}}; opacity: 0.2}
   . . .
</style>
```

Listing 6.27 Changing logo.svg (assets/image/logo.svg.tpl)

```
<style type="text/css">
   .st0{fill:{{site.Params.color | default "#4f46e5"}};}
   . . .
</style>
```

The CSS file for the Acme Corporation website uses CSS custom properties for each color component (red, green and blue) to define its theme. If we simply coded this with the color value, a string replacement of "#4f46e5" with {{site.Params.color}}) would have sufficed. For passing individual color values, we need to do a little more work. The following listing provides individual theme colors to CSS variables from Hugo.

Listing 6.28 Providing individual theme colors (assets/index.css.tpl)

A default value is needed so that it will not fail if the theme color is absent.

```
{{ $color := site.Params.color
    | default "#4f46e5" }}
{{ $b := substr $color -2 2 |
    print "0x" |
```

Extracts the last two characters for the blue value. (The hex is #RRGGBB.)

Converts the hex value to 0xBB

```
         int}}            ◁——— Parses the value as an integer
  {{ $g := substr $color -4 2
     | print "0x" | int}}       ◁—┐
  {{ $r := substr $color -6 2       │  The two characters starting 4 positions from the
     | print "0x" | int}}       ◁—┘  end are green, while the red color starts at 6.
:root {
  --red: {{$r}};        │  Passes this data to CSS
  --green: {{$g}};      │  for use as variables
  --blue: {{$b}};
}
```

The CSS file also contains background SVG images with a hardcoded background color, rgb(79, 70, 229). We should do a find and replace operation in the whole file to replace the hardcoded color value with rgb({{$r}},{{$g}},{{$b}}). We cannot use $color directly here as that would need to be URL-encoded.

Next, we need to load these files into our website via resources.ExecuteAsTemplate as shown in the following listing. We will also be piping the output through resources.minify to reduce its file size.

Listing 6.29   Parsing index.css.tpl (layouts/modern/baseof.html)

```
{{ $css := resources.GetMatch "index.css.tpl"
       resources.ExecuteAsTemplate "index.css" "nothing"
       resources.Minify }}
```

resources.ExecuteAsTemplate takes the name of the target file and the context variable to pass to the template. Like partials, a resource template executes in an isolated environment, and the $ variable consists of the data we pass directly. The reason for that is the same as that of a partial: to allow caching with maximum reuse. Because the site variable is globally available, we don't need parameters for template execution. Once this is done, we can load the logo.svg in the base template by parsing it and executing it similarly to how we did with index.css. The following listing shows this process.

Listing 6.30   Parsing logo.svg.tpl (layouts/modern/baseof.html)

```
{{ $logo := resources.GetMatch "image/logo.svg.tpl"
      resources.ExecuteAsTemplate "logo.svg" "nothing"
      resources.Minify }}
<img src="{{$logo.Permalink}}" alt="Acme Logo"
           width="48" />
```

We can update the index.css.tpl to render the background.svg template. The following listing shows how to update index.css to use the .tpl file for this.

Listing 6.31   Updating index.css for background.svg (assets/index.css.tpl)

```
{{ $background := resources.GetMatch "image/background.svg.tpl" |
   resources.ExecuteAsTemplate "background.svg" "nothing" | resources.Minify}}
background: url({{$background.Permalink}}) 0 0/cover;
```

NOTE The caching mechanism for Hugo becomes compromised if we use resources.ExecuteAsTemplate. It is strongly advised to use resources.ExecuteAsTemplate within a partial and to call it with partialCached to prevent unnecessary recalculation. We leave the task of moving logo.svg and index.css parsing into separate partials as an exercise for the reader.

CODE CHECKPOINT   https://chapter-06-15.hugoinaction.com, and source code: https://github.com/hugoinaction/hugoinaction/tree/chapter-06-15.

Now we can control the color in the website configuration (for example, to "#DC2626") to get a different theme color for the website (as shown in figure 6.4) for use in the rest of the book.

CODE CHECKPOINT   https://chapter-06-16.hugoinaction.com, and source code: https://github.com/hugoinaction/hugoinaction/tree/chapter-06-16.

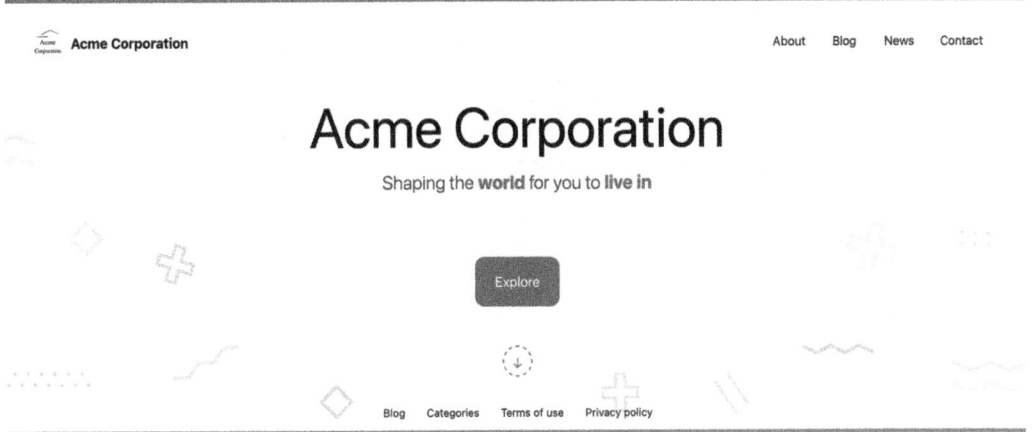

Figure 6.4 Changing the website's theme color in the configuration file to "#DC2626"

Another important feature is support for CSS concatenation. Hugo can easily merge multiple CSS files into one for release, but we cannot concatenate images. In the resources for chapter 6, you will find the file additional.css.tpl (https://github .com/hugoinaction/hugoinaction/tree/chapter-06-resources/05). We can place this file in the assets folder for consumption. Then we can concatenate it using resources.Concat. Note that resources.Concat needs valid mime types to work. Therefore, we will use index.css and not index.css.tpl for the concat API. The following listing uses this API to allow loading multiple CSS templates via a single call.

Listing 6.32   Using the concat API (layouts/partials/index.css.html)

Gets all css.tpl files

```
{{ $css := resources.Match "*.css.tpl" |
       resources.Concat "index.css" |
       resources.ExecuteAsTemplate "index.css" "nothing" |
       resources.Minify }}
```

Combines them with index.css

Processes mustaches

Minifies the generated CSS file

CODE CHECKPOINT   https://chapter-06-17.hugoinaction.com, and source code: https://github.com/hugoinaction/hugoinaction/tree/chapter-06-17.

To get a slice (array) of all files matching a glob pattern, we can use resources.Match. This way we can develop independent files and supply a merged version in production. Note that additional.css provides a subtle change in the design on the website's header, which we can use to verify the loading of this file.

Exercise 6.4

Add a hero image to the Acme Corporation website home page. The hero image is supplied as an SVG image in the chapter resources (https://github.com/hugoinaction/hugoinaction/tree/chapter-06-resources/06). The generated HTML should match https://chapter-06-18.hugoinaction.com, with the SVG image dynamically generated so that it matches the website colors. The following figure shows the home page after we add the image.

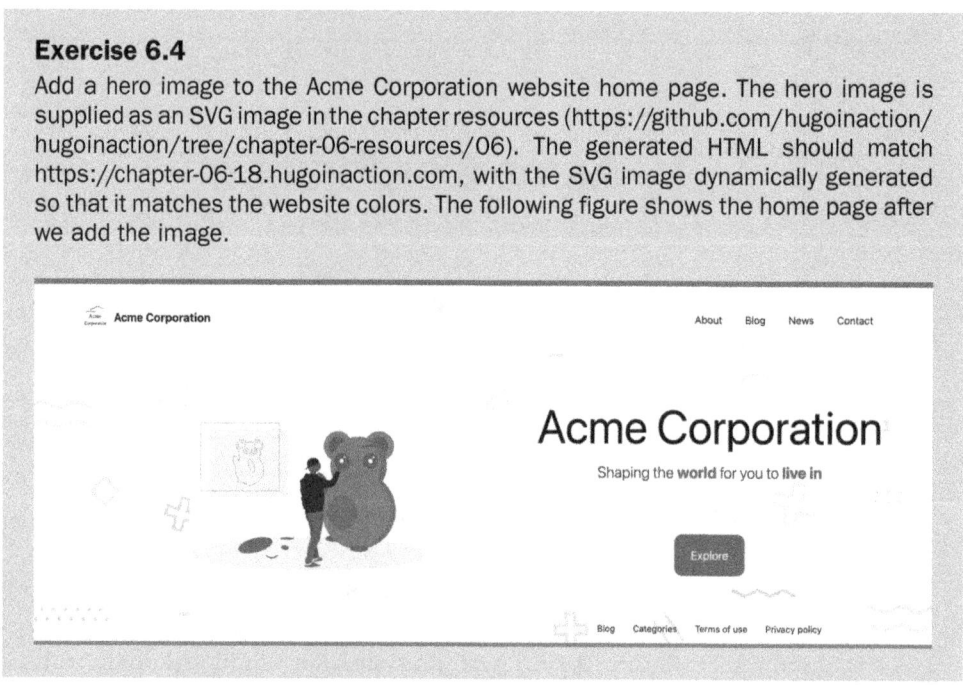

CODE CHECKPOINT   https://chapter-06-18.hugoinaction.com, and source code: https://github.com/hugoinaction/hugoinaction/tree/chapter-06-18.

6.3.2   *Handling images*

While vector graphics and SVGs are great for file sizes, not everything is easily buildable using vector graphics. Raster images like JPEGs and PNGs are significant portions of the modern web, forming the bulk of the network traffic for many websites. Hugo

Pipes broadly supports these images, including manipulations that allow us to prepare them for optimal delivery over the web. Although our blog posts have images, we do not use these on the index page of our website. Without the images, our blog posts look incomplete.

To add a cover image for blog posts, the resources in the global assets location are accessible via `resources.GetMatch`. The following listing shows how we can access the resources present in page bundles via `Page.Resources.GetMatch` to add the cover image.

Listing 6.33 Adding a cover image for blog posts (layouts/modern/index.html)

```html
<li class="post">
  <a href="{{.Permalink}}">
    {{$title :=  .Title}}
    {{with (.Resources.GetMatch "cover.*")}}
    <img alt="{{$title}}" loading="lazy"
      src="{{.Permalink}}" />
    {{end}}
    ...
  </a>
</li>
```

CODE CHECKPOINT https://chapter-06-19.hugoinaction.com, and source code: https://github.com/hugoinaction/hugoinaction/tree/chapter-06-19.

The code in the previous listing has a significant performance issue. The cover images for the blog posts are huge and have more pixels than what is needed to render them in the small view on the home page. We cannot resize them in the page bundle because the single page needs bigger images. Hugo provides support for dynamically resizing images during compilation for this use. Here are the resizing options in Hugo:

- `.Resize`—This option resizes the image. It can take parameters in the form of the desired width and height. For example, `{{ $hero.Resize "200x200"}}` resizes the hero image to 200×200 px, ignoring the aspect ratio. If we use `{{ $hero.Resize "200x"}}`, the image is resized to the width of 200 px with the height based on the aspect ratio, and `{{ $hero.Resize "x200"}}` resizes the image to the height of 200 px with the width calculated based on the original aspect ratio.
- `.Fit`—This option resizes the image to fit within the supplied box. For example, `{{ $hero.Fit "200x200"}}` ensures that either the width or the height is 200 px and the other dimension (height or width) is less than 200 px. A 1000×800 image will shrink to 200×160 while a 800×1000 image will become 160×200. This is similar to the CSS property `object-fit: contain` or `background-fit: contain`.

- .Fill—This option resizes the image to fill the supplied box while cropping the outside parts. For example, {{ $hero.Fill "200x200"}} creates a 200×200 image where the image would be resized and cropped either in the length or the breadth. This is equivalent to object-fit: cover or background-fit: cover. .Fill in Hugo can also take an optional parameter that defines the part of the image to keep. For example, if we use .Fill "200x200 left", Hugo leaves the leftmost part of the image intact. Hugo also offers an option called smart, where Hugo automatically detects the important part of the image.

Further optimizations

While Hugo processes assets as per the supplied parameters, further optimization of assets is still possible. Many developers use postprocessing on Hugo's output to optimize further. Most hosts, including Netlify, offer asset optimization as a feature of their CDN hosting.

We can include specific plugins for this processing. We can postprocess manually by taking the contents of the public or the docs folders and passing images through a tool like ImageOptim, CSS through CSSMin, and JavaScript through Terser to further optimize the generated assets. We can also use the HTML picture tag or srcset attribute in the img tag to provide the browser with options to load the correct image based on the viewport size.

The maximum size needed for the cover images on the home screen has a width of approximately 1000 px (to handle 2× scaling in high-density displays). The following listing shows how we can use the .Resize option to restrict the cover images to a shorter size. We also add loading=lazy to load these images lazily, thereby speeding up the initial rendering of the website. Note that lazy loading is an HTML and not a Hugo performance feature.

> **Listing 6.34   Resizing the cover image for blogs (layouts/modern/index.html)**

```
<img alt="{{.Title}}" loading="lazy"
    src="{{((.Resources.GetMatch "cover.*").Resize "1000x").Permalink}}" />
```

This code provides massive savings when loading the index page in terms of file size. *It is highly recommended to convert images to the WebP format, which offers further file size reductions.* We can pass webp as an option in .Resize (for example, .Resize "1000x webp"). This option converts the image to the WebP format if we use the extended flavor of Hugo. WebP has >95% browser adoption, and unless we are targeting ancient browsers, it is safe to use WebP as the only format for images on our websites. If older browser support is needed, we can use the HTML picture tag to provide both WebP and JPEG/PNG versions of the image. To keep the dependency on the extended version of Hugo optional, we are not using WebP for this book.

CODE CHECKPOINT https://chapter-06-20.hugoinaction.com, and source code: https://github.com/hugoinaction/hugoinaction/tree/chapter-06-20.

We can also provide artistic filters to the image like a blur, sepia, or grayscale. Figure 6.5 includes a list of some of these filters.

The favicon for the Acme Corporation website is still in the same color as the hardcoded "old" theme. Unfortunately, due to choppy support for SVG favicons by the various browser vendors, we need to have at least a PNG copy of the favicon linked to our website. We can use Hugo's image-processing filters to recolor our favicon, using the theme color (https://github.com/hugoinaction/hugoinaction/tree/chapter-06-resources/08).

Figure 6.5 Image processing and filter support in Hugo. Hugo supports a variety of options for resizing as well as processing images with filters (https://github.com/hugoinaction/hugoinaction/tree/chapter-06-resources/07).

Note that the math here is complicated, and while it showcases the flexibility offered by Hugo, in most cases, you do not need something this complex. We will calculate the favicon in a cached partial to prevent rerunning our math and then using it inside the head section of our website. The following listing shows how to recolor the favicon dynamically using the color present in the configuration.

Listing 6.35   Recoloring the favicon (layouts/partials/favicon.png.html)

Gets the percentage of the red color to be
suppressed between 0–1 (100% = Red)

```
{{ $color := site.Params.color | default "#4f46e5" }}          Removes RGB
{{ $b := substr $color -2 2 | print "0x" | int}}               components from the
{{ $g := substr $color -4 2 | print "0x" | int}}               provided hex color
{{ $r := substr $color -6 2 | print "0x" | int}}               (same logic as CSS)

{{$r1 := sub                          Converts the color red
    (div ($r | float) 255)            to the 0–1 interval
    1 |
    mul 100}}                         Multiplies this by 100 to get
                                      a number between 0 and 100

{{$g1 := sub (div ($g | float) 255) 1 | mul 100}}
{{$b1 := sub (div ($b | float) 255) 1 | mul 100}}
```

Reads
favicon.png

Inverts the
image. All
text is now
white on the
transparent
background.

```
{{ return(
    (resources.Get "image/favicon.png" |
    images.Filter (images.Grayscale)
                  (images.Contrast *100*)
    (images.Invert)
    (images.ColorBalance $r1 $g1 $b1)
    ).Resize "128x #FFF").Permalink }}
```

Converts to grayscale and then bumps
up the contrast to 100% to make this
black and white

Shifts the color balance
by suppressing colors
based on the calculated
percentage

Fills the transparent areas with
white and resizes to 128 px width

To understand what is happening, let's take an example. Say we want to recolor the icon to rgb(220,38,38). We first convert all the things that define this color as white, rgb(255,255,255), with the rest of the image as transparent. Next we calculate the RGB value:

```
r1 = (220/255 - 1) * 100 = -13.73%
g1 = (38/255 - 1) * 100 =  -85.10%
b1 = (38/255 - 1) * 100 =  -85.10%
```

Using these as the color-balance filter, we can now recolor our image with the new RGB values:

```
Color balance = current color + current color * balance shift

newR = 255 - 255 x 13.73/100 = 220
newG = 255 - 255 x 85.10/100 =  38
newB = 255 - 255 x 85.10/100 =  38
```

We can call this in the head section of our base template to load the favicon. The following listing shows the code for this.

Listing 6.36   Loading the favicon (layouts/modern/baseof.html)

```html
<link rel="icon"
    type="image/png" href="{{partialCached "favicon.png.html" $
    "nothing"}}">
```

CODE CHECKPOINT   https://chapter-06-21.hugoinaction.com, and source code: https://github.com/hugoinaction/hugoinaction/tree/chapter-06-21.

We can redo the products section on the index page to include a list of cards with product images rather than using a table and provide a rating for these. We have all the information already except for the product images, which are provided in the chapter resources (https://github.com/hugoinaction/hugoinaction/tree/chapter-06-resources/09). Because Acme Corporation sells the images, we do not want to expose raw images over the internet. Hugo offers support for an `Overlay` filter that we can use to provide a *watermark*. The following listing adds the watermark and then uses Unicode stars (`&star;` and `&starf;`) to provide the star ratings. Figure 6.6 shows a completed card.

Listing 6.37   Showing products as cards (layouts/modern/index.html)

```html
{{with (partialCached "products.html" "cache")}}    ⟵——— Gets the cached product list
<section id="store">
  <h1>Our Products</h1>
  <ul>                                              Loops through the keys
    {{range $name, $data := .}}    ⟵┘ and values of the map
    <li>
      <a href="#">
        {{$img := resources.GetMatch                Generates an image
          (print "image/products/" $name ".") |    ⟵┘ name dynamically
        images.Filter (images.Overlay
          (resources.GetMatch "image/watermark.")   Overlays the
          0 0 )}}                                    watermark image
      {{$img := $img.Resize "1000x"}}
        <img src="{{$img.Permalink}}" alt="{{$name}}">   Converts the data.Rating to a
        <h2>{{$name}}</h2>                               sequence to loop from 1 to
        <div class="price">$ {{$data.Price}}</div>       Rating, and then prints the
        <div class="rating">                             Unicode filled stars. The dash at
          {{range (seq $data.Rating)}}&starf;{{end -}}   ⟵ the end removes whitespace
                                                         between the stars.
```

Adds an overlay filter

Resizes to max width

Uses HTML stars to display the rating

```
          {{range seq
              (sub 5
                ($data.Rating
                | int ))}}&star;{{end}}
        </div>
      </a>
    </li>
    {{end}}
  </ul>
</section>
{{end}}
```

> **Loops from 1 to (5 minus Rating) and displays hollow stars**

We do not need to move this to a partial. Hugo does not recompute images if nothing changes. The case where cached partials are helpful is when there is a dynamic calculation, like executing the SVGs and the color calculation in the favicon.

TIP Unicode symbols provide significant savings in terms of bytes in comparison to SVGs and font icons.

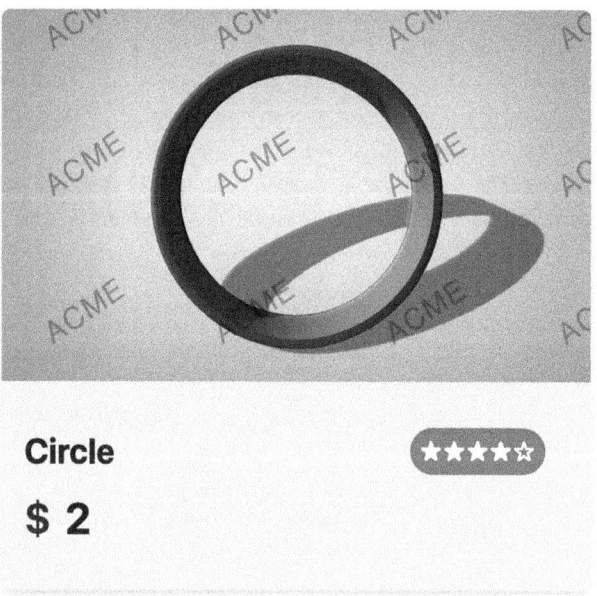

Figure 6.6   Adding a card for the products. Hugo provides support for overlaying an image onto another to create a watermark.

CODE CHECKPOINT   https://chapter-06-22.hugoinaction.com, and source code: https://github.com/hugoinaction/hugoinaction/tree/chapter-06-22.

6.3.3   *Other assets*

We can also use Hugo Pipes to access other nontextual assets like PDFs, ZIPs, or other binary content files. Although Hugo does not understand their contents, we can use accurate relative and absolute links to those files. If the files are missing, the build fails. If we delete the code that uses the file, the file does not copy over to the output directory. These features make it worthwhile to have an empty static folder and copy over content using the Hugo pipeline.

Exercise 6.5

Which of the following are the reasons to use Hugo Pipes over prebuilding content outside Hugo or using browser JavaScript? (Select all that apply.)

a. Hugo Pipes run when the user requests data and, therefore, no needless execution happens for data that is never requested.

b. Hugo Pipes have access to the website configuration and front matter where we can consolidate all the website settings like theme color, which can be passed on to the relevant JavaScript, CSS, or image code by Hugo.

c. Hugo Pipes can cache files across builds, only updating content when it changes.

d. Hugo Pipes can generate multiple sizes for images based on need, and the size requirement can be changed by a simple string replacement in code.

6.4 *Controlling Markdown rendering*

We also have images present in the Markdown documents, which we are not optimizing for production. These can also slow down loading the website. To control how Hugo renders content in the Markdown documents, Hugo provides hooks (called *render hook templates*) into the Markdown parser, where we can customize the rendering for Markdown elements. We can override the rendering of images, links, and even headings if we want. When optimizing images, we will override the image-rendering functionality in Markdown to limit the maximum size of the images to 1000 px. The following listing shows how we can add a image render hook in the modern content type, which uses the `resize` function (https://github.com/hugoinaction/hugoinaction/tree/chapter-06-resources/10).

> **Listing 6.38 Controlling image size (layouts/modern/_markup/render-image.html)**

```
<img loading="lazy" src="
{{with (.Page.Resources.GetMatch .Destination)}}
{{(.Resize "1000x").Permalink }}         ◀─────  Finds the bundled
{{else}}                                          resource and
{{ .Destination | safeURL }}      ◀──────         optimizes it
{{end}}                                  If the destination is not
                                         found, uses the URL as-is
"
alt="{{ .Text }}"
{{ with .Title}} title="{{ . }}"{{ end }}
/>
```

It is difficult to see visually if our Markdown hook was actually executed because we are not changing the image. We can view the HTML source of the web page and check for lazy loading (`loading="lazy"`) to verify.

6.5   *Using bundled templates for common work*

From the perspective of maintenance, the best piece of code is an empty file. The second best is a well-written piece of code maintained by a trusted team of experts. Hugo comes bundled with ready-to-use templates supported by its core team and used in hundreds of themes by the community. Reusing some of this makes life as a developer a lot easier.

When we added the head section of the website, we did not provide much metadata. While metadata does not change the raw contents of the web page visible to the user, that information is vital for the discoverability of the web page. The Google search bot uses microdata to identify and list pages for a Google search. Services like Facebook and LinkedIn use OpenGraph tags to provide richer experiences to users sharing the web page on these platforms. With Twitter cards, we can control how our web page looks if someone tweets the URL.

Although we can create the metadata tags manually, there is no real need to do so. Unless we need to pass specific data to any of these tags, we can use Hugo's internal templates for this task. These templates use the front matter, the summary, the site configuration, and the page bundle resources to generate HTML tags that we can place on our website. There is not a lot of wiggle room in the specification provided by these services. Therefore, it makes little sense to modify these. Hugo comes bundled with standard scripts from Google Analytics to disqus.com comments, and these can be added to the template using a single line of code.

The following listing adds Open Graph and Twitter cards to the base template for our website via internal templates. A copy of the template is also available in the chapter resources (https://github.com/hugoinaction/hugoinaction/tree/chapter-06-resources/11). The generated HTML content should have og:title and og: description along with twitter:title and twitter:description tags.

> **Listing 6.39   Adding metadata (layouts/modern/baseof.html)**

```
{{ template "_internal/twitter_cards.html" . }}
{{ template "_internal/opengraph.html" . }}
```

CODE CHECKPOINT   https://chapter-06-23.hugoinaction.com, and source code: https://github.com/hugoinaction/hugoinaction/tree/chapter-06-23.

Just like bundled templates, Hugo provides variables and functions to reduce work. One such example is automatic summarization we introduced in chapter 4. We can access the page summary by using `.Summary` in the page context. Another such method is `.TableOfContents`, which parses the headings in the Markdown document and provides a table of contents based on that. We can configure the table of contents in the global configuration. The following listing moves the definition of the body for single pages to single.html and adds a table of contents (see figure 6.7).

Listing 6.40   Table of contents in single pages (layouts/modern/single.html)

```
{{define "body"}}
<main>
  {{with .Title}}
    <h1>
      {{.}}
    </h1>
  {{end}}
  {{if .Param "toc"}}
    <h2>Table of Contents</h2>
    {{.TableOfContents}}
  {{end}}
{{.Content}}
</main>
{{end}}
```

Let's enable the table of contents for the Terms of Use page by passing toc:true in the front matter. We can also move the title from the Markdown <h1> heading to the Title attribute in the front matter.

CODE CHECKPOINT   https://chapter-06-24.hugoinaction.com, and source code: https://github.com/hugoinaction/hugoinaction/tree/chapter-06-24.

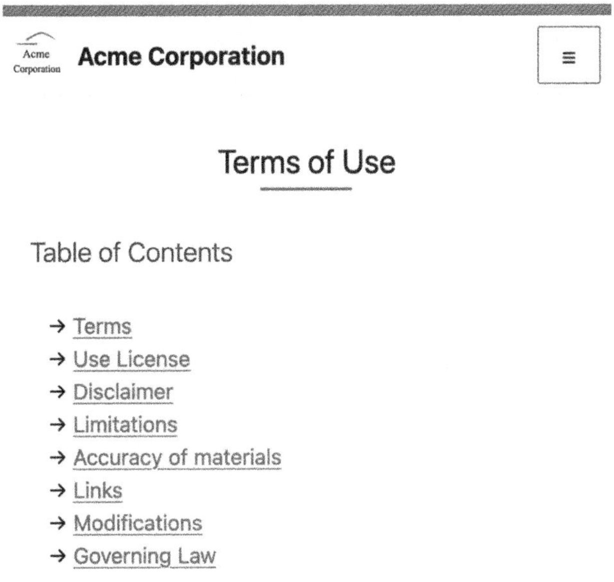

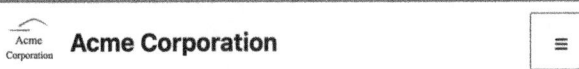

Acme Corporation   ≡

Terms of Use

Table of Contents

→ Terms
→ Use License
→ Disclaimer
→ Limitations
→ Accuracy of materials
→ Links
→ Modifications
→ Governing Law

Figure 6.7   Table of contents for the Terms of Use page is enabled by using the {{.TableOfContents}} method.

With the power of partials, Hugo Pipes, and bundled templates, we enhanced the index.html page and laid down the foundations of a new theme for the entire website. We can transfer any page to the new template by specifying its type as modern. In the next chapter, we will be moving away from the Eclectic theme to a custom theme called Acme that will power the Acme Corporation website.

Summary

- Content types in Hugo provide the means to write different, potentially independent templates for different types of content. Hugo automatically maps the section name of the branch bundle to the content type.
- We can use the base template and code blocks in Hugo to share common snippets of the Go template language via an inheritance mechanism. The base template provides snippets of default code that we can override in the specific templates.
- Partials in Hugo provide a means to encapsulate a shared code snippet in an independent file. We can cache partials for faster execution.
- Partials also act as functions that can return values to the caller.
- With Hugo Pipes, we can process textual and nontextual assets with a series of filters.
- We can write Go template code in any text-based file format from CSS and JavaScript to SVG.
- Hugo provides a variety of image manipulation functions for resizing to filtering.
- We can write custom code to control how Hugo renders the elements of the Markdown document.
- Hugo comes bundled with many reusable templates that we can add to a website with just one line of code.

Creating your own theme 7

This chapter covers

- Creating multiple layouts with shared base templates
- Using front matter cascades in Hugo
- Creating index and taxonomy pages to navigate through the website
- Converting content type to a theme
- Building content views to share content between templates

In chapter 6, we started moving away from the Eclectic theme and began to create the underpinnings for a new theme. We created a new content type called modern, which has custom template code. In this chapter, we will convert the modern content type to a complete theme (AcmeTheme). We will also focus on all types of content and how that fits together in a new theme as figure 7.1 illustrates.

In Hugo, a theme does not have a rigid definition. A set of templates that can render the content folder to a website is technically a theme. If we take the modern content type that we have so far and place it in the themes/<theme name>/_default/ folder, we could call that a theme, but it would not be a good theme. It will not render the list pages (the root pages of the branch bundle) well. The taxonomy pages will

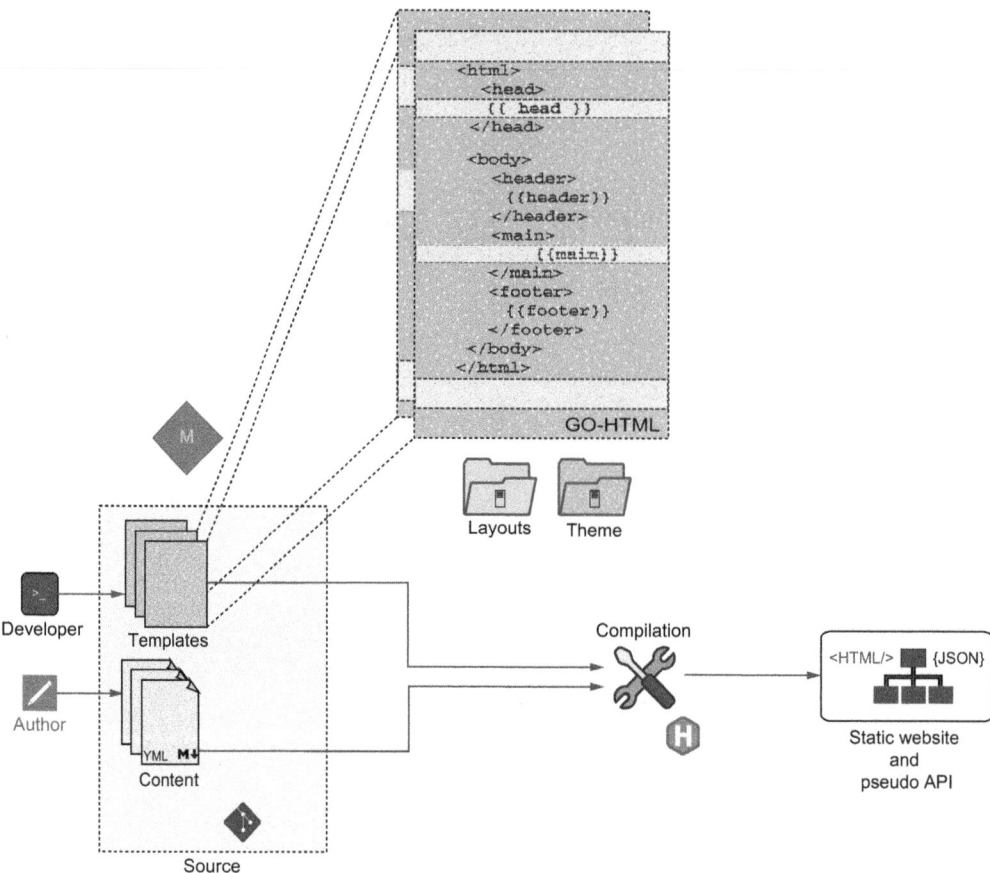

```
<html>
    <head>
        {{ head }}
    </head>

    <body>
        <header>
            {{header}}
        </header>
        <main>
            {{main}}
        </main>
        <footer>
            {{footer}}
        </footer>
    </body>
</html>
                              GO-HTML
```

Layouts   Theme

Developer   Templates

Author

YML M↓

Content

Source

Compilation

<HTML/>   {JSON}

Static website
and
pseudo API

Figure 7.1   Chapter 7 focuses on going through the breadth of the website and making sure all pages can move from the Eclectic theme to our new theme. The chapter also goes into the theme/layout split and how to get parts of the page from different areas.

also be mostly blank. A proper theme in Hugo should be able to render all the standard types of content from regular pages to list pages and taxonomy.

Currently, we depend on the Eclectic theme for a lot of pages. In this chapter, we will move the pages, one by one, to the modern content type, and once that migration is complete, we will be able to restructure that content type to become a theme.

7.1   *More ways to lay out content*

There are multiple types of pages in an application, each with a different look. A blog page, for example, typically has a sidebar with additional information about the blog post. Various types of pages can have different CSS styles and different HTML structures to accommodate their unique design.

One way to style pages differently, which we used in chapter 6, is to use a new content type for each category of page created. While content types are potent concepts that provide a mechanism to isolate the rendering code for a particular type of content, there are additional ways in Hugo to render content in a different design—parameterized front matter or a new layout. All three approaches have their use cases, advantages, and disadvantages, and we can use all of them in tandem in the same website.

For the Acme Corporation website, the web page design we used for the Terms of Use page (section 6.1.4) is pretty barebones. It does not work well with the content pages in the blog and the news sections. We need a more elaborate design for these pages. The desired changes in the News page can be achieved by CSS, while for the Blog pages, we want to add a sidebar, which involves adding HTML content. Let's see the various ways in which we can achieve this with Hugo.

7.1.1 Parameterizing front matter to differentiate the News page interface

When we have minor HTML changes between two different types of pages, we might not want to create a new content type. We can expose a variable that the template code can use to provide differentiated HTML. Using the conditional statements `if` and `else`, we can write different HTML content if needed. This way, minor HTML changes live in the same file, and we do not need to manage a separate file on disk. We can have maximum code reuse, and we do not need to split the code into partials to prevent repetition.

For the News pages on the Acme Corporation website, we do not need many changes. These pages come with cover images that we need to apply. Remember from chapter 6, the `.Resources` in the context of a page refers to the resources in the page bundle for that page. We can use a `with` or an `if` check to ensure that if the resources are not present, no additional HTML is generated. We can then add this to the existing single.html as in the following listing.

Listing 7.1 A cover image for the News page (layouts/modern/single.html)

```
{{define "body"}}
<main>
  {{$img := .Resources.GetMatch "cover.*"}}     ◁────┐ Gets the cover image
  {{ if $img }}                              ◁─────── for the page
    <img alt="{{.Title}}" width="1920" height="400"
         loading="lazy" src="{{($img.Fill "1920x400").Permalink}}">
  {{ end }}                                          Adds the image to the
  ...                                                web page if present
{{end}}
```

The pages in the news section (figure 7.2) in the Acme Corporation website have a similar HTML structure to the pages we have developed so far, and all the changes live in the CSS styling. Because the HTML is mostly the same, a conditional statement approach to switch CSS classes is better suited for this use case. Although we can take the class name from the front matter as a variable and use that by calling the `$.Param` function, there are ways with which we could get this information without needing to write anything in the content area of the website. Had we not set up the content type, we could have used the content type for this case via the `.Type` property.

Shaper

Drawing is a form of visual art in which a person uses various drawing instruments to mark paper or another two-dimensional medium. Instruments include graphite pencils, pen and ink, various kinds of paints, inked brushes, colored pencils, crayons, charcoal, chalk, pastels, various kinds of erasers, markers, styluses, and various metals (such as silverpoint). Digital drawing is the act of using a computer to draw. Common methods of digital drawing include a stylus or finger on a touchscreen device, stylus- or finger-to-touchpad, or in some cases, a mouse. There are many digital art programs and devices.

A drawing instrument releases a small

almost anything. The medium has been a popular and fundamental means of public expression throughout human history. It is one of the simplest and most efficient means of communicating visual ideas. The wide availability of drawing instruments makes drawing one of the most common artistic activities.

In addition to its more artistic forms, drawing is frequently used in commercial illustration, animation, architecture, engineering and technical drawing. A quick, freehand drawing, usually not intended as a finished work, is sometimes called a sketch. An artist who practices or works in technical drawing may be called a drafter, draftsman or a draughtsman.

Traditional drawings were monochrome, or at least had little colour, while modern colored-pencil drawings may approach or cross a boundary between drawing and painting. In Western terminology, drawing is distinct from painting, even though similar media often are employed in both tasks. Dry media, normally associated with drawing, such as chalk, may be used in pastel paintings. Drawing may be done with a liquid medium, applied with brushes or pens. Similar supports likewise can serve both: painting generally involves the application of liquid paint onto prepared canvas or panels, but sometimes an underdrawing is drawn first on that same support.

There are several categories of drawing, including figure drawing, cartooning, doodling, and freehand. There are also many drawing methods, such as line drawing, stippling, shading, the surrealist method of entopic graphomania (in which dots are made at the sites of impurities in a blank sheet of paper, and lines are then made between the dots), and tracing (drawing on a translucent paper, such as tracing paper, around the outline of preexisting shapes that show through the paper).

A quick, unrefined drawing may be called a sketch.

In fields outside art, technical drawings or plans of buildings, machinery,

Figure 7.2   The news sections are rendered with a different UI by switching the CSS styling using the section information. (Image by tookapic on Pixabay.)

We can use the folder location of the page to find its section. If we run {{path.Base (path.Dir .Page.FirstSection.File.Path)}} for the News page, we will get the news section. .Page.FirstSection points to the _index page of the news section, and we can find the folder name using the path.Dir at its path. Note that we can also use CurrentSection for the News page, but this will break the community subsection of the blog section. We can use this folder location to change the HTML class of the News page and make it different from the other pages as in listing 7.2.

> **TIP** Minimizing the need for entering data in the front matter can help keep the content area simple. When creating content, the less we have to think about front matter metadata, the better. We make a theme once, but we continuously add content to the website.

Listing 7.2   Adding the page section name (layouts/modern/single.html)

```
{{define "bodyClass"}}
   {{ path.Dir .Page.FirstSection.File.Path) }} page
{{end}}
```

> **TIP** It is good to expose one entry in the head section of the website in the define block. This can be overridden for page-specific metadata or for supplying page-specific CSS/JavaScript files, making the theme extensible. We could even have a naming convention like cover.* to load additional CSS/JS files.

The single page template can automatically find the section's name and provide the appropriate CSS class with these changes. Because this code is present in the single page template for the modern type in Hugo, we need to assign all pages in the news section to this content type. We will need to add type: modern to every page in the news section. Considering there could be hundreds of News pages, that is a lot of work. For new pages, however, archetypes (discussed in section 5.4.3) can help in predefining them, but the text will still be required, leading to the possibility of typographical errors and other mistakes.

7.1.2 Using the cascade property to apply properties to the front matter of multiple pages

One central principle in Hugo is to reduce work and prevent duplication of the code to the maximum extent possible. Having a property shared between all pages in a section is common for websites. Hugo recognizes this and provides a mechanism to write this property once and apply it to all of the pages. Hugo has a property in the front matter called cascade (figure 7.3), whose subproperties apply as front matter properties to all pages in that section.

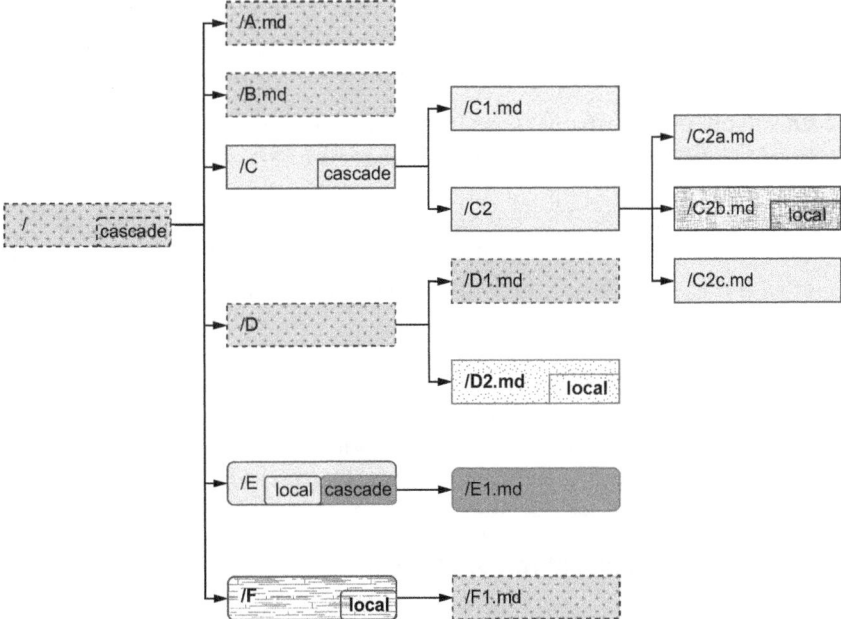

Figure 7.3 The cascade property allows us to provide values to the front matter variables, which we can use across the whole section. In the diagram, local specifies the keys in the front matter, while cascade sets the same key as a subkey for the cascade. The top-level _index file specifies a cascade that applies to that file as well as to the subsections for its child pages. /C issues a cascade override so that its subtree gets the cascade value from this section. /C2 does not use an override, and therefore, the cascade from /C carries through. In /C2b, we have a local override that takes over the property. In /D, we do not override the cascade property, but /D2 does a local override. /E has both a local override for the specific index page and a cascade for the child pages, which /E1 uses. Section /F only has a local override, and the properties from its root follow through to /F1.

The concept of *cascade* is the same as in CSS, which stands for cascading style sheets. We define a generic property at the top level and then a specific property when an override is needed. The more specific property overrides the generic one. We can even do a local override, where the cascade property applies to the subpage but not to the current page because the property present in the front matter for the current page has a higher priority.

On the _index page for the news section, let's enable the type modern via the cascade property as in listing 7.3. We will revert it for the news/_index page because the modern type does not have the HTML layout for a branch list page. By default, the cascade property applies to all pages in a section, including subsection index pages (list.html) and individual (single.html) pages.

Listing 7.3   The `modern` type in all content pages (content/news/_index.md)

```
cascade:
  type: modern
type: _default
```

> **NOTE** We could have used a garbage string in the front matter's root level type field. Hugo falls back to the _default folder to look for the layout if the type specified in the front matter is not present on the disk.

> **CODE CHECKPOINT**   https://chapter-07-01.hugoinaction.com, and source code: https://github.com/hugoinaction/hugoinaction/tree/chapter-07-01.

Every page in the news section has been assigned to the content type modern using the cascade property. Once this is enabled, we can see the child pages in the news section render with the new CSS styling for the News pages. The next set of pages that need a different design are the Blog pages.

> **NOTE** We can still override the cascade property by manually specifying it in the front matter; for example, if we put type: _default in any of the pages in the news section, that specific page renders with the default content type even if it is in the news section that has set the cascading content type modern. We can view the various permutations of cascade and overrides in figure 7.3.

7.1.3   *Providing a different layout to the blog content*

The design for the blog section includes a sidebar (figure 7.4). Over time, we expect blogs to diverge in design from the News pages or the regular web pages. Keeping the code together with unrelated pages is not a scalable solution. When we have more than a couple of conditional statements, things can get complicated, especially if the content in these conditional statements is enormous. If we want to share the base template with different generated HTML for various content, we need to create a new layout.

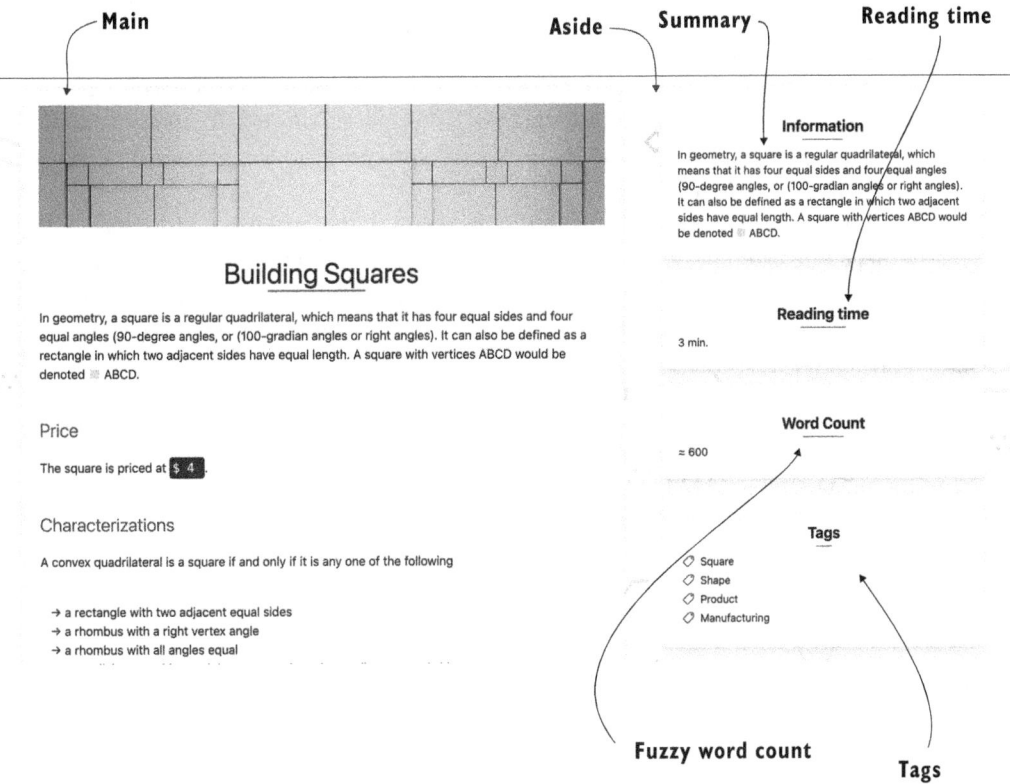

Figure 7.4 The Blog page with a sidebar was created by adding a new layout to the `modern` content type web pages. (Image by Pexels on Pixabay.)

The default layout for a web page/leaf bundle is the single layout, so we have a file called single.html. This is where we provide the overrides to the base template. But we are not restricted to that layout. We can override it to anything we desire. Layouts within a content type share all templates within the content type including render hooks. Table 7.1 compares the content type with a layout.

Table 7.1 Content type vs. layout

Area	Content type	Layout
Usage	Provides the templates for all pages within a section of the website. For example, the `blog` type represents the blog content pages and the blog index pages, and it can have multiple layouts like blog posts with and without sidebars.	Provides the template for an individual page (like a blog post with a sidebar). A blog post without a sidebar can be in a different layout.
Default mappings	The map name automatically maps to the section name. The `blog` content type automatically applies to the pages in the /content/blog folder unless overridden.	Every web page has a default layout, which is based on the template lookup order. The single and list layouts are the most common.

We want to have a sidebar in the blog section to provide more information about the blog post. We can provide information like tags in the front matter and things like summaries used in the index page and other properties in the front matter. Along with this, Hugo can generate a bunch of other metadata such as an approximate reading time with the .ReadingTime property and an approximate word count with the .WordCount property.

Let's create a new file called blog.html in the modern folder (https://github .com/hugoinaction/hugoinaction/tree/chapter-07-resources/01). In this file, we will define the body block for the Blog pages to include a sidebar. The following listing sets up a sidebar in the HTML <aside> tag that provides information generated by Hugo.

Listing 7.4   The blog layout with a sidebar (layouts/modern/blog.html)

Wrapping in a content div to differentiate from header and footer

```
<div id="content">
    <main>...</main>          ← Same main tag as in a regular singe page
    <aside>
        <section>
            <h2>Information</h2>
            <p>{{.Summary}}</p>      ← The autogenerated or manually provided summary in the sidebar
        </section>
        <section>
            <h2>Reading time</h2>
            <p>{{.ReadingTime}} min.</p>   ← Hugo calculates approximate reading time based on the word count and the character length.
        </section>
        <section>
            <h2>Word Count</h2>
            <p>? {{.FuzzyWordCount}}</p>   ← Gives an approximate word count to the user. We have an exact option as well, but that can be too much detail for the reader.
        </section>
        {{with .Params.tags}}
        <section>
            <h2>Tags</h2>
            {{range .}}
            <p>
                <a
                    href="{{"/tags/" | relLangURL}}
                        {{- . | urlize}}">   ← "{{-" ensures no space is present between /tags/ and the tag name.
                    {{. | humanize}}   ← Displays the tag name, capitalizing the first letter for human readability
                </a>
            </p>
            {{end}}
        </section>
        {{end}}
    </aside>
</div>
```

aside is a good HTML tag for a sidebar.

Loops through the supplied tags

Converts each tag path to a language-specific URL link

We will also need to specify the layout and type for the blog section via the `cascade` property as in the following listing. We use this to update the layout and content type in the blog section.

> **Listing 7.5   Updating the layout and content type (content/blog/_index.md)**

```
---
cascade:
  layout: blog
  type: modern
---
```

We have now updated all the pages in the blog folder from the single layout to the blog layout.

> **Exercise 7.1**
>
> A _____ in Hugo can share the base template and Markdown render hooks (mentioned in section 6.4) with other templates of the same content type.

7.1.4   *Cascading targets*

We also have an index page for the community subsection of the blog section. Like the News pages, we do not want the new template to override the index page for the blog section. One approach to prevent this override is to add a local override in _index.md in both of these places. However, this approach can lead to bugs when we introduce new sections and forget to apply this setting. A better solution is to scope the overwrite to the right set of pages. To do this, along with the cascades, we can provide target information in the front matter using the key `_target`. We can use this key to restrict the `cascade` option to only apply to a subpath, a specific language folder, or a specific kind of page in Hugo. To restrict the target to the non-index pages, we need to understand the concept of page kinds in Hugo.

PAGE KINDS IN HUGO

Similar to a layout, each page in Hugo has a *kind*. A kind is the internal data structure that represents a page in Hugo. The set of variables available to the template are dependent on the kind of page. For example, the taxonomy page kind always has access to the list of terms in the taxonomy, which may not be available in the other page kinds. The kind of a page cannot be changed. In Hugo, the page kind is one of the following:

- *home*—The index page of the entire website. Corresponds to index.html by default.
- *page*—A single web page. Corresponds to single.html by default.

- *section*—The index page of a website section or branch bundle. Corresponds to list.html by default (see section 7.2).
- *taxonomy*—The index page of an individual taxonomy list. Corresponds to terms.html (and not to taxonomy.html) by default (see section 7.3).
- *term*—The page for an individual taxonomy term. Corresponds to taxonomy .html (and not to terms.html) by default (see section 7.3).

Difference between theme, type, layout, and page kind

While they may seem synonymous, the theme, type, layout, and page kind are different things in Hugo:

- A *theme* represents the templates for the entire website. It contains multiple types.
- A *type* (or *content type*) represents a section of the website that can have multiple variations of content and multiple templates for generating the HTML for each of the variations. A type can have many layouts.
- A *layout* maps to a single template that can render a single design across multiple pages. Using conditionals, we can make some content different, but there has to be one template that represents a layout.
- A *page kind* in Hugo defines what variables are available to the template when it is rendered. A page kind is fixed and cannot be changed.

APPLYING CASCADE ON A PAGE KIND

Our template only targets the single pages, all of a kind `page`. We can override the type and layout for these pages by selecting them as the target in Hugo. The following listing shows this for individual pages in the blog section. With these changes, the blog and the community index pages should revert to normal, while the rest of the pages in the blog section will have a sidebar.

Listing 7.6   Targeting cascading overrides (content/blog/_index.md)

```
---
cascade:
  - _target:
      kind: page
    layout: blog
    type: modern
---
```

CODE CHECKPOINT   https://chapter-07-02.hugoinaction.com, and source code: https://github.com/hugoinaction/hugoinaction/tree/chapter-07-02.

7.1.5 *Related pages via Hugo*

In the blog section, we will like to introduce a link to more pages, relevant to the reader within the website. *Related pages* is a Hugo feature that allows us to get pages similar to the supplied page. The related pages feature encapsulates the matching algorithm for pages to achieve this complex operation, and it comes with an outstanding performance. The similarity matching is done based on the metadata, and the front matter parameters are controlled using the `related` section in the website configuration. A file named related.yaml (https://github.com/hugoinaction/hugoinaction/tree/chapter-07-resources/02) can be placed in the config folder to control how the pages are selected. The following listing shows how to use parameters to find the related pages for a given page.

Listing 7.7 Adding parameters to get related pages (config/_default/related.yaml)

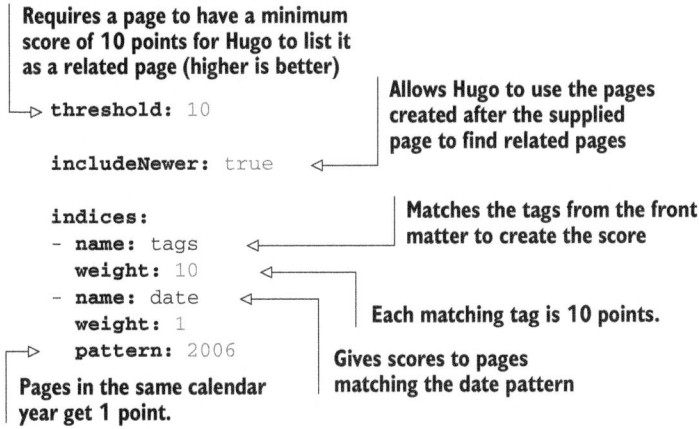

Requires a page to have a minimum score of 10 points for Hugo to list it as a related page (higher is better)

```
threshold: 10

includeNewer: true

indices:
  - name: tags
    weight: 10
  - name: date
    weight: 1
    pattern: 2006
```

Allows Hugo to use the pages created after the supplied page to find related pages

Matches the tags from the front matter to create the score

Each matching tag is 10 points.

Gives scores to pages matching the date pattern

Pages in the same calendar year get 1 point.

Note that when providing a threshold to get a list of related pages, it needs to be a number between 0 and 100. When searching for related pages, the `includeNewer` parameter can cause the list of related pages to change as we add more content.

The `site.RegularPages.Related` function takes a page as an argument and provides scores to all pages in the website related to that page and then sorts those pages. Because Hugo provides no limits, this can turn into a vast list, and therefore, it is a good idea to filter out the top few pages to show to the end user (for example, with `first 5` in the code).

The card view of the page is the same as what we used on the home page for recent blog posts (see figure 5.8). We can move it to a partial. To do that, we can use a cached partial (as discussed in chapter 6) because the rendition of a page is the same across all pages. The following listing uses `site.RegularPages.Related` to find related pages and then uses a cached partial, card.html, to render those within the current page.

Listing 7.8   Using a cached partial for the blogs (layouts/modern/blog.html)

```
{{with site.RegularPages.Related .}}
<div id="related">
  <h2>Related Pages</h2>
  <ul class="posts">
    {{range first 5 .}}
      {{partialCached "card.html" . .Permalink}}
    {{end}}
  </ul>
</div>
{{end}}
```

Caches by .Permalink to reuse the card content in all the places we need the card version of the page

CODE CHECKPOINT   https://chapter-07-03.hugoinaction.com, and source code: https://github.com/hugoinaction/hugoinaction/tree/chapter-07-03.

Exercise 7.2

Which property decides the contents and availability of variables in Hugo?

a. Type
b. Layout
c. Kind
d. Content type
e. Template name
f. Permalink
g. Containing folder

7.2   Updating the index pages by providing content and subsection lists

The index pages like /blog need to have a different interface than the regular pages. Rendering it with the blog layout renders only the Markdown content, and we lose the capability to navigate to the child pages in the section and the subsections. These pages deserve separate templates.

7.2.1   Using the list template for index pages

The index pages provide access to the content within a section. Because we have multiple content pages, the index pages have a list of pages. These are called *list pages*. Hugo allows list pages to have a different template to render content differently.

Let's create a file called list.html in the modern subfolder in the layouts directory. In the index page, we need to provide a list of pages in the section. If a page has child pages, those are available in the .RegularPages variable for the page. We can loop through these pages to provide a list of child pages for navigation (https://github.com/hugoinaction/hugoinaction/tree/chapter-07-resources/03). The following listing shows how to provide the list of pages for the Acme Corporation website.

Listing 7.9   Getting a list of pages (layouts/modern/list.html)

```
{{define "bodyClass"}}page list{{end}}
{{define "body"}}
<main>
  <h1>
    {{.Title | humanize}}          ◄──── Uses humanize to convert the
  </h1>                                    first letter to capital case
  <center>{{.Content}}</center>
  {{with .RegularPages}}          ◄────── Regular pages are all pages of the kind page
                                          in a section that removes taxonomy, section,
    <ul class="posts">                    term, and home page from this list.
      {{ range .}}
        {{partialCached "card.html" . .Permalink}}
      {{ end }}
    </ul>
  {{end}}
</main>
{{end}}
```

In blog/_index.md, we can return the modern content type for all the pages where the kind is section. The following listing sets up these pages as the list type for the Blog pages. The blog index page will then render with the list of pages directly in that section with these changes.

Listing 7.10   Setting the kind section as the list type (content/blog/_index.md)

```
---
cascade:
  - _target:
      kind: section
    type: modern
    layout: list
---
```

CODE CHECKPOINT   https://chapter-07-04.hugoinaction.com, and source code: https://github.com/hugoinaction/hugoinaction/tree/chapter-07-04.

7.2.2   Creating multiple pages to render a long list

We loop through all the pages in a section to form the index page. One problem with this approach is that all pages will render together on a single page even if we have hundreds of posts. That would turn this into a heavy web page and cause a slow down when loading. But if we restrict to a smaller number of posts (like we did on the index page using the first function), all the posts will not be navigable. We need a mechanism to provide multiple pages with all the posts generated from one template (figure 7.5). Hugo answers this problem with the Paginator object.

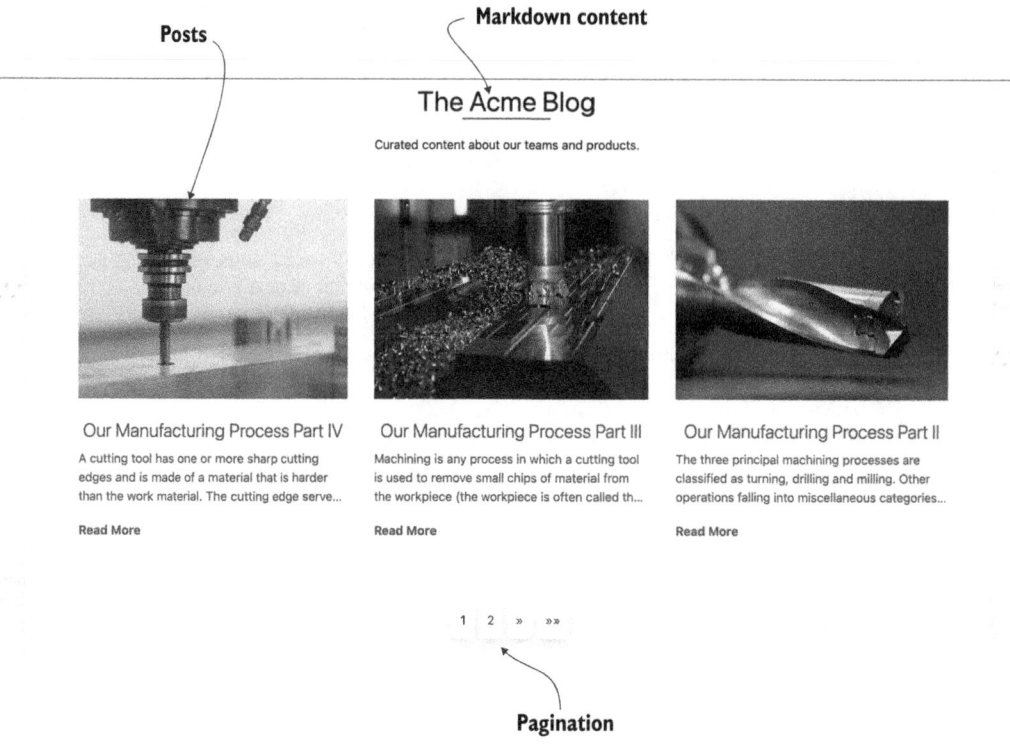

Figure 7.5   The list pages for the blog items with pagination enabled. (Images by Michael Schwarzenberger, gefrorene_wand, and Robert Wilkos on Pixabay.)

Paginator is a Hugo object used to create multiple pages from a single function call. We can use .Paginator.Pages in the loop instead of .RegularPages as in the following listing and set the pagination options in the website configuration file. The .Paginator object automatically splits the list of pages into multiple pages and supplies the right set of pages to render.

Listing 7.11   Splitting the index page (layouts/modern/list.html)

```
{{ with .Paginator.Pages }}
<ul class="posts">
```

Because we have a small number of posts, we need to change the number of posts per index page to trigger pagination. The following listing changes the number of elements in a page in config.yaml for the paginator to take effect.

Listing 7.12   Updating the pagination options (config/_default/config.yaml)

```
Paginate: 3        ◁─┐   Number of posts that Hugo should show
                     └   on a page using the .Paginator object
```

Grouping pages

Hugo supports grouping pages into arbitrary groups using the `.Pages.GroupBy` set of methods. For example, if we want to show pages with headings based on the creation year, we could use the `{{range .Pages.GroupByDate "2006"}}` and then set the year as the `.Key` and `.Pages` as all pages with that key. This sample code is not added to the chapter resources, but you can add it to layouts/modern/list.html.

```
{{ range .Pages.GroupByDate "2006" }}
Posts in year {{ .Key }}:
{{range .Pages}}
  <a href="{{.Permalink}}"> {{.Title}}</a>
{{end}}
{{end}}
```

The snippet groups all pages by year. Then it loops through the various years, providing them in the `.Key` field with the pages belonging to the year in the `.Pages` field. We can also use the `Paginator` object for page groups.

To enable page numbers, we can use the properties from the `.Paginator` object (for example, `TotalPages`, `Next`, `First`, `PageNumber`, and so on). Hugo ships with an internal template that we can also use for this task. The following listing enables the internal template, which is mostly complete and rarely overridden by themes.

Listing 7.13   Using the pagination template (layouts/modern/list.html)

```
{{ template "_internal/pagination.html" . }}
```

While the default pagination template is good, the terse pagination template (listing 7.14) builds faster and, therefore, is recommended. A copy of the template is present in the chapter resources just in case it gets modified in future versions of Hugo (https://github.com/hugoinaction/hugoinaction/tree/chapter-07-resources/04).

Listing 7.14   Using the terse format (layouts/modern/list.html)

```
{{ template "_internal/pagination.html" (dict "page" . "format" "terse") }}
```

We can now update the news index page to use the modern content type. The pagination does not show up in the news section because it has just one page.

CODE CHECKPOINT   https://chapter-07-05.hugoinaction.com, and source code: https://github.com/hugoinaction/hugoinaction/tree/chapter-07-05.

Exercise 7.3

What allows us to split a single array across multiple pages in Hugo?

- a. List template
- b. Bundle
- c. Cascade
- d. Content type
- e. Paginator
- f. Taxonomy

7.2.3   *Using a custom paginator*

The built-in .Paginator has a great set of defaults and, in most cases, suffices for the index page. We can further customize that page if needed. The community blog posts hidden away in a subsection on the Acme Corporation website do not get too many hits. Therefore, the management wants to uplevel them to the regular blog list. The default pagination does not include all child pages but only direct descendants. We need to use a custom paginator to use both the section and subsection pages as in the following listing. For this, the .Paginate function takes a list of pages.

Listing 7.15   Adding a custom paginator (layouts/modern/list.html)

```
{{$pages := .RegularPages}}
{{range .Sections}}
  {{$pages = append $pages .RegularPages}}     ⟵⎤ Appends all
{{end}}                                           ⎦ child pages
{{$pages = sort $pages "Date" "desc" }}   ⟵⎤
{{ with (.Paginate $pages).Pages }}          ⎦ Sorts the pages
                                               by creation date
```

This code reads the pages from the one-level deeper subsections and appends them to the $pages variable. If we need navigation for the entire tree, we need to write a recursive partial template. When we create a custom paginator, Hugo does not generate the default paginator.

> **NOTE**   We can override the page size specified in the configuration using the Paginate property by passing it as an additional argument to the .Paginate function. For example, .Paginate $posts 5 puts 5 posts in one page.

7.2.4   *Rendering a list of subsections*

The community blogs are a subsection of the blog section of the website. Each index page has a variable called .Sections, which gets a list of the child sections for index pages. Using this variable allows us to show the child pages for each section with the current page. Without providing a list of subsections on the list pages, we leave pages like these unreachable. In this section, we will also add a list of subsections to the first of the section pages (figure 7.6).

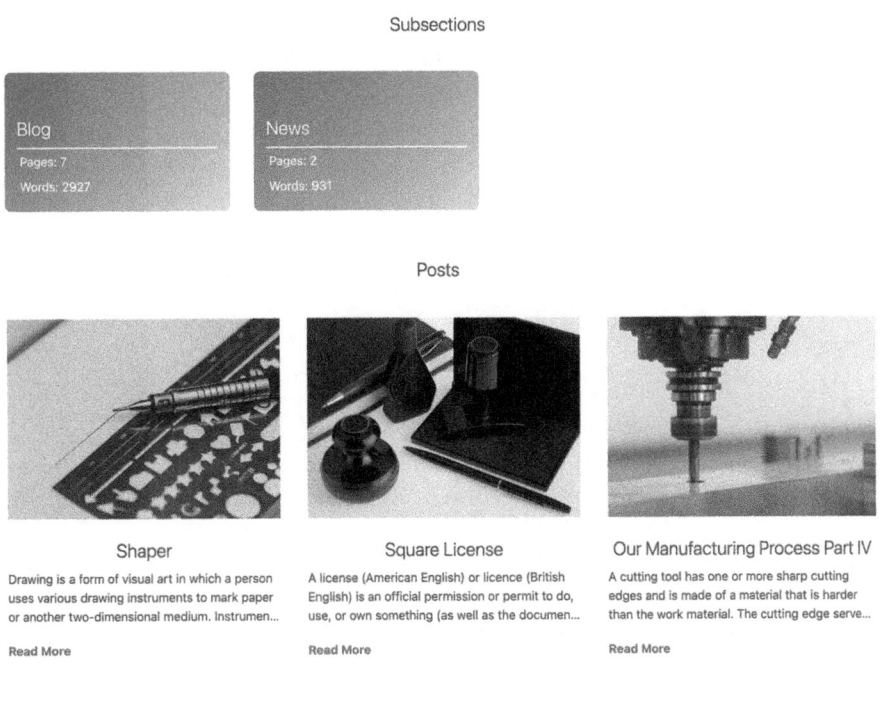

Figure 7.6　The index page for the Acme Corporation website using a list instead of an index template. (Images by tookapic, ds_30, and Robert Wilkos on Pixabay.)

We can use the `Paginator` object to detect if this is the first page (https://github.com/hugoinaction/hugoinaction/tree/chapter-07-resources/05). If the user is on page 1, we can display the header for posts (versus subsections) and the list of subsections. The following listing uses `.Sections` in the index page of a section to provide the subsections in a Hugo template.

Listing 7.16　Providing the list of subsections (layouts/modern/list.html)

```
{{ $paginator := .Paginate $pages }}
{{if and (eq $paginator.PageNumber 1)
         (gt (len .Sections) 0) }}
<h2>Subsections</h2>
  <ul class="subsections">
  {{range .Sections}}
    <li class="subsection">
      <a href="{{.Permalink}}">
        <h3>{{( default
```

Gets access to Paginator. We can also use the default .Paginator object.

Only shows subsections on the first page

Only shows titles if subsections exist

Uses the folder name to provide a reasonable default

```
      (.File.Path │ path.Dir │ path.Base )
        .Title ) │ humanize}}</h3>
      <p>Pages: {{len .Pages}}</p>
      {{$words := 0}}
        {{range .Pages}}
          {{$words = add $words .WordCount}}
        {{end}}
      <p>Words: {{$words}}</p>
    </a>
  </li>
{{end}}
</ul>
<h2>Posts</h2>
{{ end }}
{{with $paginator.Pages}}
...
```

Sums up the total word count of all child pages

CODE CHECKPOINT   https://chapter-07-06.hugoinaction.com, and source code: https://github.com/hugoinaction/hugoinaction/tree/chapter-07-06.

Something to note here is that if we have multiple subsections, we will not be able to have multiple paginators (one for pages and another for subsections). A page can have only one paginator. This limitation is present because if we have two paginations per page (for example, subsections and posts), we will need to support independent navigation (for example, post page 2 with subsection page 1, post page 3 with subsection page 1, post page 2 with subsection page 2, post page 3 with subsection page 2, and so on). Double pagination has exponential ($O(n^k)$) combinations (to n paginations and k pages each), which is slow and wasteful.

CODE CHECKPOINT   https://chapter-07-07.hugoinaction.com, and source code: https://github.com/hugoinaction/hugoinaction/tree/chapter-07-07.

7.3   *Providing the taxonomy pages*

There are two types of taxonomy pages: the *taxonomy page* (used for each taxonomy term) and the *terms page* (used for the taxonomy list). The terms pages provide a list of all the terms in the taxonomy (for example, all the tags at /tags), while the taxonomy pages list all pages with a specific term (like all posts with the tag square). Before overriding any of the pages, let's see how they look in the existing list template. Let's replace the type as a cascading property in content/categories/_index with modern and see how the pages look. The terms in a category turned into child pages for the category, while the individual posts became the child pages of each taxonomy page.

Hugo tries to ease the life of theme authors by fitting various content into the two types of pages: list page and single page. The index page, the terms page, and the taxonomy page fall back to the list page if the corresponding pages are not present (the single template is for individual pages). We can override these pages by creating a taxonomy.html and terms.html layout for the taxonomy page and a list of terms, respectively. Because the list template does not read taxonomy terms, locations like /categories will not show any content yet.

> **NOTE** A Hugo website needs only two templates: a list.html and a single.html to be complete. Remember from chapter 4, there are two types of bundles in Hugo: branch bundles and page bundles. The two templates, list.html and single .html, correspond to these bundle types, respectively. All other templates are specialized cases of the list template. If we remove index.html, Hugo selects the list.html for the website's index page. Similarly, the taxonomy pages use the list template to render unless we provide a custom template.

> **CODE CHECKPOINT** https://chapter-07-08.hugoinaction.com, and source code: https://github.com/hugoinaction/hugoinaction/tree/chapter-07-08.

7.3.1 *The terms page*

The terms page shows a list of terms in a taxonomy. We can define pages for individual terms and have content associated with them to provide summaries. It is rather rare that we need such a thing. We rarely write the summary for each hashtag that we use in the website. A better presentation would be to provide a list of tags (figure 7.7).

Figure 7.7 The terms page for the `categories` taxonomy type in the Acme Corporation website. The terms page provides unique variables to access all the terms and to use the pages in the terms if the list template does not seem the best suited for the specific page.

In layouts/modern/terms.html, we will provide the same minimal details that we used for the subsections that we will be moving to a partial (https://github.com/hugoinaction/hugoinaction/tree/chapter-07-resources/06). Note that because not all taxonomies have a file, we need to wrap the h3 in if checks in the partial. The .Data.Terms variable allows access to all the terms in the given taxonomy type. We have many options to get sorted versions of this data. Alphabetically, the one we will use in the following listing is the most popular.

Listing 7.17   Rendering a list of taxonomy terms (layout/modern/terms.html)

```
{{define "bodyClass"}}page terms{{end}}
{{define "body"}}
<main>
  <h1>
    {{.Title | humanize}}      ◁──┐  The title for the
  </h1>                             terms page
  <center>{{.Content}}</center>
  {{with .Data.Terms.Alphabetical}}  ◁──┐
    <ul class="section">                   Loops through the terms in this
      {{ range .}}                         taxonomy in alphabetical order
        {{partialCached "subsection" .Page .Page.Permalink}}
      {{ end }}
    </ul>
  {{end}}
</main>
{{end}}
```

Note that, in the previous listing, the title for the terms page comes from the website configuration (for example, categories) but can be overridden by creating a separate _index.md for the taxonomy list (for example, content/categories/_index.md). The next listing provides the subsection partial that is used to render a subsection as a card. Individual terms within a taxonomy list are rendered as a subsection.

Listing 7.18   Partial to render an individual term as a card in the taxonomy list

```
<li class="subsection">
  <a href="{{.Permalink}}">
    {{if .Title}}
    <h3> {{.Title | humanize}} </h3>
    {{else if .File}}
    <h3>{{.File.Path | path.Dir | path.Base | humanize}}</h3>
    {{end}}
    <p>Pages: {{len .Pages}}</p>
    {{$words := 0}}
      {{range .Pages}}
        {{$words = add $words .WordCount}}
      {{end}}
    <p>Words: {{$words}}</p>
  </a>
</li>
```

CODE CHECKPOINT   https://chapter-07-09.hugoinaction.com, and source code: https://github.com/hugoinaction/hugoinaction/tree/chapter-07-09.

7.3.2 *The taxonomy pages*

Most developers do not need to override the taxonomy pages because the list template works well for these pages. The list pages are so good that a great start to customizing the taxonomy pages is to take the list template and create a copy called taxonomy.html. Now we can customize the taxonomy.html template. The section associated with the taxonomy page is the terms page and has all the variables associated with terms.html accessible. We can use this to change the title of the taxonomy page as the following listing shows.

> **Listing 7.19 Changing the taxonomy title (layouts/modern/taxonomy.html)**

```
<h1>
{{$.CurrentSection.Data.Singular | humanize}}
- {{.Title | humanize}}
</h1>
```

CODE CHECKPOINT https://chapter-07-10.hugoinaction.com, and source code: https://github.com/hugoinaction/hugoinaction/tree/chapter-07-10.

NOTE Remember, in chapter 4, we provided both the singular and plural text for a taxonomy. Hugo allows access to both the strings for our use. It does not automatically convert those because that cannot be reliably done across languages (not programming but human languages) without a vast database. We can use any of the strings as we see fit in the template.

Exercise 7.4

The two most important templates in Hugo's template system that can be mapped to all other templates in a meaningful way include (select two):

    a. list.html

    b. baseof.html

    c. terms.html

    d. taxonomy.html

    e. single.html

    f. index.html

    g. hugo.html

    h. partial.html

7.4 *Creating our own theme*

Now that we have moved the significant parts of our theme onto the modern layout, we don't need Eclectic anymore. We can safely remove it from our codebase and move all the pages over to our custom theme.

7.4.1   *Moving to a new theme*

To move to a custom theme, we need to make sure we do not use any feature from Eclectic. We don't want broken pages that need more work in our new theme. Note that we do not need to replicate all Eclectic features. Just focus on what we need and then decide about content that we can remove. For verification, we will add a cascading type switch on the index page of the website to the content type modern as the following listing demonstrates.

Listing 7.20   Moving all pages to content type `modern` (content/_index.md)

```
cascade:
  type: modern
```

> **NOTE** We can use the Hugo configuration to provide the top-level cascade property as well. This lets us keep this configuration outside of content.

With this change, we have applied content type modern to all pages on the website. We can verify that the website looks good without the theme. Note that there are broken pages like data-driven.md because we did not add support for using its front matter keys to create some elements. We do not need this page in the Acme Corporation website, so we can remove the themes/eclectic folder and the theme: eclectic setting from config/_default/config.yaml.

> **CODE CHECKPOINT** https://chapter-07-11.hugoinaction.com, and source code: https://github.com/hugoinaction/hugoinaction/tree/chapter-07-11.

The next step is moving the layout to a different theme. The concept of a theme in Hugo is fluid. Websites can pick and choose parts of their template content and move that to a theme. To create a new theme, we need to create a subfolder in the themes folder with the theme's name. We can choose to name the theme whatever we want. For this book, we chose AcmeTheme as the theme name. We can move the layouts folder to the themes/AcmeTheme folder to promote the layouts as part of the theme. Next, we need to update the theme in the configuration file, config/_default/config.yaml. The following listing updates the theme.

Listing 7.21   Setting the theme to AcmeTheme (config/_default/config.yaml)

```
theme: AcmeTheme
```

> **CODE CHECKPOINT** https://chapter-07-12.hugoinaction.com, and source code: https://github.com/hugoinaction/hugoinaction/tree/chapter-07-12.

We should get the same website with all pages built using our modern type if we run the code in listing 7.21. We can then get rid of the Eclectic theme completely by deleting it from the themes folder.

7.4.2 *Aligning content with the theme*

Technically, we now have a theme. A significant conceptual difference between a content type (or any other parts of a theme that we have overridden so far) and the theme is that we build a theme for reuse across multiple websites. But now, it is tightly coupled with the content structure. If we had picked up the project after chapter 4 (using code checkpoint chapter-04-11) and had swapped its theme with the one we have right now, nothing would work. We need to provide meaningful defaults and make it easy for someone to pick up the theme with a barebones Hugo project. All added functionality can be made accessible via the configuration, front matter, or hardcoded file locations (like we have for background.svg), but the base functionality should be readily available.

The first step is to remove the requirement of the content type. To do this, we need to rename themes/AcmeTheme/layouts/modern to themes/AcmeTheme/layouts/_default, which makes our layout the default layout. The code we have should continue to work even though it references the content type modern. In the absence of a content type, Hugo falls back to the default content type. We can now remove type: modern from our codebase completely.

CODE CHECKPOINT   https://chapter-07-13.hugoinaction.com, and source code: https://github.com/hugoinaction/hugoinaction/tree/chapter-07-13.

We moved the Blog pages to a new layout called *blog*. There is a discoverability problem with layouts in Hugo. Unless someone knows about it, the likelihood of not finding a layout is high. It makes much more sense for the blog to be a new content type. Therefore, we will create a new folder called themes/AcmeTheme/layouts/blog and move themes/AcmeTheme/layouts/_default/blog.html to themes/AcmeTheme/layouts/blog/single.html. This way, all the pages in the blog folder are automatically selected with the content type blog and use the single.html template.

It is great to see the Blog pages picking up this information automatically. If a particular layout is absent, Hugo falls back to the default layout for that file. Because the single layout exists in the blog folder, the entries in that folder automatically pick this up. With this, we can remove the layout changes in the front matter of the Blog pages.

CODE CHECKPOINT   https://chapter-07-14.hugoinaction.com, and source code: https://github.com/hugoinaction/hugoinaction/tree/chapter-07-14.

When we created the blog content type, the blog's single.html template automatically picked up the base template (baseof.html) from the _default type. Even the base templates can fall back to the default type if they are not present in a specific content type. The default content type is unique in Hugo because it can provide the base template to all content types. Therefore, most default base templates are generic and extensible. That we need entirely independent HTML pages on the same website is sporadic. If we override the default content type in a theme, it is challenging for the rest of the theme to function correctly.

7.4.3 Providing theme assets

The templates defined in the theme refer to multiple assets like CSS files and images in the assets folder. We need to move these to the themes/AcmeTheme folder to make the theme independent. Although moving the CSS files is not a big issue, the logo and the products.csv file information is specific to the Acme Corporation website and does not belong to the theme. We can place the empty products.csv and the placeholder images in the theme folder to allow the website to compile and execute (https://github.com/hugoinaction/hugoinaction/tree/chapter-07-resources/07). Once we move the CSS file and provide the theme assets, the theme should potentially stand on its own.

> **CODE CHECKPOINT**　https://chapter-07-15.hugoinaction.com, and source code: https://github.com/hugoinaction/hugoinaction/tree/chapter-07-15.

> **NOTE**　You will need to change the theme name to Acme in the configuration to pick up this theme.

To check this, we can move the source code (content and config folders) from chapter 4, empty the assets and archetypes folders, and then test.

> **CODE CHECKPOINT**　https://chapter-07-16.hugoinaction.com, and source code: https://github.com/hugoinaction/hugoinaction/tree/chapter-07-16. (reverted in chapter-07-17)

The theme we have just created is ready to be used outside of our website. We can now host it independently in its own separate repository or provide it as a folder to be integrated by other websites. We can also submit this theme to the Hugo theme gallery.

> **NOTE**　Not all Hugo websites create independent themes. If you are building a theme just for your website, keeping it in this state in the themes folder may be the best approach.

Having a theme embedded in the website provides maximum ease of use as you only have to manage one code repository; you only need to cater to the content of a single website rather than a general-purpose use case for multiple. You then get all the flexibility of a theme without the overhead of multiple repositories for your code.

All themes do not need to be shared publicly. You can have multiple websites with the same shared theme used within an organization. The sales team can have their independent website with a content folder, while the documentation team can set up a separate website as well. They all can share a custom theme managed by the engineering team.

Figure 7.8 Remove the data: reusable themes make some jobs like sharing only a piece of the website simple. Alex persuades the marketing team to try this lightweight approach.

7.5 *Powering up with content views*

With a theme, we get access to multiple content types. We already saw how content types can automatically map to section names. A content type also can have content views. *Content views* are partial layouts rendered inline in another layout. Creating these is similar to creating a layout. To understand the problem content views solve, navigate to the public category page on the Acme Corporation website (http://localhost:1313/categories/public/). It contains three pages: Circle, Curve, and Shaper. Although Circle and Curve come from the website's blog section, the Shaper page comes from the news section. The news section looks different from the blog section of the website and has a separate template. But the taxonomy template is shared between these sections.

Content views are subtemplates that we can render from inside another template. We need to move the card view, themes/AcmeTheme/layouts/partials/card.html, to the default entry for the card template, themes/AcmeTheme/layouts/_default/card.html. Listing 7.22 shows how we can call this template in all referring pages via the `Page` `.Render` function. Note that in the following listing, you will need to make this change to theme/AcmeTheme/layouts/_default/taxonomy.html, theme/AcmeTheme/layouts/_default/list.html, theme/AcmeTheme/layouts/blog/single.html, and theme/AcmeTheme/layouts/_default/index.html.

Listing 7.22 Rendering the card view via a content view instead of a partial

```
{{.Render "card"}}
```

Now we can create card.html for the news section, which is different from a regular card and can uniquely identify that section (figure 7.9). Note that we will create a different content type for the News pages to map to the news section automatically.

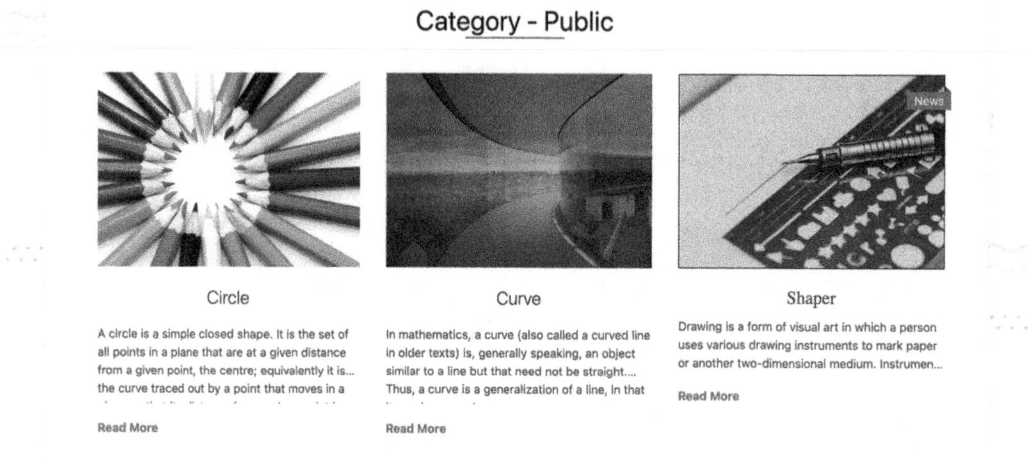

Category - Public

Circle

A circle is a simple closed shape. It is the set of all points in a plane that are at a given distance from a given point, the centre; equivalently it is... the curve traced out by a point that moves in a

Read More

Curve

In mathematics, a curve (also called a curved line in older texts) is, generally speaking, an object similar to a line but that need not be straight.... Thus, a curve is a generalization of a line, in that

Read More

Shaper

Drawing is a form of visual art in which a person uses various drawing instruments to mark paper or another two-dimensional medium. Instrumen...

Read More

Figure 7.9   The `public` **category page with a different card view for the news section, which contains a badge to highlight it. (Images by PublicDomainPictures, Free-Photos, and tookapic on Pixabay.)**

We can decide not to override any other layouts and leave those to use the default layout (https://github.com/hugoinaction/hugoinaction/tree/chapter-07-resources/08). The following listing adds a badge to news posts in the news specific card.html. With these changes, the news section should be easily identifiable everywhere as a card.

Listing 7.23   Adding a badge to news posts

```
<li class="post news-item">    ⟵—— Adds the news-item class
  <div class="badge">          Adds a badge for the
    News                       news summaries
  </div>
  ...
</li>
```

CODE CHECKPOINT   https://chapter-07-18.hugoinaction.com, and source code: https://github.com/hugoinaction/hugoinaction/tree/chapter-07-18.

Exercise 7.5

Which of the following are features of content views? (Select all that apply.)

  a. Content views are not cached and generated each time the view is used.
  b. Content views allow arbitrary arguments to be passed to the content.
  c. Content views are rendered in the same context as the parent layout.
  d. Content views can be rendered from within another layout.
  e. Content views can be overridden based on the content type.
  f. Content views can be overridden based on the layout.

Creating a theme is a significant accomplishment in a developer's journey into Hugo. A theme author masters the Go template language and understands the critical principles of laying out content and the internal features that ensure outstanding performance in a Hugo-based website. Theme authors can map any content to a website and effectively use all the power and flexibility provided by Hugo.

Summary

- We can use layouts to order different content within the same content type.
- The cascade option in the front matter allows us to share front matter properties with all pages in a branch bundle.
- The templates single.html and list.html are essential in completing a Hugo theme. They correspond to leaf bundles (or individual pages) and branch bundles, respectively.
- The index.html, taxonomy.html, and terms.html files default to list.html if any of those files are not present.
- The files taxonomy.html and terms.html provide fine-grain control over the website taxonomy.
- A Hugo theme is a collection of templates, shortcodes, assets, and other resources to render a website when provided in the content folder.
- As template authors, we should aim to create a template that can render with an arbitrary content folder. All features should be opt-in and provide sensible defaults.
- Content views are subtemplates that render in another template. They act as more flexible replacements for partials, which override content types.

Hugo Modules:
Plugins for everybody

This chapter covers

- Using Hugo Modules for distributing and using themes
- Adding dependencies in a theme or a website with Hugo Modules
- Embedding template plugins to get reusable Go template code
- Including plugins that provide configurable content

In this chapter, we will set up and utilize Hugo Modules—one of the most powerful, underrated, and underutilized features of Hugo. We have worked in isolation so far and have an independent website with no external dependency. That's an incredible feat to have in modern-day software. Lots of poorly maintained dependencies make managing software difficult. That does not mean that we should always build our website as a monolith. There are immense advantages of splitting our site into modules that can work independently. We can then reuse the theme across multiple sites. Shortcodes, debugging utilities, and certain types of content can have a life of their own.

The desire to have a low number of dependencies should not be a goal in itself. Some dependencies provide so much that it would be foolish not to use them. If we write the same code that we would have gotten by adding a dependency, it might be a waste of effort. Our custom utilities might fall short both in features and maintainability rather than well-architected and maintained external libraries. There is a tradeoff between doing it yourself versus importing third-party code. Suppose we want to split our code into modules for reuse across multiple websites or have dependencies external to our custom code that's created and managed by someone else. In that case, Hugo provides the means to manage this effectively via Hugo Modules.

Hugo Modules have been integrated tightly into Hugo, and all Hugo features are tuned to work better with Hugo Modules. With Hugo Modules, we can manage the versions of our theme better. We can move our shortcodes out for use across multiple websites, or we can pick up some built by the community to drop into our website. We may need some content across numerous websites, but copy and pasting across projects becomes a nightmare when the need to update it arises. Although, logically, Hugo creates one folder with everything needed to set up a website that is provided in the template code, physically, the files could be re-sent across various repositories that Hugo assembles for us to use (see figure 8.1).

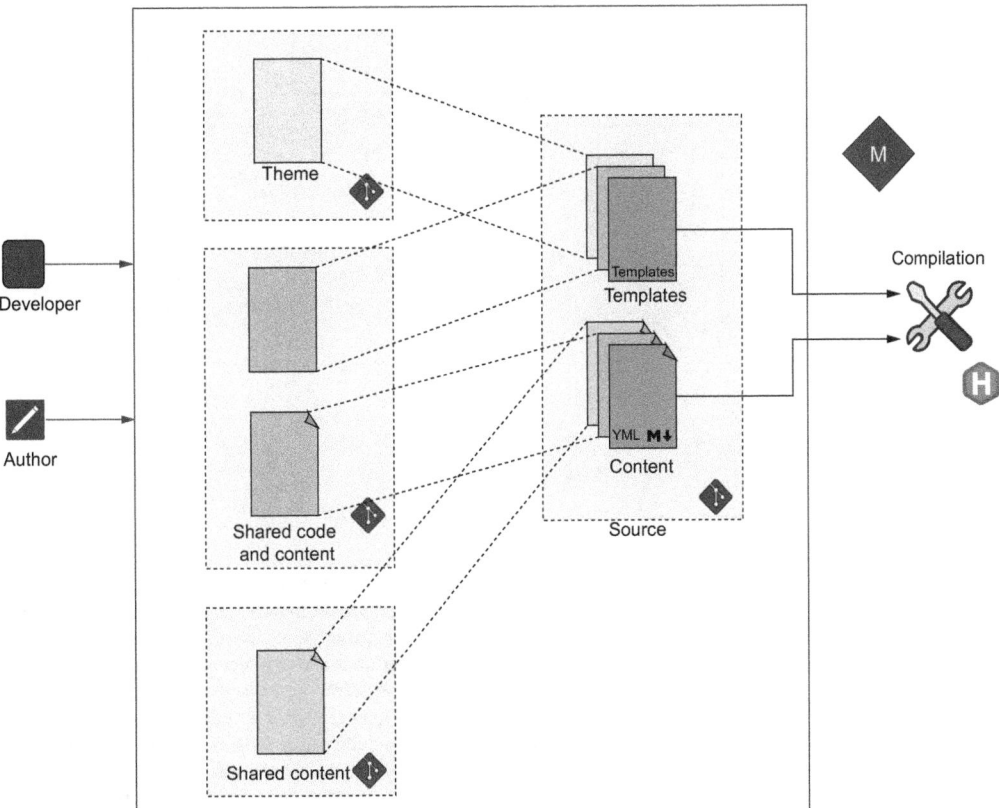

Figure 8.1 In this chapter, we separate our code into modules used by Hugo to create a logical structure with co-located files for our template code to use. In contrast, physically, this code may be present in independent repositories.

In this chapter, we will utilize Hugo Modules to import themes to our website. *Hugo Modules* are the parts of a Hugo website (including any of the folders) that are available as a reusable component. We will move AcmeTheme into a module that we can reuse across multiple websites. We will add the ability to load CSS and JS files dynamically through sources not set up as Hugo Modules. We will also include debugging utilities as an external Hugo Module and showcase how we can externalize website content by moving our Terms of Use and Privacy Policy pages to an external module that can reuse the base content of these pages across multiple websites. Figure 8.2 provides the structure of our website when we reach the end of this chapter.

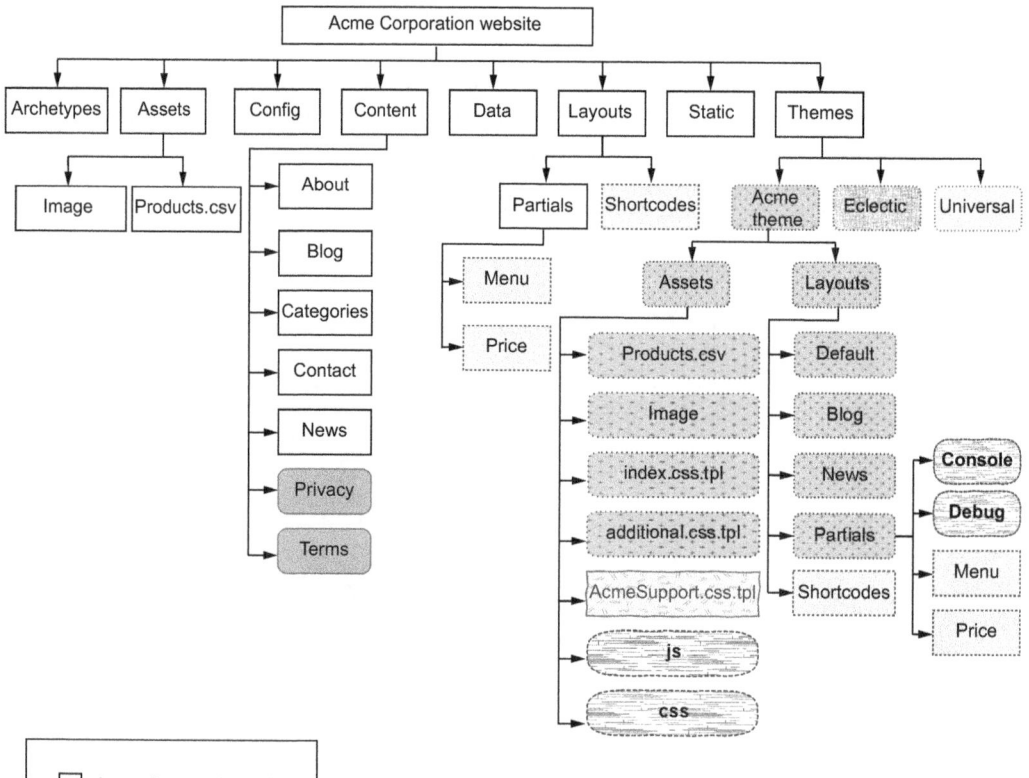

Figure 8.2   Modular structure of the Acme Corporation website that we will set up in this chapter. The Acme Corporation website will include multiple modules: AcmeTheme/Eclectic/Universal as themes; AcmeCommon for shortcodes and partials shared between the AcmeTheme and the Acme Corporation website; AcmeSupport for assets that we need to progress through in this book; hugo-debug-utils with the debug bar; and the TermsAndPrivacy module, where the content files shared between multiple websites are present. Note that this figure does not include all files, just a representative list to understand the actual filesystem used when including the modules for rendering.

8.1   Setting up Hugo Modules

Hugo Modules have a dependency on Go. You can install Go using your package manager or using the instructions at https://golang.org/doc/install. Remember that Go needs to be present in the system path to be usable by Hugo.

To verify if Go is available, run the command `go version`, which outputs the version of Go in the console. Ensure that the version of Go is greater than 1.12. Once we have a supported version of Go installed, we can forget about Go and get back to Hugo. This installation is all that we will deal with in the Go language for the entire book.

> **NOTE**   Having Go installed is essential to complete the exercises in the rest of the book. We will use Hugo Modules in the second half of the book.

The next step is to initialize Hugo Modules. Each Hugo module needs a module name. This name identifies the module. The module name is used only in the context of Hugo Modules. To initialize a module named AcmeCorporationWebsite, on the command line, run the command in the following listing.

Listing 8.1   Hugo command to create a new module

```
hugo mod init AcmeCorporationWebsite
```

This command creates a file called go.mod in the root folder. Each module has a go.mod file. This file is the entry point for Hugo Modules. It identifies the current module and stores the information about the other modules that this module links to. This file is similar in concept to Gemfile in Ruby, package.json in Node.js, and requirements.txt in Python's pip. It lists the dependencies and their versions that we can use during installation and update. We can use this file to scan the list of direct dependencies. We should check this file into version control, and in most cases in the Hugo world, we do not modify it manually.

Exercise 8.1
True or False: If we are developing a single website, there are no advantages to Hugo Modules.

Why go.mod when we have config.yaml
Hugo Modules is a unique feature in Hugo in many respects. Go needs to be installed, it has an extra initialization command, and a separate go.mod file. This separation is necessary because Hugo Modules is a lightweight wrapper over Go modules. If instead of `hugo mod init` you called `go mod init`, you would find that it behaves the same. Hugo chose the Go modules as the basis for its module system for a variety of reasons:

(continued)

- *It is a high performance, well maintained, highly flexible feature with sensible defaults.* You can link to anything from an individual file in a server repository to a folder from another module.
- *Hugo is built using Go.* This does not add a new maintainability risk (remember from section 2.5.2, every dependency can require additional maintenance) to the websites using Hugo.
- *Writing and maintaining a module system that involves managing dependencies downloaded from the internet is hard.* Apart from performance, security is a big concern. By wrapping Go modules, the Hugo team gets a powerful feature at a low cost.
- *The standard go.mod file has its advantages.* Auditors inspecting Hugo websites need one file, and vulnerability detection systems are much more likely to support the Go language than the Hugo web development framework.

Hugo's team has built some clever optimizations and tight integration into Hugo Modules. Even if you are a Go developer familiar with Go modules, Hugo Modules provides many great surprises. Hugo has personalized the Go modules by automatically filling go.mod with custom mappings for folder locations and with the ability to pick and choose plugin types. For Hugo developers, go.mod is a machine-generated file in most cases. Like the resources folder, go.mod does not need to be touched manually; just check it in with the source code. Hugo can figure out the dependencies using the configuration and create go.mod files automatically.

8.2   *Themes as Hugo Modules*

Themes are the most common shared element across multiple websites. They are the most common use case for Hugo Modules. In section 2.2, where we introduced the concept of themes, we discussed three ways to integrate themes into a website: download and copy (which we have used so far), Git submodules (not recommended anymore), and Hugo Modules (which we did not use because download and copy is easier for beginners). We used download and copy because it is easy to get started with, but it has some downsides:

- *Updates*—Distributing a theme's updates is painful. Everyone keeps a copy of the theme. Updating is a manual operation as you need to download a new version. There is no intuitive way to know of a new release, and developers are free to modify their local copies, making updates even harder.
- *Dependencies*—Although we hardcoded all our CSS and JavaScript files in the AcmeTheme module so far, it is rare to have an independent website. Chances are high that a theme might depend on a JavaScript or CSS library maintained elsewhere. If that library is downloaded and copied into the theme, then updating is also manual.
- *Size and sharing*—Keeping a copy of the theme bloats the size of our code repository. Sharing an enormous repository can be clunky. The code present in the theme can also botch a reporting build. Automated tools that modify the codebase can mess up with bundled themes, causing confusion and a waste of resources.

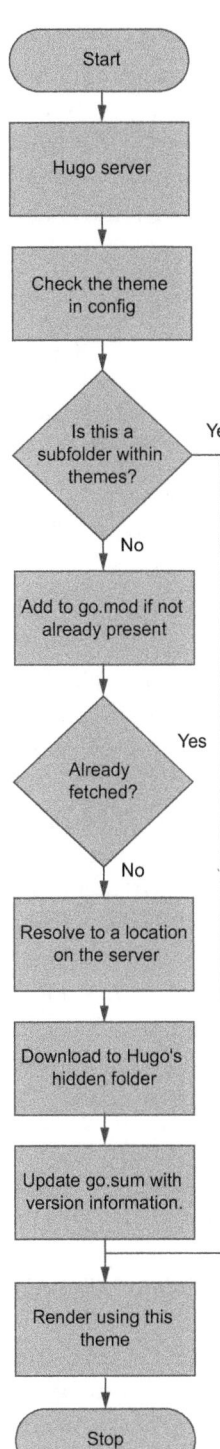

These problems are primarily caused by copying the theme's source code rather than linking to it. Linking is a much cleaner solution than downloading and copying. If we need a backup of a repository, a linked fork (copy of a Git repository that can have links to the original code) or an external archive is a much better idea than a bundled copy of the resource. That way, we make it easy to get dependencies and also to share the theme across websites.

8.3   *Importing themes*

Once we have enabled Hugo Modules, we can come back to config.yaml to manage it. If the theme is available as a Git repository on GitHub (as is the case with most Hugo themes), Hugo can do the job of fetching and setting it up for us automatically. We will be testing the waters by first importing Eclectic via Hugo Modules and then move to AcmeTheme after that. Unlike downloading the theme manually from GitHub and placing it in the themes folder, we can put `github.com/hugoinaction/Eclectic` in the theme configuration setting as listing 8.2 shows, and Hugo will do the downloading for us.

NOTE If you are working offline, read along to section 8.7, where we get back to using the theme locally, discussing how we can achieve that for other dependencies.

Listing 8.2   Adding a theme via Hugo Modules

theme: `github.com/hugoinaction/Eclectic`

That's it. The next time we run `hugo server` or push to GitHub pages or to Netlify, Hugo automatically fetches the Eclectic theme from the internet and uses that to render our website. When we run `hugo server` after linking to a GitHub repository, many things happen (see figure 8.3):

- In the background, Hugo figures out and installs the correct version of the dependency. Hugo also caches this locally for subsequent runs.
- The go.mod file is updated with the direct list of dependencies on the website.
- A new file called go.sum is created, ensuring that Hugo will fetch the correct version of the dependency specified in the go.mod file. Like Gemfile.lock in Ruby and package-lock.json in the Node.js world, this file ensures consistency and reproducibility of the build by listing exact versions of all direct and indirect dependencies.

Figure 8.3   Activities happening at launch when we load the Hugo development server with a Hugo Modules-based theme

You can push the AcmeTheme folder to a new GitHub repository and use that as the location to load the theme. You do not need to initialize the AcmeTheme repository as a new Hugo module or add any code to use it. If you specify a dependency as a theme in the configuration file, config/_default/config.yaml, there is nothing else that Hugo needs. A theme can have a go.mod file to specify its dependencies, but it is not required. Hugo will honor it if such a file exists. Hugo will read the theme if no such file exists.

> **CODE CHECKPOINT**   https://chapter-08-01.hugoinaction.com, and source code: https://github.com/hugoinaction/hugoinaction/tree/chapter-08-01.

8.4   *Enabling themes other than Eclectic*

Adding a theme to a Hugo website is as simple as replacing the URL in config.yaml, but this may not always work. Theme switching can fail for a couple of reasons:

- Some themes require unique settings in the configuration to be usable.
- The website may be dependent on shortcodes that are not available in a different theme. Hugo will fail to compile in case of a missing shortcode.

Whereas a theme causes the first reason, the content creators can unknowingly cause the second. When we moved the layouts folder to AcmeTheme, we also moved the shortcodes that our website depends on. Although those shortcodes were available in Eclectic, they are not present in other themes like Universal. Therefore, if you take the source code at checkpoint 08-1 and try to replace the theme with any other that you find in the Hugo themes showcase, it will fail to build.

To keep the content independent of the theme, we need to have a copy of all the shortcodes used in the website, bundled in its codebase or loaded module (we will do this in section 8.10). To allow other themes, we will keep a copy of the partial and the shortcode folders in the core website. Copy the two folders from the themes/AcmeTheme/layouts folder to the top-level layouts folder. Then you can use a different theme (like Universal) with the website by providing the GitHub path of the theme (for example, github .com/hugoinaction/Universal) in the theme section of the configuration. Note that because we got rid of the home page and have not configured the home page in Universal, the home page will be mostly blank at this point.

> **CODE CHECKPOINT**   https://chapter-08-02.hugoinaction.com, and source code: https://github.com/hugoinaction/hugoinaction/tree/chapter-08-02.

8.5   *Getting a specific version of a theme*

Hugo Modules has support for versions via Git tags. This allows us to link to a different version of our dependencies rather than what is the latest mainline. In many projects, *mainline* is under active development and unstable when a release version is marked separately. We will switch back to AcmeTheme with Hugo Modules. A copy of the AcmeTheme is on GitHub in the github.com/hugoinaction/AcmeTheme folder, tagged with version 0.8.0 for its contents through section 8.5 (this section) of the book.

NOTE Do not use the main branch of the Acme repository on GitHub because it points to the AcmeTheme module at the end of this book.

To get a specific version of a theme, we need to specify the theme as we did before, but instead of telling Hugo to automatically fetch the latest version via `hugo server`, we will manually tell Hugo the version to fetch. Let's start by changing our theme to the hosted AcmeTheme repository in our configuration as the following listing shows.

Listing 8.3   Switching to the AcmeTheme repository (config/_default/config.yaml)

```
theme: github.com/hugoinaction/AcmeTheme
```

NOTE The live server should not be running when updating to AcmeTheme, and we should not call `hugo server` at this point. It will lead to the installation of the main branch of AcmeTheme.

Next, we need to install the theme from the `v0.8.0` tag. There are two ways to do this: adding an entry to the go.mod file manually or running the installation command from the command line. The `hugo mod` subcommands are associated with Hugo Modules, which provide access to the management features related to Hugo Modules. We use `hugo mod init` to define a new module that makes up our website. The `hugo mod get` command fetches the module-based dependencies manually. The `-u` command-line flag overwrites the existing entry in go.mod if present. The following listing adds an entry to the go.mod file for the v0.8.0 version.

Listing 8.4   Adding a specific version of AcmeTheme

```
hugo mod get -u github.com/hugoinaction/AcmeTheme@v0.8.0
```

With this command, you should see require `github.com/hugoinaction/AcmeTheme v0.8.0 // indirect` in your go.mod file. The checksum file, go.sum, should also include "v0.8.0" as the installed version of the AcmeTheme dependency.

We can continue to use our website with AcmeTheme linked as a module in Hugo. We have completely moved off Eclectic with this change and have taken over complete control of the Acme Corporation website with every piece of code in our possession. We will not be using Eclectic or Universal in the rest of this book. We can remove the entries that were specific to these themes in the configuration (except for the color and the copyright in config/_default/params.yaml), as well delete the assets/image/background.svg, assets/image/logo.svg, content/data-driven.md, static/image/*, and static/favicon.ico files, which we do not use in the theme Acme. We can delete the themes/AcmeTheme folder if we want to, and the website will still continue to function.

CODE CHECKPOINT   https://chapter-08-03.hugoinaction.com, and source code: https://github.com/hugoinaction/hugoinaction/tree/chapter-08-03.

8.6   *Viewing the dependencies source code*

By moving to Hugo Modules, we lost the ability to inspect the source code of the dependencies. Also, because dependencies are not a part of the website's source code, our website will need internet access to be compiled. Internet dependency may turn out to be a limitation in certain use cases. If we archive our website for long-term storage, backing up a copy of the dependencies is as important as backing up the source code.

To perform this task, we can run `hugo mod vendor`. Hugo creates a folder called vendor with the source code of all the dependencies. Not only that, if this folder is present and contains the dependencies, Hugo does not go to the internet to build our website. We can check in this folder, just like the resources folder, with our source code.

> **Why not vendor by default?**
> Hugo's decision not to have the vendor folder present by default provides better efficiency. Hugo can download it only once and share it across multiple projects if two projects use the same module. Also, keeping the dependencies hidden ensures that we follow the development practices of not modifying the dependencies and getting the changes done through official means (updating the dependency version). In-place hot patches in dependencies have a high possibility of being missed in a commit to source control, leading to broken builds.

CODE CHECKPOINT   https://chapter-08-04.hugoinaction.com, and source code: https://github.com/hugoinaction/hugoinaction/tree/chapter-08-04.

8.7   *Modifying dependencies locally*

We can change the contents of the _vendor folder and view the changes live in Hugo, but this is a bad practice. The next time we update a dependency, our changes will get overridden. Pushing every commit to the theme repository can also be tiresome. Hugo has a mechanism to provide a local version of a hosted dependency for local development. We need to set up the dependency (the AcmeTheme in this case) as a Hugo module to enable this. To perform this task, go to the theme folder and run the following command:

```
hugo mod init AcmeTheme          Initializes the module with
                                 the name AcmeTheme
```

This command creates a go.mod file in the theme's folder. With this change, the module system can read the AcmeTheme as more than a folder, but as a proper Hugo module. Next, we can provide the path to this module in go.mod for the Acme Corporation website using the `replace` directive under the `require` call as the following listing shows.

```
module AcmeCorporationWebsite

...

replace github.com/hugoinaction/AcmeTheme =>
  <Absolute or relative path to the theme>.
```

With this `replace` directive, we can easily continue developing locally in an independent repository and still refer to it using Hugo Modules. In the code samples present with this book, we will use the AcmeTheme folder in the code repository to host the theme. Only the final version of the theme (at the end of the book) is pushed to the github.com/hugoinaction/Acme folder. Because the _vendor folder is present, the `replace` directive will not take effect until we delete the _vendor folder, which has higher precedence. We should use the _vendor folder for archiving and not development. Although it is good to use this when the theme does not change (only the content changes), it is a hindrance when we develop the theme, so we will delete it.

We have created a new module we plan to use outside of the Acme Corporation website. It is a good idea to declare its requirements so other places can import it. Hugo's package management needs two files: the go.mod and the config. The go.mod file lists dependencies, and the config file provides configuration and package information.

Because AcmeTheme does not have a colossal configuration yet, a config folder will be overkill. We will place a simple config.yaml in the theme's folder (https://github.com/hugoinaction/hugoinaction/tree/chapter-08-resources/01). In the configuration, we can specify the minimum and maximum versions of Hugo that this specific module depends on and whether Hugo extended is needed. Although it is not required, it is a good idea to specify a minimum version of Hugo that the theme needs. We do this in the following listing.

```
module:
  hugoVersion:
    min: 0.91.2
```

CODE CHECKPOINT https://chapter-08-05.hugoinaction.com, and source code: https://github.com/hugoinaction/hugoinaction/tree/chapter-08-05.

8.8 *Adding nested dependencies*

With Hugo Modules so far, we have been able to load the theme dynamically and provide some level of checks (like the minimum Hugo version needed) for the theme to be used correctly. The main power of Hugo Modules is the ability for the theme to have its own dependencies, which we will use now. Because turning a theme into a Hugo module makes it possible for theme-specific dependencies, these will be pulled into the website when installing the theme. In Hugo, we can have various module dependencies from templates and content to JavaScript and CSS.

We can mount dependencies from any folder in a dependency to any location in our website. Hugo Modules coupled with Hugo Pipes can act as a lightweight bundler for linking to and bringing in resources (for example, themes, layouts, assets, content) for our website as an alternative to the npm plus webpack ecosystem in JavaScript or to RubyGems Sprockets in Ruby/Rails. Unlike asset systems that force content to mount to a specific folder (for example, node_modules in JavaScript), Hugo Modules can map to anywhere in its filesystem. We can import the asset template files (*.css.tpl) into the assets folder to use them on the website.

Additional support files are present in the github.com/hugoinaction/AcmeSupport repository, so we will import those via Hugo Modules. For offline usage, the chapter resources for chapter 8 also contain the contents of this repository that we can import using the `replace` directive previously described (https://github.com/hugoinaction/ hugoinaction/tree/chapter-08-resources/02).

First, we need to add a dependency to the AcmeSupport repository. By default, Hugo imports all dependencies into the themes folder. Because themes are the most common dependency, this default allows us to import a theme by specifying a GitHub location as described in section 8.3.

Hugo mounts all modules in the /themes folder by default. The AcmeSupport repository consists of CSS template files. Therefore, we need to manually override the default location where this dependency is mounted. Hugo allows us to specify mount points in the source as well as the target repository.

The AcmeSupport repository is not a Hugo module; there is no go.mod file in it. Still, we can import it successfully. To specify its mount points, we can go in to the configuration of the integrating repository (the AcmeTheme codebase) and specify the mount points in the module section as the following listing shows. We will mount the assets folder (the source name can be anything) to the assets folder (the destination name, needs to be `assets`) in the theme repository.

> **Listing 8.7   Mounting the AcmeSupport repository (AcmeTheme/config.yaml)**

```
module:
  ...
  imports:
    path: github.com/hugoinaction/AcmeSupport
    mounts:
      - source: assets
        target: assets
```

CODE CHECKPOINT   https://chapter-08-06.hugoinaction.com, and source code: https://github.com/hugoinaction/hugoinaction/tree/chapter-08-06.

If you remember from chapter 6, we used Hugo Pipes to merge the *.css.tpl file into the CSS file used in the website. The newly added css.tpl files are automatically included with the changes we previously made and are used on the website. This CSS file (added in the AcmeSupport repository) reverses the order of the image and the text on the home page as shown in figure 8.4. The image goes to the right and the content to the left. We can use this to verify that the module is loading as expected.

Figure 8.3 Swapped image and content on the home page with AcmeSupport

If we run `hugo mod vendor` at the root (the Acme Corporation repository), Hugo creates the AcmeSupport folder in the _vendor/github.com/hugoinaction folder, which now contains the contents of the Git repository. Hugo also updates the go.sum file for the Acme Corporation website with this dependency. The go.sum file tracks dependencies as well as subdependencies used in the project. If we want to audit the dependencies of a website, the go.sum file is the right place to look.

> **Exercise 8.2**
> What information is present in the go.mod file? (Select all that apply.)
>
> **a.** Name of the module
> **b.** Version of Hugo used to create the module
> **c.** List of dependencies (both direct and indirect) of the website
> **d.** Exact hashes of each website dependency
> **e.** Mount paths for various folders in the repository

We can mount as many subfolders as we desire because the `mounts` option in the configuration file takes a list of source and target mount locations. This option allows us to import our JavaScript and CSS dependencies without needing the originating repositories to be set up as Hugo Modules or to even understand Hugo as a concept, which opens up the entire internet as a source of content for a Hugo website. Popular

JavaScript/CSS libraries like Bootstrap (https://getbootstrap.com), jQuery (https://jquery.com), etc., can be linked via this method. We could also link icon packs like FontAwesome (https://fontawesome.com) or SCSS toolkits like Bourbon (https://www.bourbon.io).

> **NOTE** Even if you plan to use the theme for a single website, using Hugo Modules provides the ability to link to dependencies outside of the theme. Linking through modules instead of copying offers the benefit of updating the dependency quickly and tracking the ownership of pieces of code better. We can also have subdependencies, which makes this very flexible.

8.9   *Modules as template plugins*

We can share Hugo's template code in the form of partials across multiple themes. These shared partials can act as plugins that wrap reusable functions. One module that can be useful when developing Hugo templates is the Hugo debug utilities, which provide the debug button we used with the Eclectic theme. We will add this module to the AcmeTheme module to be made available for all websites using this theme.

To use this module, we will import it in the config.yaml for AcmeTheme (https://github.com/hugoinaction/hugoinaction/tree/chapter-08-resources/03). Hugo supports a single module and a list in the `module: imports` section in the configuration. Because we already have a module, we will need to convert `module: imports` into a list to get multiple modules as the following listing shows.

Listing 8.8   Importing the debug utilities (AcmeTheme/config.yaml)

```
module:
  . . .
  imports:
    . . .
    - path: github.com/hugoinaction/hugo-debug-utils
```

Note that the Hugo debug utilities are already initialized as a Hugo module and provide its mounts internally. Therefore, we do not need to set the mounts for this module manually. We can start using this module in our code after inclusion. A copy of the Hugo debug utilities is also available in the chapter resources (https://github.com/hugoinaction/hugoinaction/tree/chapter-08-resources/04). In the base template, layouts/_default/baseof.html, we can add the code in the following listing to load the debug bar after defining the footer block.

Listing 8.9   Adding the debug bar (AcmeTheme/layouts/_default/baseof.html)

```
{{if not hugo.IsProduction}}          ◁──   Do not load this in production mode.
  {{ partial "debug/debug.html"              Alternatively, we can use if site.IsServer
     (dict "context" .) }}                    to check if we are in live reload mode.
{{end}}
Loads the debug partial
```

CODE CHECKPOINT   https://chapter-08-07.hugoinaction.com, and source code: https://github.com/hugoinaction/hugoinaction/tree/chapter-08-07.

If we run the live server mode by issuing `hugo server` on the command line, the module is downloaded automatically, added to the go.mod and go.sum files, and the debug button should show up. Hugo Modules makes isolating Hugo dependencies simple. To understand how this works, we can take a look at the config.yaml file present in the hugo-debug-utils modules using this code:

```yaml
module:
  mounts:
    - source: debug-bar/template
      target: layouts/partials/debug
    - source: debug-bar/css
      target: assets/css
    - source: debug-bar/js
      target: assets/js
    - source: console
      target: layouts/partials/console
```

The mounts for this module, including the JavaScript, CSS, and the partial, are specified in its configuration. The corresponding files are placed in the correct virtual locations by Hugo during website compilation.

The Hugo debug utilities also come with a `console` partial that we can use to log any Hugo variable in the browser's JavaScript console. This is extremely useful when developing templates. Say that we want to know the value of an expression. We can pass this to the `console` partial, and the value of the expression will be made available in the browser console. The following listing allows us to view the front matter parameters passed to the page (use AcmeTheme/layouts/_default/baseof.html to make these changes).

NOTE   You should only add the code in the following listing when debugging.

Listing 8.10   Passing debugging parameters the browser console

```
{{ partial "console" .Params }}
```

8.10   *Shared dependencies across the theme and website*

We copied over the partial and shortcodes into the Acme Corporation website from the AcmeTheme module to be portable across themes. That led to duplication of content, which makes it difficult to maintain. We can potentially remove the shortcodes from the theme, but the partials are needed for both the theme and for the website to function. They need to live in the theme, so that it is reusable across websites, and in the website, so we can switch themes. This dependency is the perfect use case for moving to a separate module.

We can create a new module called AcmeCommon and move shared resources needed by both the Acme Corporation website and AcmeTheme. We set up the data in the folder github.com/hugoinaction/AcmeCommon (https://github.com/hugo-inaction/hugoinaction/tree/chapter-08-resources/05). Using this shared repository in the theme and the website is an exercise for the reader. The reader should remove the shared layouts present in this repository from both repositories. You can browse the code at the code checkpoint ch08-8 to see this in action.

Versions and shared dependencies

If a Hugo-based website finds a dependency in two places, Hugo integrates only one version of the dependency even if different minor versions are present in various sources. Bundling multiple versions of a dependency is wasteful, increases bloat, and can make Hugo's caching and, thereby, its performance suffer. Hugo expects its module developers to follow the Semver guidelines (https://semver.org/) and to introduce only breaking changes in a new major build.

Hugo can use multiple versions of a dependency (for example, 1.0 and 2.0 are major version changes, and 1.2 and 1.3 are not). *It is strongly advised to remove this duplication to improve performance, disk utilization, and safety.* This prevents unknown vulnerabilities from using unsupported older versions of dependencies.

CODE CHECKPOINT   https://chapter-08-08.hugoinaction.com, and source code: https://github.com/hugoinaction/hugoinaction/tree/chapter-08-08.

NOTE   Hugo does not add the AcmeCommon module to the go.mod file of the Acme Corporation website even though it is present in the configuration. Because there can be only one AcmeCommon, there was no point in adding it twice. Hugo adds AcmeCommon to go.mod automatically when we switch to a different theme.

8.11   *Content plugins*

Template plugins are useful abstractions over template code that we can reuse. Hugo Modules also allows us to have content plugins that can package content that we can reuse across multiple websites.

One example of content shareable across numerous websites is the Terms of Use and the Privacy Policy pages. Websites from the same company share the same Terms of Use page. We can move this page to an independent module and import it across all company websites for reuse. The page can use the built-in `param` function to access site parameters from the configuration and can also bundle shortcodes to provide standardized data across the multiple websites.

We need the same Terms of Use and the Privacy Policy pages across all websites under the Acme umbrella. The Terms of Use and the Privacy Policy pages for the Acme Corporation website are also present in the repository in github.com/hugoinaction/TermsAndPrivacy (https://github.com/hugoinaction/hugoinaction/tree/chapter-08-resources/06). The menu entries are in the front matter, and the hardcoded data values, which can differ across various websites, are replaced with the `param` shortcode (for example, `{{< param "TermsAndPrivacy.company_name" >}}` for the company name). Performing these changes has been left as an exercise for the reader.

Figure 8.4 Months of work: Bob faces the brunt of the angry marketing head for not having a central place to keep the Terms of Use and Privacy Policy pages, which puts the marketing campaign at risk legally with the older Terms of Use.

We will integrate a plugin into the Acme Corporation website (and not the Acme Corporation theme) and configure it to get rid of our hardcoded Terms of Use and Privacy Policy pages. To integrate this plugin into the Acme Corporation website, we will need to perform the following steps.

1 Delete the terms.md and the privacy.md pages.
2 Update the module.yaml file in the config/_default folder with the contents in the following listing (https://github.com/hugoinaction/hugoinaction/tree/chapter-08-resources/07).

Listing 8.11 Adding a new dependency (config/_default/module.yaml)

```
imports:
  - path: github.com/hugoinaction/TermsAndPrivacy
  . . .
```

3 Add the terms and privacy parameters to the configuration for the TermsAndPrivacy repository as the following listing shows.

Listing 8.12 Adding the parameters (config/_default/params.yaml)

```
TermsAndPrivacy:
  company_name: Acme Corporation
  contact_email: contact@example.org
  website: https://hugoinaction.com
  contact_dpo_email: dpo@hugoinaction.com
  contact_dpo_phone: 9999999999
```

4 Add the menu file to bring back the footer menu entries as the following listing shows.

Listing 8.13   Restoring the footer entries (config/_default/menu.yaml)

```
footer:
  - name: Privacy Policy
    weight: 300
    url: /privacy
  - name: Terms of Use
    weight: 200
    url: /terms
```

CODE CHECKPOINT   https://chapter-08-09.hugoinaction.com, and source code: https://github.com/hugoinaction/hugoinaction/tree/chapter-08-09.

The Privacy Policy and the Terms of Use pages load from a shared content module with these changes. This module is generic, and you are free to use this for your own websites outside of Acme Corporation and *Hugo in Action*.

Exercise 8.3

Which of the following is an accurate statement about a content plugin? (Select all that apply.)

a. A content plugin creates a link to the shared content in the generated website.

b. A content plugin cannot have template code.

c. A content plugin can be used to set up access control on the content by splitting each area into a separate repository.

d. A content plugin moves the common content into a separate repository for one place of access.

8.12 *Commonly used Hugo Modules APIs*

Running hugo mod provides a great variety of subcommands that are useful in managing modules in our daily life. For example,

- hugo mod tidy—Removes unused entries from the go.sum and go.mod files (like getting rid of Eclectic).
- hug mod clean—Clears the module cache to pick up newer changes (if done locally). Sometimes, the local store may get corrupt, giving us incorrect data.
- hugo mod graph—Shows the list of dependencies of the current website or module. Understanding go.sum can be challenging, but hugo mod graph makes this file human-readable.
- hugo mod get -u—Updates all modules.
- {hugo mod get -u ./...}—Updates all modules and their dependencies.
- hugo mod get <module>@<version>—Gets a specific version of a module.

Remember that we added the Eclectic theme as a module to try it out when we started with Hugo Modules. It is still present in go.mod and go.sum. It is costing us the needless waste of bandwidth by downloading when we are not using it. We can use hugo mod tidy to eliminate unused entries from the go.mod and go.sum files.

CODE CHECKPOINT https://chapter-08-10.hugoinaction.com, and source code: https://github.com/hugoinaction/hugoinaction/tree/chapter-08-10.

After cleaning up the dependencies, the correct dependency list can be viewed with hugo mod graph as listing 8.14 shows. This command provides a list of dependencies actively used in a Hugo website.

Exercise 8.4

True or False: Hugo Modules are automatically downloaded every time we build a Hugo-based website.

Listing 8.14 Getting the Acme Corporation website's dependency list

```
> hugo mod graph
AcmeCorporationWebsite github.com/hugoinaction/
➥ TermsAndPrivacy@v0.0.0-20200223231951-1c7c1972007a
AcmeCorporationWebsite github.com/hugoinaction/
➥ AcmeCommon@v0.0.0-20210710221623-ca55f92c01bc
AcmeCorporationWebsite github.com/hugoinaction/
➥ AcmeTheme@v0.8.0 => <path>/AcmeTheme
github.com/hugoinaction/AcmeTheme@v0.8.0 github.com/hugoinaction/
➥ AcmeSupport@v0.0.0-20210710141629-d5aef37e0e9c
github.com/hugoinaction/AcmeTheme@v0.8.0 github.com/hugoinaction/
➥ hugo-debug-utils@v0.0.0-20200427035302-d4636e5c27cf
```

TIP When running the development server, if you face errors that are unrelated to the website's code, Hugo's module cache has likely gone bad. Hugo keeps its cache in the temporary data folder so that the operating system can reclaim the space if needed. Because this data is publicly accessible, it can get corrupted, leading to weird errors. When facing such issues, the best solution is to clear the cache entirely with hugo mod clean. Hugo re-fetches the data on the next launch.

This chapter completes the first part of *Hugo in Action*. In the second part of the book, we will move out of the bounds of the fully static website and see how Hugo interacts with the rest of the Jamstack. We will continue to complete the Acme Corporation website with a contact page, a JSON-based API, a small search engine, and then create an e-commerce area in our website using Hugo. We will discover some hidden gems in the Hugo template language and its features that do a lot more than what appears on the surface as we continue to introduce and learn more Hugo features to simplify web development.

Summary

- Hugo Modules is a powerful way to manage dependencies. We can mount any folder in any Git repository at any location in our project, even if the source repository knows nothing about Hugo or Hugo Modules.
- Hugo provides the means to manage dependencies in whatever approach we desire. We can keep dependencies in the vendor folder, download them on the fly from a link, or have a local copy on disk.
- We can use Hugo Modules to create themes, template plugins, and content plugins. These plugins can mount to any location in a Hugo repository and have access to the entire template language. We can override specific files in a plugin for customization.
- Modules can depend on other modules, and we can decide to use the dependencies directly.
- Hugo makes it easy to deduplicate and have one copy of a module.

Part 2

Expanding with the Jamstack: Dynamic outside, static inside

Do static websites feel, ummm . . . too static? They don't have to. We can make them as dynamic as desired without losing the performance, maintainability, and scalability of static websites. Part 2 of *Hugo in Action* shows you how to make a static web page accept dynamic input, react to change, and remain as accessible and performant as before.

In chapter 9, we will use APIs from third-party service providers to accept user input, react to change, and provide control for the content author to build a custom form-based system without recoding the site for every form. We will also set up an API for our website, which we will pick up in chapter 10, to create a search engine. Also in chapter 10, we will use Hugo's JavaScript integration features to react better to user input. We will see firsthand how Hugo enables us to tap into the vast JavaScript ecosystem when needed, while retaining the power and performance of the static site we have built so far. We will also see how Hugo can work in a hybrid website with a single-page application embedded at an endpoint.

In chapter 11, we will build custom APIs to extend Hugo and perform tasks that are not natively available in Hugo. We will embed LaTeX's mathematical rendering system to provide full support for complex mathematical equations in a Hugo website, using an approach that retains phenomenal build and run-time performance.

In chapter 12, we will change gears and switch over to a completely different web domain. We will use the learning and the code we have created thus far to build a functional e-commerce website with complete support for shopping carts, checkout, and fulfillment of digital assets.

Chapter 13 will explore some of the advanced features of Hugo and the Jamstack, including multilingual websites and scripting-based control of all the services. We will also explore libraries such as instant page and Turbo that make our already fast website even faster.

At the end of part 2, you should be comfortable with making Hugo an integral part of your web development arsenal and using it to solve any web development problem while focusing on performance and maintainability.

Accessing APIs to enhance functionality

9

This chapter covers
- Enhancing the website using APIs
- Embedding tweets into a web page
- Creating forms using third-party APIs
- Using form APIs to create dynamic forms
- Creating a JSON-based API using Hugo's output formats

In the first half of this book, we worked on the Hugo website in isolation. This chapter involves using Hugo to get access to data from outside of our website. We will also add dynamic features and learn how the Jamstack can perform tasks requiring server intervention without sacrificing the website's performance.

In this chapter, we will focus on APIs, the *A* in Jamstack. APIs are mechanisms with which systems or components in a system can interact. A service exposes certain functionality through an API, and the client can use the API to consume it. APIs are everywhere in the web ecosystem. When a web page like https://localhost:1313/index.html is requested, the web browser sends a GET API request for /index.html from the localhost server at port 1313 using the HTTPS protocol. We can use APIs in our websites to request data processing or to access information stored on a service. For example, we can access the tweet or an Instagram image using a given ID and the HTTP-based API exposed by these services. We will learn about the various ways in which we can consume APIs and write code in a Hugo-based website to consume third-party APIs (figure 9.1). We will use Hugo to embed a tweet into our website at compile time and to create contact forms, a dynamic survey generation system, and a commenting system to embed comments into our website. We will also set up a JSON-based API for our website.

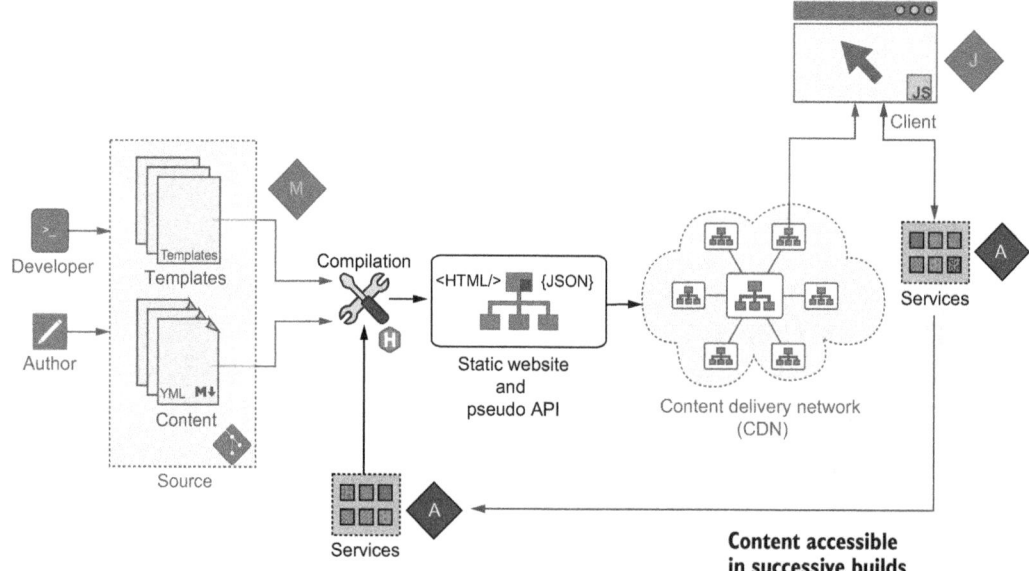

Figure 9.1   Chapter 9 focuses on the API layer of the Jamstack. We can consume APIs in Hugo at compile time from multiple services. We can also create web forms that direct their responses to services that are configured to receive them, which may feed the data back into the website on rebuilds.

9.1   *Build-time vs. run-time API access*

In most websites developed using traditional web stacks, we access third-party APIs at run time exclusively. When the user requests a web page, the server connects to various services that own the information needed to render, collects the services, and then sends them to the browser to render. There is another set of requests that come from the client. We implement these in JavaScript, which calls and assembles the data from all endpoints.

The two approaches we've discussed so far are access to an API at run time, where the user usually waits for information that needs to be filled by a spinner or a blank waiting screen, and the Jamstack-popularized processing at build time, which provides its results to all users at run time. In this case, the server requests the data when the builder (for example, Hugo) compiles the website before pushing it live. The server serves this information as-is when requested from the client statically.

We can use both build-time (or compile-time) and run-time API access inside the same website for different things, and each has its use cases. With build-time API access, the target service is called once per compilation. (Hugo offers to cache this response for a configured period, and it may not call this on every build.) This one-time compilation reduces the load on the target service and can directly save on cost. For example, many websites load maps in their contact section showing the location of their offices. Because the office location changes infrequently, we can realize massive savings by replacing the map with an image generated at compile time or one that's manually provided. The same is true when we embed specific tweets, Instagram posts, or product catalogs for a commercial website.

Apart from performance, there are other advantages for using build-time API access. When using run-time API access, we provide more information about our system to the target service than is needed. An Instagram widget provided in JavaScript leaks a lot of information about our website visitors to Instagram. Instagram can then mine all the user information and potentially share it with competitors targeting our users. Even when our server performs the API access, the load statistics leak to the API. We need to build caching for the servers to prevent this and to allow cache reuse when autoscaling (where new machines are added to the cluster dynamically). We can reuse the API response across web pages easily by compile-time API access.

Build-time API access is deterministic, testable, cheaper, and more straightforward than run-time API access. But it comes with its caveats. Updating data requires a new build to be generated and deployed. We cannot embed a running or live Twitter feed, for example. This rebuild requirement makes user-generated data, live updates, and even regular data changes harder to track. In most cases, though, the information does not change in real time. Automated continuous integration and subsecond build times (which we have with Hugo) can ease these limitations.

In Hugo websites, we can use both compile-time API access via Hugo's API access functions and run-time API access via JavaScript (more on JavaScript in chapter 10). We can use APIs provided by third parties or build our own. We can also build pseudo APIs with Hugo (see section 9.7), which act like full APIs but do not support dynamic queries to a database, and Hugo generates them while compiling.

9.2 *Embedding tweets at compile time*

In chapter 4, when introducing shortcodes, we mentioned the built-in `tweet` shortcode, which is implemented as a compile-time shortcode in Hugo. This section shows how that works and then we will replicate that functionality with compile-time API access. While Twitter provides HTML markup that we can paste into our website, there are a lot of downsides for copying and pasting that markup:

- The HTML markup embeds tweets at run time, which means an extra request goes to Twitter each time a user sees a tweet.
- The usage data for that page gets shared with Twitter.
- The design of the embedded tweet is controlled by Twitter, and we do not have a lot of customization options.

Because tweets rarely change, there is little upside to the run-time API embedding this static data. A plain copy/paste of the textual content is better than run-time access for greater performance and security. Linking allows us to have verified ownership and authenticity of the embedded content and easier access to updates if the content changes. Compile-time linking allows us to have these advantages without the downside of slow run-time access and data usage leaks.

On the home page of the Acme Corporation website are some testimonials from customers about their products. Many of the product testimonials come from social networking websites like Twitter and Facebook. While the tweet is public and embeddable via its native UI, the design of testimonials on the home page doesn't match Twitter's layout. Although we have testimonials from various sources, the home page needs to look coherent.

To embed the tweet in the format we desire, we need to get the tweet's text into a variable in Hugo. We can fetch Twitter data by accessing Twitter's public API using the getJSON function in Hugo for compile-time access. Figure 9.2 shows the tweet that we want to embed.

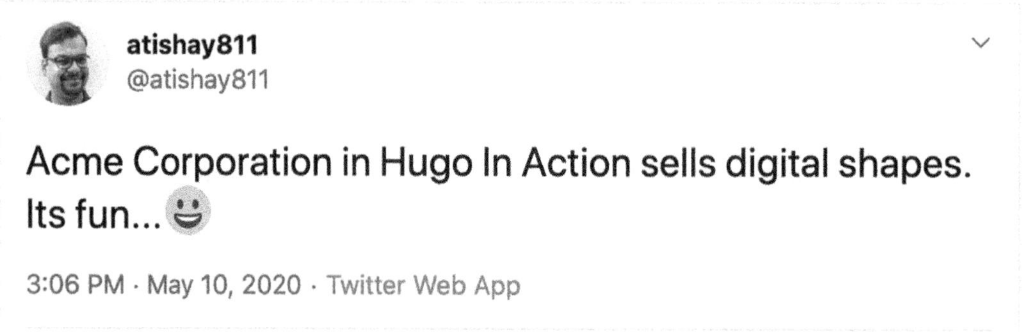

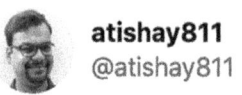

atishay811
@atishay811

Acme Corporation in Hugo In Action sells digital shapes. Its fun... 😃

3:06 PM · May 10, 2020 · Twitter Web App

Figure 9.2   The tweet to embed in the Acme Corporation website. Hugo allows us to embed tweets using both compile-time and run-time API access.

You can view the tweet online at https://twitter.com/atishay811/status/1259605801968128000. You can embed it in the Acme Corporation website using the tweet shortcode via {{<tweet user="atishay811" id="1259605801968128000">}} if you so desire.

9.2.1 Understanding the Twitter API

Twitter has a variety of JSON-based APIs to embed tweets. While most require authentication, the OEmbed API used for embedding tweets does not. The documentation for the Twitter OEmbed API is available at http://mng.bz/Ex2J. The OEmbed API takes a URL of the tweet and a bunch of options for the type of data we want to embed. By default, Twitter's widgets.js script is loaded, which renders the tweet using Twitter's CSS, and that makes it look official.

An embedded tweet supports a variety of Twitter features such as threading, embedded images, and embedded video. We don't need these because we want to style the tweet differently. We can disable images and videos by passing `hide_media` as a flag, disable threads only via `hide_thread`, and disable the widget.js JavaScript file with `omit_script`. We will also send `dnt` to tell Twitter not to track us. The following listing provides the call for the request to the Tweet API.

Listing 9.1 The Twitter OEmbed API to get a tweet

```
https://publish.twitter.com/oembed?url=
➥ https%3A%2F%2Ftwitter.com%2Fatishay%2Fstatus%2F1259605801968128000
➥ &omit_script=1&hide_media=1&hide_thread=1&dnt=true
```

You can directly open the URL in listing 9.1 in a web browser. It should return a JSON file with the tweet content, which you can download. The JSON output for the request in that listing provides the tweet metadata such as author name, author's Twitter URL, the tweet's URL, etc., along with its content. The following listing shows the metadata (beautified for readability). We will fetch this into a Hugo variable and then render the core contents.

Listing 9.2 Sample response from the Twitter OEmbed API for a tweet

```json
{
  "url": "https://twitter.com/atishay811/status/1259605801968128000",
  "author_name": "atishay811",
  "author_url": "https://twitter.com/atishay811",
  "html": "<blockquote class=\"twitter-tweet\"
➥ data-cards=\"hidden\" data-dnt=\"true\"><p lang=\"en\" dir=\"ltr\">
➥ Acme Corporation in Hugo In Action sells digital shapes. It's fun...?
➥ </p>&mdash; atishay811 (@atishay811) <a href=\"
➥ https://twitter.com/atishay811/status/1259605801968128000?
➥ ref_src=twsrc%5Etfw\">May 10, 2020</a></blockquote>\n",
  "width": 550,
  "height": null,
  "type": "rich",
  "cache_age": "3153600000",
  "provider_name": "Twitter",
  "provider_url": "https://twitter.com",
  "version": "1.0"
}
```

> ### Exercise 9.1
>
> Using compile-time API access allows us to do which of the following? (Select all that apply.)
>
> a. Provide better user performance.
> b. React to user input.
> c. Enable better tracking of users.
> d. Prevent API owners from tracking users.
> e. Enable content manipulation and reuse of data across multiple pages.

9.2.2 *Understanding Hugo's functions for compile-time API access*

To embed tweets, we need to get the API response from Twitter into Hugo. To use APIs at compile time, Hugo provides two functions, `getJSON` and `getCSV`. These methods can access any HTTP(s) service to access data delivered in JSON or CSV file formats, respectively. JSON is the most popular data interchange format on the web. At the same time, CSV can be extremely useful in reading tabular data (remember, in chapter 5, we used `resources.Get` followed by `transform.Unmarshal` to parse CSV files that provided product details). Hugo also provides `resources.GetRemote` as a generic method to fetch remote content that we will use in section 9.6.2.

Calling an HTTP service is simple. For a call to the Twitter API to fetch a specific tweet, we can use the code in the following listing.

Listing 9.3   Using `getJSON` to fetch a tweet

```
{{ $tweet := getJSON "https://publish.twitter.com/oembed?
  url=https%3A%2F%2Ftwitter.com%2Fatishay%2Fstatus%2F1259605801968128000
  &omit_script=1&hide_media=1&hide_thread=1&dnt=true" }}
```

This line calls the Twitter OEmbed API and stores the response in the `$tweet` variable. If the Twitter API is inaccessible or returns an error, the static compilation fails. This API can also join strings if passed several arguments. If the URL of the tweet is present in a variable called `$tweet_url`, we can pass it as-is. The following listing shows the code to parameterize the `getJSON` call.

Listing 9.4   Parameterizing a `getJSON` call

```
{{ $tweet := getJSON "https://publish.twitter.com/oembed?url=" $tweet_url
   "&omit_script=1&hide_media=1&hide_thread=1&dnt=true" }}
```

With the tweet info stored in `$tweet`, the author name is now available in `$tweet.author_name`, and the tweet contents are available as HTML in `$tweet.html`. We can access the URL of the tweet with `$tweet.url`. We can now use this information to render the tweet on the home page.

NOTE Nowadays, JSON is everywhere. Most services provide easy-to-use JSON APIs that we can use with Hugo. From Instagram to Google Maps, Twitter to Wikipedia, we can access anything at compile time with Hugo.

9.2.3 Rendering a tweet as a testimonial

Now that we have a tweet to match the same design, we need to update our data with what we get from Twitter. We will define a key called tweet with an URL and no other information. We can use it to fetch all the data and then render it. Let's update the testimonial with that information. The following listing uses compile-time API access to twitter.com to do just that.

Listing 9.5 Embedding tweets (AcmeTheme/layouts/_default/index.html)

The getJSON call is present in the if statement so that we call it if data from Twitter is needed.

```
{{range .}}
{{$author := default "" .author}}          Saves the data in variables so that
{{$content := default "" .content}}         we can override it from the tweet
{{$from := default "" .from}}
{{if .tweet}}
  {{$tweet := getJSON
    "https://publish.twitter.com/oembed?url=" .tweet
    "&omit_script=1&hide_media=1&hide_thread=1&dnt=true" }}
  {{$author = $tweet.author_name }}
  {{$from = "via Twitter"}}
  {{$content = $tweet.html }}
{{end}}
                                    Twitter returns HTML, unlike
                                    plain text, which Hugo should
<li>      <p>{{$content | safeHTML}}</p>    not escape.
   <div>
     <h2>{{$author | title}}</h2>          The rendering code is
     <h3>{{$from}}</h3>                     used as it was before.
   </div>
</li>
{{end}}
```

Next, we need to provide the tweet URL. The following listing sets the URL in the content/_index.html file under the testimonials section in the front matter.

Listing 9.6 Adding a tweet URL (content/_index.md)

```
testimonials:
  ...
  - tweet: https://twitter.com/atishay/status/1259605801968128000
```

CODE CHECKPOINT https://chapter-09-01.hugoinaction.com, and source code: https://github.com/hugoinaction/hugoinaction/tree/chapter-09-01.

With these changes, we have enabled support for embedding tweets into our website's testimonials section (figure 9.3), and we did it so that these tweets match the website's design! When Hugo compiles the website, missing tweets are fetched and updated. We can add new tweets easily by just editing a string in the testimonials portion of the front matter for the website's index page.

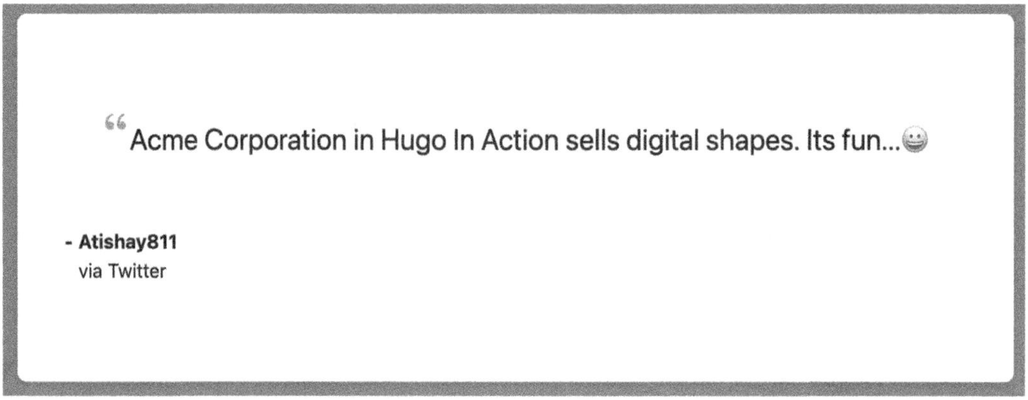

> " Acme Corporation in Hugo In Action sells digital shapes. Its fun... 😊
>
> **- Atishay811**
> via Twitter

Figure 9.3   Testimonials with embedded tweets as well as hardcoded strings presented in the same user interface

9.2.4   *Managing content lifetimes*

Although we are getting the data from Twitter successfully now, we need to ensure that our website can build if Twitter is down and that our build performance stays good. Unlike Hugo Modules, which have a strong set of versioning and content guarantees ensured by the go.sum file, HTTP(s) APIs are, in general, open. The content can change at any time, and the API does not provide any guarantees for consistency and availability. We should inspect every request that we make.

We also have a huge performance tradeoff when calling APIs. Network calls cannot provide subsecond render times. The solution for slow network calls is *caching*. Hugo can perform the network call once and keep the response on disk until changes are needed. By default, Hugo caches the downloaded resources at a hidden location, just like it does with modules. We can override both the default cache interval and the cache location using the Hugo configuration. Let's add a caches.yaml file (https:// github.com/hugoinaction/hugoinaction/tree/chapter-09-resources/01) to the config/ _default folder to control the caching of the getJSON response.

We will tell Hugo to cache the response from the getJSON function in the getJSON folder in the resources directory as listing 9.7 shows. The resourceDir variable tells Hugo to use the value of the resourceDir configuration setting, which, by default, points to the resources subfolder in the website root folder. The maxAge setting specifies the cache duration. By setting this to -1, we inform Hugo to keep the response on the disk forever. We can delete this folder or its subfolders manually if we want to update the content of the cache. The first time we build the website after updating the caching settings, the build takes a bit more time than usual to fetch the information from the network and store it on disk.

Listing 9.7   Updating the cache location (config/_default/caches.yaml)

```
getjson:
  dir: ':resourceDir/getJSON'
  maxAge: -1
```

> **NOTE** We can also override the default hidden folder for modules, which will be an alternative to the _vendor folder. We can also change the visible folder for images, CSS, and JavaScript files cached via Hugo Pipes in the caches.yaml file.

> **CODE CHECKPOINT** https://chapter-09-02.hugoinaction.com, and source code: https://github.com/hugoinaction/hugoinaction/tree/chapter-09-02.

We should see a subfolder named getJSON inside the resources folder with a single file containing the contents of the API response. The next time we run the Hugo build, it will not contact the API but will use the cached contents in this file. We can delete the cache file if we want Hugo to request the API again.

Exercise 9.2

By moving the cache location of the getJSON responses to a local folder, we (enable/disable) data reuse across our projects but (enable/disable) reuse for the same project across machines.

9.3   Hugo and REST APIs

The getJSON API that we just used is a wrapper over an HTTP GET API. The Representational State Transfer (REST) is the software architectural style built around the concept of stateless API calls using HTTP verbs like GET, POST, DELETE, HEAD, PUT, and PATCH to perform actions on resources. The main verbs in a RESTful API are as follows:

- GET downloads resources from a server at a given URL.
- POST allows us to create and send new content.
- PUT enables providing updates to an existing resource.
- DELETE removes content.

REST has other verbs that web developers use rarely. Hugo's `getJSON` sends an HTTP GET request and expects the response in the JSON format. While it primarily downloads, we can provide data via query parameters if needed. Because Hugo runs while compiling, only GET makes sense in the context of Hugo. Actions like creating or deleting need to be performed in response to user activity on the website. Therefore, the focus of Hugo is on GET and not on PUT, POST, or DELETE. PUTs and DELETEs require JavaScript to chain together retrieval and then perform the edit and delete operations.

There are definite use cases for a website developer where data needs to be edited, updated, or deleted. The Jamstack takes care of this through HTML forms and JavaScript on the client. Hugo supports the API and JavaScript layers by making it easy to operate with them. HTML forms are rich in features and powerful. Browsers perform the bulk of the work including client-side validations, data encoding, communication, and error handling. Hugo makes form generation simple, and the Jamstack provides the means to use forms with minimal work and with a low overhead. In the following sections, we will discuss how we can use Hugo to utilize HTML forms efficiently and how forms and `getJSON` can provide a lot of power.

9.4 Creating a contact page the Jamstack way

The Contact Us page for the Acme Corporation website located in the folder /contact still shows placeholder content. The Contact Us page lists the means to contact Acme Corporation and provides a Contact Us form to fill in to send a question. We will present this form in plain HTML and configure a service to handle submissions.

Forms need server-side code to handle submissions, which traditionally needed maintaining a 24/7 running server that can respond to requests. We can embed prebuilt forms hosted by Google Forms or Wufoo that perform this handling if we're looking for a simple solution. Designing these forms to match our website is not easy, and these make additional requests to the host services, adding performance penalties and leaking usage data. These prebuilt forms are not pregenerated and do not conform to the ideology of the Jamstack.

Services like Netlify forms (https://www.netlify.com/products/forms/), Formspree (https://formspree.io/), FormKeep (https://formkeep.com/), and Getform (https://getform.io/) provide us with a way to have customized forms, which we can use with our design. With these services, we can offload the cumbersome maintenance tasks of maintaining a backend to a third party and focus on our aesthetics and content. In this section, we will design a fully functional Contact Us form for our website.

9.4.1 Setting up a contact form

The Contact Us page needs different HTML than a regular page. We will define a new layout in AcmeTheme. We use a layout because the contact page is not a section, and it does not have list pages to build the page shown in figure 9.4 (https://github .com/hugoinaction/hugoinaction/tree/chapter-09-resources/02).

Image of the map   Contents of
contact/index.md   HTML-based form

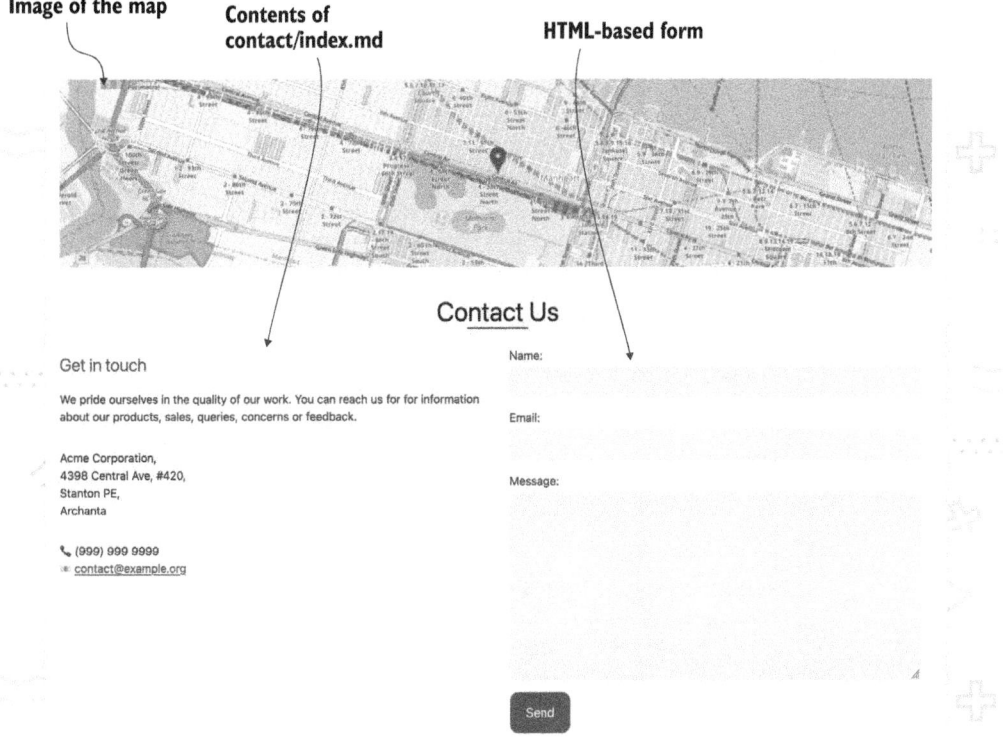

Figure 9.4 The Contact Us page with a static image for the map, a CSS-positioned marker, and a basic HTML form. (Map from OpenGeoFiction.)

Many contact pages embed a map of the office location to help readers looking for physical addresses. Embedding a live map from a mapping service has performance and privacy issues. We will use a screenshot of the map instead, which is pregenerated. Physical offices rarely change locations, and updating the image when that happens is not too hard. To begin, we will add a new layout for the contact page with the map and the form as the following listing shows. The code uses embedded images, rather than mapping to a website, and a simple CSS form that's custom styled for this page.

Listing 9.8 Creating a contact form (AcmeTheme/layouts/_default/contact.html)

```
{{define "bodyClass"}}contact page{{end}}      ◁── Adds a class to get
{{define "body"}}                                  the correct CSS
<main>
  {{$img := .Resources.GetMatch "cover.*"}}
  {{ if $img }}                                      Embeds the map as an image (cover.*)
  <img alt="{{.Title}}" width="1920" height="400"   and ensures that the image's center is
      loading="lazy"                                 visible when cropping. The address
      src="{{($img.Fill                              marker is assumed to be at the center
        "1920x400 Center").Permalink}}">             of the image.
```

```
{{ end }}
{{with .Title}}
  <h1>
    {{.}}
  </h1>
{{end}}

<div class="contact-box">
  <div class="content">
    {{.Content}}
  </div>

  <form>
    <div>
      <label for="name">Name:</label>
      <input id="name" name="name" type="text" required>
    </div>
    <div>
      <label for="email">Email:</label>
      <input id="email" name="email" type="email" required>
    </div>
    <div>
      <label id="message" for="message">Message:</label>
      <textarea name="message" cols="50" rows="10"
        required></textarea>
    </div>
    <div>
      <button type="submit">Send</button>
    </div>
  </form>
</div>
</main>
{{end}}
```

> This displays the content provided in Markdown format above the contact form.

> The form is plain HTML.

Next, we move contact.md to a page bundle and add an image and some markup content as listing 9.9 shows. The code in this listing moves the contact layout and fills the title and content with meaningful data. There are blank spaces to create a new line after each line of the address field.

Listing 9.9   Changing the contact.md file (content/contact/index.md)

```
---
title: Contact Us
layout: contact
---

Get in touch
------------

We pride ourselves on the quality of our work. You can reach us for
information about our products, sales, queries, concerns, or feedback.

Acme Corporation,
4398 Central Ave, #420,
```

```
Stanton PE,
Archanta
```

📞 (999) 999 9999
✉ contact@example.org

> **NOTE** This form is not functional yet. It does not send the data anywhere when submitted.

> **CODE CHECKPOINT** https://chapter-09-03.hugoinaction.com, and source code: https://github.com/hugoinaction/hugoinaction/tree/chapter-09-03.

> **Exercise 9.3**
> HTTP PUT requests that modify existing data are best handled at the _____ layer of the Jamstack.

9.4.2 Choosing a form provider

The form data currently is not being submitted anywhere. We have a choice to build our own service with a custom API for form handling or to choose one from a third party. Unless it is our core competency or there is a lack of good third-party options available (due to cost, features, or flexibility), *it is not recommended to build services.* We will use a third-party form provider to provide support for form APIs. When looking for a form service for a Hugo-based website, it is a good idea to look for services that have the following characteristics:

- Is stable, well-maintained, and not likely to go out of business.
- Provides support for dynamically generating forms through some API.
- Provides the ability to access form submissions through an API.
- Provides a good set of integrations with other services (e.g., email) to use the data to trigger actions easily.

There are many form providers. Each brings its own set of features for integration to other services and has different price points and features. You can get an updated list of various form providers at https://serverless.css-tricks.com/services/forms.

> **NOTE** Adding APIs increases maintenance work as the third-party APIs can change, become expensive, or go away. First-party APIs have similar risks with the underlying framework and with the hosting provider, as well as potential security risks depending on the quality of our code and its dependencies. We can also find a database as a service and a function as a service in most cloud providers and use those to create our own Jamstack-based form backend. If we use these, we will have to deal with spam submissions ourselves.

9.4.3   *Using Netlify forms for the Contact Us page*

Netlify is a one-stop-shop for Jamstack-based websites. If we are already using Netlify hosting, it does not make sense to add additional dependencies. Netlify forms provide a generous free tier, and it meets all our needs for a form solution as used in this book. For readers not using Netlify for form hosting, we will use an alternative form host in the next section.

To host our contact form in Netlify, we need to add a `netlify` attribute for our HTML form as the following listing shows. Because Netlify also provides builds and hosting support, it can parse the form and dynamically generate the form based on that data.

Listing 9.10   Enabling Netlify forms (AcmeTheme/layouts/_default/contact.html)

```html
<form netlify="true" name="Contact">
```

The `name` attribute identifies the form in the Netlify UI. Note that Netlify (figure 9.5) provides emails for form submissions as well as API and graphical access for all of them.

CODE CHECKPOINT   https://chapter-09-04.hugoinaction.com, and source code: https://github.com/hugoinaction/hugoinaction/tree/chapter-09-04.

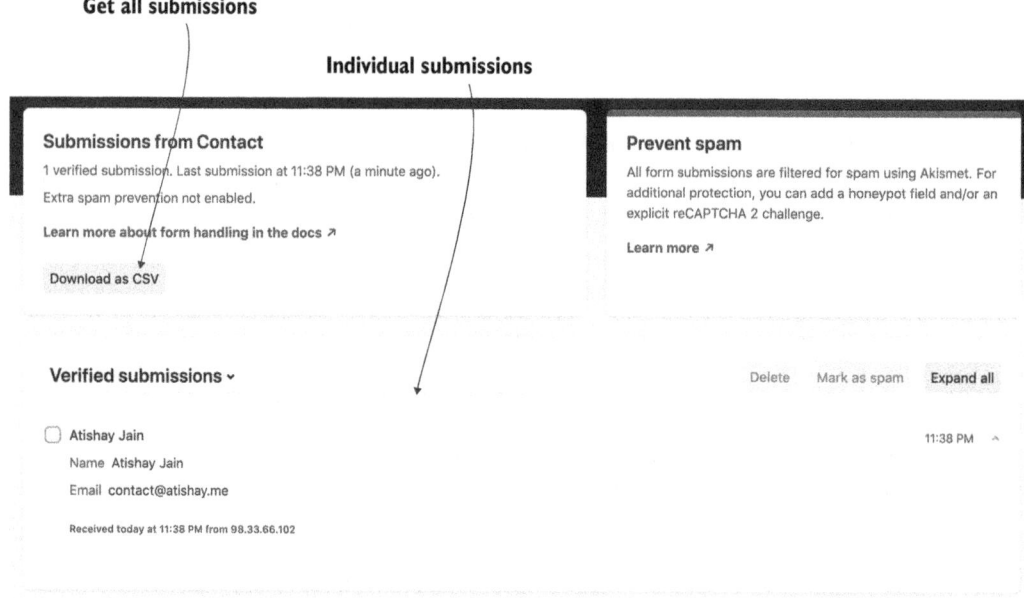

Get all submissions

Individual submissions

Submissions from Contact

1 verified submission. Last submission at 11:38 PM (a minute ago).

Extra spam prevention not enabled.

Learn more about form handling in the docs ↗

Download as CSV

Prevent spam

All form submissions are filtered for spam using Akismet. For additional protection, you can add a honeypot field and/or an explicit reCAPTCHA 2 challenge.

Learn more ↗

Verified submissions ˅

Delete   Mark as spam   Expand all

☐ Atishay Jain   11:38 PM   ˄

Name Atishay Jain

Email contact@atishay.me

Received today at 11:38 PM from 98.33.66.102

Figure 9.5   The contact form submissions with Netlify. When forms are submitted, Netlify makes them accessible on the website and can notify the creator to take action on them.

Preventing spam

If spam submissions on the forms become a problem, Netlify provides two options to work around this:

- *Captchas*—Captchas are challenges built so that humans can solve them quickly, while bots need many computational resources to do so. You can add the parameter `data-netlify-recaptcha` to the `form` tag and provide a `div` tag with the same attribute to enable captchas.
- *Honeypots*—Although captchas are a potent means to prevent spam, they are not very user-friendly. Bots that generate the most spam parse only HTML. CSS layouts are expensive, so many spambots skip CSS altogether. To identify the spam posts filled by bots, we can add a dummy field that is not expected to be filled by humans (hidden from view using CSS) but completed by the bots, which do not understand CSS. We can add an HTML attribute, `netlify-honeypot`, to a form field to make Netlify treat this as a honeypot. If your website does not have high traffic, you can try the honeypot field first to see if it meets your needs.

With these changes, we have a working contact form on the Contact Us page. Any website visitor can go to this page and fill in the form that then triggers an email to the website administrator via the Netlify Forms service. Netlify also keeps a copy of all form submissions.

9.4.4 *Using Formspree for contact forms*

An alternative to Netlify Forms is Formspree, which supports forms that we can use from any website. Formspree is an independent alternative that only focuses on forms and does not support hosting. It provides integration with services like Zendesk to create support tickets, Mailchimp to manage mailing lists, Stripe to take payments, and so on. You can also export the submissions to Google Docs or to Airtable for further processing. These integrations can save a significant amount of time while, in parallel, keeping our website lean.

Because Formspree does not compile Hugo's source code, there is no way to know automatically what and how many forms are needed. Therefore, to create forms using Formspree, we need to manually make those forms on the Formspree website. The best part of Formspree is that we need to specify minimal information when we set up a form, and everything else can be dynamic. To create a contact form with Formspree, follow these steps:

1 After creating an account, click New Form to set up a new form (figure 9.6).

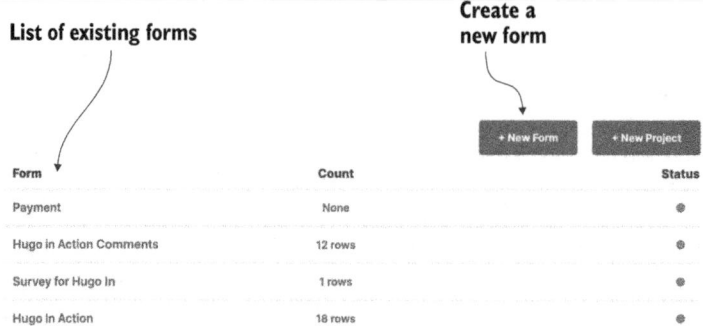

Figure 9.6   When logged into Formspree, we can click the New Form button to create a new form.

2 Fill in the Create Form dialog and click Create Form (figure 9.7).

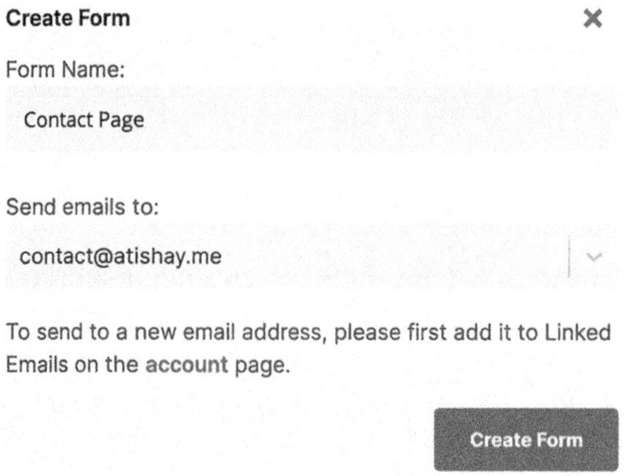

Create Form   ✕

Form Name:

Contact Page

Send emails to:

contact@atishay.me   ⌄

To send to a new email address, please first add it to Linked Emails on the account page.

                                          Create Form

Figure 9.7   The Create Form dialog asks for basic information that's required to create a form in Formspree.

3 Your form is now ready, and we can copy the form URL to use later (figure 9.8).

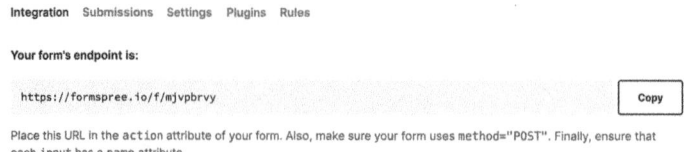

Figure 9.8   Getting the form code for Formspree for our form. The form code is a part of the form endpoint in the integration section of the form.

Once we have the URL, we can use this in our form. For the code samples with this book, we will support both Formspree and Netlify. You can choose to have just one form service. We will use Hugo's if statement to distinguish between Netlify and Formspree. (In development mode, we will exclusively use Formspree.) Hugo has a function called getenv that gets environment variables; Netlify always sets the NETLIFY environment variable in its build environment. To use the NETLIFY environment variable, we will need to enable it in Hugo's security configuration as shown in the following code snippet:

```
.Adding security config for getenv (config/_default/security.yaml)
----
funcs:
  getenv:
    - NETLIFY
----
```

The following listing shows how to add Formspree to the Contact Us form for the Acme Corporation website.

Listing 9.11 Adding Formspree (AcmeTheme/layouts/_default/contact.html)

```
{{if getenv "NETLIFY" }}                    ◁───────┐  Uses getenv to check
<form netlify="true" name="Contact">                │  environment variables
{{ else }}
<form action="https://formspree.io/f/<Your Formspree code>" method="post">
{{ endif }}
```

> **NOTE** Readers should choose one form service and stick with it. Two services are present in the book for demonstrating how simple it is to switch between services. We are adding dependencies to provide ourselves with the flexibility, should the need arise, to switch service providers, by being as close as possible to the HTML specification. You can set the NETLIFY environment variable locally. This will not break the website.

To isolate the Formspree-related changes across websites using the same theme, we should move the Formspree ID in the URL to the website configuration file and use parameters instead. The following listing shows how.

Listing 9.12 Moving a Formspree ID (AcmeTheme/layouts/_default/contact.html)

```
{{if getenv "NETLIFY" }}
<form netlify="true" name="Contact">
{{ else }}
<form action="https://formspree.io/f/{{.Param "contact"}}" method="post">
{{ end }}
```

We can provide the Contact Us URL on the contact page itself. The next listing provides the code to do this in the contact page.

Listing 9.13 Adding the Formspree code to contact (content/contact/index.md)

```
contact: <Your Formspree code>
```

Formspree also supports setting a field as a reply to the email address for any email going to Formspree. That way, we can directly reply to the sender. The following listing changes the email field to _replyto for Formspree to understand.

```
<input id="email"
 {{ if getenv "NETLIFY" }}
 name="email"
{{ else }}
name="_replyto"
{{ end }}
type="email" required>
```

CODE CHECKPOINT   https://chapter-09-05.hugoinaction.com, and source code: https://github.com/hugoinaction/hugoinaction/tree/chapter-09-05.

With this change, we are ready to receive emails from the Contact Us page via Formspree, which provides email as well as a graphical view of all submissions. Figure 9.9 shows the Submissions page on Formspree.

NOTE   The integration mechanism for most form websites is the same. If we replace Formspree with GetForm or FormKeep, we need to get the action URL for that service, and everything else should be the same.

Figure 9.9   The contact form submissions on Formspree. Formspree provides API access, a submissions page, as well as email notifications for forms. You can also use Formspree integrations to perform additional actions.

TIP We can submit Formspree forms by default from any website. We recommend that you restrict it to your domain in the form settings to prevent misuse. You can also enable captchas in Formspree, just like in Netlify.

9.5 *Building dynamic surveys*

The Contact Us form is mostly plain HTML and does not show the potential of combining Hugo's template system with the benefits of dynamically generated forms. In this section, we will see how the data-driven nature of Hugo, coupled with the dynamic form providers of the Jamstack, makes a potent combination. For this, let's look at a survey.

A *survey* usually consists of a dynamic number of questions with multiple answers or a plain text field to fill in the answers. YAML is the perfect language for creating a survey form. It keeps data together and moves the presentation logic to the template. A proper survey should have content and presentation wholly separated. The content consists of questions and answers that should be present in the markup document, whereas the layout and conversion to the final HTML form should shape the layout.

The questions in the survey content file are presented as a plain list in YAML, with options provided as an answer where available (https://github.com/hugoinaction/ hugoinaction/tree/chapter-09-resources/03). Listing 9.15 provides the code for the content file. Note that Hugo generates the survey dynamically based on the supplied data. Questions with answers turn into dropdowns, and simple text replies become text boxes.

Listing 9.15 The content file for a survey form (content/survey/random.md)

```
---
title: Random questions from Hugo In Action
survey:
- question: Do you like websites that are slow to load?
  answer: [Yes, No]
- question: Rate your confidence using Hugo to build fast websites.
  answer: [1 (Very Low),2,3,4,5 (Very High)]
- question: What is the answer to life, the universe, and everything?
- question: Any further comments?
---

Please answer a random survey we built in Hugo in Action.
```

We will create a form by looping through the list of questions and then creating a dropdown if the answer field is present and a text box if not. We could alternatively add a key called `type` to define the form element we want to use for this. Because there will be multiple surveys on the website, the natural place to put one is in a custom section with a new content type. For that, we will define a new content type called survey and place a single.html template inside it. With this template, we can loop through the questions provided in the front matter's survey section and create a dropdown when there are answers available (HTML `<select>` element); otherwise, we resort to a text box (HTML `<input>` element). The code in the following listing parses the front matter's survey parameters and runs that through a loop to create the form entries.

Listing 9.16   Form to create a survey (AcmeTheme/layouts/survey/single.html)

```
{{define "bodyClass"}} page survey{{end}    ◁——— Defines the class for CSS styling

{{ define "body" }}
<main>
  <h2>{{.Title}}</h2>          Provides Markdown content
{{.Content}}                   and a title from the header
{{if getenv "NETLIFY" }}
<form name="{{.Title}}" netlify="true">
{{ else }}
<form action="https://formspree.io/f/{{.Param "form"}}"
      method="post">
{{ end }}
  <ol>
{{ range $index, $item := .Params.survey }}
  <li>
    <label for="question{{$index}}">{{$item.question}}</label>
    {{if $item.answer}}
    <select id="question{{$index}}"
      name="question{{$index}}" required>
      <option value="" ></option>       ◁——— Does not select anything by default ...
      {{range $item.answer}}
        <option value="{{.}}" name="{{.}}">{{.}}</option>
      {{end}}
    </select>
    {{else}}                  ... else creates the
                             <input> tag for a text box.
      <input id="question{{$index}}"
        name="question{{$index}}" type="text" required>
    {{end}}
  </li>
{{ end }}
  </ol>
  <button type="submit">Submit</button>
</form>
</main>
{{ end }}
```

Creates the HTML `<select>` tag if the question has options for answers

Loops through the survey section in the front matter

With this small template, we can generate as many surveys as we want by placing Markdown documents in the survey subfolder for the content folder in our website. Note that if we use Formspree, we will need to create a new form ID for each survey and provide its code. The survey for random.md should be present at http://localhost :1313/survey/random/ (figure 9.10).

Exercise 9.4

The form service approach of the Jamstack allows us to decouple the _____, _____, and the form handling layers of the HTML form submission process.

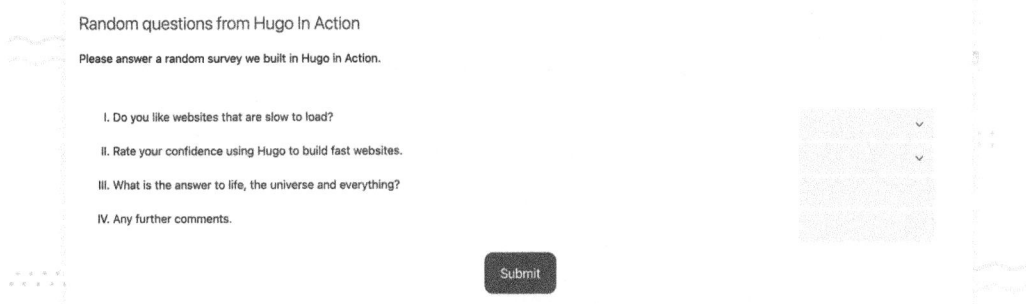

Figure 9.10 Dynamic surveys created with Hugo. Combining a backend form service, we can get dynamically generated forms, which provide a considerable amount of flexibility including creating forms like surveys based on dynamic Markdown content added by the content author.

NOTE The ability to create dynamic forms in a website is a compelling feature. A content author can create surveys using plain Markdown and YAML. The form contents are dynamic, and we can change them after publishing the form without involving a single change to the theme code.

As mentioned, to use Formspree, we will need to add the Formspree ID to the front matter. The following listing shows how to add this ID.

Listing 9.17   Adding the Formspree ID for each form (content/survey/random.md)

```
form: <Formspree id>
```

CODE CHECKPOINT   https://chapter-09-06.hugoinaction.com, and source code: https://github.com/hugoinaction/hugoinaction/tree/chapter-09-06.

Marking surveys as unlisted

Note that with this change, the survey pages now show up in the list of pages as we navigate through `site.Pages`. Survey pages are mainly unlisted. To ensure the survey pages are unlisted, we can specify build parameters to Hugo that set the `list` setting to `false` in the `Surveys` section. The following code snippet disables the index listing for the survey pages.

```
---
title: Surveys
cascade:
  _build:
    list: false        ◁─── Doesn't include any
---                          pages in the list page
                             (via cascade)

Please use the survey link provided in the email to access the survey.
```

(continued)

With this change, the survey pages will have URLs, but they will not show up in the page lists like `site.GetPage`. Note that unless the survey section is disabled in robots.txt, search engines will index the survey links. Also, if we want to have random URLs for surveys, we can use the `slug` key in the front matter to define our custom URLs.

Figure 9.11   No contest! Bob discovers the joys of the Jamstack. He moves the survey component over to this new approach and likes it so much that he declares to the management that they should move to the new stack.

9.6   Commenting using the Jamstack

We have gone through two distinct concepts around APIs so far: fetching data at compile time using APIs and submitting data at run time using a web form. The two together can provide a powerful solution to include user-generated content in a website. Let's combine a form-based API submission and a get-based API access to create a commenting system for our website.

Although Hugo provides native support for embedding the Disqus (https:// disqus.com) comment system, Disqus is not static and loads JavaScript to get the information needed to display and render comments. The flexibility of dynamic forms coupled with JSON APIs can make an effective commenting system for our websites.

9.6.1   Displaying a comment form

We will create a new partial for the comment system that will be easy-to-use across multiple types of pages (the news and blog posts, for example). The HTML comment form is similar to the Contact Us form that we had created earlier. Figure 9.12 shows the comment form we will be setting up.

The comment form is the same as the Contact Us form, but instead of including it in a new layout or type, it needs to be present in a partial. That way, we can reuse it in multiple templates.

Comments

Name:

Atishay Jain

Email:

contact@atishay.me

Comment:

Test comment

Send

Figure 9.12 The comment form can be generated using a form element in Hugo. If we want one comment form for multiple pages, we can use a hidden input field in the page's path.

Because partials cannot access variables outside their contexts, we must pass all the variables via the partial context (https://github.com/hugoinaction/hugoinaction/tree/chapter-09-resources/04). This partial can post to Netlify or Formspree depending on the environment. The following listing adds a comment partial to display a comment form on the website.

Listing 9.18 A comment partial (AcmeTheme/layouts/partials/comment.html)

```
<div class="comments">
<h2> Comments </h2>
{{if getenv "NETLIFY" }}
  <form netlify="true" name="{{.RelPermalink}}">
{{ else }}
  <form action=
  "https://formspree.io/f/{{.FormspreeCommentForm}}"
  method="post" >
{{ end }}
  <div>
    <label for="name">Name:</label>
    <input id="name" name="name" type="text" required>
  </div>
  <div>
    <label for="email">
Email:</label>
    <input id="email" name="email" type="email" required>
  </div>
  <div>
   <label for="message">Comment:</label>
   <textarea id="message" name="message" cols="50"
      rows="10" required></textarea>
```

Using RelPermalink from the params as $.Page is not available in a partial.

Gets the comment form action for form providers like Formspree

```
  </div>
 <div>
  <button type="submit">Send</button>
  </div>
</form>
</div>
```

We want to enable support for post authors to disable comments on the page. Adding this feature is straightforward. We use a parameter passed from the front matter that can prevent this form from ever being generated. The following listing disables commenting if the admin decides to do so.

Listing 9.19   Disabling commenting (AcmeTheme/layouts/partials/comment.html)

```
{{ if .Disabled }}
<div>
  Comments have been disabled by the website administrator.
</div>
{{ else }}
...
{{ end }}
```

Note that using the name .Permalink creates a new form for each page. Because Netlify can generate forms dynamically, we do not need to rely on one form to provide everything. While this is a good approach, creating lots of forms may not be desirable if our website has low volume. If we want to use a form service like Formspree, the act of creating a form for each page can be cumbersome. A simple solution is to use the same form and pass the permalink as a form parameter via hidden HTML input and then filter in Hugo. Let's see how the form section looks like now. The following listing passes the form URL to Formspree.

Listing 9.20   Passing the form URL (AcmeTheme/layouts/partials/comment.html)

```
{{if getenv "NETLIFY" }}
  <form netlify="true" name="Comments" >        ⟵┐  Uses Comments as the form name so we
{{ else }}                                          have a single form for all comments.
  <form action="https://formspree.io/f/{{.FormspreeCommentForm}}"
  method="post">
{{ end }}
                                                        ┌  Adds a hidden field
<input type="hidden" name="url" value="{{.RelPermalink}}"> ⟵┘  with the page URL
```

With this addition, we can now include this form in the Blog pages in the main section to provide the ability to send comments. This partial takes the action URL, which we can get from the front matter or the website configuration, the link to the page, and a Boolean flag to check if commenting has been disabled. The following listing loads the comment form in a blog post.

```
{{ partial "comment.html" (dict
    "FormspreeCommentForm" ($.Param "FormspreeCommentForm")
    "RelPermalink" .Page.RelPermalink
    "Disabled" ($.Param "CommentDisabled")
) }}
```

Next, we add the Formspree action URL. The following listing adds a form ID that will be converted to a URL in the template.

```
FormspreeCommentForm: <Your Formspree code>
```

Note that we can use `CommentDisabled: true` in the front matter for disabling comments on a single page. Placing it inside `cascade` in _index.md disables comments in a section or putting it in config/_default/params.yaml disables comments for the entire website.

> **CODE CHECKPOINT**   https://chapter-09-07.hugoinaction.com, and source code: https://github.com/hugoinaction/hugoinaction/tree/chapter-09-07.

9.6.2   Displaying comments

Hugo can access the comments submitted using the comment form during website compilation and place those in the associated pages. Because Hugo generates the website statically, the comment embedding process is not in real time. We can use JavaScript to fetch comments to update the list in real time. Another approach is to use a webhook by the form service, which rebuilds the website when a comment is received. We will use the webhook trigger in chapter 11.

GETTING ACCESS TO THE FORMS API

Most form services require some form of authentication to control access to the APIs. The following steps allow you to get the Netlify access token. Note that because we are building the application for a single website, a personal access token is enough for our needs.

1   Login to Netlify and click the profile image on the top right to go to the User Settings page (figure 9.13).

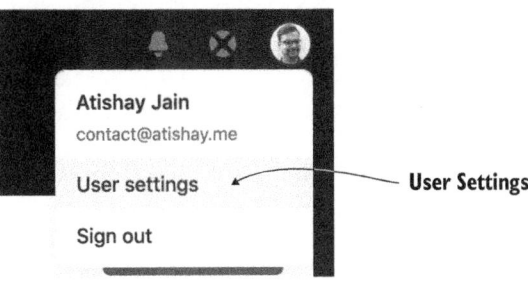

Figure 9.13   Netlify's User Settings option lets us create an access token. This setting can be reached by clicking the profile icon after logging in to Netlify.

2   Go to the Applications section and click New Access Token (figure 9.14).

1. Select the Applications tab.

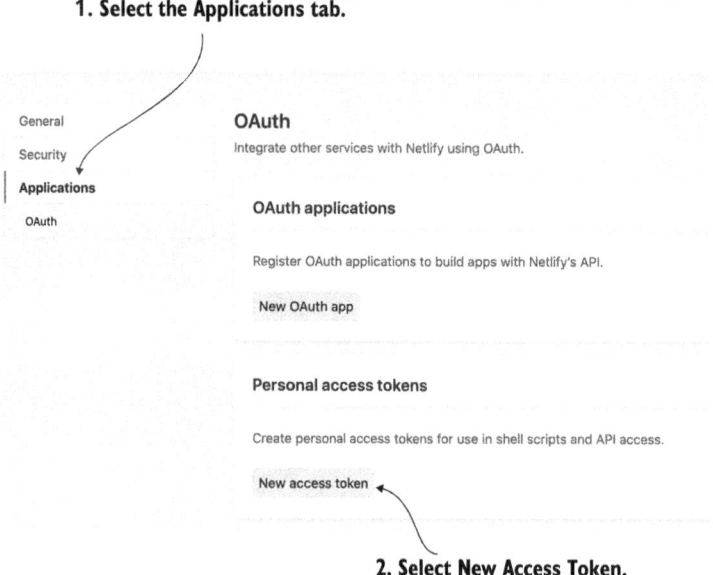

2. Select New Access Token.

Figure 9.14   From the Netlify User Settings, we can get to the Applications section, which contains the Personal Access Token subsection, where we can create new access tokens.

3   Provide a friendly name for the token and click Generate Token (figure 9.15).

Generate a personal access token

Give the token a descriptive name to help you remember what it will be used for.

Description of your token

Comments API Access   ◄─────────────── **1. Provide a name.**

Generate token   Cancel

2. Click Generate Token.

Figure 9.15   For creating an access token in Netlify, we need to provide a simple name in the Description field.

4   Copy the generated token (figure 9.16). The Netlify access token is now ready for use.

New token created

Copy the token below to your clipboard. For security reasons, after you navigate off this page, no one will be able to see the token again.

XzAdiwHbsAZ2fijQ8uWnGZ6sngRI_3sonx-6TUhb0YY

Done

Copy the generated token.

Figure 9.16 The access token from Netlify is available once we click the Generate Token button. It is not present in Netlify, which stores only its hash in its database. If a copy of the token is lost, we need to create a new token.

Formspree requires Gold membership to access its API. Once you have the Gold Membership, you can go to the form's settings and enable the HTTP API section, where you will find the read-only API key that we can copy over (figure 9.17).

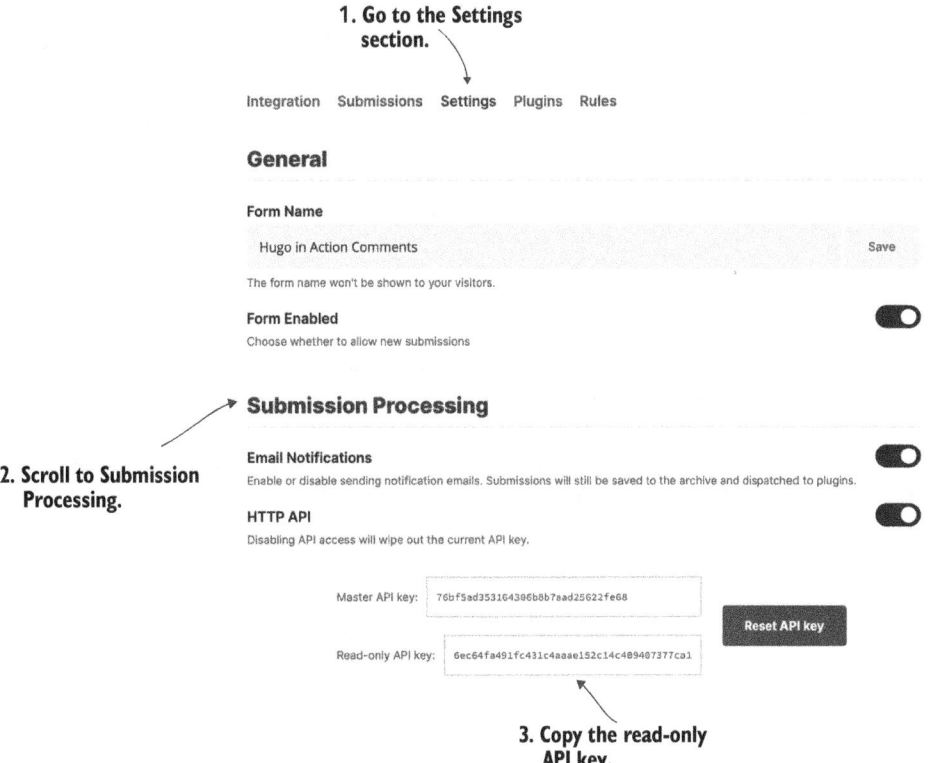

1. Go to the Settings section.

Integration   Submissions   **Settings**   Plugins   Rules

General

Form Name

Hugo in Action Comments   Save

The form name won't be shown to your visitors.

Form Enabled
Choose whether to allow new submissions

Submission Processing

Email Notifications
Enable or disable sending notification emails. Submissions will still be saved to the archive and dispatched to plugins.

2. Scroll to Submission Processing.

HTTP API
Disabling API access will wipe out the current API key.

Master API key: 76bf5ad353164306b8b7aad25622fe68

Reset API key

Read-only API key: 6ec64fa491fc431c4aaae152c14c409407377ca1

3. Copy the read-only API key.

Figure 9.17 We can obtain the Formspree API key by toggling the HTTP API option in the Settings page of a form in a Formspree Gold account. We only need the read-only API key for this book.

SECURING THE TOKENS

Best practices strongly mention keeping the API key outside of the codebase so that it's not accidentally lost or misused. Netlify allows storing secrets as environment variables via the Netlify interface. To create an environment variable in Netlify, follow these steps:

1 Go to the Settings page for the Acme Corporation website within Netlify.
2 In the Build & Deploy section, select Environment, then click Edit Variables (figure 9.18).

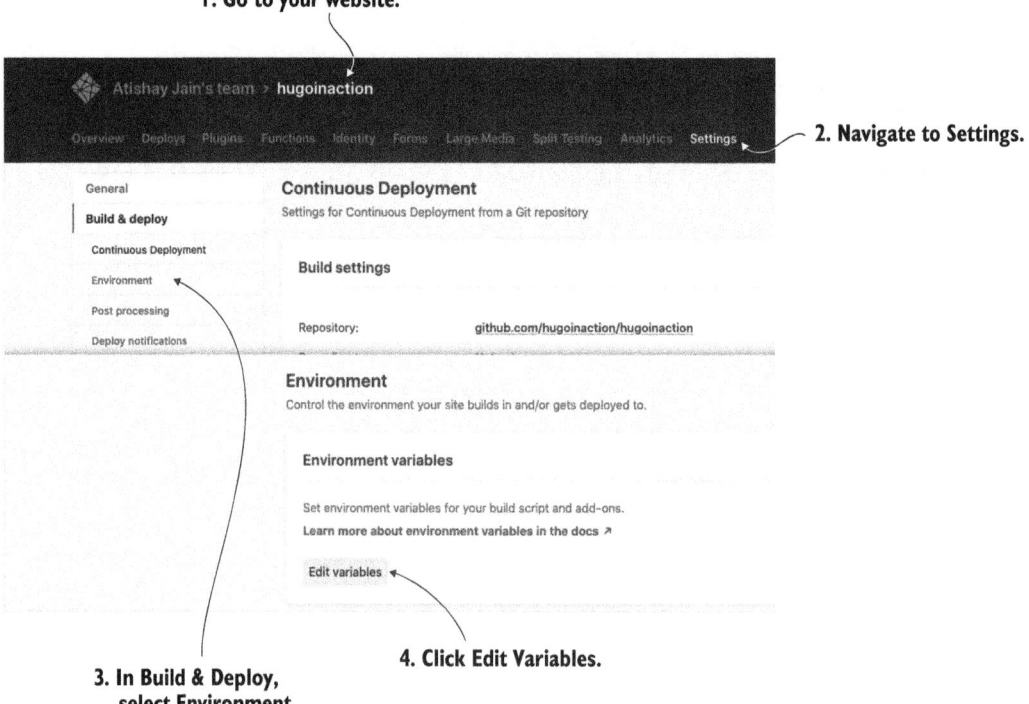

Figure 9.18   We can keep secrets outside of our code by storing them in Netlify environment variables, which we can add from the Build & Deploy section of the website settings.

3 Create a new variable named COMMENTS_TOKEN, paste the token for this variable, and click Save (figure 9.19).

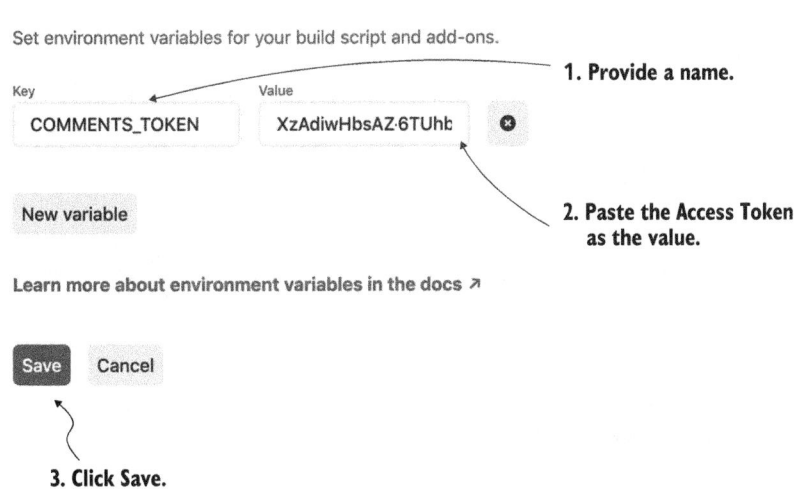

Figure 9.19   When editing environment variables in Netlify, we can add more variables like COMMENTS_TOKEN that we'll use to fetch comments.

In GitHub, we can use GitHub encrypted secrets to secure the tokens. To create an environment variable in GitHub, follow these steps:

1 In the GitHub repository's Settings page, go to the Secrets section and click New Secret (figure 9.20).

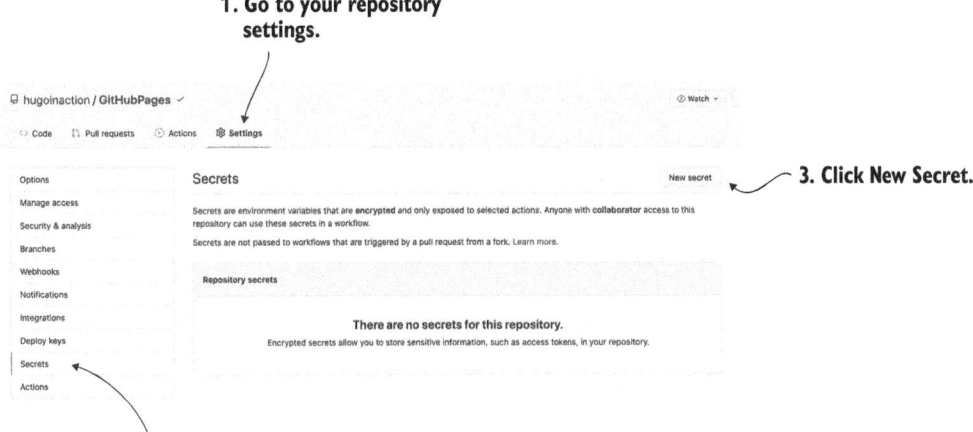

Figure 9.20   We can create GitHub secrets in the Secrets section in the repository settings.

   2 Create a new variable named COMMENTS_TOKEN, paste the token for this
      variable, and click Add Secret (figure 9.21).

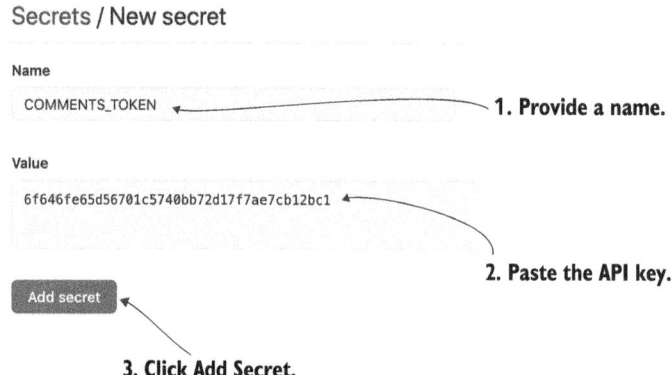

**Figure 9.21   A secret in GitHub consists of a name and a value. These secrets
are available as variables in GitHub Actions.**

   3 In the GitHub Pages build step, add an environment variable for COMMENTS
      _TOKEN. The following listing shows the code to do this.

Listing 9.23   Adding an environment variable (.github/workflows/gh-pages.yml)

```
- name: Build
  . . .
  env:
    COMMENTS_TOKEN: ${{ secrets.COMMENTS_TOKEN }}
```

For local development, we will need to set the appropriate variables for access in the
command line. For Windows, we can use the set command to set environment variables like this:

```
set COMMENTS_TOKEN="<your comments token>"
```

For macOS and Linux, we can use the export command:

```
export COMMENTS_TOKEN="<your comments token>"
```

> **NOTE** These commands set the environment variables only for the current
> shell or session. To set them permanently, you can search for "edit environ-
> ment variables <for your account>" in the Windows search box. For Linux or
> macOS, use ~/.profile (bash) or ~/.zprofile (zsh), based on your shell.

FETCHING COMMENTS

Once we have the API key, we can query the service using the getJSON API in Hugo to get all comments for all forms. Unfortunately, this API is outside of Hugo, and therefore, there is no standardization as each service has its own set of APIs. The query and parsing mechanisms for each service are different, and we will need to redo the comment-fetching code if we move to a new service.

In this section, we will create a Hugo partial that can be cached, which provides a Hugo scratch pad with a mapping from the comment page permalink to the list of comments for that page. To use Netlify to fetch comments, we need to do the following:

- To access the submissions of a form in Netlify, we need the form's Netlify ID. While we can write an API query to dynamically get a form ID because we are using a single form for all comments, putting the form ID in the front matter is more effortless.
- To get a form ID for the comment form, first publish the comment form to Netlify. After posting, the form will be available in the Forms section on the website (figure 9.22).

Figure 9.22 Netlify's Forms section contains all the active forms and provides access to the submissions. We can use the form URL of an individual form to get its identifier.

When we click the form, Netlify takes us to the Submissions page, whose URL should be something like the following:

```
https://app.netlify.com/sites/hugoinaction/forms/<form id>
```

This code provides us with the identifier (ID) of the form in Netlify. Let's add this form ID to the website configuration as the following listing shows.

> **Listing 9.24   Adding a comment form ID (config/_default/params.yml)**

```
NetlifyCommentForm: <form id>
```

To access form submissions from Netlify, we can use the form submissions API. The following listing allows us to access this API.

> **Listing 9.25   Accessing the Netlify form submissions API**

```
https://api.netlify.com/api/v1/forms/<form id>/submissions?
➥ access_token=<access token>
```

The following listing shows a sample response for submissions on the comments form.

> **Listing 9.26   Sample output from Netlify for submissions**

```
[{
  ...
  "data": {
    "url": "/blog/process-4/",
    "name": "Atishay Jain",
    "email": "contact@atishay.me",
    "message": "The quality shows. Connect a few lines and
    ➥ the shapes come out well. I think you should also sell
    ➥ shape assemblies.",
    "ip": "...",
    "user_agent": "...",
    "referrer": "https://chapter-09-07.hugoinaction.com/blog/process-4/"
  },
  "created_at": "2021-07-19T06:13:54.724Z",
  "id": "60f51822e039a4ad6c2f81c7",
  "form_id": "5f6af880fd7ebf0007984d2f",
  "site_url": "https://hugoinaction.com" ,
  "form_name": "Comments"
}, ...]
```

The response JSON schema for each form service is different. To consume it quickly, we will create partials that access this service and translate data to a standard format that makes the most sense for our use case.

NOTE You can use the Netlify APIs to fetch comments while developing locally.

To display comments, we need a map-like data structure returned from the partial that has the key as the page URL and the value as a list of all comments for that page. In Hugo, we can use a scratch pad to provide this functionality. Another thing to note is that because we are accessing all information globally available in the environment variables and the global website configuration, this partial can work without any supplied parameters. We can use the site global variable to access the site variables, and we can use the `getenv` function to provide the environment variables (https://github.com/hugoinaction/hugoinaction/tree/chapter-09-resources/05). Note that we will need to enable `COMMENTS_TOKEN` within the `funcs/getenv` section of the Hugo security configuration (config/_default/security.yaml) to use this variable. We can use the Netlify comment parsing partial, as the following listing shows, to request data for the comments form from the Netlify Forms service and provide it in a map for consumption in AcmeTheme/layouts/partials/netlifyCommentList.html.

Listing 9.27   The Netlify comment parsing partial

Creates a new scratch pad for the response

```
{{$response := newScratch}}
{{if and site.Params.NetlifyCommentForm
  (getenv "COMMENTS_TOKEN")}}

    {{$comments := getJSON
      "https://api.netlify.com/api/v1/forms/"
      site.Params.NetlifyCommentForm
      "/submissions?access_token="
      (getenv "COMMENTS_TOKEN")}}

    {{ range (sort $comments "created_at" "asc") }}
      {{if not ($response.Get .data.url)}}
        {{$response.Set .data.url (slice )}}
      {{end}}

      {{$response.Add .data.url .data}}
    {{ end }}
{{ end }}

{{return $response.Values}}
```

Uses the .Values method to convert the scratch pad to a dictionary

Only execute if all dependencies are present. We do not want to fail the build with a bad network call.

Uses getJSON to call the URL. getJSON can combine URL fragments if passed as a set of variables.

Returns a slice (array) of comments sorted by created_at to show the newest comments at the bottom

Creates a slice on first use with .url as the key to store comments.

Appends the data for the comment. This code might append additional data fields, but we can ignore them in the consumer.

In the listing, the `site` global variable is used to access the website configuration, while `getenv` provides access to the environment variables. Each element in the response has a data entry with the submitted data. We use the web page's URL as a key. Because we need to add elements to the slice (array), we need to create a new slice when we encounter the first comment.

TIP You can use debugging utilities by adding (`{{ partialCached "console" (partialCached "netlifyCommentList" "none" "cached") "netlify-Comments" }}`) to view the structure of the returned dictionary in the browser console.

Formspree's form ID was already available as `FormspreeCommentForm`, and therefore, we do not need to generate it separately. To fetch comments from Formspree, Formspree requires an `Authorization` header to connect to the Formspree API and fetch the form data. Hugo's getJSON API supports passing additional headers in the form of a dictionary. We can complete the authenticated call for Formspree by opening the URL in the following listing.

```
curl https://formspree.io/api/0/forms/<form id>/submissions -H
  "Authorization: Bearer <API Key>"
```

The following listing shows the response for the query to the Formspree form submissions API with the form submissions for the comment form.

```
{
  ...
  "ok": true,
  "submissions": [{
    "_date": "2021-07-19T14:19:12.327527+00:00",
    "email": "contact@atishay.me",
    "message": "The quality shows. Connect a few lines and the shapes
      come out well. I think you should also sell shape assemblies.",
    "name": "Atishay Jain",
    "url": "/blog/process-4/"
  }, ...]
}
```

Parsing code for the response JSON for Formspree is similar to the Netlify parser. The _date field and the headers need to be added to getJSON to sort based on these values. These minor differences are present in listing 9.30 (https://github.com/hugoinaction/hugoinaction/tree/chapter-09-resources/05). Listing 9.30 shows the comment parsing partial used to request data for the comments form from the Formspree service (Acme Theme/layouts/partials/formspreeCommentList.html) and provides it in a map for consumption.

```
{{$response := newScratch}}
{{if and site.Params.FormspreeCommentForm (getenv "COMMENTS_TOKEN")}}

    {{$comments := getJSON
        "https://formspree.io/api/0/forms/"
        site.Params.FormspreeCommentForm "/submissions"
        (dict "Authorization"
            (printf "Bearer %s"
                (getenv "COMMENTS_TOKEN")
            )
        ) }}

    {{ range sort $comments.submissions
        "date" "ASC" }}
```

The comment list is in the submissions object sorted by _date in ascending order.

Formspree requires the Authorization header.

```
{{if not ($response.Get .url)}}
  {{$response.Set .url (slice )}}
{{end}}

{{$response.Add .url .}}    ◄─┐
{{ end }}
{{ end }}

{{return $response.Values}}
```

The submission is directly available in the submissions object inside of Formspree's response, unlike Netlify, where it is nested under the data object.

> ## Exercise 9.5
> We can include user comments in our Jamstack-based website without using JavaScript at _____ time.

RENDERING COMMENTS

With comments populated in an easy-to-use map, rendering them on the web page is pretty straightforward. The form-rendering code can loop through the comments tied to the URL of the current page and display them in HTML. We can speed up processing by placing the service response code in a cached partial. Figure 9.23 shows the rendered comments.

NOTE You will need to delete the cached responses from the resources folder to see the latest comments. Because we have specified maxAge for the getJSON API as -1, Hugo does not recompute the comment submissions each time we build the website.

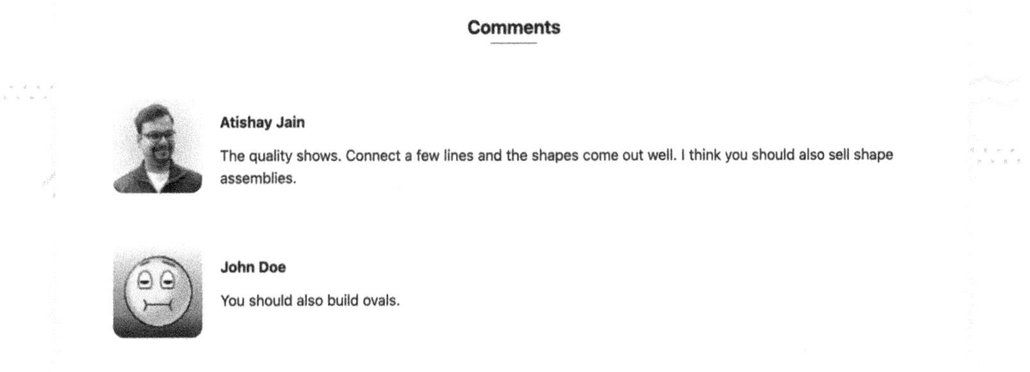

Comments

Atishay Jain
The quality shows. Connect a few lines and the shapes come out well. I think you should also sell shape assemblies.

John Doe
You should also build ovals.

Figure 9.23 Comments rendering for the form are all generated during build time when Hugo compiles the website.

We will use the Gravatar service for getting the user's avatar. Gravatar is a free service that takes the hash of a user's email address and returns a profile picture. Both Word-Press and GitHub use Gravatar and, therefore, have the avatars for a vast number of potential readers. We will be using `resources.GetRemote` API to get a remote resource (from the Gravatar service via HTTP) at compile time and caching it locally.

Based on the form service used, the `comment` partial calls the appropriate partial method to get the list of comments for the website as the following listing shows. Then the comments for the specific page are filtered and displayed to the end user.

Listing 9.31   Getting comments (AcmeTheme/layouts/partials/comment.html)

```
{{$comments := dict}}          ◁──┐  Initializes the $comments variable
{{if getenv "NETLIFY" }}          │  based on NETLIFY environment variable
  {{$comments = partialCached "netlifyCommentList.html" .}}
{{else}}
  {{$comments = partialCached "formspreeCommentList.html" .}}
{{end}}
                                      ┌  Loops through the comments
                                      │  for the current page
{{range (index $comments .RelPermalink)}}  ◁─┘
<div class="comment">
  <img width="100" height="100"
    alt="{{.name}} Avatar"
    {{with resources.GetRemote (print
      "https://www.gravatar.com/avatar/"
      ( md5 .email ) "?s=100&d=wavatar") }}    Uses the avatar image (200×200 px for
      {{ with .Err }}                          retina screens) from Gravatar, falling
        {{ warnf "%s" . }}                     back to Wavatar (generated faces with
      {{ else }}                               differing features and backgrounds) for
        src="{{ .RelPermalink }}"              unknown emails
      {{end}}
    {{end}}>
  <div class="author">{{.name}}</div>      Renders the comments
  <div class="message">{{.message}}</div>
</div>
{{end}}
```

CODE CHECKPOINT   https://chapter-09-08.hugoinaction.com, and source code: https://github.com/hugoinaction/hugoinaction/tree/chapter-09-08.

9.7   *Pseudo APIs that compile to JSON*

In this chapter, we have accessed third-party APIs by sending GET requests at compile time and POST requests from the web form. In this section, we will create custom APIs to deliver content.

Having an API for content has become an essential aspect of web development. This is due to the proliferation of native applications that rely on the same data as the website but render them using a different technology that's more suited to the hardware. The Jamstack does not prevent us from exposing APIs for our website. On the contrary, the Jamstack allows us to have the APIs hosted on a content delivery network (CDN) for greater availability and performance.

For the website serving content with no need for dynamic data processing, an API can simply be the same data from the website provided in a machine-friendly format like XML or JSON. We already handle GET requests to serve HTML so we can serve JSON from the same endpoint. While JSON cannot have the POST, PUT, or DELETE pieces, the GET portions of the API can be made very solid. I prefer to call these *pseudo APIs* to distinguish them from other APIs as these are limited to GET requests and cannot do dynamic processing on the server.

We can achieve a lot using pseudo APIs. From the perspective of the client, they are as genuine as server-related ones. Mobile apps can query to display data. Single-page applications (SPAs) rendering the website through JavaScript can use these APIs to get content. We can enhance our server rendering website fetching data dynamically through the JSON-based APIs exposed as pseudo-APIs.

GET APIs are among the most used REST-based APIs. We will create APIs for our website in this section and start using them via JavaScript in the following chapter.

9.7.1 Custom output formats in Hugo

The key to creating pseudo APIs in Hugo is to understand the concept of output formats. So far, we have generated a single HTML page from the Markdown document for each page of the website. Hugo supports much more than that. We can create as many pages from each Markdown document as we desire and in as many formats as we want. With Hugo, we can build everything from RSS (Really Simple Syndication) feeds to AMP (Accelerated Mobile Pages) to JSON APIs. Hugo comes bundled with the knowledge of many *outputs formats*, but Hugo users do not use most of them by default. To create a page in a custom output format, we need two things:

- An entry in either the front matter or the website configuration informing Hugo which output formats a specific page kind supports. (Remember in chapter 7, we learned that a page kind determines how the page is represented internally in Hugo and cannot be changed.)
- A template for rendering the page in that output format.

For example, say we want to create the AMP version of a specific blog post page. Then we need to add amp in the outputs section in the front matter for that page and create a single.amp.html template for single blog posts. Although amp is predefined, we can define custom mime types and custom formats in the website configuration, and chapter 13 shows how we can create a custom format in Hugo.

9.7.2 Creating the JSON API for the website

Although we can create a separate JSON API for each web page, we won't use that for this book. We will expose the entire website's content over a single GET request (/index.json). It may seem like an anti-pattern to reveal lots of content over a single request, but the text is surprisingly lightweight, and a 1 MB JSON response consists of a million English characters. We can split it into pages or do preprocessing as we desire. Many websites do not expose the contents of the web pages, just the title and summary over the API, and that is also an option if we are worried about file size.

To create JSON APIs for the website, enable the JSON output format for the index page. The following listing defines the custom output format.

Listing 9.32   Defining a custom output format (content/_index.md)

```
---
outputs: [html, json]
---
```

Next, we create a new template for the JSON API. This template will have a new scratch pad for storing the data we need to expose in the API and then uses the `jsonify` function to convert to JSON (https://github.com/hugoinaction/hugoinaction/tree/chapter-09-resources/07). The following listing defines the template we use to create a pseudo API for our blog. It collects the required data in a Hugo scratch pad and then uses the `jsonify` method to provide the scratch pad contents as JSON.

Listing 9.33   Creating the template (AcmeTheme/layouts/_default/index.json)

Creates a new scratch pad for storing the results

Creates an empty slice (array) to add the page contents to

```
{{ $result := newScratch }}
{{ $result.Set "pages" slice }}
{{ range site.RegularPages }}
{{ $cover := $result.Get "Null" }}
{{ with (.Resources.GetMatch "cover.*")}}
   {{ $cover =
      (.Resize "100x100 Center").Permalink}}
  {{end}}
{{ $result.Add "pages" (dict
   "url" .RelPermalink
   "content" .Plain
   "title" .Title
   "tags" .Params.Tags
   "cover" $cover)
}}
{{ end }}
{{ $result.Get ."pages" | jsonify }}
```

RegularPages is used instead of all pages to remove tags, categories, and other taxonomy-related pages from the JSON.

A roundabout way to initialize to nil

Adds a cover image with a 100 px width

Adds the page's link (RelPermalink), content in plain text format (Plain), title (Title), and tags (.Params.Tags). .Plain does not convert the content to HTML.

Converts to JSON to return result

Exercise 9.6

Which of the following is *not* a useful Hugo feature for pseudo APIs?

- **a.** Content views
- **b.** Page bundles
- **c.** Related pages
- **d.** Taxonomy
- **e.** Internal pagination template

We can create any GET API we desire using Hugo. These APIs are available over CDNs and can handle a significant load, delivering outstanding performance in terms of speed. The following listing provides a sample output from the pseudo API.

```
[{
  "content": "Acme Corporation™ is ...  Nothing else.\n",
  "cover": null,
  "tags": null,
  "title": "About Us",
  "url": "/about/"
},...]
```

Hugo as an API generator adds a whole new dimension to the use of the static site builder. From page bundles to taxonomies (chapter 4), most of its key features still make sense even in an API. We can still use partials (chapter 6) to share standard code and split functions, paginators (chapter 7) to create multiple pages, and content layouts to have different types of content. We can even use content views (chapter 7) to get custom data-specific JSON.

CODE CHECKPOINT   https://chapter-09-09.hugoinaction.com, and source code: https://github.com/hugoinaction/hugoinaction/tree/chapter-09-09.

The ability to build and access APIs moves our website to the Web 2.0 world, where readers can participate and new avenues of functionality are unlocked.

In this chapter, we discussed how Hugo interacts with the rest of the Jamstack ecosystem. We can call REST APIs like those from Twitter at compile time. The Contact Us page already sends data to a form provider. Forms can be content-driven instead of hardcoded as in the case of dynamic surveys. Data retrieval APIs allow us to display user-generated content in comment forms. With Hugo's custom output formats feature, we can expose our website over a GET-based (pseudo) API.

Summary

- The Jamstack provides an opportunity to access APIs at website compile time, enabling us to prebuild pages, thus not incurring the performance overhead and usage information leaks to third parties at run time.
- With the getJSON function, Hugo provides access to any API over HTTP. Most popular websites have a JSON-based API that we can use to get content to embed in a Hugo page.
- We can create web forms in Hugo and then use a form service like Netlify Forms or Formspree to send the form data to a third-party service that takes care of the day-to-day operations of a form backend.

- Having form generation based on markup and metadata provides the content creators a lot of flexibility with forms generated on the fly and without writing server code or HTML.
- We can combine form submissions with APIs to build a dynamic system that can feed off user-generated content.
- Using output formats in Hugo, we can build our own pseudo APIs that can serve data in any file format we desire. While those APIs cannot react to user input, we can make many applications, from mobile websites to single-page applications (SPAs).

The power of JavaScript

This chapter covers
- Evaluating JavaScript's role in a Jamstack-based website
- Building dynamic features like asynchronous form submission
- Performing fuzzy searches in the JavaScript/TypeScript ecosystem
- Embedding single page applications
- Tips and techniques for JavaScript

The definition of *dynamic* in terms of websites has changed over time. In the early days of the web, a dynamic website was the one that could have user-generated content, server-side processing, and all the great features we developed in the previous chapter (like comments and contact forms). This definition changed with the advent of web applications that redefined "dynamic" as web pages that could update on the fly without explicitly reloading the entire content. These pages can fetch content in the background and provide real-time updates without manually triggering some action. This modern definition of a dynamic website is possible with client-side processing, where a script accompanies the website content and runs on the end-user machine. JavaScript is the standard programming language used on the browser frontend, and all frameworks, including Hugo, need to play nice with JavaScript to unlock additional features.

In this chapter, we will focus on JavaScript, the *J* layer of the Jamstack. Prior Java-Script knowledge is required to be successful with this chapter. We will not use any specific JavaScript framework and will keep the JavaScript code simple. This approach does not mean that Hugo is incompatible with any of the modern JavaScript frameworks. Hugo sits on a different layer of the Jamstack than JavaScript and performs activities not associated with client-side processing. We will understand the special place Hugo has carved out for JavaScript, how to best use JavaScript in a Hugo-based website, and the set of features client-side JavaScript can enable for our website.

This chapter will show how we can use JavaScript to communicate with external and internal APIs (pseudo APIs). We will use JavaScript to control the page flow and make the server communication happen in the background without refreshing the user interface. We will also change parts of a web page dynamically for cases like search results, where all possible options are too many to be statically built and easier to do in JavaScript. Figure 10.1 describes the role of this chapter in the Jamstack.

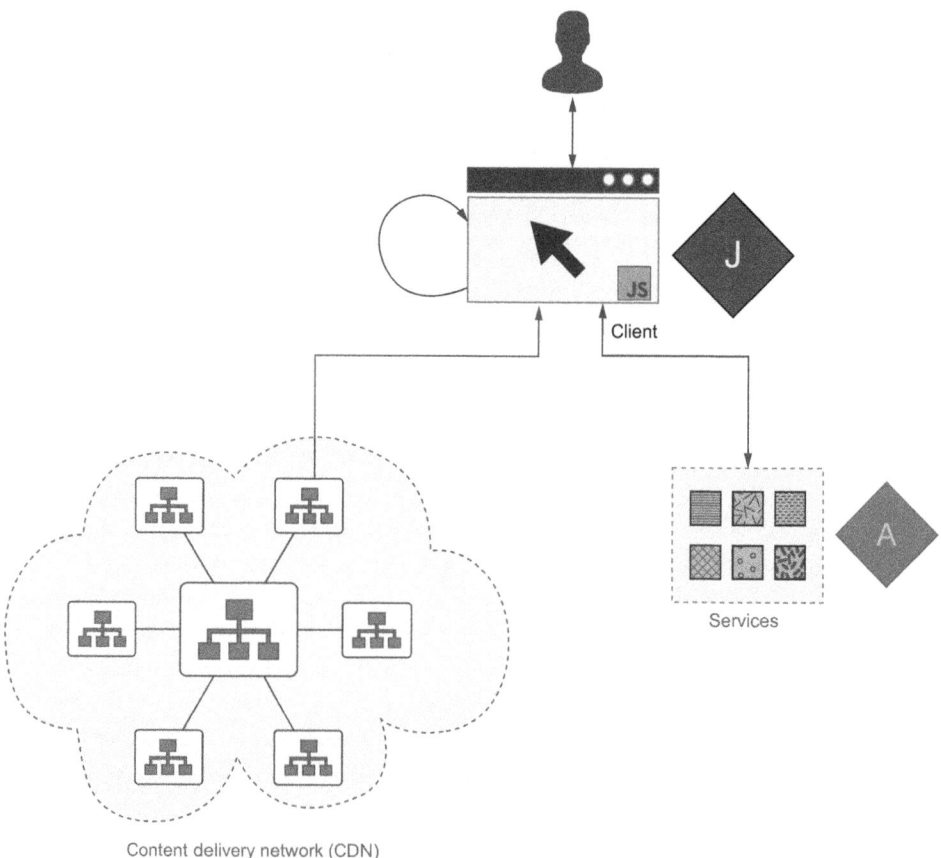

Content delivery network (CDN)

Figure 10.1   Chapter 10 focuses on the JavaScript layer of the Jamstack. We can control the flow of web pages, react to user input, have two-way communication with services, and dynamically generate portions of a web page using JavaScript.

10.1 Why use JavaScript in a Hugo project?

JavaScript is the only language that the browser natively understands. It is the only language with access to the browser's document object model (DOM), and updating it on the fly provides unique advantages for web developers. In a web page built without JavaScript, each interaction including the benign ones like clicking a search box or opening a menu item needs to go to the server. This server communication causes delay and occasionally flashes of an empty white screen in the browser. Using JavaScript, we can hide this network traffic in multiple ways, some of which include:

- We can hide the data for certain parts of the web page, such as menu items, from the user.
- We can prefetch the needed data when the user mouses over the search form as a signal to act.
- We can show a spinner only in the part of the web page we are updating while the rest continues to function.
- We can hide the entire loading activity in a client-side animation.

We cannot provide these features by using a server-side technology or a build-time solution. Another possibility enabled uniquely by JavaScript is the ability to generate web applications. Unlike web pages, web applications focus on manipulating rather than rendering content. For instance, having Microsoft Word running in the browser is not possible without JavaScript.

Hugo is built for data presentation and not manipulation. We can get close to a single-page web application in terms of behavior and performance, but a single-page application does not play to the strengths of Hugo. Suppose you have a web application built with the JavaScript framework. In that case, Hugo supports presenting and embedding the application, making a hybrid website that we will explore in section 10.6. Our focus in this chapter will be on rounding the rough edges of the Acme Corporation website with a small amount of JavaScript.

> **Progressive enhancement**
>
> Although not officially prescribed in the Jamstack or in Hugo, a guiding principle to follow in web development made simple with Hugo's approach is *progressive enhancement*. Progressive enhancement revolves around putting the web content first and then adding the styling and interactivity. The basic idea is that the plain HTML version of the website should have all the textual content that can be read without any CSS or JavaScript loaded. Then, if CSS is available, it should enhance the content with styling, and if JavaScript support is available, we should use it to add interactivity. This approach provides a great experience for users with bad network connections, older web browsers, accessibility, and perceptible performance benefits for all other regular users.

> **(continued)**
> There is a whole world of JavaScript frameworks targeting developers looking at progressive enhancement as the means to developing their websites. For example, alpine.js and Stimulus.js can generate a JavaScript model for building a web application directly from an HTML web page. This way, we can create dynamic pages or any data-based interactivity with the non-interactive pieces rendered in the template by default.

10.2 *Using JavaScript to control the page flow*

Suppose you submit a comment or the Contact Us form from the previous chapter. In that case, you might have noticed that the form redirected to the Netlify or Formspree page, which informed you about the form submission and requested that the reader return to the web page after submitting the form. Although this is functional, this page takes us out of our the website, and its design does not match what we have built in the rest of the site. Whereas Netlify allows us to define a custom form response page, an inline form submitted as a message is better because it reduces the need to generate a whole new page. Full redirect causes a flicker of whitespace, and the user temporarily loses context (like scrolling position) and cannot perform any other task on the page while the content refreshes. This experience is jarring, especially if submitting comments to an article. We can fix this by using JavaScript to make the submission and report the response inline.

10.2.1 *Handling forms in JavaScript*

The implementation of the dynamic form handler is fairly straightforward. We need to attach an event listener to the form's submit event, cancel and submit it manually, and then inform the user about its submission. Here are some of the JavaScript-based browser features we will use for this redirection:

- `event.target`—Gets an element that triggers an event.
- `FormData`—Converts a form's data to a JavaScript object.
- `fetch`—Sends HTTP(s) requests from JavaScript.
- `Event.preventDefault()`—Prevents default execution of an event.
- `submit`—Sends an event via a form when submitted by the user.
- `insertAdjacentHTML`—Adds HTML, based on an existing DOM node.

NOTE We can use a library like JQuery for this use case. JQuery takes care of a lot of best practices like event delegation, page load, and so on. It also comes with a pleasant, terse, and complete API for DOM manipulation.

For submitting forms through Formspree via Ajax, we need to pass a header informing Formspree that the response needs to be formatted in JSON format. We can transmit this information by sending the `Accept` header with `application/json` as the value. The code involves adding a top-level event listener for the submit event. We can get the submitted form data and send it via the fetch API. We will follow this up with the addition of a DOM element to inform the user of the submission (https://github.com/hugoinaction/hugoinaction/tree/chapter-10-resources/01).

Specific events vs. event delegation

The technique of adding an event listener in JavaScript at the top level rather than for each element is called *event delegation*. When an event gets fired in the web browser, it bubbles up in the DOM until the event reaches the root element. If we add an event listener to the document itself, it will catch all events anywhere in it. We can then use the `target` property to get the specific DOM element where this event occurs. This approach is, by default, the way libraries like JQuery deal with events. Event delegation has a few advantages:

- *The listeners can continue to work on elements currently not present in the DOM but added later.* The listener applies to the document and does not change until the page reloads.
- *We reduce our DOM interaction.* Only one listener can take care of all events (as in the case of forms). All DOM interactions are expensive operations, and event delegation avoids the slow ones.
- *We can add event listeners even when the page is not ready.* We do not need the page to load and render completely. Because the listeners are there even when the DOM is loading, if some part takes time to load/render, the available part can still be functional.

The delegation comes with a few disadvantages. The order of receivers for the same event may not be as apparent because there is bubbling involved. We might need to add additional code to handle that. Also, because the document doesn't clear until the DOM unloads, the event listeners need to be removed manually if they are not required. We could leak memory by keeping the listeners alive for a long time in a never-closing document in the case of JavaScript-based web applications. If we are careful with how we deploy event listeners at the root, they can improve performance and reduce the amount of code we need to manage when event handling on our website.

The JavaScript code in the following listing converts the form submission into an asynchronous operation with inline feedback. In the listing, we use an asynchronous operation rather than redirection to a different page.

Listing 10.1   Converting the form submission (AcmeTheme/assets/index.js)

```
function addFormHandler() {
    document.addEventListener('submit',        Event listener for the submit event
        async event => {                    ⟵
            if (!event.target instanceof HTMLFormElement)
            {                                          Checks if a form element
                return;                                fired the event
            }
        event.preventDefault();
```

Prevents the form's automatic submission

```
const form = event.target;
const data = new FormData(form);        ◁───  Captures the form's data via JavaScript.
const action = form.action;                   The FormData object supports the same
const method = form.method;                   mime type as an HTML form via JavaScript
const response = await fetch(action, {        and also conversion to JSON if needed.
  method,
  body: data,                                 Passes the Accept header to
  headers: {"Accept": "application/json"} ◁─  request the server to respond
});                                           in JSON format
if (response.ok) {
    form.insertAdjacentHTML('afterend',
      '<div class="success">The form has been submitted.</div>');
} else {
    form.insertAdjacentHTML('afterend',
      '<div class="error">The form could not be submitted.
      ➥Please try again later.</div>');
}
const message = form.nextElementSibling;      Empties the form after submitting
form.reset();                           ◁──   it to allow for more submissions
setTimeout(() => message.remove(), 10000);  ◁──  Clears the message
  });                                              after 10 seconds
}

addFormHandler();
```

Calls the fetch API to send data to the server

Informs if response used in both success and error scenarios

10.2.2 Building and loading JavaScript using Hugo Pipes

The next step is to make this JavaScript file available in the various web pages that need it. The index.js JavaScript file (in listing 10.1) is simple, and if we want, we could pop that into the static folder and link it from the template HTML. But that approach is fraught with problems:

- The handwritten JavaScript has extra spaces and comments that can be cleaned up and minified to reduce bundle size.
- If we add dependencies based on the npm ecosystem, we will need a bundler that converts to a single JavaScript file for hosting.

We therefore recommend using Hugo's JavaScript builder support right from the start. It is so fast that you will not notice the build times, and it also provides tons of features from shimming mount (to target older browsers) to node module bundling and TypeScript. Just as we needed `resources.ToCSS` to convert SCSS to CSS (as used in chapter 6), JavaScript compilation requires `js.Build` via Hugo Pipes.

To use Hugo Pipes with JavaScript, we can either put the JavaScript files in a page bundle or in the assets folder. Page-specific JavaScript files are rare, so for this specific use case, we will use the assets folder. We can load this script like we loaded CSS files earlier in the book using `resources.Get` and then pass it through js.Build to compile the JavaScript code. The following listing loads the JavaScript code using Hugo Pipes.

Listing 10.2   Loading JavaScript code (AcmeTheme/layouts/default/baseof.html)

```
{{ $js := resources.Get "index.js" | js.Build}}

<script type="text/javascript" src="{{ $js.RelPermalink }}" defer></script>
```

In the listing, note that we use `defer` to load the JavaScript file without blocking the HTML content rendering after the `script` tag. Also, it reads index.js and combines all the JavaScript code required by the index.js file. This code can search across the Hugo modules imported by the current project and all the node modules imported from npm. It then compiles the JavaScript code to a single file that we have linked to in the `<script>` tag.

By default, Hugo performs no minification on the file. We can supply additional options to enable minification via the `minify` flag in the argument as the following listing shows. We will not be minifying the development server to allow easier debugging.

Listing 10.3   Minifying the JavaScript (AcmeTheme/layouts/default/baseof.html)

```
{{ $js := resources.Get "index.js" | js.Build
   (dict "minify" hugo.IsProduction) }}
```

CODE CHECKPOINT   https://chapter-10-01.hugoinaction.com, and source code: https://github.com/hugoinaction/hugoinaction/tree/chapter-10-01.

Hugo and TypeScript

TypeScript is a programming language that is popular in the JavaScript ecosystem. It adds support for JavaScript data types, making tools like Visual Studio Code better able to understand the code and minimizing errors associated with data types and mistyping when writing JavaScript.

Hugo supports TypeScript by default, and we can import any .ts file just like we imported the .js file. However, Hugo does not type check like the JavaScript compiler, only doing the conversion. You can run the TypeScript compiler to check or install a plugin in your text editor while building using Hugo.

Hugo's TypeScript-to-JavaScript conversion is an order of magnitude faster than most tools, including the TypeScript compiler. We therefore recommend sticking with Hugo for the final compilation of the website. There is no need to pay the additional cost of slower JavaScript compilation when working on the website's content, HTML, or CSS portions.

10.3 *Approaches for JavaScript handling*

The previous form submission code has some issues that will come back to haunt us. These are:

- *The code acts on all HTML forms on the website.* This listener can accidentally add behavior to the forms that do not need it or to those that can get broken by this code. There should be a cleaner way to control which website forms need this code to act on when it executes.
- *The textual content becomes a part of the template, and a content editor cannot override it.* Ideally, the content should all come from the Markdown or YAML files supplied by the content editor to allow for easy overrides.
- *As we add more code, it will become unmanageable as a single file.* We need multiple files to do numerous things, each independent and loaded from an index file.

NOTE The CSS files used in this book are not as organized as they should be on a professionally developed website. Hugo offers support for SCSS and PostCSS, which provide the means to manage CSS as efficiently as desired. The CSS, HTML, JavaScript, and, in some cases, the Hugo template code used in this book are not what you would expect in a typical website. This book focuses on demonstrating and explaining the concepts of Hugo rather than building a properly engineered website theme for production usage.

There are two main approaches to using JavaScript that we can employ to gain scalability for our website: using the primary code of the website as the template logic that generates the HTML content and keeping the JavaScript code as its own entity. We discuss these approaches in the following subsections.

10.3.1 *HTML as primary JavaScript as a utility*

This approach is more traditional to website development. With this approach, the primary code of the website is the template logic that generates the HTML content, and the JavaScript pieces support the layers. The JavaScript code is generic and can activate when we set specific properties in the HTML DOM. If the corresponding DOM elements are present, the JavaScript code kicks into performing what we asked.

We can extend this approach to include CSS as a utility and focus only on HTML on day-to-day usage. Frameworks like Bootstrap (https://getbootstrap.com) and Foundation (https://get.foundation/) take this approach. They provide generic CSS and JavaScript files that we can include in our website to get a good looking and customizable user interface with added features over plain HTML. Frameworks like htmx (https://htmx.org) take this approach, providing generic support for writing logic in HTML. Let's look at some advantages and disadvantages of using this approach.

ADVANTAGES

- *The JavaScript code is scalable and reusable by default.* Any theme developer can add additional properties to a template to activate this code anywhere. We can easily expose the features to the content author, who can provide the keys to enable the components in the front matter. This flexibility provides the ability for non-developers to fine-tune the website.

- *The JavaScript code is loosely coupled and independent.* Removing one of the modules has a slight possibility of impacting other modules on the website. We can also load the modules independently on demand, reducing the bundle size and render time for the website.

- *Mixing and matching JavaScript frameworks is easy.* Because all scripts share the DOM layer and are disabled without the right trigger in the DOM, we can easily use multiple frameworks (if required) on the same website.

- *Progressive enhancement is easy with this approach.* Because the logic lies in the HTML, if the JavaScript code is not present, we can use functionality enabled by the HTML CSS.

- *The JavaScript logic is minimal and manageable.* You need to write little JavaScript code. There is no state in the frontend beyond what we can represent in the URL in many cases. The total JavaScript code written on the website can be much less in comparison to other approaches.

DISADVANTAGES

- *It is effortless to write bad or unstructured code (also called spaghetti code) with this approach.* Because nothing enforces code organization in a particular way, it is tempting to add some quick-and-dirty fix to a problem that can make mainte-nance of the website a mess. This code sprinkling can become highly annoying if the state management code is not present in a single place.

- *The approach starts to break down when the JavaScript code becomes too big.* Each check for a DOM element to enable a feature is a cost, albeit a small one. But thousands of such calls can add up and begin to show their impact on the website's perfor-mance. There is a workaround that combines some routing checks, but at that point, we are not really using JavaScript as utility code that can be reused.

- *Figuring out unused code is hard.* There is no good way to know which JavaScript code is active and which is not. Optimizing around dead code removal is difficult.

10.3.2 *JavaScript as a separate layer to HTML*

This approach is the preferred approach of websites with the single-page application (SPA) style of web development. It works best where the websites have lots of JavaScript to provide core functionality, although Hugo's approach, in general, attempts to keep the data closer to the HTML. Keeping the JavaScript code as an entity can support use cases like per-user personalization, where server-generated HTML falls short. In web-sites like these, we need to tightly couple the JavaScript code and the HTML code as we tailor the JavaScript code specifically to the HTML that accompanies it. In many cases, it is specific to the endpoint or the web page where it is loaded. Although we can reuse parts of this code as components, there has to be some page-specific JavaScript code, and in many cases, we may need state management or routing, which is not reusable.

Routing and state management in JavaScript

In an interactive website, we can manipulate a web page based on user interaction, which leads to a different page from the one sent by the server. *State* in a web page represents the changes needed to render the web page to get the form that we will display rather than the one sent by the server. In SPAs, the state is too large to be represented in the URL or set up in the cookies sent to the server. A state management library can help bridge this gap by providing a data structure in JavaScript that reflects this state and allows frameworks to update and respond to changes in this state. Although we will not use a state management library in this book, in chapter 12, we will create a shopping cart backed by a variable in JavaScript that works across tabs and relaunches, forming a rudimentary state management system.

A web browser represents all web pages with a URL. Different pieces of code need to be enabled based on the URL to render the correct page for the user. *Routing* is the concept of activating a piece of code based on the URL that is requested. In server-managed websites, the routing is server-side, either by selecting the correct file (e.g., LAMP stack) or via some function (as in Ruby on Rails or in Node.js/Express). In SPAs, this task lives in JavaScript. In the Jamstack, the routing is implicit as the contents of each valid URL are pregenerated and stored on the CDN. Note that with the Jamstack, we still expect to have the website pregenerated and ready to serve. We are not building pure SPAs where the entire HTML and CSS live in the JavaScript code, but this is the closest we can get to a SPA with generated HTML.

Hugo generates the initial HTML and presents it to the user. The JavaScript code then loads and creates a JavaScript object corresponding to the areas that need JavaScript-based interactivity, creating the controllers and components that can take over user interactivity from the pregenerated HTML. The ownership transition is automatic, and the web developer can decide the boundaries of the HTML and JavaScript code as they see fit, along with the use cases when we should load a new web page from the server versus when JavaScript should update the existing web page. Frameworks like Alpine.js (https://github.com/alpinejs/alpine/, Unpoly (https://unpoly.com), and Stimulus.js (https://stimulusjs.org/) excel in building this type of logic, which can smoothly transition from HTML to JavaScript. Let's look at some advantages and disadvantages of using JavaScript as a separate layer.

ADVANTAGES

- *We can build a highly interactive SPA for the parts of the website that form the application.* We can still use the precompiled HTML for the non-interactive pages like the Privacy Policy page using the Jamstack.

- *The JavaScript code is easier to maintain.* This is because learning from more than a decade of SPA development can be brought and applied to this setup.
- *With a proper router, we can scale the JavaScript code quickly.* This allows us to build as complex an application as needed.

DISADVANTAGES

- *The JavaScript logic can become complex.* Additionally, there is an overhead to understand the JavaScript and the corresponding template code.
- *The JavaScript code is mostly not portable across different independent web pages and websites.* It is written mainly as a one-off implementation for a specific use case. We can reuse components as modules if we so desire.
- *The code is different across different frameworks.* Although we can use two frameworks together, it might be cumbersome to do that.

10.4 Converting JavaScript to a utility controlled by the HTML code

For the form-handling use case, focusing on the HTML is more manageable than splitting it for each form and each web page. Therefore, we will stick with the first approach for keeping JavaScript as a utility.

10.4.1 Enabling dynamic forms through JavaScript

Using the JavaScript as a utility approach, we will move the content and the logic that we have built for dynamic submission into our template code, making it controllable by the developer and the content editor via the website configuration. We will enable the dynamic form submission using an attribute in the form that will trigger the JavaScript code to perform pending tasks. We also need to move the error and the success text to the markup document controlled by the content author (see figure 10.2). A default value of the count, though, should be baked into the template (https://github.com/hugoinaction/hugoinaction/tree/chapter-10-resources/02).

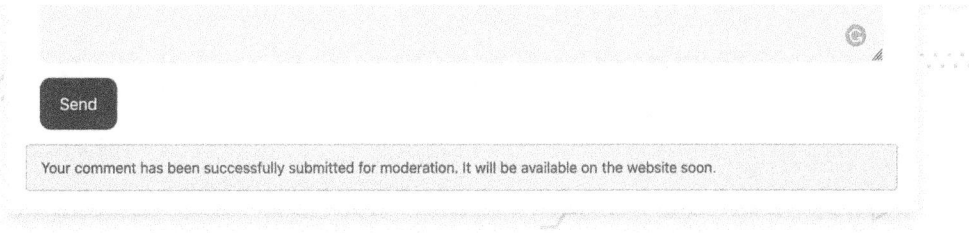

Figure 10.2   Submission success message that the JavaScript renders after asynchronous submission of the form

The template is explicitly marked with a `data-dynamic-form` attribute to tell the JavaScript code to convert this form to a dynamic one as the following listing shows. We also provide the success and error messages inline.

Listing 10.4   Converting the form (AcmeTheme/layouts/partials/comment.html)

```
<template id="comment-success">     ⟵──── Template for the success message
<div class="success">
{{default "Your comment has been successfully submitted
⟹ for moderation. It will be available on the website
⟹ soon." (site.Param "comment-success")}}     ⟵────
</div>
</template>                          Template for the
<template id="comment-error" >  ⟵──┘ error message
<div class="error">
{{default "We are facing an issue submitting the comment.
-->  Please try again later."
-->   (site.Param "comment-error")}}     ⟵───
</div>
</template>
<form data-dynamic-form
  data-success=" comment-success"
  data-error="comment-error" ...>     ⟵───
...
</form>
```

> Uses the default function to provide default data for a comment form and the $.Param function to allow reading from front matter, falling back to the website configuration if needed

> Uses the default function to provide default data for a comment form and the $.Param function to allow reading from front matter, falling back to the website configuration if needed

> Updates the form with the data-* properties meant to be read by JavaScript

We need similar changes on the contact form. This is an exercise for the reader. The code is provided in the chapter resources (https://github.com/hugoinaction/hugoinaction/tree/chapter-10-resources/02).

Next, we need to update the JavaScript code so that it does not take all the forms but uses the data from the labeled ones instead. The code in listing 10.5 reads all forms marked with data-dynamic-form and converts those to asynchronous requests, taking the post submission messages from the data-success and data-error fields associated with the form. This allows us to dynamically handle form submissions with form selection and handling controlled by the HTML code. We will read the various variables from the DOM itself.

Listing 10.5   Restricting the JavaScript code (AcmeTheme/assets/index.js)

```
function addFormHandler() {
  document.addEventListener('submit', async event => {
    if (event.target?.dataset?.dynamicForm
      === undefined) {          ⟵───
      return;
    }
    ...
    if (response.ok) {
        form.insertAdjacentHTML('afterend',
          document.querySelector(form.dataset.success)
            .innerHTML);          ⟵───
    } else {
      form.insertAdjacentHTML('afterend',
        document.querySelector(form.dataset.error)
          .innerHTML);          ⟵───
```

> Uses only the elements with the attribute data-dynamic-form

> Uses data-success and data-error attributes to get data from the form

```
    }
    ...
  }));
}
```

...

> **NOTE** If the backend is acting slow, the form should be disabled to prevent resubmission, and we should inform the user that some activity is in progress with a UI affordance like a spinner (not implemented in this book).

> **CODE CHECKPOINT** https://chapter-10-02.hugoinaction.com, and source code: https://github.com/hugoinaction/hugoinaction/tree/chapter-10-02.

10.4.2 *Splitting JavaScript into multiple files*

Our JavaScript code, although still small and manageable, needs some organization. If we plan to have more JavaScript code, now would be a good time to think about organizing it into multiple files. We can split the form-handling code into two separate files and the form and initialization into individual files. The following listing splits the code into multiple files, then the index file for the entire project initializes all the modules rather than focusing on the contents of a single module.

> **Listing 10.6   Organizing JavaScript code (AcmeTheme/assets/index.js)**

```
import FormHandler from "./formHandler"

function init() {
  FormHandler.init();

}

init();
```

We can use the index file to initialize multiple modules that live in their independent files. The following listing moves all the code for the form handler to the formHandler .js file.

> **Listing 10.7   Moving JavaScript code (AcmeTheme/assets/formHandler.js)**

```
export default {
  init() {
    document.addEventListener('submit', async event => { ... }
  }
}
```

> **CODE CHECKPOINT** https://chapter-10-03.hugoinaction.com, and source code: https://github.com/hugoinaction/hugoinaction/tree/chapter-10-03.

Hugo's build pipeline takes care of taking these JavaScript files and converting them to an optimized bundle for use in the website. With these changes, we can forget about the JavaScript code and focus on the website's contents instead.

10.4.3 *Passing variables when building JavaScript*

JavaScript can also get variables and compilation parameters directly from js.Build so we can tailor our JavaScript code based on these. One such example is the `defines` key in the JavaScript build configuration. We can use this to expose the option in the website configuration to not display the form again after submission.

We can potentially expose this as an HTML property as well, but that comes with a drawback. If we do not want to use a feature, the code for that feature is still present in our JavaScript bundle, wasting bandwidth to download it for our use and to verify it with another DOM property for accessing it. Although the form removal code is minimal, the concept applies to large pieces of JavaScript code used for any custom feature that we need to turn off until it is ready to be released or included by the website admin. Because Hugo is all about compile-time optimization, removing unused code during compilation would be ideal.

Let's start by adding the code to remove the form after submission. We can replace `form.reset` with `form.remove` in our JavaScript code to perform this task. The following listing removes the form on submission if `REMOVE_FORM_ON_SUBMISSION` is passed as true.

Listing 10.8   Removing the form (AcmeTheme/assets/formHandler.js)

```
if (REMOVE_FORM_ON_SUBMISSION) {
  form.remove();
} else {
  form.reset();
  setTimeout(() => message.remove(), 10000);
}
```

Next, we need to pass the value of the `REMOVE_FORM_ON_SUBMISSION` variable from the website configuration during compilation. We can use the `defines` option in Hugo's js.Build to achieve that task as the following listing shows. You'll need to add the code in this listing to AcmeTheme/layouts/default/baseof.html.

Listing 10.9   Passing `REMOVE_FORM_ON_SUBMISSION`

```
{{ $defines := dict "REMOVE_FORM_ON_SUBMISSION"
  (default "false"
    (site.Param "RemoveFormOnSubmission")
  )
}}

{{ $js := resources.Get "index.js"
  | js.Build (dict "defines" $defines
                   "minify" hugo.IsProduction )}}
```

We can control the code to either reset or remove the form after submission in the Hugo configuration with this small change. The best part about this is that not even a trace of another piece of code that's turned off remains in the compiled JavaScript once it goes through the minifier in the production build. To test this, we can set `RemoveFormOnSubmission` to `true` in the config/_default/params.yml file, which returns a view similar to figure 10.3. The following listing enables form removal on submission from the Hugo configuration.

Listing 10.10   Enabling form removal (config/_default/params.yaml)

```
RemoveFormOnSubmission: true
```

CODE CHECKPOINT   https://chapter-10-04.hugoinaction.com, and source code: https://github.com/hugoinaction/hugoinaction/tree/chapter-10-04.

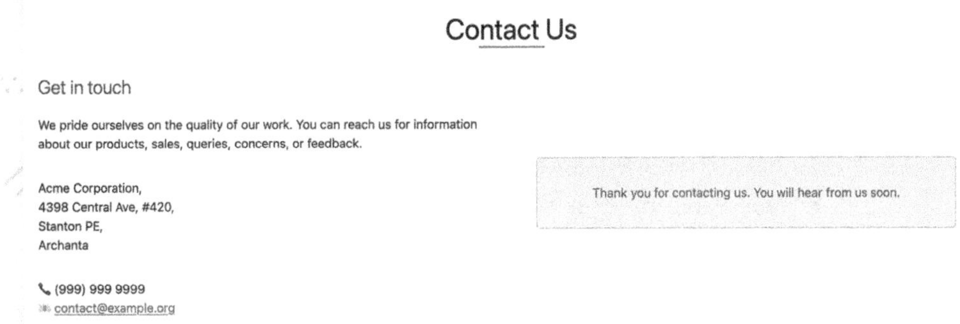

Contact Us

Get in touch

We pride ourselves on the quality of our work. You can reach us for information about our products, sales, queries, concerns, or feedback.

Acme Corporation,
4398 Central Ave, #420,
Stanton PE,
Archanta

Thank you for contacting us. You will hear from us soon.

📞 (999) 999 9999
✉ contact@example.org

Figure 10.3   Removal of the form on submission from the Contact Us page is achieved with JavaScript, replacing the form with a message post submission.

More options to customize js.Build

Hugo's js.Build exposes a lot of options to customize JavaScript compilation. Here is a subset of the options that are most useful for our daily use:

- `params`—Like defines, there are parameters that are available as variables (think about the default values for the configuration). The JavaScript code can supply these. Unlike defines that find and replace and need unique names, parameters participate as valid JavaScript values in the parser and minifier.
- `sourceMap`—Enables source maps for debugging JavaScript code from the minified output.
- `target`—Targets older browsers. The JavaScript compiler can convert modern JavaScript to older formats automatically for compatibility.

(continued)

■ externals—Ignores specific packages that can be assumed to be loaded by a CDN.

Full configuration options for js.Build are available on Hugo's JavaScript Building page at https://gohugo.io/hugo-pipes/js/.

10.5   Enabling client-side search

Just like dynamic form submissions, a search widget with real-time results as you type requires JavaScript. Now that we have a skeleton structure of the JavaScript code and JSON-based pseudo API for the website ready, we can use a search widget to provide client-side searching.

10.5.1   Concept of a client-side search

In traditional systems, search is server-based, where the keyword supplied by the client maps to values in a search index that provides the best ranking pages for the keyword. A client-side search is a concept where the server supplies this index to the client (or the client builds it dynamically), and the mapping happens on the client. Client-side search has many advantages over server-based search:

- The search index is static (like everything else in the Jamstack). It can be distributed over a CDN and provide all the advantages of caching and performance that a CDN has to offer.
- The search index is pushed to the client on demand or even preloaded. No roundtrip time is lost in sending keystrokes to the server, so the search becomes faster.
- There is no additional server to maintain and keep in sync with the database. The user's machine supplies the resources required to perform the search.
- The search can work even if the user goes offline after loading the initial web page.

The significant limitation of the client-side search is the size of the index. If we have an extensive index, preloading the search index can prove to be too bandwidth-intensive to be of any practical use. We can split the index and load it in parts on demand, but stretching that approach goes back to the world of having the entire index maintained by the server.

For most websites, the textual content is not huge from the eyes of the modern web; 2 MB of data can store 2 million characters. That number is considerable for a text-based search index but is not a massive overhead for a web page where we often have images of this size on websites. Although we can create a more optimized and robust search index in Hugo, the amount of data in the Acme Corporation website is so tiny that we will supply all of it via the JSON pseudo API. We can even move the search index creation to JavaScript if we want.

10.5.2 *Showing the search box in the header*

A search widget consists of an input box and a dropdown to show results from partial queries. The following listing adds this widget to the website header.

Listing 10.11   Adding a search form (AcmeTheme/layouts/_default/baseof.html)

```
<header>
  ...
  <span id="search">        ◁──┐ Wrapper div that contains
    <input type="search" placeholder="Search">        the search form and the list
    <div></div>        ◁──┐        Actual search form
  </span>              │        for the website
                       │ Placeholder for search results
{{ partialCached "menu.html" ... }}
  ...
</header>
```

That is all that is needed. Next, we will use JavaScript to make this search field active.

10.5.3 *Loading the website data*

To fill the search results in JavaScript, we need to load the website content from the pseudo API and create a search index. We can use JavaScript's fetch function to push the website data into a variable (https://github.com/hugoinaction/hugoinaction/tree/chapter-10-resources/03). The following listing loads the website data using this function.

Listing 10.12   Loading the website data (AcmeTheme/assets/search.js)

```
export default {
  async init() {
    try {
      const response =
        await window.fetch("/index.json");        ◁── Uses fetch() to download
      if (!response.ok) {        ◁────┐                 the index file with all the
        this.removeSearch();            │                 website content
        return;
      }
      let data = await response.json();        In case of error, removes
      // Just for now.                         the search box
      console.log(data);
    } catch(e) {
      this.removeSearch();        ◁────┘
    }
  },

  removeSearch() {
    document.querySelector("#search")?.remove();
  }
}
```

Gets the response data from JSON as an object

The previous code has one problem that will break the website if hosted in a subfolder in GitHub Pages. This code assumes the root directory, /index.json, is where the JSON version of the code lives. Listing 10.13 passes site.BaseURL as another variable to defines to fix this. This value needs to be surrounded by quotation marks to be valid JavaScript. (We could use params instead of defines, which does not have this limitation.)

Listing 10.13   Adding the `BaseURL` (AcmeTheme/layouts/default/baseof.html)

```
{{ $defines := dict
  "REMOVE_FORM_ON_SUBMISSION" (default "false"
        (site.Param "RemoveFormOnSubmission"))
  "BASE_URL" (print "\"" site.BaseURL "\"") }}
```

Surround with quotes to make this a valid JavaScript string

We will also need to fix our JavaScript code. The following listing adds BASE_URL to ensure that the search always picks up from the correct endpoint.

Listing 10.14   Adding BASE_URL (AcmeTheme/assets/search.js)

```
const response = await window.fetch(BASE_URL + "/index.json");
```

Next, we will invoke the init method of the search form from the index as listing 10.15 shows. Even though the function is asynchronous, we can call it without using await if we do not need to wait for it to return a valid value. This code should log the entire contents of the website in the browser console.

Listing 10.15   Initializing the search query (AcmeTheme/assets/index.js)

```
import Search from "./search"

function init() {
  ...
  Search.init();
}
```

Handling CORS errors

If we read index.json from a different website in a different domain than the current website, a header Access Control Allow Origin with the value of * is required for the browser to allow cross-origin access. If this is not present, a cross-domain request will fail with an error similar to the following:

```
No 'Access-Control-Allow-Origin' header is present on the requested
resource. If an opaque response serves your needs, set the request's
mode to 'no-cors' to fetch the resource with CORS disabled.
```

Cross-origin resource sharing (CORS) is the standard we need to implement if we want resources accessible across domains. For this, GitHub Pages provides Access-Control-Allow-Origin by default, but for Netlify, we need to configure it. As of writing this book, Netlify did not expose this option in the UI, though we can enable it through the Netlify configuration.

If you are using pull request previews in Netlify, you are likely to hit this error. A sample configuration file (netlify.toml) is provided in the chapter resources (https://github.com/hugoinaction/hugoinaction/tree/chapter-10-resources/04).

CODE CHECKPOINT   https://chapter-10-05.hugoinaction.com, and source code: https://github.com/hugoinaction/hugoinaction/tree/chapter-10-05.

Exercise 10.1

Why is Hugo a good choice as a static site builder even for heavy JavaScript-based projects? (Select all that apply.)

- a. Hugo is written in Go and, therefore, causes less confusion.
- b. Hugo has great support for playing nicely with client-side JavaScript with a well-defined interface for transferring compile-time data.
- c. Hugo can cross-compile to JavaScript and run in a web browser.
- d. Hugo provides a clear, well-defined separation of concerns for build-time and run-time processing.
- e. Hugo Pipes delivers a rich, powerful, and extremely fast JavaScript builder.

10.5.4   *Importing a search library*

When the data on the website is small, we can use regular expressions and loop through the content to find results. It may work, but an excellent full-text search library can be helpful when we need features like *fuzzy matching* (which allows for results with partial terms and autocompletes) and properly weighted scoring of search results. The Java-Script ecosystem has many ready-to-use libraries, which are well-maintained, easy-to-use, and readily available. Node.js (https://nodejs.org) needs to be installed (we can use any stable version) on the machine for getting community modules. Once Node.js is available, we can use the npm (node package manager) command line.

Before installing a Node.js dependency, we need to initialize it for our project. We have multiple projects on our website: the AcmeTheme project and the Acme Corporation website project. Because the search code lives in AcmeTheme and is shared, we need to initialize Node.js in the AcmeTheme project as the following listing shows. To do that, we will run npm init to get a package.json file that can list our JavaScript-based dependencies.

Listing 10.16   Initializing Node.js (in AcmeTheme/)

```
npm init
```

Next, we need to search for and download a Node.js module to help users with fuzzy searches. To find a library, you can use the `npm search` command as shown in listing 10.17; listing 10.18 shows the results.

Listing 10.17   Searching for a fuzzy search library

```
npm search fuzzy search
```

Listing 10.18   Search results for `fuzzy search`

```
> npm search fuzzy search
NAME                    | DESCRIPTION             | AUTHOR             | DATE        |
fuse.js                 | Lightweight...          | =krisk            | 2021-01-05|
fastest-levenshtein     | Fastest Levenshtein...  | =ka-weihe         | 2020-08-07|
fuzzy-search            | Simple fuzzy search     | =wouter2203       | 2020-02-20|
feathers-mongodb-f...   | hook which adds...       | =arve0            | 2020-09-13|
minisearch              | Tiny but powerful...    | =lucaong          | 2021-06-25|
mongoose-fuzzy-sea...   | Mongoose fuzzy...       | =vspallas         | 2020-11-03|
fuzzy-tools             | Functions for fuzzy...  | =axules           | 2021-04-18|
fuzzy                   | small, standalone...    | =mattyork         | 2016-10-01|
leven-match             | Return all word...      | =eklem            | 2021-06-11|
fuzzysearch             | Tiny and...             | =bevacqua         | 2015-03-06|
mongoose-fuzzy          | Mongoose fuzzy...       | =pabloc           | 2020-07-28|
scored-fuzzysearch      | Tiny and...             | =jhudson          | 2020-07-31|
neofuzzy                | Quick fuzzy search...   | =jeanno           | 2020-11-26|
fuzzy-search-mongo...   | Fuzzy search            | =piotreksl        | 2020-09-28|
vue-fuse                | A Vue.js pluggin...     | =shayneosulli...  | 2021-07-02|
liblevenshtein          | Various utilities...    | =dylon.edwards    | 2015-07-04|
fuzzy-pop               | Simple fuzzy search...  | =yoshokatana      | 2015-05-05|
fast-fuzzy              | Fast and tiny...        | =ethanrutherf...  | 2021-05-19|
react-fuzzy-picker      | Search through a...     | =1egoman          | 2019-09-29|
```

Here the root command passed to npm is `search`; we are searching for a library that provides `fuzzy search`. The top result from npm is Fuse.js. A quick check over the internet shows us that Fuse.js has an Apache license, reasonably small (< 50 KB), has no other dependencies, and has been maintained regularly for almost a decade with regular releases along with having a lot of downloads and packages that depend on it.

To add a dependency, we can use the `npm install` command. The `--save-dev` flag saves the development dependency in package.json so that it is available for use if we run `npm install` on a new machine. A *development dependency* means that it is used only during development and is not required in the released website. Because we compile our dependencies, we do not need them at run time. For the sake of maintaining compatibility in the book, we would recommend using version 6 of Fuse.js. The following listing adds this as a dependency.

Listing 10.19   Adding Fuse.js as a dependency (in AcmeTheme/)

```
npm install --save-dev fuse.js@6
```

This command generates a file called package-lock.json along with a node_modules folder at the root directory in parallel to package.json. The package-lock.json is equivalent to go.sum in Netlify and holds the checksums to ensure the integrity of our dependencies. The node_modules folder is similar to the _vendor folder, which stores our dependencies. Note that npm does not create a hidden folder for the dependencies.

10.5.5 *Updating our build systems to support npm*

Unless archiving, it does not make sense to submit the node_modules folder to source control. But that may be easier said than done because we need to run `npm install` from the AcmeTheme module to get its contents. And, running `npm install` from the AcmeTheme module may not be possible because Hugo, by default, puts modules in a hidden folder. Therefore, we need a way to get the Fuse.js dependency exposed to the top-level AcmeCorporationWebsite project.

To perform this task, we need to rename package.json in the AcmeTheme module to package.hugo.json. If there is a package.hugo.json file present in a Hugo module, Hugo understands that this module depends on npm, and Hugo is allowed to copy its dependencies to the top-level project. To transfer our dependency to the top-level project for the Acme Corporation website, we can run the command in the following listing to pack all the module packages in the website root folder.

Listing 10.20 Generating the top-level package.json

```
hugo mod npm pack
```

After we run this command, Hugo initializes the top-level project for the Acme Corporation website as an npm-based project and creates a package.hugo.json and a package.json. Now we can run `npm install` at the top-level project to get the node_modules and package-lock.json files in that folder. The ones in the AcmeTheme project are redundant, and we can delete them. If we ever add a new dependency to the Acme-Theme project, we need to add it to the package.hugo.json file and run the `hugo mod npm pack` command again.

Next, we need to update our build script to install npm-based dependencies. For this to work, we need the `npm install` command installed on the build machines. Netlify's build machines come preinstalled with npm, although for GitHub Actions, we need to add a step. (Note that `npm i` is shorthand for `npm install`.) There is also an `npm ci` command that ensures the dependencies match package-lock.json, but it deletes the already installed node_modules and can cause builds to take longer.

Note that because we have the same version of our Hugo Modules-based dependencies in go.sum, the npm-based dependencies of Hugo Modules cannot change across builds. Therefore, we need to run `hugo mod npm pack` when we change our modules and check in the generated package.json in source control.

UPDATING NETLIFY

We can update the build command in Netlify from the Site Settings > Build & Deploy > Continuous Deployment > Build Command section. Because the Netlify UI takes only one text box for the build command, we can use the && operator to pipe commands as the following listing shows to ensure both commands succeed to call the build a success.

Listing 10.21   Setting up npm dependencies to build the website using Hugo

```
npm i && hugo --minify --baseURL $DEPLOY_PRIME_URL
```

Older commits and build machine changes

If we change the build settings, our older commits where package.json is not present will not build on Netlify. Although that is rarely a problem, it is good to have the older builds deployable. The ideal solution is to move the Netlify configuration from the UI to a file as discussed in chapter 13. If we want to continue using the Netlify UI, we can change the build script to run npm i only if a package.json file is present and, otherwise, skip npm i. The following test command checks if package.json exists and runs npm i if it does. Irrespective of what happens, hugo is run after that:

```
(test -f package.json && npm i || true ) &&
   hugo --minify --baseURL $DEPLOY_PRIME_URL
```

Exercise 10.2

We can use _____ as a means to expose the data available to the static site builder and the run-time processing code that needs it.

UPDATING GITHUB ACTIONS

For GitHub Pages, we need to add a set of build steps in gh-pages.yml to set up Node.js and then run npm i. The code in the following listing makes these changes to GitHub Actions to install npm and npm-based dependencies.

Listing 10.22   Changes to GitHub Actions (.github/workflows/.gh-pages.yml)

```
jobs:
  deploy:
    steps:
      ...
      - name: Use Node.js
        uses: actions/setup-node@v1
        with:
```

```
  node-version: '16.x'

  - name: Install NPM Dependencies
    run: npm i
```

With these changes, we have the Fuse.js search library ready to use in our JavaScript code.

10.5.6 *Creating a search index*

We can import Fuse.js by using the `import` statement in JavaScript. After fetching the website data, we need to pass this to Fuse.js to create a search index. We will be making a weighted search index that allows for having the word in the web page title given a much higher value than one that's present in the web page content. The title gets a weight of 20, a tag score of 5, and the content gets a weight of 1.

We store the search index as a local variable of the module. This way, it can be used by all methods in the modules. Because search is not a class and we expect only one instance, a local variable of the module acts like a private variable that's not accessible outside of this file. Listing 10.23 imports the Fuse.js library to perform a search with JSON-based content. Fuse.js provides support for fuzzy matching and weighted searches to provide a great searching experience. Running this in JavaScript makes the search responsive and fast.

Listing 10.23 Importing the Fuse.js library (AcmeTheme/assets/search.js)

```
import Fuse from 'fuse.js'          Creates a module variable to
                                    store the index to use in all
let index = null;        ◄———————— functions
export default {
  init() {
    ...

    let data = await response.json();
    index= new Fuse(data, {         ◄——— Creates a Fuse.js index
      keys: [{
        name: 'title',      ◄——┐
        weight: 20            │   Adds title with
      }, {                        a weight of 20
        name: 'tag',
        weight: 5
      }, {
If not      name: 'content'
provided,   }]
weight is  });
treated as 1.                                When developing, leaving a test
    // Just to test. Do not leave in code.   query can help. We log the search
    console.log(index.search('acme'));  ◄——— results to the browser's console.
  }
}
```

NOTE If we have a lot of data on a website and think that index.json is too big, we can process the file in Hugo and remove common words like "and", "or", and so forth that we do not care about in the search index.

CODE CHECKPOINT   https://chapter-10-06.hugoinaction.com, and source code: https://github.com/hugoinaction/hugoinaction/tree/chapter-10-06.

10.5.7 Getting search input and showing results

With the search input box and the search method ready, the next step is to link the two together. The first thing we need to do is listen to the input event on the search box. We will run a search query as soon as the user enters a single character in the search box and display the page title in the `result div`. If the user presses the Enter key, we will navigate to the first search result. We will also limit the number of search results to a reasonable number.

We also need to show the search result dropdown when the user moves the focus to the search box and remove it when the user clicks outside. Listing 10.24 shows the search results inline via a dropdown. The code is relatively straightforward. We use the `input` event to take keyboard and context menu entries. The input event is the best one for a text box because it handles uncommon cases like copy and paste via mouse as well as regular keyboard presses. The full file after this change is present in the chapter resources (https://github.com/hugoinaction/hugoinaction/tree/chapter-10-resources/05).

Listing 10.24   Showing the search results (AcmeTheme/assets/search.js)

```javascript
import Fuse from 'fuse.js'

let index = null;
const MAX_SEARCH_RESULTS = 5;

export default {
  init() {
    ...
    document.addEventListener("input",          Adds the
        this.showResults);                      input event
  }

  showResults(event) {
    const searchBox = document.querySelector("search input");
    if (event.target !== searchBox) {
      return;
    }                                                    innerHTML replaces
    const result = document.querySelector("#search div");  the contents of the
    result.style.display = "block";                      dropdown. We can
    if (searchBox.value.length > 0) {                    update existing DOM
      const results = index.search(searchBox.value);     elements instead if
      result.innerHTML = results       ◁──────────       performance is a
                                                          concern.
```

```
      .slice(0, MAX_SEARCH_RESULTS)          ◄─┐  Limits the number of search results
      .map(x => `<a href="${x.item.url}">        │  to MAX_SEARCH_RESULTS
        <img src="${x.item.cover || ""}"
          width="40" height="40">
        <h3>${x.item.title}</h3>
        <span>${x.item.content.substr(0,40)}</span>
      </a>`)          ◄────────┐  Provides a rich dropdown experience
      .join("");               │  with an image and accompanying text
  } else {
    result.innerHTML = '';
  }
},
...
}
```

CODE CHECKPOINT   https://chapter-10-07.hugoinaction.com, and source code: https://github.com/hugoinaction/hugoinaction/tree/chapter-10-07.

Note that the variable MAX_SEARCH_RESULTS can come from the Hugo configuration as define or as param. With these changes, we have a working search box (figure 10.4) in our website to help users navigate the entire content. The GitHub Pages repository with the npm changes is present at https://github.com/hugoinaction/GitHubPagesNpm.

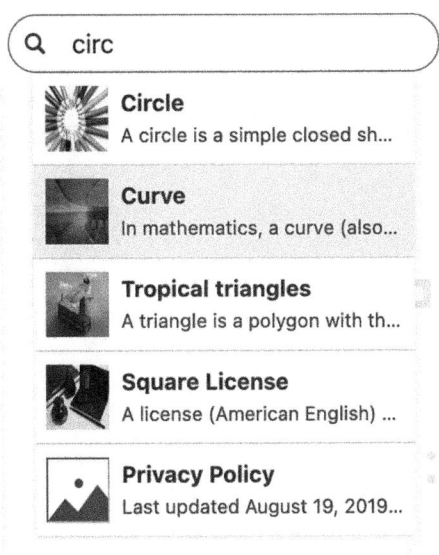

Figure 10.4   The search box with a results dropdown in the Acme Corporation website. The search box can be added in Jamstack-based websites using a pseudo API to get all contents and then using JavaScript to filter it.

10.5.8 Using Hugo modules with JavaScript

Although using npm is straightforward, we can continue to use Hugo modules to load dependencies. Hugo Modules allow dependencies to provide template code, bundled content, and other Hugo-specific data alongside JavaScript. The assets folder in a Hugo module acts as the node_modules folder in Node.js.

We did not add any keyboard handling in our search handler. We will import a Hugo module called AcmeSearchSupport (https://github.com/hugoinaction/hugoinaction/tree/chapter-10-resources/06) to perform this task. Let's start by adding this as a dependency to the AcmeTheme project in listing 10.25.

Exercise 10.3

Although npm is a huge ecosystem and has many times more content than that of Hugo Modules, we can choose to use Hugo Modules due to the ability to load Hugo-specific _____.

Listing 10.25   Adding AcmeSearchSupport (AcmeTheme/config.yaml)

```yaml
module:
  ...
  imports:
    ...
    - path: github.com/hugoinaction/AcmeSearchSupport
```

Next, we load this module as our search.js and call it during initialization. The following listing loads the JavaScript code from Hugo Modules, which is compiled by js.Build.

Listing 10.26   Loading JavaScript code (AcmeTheme/assets/search.js)

```javascript
import AcmeSearchSupport from "SearchSupport"
...
export default {
  async init() {
  ...
    try {
      ...
      AcmeSearchSupport();
    } catch (e) {
      this.removeSearch();
    }
  },
  ...
}
```

CODE CHECKPOINT   https://chapter-10-08.hugoinaction.com, and source code: https://github.com/hugoinaction/hugoinaction/tree/chapter-10-08.

10.6 *An SPA in a Hugo website*

Hugo does not target the creation of SPAs. The whole concept behind Hugo is getting a static website with content built from text stored as markup-based documents on disk. Hugo is not the right technology if we want to create an SPA like Google Docs. A JavaScript-based frontend framework may be a better choice for this use case.

That does not mean that Hugo has nothing to offer for single-page scenarios. An SPA also needs a content-based website like some help or documentation pages, a privacy policy page, (optionally) a landing page used for introducing the users to the product, and (maybe) a blog. Adding those pages with the technology used to build SPAs is not the best strategy. SPAs are difficult to index by search engines. SPAs require a time-consuming download, the execution of vast blobs of JavaScript, and are not great citizens of the document-based web. They need to manually handle use cases like the mouse middle click and the browser back icon.

One advantage of using Hugo with an SPA is clear demarcation of the prebuilt and run-time code. Because Hugo is agnostic of a JavaScript framework and all the logic resides entirely in the build process, there are minimal chances of collisions with the JavaScript code and framework used for the SPA.

This section creates a new web page for the Acme Corporation website that will be a single-page application, which provides an SVG shape editor for its users. This page will share a header generated and managed by Hugo, and the contents will come from JavaScript as an SPA. We will use the EasyLogic editor (https://editor.easylogic.studio/) as the SPA embedded in the web page. The EasyLogic editor is MIT-licensed and is available as a packaged npm module that we can import into our website. This editor will be managed as an independent SPA outside the website but will be assembled at the right endpoint by Hugo and fully functional and integrated into the website.

10.6.1 *Importing a node module in the root project*

The EasyLogic editor is available as an npm-based node module that we will import into our project. Because we do not want to expose this editor to AcmeTheme, we will import this directly into the Acme Corporation website. We need to convert the website into a Node.js project as well, and we will need to run `npm init` and set up package.json like we did in the AcmeTheme repository. Next, we can install the EasyLogic editor via npm (using 0.10.72 for compatibility with the book). To do that, we can update package.hugo.json with this new dependency as shown in the following listing.

> **Listing 10.27 Adding the EasyLogic editor as a dependency (package.hugo.json)**

```
{
  ...
  "devDependencies": {
    "@easylogic/editor": "0.10.72"
  }
}
```

Then after we update the dependency, we run `hugo mod npm pack` and `npm install`:

```
hugo mod npm pack
npm i
```

The final generated package.json is provided in the chapter resources (https://github.com/hugoinaction/hugoinaction/tree/chapter-10-resources/07).

10.6.2 *Creating a template for the SPA*

We can put an HTML file directly in our content folder, but if we need to use Hugo's variables, we will need to create a template. Using a Hugo template, we can control information with the configuration and front matter, reuse the shared code to create the header, and have tighter integration with the rest of the website.

Let's create a new layout called "editor" in the default layout folder. We do not need a new content type as we are not making a section but instead a single page. In this new layout, we will leave the website's header intact, replacing the body section with the SPA that we need to display. For the SPA, we will create a new JavaScript file in the assets folder. Because the editor has a large JavaScript file, we do not want to load this on every web page, so we will leave this independent. Let's call this Editor.js and load the file in the new template as the following listing shows. We will give the editor layout the editor class for the body tag.

> **Listing 10.28 Loading Editor.js (layouts/_default/editor.html)**

```
{{define "bodyClass"}}editor{{end}}
{{define "body"}}
{{ $js := resources.Get "editor.js" | js.Build }}
<div id="app">
  <div class="loader"></div>
</div>
{{end}}
```

> **NOTE** If we want to import the JavaScript files to the <head> section of our website, we will need to create a new block in the base template.

In Editor.js, we will import the EasyLogic editor. The following listing shows how to do this.

> **Listing 10.29 Importing the EasyLogic editor (assets/editor.js)**

```
import EasyLogic from "@easylogic/editor";

const app = new EasyLogic.createDesignEditor({
  container: document.getElementById('app')
});
```

Because the editor is packaged and ready-to-use, we do not need to configure it for it to work. It does not require any initialization to function.

> ### Exercise 10.4
> Hugo (is/is not) a great tool for building a single-page application (SPA). If we build the SPA in a different framework Hugo (can/cannot) play nicely with it.

Figure 10.5   It's a win-win! Engineering plans to shift to the Jamstack, and management gets huge savings for the release schedule.

10.6.3 *Importing CSS*

The EasyLogic editor calls for a CSS file that needs to be loaded. Although CSS does not come with its module system, developers have used npm to export CSS files. Hugo does not support the resolution of CSS files in the JavaScript code as of version 0.91.2. We need to use either PostCSS or SCSS to import the CSS file outside of the assets folder. PostCSS and SCSS (via a plugin) support @import statements to import external SCSS or CSS files into an existing file. Alternatively, we can use a readFile to read the CSS file and import it into Hugo directly. We will use the readFile solution as it is the simplest for our use case. The following listing reads the EasyLogic CSS file and embeds it in the editor page.

Listing 10.30   Reading the EasyLogic CSS file (layouts/default/editor.html)

```
{{define "body"}}
...
{{ $style := readFile "node_modules/@easylogic/editor/dist/editor.css" |
  resources.FromString "editor.scss" | toCSS | minify }}          ◁─────
<link rel="stylesheet" href="{{ $style.Permalink }}">
<div id="app"></div>
{{end}}                              Uses the shorthand toCSS for resources.ToCSS,
                                     which is available in each resource object
```

10.6.4 *Creating a web page*

Once we have a working template, we need to create a markup document to use the EasyLogic editor. We will add editor.md to the content folder with this new layout. We will also add an entry to our top menu for the editor endpoint as the following listing shows.

Listing 10.31   Creating a markup page for the editor (content/editor.md)

```
---
layout: editor
menu:
  main:
    name: Editor
    identifier: editor
    weight: 130
    post: Build it your way
---
```

CODE CHECKPOINT   https://chapter-10-09.hugoinaction.com, and source code: https://github.com/hugoinaction/hugoinaction/tree/chapter-10-09.

With these changes, we now have a shape editor (figure 10.6) built into the Acme Corporation website, loaded as an SPA, and managed in JavaScript. Although decoupled from the Hugo website, it still uses Hugo for the website's content, which supports the SPA.

Figure 10.6   The EasyLogic editor is embedded in the Acme Corporation website, converting it into a hybrid website with an SPA in a Hugo website.

JavaScript, just like an API, is such a vast topic that even an entire book is not enough to cover it completely. In this chapter, we focused on Hugo's touchpoints to interact with JavaScript to have the Acme Corporation website delve into the entire Jamstack. In the next chapter, we will be showing some advanced features enabled by creating custom APIs to extend the power of Hugo, keeping in alignment with the principles of website compilation that form its founding guidelines.

Summary

- JavaScript is one of the three pillars of the Jamstack for a simple reason: the browser reserves some web features to be available only to the client-side JavaScript language.
- Hugo has built a unique pipeline to play nicely with the JavaScript ecosystem and goes to great lengths to ensure that we can achieve the full capabilities that we desire from our JavaScript code.
- When building its JavaScript integration, the Hugo team reinforced its performance objectives, ensuring that Hugo has one of the fastest JavaScript builders with full support for interacting with the Node Package Manager (npm) and the entire JavaScript/TypeScript ecosystem.
- We can use JavaScript to reload parts of a web page and submit forms dynamically to a website.
- JavaScript can do calculations on the client, providing cheaper, faster, and easier-to-maintain versions of what used to be server-bound features such as search.
- We can build a decoupled single-page application (SPA) in a Hugo website and have a good division of responsibilities, where JavaScript is responsible for the interactive pieces. At the same time, Hugo focuses on the content-based parts of the entire web-based solution.

11

Breaking barriers with custom APIs and webhooks

This chapter covers

- Creating custom API endpoints and hosting them as cloud functions
- Creating and calling APIs to extend Hugo's core functionality
- Adding compile-time LaTeX
- Hooking up webhooks with APIs to automate manual tasks

APIs are marvelous. We can encapsulate the most complicated functionality behind an easy-to-use API, and its users don't need to know the logic or the details of how an API works. Chapter 9 went over some APIs provided by third parties, which worked for us. But it is not always possible to get APIs for everything we need. Some functionality might be particular to our website or be our secret sauce. We need to write this ourselves. The Jamstack identifies that as a valid and practical use case and provides support for this functionality.

In this chapter, we will go over some of the means that the Jamstack provides to handle cases where Hugo might not have the features we need (figure 11.1). We will embed LaTeX-based math inside our project—the Jamstack way—compiled during the build and delivered without any excess JavaScript or additional network request. The conversion from textual to a visual representation of the mathematics will be done outside Hugo and integrated into the web page at build time. We will also look at the concept of webhooks and how we can use them to link together independent services.

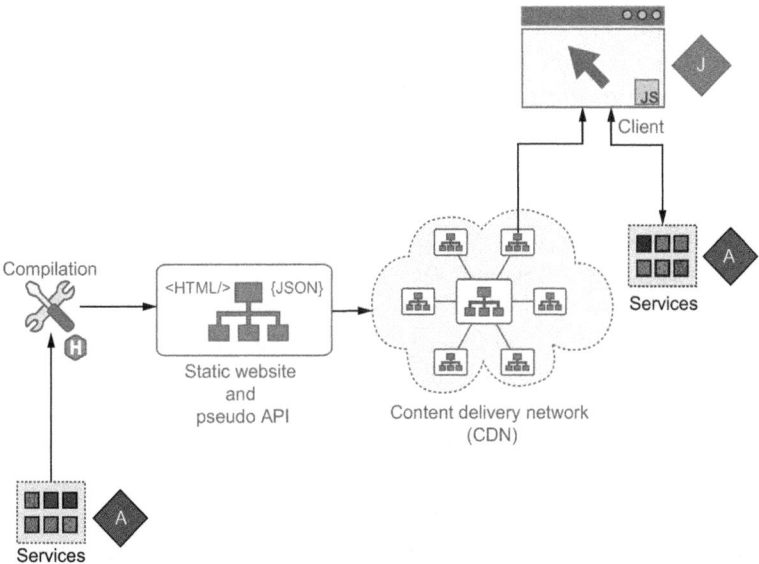

Figure 11.1   Chapter 11 enables us to build custom APIs using some Jamstack-based services to keep maintenance low and to provide the same high-speed experience we expect from the Jamstack.

11.1   Building custom APIs

Third-party APIs have their distinct advantages: we do not have to maintain them on a day-to-day basis. We pay for the maintenance overhead and enjoy a safe, functional, and improved service. But they come with their caveats. Third parties may not provide the precise service we need. Third parties can also change their terms of service, pricing, or availability on short notice. Considering the tradeoffs, it may make sense to build custom APIs for specific use cases.

11.1.1   Choosing the layer of the application stack

When we build custom APIs, we need to decide which layer from a third-party provider to rely on. It is impractical to create everything needed to get our APIs up and running ourselves. Most companies do not build the lowest layer: the hardware, operating system, and programming language toolchain. But maintaining hardware is a huge undertaking and requires constant struggles. It is worth paying a third party for this work.

Cloud vendors can provide API encapsulations over hardware in an infrastructure as a service (IaaS) system. We can move a layer up if we desire to platform as a service (PaaS), where the operating system and the programming toolchain are kept up-to-date and managed by the service provider. A blurred line separates PaaS from FaaS (function as a service), where the service provider encapsulates everything until the invocation of our code. All we need to do is provide our code and see it in action.

This chapter uses Netlify Functions (an FaaS) to host the cloud functions for the Netlify-hosted website. We advise relying on the FaaS and PaaS layers and building our secret sauce rather than redoing tasks like managing hardware that others do best. The cloud vendors that we already rely on for hosting our websites can also host our cloud functions, so we do not have any additional dependencies. In this chapter, we will also look at Heroku (https://www.heroku.com/), a popular PaaS platform that provides a generous free tier, which is more than enough for our simple use case.

As a user, FaaS solutions benefit from writing the absolute minimum code we need to get some functionality. All scaling is automatic. The billing is granular, sometimes up to a millisecond of invocation. This power does come at a cost. FaaS solutions, by nature, are tied to a vendor, and there is some degree of vendor lock in involved. If the function runs continuously due to our load on them, FaaS can be a lot more expensive than PaaS. Apart from being vendor-neutral, PaaS solutions leave a lot more control in the developer's hands from managing the load, providing the ability to cache, preconnecting to other services, and precomputing data based on some expected user state. FaaS may be a better choice until we have a certain load threshold, after which switching over to PaaS or even IaaS may make more sense.

11.1.2 Monoliths vs. microservices

Another significant consideration to make when building custom APIs is the monolithic services versus microservices debate. A *monolithic service* is one where one codebase performs all the functions needed by the website, which are all hosted together, exposing multiple endpoints that perform numerous tasks. A monolithic service allows for maximum code sharing and reuse. It also enables smoother caching and handoff where one API request can trigger a pre-emptive cache warmup for another. This increases the perceived performance of a second API request. A monolithic service has fewer moving parts and may be easier to manage by an individual or a small team.

A *microservice* takes the opposite approach, where each endpoint is separate. The objective of the microservice architecture is to decouple independent tasks from one another where one change cannot take down the whole system. If some services are stable and do not change regularly, it may be better to siphon the code off to a separate microservice that keeps chugging along without bothering us. Microservices can become simpler to manage than monolithic ones if they combine with PaaS or FaaS platforms where the service provider handles the ongoing maintenance.

The Jamstack advocates using microservices for building APIs. Because most of the jobs are handled at compile time or by third-party services, the code in the API layer is relatively small and does not change frequently. FaaS solutions don't cater to monolithic services. With microservices, it is much easier to live the dream of having a low-maintenance system where we can get good up time and an acceptable performance all around the planet.

Function-based microservices

In the broad definition of microservices, there is no definite specification of the size of the service and its boundaries. In general, if breaking away from an extensive monolithic application, the developer decides how many services to employ. FaaS stretches this definition, where each function or API in our code is a small microservice that focuses on handling responses for a particular type of request. The Jamstack aligns well with this but allows scope for having some looser versions, as well as where we can club group path functions associated with the same data into one microservice.

PaaS is a lot more nuanced than FaaS. We can define whole services, but we have to be careful to split them into smaller ones at the appropriate places.

Exercise 11.1

To keep maintenance low, which of the following act as good practices at the start of a project?

- a. Opting to build custom APIs even if the exact functionality required is readily available via multiple third-party, industry-standard service providers.
- b. Building a data center to host physical machines to perform custom tasks.
- c. Using a function as a service (FaaS) solution and only writing our core business logic.
- d. Investing in a custom flavor of Linux, which is more optimized for our use case.
- e. Using an infrastructure as a service (IaaS) solution and building our database schemas and application servers, and then investing in scaling and DevOps.
- f. Keeping processes manual and hiring contract firms to do things for us.

11.2 Adding LaTeX rendering to our website

Acme Corporation is all about digital shapes. Shapes as a concept interlink with geometry, and we need to reach into the arsenal of mathematical notations to express and understand them better. We will use this as the means to render LaTeX to represent mathematical notations in our markup. The end goal of this section is to create a shortcode like `{{<latex>}}\frac{a}{b}{{</latex>}}` that can be placed anywhere in Markdown for a page that will render appropriately as mathematical. We will use this to render complicated LaTeX equations like the own shown in figure 11.2.

$$\mathbf{B}(t) = \sum_{i=0}^{n} \binom{n}{i} (1-t)^{n-i} t^i \mathbf{P}_i$$

Figure 11.2 Sample rendering for a complex LaTeX string: \mathbf {B} (t)&=\sum +_+{i=0}^{n}{n \choose i}(1•t)^{n•i}t^{i}\mathbf {P} +_+{i}. We will look at LaTeX equations in this chapter.

11.2.1 *What is LaTeX?*

LaTeX is a markup language that has great support for defining mathematical notations. It is prevalent in the academic and scientific world as a typesetting system for paper publications and books. The mathematical notations described in LaTeX have been standardized and used in various scenarios outside of the LaTeX typesetting system. LaTeX is text-based and, therefore, a great fit for the Jamstack. For example, for a fraction with a numerator *a* and denominator *b*, we can write \frac {a}{b} in LaTeX. The full LaTeX specification is out of scope for this book, but you can read about it at https://www.latex-project.org. As of v0.91.2, Hugo natively does not support rendering LaTeX.

> **NOTE** If future Hugo versions support LaTeX natively, there will be use cases that Hugo does not support for which the exercises in this chapter will be applicable.

11.2.2 *How can we render LaTeX?*

Although we can use the official TeX system to render LaTeX, it is geared towards full documents and is not friendly to embedding. Therefore, it's not suitable for our use case. A JavaScript library called MathJax (https://www.mathjax.org/) supports rendering LaTeX-based mathematical notations in the web browser. The library is very popular. It works similarly to how we implemented the search box in chapter 10. It scans the LaTeX-based mathematical expressions on the web page and replaces them with the equivalent SVG rendition. *SVG* is an image format that web browsers natively support. It is lightweight and does not lose its quality on zoom. This ability makes it a perfect image format for mathematical equations. Although using MathJax directly is the easiest solution to getting mathematical notations on our websites, it has its drawbacks:

- *MathJax is large.* Although it does code splitting and tries to get the minimal payload to render what is needed, additional JavaScript still needs to be downloaded by and run on every customer's machine.
- *MathJax does not add any interactivity to our website.* The output is a static image, and there is no advantage of doing this in the browser. Rendering math on the server is more performant and faster than adding the extra hop to download this library and then performing the calculations and updating the image.

- *MathJax output is difficult to cache.* Because it needs to do all the work on demand, we cannot pre-generate the images for our mathematical symbols and save them.

11.2.3 Server-side LaTeX rendering

It is a superior user experience if we can move mathematical rendering to the server and cache the results across page loads or even website rebuilds. This caching follows the Jamstack approach of compiling the content when publishing without wasting time when the data is requested. Because Hugo does not understand LaTeX and does not have an external helper to communicate with MathJax, we will create a separate API to perform this task. Instead of relying on a third-party API, we will create custom APIs to convert LaTeX to SVG. Here are the steps required to do this:

1. Create a function to convert the LaTeX string to an SVG image.
2. Host this function on the cloud to get an HTTP API.
3. Call the HTTP API in Hugo and embed the generated SVG in our website.
4. Create a shortcode in Hugo to allow content authors to use this functionality.

> **Exercise 11.2**
> True or False: LaTeX meets the definition of a markup language of the Jamstack.

11.2.4 Writing the code to render LaTeX

Because MathJax is a JavaScript library, we will use Node.js to interface with it. We will start by installing the Node.js version of MathJax as a dependency on our website by adding `mathjax` to package.hugo.json (set up in the previous chapter) as listing 11.1 shows. We will use the `dependency` and not the `devDependency` attribute in package .hugo.json as we need this when live. For this book, we use version 3.2.0 of MathJax.

> **Listing 11.1   Adding MathJax as a dependency (package.hugo.json)**

```
{
  . . .
  "dependencies": {
    "mathjax": "3.2.0"
  }
}
```

Next, we need to regenerate package.json via Hugo and then install it as a dependency. Marking it as a dependency ensures that it will be available in production when deployed (instead of devDependency, which we can remove). This command downloads MathJax as a dependency for our website:

```
hugo mod npm pack
npm i
```

Next, we will create a tex2svg folder that contains the code to convert LaTeX to SVG. This task involves initializing MathJax, taking the LaTeX string as an input, defining the parameters that we can use to perform the SVG conversion, and then returning the output as a string. We will save our API code to a folder called api, with a subfolder called tex2svg that exposes this function. Inside tex2svg, the file called index.js will export this as a cloud function.

Instead of creating an arbitrary function with custom arguments, we'll use `exports.handler = async function(event, context){}`, which is the format AWS Lambda and Netlify functions employ for this method (see http://mng.bz/M2g7 for more information). This format is required if we want to use Netlify to host this function. This function takes two parameters, `event` and `context`. The event object has the following properties:

- `path`—Path to the request (e.g., `/latex2svg`)
- `httpMethod`—Incoming request's method name (GET, POST, PUT, etc.)
- `headers`—Incoming request headers (e.g., `{'Content-Type': 'application/json'}`)
- `queryStringParameters`—The query string parameters (e.g., `{tex: '\frac{1}{2}'}`)
- `body`—A JSON string of the request payload (empty in a GET request)
- `isBase64Encoded`—A Boolean flag to indicate if the applicable request payload is in Base64 format

NOTE We will wrap this function in an HTTP server to create a RESTful API layer for use outside of Netlify.

The code for this script is shared in the chapter resources (https://github.com/hugoinaction/hugoinaction/tree/chapter-11-resources/01). In this code, we initialize MathJax and then pass the supplied LaTeX code through it, along with the `display` parameter for inline rendering (versus block rendering). We output the JSON string instead of the SVG to get this in to Hugo as a JSON object via `getJSON`. We can alternatively output as SVG and use `resources.GetRemote` to fetch this file. We can pass additional information (if required) to Hugo in the response JSON. The following listing shows the source code for the cloud function to convert LaTeX to SVG.

Listing 11.2 Converting LaTeX to SVG (api/latex2svg.js)

```
const MathjaxModule = require("mathjax");          ◁──┐ Imports the MathJax
                                                       │ dependency
let MathJax = null;
module.exports = {
  async handler(event, context) {
    if (!event.queryStringParameters ||
      !event.queryStringParameters.tex) {          ◁──┐ Ensures that the tex
      return {                                         │ parameter is available
        statusCode: 400,
```

```
      headers: {'Content-Type': 'application/json'},
      body: JSON.stringify({
        error: "The required `tex` parameter not supplied.",
      })
    }
  }
  if (!MathJax) {
    MathJax = await MathjaxModule.init({
      loader: { load: ['input/tex', 'output/svg'] }
    });
  }

  const svg = MathJax.tex2svg(
    event.queryStringParameters.tex, {
      display: event.queryStringParameters.display
    });

  return {
    statusCode: 200,
    headers: {'Content-Type': 'application/json'},
    body: JSON.stringify({
      data: MathJax.startup.adaptor.outerHTML(svg)
    })
  };
  },
}
```

Initializes MathJax only if needed. It takes input as LaTeX and outputs SVG.

Passes all parameters from the query string to MathJax

Returns the status code 200 with the results as JSON

We can deploy this code to a FaaS solution like AWS Lambda or Netlify Functions. For PaaS solutions, we need a little more work.

Child processes vs. APIs

Theoretically, running additional code associated with a project as a subprocess is more manageable, and this has been the go-to mechanism of interfacing with other tools everywhere. Hugo calls external helpers like AsciiDoc (chapter 3) and tools like PostCSS (chapter 6) via the command line. But this is not available for generic use. Child processes have a nasty habit of getting the full credentials and then control of the parent process that launched them. This means any malware can easily hide in a module or some sample source code and do immense damage to a system if run via a child process.

APIs accessed over HTTP are present in a sandbox by running in a different machine. Keeping extensibility via APIs makes the Hugo ecosystem secure. Although you need to be careful running `npm install` to make sure you do not run into malicious software, running the Hugo command is unlikely to cause any damage to your machine. Hugo cannot write outside of the public directory, and this makes everything safe. As a bonus, creating APIs promotes reuse across multiple systems because these APIs form microservices that are loosely coupled and are available at both compile time and run time.

11.2.5 Adding a HTTP server to call this function

To execute this function on our developer machine, we need to convert it to an HTTP API. Whereas Netlify provides Netlify Dev, we will instead opt to create a custom HTTP server. This approach will make our code portable outside of Netlify, and for readers who are not using Netlify for hosting, we will still be able to use the cloud function we just wrote. We will, instead, host this on Heroku, a PaaS solution. PaaS solutions do not take a function but the entire Node.js application.

> **NOTE** Although you do not need to create this file if you use Netlify for hosting, this can be useful in testing locally if not using Netlify Dev.

Exercise 11.3

Calling _____ at build time provides us with the ability to extend Hugo and to keep integration minimal and implementation sandboxed.

Let's create a new file, api.js, at the root of our project (creating it in the API folder makes Netlify treat that as a function) with a simple Node.js-based HTTP server that responds to HTTP requests and calls this method (https://github.com/hugoinaction/hugoinaction/tree/chapter-11-resources/02). The following listing creates the Node .js-based HTTP server, which routes requests to the proper functions for handling in a PaaS solution.

Listing 11.3 Creating a Node.js-based HTTP server (api.js)

```
const http = require('http');
const querystring = require('querystring');
const latex2svg = require('./api/latex2svg');          Asks for the port from the
                                                        environment variables or
const port = process.env.PORT || 3000;          ◁────  defaults to 3,000
const server = http.createServer().listen(port);

                                                        Sets up an HTTP server
server.on('request', async function (req, res) {  ◁──
    const url = new URL(req.url, `http://${req.headers.host}`);
    const queryStringParameters = url.search &&
                        querystring.parse(url.search.slice(1));
    const request = {          ◁──
      queryStringParameters,          Creates a request object
      path: url.pathname,             compatible with AWS Lambda
      httpMethod: req.method,
      headers: req.headers,
      body: req.body
    }
    let response = {      ◁────  Creates a default response
      statusCode: 404,
      headers: { 'Content-Type': 'application/json'},
      body: JSON.stringify({error: "Page not found"})
    }
```

```
    try {
      switch (url.pathname) {    ⟵—— Creates a lightweight router
        case '/latex2svg':
          response = await latex2svg.handler(request);
          break;
      }
    } catch(e) {                 ⟵—— Gracefully handles exceptions
      response.statusCode = 500;
      response.body = JSON.stringify(e);
    }

    response.headers = response.headers || {};                Allows cross-origin access
    response.headers['Access-Control-Allow-Origin'] =         to prevent blockage to
                       '*';                    ⟵————           Heroku from our website
    res.writeHead(response.statusCode,
                  response.headers);    ⟵——  Returns the response
    res.end(response.body);                    to the client
});

console.log(`Listening on port ${port}`);
```

We can run this code by calling node api at the root of our project. We can navigate to http://localhost:3000/latex2svg?tex=%5Cfrac%7Ba%7D%7Bb%7D to get the JSON output for the inline version of the \frac{a}{b} LaTeX string. We can append &display =true to get the display version.

At this point, we should update the entry for main in package.json to point to api.js. This allows running our API as a valid project in the JavaScript ecosystem. We will also add a start script to run our API server when we write npm start. We need to update package.hugo.json and run hugo mod npm pack as the following listing shows.

Listing 11.4 An initialization script to run the API (package.hugo.json)

```
{
  ...
  "main": "api.js",
  "scripts": {
    "start": "node api.js"
  }
}
```

Listing 11.5 shows the JSON response. The LaTeX-to-SVG conversion API takes the input as a query parameter (called tex) along with other parameters like display to generate an SVG version of the supplied LaTeX string and return that in the key called data.

Listing 11.5 JSON response for the LaTeX-to-SVG conversion API

```
{ "data": "<mjx-container class=\"MathJax\" jax=\"SVG\"
➥ display=\"true\"><svg ...>...</svg></mjx-container>" }
```

11.2.6 *Adding some security to prevent unauthorized access*

Although our function is ready to be hosted on the cloud, we do have one problem. It will be available on the public internet, and anyone can call it even from outside our website. We do not want to pay for that additional load by an unauthorized website. A simple solution to prevent this is to add a password requirement for using our function. Checking in a password with our source code is a flawed approach. Instead, we will place the password in an environment variable in Netlify (and Heroku) and access it dynamically.

> **NOTE** A better solution for compile-time API access is to have an internal service hosting this API and not expose it to the internet. This requires support from cloud providers like Netlify or GitHub Pages to provide such a feature.

In latex2svg.js, before checking for the `tex` query parameter, we should check for the `password` query parameter and return an access denied error without it. The following listing performs this check to prevent unauthorized access.

Listing 11.6   Adding a password to our API (api/latex2svg.js)

Disallows a blank **LATEX2SVG_PASSWORD**

```
...
async handler(event, context) {
  if (!event.queryStringParameters ||
      !process.env.LATEX2SVG_PASSWORD ||
      event.queryStringParameters.password !==
          process.env.LATEX2SVG_PASSWORD) {
    return {
      statusCode: 401,
      headers: {'Content-Type': 'application/json'},
      body: JSON.stringify({
        error: "Access Denied.",
      })
    }
  }
  ...
}
```

Uses HTTP 401 if the password is incorrect. If the password is correct, and the user still does not have access, HTTP 403 would be the correct error code.

For testing locally, we can expose `LATEX2SVG_PASSWORD` as an environment variables for our system. We can configure the cloud provider to pass this on to both Hugo and our cloud function.

11.2.7 *Deploying to the cloud via Netlify Functions*

After setting up and verifying the function using local execution, we need to get it to the cloud. Netlify offers a service, called Netlify Functions, where we can build custom APIs managed by Netlify. We need to provide the source code as a file along with the rest of the website. Netlify packages it as a cloud function and makes it live. Because we have already built the function in the Netlify format, there isn't much work needed to deploy it to Netlify. The first step is to tell Netlify the location of the functions folder. To set up a folder for Netlify functions,

1 Go to Site Settings > Functions > Deploy Settings and click Edit Settings (figure 11.3).

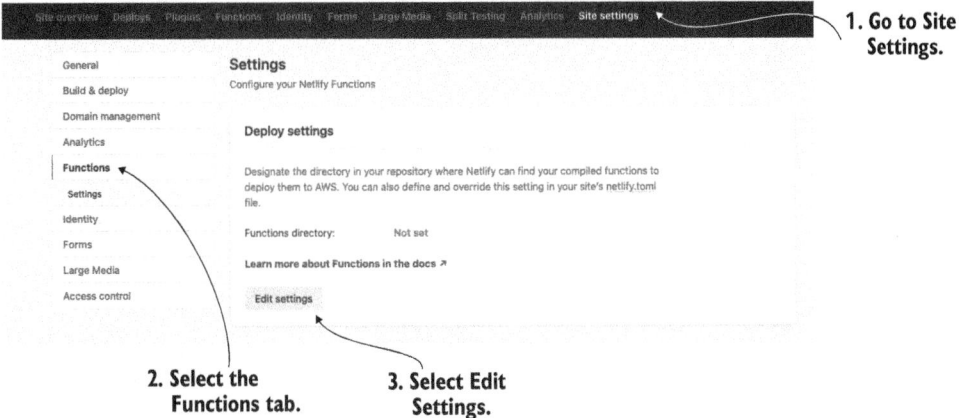

Figure 11.3 Settings for Netlify functions to specify the folder location where the website's source code is present

2 Specify `api` and click Save (figure 11.4).

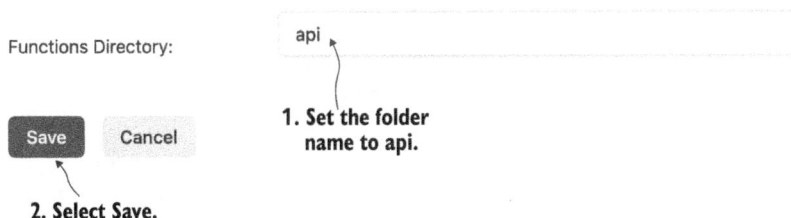

Figure 11.4 Specifying the directory for Netlify Functions in the deployment settings

We also need to add the `LATEX2SVG_PASSWORD` variable in the environment. The steps are the same as we used in setting the `COMMENTS_TOKEN` earlier in chapter 9. Go to Site Settings > Build & Deploy > Environment > Environment Variables. Click Edit Variables > New Variable (see figure 11.5). Add a complex password for `LATEX2SVG_PASSWORD` and click Save. We only need this password to test Netlify Functions after deployment. You do not need to remember this password.

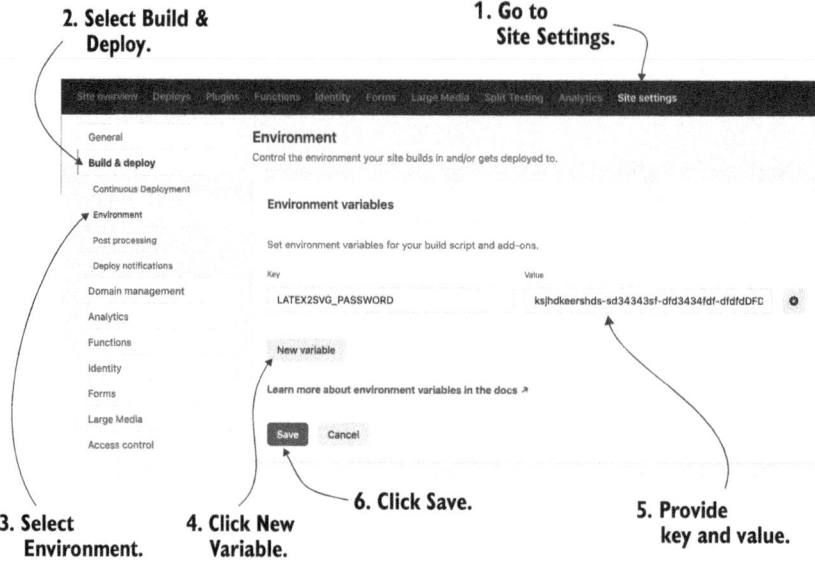

Figure 11.5   Storing the password for limiting unauthorized access to our function. Environment variables are a great way to keep passwords out of our codebase.

Next, we can push our code to Netlify to try out Netlify Functions. After the code goes live, we can call the `https://<endpoint>/.netlify/functions/latex2svg` endpoint with `?tex=%5Cfrac%7Ba%7D%7Bb%7D&password=<password>` as the argument to get the same response that we got previously when we ran locally.

We can also view our function in the Functions tab of the Netlify website. Here we can get debugging logs to figure out what happened on each invocation (figure 11.6).

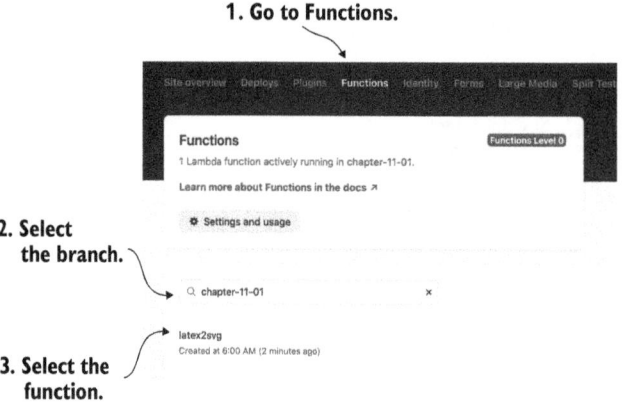

Figure 11.6   Accessing debugging logs for Netlify Functions. The Functions tab in Netlify provides access to Netlify parts, which we can use to see all the functions active in our website and then debug the errors associated with them.

Netlify automatically reports all errors. We can put the console.log statements in our JavaScript code and view the logs in this summary page (figure 11.7).

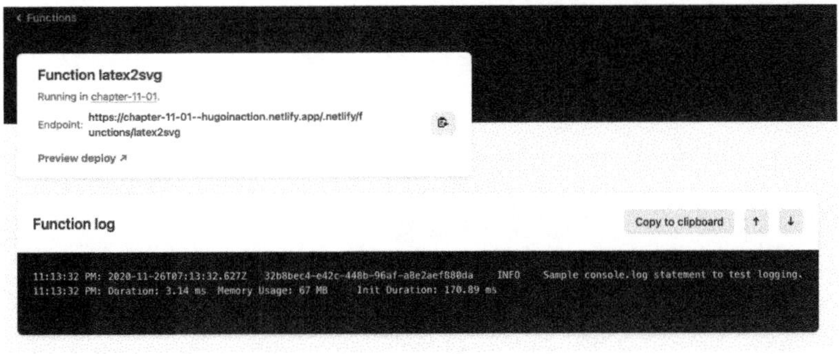

< Functions

Function latex2svg

Running in chapter-11-01.

Endpoint: https://chapter-11-01--hugoinaction.netlify.app/.netlify/f
unctions/latex2svg

Preview deploy ↗

Function log   Copy to clipboard ↑ ↓

11:13:32 PM: 2020-11-26T07:13:32.627Z   32b8bec4-e42c-448b-96af-a8e2aef880da   INFO   Sample console.log statement to test logging.
11:13:32 PM: Duration: 3.14 ms Memory Usage: 67 MB   Init Duration: 170.89 ms

Figure 11.7   Detailed logs in this summary page are available for each function in Netlify.

CODE CHECKPOINT   https://chapter-11-01.hugoinaction.com, and source code:
https://github.com/hugoinaction/hugoinaction/tree/chapter-11-01.

11.2.8 *Deploying to the cloud via Heroku*

In case you are not using Netlify, you need to select a vendor to host APIs. Many cloud vendors support both the PaaS and the FaaS models, and we are free to decide what approach we want to take to deploy our website. Because Netlify uses the FaaS solution, which we already discussed, we will demonstrate a PaaS solution.

Heroku is used as the PaaS platform, although we use little of its features, so the the code should work in any PaaS platform we choose. Heroku provides integrations with both the Node.js ecosystem and GitHub, making the deployment job easy. Heroku also provides continuous integration and deployment for our code without us having to write anything in our GitHub actions. This makes our job easier. Once configured, we just need to push the code to GitHub to get it live in Heroku.

1 When you sign up for Heroku, you will land at https://dashboard.heroku.com/
   apps. Go to New > Create New App to create a new application (figure 11.8).

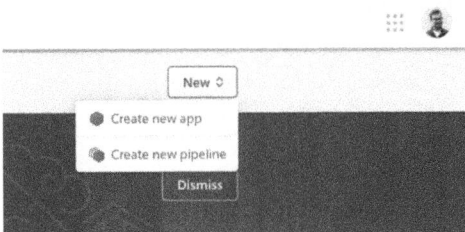

Figure 11.8   Creating a new application in Heroku to host our APIs

2 Give the application a name. Application names are unique in Heroku. This book has reserved `latex2svg`. You will need to provide a unique name for your API (figure 11.9).

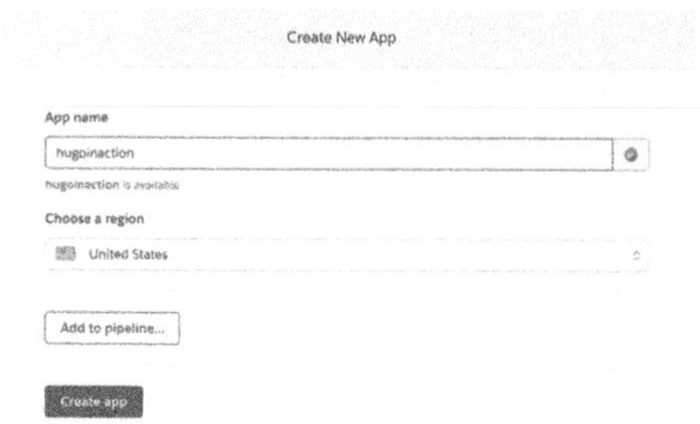

Figure 11.9   Naming an application in Heroku

3 We can now decide the mode of integration. Direct GitHub integration is the easiest, and we will use that for our use case. To connect to GitHub, you can go to Deploy > Deployment Method > GitHub and then click Connect to GitHub (figure 11.10).

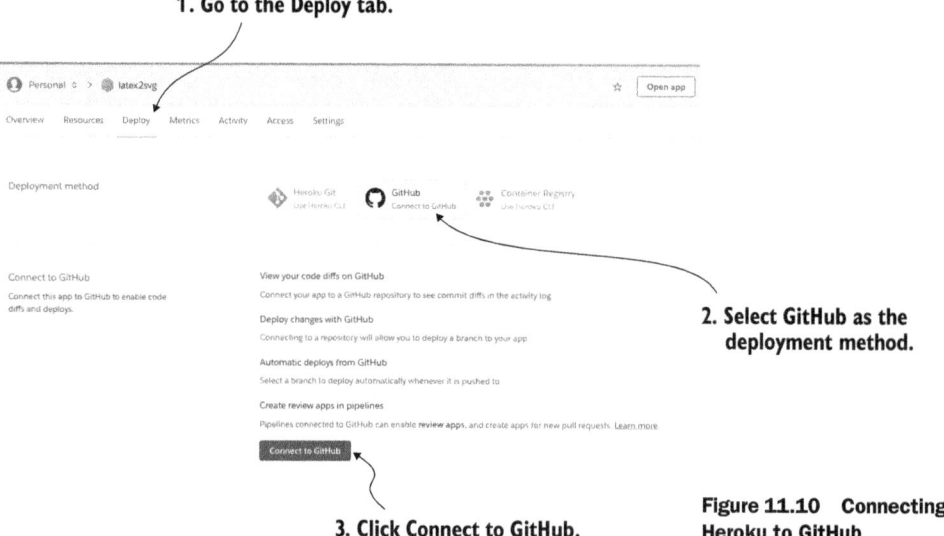

1. Go to the Deploy tab.

2. Select GitHub as the deployment method.

3. Click Connect to GitHub.

Figure 11.10   Connecting Heroku to GitHub

4 After providing credentials, we can search for repositories to connect to Heroku. Select the correct Git repository and click Connect (figure 11.11).

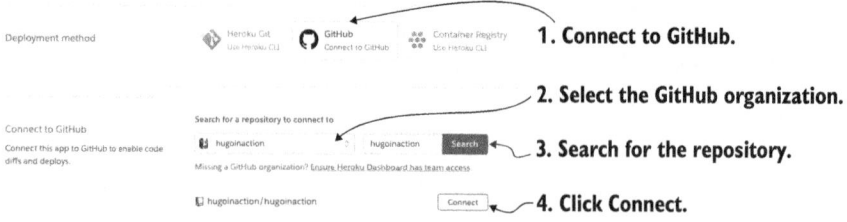

1. Connect to GitHub.

2. Select the GitHub organization.

3. Search for the repository.

4. Click Connect.

Figure 11.11   Finding and connecting the right repository from GitHub to Heroku

5 Before triggering the deployment, we need to go to the Settings tab (figure 11.12). In the Buildpacks section, click Add Buildpack.

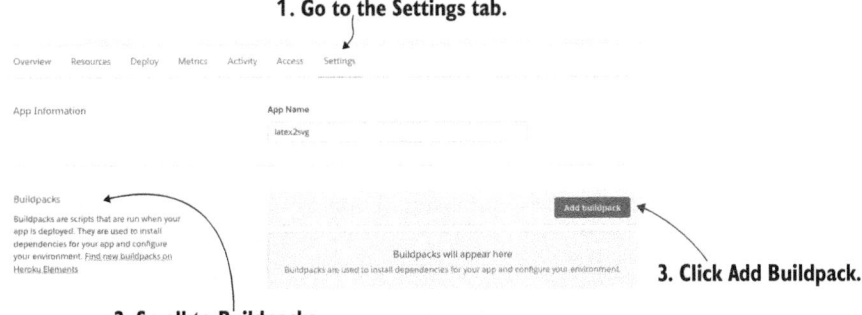

Figure 11.12 The Settings tab of Heroku contains Buildpacks, which is the configuration for the programming platform for Heroku.

6 In the Add Buildpack dialog, select nodejs (figure 11.13). (Because we have both go.sum and package.json, Heroku can get confused.) We need the Node.js buildpack for our APIs. This allows us to run the MathJax code.

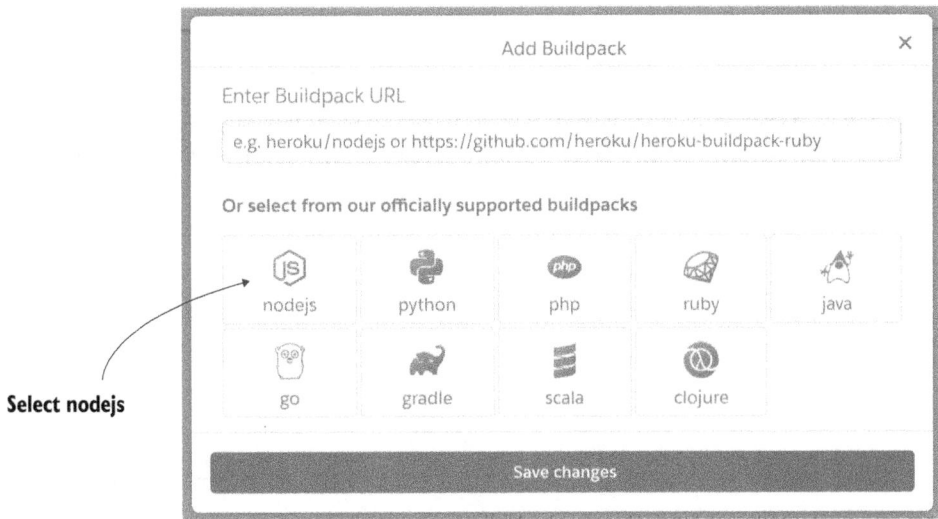

Figure 11.13 Heroku supports multiple platforms to deploy our applications. Node.js is the one we need to get our MathJax code up and running.

7 In Settings, there is also a Config Vars section to define our environment variables. We need to define `LATEX2SVG_PASSWORD` to get a password to restrict access (see figure 11.14).

1. Go to the Settings tab.
Overview
Resources
Deploy
Metrics
Activity
Access
Settings
Config Vars
Config vars change the way your app behaves. In addition to creating your own, some add-ons come with their own.
Hide Config Vars
LATEX2SVG_PASSWORD
KEY
VALUE
Add
2. Scroll to Config Vars.
3. Add the variable.

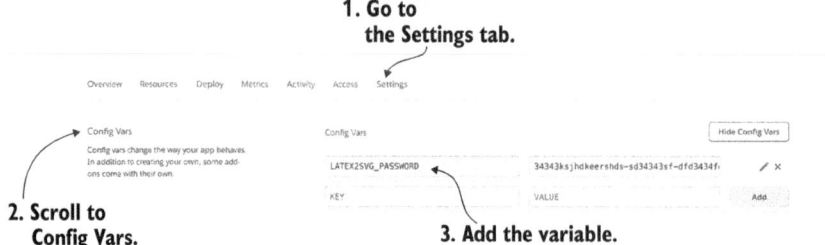

Figure 11.14 Configuration variables in Hugo are passed as environment variables to the running code.

Now we can trigger the deployment from Deploy > Manual Deploy (figure 11.15). We should do a manual deployment first for verification that everything is correct and then switch to automatic.

1. Go to the Deploy tab.
Overview
Resources
Deploy
Metrics
Activity
Access
Settings
2. Scroll to Manual Deploy.
Manual deploy
Deploy the current state of a branch to this app.
Deploy a GitHub branch
This will deploy the current state of the branch you specify below. Learn more.
Enter the name of the branch to deploy
chapter-11-01
Deploy Branch
3. Type the branch name.
4. Click Deploy Branch.

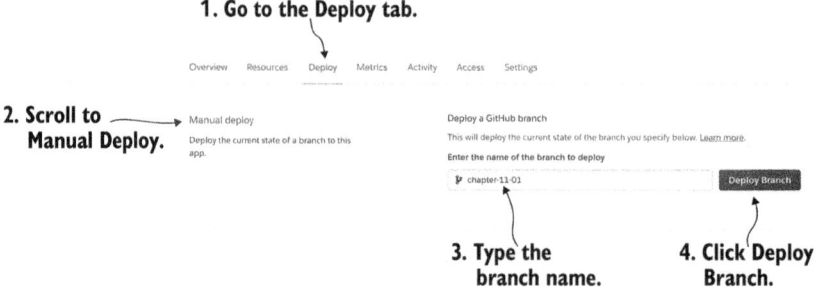

Figure 11.15 Manual and automatic deployments in Heroku. We should use Manual Deploy for verification, and once we know everything is working, we can use the automatic deploy option.

Hugo provides step-by-step progress of the deployment as it happens (figure 11.16). After the code goes live, we can call `https://<endpoint>.herokuapp.com/latex2svg` with `?tex=%5Cfrac%7Ba%7D%7Bb%7D&password=<password>` to get the same response that we got locally.

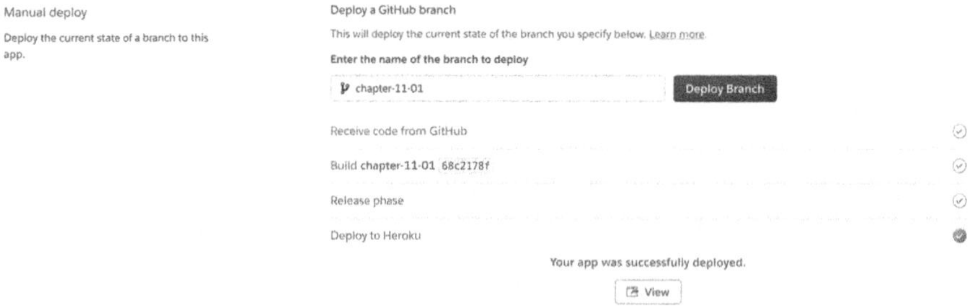

Manual deploy
Deploy the current state of a branch to this app.
Deploy a GitHub branch
This will deploy the current state of the branch you specify below. Learn more.
Enter the name of the branch to deploy
chapter-11-01
Deploy Branch
Receive code from GitHub
Build chapter-11-01 68c2178f
Release phase
Deploy to Heroku
Your app was successfully deployed.
View

Figure 11.16 When we trigger manual deployment in Heroku, Heroku provides step-by-step progress (the checkmarks on the right) until everything is ready.

We can troubleshoot any issues by looking at the application logs, which are present in the More menu on the top right (figure 11.17). Here we can click on View Logs to display the run-time logs in a separate web page (figure 11.18).

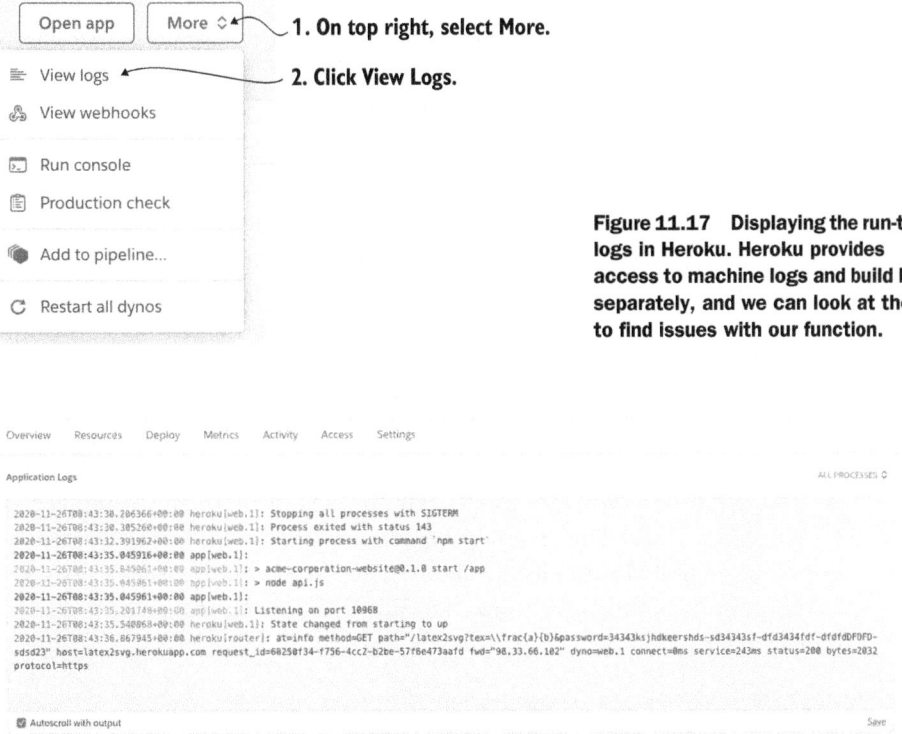

Figure 11.17   Displaying the run-time logs in Heroku. Heroku provides access to machine logs and build logs separately, and we can look at those to find issues with our function.

Figure 11.18   Viewing a sample log from the Node.js process running in Heroku. We can use this console log to get all the logs from Node.js. All crashes and error logs are also available.

Monorepo vs. separate repositories for APIs and markup

We decided to use the repository that we used for the website for the API code as well. This approach has a clear disadvantage of pushing the needless markup code to Heroku and rebuilding the Heroku-based APIs each time a markup-based document changes. If this becomes a big problem, we can choose a separate branch for the API or a separate repository. We can also change our integration to happen via GitHub Actions instead of the direct Heroku import, where we can recognize whether the API has changed. We can also move to manual deploys if the APIs change infrequently.

The choice of a monorepo has nothing to do with Hugo or the Jamstack. It is a matter of personal preference. Netlify works better with one repository and manages the changes across APIs. Its invocation in the core template code may be more straightforward using a monorepo, however.

11.2.9 Creating shortcode to render LaTeX

We need to call this API from our Hugo website to be able to use it. To make LaTeX rendering available as a feature to our content authors, we will create a shortcode.

> **NOTE** Although we are using the APIs at compile time, if we want to use them at run time, the steps to set up the APIs will be precisely the same. For example, instead of calling the API via Hugo in chapter 10, we could have used the `fetch` function for getting the content for our search widget.

In the shortcode, we will use the LaTeX code as the inner content of the shortcode and then call the latex2svg API to get the SVG version of this LaTeX document. We can convert that to a resource using `resources.FromString` or render it inline as an SVG document. We will provide the SVG inline for our use case.

Although we can use the `site.baseURL` in the endpoint if we use Netlify, it does not work for compile-time API access when the website has never been pushed live before. The compile-time need for a run-time function causes us to deploy twice: once to get the function up and the second time to call it. *Unless you use JavaScript, it is advisable to have a static URL for the API present in the configuration.* Note that we will also need to enable `LATEX2SVG_PASSWORD` within `funcs/getenv` of the Hugo security config (config/_default/security.yaml) to fetch the value from the environment variables.

We can convert the `display` parameter of the API into arguments for the shortcode as the following listing shows. The corresponding file is also present in the chapter resources (https://github.com/hugoinaction/hugoinaction/tree/chapter-11-resources/03).

Listing 11.7 Shortcode to render LaTeX as SVG (layouts/shortcodes/latex.html)

```
{{/*  a Boolean specifying whether the math is in
    display-mode or inline mode */}}
{{ $display := true }}                          ◁————————————  Sets up the parameters
{{ with .Get "display" }}{{ $display = . }}{{ end }}            with meaningful defaults

{{ if (and site.Params.Latex2Svg                     Disallows calling the server if there
        (getenv "LATEX2SVG_PASSWORD") ) }}     ◁—    is no LATEX2SVG_PASSWORD or the
  {{ $json := getJSON site.Params.Latex2Svg "?"      endpoint is not defined
    (querify "tex" .Inner)
    "&password=" (getenv "LATEX2SVG_PASSWORD")
    "&display=" $display}}
  {{ with $json.data }}
  {{. | safeHTML}}        ◁——┐ Embeds the data without
{{ end }}                     escaping the SVG content inline
{{ end }}
```

Next, we need to enter the `Latex2Svg` endpoint in the website configuration, depending on whether you used Heroku or Netlify for deployment. The following listing adds the path for this endpoint.

Listing 11.8   Adding latex2svg path (config/_default/params.yaml)

```
Latex2Svg: https://<endpoint>.herokuapp.com/latex2svg
 or
Latex2Svg: https://<endpoint>/.netlify/functions/latex2svg
```

If we do not want to call the cloud service, we can use `http://localhost:3000/latex2svg` as the URL in config/development/params.yaml. We can also disable the call during development by setting this to blank.

11.2.10   Adding some LaTeX to our website

Now we can finally have mathematical functions on our website! Let's use our shortcode to add some math to our website. In our blog, we have a page about triangles. Listing 11.9 adds the formula for the area of a triangle to the Tropical Triangles page. Then listing 11.10 does the same for a circle.

Listing 11.9   LaTeX for triangles (content/blog/tropical triangles/index.md)

```
Equation
---------

{{<latex>}}\text{Area} = \frac{b \times h}{2}{{</latex>}}
```

Listing 11.10   LaTeX for circles (content/blog/community/circle/index.md)

```
Equation
--------

{{<latex>}}\text{Area} = \pi r^2{{</latex>}}
```

We can also do complex mathematical equations to get the SVG rendering. For example, figure 11.19 shows the mathematical definition of a Bézier curve. The following listing adds that equation to index.md.

Listing 11.11   The Bézier curve equation (content/blog/community/curve/index.md)

```
Equation
---------

{{<latex>}}
\mathbf {B} (t) = \sum __{i=0}^{n}{n \choose i}(1-t)^ {n-i}t^ {i}\mathbf {P}
    __{i}
{{</latex>}}
```

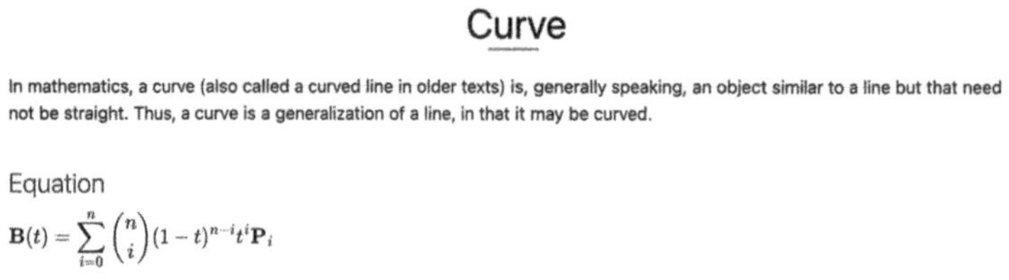

Curve

In mathematics, a curve (also called a curved line in older texts) is, generally speaking, an object similar to a line but that need not be straight. Thus, a curve is a generalization of a line, in that it may be curved.

Equation

$$\mathbf{B}(t) = \sum_{i=0}^{n} \binom{n}{i} (1-t)^{n-i} t^i \mathbf{P}_i$$

Figure 11.19   LaTeX is rendered as SVG on the Curve web page. Using compile-time API access, we can convert LaTeX to SVG without requiring any JavaScript on the client.

We can do inline LaTeX as well. The following listing adds inline LaTeX to the Circles page.

Listing 11.12   Adding inline LaTeX (content/blog/community/circle/index.md)

```
The area of a circle is {{<latex display="false">}}
\pi r^2 {{</latex>}}
```

CODE CHECKPOINT   https://chapter-11-02.hugoinaction.com, and source code: https://github.com/hugoinaction/hugoinaction/tree/chapter-11-02.

Figure 11.20   Uptime: Bob is confident about the freedom obtained by handing over up-time management to a FaaS hosting provider.

11.3   *Using webhooks to rebuild automatically*

When someone submits a comment to our website, the current approach is to rebuild it to make it available to the readers manually. This section will automate that rebuild so that the comments get posted by themselves when submitted.

So far, in this book, we have seen APIs called manually, either from the build system (through Hugo) or via JavaScript (through `window.fetch`). Services can also contact an API in response to some action (including actions from the users). *Webhooks* are invocations of a web URL from within a service. When an event happens, any service (first party or third party) can send an HTTP request (via a preconfigured URL) and the payload format to another service, causing some other linked action. With webhooks, we can connect services to perform tasks across multiple service boundaries without writing explicit code. Services like Heroku, which we have used so far, automatically configure webhooks for determining repository changes (figure 11.21).

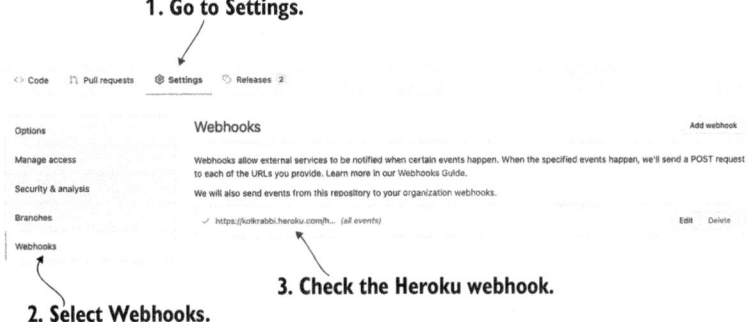

Figure 11.21 A webhook registered by Heroku notifies GitHub when changes are pushed to our repository to rebuild Heroku.

Both Formspree and Netlify support webhooks for form submissions. We can use these to rebuild our website when a comment is submitted to remove the need for manual moderation. When users submit comments, the website rebuilds, and the comment is made available on the website.

NOTE Webhooks are used extensively in the modern web. When we push a change to GitHub, GitHub invokes a webhook that notifies Netlify or Hero to rebuild. When we give Netlify or Heroku access to our GitHub account, the services register their webhooks at that time, which GitHub invokes on specific actions. (The webhooks in GitHub can be at the repository or organization level. GitHub also has the concept of GitHub Apps, which get a single webhook for multiple actions across multiple repositories and support login via GitHub.) All this happens behind the scenes, and the two services work seamlessly together due to this integration.

11.3.1 Creating a webhook for Netlify rebuilds

To create a webhook in Netlify, you need to go to Site Settings > Build & Deploy > Continuous Deployment > Build Hooks and click Add Build Hook (figure 11.22). We need to name the build hook and select the branch that you want to build (figure 11.23).

The build hook is a URL like `https://api.netlify.com/build_hooks/<hook hash>`. We can call `curl -X POST -d {} <url>` in the command line and then go to the deploy tab to see the build hook triggered.

> ### Exercise 11.4
> Webhooks are APIs that enable a server to _____ communication.

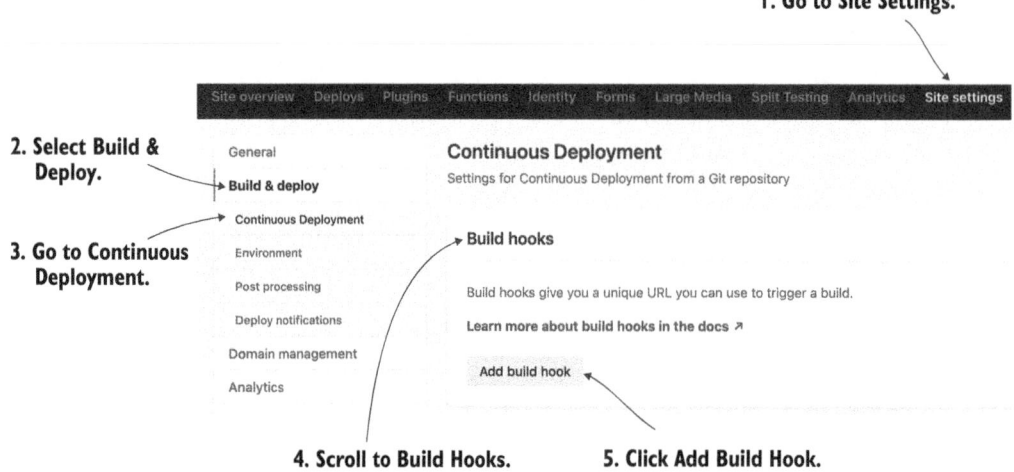

Figure 11.22   The Build Hooks section on the Netlify website. Build hooks allow triggering the deployment of a Netlify website from anywhere by just opening a URL.

Figure 11.23   Creating build hooks on the Netlify website. A build hook needs a name and the default branch to build. We can override both of these when calling the build hook if we want.

11.3.2 Adding the webhook to Netlify Forms

We can add the webhook in Netlify Forms to rebuild the website when a new comment is posted. We can create this webhook by going to Site Settings > Forms > Form Notifications, click Add Notification to the right of Outgoing Notifications, and then select Outgoing Webhook (figure 11.24).

From the Event to Listen For dropdown, we can select the form whose submission should trigger the webhook. Then we can enter the corresponding URL and click Save (figure 11.25). The webhook is triggered when the comments form is submitted.

With these steps, every comment submission should trigger a rebuild of our website. This deploys the comment to our website within a few minutes.

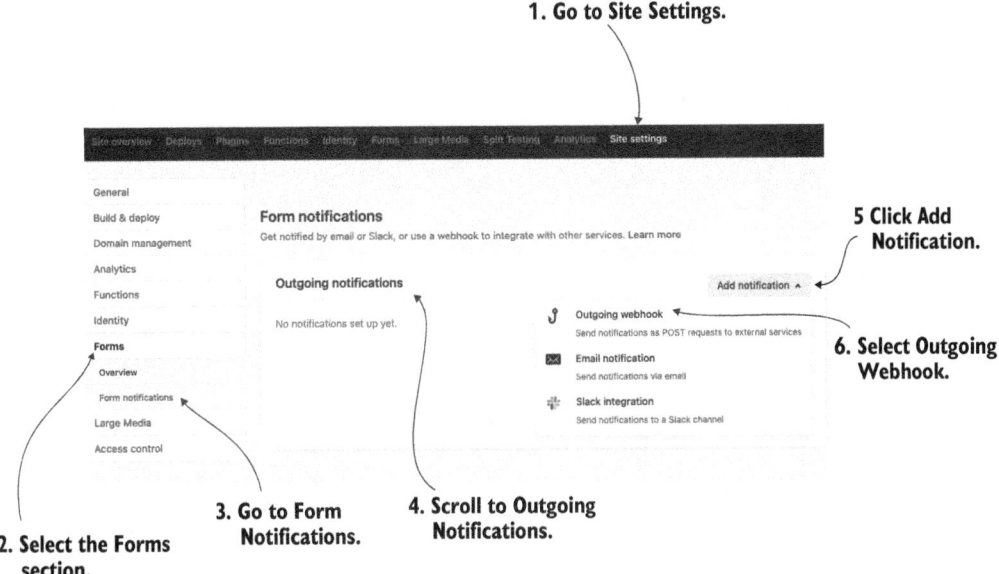

Figure 11.24 Adding an outgoing webhook to Netlify Forms involves going to the Site Settings page and adding an entry.

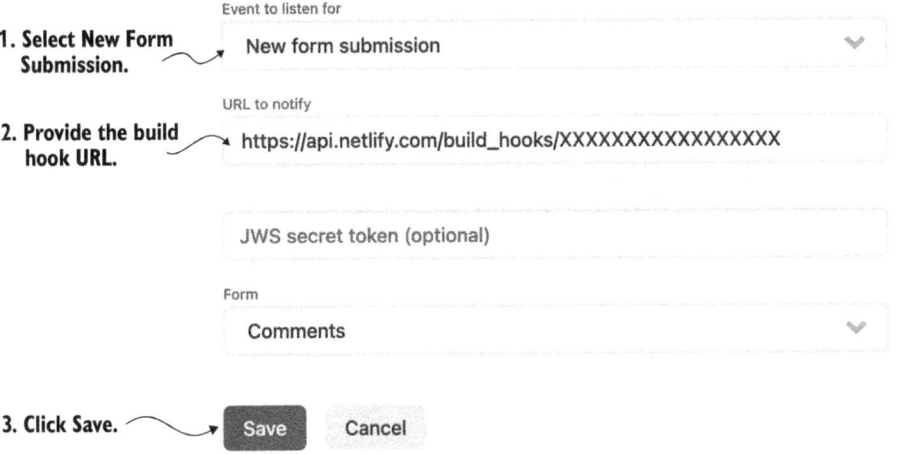

Figure 11.25 Outgoing webhook screen showing the details when adding a webhook to Netlify. We want to trigger the most fine-tuned webhook to prevent excessive builds by selecting the right form.

Triggering via IFTTT or Zapier

Many form services including Netlify Forms and Formspree integrate piping services. Piping services like IFTTT or Zapier support taking webhook data and converting it into another format to trigger an API in another service. These services act like hubs that connect to hundreds of services initiated from a webhook, most of them with no code at our end.

11.3.3 *Preventing abuse*

Although we have a functional setup, where a comment issues a retrigger, we have added a cost risk to our website. Netlify charges its users for build minutes beyond its free tier. We have opened ourselves to the potential of many expensive rebuilds by triggering it on form submission, especially if we get a sudden influx of users or bots who leave comments on our website. It is always a good idea to keep tabs on the expensive operations on the website. We can turn them off when required, but we must safeguard against malicious actors on the open internet by default.

TIP Investigate your build costs before adding abuse prevention. This additional work is unnecessary for most use cases.

To add this layer of additional security, we can limit deployments to once per minute, once per hour, or even once per day, depending on the time a rebuild consumes and the website's requirements. For this, we will need to create another Netlify function that queries the Netlify API to get the last build time and to react based on its value.

To query the Netlify API for the last build time, we first need to get the API ID of the website. This ID is available in Site Settings > General > Site Details (figure 11.26). We can store this API ID in an environment variable called NETLIFY_SITE_ID. We can now call the Netlify deploys API (https://api.netlify.com/api/v1/sites/#{site_id}/deploys) to get the last deployment time and trigger deployment if it is more than the

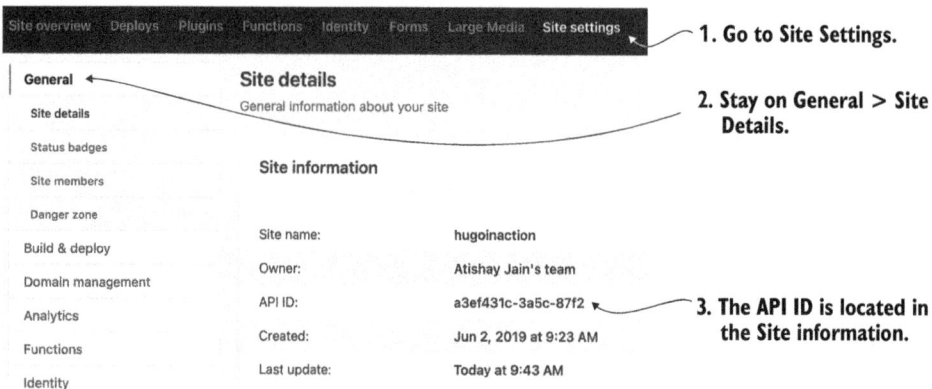

Figure 11.26   Getting the API ID of a Netlify website. We can use the API ID to contact the Netlify API to get further details about the site.

configured rebuild time. We should also store the ID of the webhook in BUILD
_HOOK_ID to keep it out of our codebase. In parallel, we will be password-protecting
this API similar to the latex2svg API via the REBUILD_PASSWORD environment variable.

> **NOTE** Because the sample code hosts multiple branches, we need to perform
> many rebuilds on each comment submission. Additional checks like captchas
> can be added, or webhooks can be disabled if the API gets a lot of abuse.

We will also need to add a dependency on node-fetch to call the fetch function from
Node.js, which is used to call the Netlify API. The following listing adds this dependency.

Listing 11.13 Adding `node-fetch` as a dependency (package.hugo.json)

```json
{
  ...
  "dependencies": {
    ...
    "node-fetch": "2.6.1"
  }
}
```

We now need to call hugo mod npm pack and npm install. The rebuild code for calling
to Netlify is fairly simple. We can directly call the build hook API and share its results
with the caller for our webhook (https://github.com/hugoinaction/hugoinaction/
tree/chapter-11-resources/04). The following listing shows the core rebuild functionality via a webhook that forwards requests to the Netlify API.

Listing 11.14 Core rebuild functionality (api/rebuild.js)

```js
const fetch = require("node-fetch");
module.exports = {
  async handler(event, context) {
    const rebuild = await fetch(
        "https://api.netlify.com/build_hooks/" + process.env.BUILD_HOOK_ID,
        { method: 'POST' });
    if (rebuild.ok) {
      return {
        statusCode: 200,
        headers: { "Content-Type": "application/json" },
        body: JSON.stringify({response: "Triggered successfully"})
      };
    } else {
      return {
        headers: rebuild.headers,
        statusCode: rebuild.status,
        body: await rebuild.text()
      };
    }
  }
}
```

We will use `NETLIFY_SITE_ID` and `COMMENTS_TOKEN` to call the deploys API. If the deploy is old enough to allow rebuilds, we'll need to trigger the build hook. The following listing does this and then checks if the last deployment was within the `DEPLOY_MIN_INTERVAL`. If so, the deploy action is ignored, and we return HTTP 429 (Too Many Requests).

Listing 11.15   Calling the deploys API from Netlify (api/rebuild.js)

```
const DEPLOY_MIN_INTERVAL = 60 * 1000; // 1 minute
...
module.exports = {
  async handler(event, context) {
    if (process.env.NETLIFY_SITE_ID && process.env.COMMENTS_TOKEN) {
      const deploys = await fetch(
        "https://api.netlify.com/api/v1/sites/" +
        process.env.NETLIFY_SITE_ID + "/deploys?access_token=" +
        process.env.COMMENTS_TOKEN);              ⟵─────  Fetches the list of
                                                          deploys from Netlify
      if (deploys.ok) {
        const list = await deploys.json();
        if ( Array.isArray(list) && (!list[0]             Checks if it exceeds
            || new Date().getTime() -                     DEPLOY_MIN_INTERVAL
            new Date(list[0].created_at).getTime()        since the last trigger
            > DEPLOY_MIN_INTERVAL)
        ) {

          ... // Rebuild code
        } else {
          return {
            statusCode: 429,
            headers: {
              'Retry-After': Array.isArray(list) &&
                list[0] ? (DEPLOY_MIN_INTERVAL -
                  new Date().getTime() +
                  new Date(list[0].created_at).getTime()
                )/1000   : 1,              ⟵─────  Retry-After tells the server
            }                                      to try again at a specific
          }                                        time in the future.
        }
      }
    }
    return {
      statusCode: 400,
      headers: { "Content-Type": "application/json" },
      body: JSON.stringify({
        error: "Missing data.",
      }),
    };
  }
}
```

We will also add a password check and surround our code with a `try..catch` block to prevent accidental crashes. The following listing adds these measures to ensure that the code is safe to be deployed from crashes and adds a rebuild password security check.

```
...
  async handler(event, context) {
    try {
      if (
        !event.queryStringParameters ||
        !process.env.REBUILD_PASSWORD ||
        event.queryStringParameters.password !== process.env.REBUILD_PASSWORD
      ) {
        return {
          statusCode: 401,
          headers: { "Content-Type": "application/json" },
          body: JSON.stringify({
            error: "Access Denied.",
          }),
        };
      }
      ...
    } catch (e) {
      return {
        statusCode: 500,
        headers: { "Content-Type": "application/json" },
        body: JSON.stringify({
          error: "Please try again later.",
        }),
      };
    }
  }
...
```

Because this code does not trigger rebuilds after every comment, not all comments may be available on the website. We might have to manually rebuild if no build happens after a particular comment. We recommend keeping the throttle duration short to provide a good user experience.

Triggering builds on multiple branches

Although Netlify supports building one branch with a single build hook call, it is straightforward to trigger multiple branch builds with a hook. A hook can optionally take a branch name to build and a message to associate a trigger with. The following code snippet creates a Netlify function that goes in a loop to trigger rebuilds of all the branches we desire:

```
(continued)
const branches = [...];
let rebuild = {ok: false, status: 400};
do {
  const branch = branches.shift();
  rebuild = await fetch(
    "https://api.netlify.com/build_hooks/" +
      process.env.BUILD_HOOK_ID + "?trigger_branch=" + branch,
    { method: 'POST' }
  );

} while(rebuild.ok && branches.length > 0);
```

The sample website for this book uses multiple branches to host various checkpoints. After the abuse prevention function, this code will trigger rebuilds on all relevant branches.

CODE CHECKPOINT   https://chapter-11-03.hugoinaction.com, and source code: https://github.com/hugoinaction/hugoinaction/tree/chapter-11-03.

11.3.4 Creating a GitHub Pages rebuild webhook

In GitHub, webhooks to trigger GitHub actions are called *workflow dispatch events* or *repository dispatch events*. Workflow dispatch events start a single workflow, and repository dispatch events trigger multiple workflows in a single repository. We will use the workflow dispatch event (also used for manually triggering rebuilds) set up in chapter 2 as the following listing shows.

> **Listing 11.17   The `workflow_dispatch` property (.github/workflows/gh-pages.yml)**

```
name: GitHub pages

on:
  push:
      branches:
        - main
  workflow_dispatch: # Kept empty. Can have parameters if needed.
```

> **Scheduling rebuilds**
> GitHub also supports the `cron-job` syntax to schedule builds to run at specified intervals. We can use these to update our builds regularly.

11.3.5 Creating a function to trigger GitHub webhooks

To trigger a workflow in GitHub, we need to provide the corresponding branch and the workflow's name to the fixed workflow dispatch endpoint. Because Formspree does not support sending an arbitrary payload to a workflow, we need a function to perform this task. This function will also perform abuse filtering in GitHub Actions and limit the number of rebuilds that happen within a short duration on GitHub.

We need a personal access token from GitHub to trigger builds. To get a personal access token, in GitHub, click the Profile icon on the top right, go to Settings. Then in the left-hand menu, click Developer Settings (figure 11.27) followed by Personal Access Token.

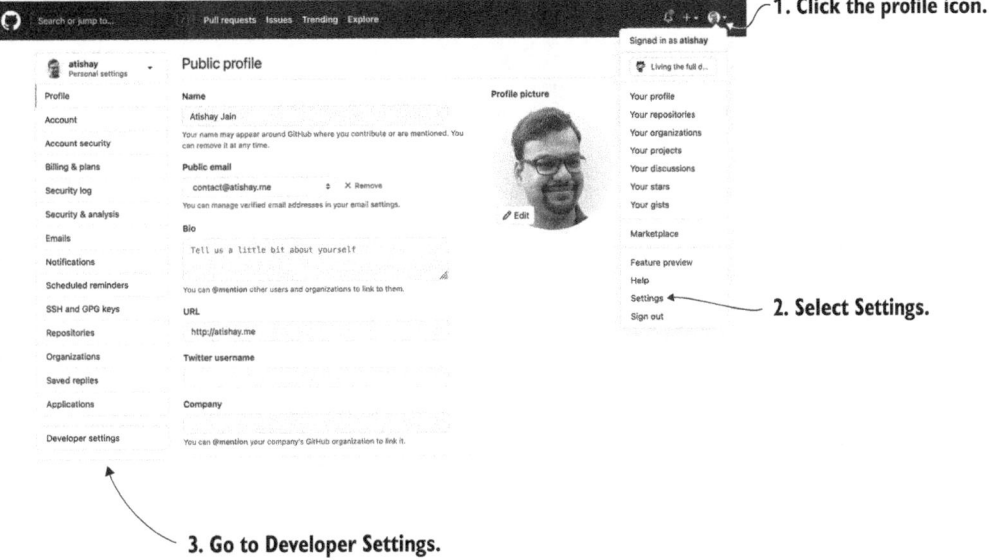

Figure 11.27 Getting to Developer Settings on GitHub to create a personal access token

In the Personal Access Token area, we can click Generate New Token to get a new token (figure 11.28).

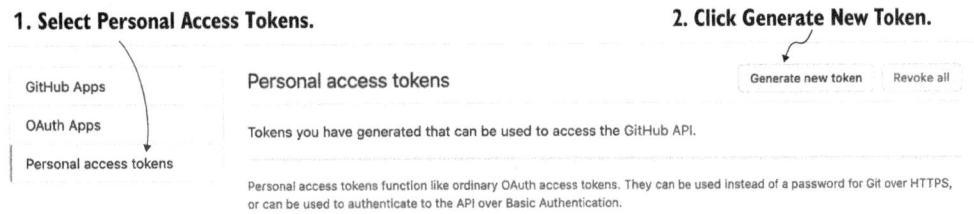

Figure 11.28 The Personal Access Token area in GitHub settings to generate a new access token

The access token needs workflow permissions to access and trigger workflows associated with GitHub actions. Figure 11.29 shows the steps to take for this.

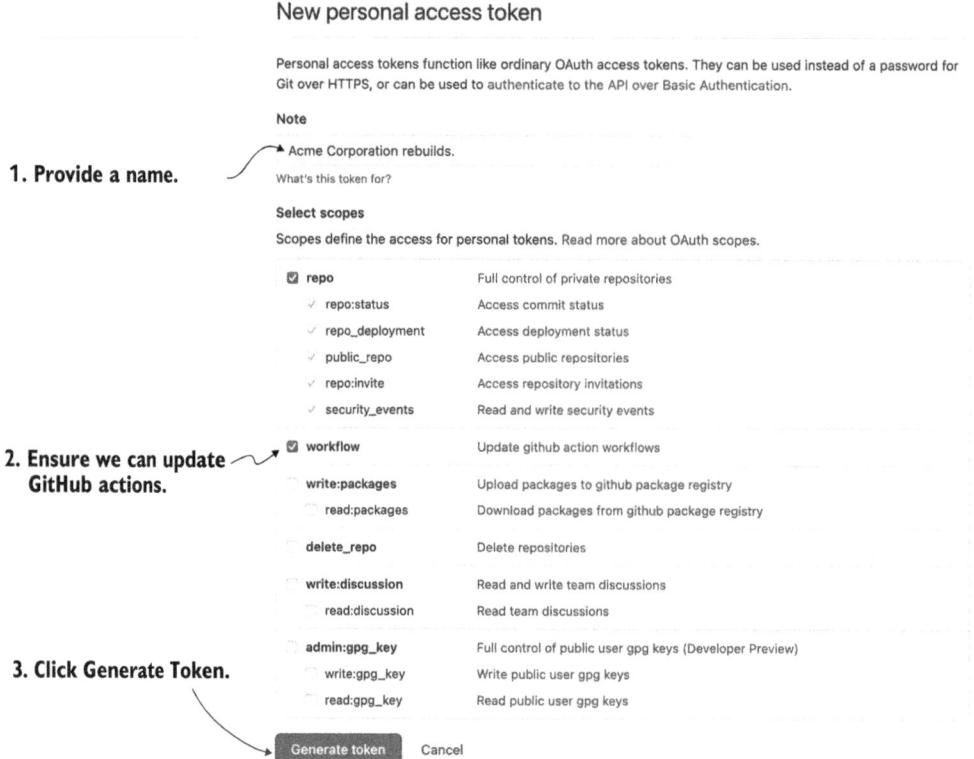

1. Provide a name.

2. Ensure we can update GitHub actions.

3. Click Generate Token.

Figure 11.29   The Personal Access Token area in GitHub settings to generate a new access token

Once generated, copy the access token and save this to the environment variables in Heroku as GITHUB_ACCESS_TOKEN. We can use this token to access the GitHub API. There are two APIs we will use to trigger a workflow:

- *GET /repos/:owner/:repo/actions/workflows/:workflow_id/runs*—This API provides the last run of a workflow with the provided name. We can use this to get the created_at date from the deploys API for Netlify. In our case, the workflow_id is the filename in the .github/workflows subfolder, gh_pages.

- *POST /repos/{owner}/{repo}/actions/workflows/{workflow_id}/dispatches*—This API triggers an action.

We will use the function to trigger rebuilds as we used for Netlify. As with NETLIFY _SITE_ID, we will check for GITHUB_ACCESS_TOKEN to see if this is a GitHub Pages deployment. We have to set up a new repository, GitHubPagesRebuild, for this deployment as listing 11.18 shows. GitHub provides APIs to programmatically invoke dispatches on workflows where we can rebuild the website. We can use the workflow runs API from GitHub to get the previous workflow runs to figure out if we need to throttle rebuilds.

Listing 11.18 Triggering rebuilds on GitHub Pages (api/rebuild.js)

```
if (process.env.GITHUB_ACCESS_TOKEN) {
  const response = await fetch(
    "https://api.github.com/repos/hugoinaction/" +
    "GitHubPagesRebuild/actions/workflows/gh-pages.yml/runs", {
    headers: {
      'Accept': 'application/vnd.github.v3+json',
      'Authorization': `token ${process.env.GITHUB_ACCESS_TOKEN}`
    }
  });
  if (response.ok) {
    const data = await response.json();
    const list = data.workflow_runs;
    if (Array.isArray(list) && (!list[0] ||
      new Date().getTime() - new Date(!list[0].created_at).getTime()
          > DEPLOY_MIN_INTERVAL)) {
      const rebuild = await fetch(
        "https://api.github.com/repos/hugoinaction/" +
        "GitHubPagesRebuild/workflows/gh-pages.yml/dispatches", {
        method: 'POST',
        headers: {
          'Accept': 'application/vnd.github.v3+json',
          'Authorization': `token ${process.env.GITHUB_ACCESS_TOKEN}`
        },
        body: JSON.stringify({
          "ref": "main",
        })
      });
      if (rebuild.ok) {
        return {
          statusCode: 200,
          headers: { "Content-Type": "application/json" },
          body: JSON.stringify({response: "Triggered successfully"})
        };
      } else {
        return {
          headers: rebuild.headers,
          statusCode: rebuild.status,
          body: await rebuild.text()
        };
      }
    }
  }
}
```

Annotations:
- **Fetches the list of runs for the gh-pages workflow in hugoinaction/hugoinaction on GitHub**
- **Tells GitHub we want to use the V3 API**
- **Posts a new dispatch to the gh-pages workflow**

We also need to update api.js to handle the `rebuild` workflow. The following listing provides the code for this update. With this change, the rebuild API is ready to handle rebuilds from the comments form.

Listing 11.19   Providing an endpoint for the rebuild API (api.js)

```
const rebuild = require('./api/rebuild');

switch (url.pathname) {
  case '/latex2svg':
    response = await latex2svg.handler(request);
    break;
  case '/rebuild':
    response = await rebuild.handler(request);
    break;
}
```

11.3.6 Adding a webhook to Formspree to rebuild the website

The final step is updating Formspree to submit a request to our rebuild API when a new comment is submitted. Go to the Plugins tab in the Formspree Form Details page for the Hugo in Action comments and select Webhook (figure 11.30).

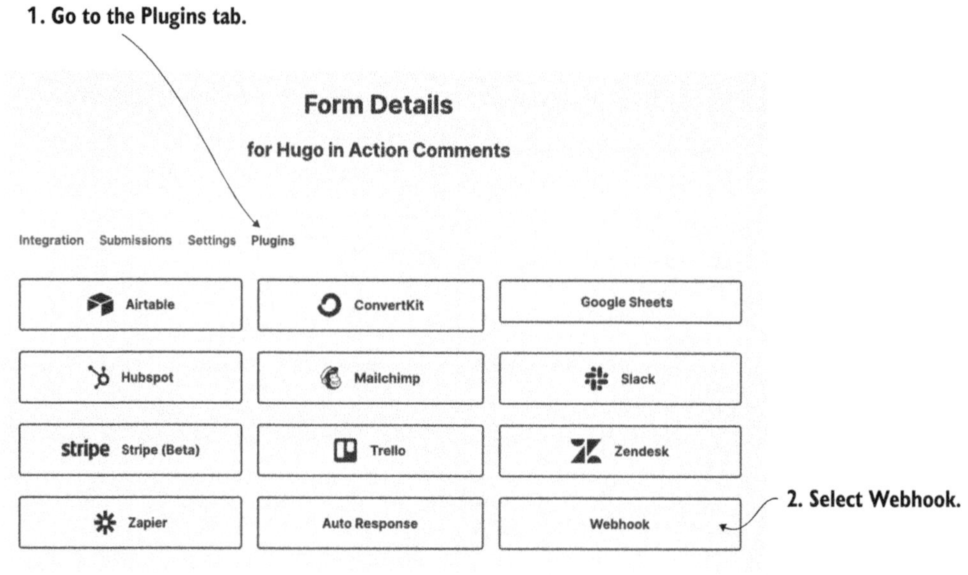

Figure 11.30   Creating a webhook in Formspree. Each form has a plugins page from where we can create a webhook in Formspree.

We will use the build hooks version of the webhooks. We do not need the information submitted in the form to trigger a rebuild (figure 11.31).

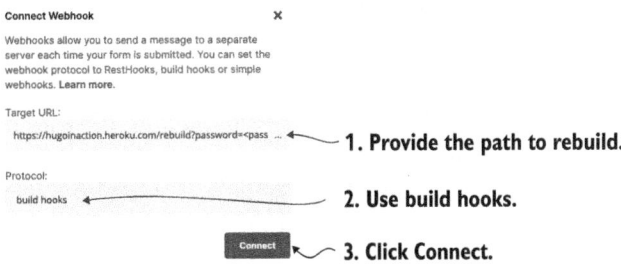

Figure 11.31 Formspree needs the endpoint and the type of webhook we want to create to render it. The build hook is the simplest because it requires no pre-registration and no data.

1. Provide the path to rebuild.

2. Use build hooks.

3. Click Connect.

We can then click the webhook again to get to the Webhook Settings page. Once there, we can test our webhook (figure 11.32).

Figure 11.32 Validating a webhook in Formspree involves going to the Webhook Settings page and clicking Send Test.

Do rebuilds get us to the same architecture as a traditional web app in a roundabout way?

With the changes we have done to perform rebuilds, it may appear that we have gone back to the same architecture as we had in traditional application layers, but worse! We have added long delays to trigger rebuilds. Even if we wanted to put the CDN layer with the traditional stacks, we could fine-tune the invalidation logic to the specific change needed. We do not need to rebuild the whole website again.

This observation is correct and valid. Rebuild is more of a hack for getting dynamic behavior rather than a perfect solution. Another solution is to build a service that does commenting and exposes them through a JavaScript-based API. (We could potentially use the Netlify forms API on the client side.) This causes a lot more load on the forms retrieval service and incurs the most cost, especially if the creation of new comments is rare. There will also be a performance penalty for the client-side API communication. This tradeoff of dynamic behavior and cost is something to consider on a case-by-case basis. The Jamstack allows for the low-cost approach of rebuilds that we just did as well as an API-based solution that offers more dynamic behavior at a potentially higher cost.

CODE CHECKPOINT   https://chapter-11-04.hugoinaction.com, and source code: https://github.com/hugoinaction/hugoinaction/tree/chapter-11-04.

11.3.7 Updating the JavaScript code for some immediate feedback on the comment submission

With automatic rebuilds, we have removed the moderation step before taking the website live. Therefore, we can immediately show the comment to the user that posted the comment via JavaScript. At the same time, the rebuild takes place behind the scenes. Waiting for the comment to be made available causes needless worry, especially in the most likely case where the comment is present in the next build.

To match the JavaScript-as-utility architecture used with comments, we can add another template, called `comment-pre`, and another property, called `data-pre`. We will use placeholders for the `name` and `message` fields, which we will fill up with JavaScript. Listing 11.20 shows a sample template to render comments as soon as they are submitted, using `comments-pre` as an identifier to be picked up by JavaScript. We use `[[key]]` as the syntax for placeholders to disambiguate from Hugo template markers (`{{key}}`).

Listing 11.20   Template for comments (AcmeTheme/layouts/partials/comment.html)

```
<template id="comment-pre">
  <div class="comment" >
    <img alt="[[name]] Avatar"
      src= "https://www.gravatar.com/avatar/
      ⮡ [[emailhash]]#?s=100&amp;d=wavatar"
      width="100" height="100">
    <div class="author">[[name]]</div>
    <div class="message">[[message]]</div>
  </div>
</template>

. . .

<form data-pre="#comment-pre" ...>
```

> Uses [[key]] for placeholders. If we want double brackets, we need to use {{ "{{title}}" }} to override Hugo's template system that uses the same syntax.

> Adds email hash via JavaScript code

Next, we can update our JavaScript code. We need an md5 library to calculate the md5 in JavaScript. md5 with npm is small and well used. The following listing adds this as a devDependency.

Listing 11.21   Adding a dependency on the md5 library (package.hugo.json)

```
. . .
"devDependencies": {
  . . .
  "md5": "2.3.0"
}
```

Exercise 11.5

Immediate feedback via _____ is a critical element in making the Jamstack-based websites feel dynamic, fast, and modern.

Now we can load the content marked with `data-pre` when submitting a form, placing it before the form. The following listing uses JavaScript to accomplish this.

Listing 11.22 Moving content before the form (AcmeTheme/assets/formHandler.js)

```
import md5 from "md5"

...
if (response.ok) {
  if (form.dataset.pre) {                              ⟵  Checks for the existence
    let content = document.querySelector(form.dataset.pre).innerHTML;    of the data-pre property
    for (let pair of  data) {                                            in the form
      let key = pair[0], value = pair[1];       Specifies a simple key-value
      content = content.replaceAll(             replacement in the template
        `[[${key}]]`,value);   ⟵                exposed to JavaScript
      if (key === "email") {
        content = content.replaceAll(
          `[[emailhash]]`,md5(value));
      }
    }
    form.insertAdjacentHTML('beforebegin', content);   ⟵  Inserts the predata
  }                                                         before the form
  ...
}
```

Adds support for the email hash needed for Gravatar — points to the `[[emailhash]]` line.

NOTE We will remove the cached file in the resources folder associated with comments from the commit to update comments on rebuild.

CODE CHECKPOINT https://chapter-11-05.hugoinaction.com, and source code: https://github.com/hugoinaction/hugoinaction/tree/chapter-11-05.

Eventual consistency and instant gratification

It is a form of cheating to show the readers the comment inline. Even if we ignore the time it takes to rebuild, we will need network communication between the user submission and the availability of the comment. This limitation does not come from the Jamstack but from fundamental physics. It does take time even for network traffic to travel throughout the planet. Traditional stacks solve this problem with the concept of eventual consistency. The write API records the data, but it may not instantly appear with a read request because updating the data through a network takes time. Rebuilds in the Jamstack do the same thing.

Once the user has submitted a comment and received a 200 series HTTP response, the backend service records the comment. At this point, there is nothing the user can do to prevent it. If we wait for the comment to be made available, it might take several seconds, which can cause a horrible user experience. To provide immediate feedback for the audience looking for instant gratification, we can send the comment early because we as the client have everything we need.

> **(continued)**
>
> This technique is not new and has been popular over the internet for a long time. In the early days, unconfirmed data used to be shown as grayed out, switching to the regular color when we received confirmation. This approach used to cause a lot of confusion and often blame for a slow service. Many modern applications still follow this show approach and then apologize in case of failure. The failed use cases are rare, and the developer should actively work to fix them. The majority of the users don't need to know about this and do appreciate instant gratification for their effort.
>
> Note that we can make this round trip faster if we move the comments out of the deploy layer to JavaScript, calling the API to fetch the comments. This approach comes with the disadvantage of additional requests, which can cause both performance compromises for the end user and extra costs for the developer.

APIs are such a vast subject that we can dedicate entire books to them, and we still keep learning something new. This chapter explored ways to use APIs that are not commonly used in most traditional web architectures but that are staples in the Jamstack world. We can also use all the other techniques used in communication with a regular website with the Jamstack.

In this chapter, we completed the introduction to the Jamstack and Hugo's support for close interaction with advanced APIs. In the next chapter, we will take what we've learned from this website and apply that to a different type of website—e-commerce.

Summary

- There is always a tradeoff we must make when choosing between a third-party API and developing our own. From additional work to ongoing maintenance, there is more to do when we create custom APIs. Still, we do get to control its feature set or price, and we don't have the assurance that it will not change its business model or go out of business outside of our control.
- In case we need to make a custom API, the Jamstack suggests using a function as a service (FaaS) model or a platform as a service (PaaS) model to keep our day-to-day maintenance work low.
- Netlify provides Netlify Functions as an FaaS solution, which we can use to customize processing such as converting LaTeX text to SVG.
- We can use a PaaS provider like Heroku if we are looking for an independent solution for our API hosting needs.
- Hugo can consume the first-party APIs by the same means as we used for third-party APIs, both at build time and at run time. We can wrap APIs in partials or shortcodes, which can act like plugins to Hugo with additional safety safeguards, thanks to running in an external service.
- Webhooks are the means for service-to-service communication. We can configure webhooks in most Jamstack services to transfer data.

- Many services from GitHub to Netlify can consume webhooks directly. We can also write custom handlers to react to a webhook.
- Jamstack-based websites can be rebuilt using a webhook that gives us the best of both worlds: reaction to user feedback on the website and low maintenance, high performance CDN-based hosting.
- Although actions like rebuilds take time, we can do some preprocessing and rendering in JavaScript to provide the user with instant gratification for an effort that might take some processing time.

Adding e-commerce capabilities using the Jamstack

This chapter covers

- Creating product pages for an e-commerce website
- Adding a shopping cart via JavaScript
- Using APIs to handle payments
- Fulfilling a purchase using a webhook in a cloud function

After 11 chapters on Hugo and the Jamstack, we have a complete, fast, and modern corporate website. We can use it to present any content, authored and managed as Markdown documents, with a custom theme. We can offer dynamic surveys, a fuzzy search on the client with support for comments, a contact form, and an embedded single-page application (SPA).

Hugo is applicable in a much wider variety of use cases. A documentation website is relatively static. A portfolio page or a media website needs image manipulation (Hugo Pipes), and the rest is all static content. An educational website is all about presenting content. This chapter will use what you've learned to build another website domain suited for the Jamstack—e-commerce. An e-commerce domain has many static pieces like product pages that need to provide excellent load performance and require user-specific shopping cart management. This makes it an ideal use case for utilizing the entire Jamstack.

In this chapter, we will add a functional e-commerce section to our existing website using the entire Jamstack. We will have separate product and index pages, operational checkout, and email-based purchase fulfillment. We will reuse many skills we have developed in this book and understand how to apply them to a different domain.

NOTE This chapter runs at a much faster pace than the previous chapters. Some readers may need to go to the official Hugo documentation (https://gohugo.io/documentation/) to understand the solutions as well as the services presented. Some prior experience with Hugo might be necessary to get comfortable with the contents of this chapter. This chapter will not introduce any new Hugo or Jamstack concepts. This chapter presents an alternate way to bring together the elements of the Jamstack.

12.1 Creating e-commerce pages

The most elaborate element in an e-commerce website is the product information pages that allow the customers to decide on what they want to purchase. An e-commerce system can have hundreds to thousands of pages based on the number of products. In a Hugo-based website, each product page has two parts: the content type or layout for the single page and the markup document for its description.

12.1.1 Creating the product content view

We already have the view of the product listing present on the home page of the website (in the Our Products section). We will move the various product assets from the assets folder to a new subfolder called store within the content folder. We will also add description pages for these products. The pricing will continue to come from the products.csv file. This way, the rarely changing description is stored away from regularly changing inventory and pricing information. Note that these prices could potentially come from an API call as well. The sample content for the product pages is present in the chapter resources (https://github.com/hugoinaction/hugoinaction/tree/chapter-12-resources/01). The completed view should look like figure 12.1.

Next, we will refactor the product's HTML from the home page to a content view for reuse across different pages. Although keeping the rest of the content the same, we will add an Add to Cart button and a color selector to allow the users to take action on the

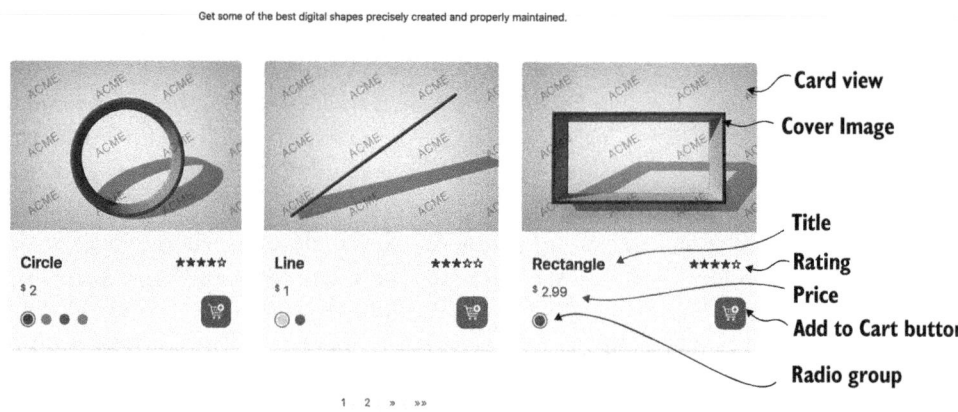

Figure 12.1   A content view allows us to reuse the logic to render the list page from the other sections to the store.

product list across the website (https://github.com/hugoinaction/hugoinaction/tree/chapter-12-resources/02). With the changes from the following listing, the list page for the store renders appropriately.

Listing 12.1   Content view for a store (AcmeTheme/layouts/store/card.html)

Gets the product information from the partial

```
{{$products := (partialCached "products.html" "cache")}}
{{$data := index $products .Params.product}}
<li class="product" >
  <a href="{{.Permalink}}">
    {{with (.Resources.GetMatch "cover.*")}}
    {{$img := . | images.Filter
      (images.Overlay (resources.GetMatch "image/watermark.*") 0 0 )}}
    {{$img := $img.Resize "1000x"}}
    <img loading="lazy" src="{{$img.Permalink}}" alt="{{$.Title}}">
{{end}}
    <h2>{{.Title}}</h2>
    <div class="price">$ {{$data.Price}}</div>
    <div class="rating">
      {{range (seq $data.Rating)}}&starf;{{end}}
      {{- range seq (sub 5 ($data.Rating | int))}}&star;{{end}}
    </div>
  </a>
  <form>
    <input type="hidden" name="name" value="{{.Title }}">
    <div class="colors">
    {{range $i, $c := split $data.Colors ","}}
      <label>
        <input type="radio" name="color"
        value="{{trim $c " "}}"
        {{if eq $i 0}}checked{{end}}>
```

- **The product class designs this card's layout CSS.** (annotation for `<li class="product" >`)
- **Uses the cover image from the page data** (annotation for `{{with (.Resources.GetMatch "cover.*")}}`)
- **Adds the purchase options and button** (annotation for `<form>`)
- **Adds a hidden field to submit the product name as form data** (annotation for the hidden input)
- **Selects the first color by default** (annotation for `{{if eq $i 0}}checked{{end}}>`)

```
      <span class="sr-only">{{$c}}</span>
    </label>
  {{end}}
  </div>
  <button class="addToCart" type="submit">Add to Cart</button>
  </form>
</li>
```

Next, in the index layout, we can swap over the logic to use this content view. The code is similar to what we used for rendering the blog section pages. Listing 12.2 shows the HTML for a sample page for an individual product sold in the store.

Listing 12.2   Sample product page (AcmeTheme/layouts/_default/index.html)

```
{{with (where site.RegularPages ".Section" "store")}}
<section id="store">
  <h1>Our Products</h1>
  <ul class="products">
  {{ range first 5 .}}
    {{.Render "card"}}
  {{ end }}
  </ul>
</section>
{{end}}
```

CODE CHECKPOINT   https://chapter-12-01.hugoinaction.com, and source code: https://github.com/hugoinaction/hugoinaction/tree/chapter-12-01.

12.1.2 *Building a single product page*

The single page using the default layout does not have purchase buttons for the product. We will redesign this page to be more suited to our e-commerce needs (figure 12.2).

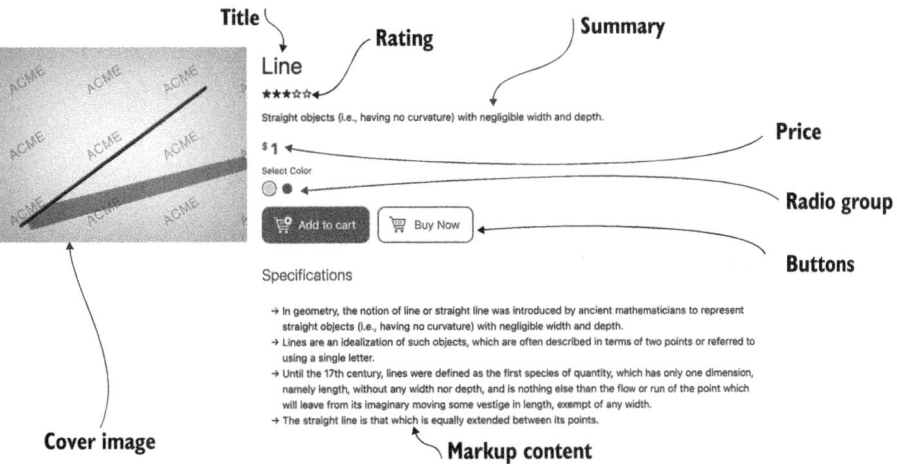

Figure 12.2   Core part of the single product page (related pages and comment section are not shown here). The single product page has an image in a sidebar along with purchase buttons and details on the right.

We can reuse the comment and the related page code from the Blog page, adding only the core product information and the purchase buttons (https://github.com/hugoinaction/hugoinaction/tree/chapter-12-resources/03). In the following listing, we use a new body class called store to identify the product page via CSS.

Listing 12.3   A single product template (AcmeTheme/layouts/store/single.html)

```
{{define "bodyClass"}} store page {{end}}   ◁─── Adds a class for the CSS

{{define "body"}}
{{$products := (partialCached "products.html" "cache")}}
{{$data := index $products .Params.product}}
 <main>
  {{with (.Resources.GetMatch "cover.*")}}          ◁─
    {{$img := . | images.Filter (images.Overlay
      (resources.GetMatch "image/watermark.*") 0 0 )}}
    {{$img := $img.Resize "1000x"}}
    <img loading="lazy" src="{{$img.Permalink}}"
      " alt="{{$.Title}}">
  {{end}}
  <div>
    <h1>{{.Title}}</h1>
    <div class="rating">                            ◁─
      {{range (seq $data.Rating)}}&starf;{{end}}
      {{- range seq (sub 5 ($data.Rating | int))}}&star;{{end}}
    </div>
    <p>{{.Summary}}</p>
    <div class="price">$ {{$data.Price}}</div>
    <form>
      <input type="hidden" name="name" value="{{.Title }}">
      <label for="color-selector">Select Color</label>
      <div class="colors" >                         ◁─
      {{range $i, $c := split $data.Colors ","}}
        <label>
          <input type="radio" name="color" value="{{trim $c " "}}"
            {{if eq $i 0}}checked{{end}}>
          <span class="sr-only">{{$c}}</span>
        </label>
      {{end}}
      </div>
      <button class="addToCart" type="submit">
        Add to Cart
      </button>
      <button class="buyNow" type="submit">
        Buy Now
      </button>
    </form>
    <h2>Specifications</h2>
    {{.Content}}
  </div>
</main>
```

Contains the same logic as the card view

Introduces a Buy Now button

We can also reuse the comments and the related pages from the Blog page for the store pages. The following listing shows the code for this step.

Listing 12.4 Reusing blog components (AcmeTheme/layouts/store/single.html)

```
{{with where (site.RegularPages.Related .)     Only allows related pages
  ".Section" "store"}}                          from the store section
<div id="related">
  <h2>Related Products</h2>
  <ul class="products">
    {{range first 3 .}}
      {{.Render "card"}}
    {{end}}
  </ul>
</div>
{{end}}
{{ partial "comment.html" (dict
  "FormspreeCommentForm" ($.Param "FormspreeCommentForm")
  "RelPermalink" .Page.RelPermalink
  "Disabled" ($.Param "CommentDisabled")
)}}
{{end}}
```

CODE CHECKPOINT https://chapter-12-02.hugoinaction.com, and source code: https://github.com/hugoinaction/hugoinaction/tree/chapter-12-02.

12.2 Creating a shopping cart

A *shopping cart* in an e-commerce website is a data structure that holds a list of all the items the user intends to purchase. It also provides a user interface to add or remove items and to navigate to the Checkout page where the actual billing information is present. The ideal shopping cart should work across user sessions carrying the information until they manually remove it or checkout. We can decide to use either a service-side technology to store a user's shopping cart (which would require us to force the user to login to purchase), or use the browser's local storage (which does not work across machines). For small websites, a login requirement is a huge hurdle and more challenging to implement, so we will use local storage.

12.2.1 Creating a cart button in the header

The shopping cart is a button in the header whose implementation is similar to the search box. When the user hovers or taps the cart icon, the cart should open with the list of items and the checkout option. The following listing adds the shopping cart to the Acme Corporation website header.

Listing 12.5 Adding a shopping cart (AcmeTheme/layouts/_default/baseof.html)

```
<span id="search">
  ...
</span>
```

```
<span id="cart">
  <button>
    Cart
    <div class="badge"></div>          ◁──┐
  </button>
  <div>
    <div class="empty">
      Please add some items to the cart.
    </div>
  </div>
</span>
```

A badge indicates the number of items in the shopping cart.

The empty container for a user without content in the cart. This text ensures the cart button is always usable.

Exercise 12.1

Which of the following Hugo features apply across domains like blogs, business websites, and e-commerce applications? (Select all that apply.)

- **a.** Taxonomy
- **b.** Page bundles
- **c.** Related pages
- **d.** Menus
- **e.** Custom output formats (JSON pages)
- **f.** Cascade

12.2.2 Creating the cart in JavaScript

The shopping cart needs to be filled by the website users in their browsers. Therefore, the cart cannot be processed at compile time and requires some JavaScript.

MANAGING SHOPPING CART ACROSS TABS

We will create a new file, store.js, to handle all the user interactions within the store section. We will use the localStorage API to store the cart locally to ensure the store is workable across browser sessions. We will also use a `storage` event from the `window` object to keep the cart in sync across all tabs. The completed store.js for the entire cart creation is present in the chapter resources (https://github.com/hugoinaction/hugoinaction/tree/chapter-12-resources/04). The following listing shows the code associated with the management of the shopping cart on local storage.

Listing 12.6   Managing the shopping cart (AcmeTheme/assets/store.js)

```
let cart = [];          ◁──┐   One way to use private variables is to move
export default {                them out of scope. We can also use a more
  async init() {                modern this.#store as a variable.
    window.addEventListener('storage',
      this.updateCart.bind(this));   ◁──┐
    this.updateCart();                    Updates if the user changes local
  },                                      storage by using a different browser
```

```
  updateCart() {
    const disk = JSON.parse(
      window.localStorage.getItem("cart")
      || "[]");
    cart = Array.isArray(disk) ? disk : [];
  },
  save() {
    window.localStorage.setItem("cart", JSON.stringify(store));
  },
}
```

> Reads the data from local storage and ensures that it is in the correct format before updating the store object

Next, we initialize the store in index.js. The following listing shows the code to do this.

Listing 12.7 Initializing the store module (AcmeTheme/assets/index.js)

```
...
import Store from "./store"
...
Store.init();
...
```

ADDING DATA WHEN CLICKING ADD TO CART

When stored in local storage, the shopping cart has no access to the backend. If details like price and availability change, we should not hold on to cached values. Therefore, it is advisable to store just the id and always fetch the information from the server. The Add to Cart button takes the form data and saves it in local storage instead of submitting it to a server.

Most commerce solutions have *stock-keeping units* (SKUs) used to identify any product uniquely, which provide all variations a unique ID. In Acme Corporation, a combination of name and color is enough to identify a product uniquely. As the following listing shows, we will use the combination as the unique set of keys to identify the product in the cart.

Listing 12.8 Add products on Add button click (AcmeTheme/assets/store.js)

```
...
export default {
  async init() {
    document.addEventListener("click",
      this.handleClick.bind(this));
    ...
  },
  handleClick(event) {
    if (event.target
      .classList.contains("addToCart")) {
      event.preventDefault();
      this.addToCart(event.target.form);
    }
  }
  addToCart(form) {
```

Adds a click handler ▷ (points to `this.handleClick.bind(this)`)

Gets the form associated with the button ▷ (points to `this.addToCart(event.target.form)`)

Handles the click event for each Add to Cart button ← (points to `if (event.target .classList.contains("addToCart"))`)

Prevents the default action of the form (submit or reset) ← (points to `event.preventDefault()`)

```
                    const data = new FormData(form);
                    const name = data.get("name");
                    const color = data.get("color");
                    if (!cart.find(x =>
                        x.name === name &&
                        x.color === color)) {
                        cart.push({ name, color });
                    }
                    this.save();
                },
            }
```

Gets the values of all the elements in the HTML form for the product added to the cart (annotation pointing to the first three `const` lines)

Adds name and color to the cart (annotation pointing to `cart.push({ name, color });`)

Ensures that we do not add the same item twice. Because we sell digital items, we do not need to provide duplicate copies. (annotation pointing to the `if` block)

CREATING AN API FOR PRODUCT INFORMATION

Because only the identifying information (name and color) is present in the cart, we need an API to fetch the rest of the product information to render the cart correctly. We have all the information available at compile time, so we will create a pseudo API for this use case.

In this pseudo API, we will use the scratch data structure to create JSON output containing all the pages present in our store. The following listing creates a JSON pseudo API to provide the product details in the shopping cart. This API automatically hides products that do not have web pages and, if they do, includes data from the web page associated by using a loop through the .Pages variable of a section.

Listing 12.9 Providing product details (AcmeTheme/layouts/store/list.json)

```
{{$values := newScratch}}
  {{range .Pages}}          ◄──── Loops through all pages
    {{if .Params.product}}
      {{$values.Add .Params.product
        (index
          (partialCached "products.html" "nothing")
          .Params.product)}}            ◄──── Calls the product partial and
                                               adds the returned information
                                               to the values scratch
      {{ if (.Resources.GetMatch "cover.")}}
        {{$img :=
          (.Resources.GetMatch "cover.") |
          images.Filter (images.Overlay
            (resources.GetMatch "image/watermark.*")
            0 0 )
        }}
        {{$values.SetInMap .Params.product
            "Cover" ($img.Fill
                "80x80 center").Permalink}}   ◄──── Adds the product's
                                                    image, reducing its
                                                    size with Hugo Pipes
      {{end}}
    {{end}}
  {{end}}
{{$values.Values | jsonify}}      ◄──── Uses the Values property to convert
                                         a scratch to a map that can be
                                         converted to JSON using jsonify
```

Next, the following listing enables this output format within the store's list page (via `outputs`). We can specify new output formats on individual pages by using the output front matter property.

Listing 12.10 Enabling JSON APIs (content/store/_index.md)

```
---
outputs: [html, json]
---
```

Exercise 12.2

Which of the following is a limitation of the client-side storage model? (Select all that apply.)

    a. It costs more at the server.

    b. It requires a powerful client machine.

    c. It does not sync across multiple machines.

    d. It is less reliable for both persistence and accuracy than a server-side storage model.

    e. It is has major performance bottlenecks even for a small amount of data.

RENDER THE SHOPPING CART

We have all the requirements to render the shopping cart: a variable in JavaScript with the cart's contents, the HTML template used to view the cart, and all the data associated with it. We can now write a function to render it in DOM. Then we can call this from within the `init` function. Clicking the Add to Cart button renders the UI correctly. The completed cart is shown in figure 12.3.

Figure 12.3 The rendered shopping cart on hovering over the cart icon in the header in the store section of the website

Before rendering, we need to fetch the product information from the pseudo API that we just created in the previous section. The following listing uses the fetch HTTP API (just like we used to get the search index) to do this.

Listing 12.11   Fetching the product information (AcmeTheme/assets/store.js)

```
...
let products = {};
export default {
  async init() {
    ...
    await this.productInfo();
    this.updateCart();
  }
  async productInfo() {
    const response = await window.fetch(BASE_URL + "/store/index.json");
    if (response.ok) {
      products = await response.json();
    }
  },
}
```

We will use the render function to update the badge next to the cart button. We have added a Delete button to remove the element from the cart as well. The following listing renders the shopping cart, then takes the template to fill up the data from the cart object present in local storage with details for each item fetched via the pseudo API.

Listing 12.12   Rendering the shopping cart (AcmeTheme/assets/store.js)

```
export default {
  ...
  render() {
    let badge = document.querySelector("#cart .badge");
    let itemList = document.querySelector("#cart > div ");
    if (badge) { badge.innerText = cart.length || ""; }           Updates the badge
    if (!products || !Object.keys(products).length) { return; }   with the number of
                                                                   items in the cart

    const info = cart.map(x => ({
      ...x, price: parseFloat(products[x.name].Price),            Creates the data used
      cover: products[x.name].Cover                              to render the shopping
    }));                                                          cart

    if (itemList) {
      itemList.innerHTML = info                Do not update the shopping
        .map(x => `<div class="item">          cart if it doesn't exist.
          <img src="${x.cover}" lazy="true" width="40px">
          <div class="details">
            <h3> ${x.name} </h3>
            <div class="color ${x.color}"></div>
            <a class="delete" data-name="${x.name}"
              data-color="${x.color}"> Delete </a>    Adds a Delete button
          </div>
```

```
      <div class="price">
       $${x.price.toFixed(2)}
      </div>
    </div>`).join("\n")
    +
    `<div class="empty">
      Please add some items to the cart.
    </div>`;
  }
 }
 ...
}
```

The render method can be called from multiple places when the shopping cart changes. The following listing calls it on init so that it is up and ready.

Listing 12.13 Calling render for cart changes (AcmeTheme/assets/store.js)

```
addToCart() { ...
  this.render()
  this.save();
},
async productInfo() { ...
  this.render();
}
updateCart() { ...
  this.render();
}
```

Next, we add an onDelete handler that removes the element from the cart, saves the information, and re-renders the cart. The following listing shows how this is done.

Listing 12.14 Removing an item from cart (AcmeTheme/assets/store.js)

```
handleClick(event) {
  ...
  else if (event.target.matches(".cart .delete")) {
    this.onDelete(event);
  }
},
onDelete: function (e) {
  cart.splice(cart.findIndex(x =>
    x.name == e.target.dataset.name &&
    x.color === e.target.dataset.color), 1);
  this.render();
  this.save();
},
```

CODE CHECKPOINT https://chapter-12-03.hugoinaction.com, and source code: https://github.com/hugoinaction/hugoinaction/tree/chapter-12-03.

12.3 Checkout support

With a functional shopping cart, we need to get the user to a purchase page to get the payment details and complete the purchase. Let's look at what it takes to do this.

12.3.1 Setting up the billing provider

The purchase workflow has many moving parts with currencies and payment methods. Creating the infrastructure to take payments is a lot of work without relying on an external payment processor. Most of the traditional websites rely on a third party to provide this support. We will use Stripe (https://stripe.com/) as our payment processor due to its simple developer-friendly API and fantastic debugging support. We can use the techniques discussed in this section for other payment providers like Authorize.net, PayPal, and Amazon Pay.

When you log in to Stripe for the first time, it provides a checklist to enable test mode (figure 12.4). The checklist goes through the steps to activate and accept payments.

Get started with Stripe, Atishay

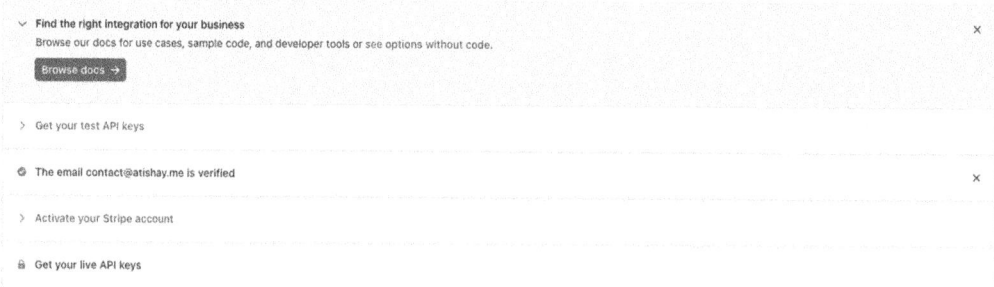

Figure 12.4   Checklist for using with Stripe when we log in for the first time

A single Stripe account can have multiple stores. Use the menu on the top left of the Stripe dashboard (which opens when you log in) to create a new store in Stripe to accept payment (figure 12.5 shows that Hugo In Action is already created) or switch to a different store using the header on the top left. Copy the test API keys. We will use both the publishable and the secret keys and store the secret key in Netlify/Heroku as an environment variable named `STRIPE_PRIVATE_KEY`.

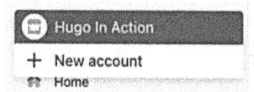

Figure 12.5   Creating and switching stores on Stripe

We can use the Settings > Branding screen in Stripe to upload our logo and set up colors to customize the generated checkout form so it looks closer to our website's theme (figure 12.6). Stripe will show these branded pages to the end users.

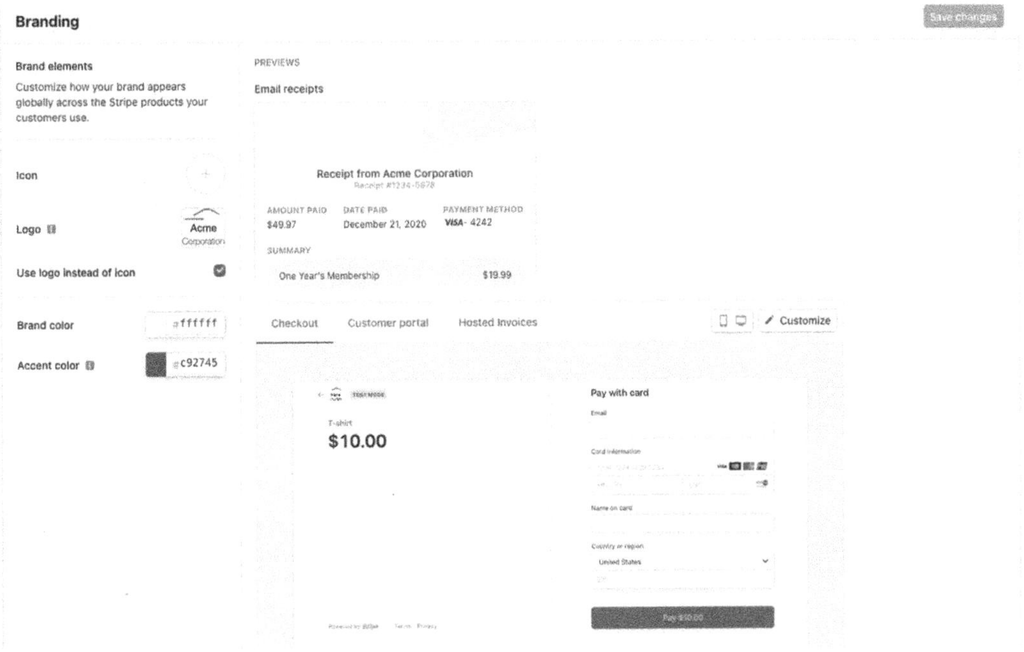

Figure 12.6   Controlling the branding of our web pages through Stripe's Branding screen

12.3.2 *Creating a checkout session*

There are multiple ways to use Stripe on our website. We will use the most straightforward approach, where the Checkout page is present on Stripe's website. We will pass Stripe the cart information, and it will come back to us after payment. This solution for accepting payments is present, step by step, in Stripe's official documentation at https://stripe.com/docs/payments/accept-a-payment.

Alternatively, some mechanisms are available to perform purchases within our website, fully controlling the UI and then sending the details to Stripe to execute the payment. That approach is more involved and beyond the scope of this book. The following lists the required steps to set up checkout using the hosted approach via Stripe:

1 Create a shopping cart and pass that information to the server.
2 Create a checkout session on the server, providing the necessary product details for purchase directly to Stripe.
3 Pass the checkout ID to the client and call the Stripe JavaScript library to navigate to Stripe to complete the purchase.
4 Handle the success/cancel navigation on the supplied URLs.

Stripe cannot work purely with a frontend (JavaScript) and needs a server API to perform the purchase so that no client can meddle with the data sent to Stripe. The Stripe server API needs the Stripe secret key that we copied in the previous section for it to function.

Before adding a Checkout button, we need to create a cloud function for step 2. In the checkout server-hosted function, the frontend passes us the product identifying information. We can then calculate the price and hand it to Stripe to create a checkout session. The cloud function gets its price from outside the caller to ensure that a client does not have the power to manipulate those values and inject custom prices during checkout. Because the backend exposes the prices via a JSON pseudo API over HTTPS, we can reuse that to get the price information.

To call the Stripe API, we need to add a dependency on Stripe's Node.js SDK. The following listing runs `hugo mod npm pack` to add this dependency to package.hugo .json, followed by `npm install` to make this available locally.

> **Listing 12.15   Adding a dependency to Stripe's Node.js SDK (package.hugo.json)**

```
{
  ...
  "dependencies": {
    ...
    "stripe": "8.169.0"
  }
  ...
}
```

A checkout function also takes the success and error paths to pass to Stripe. We will also provide the Stripe checkout API (http://mng.bz/J11o) product images and individual prices to track the receipt easily. For security reasons, we will use only URLs relative to the base URL of the website, which will be hardcoded in the function. The code for the checkout function is present in the chapter resources at (https://github .com/hugoinaction/hugoinaction/tree/chapter-12-resources/05).

Before calling Stripe to show a Checkout page, we need to create a checkout session from the server with the exact details of the items in the cart. We recommend passing only the product IDs to this backend function, which should fetch the product details and price internally to prevent manipulation. The skeleton code in the following listing ensures that the parameters are passed correctly and that meaningful error messages are sent.

> **Listing 12.16   Creating a checkout session (api/checkout.js)**

```
const stripe = require('stripe')              Passes the Stripe private key
  (process.env.STRIPE_PRIVATE_KEY);     ◁──   to initialize the Stripe API
const fetch = require("node-fetch");
const endpoint = "<Your website endpoint>"    ◁──┐ Hardcodes the
const origin = new URL(endpoint).origin;           │ website endpoint
```

```
module.exports = {
  async handler(event, context) {
    if (
      !event.queryStringParameters ||
      !event.queryStringParameters.products
    ) {
      return {
        statusCode: 400,
        headers: { "Content-Type": "application/json" },
        body: JSON.stringify({ error: "No products supplied." }),
      };
    }

    let error = "Unknown error";
    try {
      let products = event.queryStringParameters.products;
      if (!Array.isArray(products)) {
        products = products.split(",");
      }
      ...
      } else {
        error = `Could not fetch pricing table due to ${
          await data.text()} ${data.statusCode}`;
      }
    } catch (e) {
      error = e.message;
    }
    return {
      statusCode: 500,
      headers: { "Content-Type": "application/json" },
      body: JSON.stringify({error}),
    };
  },
};
```

Ensures there are some products to buy

Supports supplied parameters about product details in both an array and a comma-separated string

In the listing, passing the Stripe private key initializes the Stripe API. All variables set in the Netlify UI are available in the cloud functions. Always use the hardcoded website endpoint as the base to prevent a malicious user from pointing to a different endpoint with a changed price. This function accepts multiple products as a JSON array and also as a comma-separated string. Commas are converted to an array via `products.split`.

NOTE Netlify environment variables do not work in Netlify functions. The code present in the code checkpoints accompanying this book uses a post-install script to dump the variables in a file, which the function reads at run time. The readers are advised to hardcode these values in checkout.js for simplicity. Hardcoding is safe because a function's source code is not publicly exposed.

The checkout core implementation includes calling the same index API used in the shopping cart and creating `stripeData` for Stripe support as listing 12.17 shows. This involves sending the product information to Stripe to get a session ID. Stripe sends back the session ID, which we can then pass on to the JavaScript layer. Each product ID is in the name/color format, and we will use that to split out the name and color to get the price and image to add to the Stripe line items.

Listing 12.17 **Implementing checkout using Stripe (api/checkout.js)**

```
const data = await fetch(`${endpoint}/store/index.json`);
if (data.ok) {
  const table = await data.json();
  const stripeData = {                        ◁──┐  Sets up the data that we send
    payment_method_types: ['card'],                │  to create a checkout session
    line_items: [],
    mode: 'payment',
    success_url: `${origin}${decodeURIComponent(
      event.queryStringParameters.success)}`,
    cancel_url: `${origin}${decodeURIComponent(
      event.queryStringParameters.cancel)}`,
    metadata: { }
  };

  products.forEach((x, i) => {                        Splits out the name and color
    const name = x.split("_")[0].trim();    ◁──┐     to get the price and image for
    const color = x.split("_")[1].trim();          │  each product ID
    stripeData.line_items.push({
      price_data: {
        currency: 'usd',
        product_data: {
          name: `${name}(${color})`,
          images: [table[name].Cover],
        },
        unit_amount: parseFloat(table[name].Price.trim()) * 100,
      },
      quantity: 1,
    })
  });

  const session = await                        Calls Stripe to create
    stripe.checkout.sessions.create(stripeData);  ◁──┐  a checkout session
  return {
    statusCode: 200,
    headers: { "Content-Type": "application/json" },
    body: JSON.stringify({
      sessionId: session.id, stripeData, products
    }),
  };
```

The GitHub pages sample with checkout support is present at https://github.com/ hugoinaction/GitHubPagesStore. For supporting a PAAS like Heroku, we need to invoke this from the api.js file as the following listing shows.

Listing 12.18 Integrating checkout with a PAAS API (api.js)

```
...
switch (url.pathname) {
    ...
    case '/checkout':
      response = await checkout.handler(request);
      break;
  }
```

We can now add a Checkout button to our shopping cart and then pass the product information in the cart to the server to create a checkout session. When the user clicks the Checkout button, we can call the checkout server function we just built to get the checkout session ID. We then load the Stripe JavaScript SDK, using the publishable key to initialize it. Using the Stripe API, we can redirect the user to the checkout session. Because we are using the hosted Stripe solution, we need to pass the success and error URLs to allow Stripe to send the user back to our website after checkout or before as needed. The following listing loads the Stripe JavaScript library (SDK), adds a Checkout button, and then calls checkout at the appropriate time.

Listing 12.19 Completing a purchase (AcmeTheme/assets/store.js)

```
...
let stripe = undefined;

export default {
  async init() {
    const s = document.createElement('script');
    s.setAttribute('src', "https://js.stripe.com/v3/");     ⟵ Asynchronously loads
    s.onload = () => {                                          the Stripe JavaScript
      stripe = Stripe("<Your Stripe publishable key>");        SDK and initializes with
    };                                                         the publishable key
    s.defer = true;
    document.body.appendChild(s);
    ...
  },
  handleClick(event) {
    ... else if (event.target.id === "checkout") {
      this.onCheckout();            ⟵┐ Adds an event handler for the click
    } ...                            │ event on the Checkout button
  }
  render() {
    ...
        `<div class="empty">
          Please add some items to the cart.          ┌ Adds a Checkout
        </div>                                         │ button at the end of
          <button id="checkout">Checkout</button>`  ⟵─┘ the shopping cart
    }
    ...
  },
}
```

The checkout call to the Stripe JavaScript SDK involves getting the session ID and passing that along with the return URLs for both success and failure. The following listing implements this call, redirecting to the Checkout page.

Listing 12.20   Getting the session ID (AcmeTheme/assets/store.js)

```
async onCheckout() {
  try {
    const url = NETLIFY ? new URL(window.location.origin
      + "/.netlify/functions/checkout")          Gets the location of
      : new URL(                                  the server-hosted
      "https://hugoinaction.herokuapp.com/checkout");   cloud function
    cart.forEach(x =>
      url.searchParams.append("products",          Converts cart information
        `${x.name}_${x.color}`));                  into a list of product IDs to
                                                   be sent to the server
    url.searchParams.append("success",
      encodeURIComponent(window.location.pathname +
        "?purchase=success"));
                                                   Adds success and cancel
                                                   links to return to the
    url.searchParams.append("cancel",             current page to continue
      encodeURIComponent(window.location.pathname +   the user session
        "?purchase=cancel"));

    const response = await window.fetch(url.href);
                                                   Calls the checkout function
    if (response.ok) {                             to get the checkout session
      const resp = await response.json();          to launch
      stripe.redirectToCheckout({
        sessionId: resp.sessionId
      });                                          Launches the checkout
    }                                              session using the official
                                                   Stripe JavaScript API
  } catch (e) {
    console.log("Error", e);
  }
},
```

The code in the listing needs us to expose a variable named NETLIFY from Hugo into JavaScript. We can do this with `defines` just like we did with the REMOVE_FORM_ON _SUBMISSION option in chapter 10.

Exercise 12.4

Stripe requires us to create a checkout session on the server because the client-side data cannot be trusted and the _____ need to be provided by a trusted server.

Sharing the cloud function code via the theme

We kept the store inside the AcmeTheme template and, ideally, should have all the checkout code used in Netlify functions controlled by Heroku via AcmeTheme and reused across websites that use the theme. Because Netlify does not understand Hugo's virtual filesystem, using Hugo Modules path mapping does not work. A better solution is to convert these functions into node modules and use Hugo's npm integration to provide them from the theme to the website project. With this approach, we can turn the code for the checkout function into its own npm module with an independent package.json, whose `main` entry point is the function script.

The following code snippet shows how to create a checkout npm module in package .json:

```
{
  "main": "checkout.js"
}
```

Then in package.json in our AcmeTheme template, we can add this new module as a dependency:

```
{
  "dependencies": {
    "acme-theme-checkout": "https://github.com/<path to checkout
        repository>"
  }
}
```

Now in the Acme Corporation website repository (api/checkout.js), we can call directly into this module via the `require` statement:

```
module.exports = require("acme-theme-checkout");
```

With these changes, the store section of the website is usable. The readers can purchase products, and we can access Stripe to get the customer's information and fulfill it manually. In the case of physical products ordered through the store, this is all that's needed to run the store effectively. Stripe provides a mechanism to send a payment receipt to the end user, collect shipping addresses, process refunds, and manage users.

CODE CHECKPOINT https://chapter-12-04.hugoinaction.com, and source code: https://github.com/hugoinaction/hugoinaction/tree/chapter-12-04.

12.3.3 *Handling success and failure*

When a user completes a successful purchase, we should inform the user that the items purchased are on their way. Also, we should clear the cart of the purchased products. If the user cancels the purchase, however, the cart should stay intact so that the user can continue shopping and checkout later if desired. To enable the users not to lose context, we can add support in Stripe to return to the same URL that sent the users to checkout with additional parameters, which allows us to react to the actions during checkout.

During the initialization of the store component, we will parse the supplied parameters for a success page. There is nothing to do if the user cancels the purchase. If there is a successful purchase, we need to perform these two associated tasks: clearing the cart and showing a message. The `init` method also updates the URL to ensure that, if the user accidentally lands on this page via the browser's Back button, we do not clear the cart.

> **Listing 12.21   Completing a successful purchase (AcmeTheme/assets/store.js)**

```
...
async init() {
  ...
  const location = new URL(window.location.href);
  if (location.searchParams.get("purchase") === "success") {
    cart.length = 0;                    ←┐   Empties the cart
    this.save();
    document.body.insertAdjacentHTML("beforeend", `
    <div class="alert success">
      <div class="head">Order Confirmed.</div>
      Your product will be e-mailed soon.
      <a href="close">Close</a>
    </div>`);
    location.searchParams.delete("purchase");
    window.history.replaceState(null, "", location);
    document.querySelector(".alert.success .close")
      .addEventListener("click", e => {
      document.body.removeChild(document.querySelector(".alert.success"));
      e.preventDefault();
    });                    ←——— Makes the Close button functional
    setTimeout(() => {
      document.body.removeChild(document.querySelector(".alert.success"));
    }, 5000);              ←┐
  }                           Autohides the notification after 5 seconds
}
```

Adds some messages on the top of the page for the customer — points to `</div>`);

Removes the purchase property from the URL to prevent clearing the cart with an accidental browser Back button click

NOTE Using Stripe test accounts on our sample website, we do not need to enter an actual credit card number for a purchase. The dummy credit card number is 4242-4242-4242-4242 with a random zip code and random expiry date. These are valid for testing purposes.

12.3.4 *Enabling the Buy Now button*

The Buy Now button is a minor addition to the cart feature. Clicking Buy Now directly sends the current item to checkout, and we don't need to clear the cart upon return. In the store module, we can add a click handler to the Buy Now button and send the current item to checkout via the existing mechanism used in the cart-based checkout. The shopping cart should not be cleared on success with a Buy Now action. This functionality is an exercise for the reader. You can look at the code checkpoint for assistance.

CODE CHECKPOINT https://chapter-12-05.hugoinaction.com, and source code: https://github.com/hugoinaction/hugoinaction/tree/chapter-12-05.

12.4 Fulfillment

Acme Corporation is a digital company; its products are not physical goods shipped by regular mail. Because these are digital entities, these can be supplied to the end user by a password-protected page, a logged-in account, or an email directly on purchase.

It may seem easier to provide downloads for the purchased product on the success page itself, but that is not a good idea. The purchase result page is public, and security by having an obscure URL is no security. Purchases can take time in some instances. It is safer to provide instant information about a purchase coming asynchronously rather than having a bad user experience in some edge cases. When money gets involved, lapses in the user experience can evoke a stronger reaction than in other cases.

12.4.1 Receiving and verifying webhooks

Stripe provides the ability to register a webhook that can be called when a purchase succeeds. This webhook has access to all the information taken from the user during the purchase and any metadata that we supply. We can react to the purchase from within this webhook.

We will create a new webhook to handle successful purchases, where we will parse the user information and then send the user their purchased product(s) as an attachment over email. We already saved the Stripe private key (as STRIPE_PRIVATE_KEY) in Heroku/Netlify, so we can use that to verify that the webhook came from Stripe. Stripe webhooks come with a signature that we can use to verify the origin. This signature is what we can use to weed out fake webhook calls. The following listing provides the code to require this signature.

Listing 12.22 Verifying Stripe's webhook (api/webhook.js)

```
const stripe = require('stripe')(process.env.STRIPE_PRIVATE_KEY);

module.exports = {
  async handler(event, context) {
    const sig = event.headers['stripe-signature'];
    let stripeEvent = {};
    try {
      stripeEvent = stripe.webhooks            Calls the construct event API to
        .constructEvent(event.body,            verify the event's signature and
        sig, process.env.STRIPE_SIGN_SECRET);  ensures that it came from Stripe

    } catch (err) {         ⬅              Handles errors if the event
      return {                             came from elsewhere
        statusCode: 400,
        err: JSON.stringify(err)
      }
```

```
    }
    console.log('Received webhook with data: ',
        JSON.stringify(stripeEvent, null, 2))
    return {
        statusCode: 200
    };
    },
};
```

Logs the details for now. Note that the event details are also available in the Stripe user interface.

Calls the construct event API to verify the event's signature and ensures that it came from Stripe

TIP If we keep getting the non-success error codes, Stripe provides us with the ability to retry a webhook in its user interface. When testing, this can come in handy because we do not need to go through the entire workflow of checking something to call the webhook correctly.

For supporting PAAS like Heroku, we need to invoke the webhook endpoint within api.js. The following listing shows how this is done.

Listing 12.23   Exporting the webhook endpoint (api.js)

```
...
switch (url.pathname) {
    case '/webhook':
        response = await webhook.handler(request);
        break;
}
```

Next, we need to enable webhooks using Stripe's Add a Webhook Endpoint page. To get to this page, select Developer > Webhooks and then click Add Endpoint (figure 12.7).

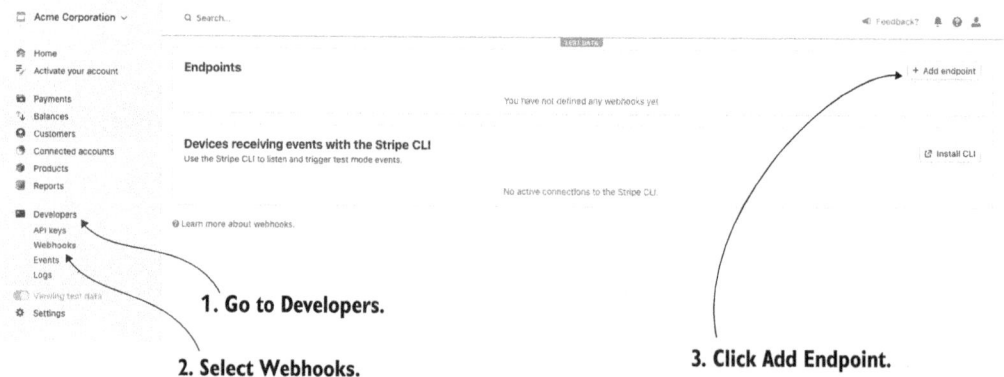

Figure 12.7   Webhooks are available in the Developer section in Stripe. These allow us to listen to events in Stripe.

Provide the details of the endpoint just created. Then select the checkout.session .completed event to listen to completed checkouts (figure 12.8).

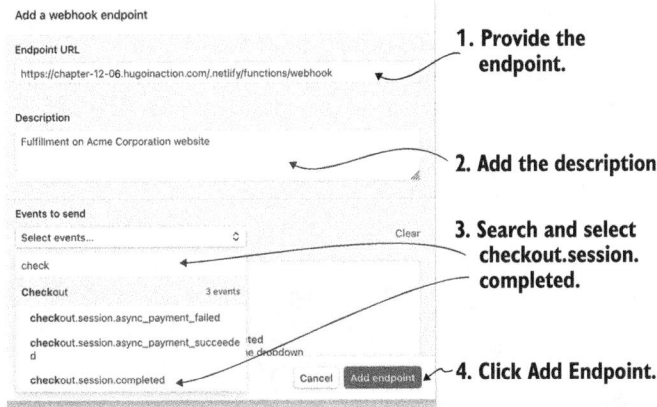

Figure 12.8 The checkout.session.completed event is triggered when checkout is complete. We can listen to it in our webhook.

We can use the webhook interface to send test webhooks and to view historical webhooks. We can then act on the failed webhooks (figure 12.9).

Note that the test webhooks sent by the Stripe interface do not contain all the data we need. We will, therefore, need to use proper webhooks via a checkout and utilize test mode to get the correct data.

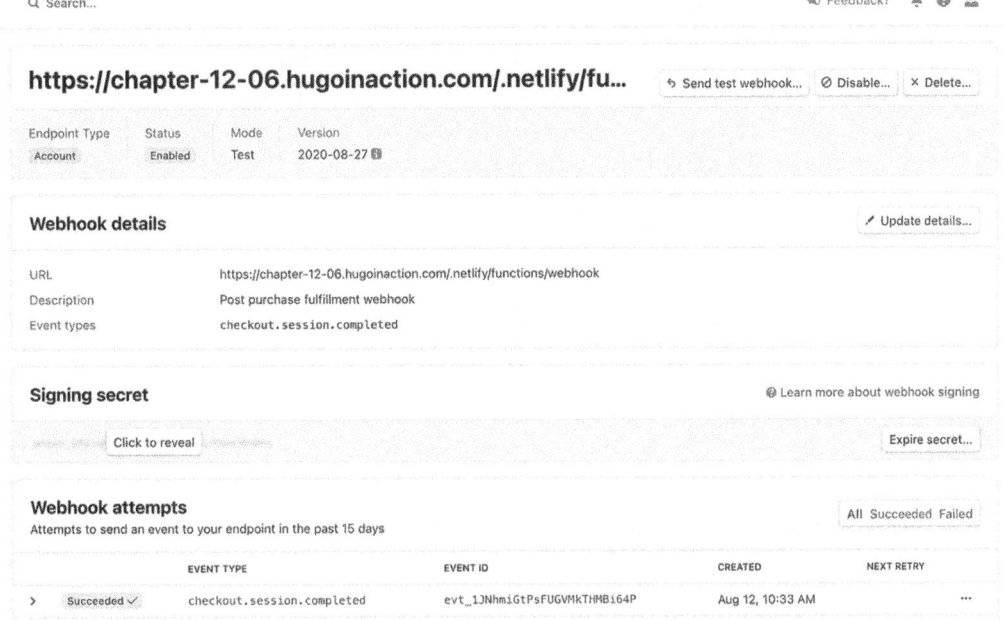

Figure 12.9 The Stripe Webhook Details page provides all the information about a webhook and the actions. This allows us to test the webhook without going through the entire flow.

TIP   For testing locally, Stripe provides a mechanism via its command-line tool to listen to and forward the webhook to a local server for verification. This tool comes in handy when debugging. Read more about it in the official Stripe documentation at https://stripe.com/docs/stripe-cli/webhooks.

Figure 12.10   All the way: Alex and Bob realize that Jamstack is not a toy anymore—it can do all that they need!

12.4.2 Getting purchase details

The Stripe webhook gives specific information about the event, but that may not be complete for our use case. We can ask the Stripe API for additional information about the event. Stripe has a concept of expandable fields, which by default are returned as an ID but can be expanded to full details if needed. We will use this to get the customer's email address and then the name used for the credit card to personalize the email to the customer. The following listing uses expandable fields to fetch the payment details as well as the additional context information.

Listing 12.24   Getting customer details (api/webhook.js)

```
try {
    stripeEvent = ...
} catch(e) {
}
try {
const session = await stripe.checkout.sessions.retrieve
    (stripeEvent.data.object.id, {
    expand: [
        'customer',
        'payment_intent',
        'payment_intent.payment_method'
    ],                                      Asks for all relevant
});                                         information from Stripe
```

```
if (!(session.customer && session.customer.email &&
        session.payment_status === 'paid' &&
        Object.values(session.metadata || {})
          .length > 0)) {
    throw new Error(
      "Could not get customer or payment information.");
}
const name = session.payment_intent &&
             session.payment_intent.payment_method &&
             session.payment_intent.payment_method.billing_details &&
             session.payment_intent
               .payment_method.billing_details.name;
const email = session.customer.email;
  } catch (e) {
  return {
    statusCode: 500,
    err: JSON.stringify(e)
  }
};
```

Ensures that the event is actionable

Gets the customer name (but prepares for the fact that it may not be present)

Always handles failures gracefully

12.4.3 Setting up an email provider

Just like billing, modern email implementation is complicated. From having a reputed IP address to following the various authentication schemes, it is better to rely on a third party unless your core product is sending emails. We use SendGrid in this book, but the steps to send emails are similar in other email providers like MailGun, Amazon SES, and Mandrill. Any provider that provides a REST-based API to send emails makes our life as developers easier.

After signing up for SendGrid (https://sendgrid.com/), you will land at a Getting Started page, which takes you through the account setup and verification before you can send an email (figure 12.11).

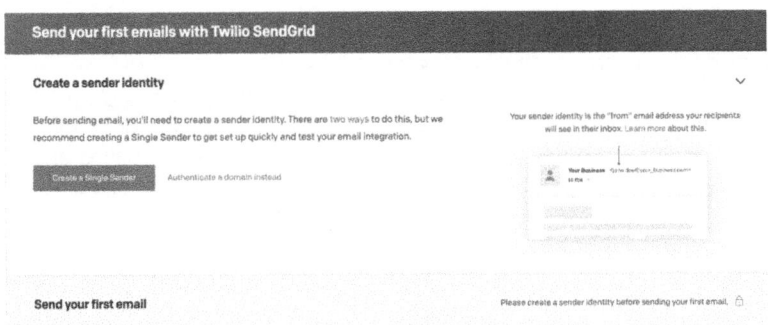

Figure 12.11 SendGrid has an onboarding guide that helps new users set up a sender that we can use to send emails.

There are two sets of steps needed to enable SendGrid: account validation and sender validation. Account validation involves verifying your account email address and setting up two-factor authentication along with a payment method if you plan to use more than the free tier of emails. With sender validation, you can use single sender or domain-based verification. When using single sender verification, you need to fill in a small form and click an email verification link (figure 12.12).

Domain-based validation requires setting up a few entries in the DNS records of the domain. Full text of these entries is available on the SendGrid website at http://mng .bz/wnnO. In case you are using Netlify DNS, the DNS settings can be updated via Site Settings > Domain Management > Options > Go to DNS Panel and then clicking the Add New Record button.

After verifying a sender, you will need to create an API key in SendGrid to send emails. The API key should be saved to environment variables in Heroku and Netlify as SENDGRID_API_KEY (figure 12.13).

Create a Sender

You are required to include your contact information, including a physical mailing address, inside every promotional email you send in order to comply with the anti-spam laws such as CAN-SPAM and CASL. You'll find replacement tags for this information in the footer of all the email designs SendGrid provides. Learn more

From Name •

From Email Address •

Reply To •

Company Address •

Company Address Line 2

City •   State
                          Select State

Zip Code   Country •
                          Select Country

Nickname •

Nickname is for your reference only; this field will not be displayed to recipients.

Cancel   Create

Figure 12.12   Single sender verification in SendGrid involves filling in a short form and then verifying the ownership of an email address by clicking a link sent via email.

Public clouds provide a single place for all APIs

If your workflow involves many third parties to handle different parts of your infrastructure, a public cloud may be a better place to access third-party dependencies. The big cloud providers have equivalents to most services under one billing and management system. For example, AWS Amplify is a Netlify hosting equivalent with AWS Lambda for functions. We can use Amazon Pay for payments and Amazon Simple Email Service for Email.

One significant disadvantage of a public cloud is the added complexity of services due to interoperability support and the management of services that we might not even be using. Another disadvantage is the service quality itself. Although some services like AWS Lambda receive a lot of love from Amazon, other services like a simple email service might not be as friendly and up-to-date as third parties, especially for less technical audiences.

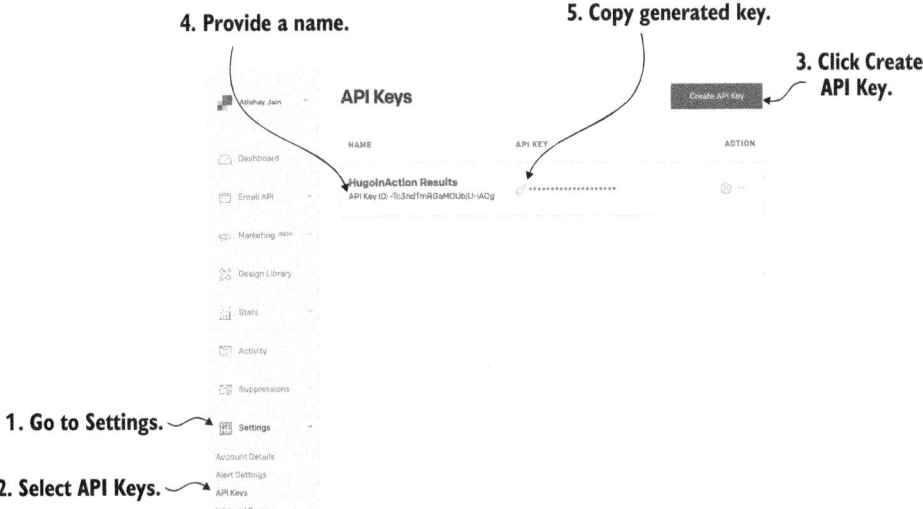

4. Provide a name.

5. Copy generated key.

3. Click Create API Key.

1. Go to Settings.

2. Select API Keys.

Figure 12.12 API keys are needed to send emails from SendGrid. We can create API keys in the Settings > API Keys section of SendGrid.

12.4.4 Sending emails

After a successful purchase, the objective of email is to provide access to the digital assets that the user has purchased. Before providing access, however, let's use the SendGrid API to verify that we can send a purchase confirmation email to the end user from our webhook. To access the SendGrid API, we need to add that dependency to package.hugo.json and run npm mod hugo pack and npm install. The following listing sets up the dependency.

Listing 12.25 Adding a dependency for SendGrid (package.hugo.json)

```
{
  "dependencies": {
    "@sendgrid/mail": "7.4.6",
    ...
}
```

Now we can use the SendGrid mail API to send an email to the end user. This API requires all the parameters to create a valid email including the from, to, and subject lines and, of course, some text. We can also supply the email message in HTML format if we so desire. The following listing sets this up for us.

Listing 12.26 Sending an email via SendGrid (api/webhook.js)

```
...
const email = session.customer.email;

sgMail.setApiKey(process.env.SENDGRID_API_KEY);
```

```
const msg = {
  to: session.customer.email,
  from: 'noreply@hugoinaction.com',
  subject: 'Your purchase with Acme Corporation (Hugo In Action)',
  text: `Dear ${name || "User"},

Thank you for purchasing digital shapes from the Acme Corporation.`,
};

await sgMail.send(msg);
...
```

12.4.5 *Preparing content to send to the users*

One way to send the purchased assets is to provide a signed link to the assets (with a one-time password or a multi-use password). Services like Netlify provide password-protected pages where you can host the content on the CDN with a password. Alternatively, you can host a password-protected archive on the regular website and share the link and the password to it via email. You can also encrypt the content and provide its path with a password as a URL parameter over email and decrypt the content using JavaScript on the client. Another option is to attach the purchased assets to the email itself. This way, there is no hosting involved, and in case the user has purchased multiple files, we can provide them together rather than asking the user to download and decrypt each file one by one.

In this section, we will use the second approach for our use case because the images are small enough to be linked to the email. This provides the added benefit of not worrying about keeping the website online for users who would expect the links to work in the far future.

The images sold through the Acme Corporation website are present in PNG format in the chapter resources. Because SendGrid takes photos in Base64 file format to create attachments, it is a good idea to adhere to the Jamstack principles of preparing the Base64 versions of the images at compile time. The npm command provides a handy way to run a script at installation time. We can add entries in the scripts section for preinstall, install, or postinstall to run custom scripts with npm. The following listing adds a postinstall script in package.hugo.json to prepare the Base64 version of all images.

> **Listing 12.27 Adding a postinstall script (package.hugo.json)**

```
{
  ...
  "scripts": {
    "postinstall": "node api/postinstall.js"
  }
}
```

Next, we run `hugo mod npm pack` to get this into package.json. Finally, we can fill in the postinstall script, which reads each image from the api/assets folder and creates a Base64-encoded version of it that we will send via SendGrid as an attachment. We will then save the entire set as a map in result.json. The following listing uses a postinstall hook in node.js to preprocess the data.

Listing 12.28 Converting images to Base64 (api/postinstall.js)

```
#! env node                              ◁──────────  Uses a hash bang to identify
                                                      the file to run directly
const fs = require('fs').promises;
const path = require('path');
                                         Creates a self-executing function to allow using
(async () => {                   ◁────── await at the top level. (This limitation is not
  const data = {};                       present if using Node.js v.14.8+.)

    const images = await fs.readdir(             Reads through all the
      __dirname + "/assets");                    files in the assets folder
    await Promise.all(images.map(async image => {
    const extname = path.extname(image);
      if (extname === '.png') {                  Reads images whose
    const buffer = await                         extension is png
        fs.readFile(__dirname + "/assets/" + image);
        data[path.basename(image, path.extname(image))] =
          buffer.toString('base64');                      Adds the image name
      }                                                   without the extension as
  }));                                                    the key and the Base64
                                                          version as the value

    await fs.writeFile(dirname +__ "/result.json",
        JSON.stringify(data, null, 2));    ◁──┐ Saves this to result.json. Note the additional
                                              parameters passed to JSON.stringify format
})();                                         the JSON into a more readable way.
```

12.4.6 Attaching files to email

With the data available in Base64 format, adding it to the email is relatively straightforward. We will read the result.json file, and for each entry in the metadata, we will attach the file corresponding to the supplied name. The following listing shows how digital orders can be fulfilled via email and sent as an attachment. With these changes, we will receive an email with the purchase contents soon after checkout.

Listing 12.29 Fulfilling digital orders via email (api/webhook.js)

```
const result = require('./result.json');
...
const msg = {
  to: email,
  from: 'noreply@hugoinaction.com',
  subject: 'Your purchase with Acme Corporation (Hugo In Action)',
  text: `Dear ${name || "User"},
```

```
                Thank you for purchasing digital shapes from the Acme Corporation.
                Your purchased shapes are attached to this email.`,
                   attachments: Object.values(session.metadata).        ◁──── Reads the metadata
Uses the        filter(img => result[img])                      ◁┐
Base64           .map(img => ({                                   Removes all metadata where
content          content: result[img],                           we do not have an image
of the file      filename: img + '.png',             ◁
                 type: "image/png",                   Gives it a good filename
                 disposition: "attachment"      ◁┐
              })                                  Marks it as an attachment
            )
        };
```

CODE CHECKPOINT   https://chapter-12-06.hugoinaction.com, and source code:
https://github.com/hugoinaction/hugoinaction/tree/chapter-12-06.

In this chapter, we used what you learned from the entire book to build a whole
e-commerce application. We created custom product pages, product lists, shopping
cart, checkout, and email-based fulfillment of a digital purchase on the Acme Corporation website. We saw how the various concepts of Hugo and the Jamstack can come
together in a completely different context. We also witnessed the modularity of
Hugo's approach, where we use a lot of existing pieces (like a comment form) as-is in a
different context. The next chapter will discuss some of Hugo's more advanced features
that we can use in particular circumstances and other essential areas in the Jamstack.

Summary

- We can use Hugo in different contexts outside of a regular blog or website. This
  includes portfolios, media, or educational websites.
- In an e-commerce application, the single pages reflect the product details, and
  the list pages can become the product lists.
- The JavaScript layer of the Jamstack coupled with the browser's localStorage
  can provide the means to customize and personalize the website. Using this
  layer, we can also store user-specific data (like a shopping cart) and provide
  user-specific pages.
- Third-party APIs are available in a developer-friendly format for complex tasks
  such as billing management or email delivery. These provide advanced functionality in a developer-friendly solution that can be picked up off the shelf and
  reused.

This chapter covers

- Building special pages and multilingual websites
- Speeding up our website with Turbo, instant pages, and service workers
- Learning about CLIs, configurations as files, and other ways to automate the Jamstack
- Getting help from the Hugo community, showcasing your work, and contributing to Hugo

Hugo websites have handled many use cases, some of which are more complicated than the examples discussed in this book. The core features of Hugo, such as page bundles, taxonomies, and its template lookup order, form the building blocks of any Hugo-based website. But there is a lot more that you might want to consider once you go one step deeper into a more complex website. There are features within Hugo that enable advanced functionality as well as modern web development practices that can make our websites faster and more complete. In this chapter, we will go over some of the obscure features of Hugo and the Jamstack, which are essential to complete and maintain a modern website.

> **NOTE** This chapter introduces a lot of unrelated features with short examples to provide a starting point for building further ahead.

13.1 *Developing multilingual websites*

As soon as you add the need for more than one language (human language and not programming language) into a web development system, things get a lot more complex. Hugo embraces *multilingual* websites and handles the complexity right from the start with proper forethought. To enable new languages, we need to update the global website configuration to be language-specific in the `languages` section. We can then create a file called languages in the config folder to provide language-specific preferences.

In the `languages` section, each key becomes a new language. The list of values for the key acts as overrides to the default values provided in the configuration. We can override all `params` and top-level textual properties such as title. Even the `baseURL` can have different domains such as example.com for English and example.com.fr for French. The default language is English, though we can override it by setting `defaultContentLanguage` in the configuration.

> **NOTE** For Hugo, the language name is just a string. This string can be anything as far as Hugo is concerned. For example, we can define a language called `elvish` if we so desire or a language called `abcd` and Hugo does not care. It creates an endpoint at /elvish or /abcd as specified and assigns markup files as .elvish.md or .abcd.md to those specific languages.

13.1.1 *Overrides and defaults for content in a multilingual website*

One important thing to note is to understand how overrides and defaults for the website's content work in a multilingual Hugo website. It is essential to know that textual content is the only difference between a localized website and the default language. Some images or settings may differ, but in most cases, the configuration and assets are the same across multiple languages in a website. This section provides a few things to remember when building a multilingual website.

First, all languages share all the configurations present on the website apart from the `languages` section. Because a configuration is simply a setting, by default Hugo shares them across all languages. Hugo reuses the themes, configurations, and variables, so we can get up and running with a new language in seconds. We can also use the configuration to provide localized data. To do this, we need to override the defaults in the language-specific section (https://github.com/hugoinaction/hugoinaction/tree/chapter-13-resources/01).

The following listing provides the configuration to enable the French language. We customize the copyright text for French, and update the menu within the French version of the website.

> **Listing 13.1   Configuration to enable French (config/_default/languages.yaml)**

```
en:
  params:
fr:
  params:
```

```
   copyright: "droits d'auteur &copy; 2022 Acme Corporation.
              Tous les droits sont réservés."
menu:
  main:
    - identifier: about
      name: À propos
      url: /about
      weight: 100
      post: Nos origines fascinantes
    - identifier: contact
      name: contact
      url: /contact
      weight: 200
      post: A votre service
  footer:
    - name: Politique de confidentialité
      weight: 300
      url: /privacy
    - name: Conditions d'utilisation
      weight: 200
      url: /terms
```

NOTE The endpoint for the default language is / instead of /en, but we can override it using defaultContentLanguageInSubdir in the configuration.

Second, all markup-based content that is not assigned a language belongs to the default language. The content documents and bundles are language-specific. If we were to render the website right now, there would be no pages in the French section due to a lack of French content. This default language logic is present in Hugo because the markup content of the web pages needs localization. The individual markup document decides both the existence of the web page and its content.

To create language-specific web pages for the French language, we need to create the files _index.fr.md (branch bundle), index.fr.md (in a leaf bundle), or about.fr.md (as a top-level Markdown document), where "fr" is the name specified in the language's configuration. If a language-specific page is not present, Hugo does not render the corresponding web page in the language-specific website.

Language-specific versions of the various pages in our website are present in the chapter resources. (For French readers, we use an online translation website that may not appropriately translate contents.) Note that localized content is entirely independent of the content in the default language. We can remove sections (like news), remove or add pages (like blog, process-3, or shape), change parts of the content or front matter, and or anything else we have linked in the content folder (https:// github.com/hugoinaction/hugoinaction/tree/chapter-13-resources/02). Figure 13.1 shows the French version of the home page.

Third, assets like images present in the page bundles are automatically available for translated content and shared across all languages. Images are rarely localized. Add to that, they are not independent entities. Therefore, by default, they are shared

Figure 13.1   French version of the home page Acme Corporation website. We can create multilingual websites in Hugo by specifying a languages configuration and providing localized content files like `_index.fr.md`.

across all languages. For example, the image for draw.jpg is available with the French translation for the About page.

> **CODE CHECKPOINT**   https://chapter-13-01.hugoinaction.com, and source code: https://github.com/hugoinaction/hugoinaction/tree/chapter-13-01.

If we want, we could create draw.fr.jpg (https://github.com/hugoinaction/hugoinaction/tree/chapter-13-resources/03) that would override draw.jpg. If draw.fr.jpg is present, the French page should link to that by convention and not to draw.jpg. The index.fr.md file needs to change if we add draw.fr.jpg. We should also do the same with the `productInfo` shortcode.

> **CODE CHECKPOINT**   https://chapter-13-02.hugoinaction.com, and source code: https://github.com/hugoinaction/hugoinaction/tree/chapter-13-02.

We can also create draw.en.jpg for English-specific overrides. We can also decide the priority for overrides if an asset is not present. In the `languages` section of the configuration, we can pass a property called `weight`. For the fallback, Hugo sorts the languages by weight. Hugo selects the language with the highest weight where the asset is present and uses it for all languages without it.

Finally, it is easier to manage separate content directories for separate content. Although creating localized files in the content directory is functional, this can become an organization and management headache. There is no easy way to know which pages have a French variant. There might be different teams working across languages, and bundling them all together is likely to be confusing.

The following listing sets `contentDir` to `contentFr` in the `fr` configuration. Then we can move the French-specific files to a separate folder called contentFr. If we want, we can rename draw.fr.jpg to draw.jpg in the contentFr/about folder.

Listing 13.2 Moving the French content (config/_default/languages.yaml)

```
...
fr:
  contentDir: contentFr
  ...
```

CODE CHECKPOINT https://chapter-13-03.hugoinaction.com, and source code: https://github.com/hugoinaction/hugoinaction/tree/chapter-13-03.

13.1.2 Accessing strings within the theme

Not all strings come from the content in the content folder. We have hardcoded text (for example, "search") inside the search box and the comment form in the theme. One way to work around this is to use the front matter and site configuration to provide the strings for these fields. The significant disadvantage of this approach is the inability to provide reasonable defaults and the clunky way the language-specific and default values need to be set up in the configuration. Localized strings are different from settings, and conflating the two into the configuration options is a recipe for confusion. Hugo provides an easy means of externalizing the strings into separate files for these labels, which can be kept in the individual files and then requested via a function in code.

We can create a top-level folder called i18n (short for internationalization) inside our website or in the theme. Inside this folder, we can add the files en.yaml for English strings and fr.yaml for French translations. (Note that JSON and TOML are also supported.) The following listing adds IDs and translations for various string labels used on the French website to these files (https://github.com/hugoinaction/hugoinaction/tree/chapter-13-resources/04).

Listing 13.3 Adding a translation string (AcmeTheme/i18n/fr.yaml)

```
- id: search
  translation: chercher
...
```

Then we can access these values using a function called i18n. For example, {{i18n "search"}} gives us the translation for the word "search" from the i18n files. Hugo also provides a language fallback to the default language (hugo --i18n-warnings) and placeholder support via enableMissingTranslationPlaceholders in the configuration to determine which words we have not translated. Playing with this configuration option is an exercise for the reader.

Some strings may be present in the JavaScript file, where we either need to pass all languages to JavaScript or move them over to HTML. Additionally, it is good to bundle some i18n strings for all keys in the theme for portability. The user can override these by creating the i18n folder at the website level and using the same key with the overridden value.

NOTE We can also use Hugo's mustaches in the translated string inside fr.yaml. For example, `Welcome to {{.Title}}` is a supported translation. We need to pass a variable with a `Title` property like `{{i18n "search" $.Page}}` (`$.Page` has a `$.Page.Title`) for this to work.

Hugo also supports having different strings for singular and plural forms of content. If the parameter passed to the i18n function is a map or a variable with a property called `Count`, we can use one instead of `translation` as the key to get a singular version of the string, and `other` would give us the plural version. Most Hugo variables like `Pages` already have the `Count` property that we can use for this purpose. The following listing provides an example of singular and plural content.

Listing 13.4   Localized content (not to be used in Acme Corporation website)

```
- id: pageKey
  one: page
  other: pages
```

Exercise 13.1

Which of the following is, by default, not considered language-specific in Hugo? (Select all that apply.)

   a. Markup

   b. Images

   c. JavaScript

   d. Front matter

   e. Templates

   f. Config

13.1.3 *Linking to translated pages*

Most of the Hugo functions that we use, like `Permalink`, automatically localize. We should stop using `absURL` or `relURL` but instead use `absLangURL` or `relLangURL` to get the localized URLs of the web pages. No other APIs require this language change as of Hugo v0.91.2. We should also avoid direct URL linking and use variables instead.

A variable called `Translations` is available on our web page. We can use this variable to figure out the translations available for the page. This variable has a list of languages that we can use to link to language-specific pages if needed. One place to add the list of translations available for a web page is in the website footer. The following listing adds this link to the translated versions at the bottom of the page in AcmeTheme/layouts/_default/baseof.html.

Listing 13.5   Adding a link to the translated versions

```
{{ if .IsTranslated }}
  <ul>
      <li>{{i18n "translations"}}:</li>
      {{ range .Translations }}
       <li>
          <a href="{{ .Permalink }}">{{ .Lang }}</a>
       </li>
      {{ end }}
  </ul>
{{end}}
<div>{{.Param "copyright" | markdownify}}</div>
```

NOTE   The Universal theme used in this book supports multilingual websites.

CODE CHECKPOINT   https://chapter-13-04.hugoinaction.com, and source code: https://github.com/hugoinaction/hugoinaction/tree/chapter-13-04.

13.2   *Special pages*

Apart from regular HTML content, there are non-HTML pages that a website needs to serve to be correctly indexed by search engines and social bots and to be successful on the modern web. The following sections cover two such pages: sitemaps and the file, robots.txt.

13.2.1   *Sitemaps*

Websites need a *sitemap* in XML format to submit to various search engines and to bots to access and index all the pages on the website. In Hugo, the sitemap is a top-level template (a new Hugo Kind parallel to page and taxonomy). Sitemaps have their own set of variables that we can use to customize them in the Hugo configuration or use within our template. Hugo comes bundled with a sitemap, and unless we are doing something special, there is no need to meddle with that sitemap. We can place a sitemap template in layouts/sitemap.xml, in layouts/_default/sitemap.xml in the theme, or directly on the website.

Suppose we want to disable the store and survey sections from being submitted to search engines. For that, we can create a sitemap template using the code in the following listing   (https://github.com/hugoinaction/hugoinaction/tree/chapter-13-resources/5). We should add this code to AcmeTheme/layouts/sitemap.xml.

Listing 13.6   Excluding sections from the sitemap

```
{{ printf "<?xml
version=\"1.0\"" "encoding=\"utf-8\" standalone=\"yes\" ?>"
  | safeHTML }}

<urlset xmlns="http://www.sitemaps.org/schemas/sitemap/0.9"
  xmlns:xhtml="http://www.w3.org/1999/xhtml">
  {{ range (where .Data.Pages "Section"
            "not in" (slice "store" "survey") )}}
  <url>
```

```
  <loc>{{ .Permalink }}</loc>
  {{ if not .Lastmod.IsZero }}
   <lastmod>{{ safeHTML
      ( .Lastmod.Format "2006-01-02T15:04:05-07:00" ) }}
   </lastmod>
  {{ end }}
  {{ with .Sitemap.ChangeFreq }}
  <changefreq>{{ . }}</changefreq>
  {{ end }}
  {{ if ge .Sitemap.Priority 0.0 }}
  <priority>{{ .Sitemap.Priority }}</priority>
  {{ end }}
  {{ if .IsTranslated }}
   {{ range .Translations }}
    <xhtml:link          rel="alternate"
      hreflang="{{ .Lang }}"
      href="{{ .Permalink }}"
      />
   {{ end }}
   <xhtml:link
      rel="alternate"
      hreflang="{{ .Lang }}"
      href="{{ .Permalink }}"
      />
   {{ end }}
 </url>
 {{ end }}
</urlset>
```

For multilingual websites, Hugo has the sitemapindex.xml template for the top-level sitemap.xml. This links to the other sitemaps on the website.

Automatically submitting sitemaps

Using the Jamstack, we can automatically submit sitemaps on each build to the search engines if we desire. We can write a webhook from Netlify or GitHub in response to a build event to reach the search engines directly. For example, to submit to Google, we can call the API https://www.google.com/ping?sitemap=https://example.com/sitemap.xml.

Netlify provides webhooks in Settings > Build & Deploy > Deploy Notifications and then click Add Notification > Outgoing Webhook to put the URL in the Deploy succeeded event. Alternatively, we can add a new step in the gh-params.yml with a custom script to call this URL for GitHub pages. Because this step happens after the website goes live, it acts as a webhook.

13.2.2 *robots.txt*

Like sitemaps, we have *robots.txt*, a file that tells bots what pages they are allowed and disallowed to index. Although bots can ignore or misuse this request, most do honor it. The robots.txt file is also a template that can access all page variables.

To use robots.txt as a template, we need to enable it on the website configuration (https://github.com/hugoinaction/hugoinaction/tree/chapter-13-resources/06) as the following listing shows.

Listing 13.7 **Enabling robots.txt (config/_default/config.yaml)**

```
enableRobotsTXT: true
```

There is rarely a use case that needs to list all disallowed pages because we can directly disallow sections. In case we wanted to, though, we could write the template in the following listing, which disallows robots from accessing the pages in the store and survey sections. In the listing, we could also use `Disallow: /store/` to disallow everything, which does not list the disallowed URLs in the store for malicious actors to find.

Listing 13.8 **Disallowing access to robots (AcmeTheme/layouts/robots.txt)**

```
User-agent: *
{{ range (where .Data.Pages "Section" "in"        ◄── Loops through all the pages in
  (slice "store" "survey") )}}                         the store and survey sections
Disallow: {{.RelPermalink}}    ◄─── Disallows the main URLs. We should
{{end}}                             ideally disallow all aliases as well.
```

NOTE The sample code with this website has an additional file, static/robots.txt, that disables all search engine indexing. This file overrides the one generated by this page.

CODE CHECKPOINT https://chapter-13-05.hugoinaction.com, and source code: https://github.com/hugoinaction/hugoinaction/tree/chapter-13-05.

Figure 13.2 **Promise? Gabby shares the news, now management needs to honor its promise.**

13.3 *Different versions using different output formats*

We briefly touched on custom output formats in chapter 9 when we built our JSON pseudo API. In Hugo, we can use as many output formats as we desire and have different templates to render the same content in different ways. This way, we can build a mobile version of the website with the /m endpoint, which can have a different layout but render the same content for mobile, or create a version for Accelerated Mobile Pages (AMP) with /amp. We can keep the same endpoint and have a different file extension much like how we did with JSON.

> **NOTE** We can have our hierarchy of content types and layout templates for each output format, including the baseof template that supports creating placeholders.

13.3.1 *Built-in RSS formats*

The most popular custom output format is the *RSS format*, which provides the website content in an XML feed that various RSS readers can parse. RSS is a popular XML-based format for website content that's readable by multiple clients. Hugo, by default, enables the RSS output format for most pages and bundles a template to convert the page data to RSS format. If you go to http://localhost:1313/blog/index.xml, you should be able to see the RSS output for the blog's index page.

The RSS format has more options than what is provided by default with Hugo. If a custom template is required, you can create list.rss.xml or single.rss.xml for the list and single pages, respectively. We can disable the RSS rendering by overriding the output formats in the website settings or in an individual page's front matter.

> **Multilingual website vs. custom output formats**
>
> The two features to generate multiple versions of the same page, multilingual pages and custom output formats, seem to be similar but are distinct and different. In multilingual pages, the layout and the theme across pages are the same, but the content changes, whereas in custom output formats, the content remains the same, but the layout and the theme are changed.

Each page variable has a property called OutputFormats, which lists all output formats for the page including the current format, and AlternativeOutputFormats, which excludes the current format. We can also search for alternate output formats for a page using the OutputFormats.Get function. The following listing includes a link to the RSS version of a web page in its content.

Listing 13.9   Adding RSS feeds (AcmeTheme/layouts/_default/baseof.html)

```
{{ with .OutputFormats.Get "RSS" }}
  <li>
    <a href="{{ .RelPermalink }}" aria-label="RSS" target="_blank">
      <i class="icon-rss"></i>
```

```
      </a>
    </li>
{{end}}
{{with site.Author.facebook}}
```

13.3.2 *Creating our own output format*

Using a new output format, we will offer a simplified version of our website and blog (with just text from Markdown and no styling) that's more akin to the reader view in the browser. For that, we will define a custom output format using a configuration setting called outputFormats (or by creating outputFormats.yaml in the config/_default folder). This defines new format names along with the media type, and the URL path where Hugo will host the content.

Let's create an output format called Plain that will host the website's plain version (figure 13.3). The plain version of the Acme Corporation website is like browser

Acme Corporation

About us   Blog   News   Editor   Store   Contact us

Acme is the best

The finest in this field

Acme Corporation™ is the *world's leading manufacturer of digital shapes*. From squares and circles to triangles and hexagons, we have it all. Browse through our collection of various forms with different thicknesses and line styles.

About Us

Personalized especially for you

We convert dreams into designs. Our artists are one of a kind. We provide full support for customizing your designs with multiple contact sessions to understand your problems and get a satisfying result.

Talk to us today

Pages

- About us
- Credits
- Editor
- Markdown
- Contact us
- Privacy policy
- Template page
- Terms of use

Subsections

- Blog
- News
- Our store

Categories   Terms of use   Privacy policy

Copyright © 2021 Acme Corporation. All Rights Reserved.

Figure 13.3 We can create different versions of a website in Hugo with custom output formats, including the plain version shown here. We have used minimal HTML styling to present the content in a straightforward layout.

reader mode with minimal styling and mostly text content. The template files for this version are present in the chapter resources (https://github.com/hugoinaction/hugoinaction/tree/chapter-13-resources/07), and listing 13.10 provides the configuration. Once defined, an output format is available to be included in the list of outputs in the front matter or in the global configuration for all pages.

> **Listing 13.10 Adding a `Plain` output format (config/_default/outputFormats.yaml)**

```
Plain:
  mediaType: text/html
  isHTML: true
  name: plain
  path: plain
```

Exercise 13.2

Suppose you want to make a set of websites for a conglomerate of companies, each with its own logo. You want to have a set of pages for each company that are different but conform to the same theme, each with their own home page, blog section, news section, and so on. You need to host all of these versions within the same website under different URLs (e.g., conglomerate.com/company1, conglomerate.com/company2, conglomerate.com/company3, etc.). What approach would not be able to solve this use case?

a. Creating a new output format for a subwebsite.
b. Creating a section for each company with different layouts for each page type and applying the cascade option.
c. Creating separate websites for each company with a shared theme and a different base URL.
d. Creating a new language for each company and supplying content in separate folders.

We can add the templates for the plain output format. The plain format does not need to go into the AcmeTheme template as we will add this to the simple version of the website. (These templates are available in the chapter resources.) We will also update the default outputs to enable plain formats everywhere as the following listing shows.

> **Listing 13.11 Adding default output formats (config/_default/outputs.yaml)**

```
home: [HTML, PLAIN, JSON]
page: [HTML, PLAIN]
section: [HTML, RSS, PLAIN]
```

We have not added the JSON output format to the global section configuration because we do not have JSON templates for all sections. Instead, in the front matter for content/store/_index.md, the following listing adds an entry for JSON in the output formats for the store section. We also need to remove the `outputs` front matter entry from _index.md and contentFr/_index.md.

Listing 13.12   Adding JSON output format (content/store/_index.md)

```
---
outputs: [html, json, rss, plain]
---
```

We can also link to the `Plain` format in the footer of the website inside the regular website pages. The following listing shows this syntax in HTML mode.

Listing 13.13   Links in HTML mode (AcmeTheme/layouts/_default/baseof.html)

```
{{ with .OutputFormats.Get "Plain" }}
  <li>
    <a href="{{ .RelPermalink }}"
      aria-label="Reader Mode" target="_blank">
      <i class="icon-reader"></i>
    </a>
  </li>
{{end}}
{{ with .OutputFormats.Get "RSS" }}
```

> **CODE CHECKPOINT**   https://chapter-13-06.hugoinaction.com, and source code: https://github.com/hugoinaction/hugoinaction/tree/chapter-13-06.

13.4   *Service workers in progressive web apps*

The default Hugo website is fast. HTML with minimal JavaScript and CSS is hard to beat when it comes to performance. With the ever-increasing need to make websites faster, both browser vendors and web developers have devised clever techniques and features that can help to increase the perceived performance of the website. Whereas many of these are transparent to developers (like HTTP v2.0/v3.0 or new image formats automatically handled by many CDNs), some need additional work.

Progressive web apps (PWAs) are websites that can act like regular applications when installed. They can have icons in the operating system and work indistinguishably from a native application. These websites use a service worker to handle intermittent networks and offline behaviors. *Service workers* are special scripts that act as a layer between the website and the internet and control the network access. These scripts can prefetch and cache certain assets and use them if network access is not present.

Although service workers and PWAs do not target the regular content-based websites that Hugo builds, they have improved the perceived performance of the website with a more refined control on the caching behavior in the client. A service worker does not need any support from Hugo, and from the perspective of Hugo, it is just another asset file that needs to be built with the website.

The completed script for the service worker is available in the chapter resources (https://github.com/hugoinaction/hugoinaction/tree/chapter-13-resources/08).   A typical service worker for a website has the following parts: install functions, activation functions, and request handlers.

13.4.1 Install functions

The browser calls an `install` function when it creates the service worker and installs it. This script typically decides which files need to be prefetched and cached by the web browser. The following listing shows a sample `install` function that executes during installation. We can use this to specify the list of resources needed for offline access.

Listing 13.14   `install` function (AcmeTheme/assets/serviceWorker.js)

```
(function () {
  const staticCacheName = 'static';
  const version = 'v1::';
    function updateStaticCache() {
      const urls = [...];
      return caches.open(version + staticCacheName)
        .then((cache) => cache.addAll(urls))
        .catch(e => {
          console.log("Error", e);
        });
    }
    self.addEventListener('install', (event) =>
      event.waitUntil(updateStaticCache()));
})();
```

Updates version if you need to refresh the cache

Lists the files that the browser should cache to launch this website in offline mode

Adds all files to the cache

Uses explicit naming and versioning of the cache

The install event fires on self.

The list of files that the browser needs to cache to launch the website in offline mode should also include all the images loaded by the theme. Typically, the home page of the website and some other crucial pages can be cached. We should use explicit naming and versioning of the cache as well. Mistakes here can leave the browser cache in a broken state. For the install event in a service worker context, `self` is the global variable we should use instead of `window`.

13.4.2 Activation functions

When updating a service worker, the newer version of the service worker gets installed. The next time we launch the website, it gets activated. This is when we can safely remove the older version's cache. We can call the `activate`/`deactivate` event handler during the transition of the service worker across versions as the following listing shows.

Listing 13.15   Executing `activate` (AcmeTheme/assets/serviceWorker.js)

```
self.addEventListener('activate', function (event) {
  event.waitUntil(
    caches.keys()
```

```
    .then(function (keys) {
      return Promise.all(keys
        .filter((key) => key.indexOf(version) !== 0)
        .map((key) => caches.delete(key))
      );
    })
  );
});
```

Removes the cache whose name is no longer valid

13.4.3 Fetching resources

The *request handler* sits between the network and the website. This handler is where the logic resides to decide what to do when a request comes in for an asset. This code has three parts: the non-GET requests, the GET requests for HTML/JavaScript/CSS, and the GET requests for the images. The non-GET requests like POST and DELETE perform server actions and, therefore, cannot be conducted offline and cannot be cached. The following listing fetches the resources for offline access.

Listing 13.16 Fetching resources (AcmeTheme/assets/serviceWorker.js)

```
const OFFLINE_URL = "/offline";
function offline(status = 200) {
  return caches.match(OFFLINE_URL)
  .then(x => x.text())
  .then(y =>
    new Response(y,
      {
        status,
        headers: {
          'Content-Type': 'text/html'
        }
      }));
}
self.addEventListener('fetch', function (event) {
  const request = event.request;
  if (request.method !== 'GET') {
    return event.respondWith(fetch(request)
    .catch(() => offline(400)));
  }
}
```

Creates a unique layout and a particular page to show to the users when offline

Always fetches non-GET requests from the network

When creating a unique layout and a particular page to show to the users when offline, make sure that it is present in the default list of pages for the website. When asked for an offline page, it is presented from the cache. We need to have different handling for different types of resources. The following are the steps to setup the service worker:

1 *Fetch the HTML/JavaScript/CSS resources.* When fetching resources, the HTML content needs to come from the server first so we can update the content on the server, and we want to serve the latest content. The following listing fetches the HTML/JavaScript/CSS content from the server first and then caches it. If

not available, we need to fall back to the local version. You'll add this code to AcmeTheme/assets/serviceWorker.js.

Listing 13.17   Fetching HTML/JavaScript/CSS content

```
...
self.addEventListener('fetch', function (event) {
  ...
  if (request.headers.get('Accept').indexOf('text/html')
    !== -1 || request.url.match(/\.(js|css)$/ */) {
    event.respondWith(
      fetch(request)                              For HTML/JavaScript/CSS requests, tries
        .then(function (response) {               the network first
          const copy = response.clone();
          caches.open(version + staticCacheName)  Saves every visited page
            .then(function (cache) {              in the cache for reuse
              cache.put(request, copy);           (the limitations follow)
            });
          return response;
        })
        .catch(function () {                      If the HTML request fails or is unavailable,
          return caches.match(request)            falls back to the cached page
            .then(function (response) {
              return response ||                  If the cached page is not
              (request.url.match(/\.(js|css)$/ */) ?   available, serves empty
              new Response('') :                  JavaScript/CSS files
              offline(200))      ◁─────┐
            })                          │  If a cached HTML page is not available,
        })                             │  shows the bundled offline page
    );
    return;
  }
  ...
});
```

Browsers have a maximum size for cache pages. The generally accepted maximum that a website can store is 50 MB, after which cache.put will start to fail. If we are concerned about the cache size, we should not put non-essential files in the cache. The browser automatically uninstalls the service worker and clears the cache when the machine runs out of disk space.

2   *Fetch the images, JavaScript, CSS, and other assets.* In the case of assets when fetching resources, Hugo Pipes generates a unique URL that changes as the content changes. Therefore, we can serve the cached image without going to the server if it's available. The following listing shows how to do this.

Listing 13.18   Serving cached assets (AcmeTheme/assets/serviceWorker.js)

```
...
self.addEventListener('fetch', function (event) {
```

```
event.respondWith(
    caches.match(request)
        .then(function (response) {
            return response || fetch(request)
                .catch(function () {
                    if (request.url.match(
                        /\.(jpe?g|png|gif|svg)$/)) {
                        return new Response(`<svg role="img"
                        aria-labelledby="offline"
                        xmlns="http://www.w3.org/2000/svg"
                        width="100%" height="100%">
<defs>
    <pattern id="textstripe"
             patternUnits="userSpaceOnUse"
             width="200" height="150"
             patternTransform="rotate(-45)">
        <text y="100" fill="rgba(0,0,0,0.33)"
              font-size="40">Offline</text>
    </pattern>
</defs>
<rect width="100%" height="100%"
    fill="rgba(145,145,145,0.5)"
    stroke="rgba(0,0,0,0.33)"
    stroke-width="3"/>
<rect width="100%" height="100%"
    fill="url(#textstripe)" />
</svg>`,
{ headers: {
  'Content-Type': 'image/svg+xml' } });
                    }
                    return new Response('');
                });
        })
    );
    ...
});
```

For non-HTML requests, looks in the cache first, then falls back to the network

For images, the offline image is provided inline as a simple SVG.

NOTE The Eclectic theme used in the book's early chapters offers an offline version of the website via this technique.

Exercise 13.3

Which of the following is true about service workers? (Select all that apply.)

a. Service workers can speed up a website by prefetching content heuristically.

b. Service workers need to be downloaded each time to run.

c. Service workers are not compatible with AJAX and the fetch API.

d. Service workers like web workers run in a separate context from the main page JavaScript.

3   *Create a page for offline scenarios.* As we're fetching resources, sometimes we may first need to inform the user that an internet connection is required. The following listing creates a minimal offline page to do just that.

Listing 13.19   Adding an offline page (content/offline.md)

```
---
title: Offline
CommentDisabled: true
---

Please connect to the internet to view this page.
```

4   *Compile the service worker (Hugo Pipes).* Although the service worker script is available, we need to compile it as a separate file in Hugo. We also need to supply the URLs of the various static resources. The service worker depends on the availability of the index.js path, and index.js needs to have the service worker path to register it. To break this cyclic dependency, we can provide the service worker path in the DOM. The service worker during compilation needs the path to all the resources we want it to cache. The number of resources in the cache needs to balance space consumption and website usability when offline.

Listing 13.20 adds the core resources (logo, background, CSS, and JavaScript files) and the offline page as a list of pages to load offline and sends them over to the service worker that is compiled into a separate JavaScript file. These file paths are built at compile time and assembled via js.Build (Hugo Pipes). The service worker file allows the worker to be loaded and updated independently outside of the browser's cache. You'll need to add this code to AcmeTheme/ layouts/_default/baseof.html. The link to the background SVG is present in index.css.tpl, which we need to move to a separate partial and reuse in the service worker registration. The background SVG move is a task for the reader.

Listing 13.20   Compiling the service worker into a separate JavaScript file

```
{{ $favicon := partialCached "favicon.png.html" $ "nothing"}}
{{ $logo := partialCached "logo.svg" $ "nothing"}}
{{ $background := partialCached "background.svg.html" $ "nothing" }}
{{ $hero := partialCached "hero.svg.html" $ "nothing" }}
{{ $css := partialCached "index.css.html" $ "nothing"}}

... {{ $js := resources.Get "index.js" | js.Build
      (dict "defines" $defines "minify" hugo.IsProduction )}}

{{$params := dict "pages" (slice
  "/"
  "/offline"
  $favicon
```

Passes all resources that need to be cached, including the page at /offline

```
$logo
$background
$hero
$js.Permalink
$css )}}

{{ $sw := resources.Get "serviceWorker.js" |
       js.Build (dict "minify" hugo.IsProduction "params" $params)}}


<template id="js-strings">
    {{ dict
       ...
       "serviceWorker" $sw.Permalink    <──┐
       | jsonify
    }}
</template>
```

> **Includes the script as a comment to ensure that Hugo compiles it and includes it in the output folder**

5 *Add an entry to register the service worker.* We can register the service worker after ensuring that the service worker is available and its code looks correct. The following listing informs the browser of our service worker file via JavaScript. For localized websites, you might want to have different service workers for each language. For this example, we use one for the entire website by setting the scope to / (website root).

Listing 13.21 Registering the service worker (AcmeTheme/assets/index.js)

```
if ('serviceWorker' in navigator &&
    window.location.pathname !== '/offline') {
    const strings = JSON.parse(document.getElementById("js-strings")
        .content.textContent);
    navigator.serviceWorker.register(     <──┐  Calls the navigator to
    strings.serviceWorker,                     register the service worker
    {scope: '/'});                 <──┐
}                                       Uses a service worker
                                        for the entire website
```

6 *Create the application manifest.* If we want to convert to a complete PWA, we also need a *web app manifest* that tells the browser how to install the website. This manifest is a JSON file with some information about the application generated from the base template. Because all the options in this file are beyond the scope of this book, we have created a sample file to allow us to create a PWA. The following listing shows the contents of such a file.

Listing 13.22 A web app manifest file (AcmeTheme/layouts/_default/baseof.html)

```
{{$manifest := (dict
  "name" (default site.Home.Title site.Title)
  "display" "minimal-ui"
```

```
        "icons" (slice (dict
                        "src" $logo
                        "type" "image/svg+xml"
                        "sizes" "155x155"))    "start_url" "/"
        ) }}
    {{ $manifestFile := ($manifest | jsonify
        | resources.FromString "/manifest.webmanifest")
        .Permalink }}
  <link rel="manifest" href="{{$manifestFile}}">
    ...
  {{$params := dict "pages" (slice
    $manifestFile
      ...
```

Provides the data to create a web app manifest → (points to the icons/dict block)

Generates a file from this data and stores it on disk → (points to `$manifestFile :=` block)

Adds a link to every page for the app manifest → (points to `<link rel="manifest">` line)

Caches the manifest in the service worker → (points to `$manifestFile` line)

With this, we can now use the website when offline. You can test this out by disconnecting from the internet and going to the website URL. The contents should show up, although placeholders will replace some images, and some pages will request us to go back online.

CODE CHECKPOINT   https://chapter-13-07.hugoinaction.com, and source code: https://github.com/hugoinaction/hugoinaction/tree/chapter-13-07.

13.5 *Prefetching on hover*

When you navigate from one page to another, the click event requires a hover, a mouse down, and a mouse up. The engaged link reports that you've clicked the touch screen when you move your finger back up after touching the link. The first interaction with a link and the final click takes a minimum of 200 ms for the average user to complete. This 200 ms is a lot of time in the world of the web.

We can utilize this time to prefetch the page and render an instant page immediately after the click completes. If the user decides to cancel the operation by not issuing a mouse down event or dragging away after touching, we can throw the prefetched page away. The likelihood of users goofing around with links is rare, so a single web page's bandwidth costs are small enough to warrant the prefetch. Note that our prefetch request is just an indication to the browser, which can ignore it in cases like a low device battery or a metered connection.

The best part about enabling instant pages on our website is that we already have a Hugo module under the official Hugo GitHub umbrella with a total of two lines of code to integrate. Listing 13.23 loads the instant page module in our `imports` section and places the script in our `body` tag. Then listing 13.24 loads the instant page.

Listing 13.23   Adding dependencies for an instant page (AcmeTheme/config.yaml)

```
module:
  imports:
    ...
      - path: github.com/gohugoio/hugo-mod-jslibs/instantpage
```

```
. . .
{{ partialCached "jslibs/instantpage/script-src.html" "-" }}
</body>
```

This code adds a separate JavaScript file to our website. If we prefer to have the instant page code bundled with our main website, we can install the instant page plugin via npm and add this to our JavaScript file.

> **CODE CHECKPOINT**   https://chapter-13-08.hugoinaction.com, and source code: https://github.com/hugoinaction/hugoinaction/tree/chapter-13-08.

13.6 *Cleaner navigation with the Turbo JavaScript library*

When the user clicks on a link, the current page becomes invalid while the new one is loaded and rendered. We often see a flicker of white when this happens. *Turbo* is a set of techniques and libraries that can write web applications that are light on JavaScript.

Turbo Drive keeps the current page active by overriding the navigation mechanism in the browsers with a background fetch. It then replaces the contents of the DOM with the new page. This way, the users never see a flicker, and the web page is functional even during navigation! This advanced library's feature allows us to prevent parts of the web page from reloading when navigating away, thereby maintaining the state of text boxes, scroll position, and other web page characteristics when reloaded. It makes page transitions and loading possible for websites where the server sends HTML rather than building the HTML in JavaScript. We will enable Turbo Drive in this section, albeit in the bare minimum state, and will not do partial page reloads. The term Turbo from here on will refer to the Turbo Drive part of the Turbo libraries.

> **Instant page vs. Turbo Drive**
>
> Instant page and Turbo Drive are complimentary and not colliding techniques. Instant page tries to prefetch the page and make sure it is loaded from the internet early, and Turbo Drive ensures that the current page is active until the new page is ready.
>
> A good analogy to understand this comes from the field of medicine. Instant page is like the technology that puts you in the queue for a kidney transplant based on the lab results, even before your kidneys fail. Turbo Drive is the dialysis machine that keeps you running until the transplant is successful and the new kidney takes over. Unlike kidneys, network bandwidth is cheap, and a little wastage is acceptable for better performance.

13.6.1 *Adding Turbo Drive to the template*

In listing 13.23, we added the instant page plugin as a Hugo module. We could have used npm for that use case as well. For Turbo Drive, we will use npm. The following listing adds Turbo as a devDependency in package.hugo.json. Then we need to run hugo mod npm pack followed by npm i to install it.

> **Listing 13.25 Adding Turbo as a dependency (AcmeTheme/package.hugo.json)**

```
{
  "devDependencies": {
    ...
    "@hotwired/turbo" :"7.0.0-rc.1"
  }
  ...
}
```

After installing Turbo, we can load this on the index page of our website. The following listing provides the code to do this. This snippet also instantiates Turbo on the website.

> **Listing 13.26 Adding Turbo to the index page (AcmeTheme/assets/index.js)**

```
import * as Turbo from "@hotwired/turbo"

...
function init() {
  ...
  Turbo.start();
}
```

13.6.2 *Handling JavaScript-based navigation*

Although Turbo handles HTML-based changes automatically, any JavaScript modifications done to the DOM could get lost. Turbo does not work well with relative links as the base URL is different when the preloading occurs. The solution to this problem includes the following:

1 Tell Turbo to deactivate for certain links by adding the data-turbo="false" attribute to the links.
2 Leave a portion of the page untouched by Turbo by adding the data-turbo-permanent attribute to the element.
3 Handle these conditions manually by calling turbo:load event.

The first approach lowers performance. Because we do not have permanent portions of a page on our website (due to localization), manual handling works best for us. Although the template links are absolute, we added manual HTML (draw.jpg in the About page) with a relative link in the content. The following listing uses the ref shortcode to prepend the link to the base URL of the current page, thus hardcoding the image URL.

Listing 13.27   Making hardcoded image URLs absolute (content/about/index.md)

```
<img style="float:right; margin: 20px;" src="{{<ref "about">}}/draw.jpg">
```

Next, we will render the cart when Turbo replaces the HTML of the web page. The following listing shows how to do this.

Listing 13.28   Re-rendering the cart (AcmeTheme/assets/store.js)

```
...
function init() {
   ...
   document.addEventListener("turbo:load",      │ Refreshes the cart
      this.updateCart.bind(this));         ◁────┘ on page load
   ...
}
```

CODE CHECKPOINT   https://chapter-13-09.hugoinaction.com, and source code: https://github.com/hugoinaction/hugoinaction/tree/chapter-13-09.

Event delegation and Turbo

Turbo loves the concept of event delegation that we introduced in chapter 10. Because the DOM loads only once, Turbo also runs the JavaScript code once. When we attach event listeners (to forms, for example) and the browser adds elements dynamically, the event handling continues to work due to delegation.

For example, suppose we need an event handler for the contact form. When the JavaScript code executes on the home page, it can add event listeners for the Contact Us form even though it is not loaded until the user navigates to that page. Turbo can replace the DOM contents without re-running all the JavaScript code when the user loads this page. The event handling for the Contact Us form continues to work automatically. With less JavaScript code running on navigation, our website becomes faster.

With the changes to include Turbo and Instant Page, we should be able to see much better page transitions on our website. Now let's look at more best practices, tools, and services that we can use across a wide variety of domains in the following section.

13.7   *More Jamstack tooling and services*

Using the Jamstack across the whole set of problems it can tackle, and the type of services that are present and evolving will require multiple books to understand. In this book, we have established a general framework of using a third-party API as we did with Netlify forms and functions, Formspree, Heroku, Stripe, and SendGrid, but there's more to the Jamstack.

13.7.1   *CLI, SDKs, configurations, and additional automation SDKs (software development kits)*

Most Jamstack services come with a command-line interface (CLI) to configure, launch, and locally test the code we write for the website. Instead of going to the website and doing this, we recommended using a command-line tool or a script. This approach provides a lot of flexibility and power. Some services work with configuration files where all the settings can be dumped and then updated on the server with the CLI. Here are several good reasons to use the CLI:

- *We can store the CLI invocations along with our code.* This storage provides proper version control and repeatability for all our configurations. We can go back in history and try out older builds with other settings for the cloud services we've used. Additionally, history searches let us fix injections or mistakes that creep in after initial testing.

- *We can track changes in the cloud services better with the CLI.* If the same command does something different than the last time it was issued, we have some assurance that the issue is on the vendor side, and we need to reach out to customer support.

- *We can automate configurations.* If you have hundreds of surveys to create, doing it manually on the Formspree interface is a lot of work that we can do via a script running via a CLI.

- *We can use the command line for replicating or synchronizing the configuration across multiple accounts.* This allows us to have different setups for development, staging, and production environments.

- *The textual configuration is faster to read and navigate.* CLIs use textual configuration by default. In many cases, it also exposes more features than what is possible in the website.

- *We can control the invocation time for the script.* This is a lot easier than manually clicking the user interface.

The big downside of the CLI is that it is more technical than a GUI and will most likely take extra effort initially to set up. That is the reason this book goes through the GUI wherever and whenever possible. We believe that this effort pays off in the long run.

A general rule of thumb with scripting is that you need to start with the graphical interface to understand the service better and to do the initial setup. Then, it is best to move off the graphical interface, but keep the version history as soon as it's time for the first revision. All services used in this book, from Netlify to SendGrid, offer either a CLI, set up with a configuration, or both. Most of the CLIs are open source and involve an SDK that we can use to invoke the commands programmatically.

> ### Exercise 13.4
> Select the statement about CLIs, SDKs, and configurations that is true.
> - **a.** CLIs cause vendor lock-in and should be avoided for better maintainability.
> - **b.** We can use SDKs within a cloud function to affect its own state.
> - **c.** If one of the service providers is a CLI or SDK, it does not make sense to use the CLI for anything because everyone provides a GUI.
> - **d.** GUIs are always faster to learn and use than CLIs.

13.7.2 *Authentication, storage, and other pieces of the puzzle*

Some functional necessities for most modern websites that we did not tackle in this book include authentication and storage. These form the building blocks of most complex applications and, on the surface, seem harder for a static website to do than something that uses a server. With the widespread use of social login buttons from big corporations like Google, Facebook, Apple, and Microsoft, and their acceptance by the general public, authentication has become commoditized. We can write a login helper using the APIs for these providers purely in the JavaScript layer and then use session storage or local storage to manage the user state. Cloud functions can validate tokens if we need to provide access to restricted resources. There are also services like Netlify Identity and Auth0, where we can add social logins and build a custom login system in pure JavaScript code and let the vendors perform user management.

There are many types of and use cases for storage. This is needed to store some user data for personalization as well as aggregation or publishing. All use cases have different potential solutions. If the data is user-generated and is needed personally by the user, we can use third-party services like Dropbox, Google Drive, or even GitHub to store this data. With these services, the cost of storage and the burden of backup and maintenance is not ours. We have already used form services to store data for aggregation. Based on our use cases, if our needs are different, we can use PAAS solutions from Heroku Dynos to AWS DynamoDB or S3. The deeper we dive into the application server layers, the more work we need to do.

Another vital piece of the modern web is notifications. Luckily for the Jamstack, these are built-in. Almost all services offer both inbound and outbound webhooks to communicate with one another, and we can add custom cloud functions to perform any missing tasks for ourselves. The second set of notifications are for the end user. Services like Twilio (owners of SendGrid), Firebase, and PubNub offer the ability to send real-time messages to the end users.

13.8   *The Hugo community*

Hugo is primarily a community-driven project. This ownership has allowed the tool to develop a passionate community of users, developers, and followers. Most Hugo users are developers, and many have personal websites where they share tips, tutorials, and sample code under a permissive license such that we can take it and make it our own.

Being a community-led and not a corporation-led effort is one of the critical benefits of Hugo. Anyone can suggest changes and influence the direction of Hugo. If you are not happy with where it is going, you have the right to fork the project and build a custom copy. Suppose you are trying to solve a problem or perform some task via Hugo that you do not understand. In that case, you can post it in the Hugo forums and be dazzled by the creativity of the Hugo community to solve the problem.

13.8.1   *Asking for help*

Hugo has a robust set of community forums at https://discourse.gohugo.io/. The community is very responsive, and you might find proper usable code as answers to your queries. The biggest thing to note is that Hugo expects that you do some homework before asking questions. Search the previously answered questions, or check in Hugo's documentation (https://gohugo.io/documentation/) and on GitHub (https://github.com/gohugoio/hugo) before raising a question. A lot of these are already solved and answered multiple times. A quick Google search can also reveal blog posts by Hugo users solving problems they've encountered when building their websites with Hugo.

We can also use GitHub Issues to ask for feature requests and changes to Hugo. Generally, use GitHub Issues if you find bugs and have well-defined feature requests. For general questions, it is better to start a discourse and graduate to GitHub Issues if the request is a new feature or a discovered bug. When reporting a bug, it is a good idea to share sample code and provide environment details and sample data to reproduce the bug.

Being civil and patient in the forums is essential to getting help. The other community members are answering their questions voluntarily without any remuneration. Although they love Hugo and are putting in the effort to see it succeed and to help you succeed with it, there is still an expectation of an intelligent inquirer who has done their homework before asking for help.

13.8.2   *Showcasing your work*

It is a proud moment to have accomplished something using Hugo, whether discovering a new trick or creating a module. We can also build entire themes that we would like to sell or give away. The Hugo community forums (https://discourse.gohugo.io/) are great places to share new modules and tricks. The community forums have two sections (Tips & Tricks and Showcases) entirely dedicated to showing off stuff from the community. The Hugo website takes pull requests, and if your work is worthy, it could land on Hugo's website itself.

Hugo also has a themes repository for user-created themes at https://github.com/gohugoio/hugoThemes, where we can send a pull request to display our theme on the Hugo website. Setting up a theme requires setting up an example website and ensuring some level of portability of content across themes. If you have created a theme, setting up a sample website to showcase its top feature should not be difficult.

A much better place to showcase your work is in your website itself. If you have a personal website on the World Wide Web, that is the best place to write about your work. Personal websites give maximum flexibility on what and how to present your work. Your website can get backlinks that provide SEO advantages for a job well done, and you have something to write about.

13.8.3 Contributing

Hugo is an open source project with all its code, plans, and documentation available for the community to peruse, improve, and fix. Users can request changes via pull requests to the core code as well as documentation. The steps for contributing code to Hugo are provided at https://gohugo.io/contribute/development/ and are up-to-date with changing build environments and support matrices.

Hugo uses the Go programming language, and knowledge about how Go works is essential to add features successfully to Hugo. That does not mean that it's the only way to contribute. We can contribute to documentation, provide themes, and help others, tasks that do not require additional knowledge outside of using Hugo that you should be comfortable with after reading this book.

13.9 The future of Hugo

Both Hugo and the Jamstack are rapidly evolving. More and more problems traditionally solved during run time are moving to the compilation layer. Hugo is stepping up to define the best practices for maintaining performance and ease of use with new use cases that emerge for the Jamstack and the web. Hugo just had three releases in 2013 and two in 2014. In 2020, Hugo had almost 50 releases, including features like js.Build, Babel, and PostCSS, along with significant changes to the new Markdown rendering engine and Hugo Modules, which came in 2019. 2021 saw new features released continuously, from faster builds on Mac ARM to `resources.GetRemote`.

Most Hugo features are added based on user requests and feedback. This community project does not have a corporate direction to cater to, just feasibility, maintainability, and performance to decide whether to add a new feature. Most features that come to Hugo are feature requests from end users. There have been multiple attempts to get a 1.0 vision and roadmap, but the needs keep evolving with time, and we cannot foresee what new releases will bring. Hugo is not going away, and its features will continue to work so we can continue to use the version of Hugo we have (unless we need something that the new versions bring in). The Jamstack is also evolving rapidly and picking up support for a wide variety of use cases. With Hugo, we can build websites that provide outstanding performance and stay live on the internet for a long time without much maintenance.

Summary

- Hugo offers a set of advanced features around creating multiple versions of a web page. These include multilingual websites and custom output formats.

- Hugo supports creating websites in multiple (human) languages, where we can provide language-specific content without necessarily redoing all the settings and images for the website.

- With custom output formats, we can design different layouts and templates for the same content to present it differently, including different mime types like RSS or JSON to different types of UIs like AMP or plain HTML.

- Hugo offers sitemap and robots.txt templates, which we can optionally use. With great defaults and simple requirements, there is rarely a need to set these up.

- Although Hugo-based websites are fast by default, we can make them faster by using techniques like Instant page or Turbo to take advantage of the capabilities of the modern web.

- With CLIs and configuration files, Jamstack is very friendly to the developer. After a certain point, keeping the configuration for the various services and the source code gets easier.

- Hugo has a vibrant community that is eager to help, provided that we have done our homework and are polite and respectful in asking for help.

appendix A
Getting up and running with Hugo

A.1 System requirements

Hugo runs on a standard version of all major desktop operating systems, including Windows, macOS, and the various flavors of Unix. The following lists additional system requirements:

- *Go needs to be installed to use Hugo Modules (chapter 8+).* Package managers that install Hugo take care of installing Go as well. The installation instructions for Go are located at https://golang.org/doc/install. You do not need to learn Go or use it directly within Hugo.
- *Although Git is not required to use Hugo, if Git is the version control system, Hugo provides access to the metadata in the templates.* Hugo can also use Git metadata in its page rendering. (For example, the date last modified for a page is safer in Git than in the OS, where each time the code is downloaded, the modified date may get changed.) Git is available in all package managers by running `git`. You can also get Git from https://git-scm.com/. You can learn more about Git from the book by Mike McQuaid, *Git in Practice* (Manning, 2014), or the book by Rick Umali, *Learn Git in a Month of Lunches* (Manning, 2015).

Hugo also integrates with the Node.js ecosystem and npm, which we utilize in chapters 10+. Node.js and npm are not required to use Hugo but are helpful if you write frontend JavaScript code to support your Hugo-based website. You can install Node.js and npm from the official website at https://nodejs.org/ or from any package manager.

A.1.1   *Hugo flavors*

Hugo comes in two flavors: standard and extended. The extended flavor of Hugo adds support for the SCSS, a language that compiles to CSS. SCSS provides support for functions, nested classes, and compile-time variables. It gels well with the core concept of the Jamstack, which prefers compilation-based processing over run-time processing in the client.

> **NOTE**   The SCSS language is beyond the scope of this book. It is not needed for learning and using Hugo.

Sass ships as two compilers: the LibSass compiler, which is bundled into Hugo extended, and the Dart Sass compiler, which needs to be installed as an external dependency if we want to use it with Hugo. Future versions of Hugo will move to Dart Sass as LibSass is deprecated. Also, there might not be an extended flavor of Hugo in the future.

A.1.2   *Hugo versions*

You can use the `hugo version` command to get the current version of Hugo installed on your machine. Hugo is relatively stable, and most Hugo-based websites do not have any other dependency apart from Hugo, making maintenance easy. Hugo is not at version 1.0 yet, and the core team does not guarantee backward compatibility. The release notes do have migration instructions that are specific and can be completed by a find-and-replace operation in your codebase. The Hugo community is open and inviting. If you have trouble migrating to a newer version, you will be pleasantly surprised by the effort the community will take to help solve your problem.

Note that, with the absence of intrusive plugins and the presence of hundreds of themes and websites with thousands of pages, the core team tries its best to maintain compatibility. Most breaking changes come when a significant change is involved in creating a new feature or cleaning up a substantial portion of the codebase. Usually, these changes come with steps on migration from the older way of doing things. There is no long-term support version of Hugo, and the core team does not patch older versions. Only the latest version gets bug fixes and updates.

Updating Hugo websites

You do not need to have the latest version of Hugo or its theme. Your website's contents are perfectly safe if generated by an older version of the theme or by Hugo. The patches are recommended and helpful only for updates, but you can do them at your own pace and at your own time.

The generated website can run forever without needing security updates or patches. You can keep adding content with the older version of Hugo if you are comfortable with that and you do not need new features, so there is no need to update. Hugo version 0.91.2 is used for this book.

A.2 Installing Hugo

Hugo is available on all major platforms, and there are many ways to install Hugo: from package managers to direct compilation. The following sections describe the installation process for these options.

A.2.1 System package managers

Hugo is available with the name "hugo" in most standard package managers. You do need to pass additional flags to install Hugo extended in some of them. The extended flavor of Hugo has more features, and we recommend using it. The following listing provides the commands to use for various package managers.

Listing A.1 Installation commands for Hugo

```
brew install hugo          ◁─── For MacOS, Homebrew at https://brew.sh/

sudo port install hugo +extended     ◁─── For MacOS, MacPorts at https://www.macports.org/

choco install hugo-extended -confirm  ◁─── For Windows, Chocolatey at https://chocolatey.org/

scoop install hugo-extended    ◁─── For Windows, Scoop at https://scoop.sh/

snap install hugo --channel=extended   ◁─── For Linux, Snap at https://snapcraft.io/

sudo apt-get install hugo    ◁─── For Ubuntu, Apt at https://wiki.debian.org/Apt

sudo pacman -Syu hugo     ◁─── For Arch Linux, pacman at https://www.archlinux.org/pacman/

sudo dnf install hugo    ◁─── For Fedora, DNF at https://fedoraproject.org/wiki/DNF

sudo yum install hugo    ◁─── For Fedora, yum at https://fedoraproject.org/wiki/Yum

sudo pkg_add hugo    ◁─── For OpenBSD, pkg at https://man.openbsd.org/pkg_add
```

A.2.2 Direct download

You can also download the precompiled Hugo binary file from Hugo's GitHub repository at https://github.com/gohugoio/hugo/releases. This page also provides release notes for the various releases and access to the older versions of Hugo. The specific version used in this book is present at https://github.com/gohugoio/hugo/releases/tag/v0.91.2. Make sure that you download the extended version for the release.

Once downloaded, you can extract Hugo to access the file hugo.exe (on Windows, it might be just hugo if the OS hides path extensions) or the file hugo (on Linux/macOS) that you can use to run the program. The Hugo binary needs to be present in the system path to be available directly in the command line:

- For Windows, see https://gohugo.io/getting-started/installing/#for-windows-10-users
- For macOS/Linux, move the hugo file to /usr/bin via sudo mv hugo /usr/bin/

Because Hugo is a single binary file and not a folder where we have multiple files to copy, this makes it easy to submit the Hugo binary to source control or save it for archival purposes. However, because the package managers support getting older versions of the hosted software, there is no real need to archive Hugo, and you do not need to keep Hugo's binary file in your version control system. The only use case for storing this binary is long-term archival.

> **NOTE** Step-by-step video guides to install Hugo are available at https:// gohugo.io/getting-started/installing/.

A.3   Code editors

Hugo does not need a specialized development environment. A text editor is enough. Sublime Text and Visual Studio Code have good syntax highlighting extensions for Hugo. A plugin is available for the Prettier code formatter to automatically manage the formatting of Go template code and is compatible with Hugo.

A.4   Troubleshooting

While there are a small number of steps involved in setting up Hugo, it might not be clear from the error code what the real cause is. Searching for the error message through Hugo's forums and GitHub repository is of great help in figuring out solutions to issues. This section describes some common problems you might encounter when using Hugo with the source code of this book.

A.4.1   Making sure Hugo runs

This error is frequent if you download Hugo from the source. Make sure your system path has Hugo. Adding the Hugo binary folder to the system path or moving Hugo to a folder present in the system path enables the Hugo command line. Also, Hugo comes as both 32-bit and 64-bit, and to run Hugo, you need to use the right combination for your operating system.

A.4.2   Installing the right version

You can use the `hugo version` command to get the current version of Hugo installed on your machine. This book uses Hugo's 0.91.2 version. The code associated with this book does not work with older versions. If you have problems building some code, it is a good idea to switch to Hugo 0.91.2 and try out the sample code with that version. Older versions can show various errors in the console, including `Unable to find theme Directory`.

A.4.3   Getting Hugo extended

Running `hugo  version` also prints the flavor of Hugo to the console. If it is not extended, than you will need to install Hugo extended. Installing the wrong flavor of Hugo can return weird errors, including:

```
WARN 2021/03/18 11:19:02 found no layout file for "HTML" for "page":
You should create a template file which matches Hugo Layouts Lookup Rules
for this combination.
```

A.4.4 *Fixing Hugo Modules*

The local cache for Hugo Modules can go out of sync with the internet and cause problems. A common error with Hugo Modules is a checksum mismatch with the following signature:

```
Error: failed to download modules: go command failed: verifying <name>:
checksum mismatch
downloaded: h1:VMeQ8LUaRmZNBFFmM3mf24H8Mf769mF2w6jqZQwxGhA=
go.sum:     h1:kX8dz4A9W9OxTHPprCPKRq3Jv2567iAGKNol4UNz8kc=
```

This mismatch can be caused by a genuine attack on the module or the module author not being careful with its content (for example, a force push on Git). Other errors associated with Hugo Modules include cases where the modules fail to download or the website fails to launch due to weird errors. In cases like this, we need to clear the module cache:

```
hugo mod clean --all
```

We should check the new version of the module and ensure our code is still compatible if the checksum has changed.

appendix B
TOML and
JSON for metadata

While we use YAML throughout the book for metadata and configuration, TOML is the default in Hugo and continues to gain popularity. JSON is more straightforward for the machine to read, and JSON generation is popular in content management systems that build over Hugo.

B.1 *Tom's Obvious, Minimal Language (TOML)*

TOML is the default metadata language in Hugo. Most of the community uses this language, and you will find most of the documentation in TOML.

Unlike YAML, the objective of TOML is to have clarity of representation (and machine readability) over human readability. TOML has stricter data types than YAML. For example, YAML automatically coerces true and false to Boolean. We need to wrap true and false in quotes to convert these words into strings, but yes and no are directly strings. The YAML parser sniffs the content for true and false to do the Boolean conversion. This type of "sniffing" magic makes writing a parser difficult. TOML avoids these cases by requiring all strings to be enclosed in quotes. TOML is more verbose than YAML. It is string-based and human-readable and does not have a lot of edge cases. It has first-class support for dates, which is the only significant data type difference with YAML.

TOML is not as popular as YAML and may be intimidating to newcomers. Knowing TOML, however, can help in the interactions with the Hugo community. TOML uses the equal sign (=) instead of YAML's colon (:). It is sensitive to the new line but not to indentation, unlike YAML. To place TOML content in the front matter of a page, we need to wrap it with three plus signs (+++) and place it at the top of the page. The three plus signs identify TOML as the content metadata language. TOML has all the same elements as YAML.

B.1.1 Comments

TOML, just like YAML, uses hashes (#) for comments. Here's an example:

```
# Comment in TOML
```

B.1.2 Basic data types

TOML has properly defined content types. It does support dates natively and does not have a `null` type. Here's a quick primer:

TOML requires strings to have quotes around them.

```
key = "value"
```

Pressing the Enter key (newline) declares new keys. This has a float value.

```
key2= 12.0
```

```
key3= 10
```
TOML recognizes floats, integers, Booleans, and dates.

```
key4= 2020-01-01T00:00:00Z
```
TOML understands dates natively.

```
     key5= "hello"
```
No new lines but indentation allowed.

```
# key6
```
TOML does not support null values.

```
key7 = false
```
The Boolean type, false

B.1.3 Multiline strings

TOML uses three quotes, both single like `'''` and double like `"""`, to wrap multiline strings. The strings are sensitive to newline characters. You can use escape characters like \n for new lines although the escaping only works within double quotes. The following code snippet provides some examples for multiline strings:

```
key1= """
   This is a multiline string
   where newline characters are valid.

   Multi line strings end by three quote(") symbols
   """
key12= '''
   String single quotes, single lines, and multiline display as is.
   Not an event a backslash(\) can escape text.
   '''
```

B.1.4 Lists

Lists in TOML can be declared using square braces. The following shows two ways that you can add lists:

```
key1= ["d", "e", "f"]
```
All spacing and indentation is optional.

```
key2= ["d",
       "e",
       "f"]
```

B.1.5   Dictionaries

In TOML, double square braces `[[]]` declare dictionaries. All the key-value pairs after the square braces become a part of the dictionary. Here's an example:

```
[[key12]]            ◁─────┐  Dictionary, map, and key-value pairs
   key13= 'value13'  ◁──── The indentation is optional.
   key14= [          ◁────
       "List \" Item 1",    Order of elements in the dictionary does not matter.
       "List Item 2"
   ]
   key15 = 10
```

B.1.6   Front matter

The wrapper for TOML content is three plus signs(+++) in the front matter. You can see this in the following:

```
+++                      ◁─────┐
<metadata section>       Three plus signs wrap
                         TOML-based front matter.
+++                      ◁─────┘
<data section>
```

REVISITING CONFIG.YAML

Here is what the configuration (config.toml) would look like if written in TOML:

```
baseURL = "http://acme.hugoinaction.com/"
languageCode = "en-us"
title = "Acme Corporation"
theme = "eclectic"

[author]
facebook = "https://facebook.com/test"
twitter = "https://twitter.com/test"
email = "contact@example.org"
name = "Acme Corporation"
location = "New York"
phone = "(999) 999-9999"
hours = "Mon-Fri: 9:00AM - 6:00PM, ET"

[menu]

   [[menu.main]]
   identifier = "about"
   name = "About"
   url = "/about"
   weight = 100

   [[menu.main]]
   identifier = "contact"
   name = "Contact"
   url = "/contact"
```

```
weight = 200

[params]
color = "#4f46e5"
copyright = "Copyright &copy; 2022 Acme Corporation. All Rights Reserved."

    [[params.footer]]
    title = "About"
    content = """
    Acme Corporation is the world's leading manufacturer of digital
    shapes. From squares and circles to triangles and hexagons, we have it
    all. Browse through our collection of various forms with different
    thicknesses and line styles. We shape the world. You live in it.
    """

    [[params.footer]]
    title = "Recent Blog Posts"
    recents = "blog"
    recentCount = 7.0

    [[params.footer]]
    title = "Contact Us"
    contact = true
```

B.2   JavaScript Object Notation (JSON)

JSON is a standard information exchange format prevalent on the web. Most services expose their functionality via JSON-based APIs. The objective of JSON is machine readability and efficient transmission over the network. Human readability is a bonus. Although JSON is more human-readable than binary formats, JSON has strict language rules to allow writing a parser more easily, which may come from the way of reading JSON. JSON is insensitive to spaces and new lines and relies on explicit markers for content. To place JSON content in the front matter of a page, we need to wrap it with curly braces({}) and place it at the top of the page. The curly braces identify JSON as the content metadata language.

B.2.1   Basic data types

JSON supports numbers, strings, and Booleans. Colons separate keys and values (:), and commas (,) separate elements. For example,

JSON groups are
wrapped in curly braces.
⌐▷ {

    All keys in JSON are strings. All
strings have double quotes.

    "key": "value",   ◁─── All keys are separated by
commas except the last one.
New lines are not important.

    "key2": 12.0,   ◁───

    "key3": 10,   ◁─── JSON uses the number type
for both integers and floats.

    "key4": null,   ◁───

    A null value is supported.

```
"key5": false,        <──── Boolean false

    "key6": "hello", "key7":7,   <──── All indentation, spacing and new lines are optional.

"key7":    <────┐
                │  JSON is insensitive to new lines and indentation
      "hello"  <┘  even in between the key and the value.

}   <────  The last element cannot be followed by a comma.
```

B.2.2 Multiline strings

JSON does not have multiline strings. You should use newline characters instead. Here's an example:

```
{
"key1": "Multiline strings need \n (newline characters).
--> No single quotes or special modes available."
}
```

B.2.3 Lists

Lists in JSON can also be declared using square braces. For example,

```
{         <──  Lists can be added via []
              (square braces).

"key3":  [   <──  All list elements need
    1,       <──  not be of the same type.
    "b",
    "c"      <──  All list elements are separated by
    ],           commas except the last element.
"key4": ["d", "e", "f"]   <──
                             All spacing and
}                            indentation is optional.
```

B.2.4 Dictionaries

In JSON, curly braces create dictionaries. The following code snippet shows how to create these:

```
{           <──  Dictionary, map,
                 key-value pairs

       "key1": {   <──
Order of    "key11": "value13",   <──── The indentation is optional.
elements  ─> "key12": [
in the          "List \" Item 1",   <──── Quotes in strings can be escaped.
dictionary      "List Item 2"
does not     ],   <──  No comma after the last item.
matter.      "key13": 10   <──
       }              <──── Closes the dictionary

}   <────  Closes the JSON section
```

B.2.5   *Front matter*

Brackets in JSON delineate the front matter. Here's how:

```
{
  <JSON configuration>
}
```

B.2.6   *Revisiting the config file*

The JSON version of the Hugo configuration file is as follows:

```
{
  "baseURL": "http://acme.hugoinaction.com/",
  "languageCode": "en-us",
  "title": "Acme Corporation",
  "theme": "eclectic",
  "author": {
    "facebook": "https://facebook.com/test",
    "twitter": "https://twitter.com/test",
    "email": "contact@example.org",
    "name": "Acme Corporation",
    "location": "New York",
    "phone": "(999) 999-9999",
    "hours": "Mon-Fri: 9:00AM - 6:00PM, ET"
  },
  "menu": {
    "main": [
      {
        "identifier": "about",
        "name": "About",
        "url": "/about",
        "weight": 100
      },
      {
        "identifier": "contact",
        "name": "Contact",
        "url": "/contact",
        "weight": 200
      }
    ]
  },
  "params": {
    "color": "#4f46e5",
    "copyright": "Copyright &copy;
       2022 Acme Corporation. All Rights Reserved.",
    "footer": [
      {
        "title": "About",
        "content": "Acme Corporation is the world's leading manufacturer of
       digital shapes. From squares and circles to triangles and hexagons,
       we have it all. Browse through our collection of various forms with
       different thicknesses and line styles. We shape the world. You live
       in it."
      },
```

```json
    {
      "title": "Recent Blog Posts",
      "recents": "blog",
      "recentCount": 7
    },
    {
      "title": "Contact Us",
      "contact": true
    }
  ]
 }
}
```

Even pure JSON files require curly braces to mark JSON objects. The objective of JSON is interoperability. The verbosity comes at a cost to human readability. JSON has a lot of quotes, strict commas, and brackets, with no regard for new lines.

appendix C
A GUI-based admin
section with Netlify CMS

Many nontechnical users coming to the world of static site builders like Hugo miss the admin interface from where they can create content. This interface typically comes with a WYSIWYG editor to create content and a one-button upload to upload images. Because it is hosted, in most cases, we do not need to worry about setting up the whole website to use this. While GitHub provides such an interface, it may be incomplete or too complicated for nontechnical team members. They may not understand the concept of branching and version management in Git and want to continue with the simplicity of a web-based GUI to create content.

There are multiple content management system (CMS) wrappers available in the market to perform this task. Netlify CMS is among the most popular, is open source, and is compatible with Hugo. This appendix provides the minimal setup for our website from code checkpoint chapter-04-03 using Netlify CMS.

C.1 Loading Netlify CMS

The easiest way to add Netlify CMS is via the unpkg content delivery network (CDN). To get Netlify CMS, create a subfolder called admin in the static folder. Inside it, add index.html, which loads Netlify CMS. The following listing uses a script to get Netlify CMS from unpkg.

> **Listing C.1 HTML content for Netlify CMS (static/admin/index.html)**

```
<!doctype html>
<html>
<head>
  <meta charset="utf-8" />
```

415

```
<meta name="viewport"
        content="width=device-width, initial-scale=1.0" />
  <title>Content Manager</title>
</head>
<body>
  <script src="https://unpkg.com/netlify-cms@^2.0.0/dist/netlify-cms.js">
  </script>
</body>
</html>
```

C.2   Configuring Netlify CMS

Next, add the Netlify CMS configuration. The following listing shows a sample configuration. In this configuration, we specify where to create Markdown files and the look for the front matter contents.

Listing C.2   Netlify CMS Configuration to load the Acme Corporation website

Path to your GitHub repository

```
backend:
  name: github                          The branch to use in Netlify CMS
  repo: hugoinaction/hugoinaction       The workflow to use
  branch: chapter-04-03                 Path to store the media files
publish_mode: editorial_workflow
media_folder: "static/images/uploads"   The src attribute for the uploaded
public_folder: "/images/uploads"        media begins with /images/uploads.
collections:
  - name: "blog"          A collection of Netlify CMS corresponds
    label: "Blog"         to a section or branch bundle in Hugo.
    folder: "content/blog"                           Each collection needs a
    create: true                                     target folder location.
    slug: "{{slug}}"      Specifies the file name
    fields:               Adds the fields for the front matter
      - {label: "Title", name: "title",
        widget: "string"}
      - {label: "Publish Date", name: "date",
        widget: "datetime"}
      - {label: "Body", name: "body",
        widget: "markdown"}
  - name: "news"
    label: "News"          Each collection needs a
    folder: "content/news"   target folder location.
    create: true             Specifies the file name
    slug: "{{slug}}"
    fields:                  Adds the fields for the front matter
      - {label: "Title", name: "title",
        widget: "string"}
      - {label: "Publish Date", name: "date",
        widget: "datetime"}
      - {label: "Body", name: "body",
        widget: "markdown"}
```

Allows file creation, which causes a pull request

Allows file creation, which causes a pull request

Note that the editorial workflow in Netlify CMS adds support for drafts and previews for content before going live. Also Netlify CMS stores media files in the repository under static/images/uploads. Netlify CMS does not support Hugo Pipes or page bundles.

Before we can use the code in the previous listing, we need to allow the Netlify CMS to connect with GitHub. To be able to authenticate with GitHub, GitHub requires a server. Because we do not want to manage a server with the Jamstack, we can use Netlify's GitHub OAuth support for connecting to GitHub. (Netlify CMS supports other OAuth brokers as well.)

Netlify is the default OAuth backend for GitHub support in Netlify CMS, so we do not need to update any configuration. We can start by going to the GitHub Developer Settings page at https://github.com/settings/developers. Figure C.1 shows what the page looks like.

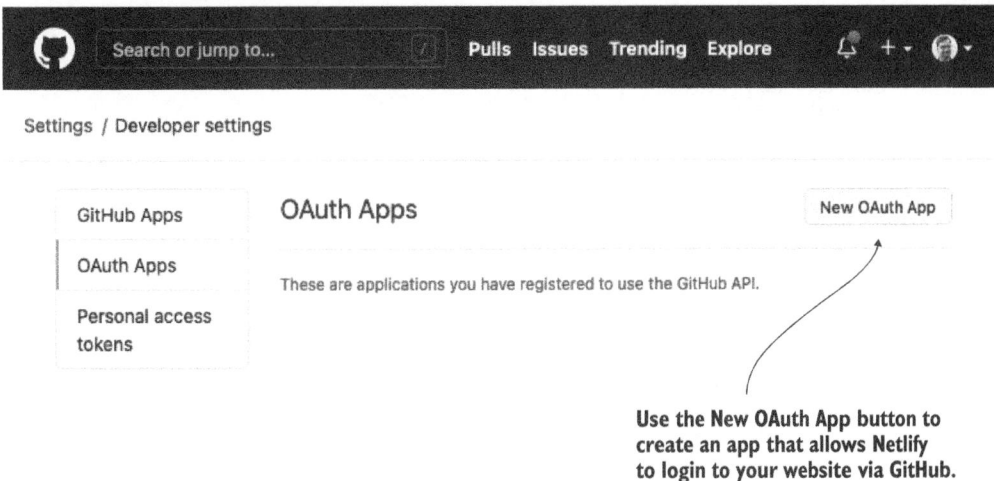

Figure C.1 Creating a new OAuth Application in GitHub Developer Settings

On the next page, we need to provide the authorization callback URL as https://api.netlify.com/auth/done. We can fill the rest of the fields with any details of our application (figure C.2).

Figure C.2   Provide the details of the OAuth application to GitHub, including the Netlify endpoint, to register the application for authentication.

Once done, we need to copy the client ID, then click Generate a New Client Secret (figure C.3), and paste the client secret in the box that appears, which we need to supply to Netlify (figure C.4).

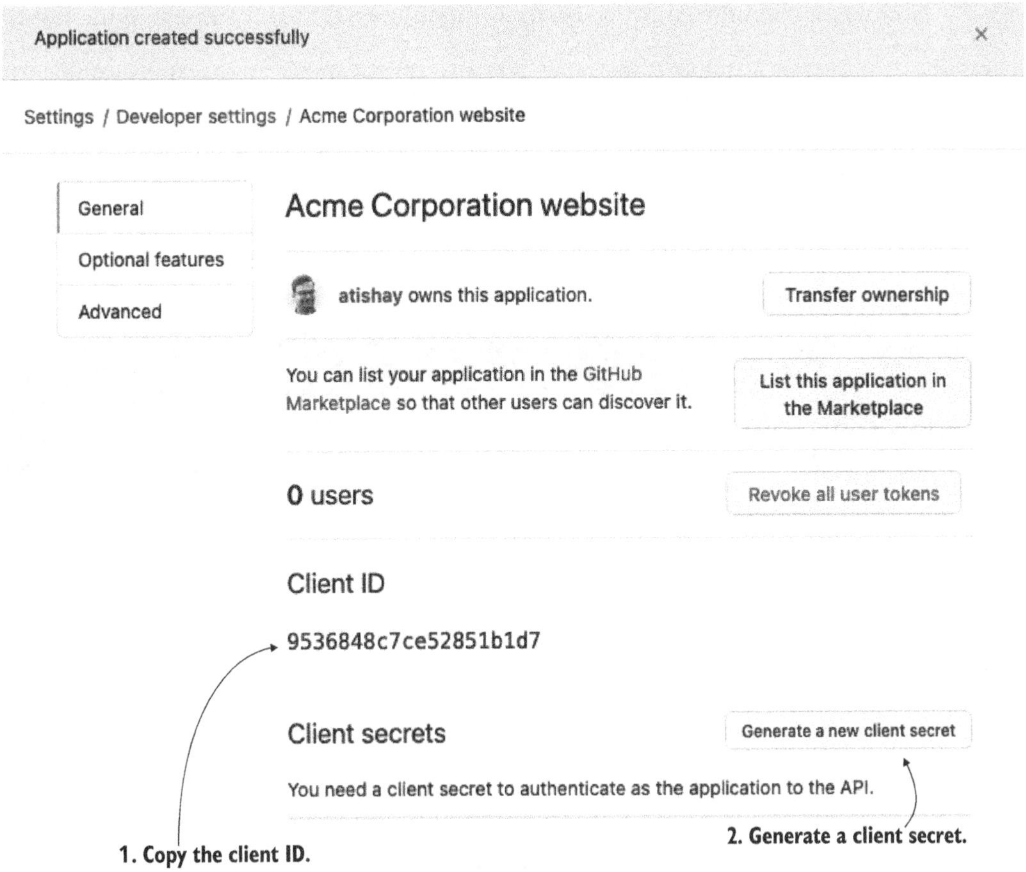

Application created successfully   ✕

Settings / Developer settings / Acme Corporation website

| General |
| Optional features |
| Advanced |

Acme Corporation website

atishay owns this application.   [Transfer ownership]

You can list your application in the GitHub
Marketplace so that other users can discover it.   [List this application in
                                                        the Marketplace]

0 users   [Revoke all user tokens]

Client ID

9536848c7ce52851b1d7

Client secrets   [Generate a new client secret]

You need a client secret to authenticate as the application to the API.

1. Copy the client ID.   **2. Generate a client secret.**

Figure C.3   Getting the client ID and creating a client secret from the GitHub Developer Settings

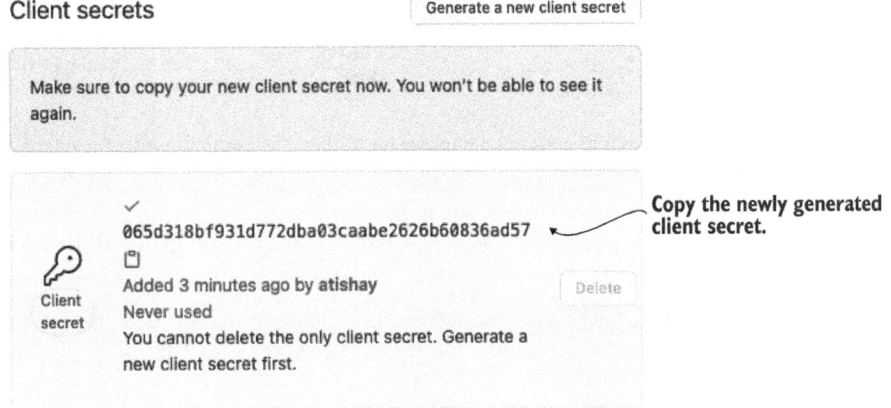

Client secrets   [Generate a new client secret]

Make sure to copy your new client secret now. You won't be able to see it
again.

✓
065d318bf931d772dba03caabe2626b60836ad57   **Copy the newly generated
                                                    client secret.**

🔑   Added 3 minutes ago by **atishay**   [Delete]
Client   Never used
secret   You cannot delete the only client secret. Generate a
          new client secret first.

Figure C.4   Getting the client secret for Netlify

Now we can add this information to Netlify (figure C.5) by completing the following steps:

1   Go to Site Settings > Access Control > OAuth.
2   In the Authentication Providers section, select Install Provider.
3   Select GitHub and fill in the Client ID and Client Secret fields, then click Save.

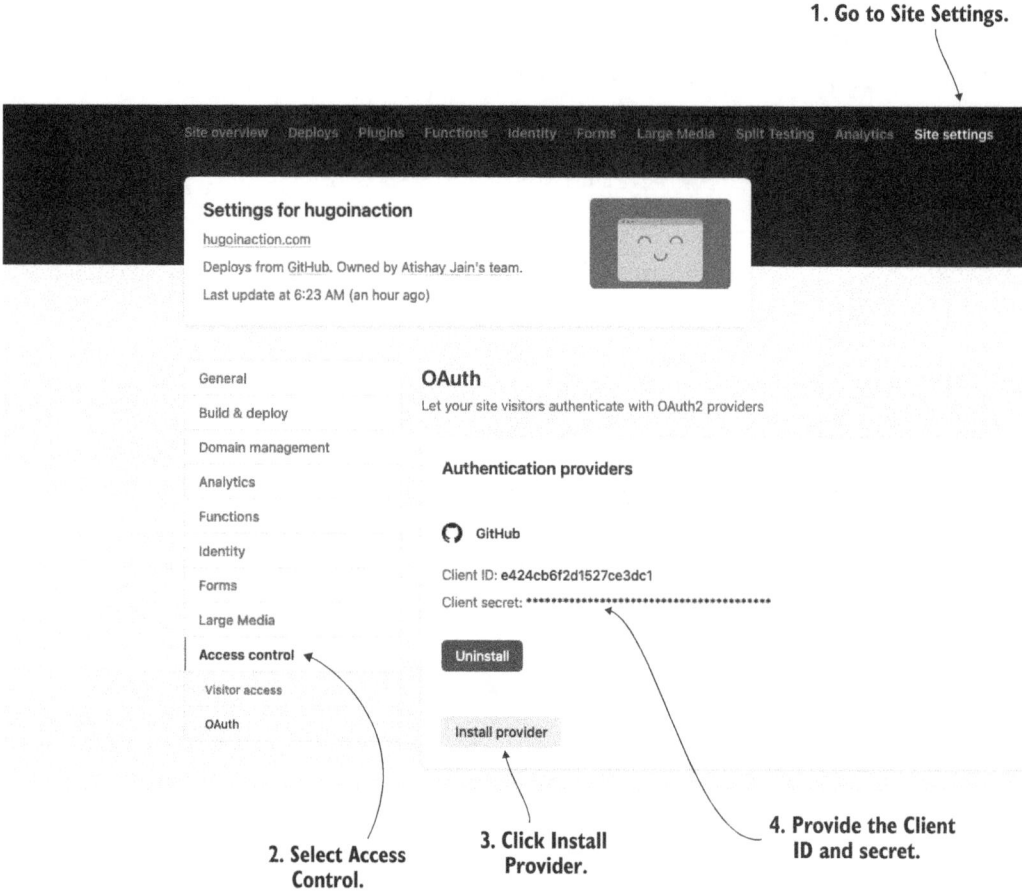

Figure C.5   Adding GitHub as an authentication provider for Netlify. The authentication Provider allows logins from GitHub to work in the Netlify CMS.

Now we can navigate to https://localhost:1313/admin to be greeted with Netlify CMS after we log in.

C.3 Using Netlify CMS

In the Netlify CMS UI, you can see all the News and Blog section contents and edit them. We can go to the Media tab to manage assets or head over to the Workflow tab to manage the editorial workflows (figure C.6).

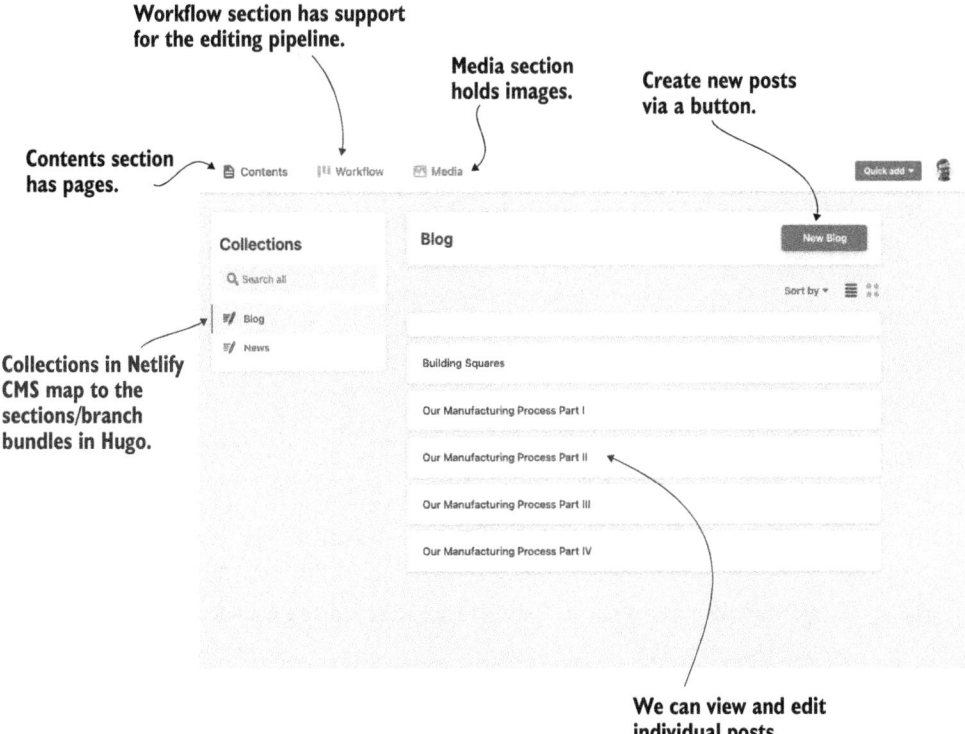

Figure C.6 Netlify CMS provides a graphic list of all the content within the website and has tabs for managing assets and the editorial workflow (draft, review, and publish graphically).

Netlify CMS provides a graphical editor for all the website content with support for live preview, major Markdown features, and front matter entries (figure C.7).

The Netlify CMS workflows map to GitHub automatically. User management happens via permissions to the repository on GitHub. Netlify CMS creates pull requests for new content, marks the various stages of the workflow as tags on GitHub, and merges the pull request during the publish action (figure C.8).

With Netlify CMS, we can hide the complexity of Git and Markdown from the less technical members of the team but keep the flexibility the developers need to provide outstanding performance and complete customization for the website.

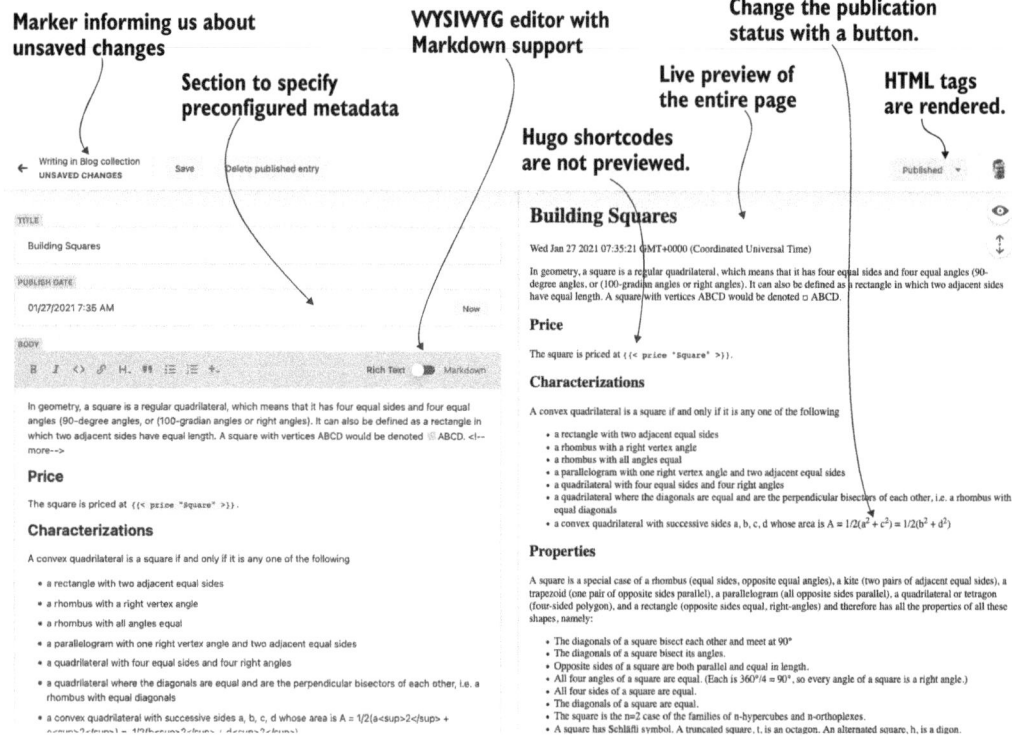

Figure C.7   Netlify CMS provides a graphical environment for handling Markdown.

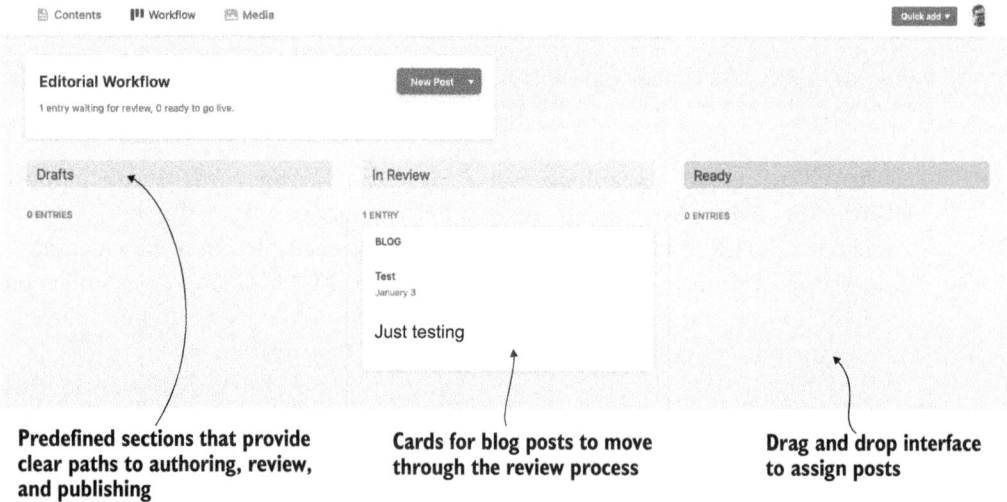

Figure C.8   Managing the editorial workflow in Netlify CMS. Netlify CMS provides complete control over the editorial process both within its GUI and within GitHub, creating pull requests, updating tags and merging them from its UI, and synching the state from GitHub if we take action there.

appendix D
The Go template language

The Go template language is a language specifically designed to fill templates for the Go programming language. Hugo builds upon the Go template language and adds more variables and functions to provide additional functionality. This appendix provides an overview of the Go template language features, which form the building blocks of the website template.

The Hugo documentation provides a ready reference for all the possible variables and functions that exist in Hugo at https://gohugo.io/variables/ and https://gohugo.io/functions/, respectively. Note that this appendix's code resources are present as a part of chapter 5 and chapter 6 resources for this book.

D.1 Basic usage

Accessing the Go template language inside Hugo requires two curly braces, {{...}}, anywhere within the template file. Hugo parses the files looking for these template markers and executes the Go Template script within these tags. All HTML and text apart from that inside the braces is considered as data for Hugo. Each page in Hugo is rendered separately in parallel to others. We can share pieces of generated content across pages. All pages have access to all other pages via variables.

D.1.1 Comments

Although we are free to use HTML comments in Hugo templates, in development mode, Hugo passes on these comments to the generated HTML. Minification can remove them. Template authors should use comments to guide the JavaScript or CSS developers. If we use template code inside an HTML comment, Hugo will execute it. We can also use Hugo comments that are present only in the file and not in the generated HTML. These are ideal for template authors. The following listing provides some ways to use comments.

Listing D.1   Comments in various forms

```
<!-- A HTML comment. Renders unless stripped during minify -->


{{/* A Hugo comment. Does not render at all */}}


<!-- Even though its result might be commented, {{.}} is still executed -->
```

D.1.2   *Whitespace removal*

Hugo templates turn into rendered content on processing, but the surrounding whitespace, which we might have used for formatting, is left behind. We can begin a template with {{- for trimming whitespace to the left and -}} for cutting spaces to the right in the executed template code. Minification also shrinks the whitespaces, leaving only one as understood by HTML. It is a personal choice whether to care about whitespace during development and trimming to properly show generated output or to use a browser plugin to beautify HTML during development and let the minifier clean it up in production. The benefit of trimming inline with the {{- or the -}} tags is better control over when the spaces get trimmed to get better looking debugging output. Because it does not matter in production and with browser plugins, we can reformat the result the way we want, and many users don't care to have clean spacing in the debugging output.

D.1.3   *Errors*

Hugo reports errors to the console and the web interface if we have improper template code (figure D.1). For example, if we use opening template brackets and don't close them, Hugo complains about using unknown variables in the template parameters. With live reload support in development mode, as soon as we fix the error and save the file, the website goes back to normal. The speed of Hugo compilation enables instant gratification for template developers. Hugo renders the page as soon as the developer completes its code.

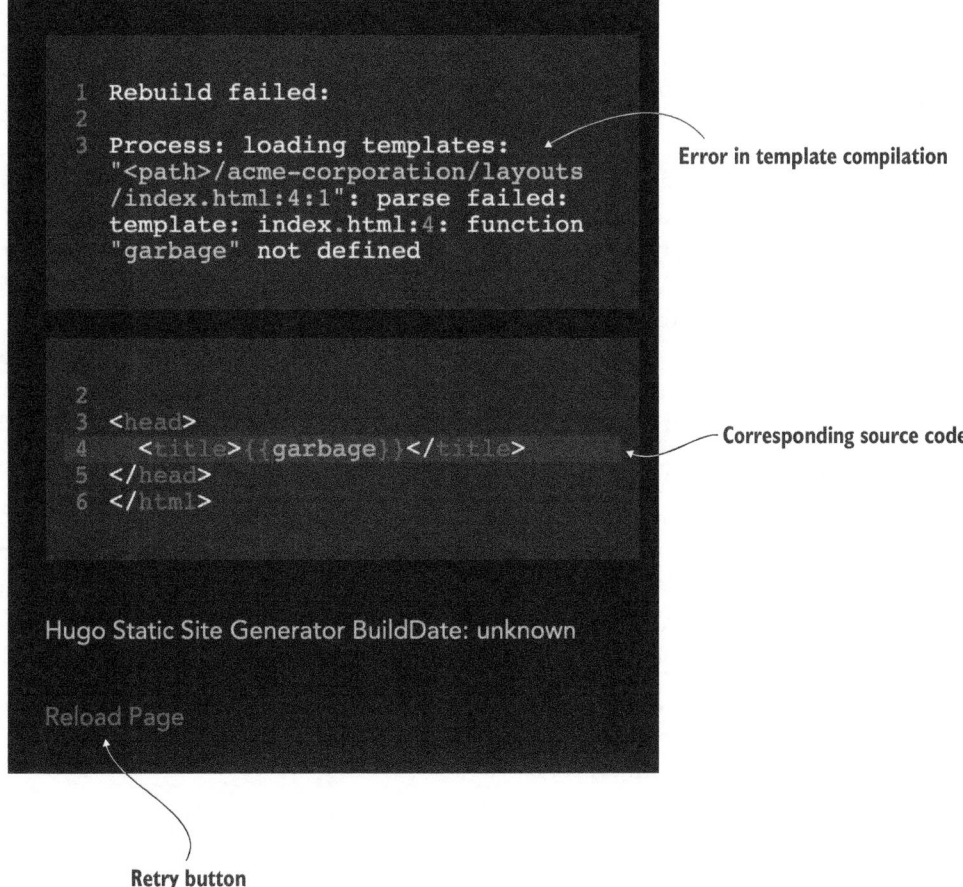

```
1  Rebuild failed:
2
3  Process: loading templates:
   "<path>/acme-corporation/layouts
   /index.html:4:1": parse failed:
   template: index.html:4: function
   "garbage" not defined
```
Error in template compilation

```
2
3  <head>
4    <title>{{garbage}}</title>
5  </head>
6  </html>
```
Corresponding source code

Hugo Static Site Generator BuildDate: unknown

Reload Page

Retry button

Figure D.1   Error reporting for Hugo templates. When we use incorrect template code, Hugo provides us with the exact line number where things went wrong during rendering.

D.2   Variables

Hugo provides a number of built-in variables. If you want, you can also define your own custom variables. This section looks at both predefined and custom variables.

D.2.1   Built-in variables

Everything that gets rendered as a context variable is accessible via the dot (.) operator in the template. The context variable can be loosely compared to the this variable in an object-oriented language. We can override (change) the context variable in a code block using statements like with and range.

The top-level context variable contains two useful subvariables: the global site and the page-level .Page variables. Variables like .File provide filesystem information, and .GitInfo gets the information from the Git version control system. Apart from these, pages such as sitemaps and taxonomies have separate variables.

The site variable has all the properties that are global to the website. We can use site.Description to access the website description and site.Title to access the website title. We can also use the global site variable to access all the Hugo website data including sections, menus, taxonomies, parameters with the configuration, and other features like data templates and multilingual content, which we have not gotten to yet. The site variable is also available as a global variable in all templates.

The .Page variables have access to the page's front matter, its content, and the generated metadata about the page such as the summary and the reading time. It has navigational variables like the NextInSection and Next and navigation support for going through the section hierarchy that leads to the current page.

The site and page variables are available outside of the context variable as $.Site and $.Page. These can be useful to get access to information from a deeply nested location within the template. The site variables are available globally as site as well.

D.2.2   *Custom variables*

We can declare our custom variables to live within a part of a page or the whole page. These can have values based on computation using conditionals and functions from the various in-build variables. All custom variables in Hugo start with a dollar sign ($). We can declare a custom variable using the := operator and modify its value using the = operator. The following listing shows different ways to customize variables.

Listing D.2   Defining a custom variable

```
{{$mycustom := site.Title}}
...
{{$mycustom = .Page.Title}}     ←———| Overrides
                                     | $mycustom
```

D.3   *Data types*

Hugo variables can have dictionaries, time objects, and slices, apart from the strings, Booleans, floating-point, and integral numbers. Dictionaries are key-value pairs, and slices are lists of objects (like arrays). Time objects are types that represent a date and a time value. Slices have read/write support; dictionaries are read-only. The following listing shows how we can render a regular variable on a page by placing it in double curly braces ({{…}}).

Listing D.3   Data types

```
Integer: {{2}}
Float: {{3.14}}
Boolean: {{false}}
String: {{"hello"}}

Slice: {{slice "foo" "bar" "buzz"}}
Dict: {{dict "key1" "val1" "w" 10 "h" 20}}
Time: {{time "2020-01-01T00:00:00+08:00"}}
```

Hugo also has a `scratch` variable to create a scratch pad that can store content (listing D.4). We use scratch pads to store and manipulate all data types and to build editable dictionaries and slices. Note that a scratch pad is not needed on a daily basis, but these can be extremely useful when doing complicated calculations. For example, templates used for creating tag clouds or usage graphs may need a scratch pad. (We do not use the `scratch` variable anywhere in the book.)

Listing D.4 Adding scratch pads

```
{{ $scratch := newScratch }}
{{ $scratch.Set "message" "Hello" }}
Scratch: {{ $scratch }}
Getter: {{ $scratch.Get "message" }}

{{ $scratch.Add "message" " World" }}          Scratch.Add appends a
Updated: {{$scratch.Get "message"}}            string, adds a number, and
                                               inserts a message in a slice.

{{ $scratch.SetInMap                           We can also create a
      "message" "english" "Hello World" }}     dictionary in a scratch pad.
{{ $scratch.SetInMap "message" "french" "Bonjour le monde" }}
```

Each page and shortcode rendering context in Hugo comes with a central scratch pad that we can access via `.Scratch`. Hugo also has resources (including images, CSS, JavaScript, PDF files) that we can use as data types.

D.4 Functions for operators

Hugo uses functions for all operations. These have spaces instead of brackets or commas as delimiters. Most programming languages declare a function as `add(5, 3)`, for example, but Hugo writes this as `{{add 5 3}}`. We can also use curly braces for nested functions. Go Template code is present in the double curly braces (`{{..}}`). Listing D.5 uses operators as functions.

The data sources for functions vary. These can be user-generated (the content, front matter, configuration, etc.), tool or system information (Git information, filesystem, date), or Hugo-generated (the summary, word count, or similar page list).

Listing D.5 Operators as functions

```
Boolean Functions
5 > 3 : {{lt 5 3}}
5 < 3 : {{gt 5 3}}
5 ≥ 3 : {{ge 5 3}}
5 ≤ 3 : {{le 5 3}}
5 = 3 : {{eq 5 3}}
5 ≠ 3 : {{ne 5 3}}

Logical Functions
true and false : {{and true false}}
true or false : {{or true false}}
not true : {{not true}}
```

```
Arithmetic Functions
2 + 3 : {{add 2 3}}
2 - 3 : {{sub 2 3}}
2 x 3 : {{mul 2 3}}
2 ÷ 3 : {{div 2 3}}      ◁───── Int types
2 ÷ 3 : {{div 2.0 3}}    ◁──────┐
2 % 3 : {{mod 2 3}}             │ Float types
2 % 3? : {{modBool 2 3}}
```

These operators come in handy with things like post counts, taxonomy counts, and list lengths. Developers use Booleans extensively with `if`/`else` and `with` statements.

Int vs. float

Integer versus floating-point types may feel new to many developers from a language like JavaScript, where there is a single number type. Many languages closer to the hardware (and therefore faster) need to make a tradeoff when storing numbers. Suppose they represent numbers as plain integers in RAM and truncate the part after the decimal in a float. In that case, those integers occupy significantly less storage than the counterparts, where this additional information needs to be stored. This is, in many cases, zero. Therefore, they expose two data types for their users: integers for integral numbers and floating-point numbers for decimals.

There is truncation with integers, and if we need decimal support, we can manually convert a number to a floating point. For this, Hugo offers the *type cast* function `float` (for example, `{{float 1}}` converts the integer 1 to a float 1.0).

We call floats floating-point numbers because they do not represent the numbers as two individual integers in RAM. While that naive approach works for smaller numbers like 1.0, this would be prohibitively expensive for numbers like 0.6666666666666666, which we got in listing D.5. Floating-point numbers follow the IEEE 754 specification, which allows them to represent a vast range of numbers. They have a tradeoff for accuracy versus precision and weird edge cases, some of which we sometimes encounter in our daily use. Most major programming languages, from C to JavaScript, use floating-point numbers, and so does Hugo.

D.5   Nesting and piping

Hugo supports both nesting and piping functions, not just for the operators. With nesting and piping, we can get the advantage of obtaining multiple function calls in one line of code and the removal of needless variable creations. The following listing shows some examples.

Listing D.6   Nesting and piping

```
Nested Functions
5/(2 + (3 x 2.0)) : {{div 5 (add 2 (mul 3 2.0))}}

Piped Functions
```

```
5/(2 + (3 x 2.0)) : {{mul 3 2.0 | add 2 | div 5}}
```
Nested + Piped Hybrid
```
5/(2 + (3 x 2.0)) : {{div 5 (mul 3 2.0 | add 2)}}
```

In nested functions, we take an inner function call, surround it with parentheses ((…)), and then use that where we would have used its output. Hugo processes the inner function first and passes its result to the outer one.

In the case of piped function calls, we have a pipe operator (|) that takes the function's output before the operator and passes the output as the last argument to the function after the pipe operator. Using the pipe operator is more restricted than a nested function call because we cannot pass the output before the pipe to the first argument. Also, piped function calls cannot have multiple nested expressions. For example, (2 + (3 x 2.0)) / 5 and 5 / ((2 x 3.0) + (3 x 2.0)) cannot be represented as a single piped expression without nesting.

Nested and piped expressions can live simultaneously in a statement as in the hybrid example shown in listing D.6. The developer can chose whether to use nested or piped formats. Piped expressions are more readable than nested expressions when transforming files and strings, especially with functions that take single arguments. Because template generation involves many string manipulations, pipes are readily available and extensively used in Hugo.

D.6 *Conditional expressions*

Hugo supports conditional expressions for branching code. The following listing uses a conditional expression with the if/else statement. The else statement is optional.

Listing D.7 Condition via `if/else`

```
{{if $condition}}
  {{$condition}}
is true.
{{else}}
  {{$condition}}
is false.
{{end}}
```

We can also use with like if for conditional branching, especially if we need existence checks. The following listing shows an example of a condition using a with statement to override context.

Listing D.8 Condition via `with`

```
{{with $condition}}
  {{.}}
is the value of the condition
{{else}}

Condition is not defined.
{{end}}
```

Hugo also provides a {{isset <variable> <key>}} function to check the existence of a variable. We can use this in the if statement.

Both if and with have different use cases; with is also a conditional like if but only works for existence checks. The with statement switches the context variable . to the selected variable. Many Hugo variables are deeply nested, and with allows us to focus on generating HTML for a particular variable and providing the fallback HTML in the {{else}} block. All the front matter variables and most configuration variables are optional in Hugo, and if the content author does not provide them, Hugo will not set the corresponding property. Although printing an empty property would not fail the build process, we might generate blank HTML tags in those cases, which would not look good. The with statement comes in handy in dealing with these cases.

Hugo also supports the cond function. This gives us a straightforward way to provide a value based on a condition; for example,

```
{{cond (eq $count 1) "page" "pages"}}
```

D.7 Loops

Loops are available in Hugo for navigating through slices. Hugo provides a range function to loop through some variables as the following listing shows.

Listing D.9   Ranges for loops in the Go HTML templates

```
All website pages:
{{range site.Pages}}
* {{.Title}}
{{end}}
```

Just like with, the range function also switches the context. The . variable changes to the variable within the slice, and we can then access its contents. We can carry forward any variables from the previous context by assigning them to custom variables. For example, if we need the website title inside of the range, we need to store it in a variable like $title to access it as the following listing shows.

Listing D.10   Keeping variables out of context for ranges

```
{{$title := site.Title}}
{{range site.Pages}}
* {{.Title}} @ {{$title}}
{{end}}
```

If we do not want to override the context (.), we can provide a variable to range. The following listing shows this approach.

> **Listing D.11 Ranges without overriding context**

```
{{range $page := site.Pages}}
* {{$page.Title}} @ {{site.Title}}
{{end}}
```

The range function can also provide an index for an array and the key of a dictionary. The following listing shows this use.

> **Listing D.12 Getting the loop index from the range**

```
{{ range $index, $page := site.Pages }}
{{$index}}. {{$page.Title}} @ {{site.Title}}
{{ end }}
```

Unlike traditional loops, range uses the else keyword to provide content if no elements are present. The following listing shows how.

> **Listing D.13 Using else with range**

```
{{ range $index, $page := site.Pages }}
{{$index}}. {{$page.Title}} @ {{site.Title}}
{{ else }}
No pages present
{{ end }}
```

Viewing and debugging template variables

If you are unsure about the value of a variable, you can print it to the DOM to view it using the {{$variable}} method. If the variable is of a complex type, you can use {{ printf "%#v" $variable }} to output a variable to the DOM. The print function supports a wide range of formats for printing variables to the DOM. It can interlace strings, change formatting, and cast variables from one type to another. Specifying the %#v format outputs the value of $variable in Go syntax form, which includes the entire value tree for dictionaries and slices.

We can also use {{ jsonify . }} to convert a variable to JSON format, which we can then export to a script tag in the output HTML. If we use the following script, we will see the variable contents in the browser console:

```
<script>
  console.log('Hugo Debug: ', JSON.parse({{ jsonify . }}))
</script>
```

D.8 Standard library

Hugo has a huge and growing standard library of functions that we can use to access and manipulate data. The following sections describe the top categories of methods that Hugo provides.

D.8.1   *String conversions*

Web output consists of various formats from languages like HTML, CSS, and Java-Script to components like URL and HTML attributes. Hugo provides automatic conversion to these formats appropriately. For example, when writing to an HTML template, Hugo automatically escapes the HTML. We have the option to opt out via the `safeHTML` function. Hugo also has methods to interconvert between other languages like JSON and Markdown and the GO template variables. These include the `safe*` methods like `safeHTML`, `safeCSS`, and so forth, as well as the `*ify` methods like `markdownify`, `jsonify`, `emojify`, `plainify`, and others.

D.8.2   *String creation and manipulation*

Data used in Hugo templates comes from the front matter and the configuration in the form of slices, dictionaries, and variables. These need to be used in various places from the human-readable text in the web pages to URLs and anchor tags (used to access data) and API formats like XML (for example, in sitemaps) and JSON (JSON-LD can be used for rich metadata snippets understood by Google). Human readable formats require us to capitalize the first letter, lowercase URLs, and CamelCase hashtags for Twitter.

Hugo provides string manipulation functions to convert data to all these formats and to custom ones as well, not only from strings but also from slices, dictionaries, and other data types. These string manipulation functions include a variety of methods like `chomp`, `humanize`, `print*` and `replace*`.

D.8.3   *List and map manipulation and filtering*

Lists are another common type of data that we will encounter when building web pages via Hugo templates. Accessing parts of these, then filtering and selecting are other typical operations where Hugo's standard library provides much functionality. This includes a wide variety of methods from `first` and `last` to `slice` and `join`. We can also use set functions such as `complement` and `intersect`.

D.8.4   *The web and Hugo-specific tasks*

Hugo also has utilities to perform Hugo-specific and web-specific tasks like finding URLs, accessing parameters from the front matter, and getting pages. These methods help us shorten the amount of template code required for day-to-day Hugo needs. These include `ref`, `param`, `.GetPage`, `.HasMenuCurrent`, and others.

D.8.5   *Resource access and manipulation*

Another common task for the web workflow is accessing and manipulating resource files like image, SCSS or CSS, and JavaScript files. Hugo provides a range of functions for path manipulation, resource manipulation, image processing, content minification, and hashing (for both MD5 and SHA). These include `+path.*` for path utilities, `resource.\*` for resource manipulation, and `` `transform.*` `` for file transformation.

D.8.6   *Language features*

From type casting and reflection to partials, Hugo provides many language features as functions. We can convert from integers to floats via `float`, write partial templates with `partial`, and check if a variable is a map using `reflect.IsMap`.

D.8.7   *File handling and network access*

Functions like `readFile` provide direct access to the filesystem. We can also use methods like `getJSON` to provide support for getting JSON-based data both from the filesystem and a HTTP-based web service.

D.8.8   *Resource manipulation and Hugo Pipes*

Functions like `resources.GetMatch` allow access to assets files, both for linking and manipulation.

We do not need to know all the functions to be successful with Hugo. But it is a good idea to keep the function reference (https://gohugo.io/functions) handy when writing templates. The chances are, if we want to do some manipulation, it might be natively available in Hugo rather than us reinventing the wheel.

appendix E
Answers to exercises

Chapter 1

- Exercise 1.1: c (compiled templates)
- Exercise 1.2: a (markup)
- Exercise 1.3: b (a shopping website)
- Exercise 1.4: Go (or Golang)
- Exercise 1.5: False. You can write locally in the markup language and directly check that in to source control, or you can use admin tools like Netlify CMS.
- Exercise 1.6: Markup

Chapter 2

- Exercise 2.1: d (all of the above)
- Exercise 2.2: c (content)
- Exercise 2.3: 1 (YAML) and d (config); 2 (Markdown) and c (content); 3 (PDF) and b (static); 4 (HTML) and e (themes); 5 (CSS) and a (assets)
- Exercise 2.4: 1313
- Exercise 2.5: `hugo serve` or `hugo server`
- Exercise 2.6: a (baseURL)
- Exercise 2.7: b (index)
- Exercise 2.8: c (compare performance across multiple builds of our website and multiple builds of Hugo to find faulty behavior)

Chapter 3

- Exercise 3.1: c, d, and f (a hyphen/dash (-), an equal sign (=), and a hash (#))
- Exercise 3.2: b (smaller font size)
- Exercise 3.3: a (date)

- Exercise 3.4: slug
- Exercise 3.5: True. Although suboptimal, we can provide everything as data to make a data-driven website.

Chapter 4

- Exercise 4.1: production
- Exercise 4.2: b (front matter)
- Exercise 4.3: a (the logo of a section)
- Exercise 4.4: b (taxonomy term)
- Exercise 4.5: layouts, content

Chapter 5

- Exercise 5.1: a (the shortcode)
- Exercise 5.2: default
- Exercise 5.3: e (both b and c). We can use `with` to check the existence of a value and to provide a default behavior or value if absent. We can also use `with` to update the context to write less code if it relies only on the subproperties of a variable.
- Exercise 5.4: See https://github.com/hugoinaction/hugoinaction/tree/chapter-05-resources/05
- Exercise 5.5: a, d, and e (music playlists, list of top ten most liked blog posts, and affiliate link to the product in review)
- Exercise 5.6: developer, author/editor

Chapter 6

- Exercise 6.1: c (baseof.html)
- Exercise 6.2: single.html
- Exercise 6.3: False. Blocks execute for each page. Only cached partials are shared.
- Exercise 6.4: See https://github.com/hugoinaction/hugoinaction/tree/chapter-06-19 See layouts/modern/index.html
- Exercise 6.5: b, c, and d. Hugo Pipes can use website configuration and front matter, cache files across builds, and generate multiple image sizes as needed using code.

Chapter 7

- Exercise 7.1: layout
- Exercise 7.2: c (kind)
- Exercise 7.3: e (paginator)
- Exercise 7.4: a and e (list.html and single.html)

- Exercise 7.5: a, d, and e. Content views are not cached and generated each time the view is used. They can be rendered from within another layout, and can be overridden based on the content type.

Chapter 8

- Exercise 8.1: False. We can use Hugo Modules to share dependencies and import third-party content.
- Exercise 8.2: a and c (name of the module, and list of website dependencies, both direct and indirect)
- Exercise 8.3: c and d. A content plugin can be used to set up access control on the content by splitting each area into a separate repository. It can also move the common content into a separate repository for one place of access.
- Exercise 8.4: False. Hugo caches modules as temporary files for faster rebuild and offline support.

Chapter 9

- Exercise 9.1: a, d, and e (provide better user performance, prevent API owners from tracking users, enable content manipulation and reuse of data across multiple pages)
- Exercise 9.2: disable (across projects), enable (across machines)
- Exercise 9.3: JavaScript
- Exercise 9.4: data/content, presentation/layout
- Exercise 9.5: e (internal pagination template)

Chapter 10

- Exercise 10.1: b, d, and e (Hugo has great support for playing nicely with client-side JavaScript, with a well-defined interface for transferring compile-time data. Hugo provides clear, well-defined separation of concerns for build-time and run-time processing. Hugo Pipes delivers a rich, powerful, and extremely fast JavaScript builder.)
- Exercise 10.2: Pseudo-APIs/APIs
- Exercise 10.3: Templates/Go templates/layouts/themes
- Exercise 10.4: is not, can. Hugo cannot build SPAs but plays nicely with them.

Chapter 11

- Exercise 11.1: c (using a function as a service (FaaS) solution and only writing our core business logic)
- Exercise 11.2: True. In the universe where we do not need to output HTML but PDFs, LaTeX is used similarly as Markdown in the Jamstack.
- Exercise 11.3: APIs
- Exercise 11.4: server
- Exercise 11.5: JavaScript

Chapter 12

- Exercise 12.1: a, b, c, d, e, and f. All features can be used across domains and provide value.
- Exercise 12.2: c, d. The client-side storage model does not sync across multiple machines, and it is less reliable for both persistence and accuracy than a server-side storage model.
- Exercise 12.3: user
- Exercise 12.4: prices
- Exercise 12.5: d. If fulfillment happens in case of false positive, there is undoable financial loss. The stakes are much higher in case of purchases and we cannot work with guesses.

Chapter 13

- Exercise 13.1: b, c, e, and f (images, JavaScript, templates, and config)
- Exercise 13.2: a. Creating a new output format for a subwebsite. Different output formats share content.
- Exercise 13.3: a and d. Service workers can speed up a website by prefetching content heuristically, and like web workers, they run in a separate context from the main page JavaScript.
- Exercise 13.4: b. We can use SDKs within a cloud function to affect its own state. We used the Netlify API in the rebuild webhook but could have used the SDK as well. Rebuilds can affect Netlify functions.

index

RELATED MANNING TITLES

The Jamstack Book
by Raymond Camden and Brian Rinaldi

ISBN 9781617298882
250 pages *(estimated)*, $49.99
April 2022 *(estimated)*

Svelte and Sapper in Action
by Mark Volkmann

ISBN 9781617297946
456 pages, $59.99
September 2020

React Hooks in Action
by John Larsen

ISBN 9781617297632
376 pages, $49.99
March 2021

For ordering information go to www.manning.com

Web Design Playground
by Paul McFedries

ISBN 9781617294402
440 pages, $39.99
April 2019

CSS in Depth
by Keith J. Grant
Foreword by Chris Coyier

ISBN 9781617293450
472 pages, $44.99
March 2018

Testing Web APIs
by Mark Winteringham

ISBN 9781617299537
325 pages (estimated), $59.99
Summer 2022 (estimated)

For ordering information go to www.manning.com

A new online reading experience

liveBook, our online reading platform, adds a new dimension to your Manning books, with features that make reading, learning, and sharing easier than ever. A liveBook version of your book is included FREE with every Manning book.

This next generation book platform is more than an online reader. It's packed with unique features to upgrade and enhance your learning experience.

- Add your own notes and bookmarks
- One-click code copy
- Learn from other readers in the discussion forum
- Audio recordings and interactive exercises
- Read all your purchased Manning content in any browser, anytime, anywhere

As an added bonus, you can search every Manning book and video in liveBook—even ones you don't yet own. Open any liveBook, and you'll be able to browse the content and read anything you like.*

Find out more at www.manning.com/livebook-program.

*Open reading is limited to 10 minutes per book daily